Time Out

San Francisco

Penguin Books

PENGUIN BOOKS

Published by the Penguin Group
Penguin Books Ltd, 27 Wrights Lane, London W8 5TZ, England
Penguin Books USA Inc., 375 Hudson Street, New York, New York 10014, USA
Penguin Books Australia Ltd, Ringwood, Victoria, Australia
Penguin Books Canada Ltd, 10 Alcorn Avenue, Toronto, Ontario, Canada M4V 3B2
Penguin Books (NZ) Ltd, 182-190 Wairau Road, Auckland 10, New Zealand

Penguin Books Ltd, Registered Offices: Harmondsworth, Middlesex, England

First published 1996
Second edition 1998
Third edition 2000
10 9 8 7 6 5 4 3 2 1

Colour reprographics by Precise Litho, 34-35 Great Sutton Street, London EC1
Printed and bound by William Clowes Ltd, Beccles, Suffolk NR34 9QE

Edited and designed by
Time Out Guides Limited
Universal House
251 Tottenham Court Road
London W1P OAB
Tel + 44 (0)20 7813 3000
Fax + 44 (0)20 7813 6001
Email guides@timeout.com
www.timeout.com

Editorial
Editor Caroline Taverne
Consultant Editor Colin Berry
Deputy Editor Lily Dunn
Researchers Laurie Amat, Catherine Guthrie
Proofreader Rosamund Sales
Indexer Richard Wright

Editorial Director Peter Fiennes
Series Editor Caroline Taverne

Design
Art Director John Oakey
Art Editor Mandy Martin
Senior Designer Scott Moore
Designers Benjamin de Lotz, Lucy Grant
Picture Editor Kerri Miles
Deputy Picture Editor Olivia Duncan-Jones
Picture Admin Kit Burnet
Scanning & Imaging Chris Quinn

Advertising
Group Advertisement Director Lesley Gill
Sales Director Mark Phillips
Advertisement Director North American Guides
Liz Howell (808 732 4661)
Advertising co-ordinated in the US by
Time Out New York:
Alison Tocci (Publisher), Andy Gersten (Advertising Production Manager), Tom Oesau (Advertising Production Co-ordinator), Claudia Pedala (Assistant to the Publisher)

Administration
Publisher Tony Elliott
Managing Director Mike Hardwick
Financial Director Kevin Ellis
Marketing Director Gillian Auld
General Manager Nichola Coulthard
Production Manager Mark Lamond
Accountant Bridget Carter

Features in this guide were written and updated by:
Introduction, **History**, **San Francisco Today**, **Architecture**, **Literary San Francisco**, **San Francisco by Season**, **Sightseeing**, **Museums & Galleries** Colin Berry. **Accommodation** Matthew Poole. **Restaurants & Cafés** Colin Berry, J Poet (The greens scene), Michael Stabile. **Bars** Colin Berry, Michael Stabile, Danielle Svetcov (Hipper than thou). **Shops & Services** Deborah Bishop. **Children**, **Film**, **Gay & Lesbian San Francisco**, **Media** Colin Berry. **Nightlife** Colin Berry, Scott Capurro (The last laugh?). **Performing Arts**, **Sport & Fitness** Colin Berry. **Trips Out of Town** Victoria Maitland-Lewis. **Directory** Colin Berry.

The editor would like to thank the following:
Adam Coulter, Sarah Guy, Ruth Jarvis, Julie Soller and Dayna Nelson at the San Francisco Convention & Visitors Bureau, Patrick Sampson at Personality Hotels of Union Square, Sharon Wright at Virgin Atlantic.
The Editor flew to San Francisco with Virgin Atlantic (reservations UK 01293 747 747; US 1-800 862 8621)

Map on pages 292-93 by Reineck & Reineck; **maps on pages 294-305** by Mapworld, 71 Blandy Road, Henley-on-Thames, Oxon RG9 1QB; **map on page 306** by JS Graphics, 17 Beadles Lane, Old Oxted, Surrey RH8 9JG.

Photography by Sara Hannant except: p7 Sonoma Valley Visitors Bureau; p9 AKG; p12 Associated Press; p23 Tony Gibson; p27 San Francisco Examiner/Katy Raddatz; p31 Katinka Herbert; p73 San Francisco Conference & Visitor's Bureau; p155 Steven Dorlan Miner; p183 Larry Merkle; p192 Warner Brothers; p223, 225 David Allen; p226 Marit Brook-Kothlow; p227 Jamie Smith; p232 SF Giants; p234 San Francisco 49ers; p242, 255 Santa Cruz County Conference and Visitors Council; p242 Grey Crawford; p247 Marine Mammal Center; p248 Verne Paule; p241, 256 Telegraph Colour Library; p259 Catherine Karnow; p262-263 Heavenly Ski Resort/Chaco Mohler; p263 Peaché. The following photographs were supplied by the featured establishments: pages 89, 93, 153, 117, 227, 250. The photo on p80 was reproduced by kind permission of the artist.

Contents

About the Guide

The *Time Out San Francisco Guide* is one of an expanding series of city guides produced by the people behind London and New York's successful listings magazines. Our hard-working team of resident writers has given the third edition a thorough overhaul in order to provide you with the most up-to-date information you'll need to take on one of America's most exciting and culturally diverse cities. Some chapters have been rewritten from scratch; our restaurant coverage has been expanded and we've also added lots of new shops, sights and clubs, to keep up with the ever-changing city scene. At the end of each chapter, we've included 'out of town' round-ups for the whole of the Bay Area.

ABOUT OUR LISTINGS

Addresses, telephone numbers, transport details, opening times, admission prices, credit card details and websites have all been included in our listings. We've also cross-referenced each venue to the colour maps of the city that appear on pages 293-306. And, as far as possible, we've given details of facilities, services and events, all checked and correct at the time we went to press. But owners and managers can change their arrangements at any time. Before you go out of your way, it's always best to telephone and check opening times, dates of exhibitions and other details.

For important information on disabled access, as well as details of California's rigorous anti-smoking laws, turn to the **Directory** chapter. It also lists a host of other practical information, from using public transport to advice on tipping.

ADDRESSES

Apart from the area around Twin Peaks and the outer neighbourhoods, most of San Francisco is laid out on a grid plan, with Market Street bisecting it into north and south segments from the Embarcadero to the Castro. Each block increases its numbering by 100, but we have included cross streets in all our addresses, so you can find your way about more easily.

Streets have both names and numbers; it's important not to confuse the numerical avenues (to the west) with the streets (which start at the Embarcadero, in the east). It is also worth noting that in the US, the ground floor of a building is what would be called the first floor in the UK, which makes the first floor the second, and so on.

PRICES

The prices we've supplied should be treated as guidelines, not gospel. Fluctuating exchange rates and inflation can cause prices, in shops and restaurants particularly, to change rapidly. If prices vary wildly from those we've quoted, ask whether there's a good reason. If not, go elsewhere. Then please write and let us know.

CREDIT CARDS

The following abbreviations have been used for credit cards: **AmEx**: American Express; **DC**: Diners' Club; **JCB**: Japanese credit cards; **MC**: Master-card (Access); **V**: Visa (Barclaycard). Most shops, restaurants and attractions will accept dollar travellers' cheques issued by a major financial institution.

TELEPHONE NUMBERS

There are three area codes that serve the Bay Area: 415 for San Francisco and Marin County, 510 for Berkeley and Oakland, and 650 for the peninsula cities. All telephone numbers printed in this guide take the 415 code, unless otherwise stated. Numbers preceded by 1-800 can be called free of charge from within the US.

RIGHT TO REPLY

It should be stressed that the information we give is impartial. No organisation has been included in this guide because its owner or manager has advertised in our publications. We hope you enjoy the *Time Out San Francisco Guide*, but we'd also like to know if you don't. We welcome tips for places that you think we should include in future editions and take notice of your criticism of our choices. There's a reader's reply card at the back of this book.

There is an online version of this guide, as well as weekly events listings for other international cities, at http://www.timeout.com

Introduction

Bookended by majestic bridges and wrapped in a stole of fog, San Francisco may be one of the most contradictory cities you'll ever visit. Meteorologically, politically, even geographically, the City by the Bay is the embodiment of quirky contrasts, cheerful reversals and impossible opposites.

Take the weather. Cold and foggy in the summer months, San Francisco turns balmy in autumn, warming the pale souls who trek to her parks between Labor Day and Hallowe'en. Rainy in winter, the city blossoms in spring – but only for a few weeks, before the fog and wind return to chill the populace and send them diving for their warm coats.

Similarly, the city's footprint, when seen on a map, is an expanse of neat, gridded streets and predictable right angles – a complete misrepresentation of the ridiculous inclines and declines one must actually traverse on the way across town. Even the landscape is contrary, crowding certain neighbourhoods – Pacific and Bernal Heights and aptly-named Telegraph, Russian and Nob Hills – with clusters of bluffs, and leaving others – the Mission, Sunset and Richmond districts – flat and topographically nondescript.

San Francisco's contrary nature is evident in other ways. Its reputation as a liberal epicentre, for example, is diffused by a seam of conservatism that pervades the politics within City Hall, the artwork in the museums and the programmes performed by the symphony, ballet and opera. Its residents are Californian coast-dwellers, to be sure, but they don't much care for the beach; they fear earthquakes, but do little or nothing to prepare for them mentally.

Perhaps the most striking contradiction is the way in which the city views itself as a metropolitan centre in a league with New York, Paris or London. It does indeed boast world-class restaurants and museums, a soigné performing arts scene and an elegant populace who can appreciate Mozart, Moët and Mondrian all in the same evening. A tour of several neighbourhoods bears this perception out: in the Financial District, bank headquarters stand shoulder-to-shoulder with international clothiers, telecommunications giants and five-star hotels; in the Civic Center, heads of government work inside the nation's most technologically sophisticated (and visually impressive) City Hall. South of Market Street, SFMOMA, the Yerba Buena complex and other art galleries define the cultural standards, while Internet and digital start-ups set the pace for twenty-first century business.

Yet in many ways the city – comprising just over 46 square miles and nearly three-quarters of a million in population – is still a small town. Some neighbourhoods feel downright rural: Hayes Valley, for instance, feels like the Main Street of a much smaller municipality – albeit one selling rare books, eco-friendly gifts and designer shoes. Other factors contribute to this sense of simplicity: relatively safe streets, well-manicured parks and playgrounds, bartenders and shopkeepers who recognise you on sight – all undermine San Francisco's potential for chilly urbaneness in the best possible way. Even Pacific Bell's new ballpark feels more *Field of Dreams* than *The Natural*.

But the small town is not without big city problems – a population of nearly 14,000 homeless, the increasing unreliability of the city's once-proud public transport system, gridlocked traffic, skyrocketing housing prices and the continuing Aids epidemic among them.

A complex city with complex character, thus does San Francisco flash its many facets, reveal its diverse personalities and contradictory nature. Perhaps the key to reconciling it all comes from recalling that since the Barbary Coast era, San Francisco has had a reputation for both great riches and ragged poverty, for high culture and low humour, for ethnic, culinary and cultural diversity in contrast with the homogeneity to be found in the rest of America. It has it all today, as it did then, in careful balance.

Colin Berry

In context

Key Events

10,000 BC The Ohlone and Miwok – or 'Costanoan' – Indians begin to settle the Bay Area.

1542 Juan Cabrillo sails up the California coastline.

1579 Francis Drake lands north of San Francisco Bay, claiming the land he finds for Elizabeth I as New Albion.

1769 Gaspar de Pórtola and Father Junípero Serra lead an expedition overland of 300 men to establish a mission at San Diego. An advance party is sent to scout out the coast and they become the first white men to see San Francisco Bay.

1775 The *San Carlos* is the first ship to sail into the Bay.

1776 On 4 July, 13 American colonies declare their independence from Great Britain. In the autumn, a Spanish presidio (military fort) is founded near Fort Point and Father Junípero establishes the Mission Dolores to convert the Ohlone to Christianity.

1821 Mexico declares its independence from Spain and annexes California.

1828 Fur trapper Jedediah Smith becomes the first white man to reach California across the Sierra Nevada mountain range.

1835 English-born sailor William Richardson establishes a trading post and calls it 'Yerba Buena'.

1846 The 'Bear Flag Revolt' takes place against Mexican rule in California.

1847 Yerba Buena is renamed San Francisco. It has 800 inhabitants.

1848 A US-Mexican treaty confirms American dominion over California; Gold is discovered in the low Sierras near Sacramento.

1849 The Gold Rush swells the city's population from 800 to 25,000 in less than a year. On Christmas Eve a huge fire levels the tent city.

1850 California becomes the 31st State of the Union. But lawlessness still rules in San Francisco.

1851 At a 'necktie party', vigilantes hang four men in Portsmouth Square.

1859 The Comstock Lode is discovered in western Nevada, triggering the Silver Rush.

1861 Civil War breaks out between the Union and the Confederacy in the US. Being so far west, California remains largely untouched by hostilities.

1868 The University of California is established at Berkeley.

1869 The Central Pacific Railroad reaches San Francisco.

1873 Andrew Hallidie builds the first cable cars.

1906 The Great Earthquake strikes and the fire that follows razes the city. Several thousand lose their lives, and over 3,000 acres of buildings are destroyed.

1913 The Los Angeles aqueduct opens.

1915 San Francisco celebrates the opening of the Panama Canal with the Panama-Pacific Exposition.

1932 San Francisco Opera House opens.

1934 On 'Bloody Thursday', police open fire on striking longshoremen, leaving two dead, and prompting a three-day general strike that brings the Bay Area to a standstill.

1936 The Bay Bridge is completed.

1937 The Golden Gate Bridge is completed.

1941 The Japanese attack Pearl Harbour and America enters World War II.

1945 Fifty nations meet at San Francisco Opera House to sign the United Nations Charter.

1955 Allen Ginsberg reads *Howl* at the Six Gallery on Fillmore Street, with other members of the Beat Generation cheering him on. The first Disneyland opens in California.

1961 UC Berkeley students stage a sit-in protest against a closed session of the House of Representatives Un-American Activities Committee at City Hall.

1964 Student sit-ins and mass arrests grow as the civil rights, free speech and anti-Vietnam war movements gain momentum. John Steinbeck receives Nobel Prize for literature.

1967 The Human Be-in, organised by Ginsberg, marks the start of the Summer of Love. The San Francisco sound is defined by groups like Jefferson Airplane and the Grateful Dead.

1968 Seventeen-year-old Bobby Hutton is killed in a Black Panther shoot-out with Oakland police.

1972 The Bay Area Rapid Transit (BART) transport system opens.

1978 Gay supervisor Harvey Milk and Mayor George Moscone are shot and killed by former supervisor Dan White. Dianne Feinstein becomes Mayor.

1981 The first cases of AIDS are recorded.

1989 An earthquake measuring 7.1 on the Richter scale strikes San Francisco.

1992 Fire sweeps through the Oakland hills killing dozens and destroying 3,000 homes.

1995 Jerry Garcia, icon of the Grateful Dead, dies. Willie Brown Jr becomes the city's first African-American mayor. The San Francisco 49ers win their fifth Super Bowl.

1996 Engineers announce the Bay Bridge needs a $1.3 billion seismic retrofit.

1997 Herb Caen, longtime *Chronicle* columnist, dies at 80.

1998 The War Memorial Opera House, damaged in the 1989 quake, re-opens in Civic Center.

1999 City Hall re-opens after a $300 million retrofit; the Metreon, Sony's flagship 15-screen movie and entertainment mall, opens.

2000 Pacific Bell Park, the San Francisco Giants' new 40,800-seater baseball stadium, opens.

History

From colonisation to counter-cultural revolution.

The Ohlone Age

San Francisco Bay began to take shape through the melting of the last glacial ice sheet a couple of millennia ago. The swelling waters of the Sacramento River and successive earthquakes created what we now call Northern California, giving it roughly the outline it has today. Forty-three prominent hills jostle around two sandy peninsulas that almost meet at either end of the Golden Gate, like a forefinger and thumb hooked towards each other. This natural bay protects three islands – Alcatraz, Angel and Yerba Buena.

DANCING ON THE BRINK OF THE WORLD

Until the eighteenth century, the sand-swept, fault-striped peninsulas and surrounding area had scarcely changed in thousands of years. After the Ice Age had scooped out the deep gouge of the Bay and dappled the marshes with reeds and the hilly banks with meadows, the area came to sustain more than 10,000 Northern Californian Indians of different tribes, collectively known as the Costanoans – or 'coast dwellers' – as they were later dubbed by the Spanish.

The people who inhabited the site of the future San Francisco were the Ohlone. They apparently lived in harmony both with their Miwok neighbours and the land, which provided them with rich pickings of game, fish, shellfish, fruit and nuts – a land of 'inexpressible fertility' in the words of a later French explorer.

Protected by the Bay's seeming inaccessibility, the Ohlone and their neighbours lived a successful hunter-gatherer existence – 'dancing on the brink of the world,' as an Ohlone song went – until their disastrous introduction to 'civilisation' with the arrival of Spanish missionaries. Their previous rare contacts with Europeans had been friendly and travellers had been impressed by the welcome the Costanoans gave them. But the Spanish brought with them the dubious gifts of Christianity, hard labour in the fields and diseases like smallpox, which would all but annihilate the tribes in a matter of 200 years.

The destruction of their culture has been largely ignored because the Ohlone and other tribes had no tradition of recording their history, orally or otherwise. Malcolm Margolin's *The Ohlone Way* is an attempt to trace the lost culture of Northern

The Golden Gate Bridge now spans the entrance to the bay missed by several explorers.

Californian Indians; today the only surviving traces of the Costanoans feature in the records of their colonisers and destroyers.

In search of El Dorado

Looking at the Golden Gate Bridge today, it's hard to imagine how anyone could miss the mile-wide opening into a bay that was twice as large back then as it is now. But the Bay and its Indians were hidden from view by 'stynkinge fogges' (as Drake later complained) and a lush green island.

COLONISING CALIFORNIA

An early series of Spanish missions – sent up the coast by Hernán Cortés, notorious conqueror of Mexico and the Aztecs – never got as far as Upper California. In 1542, under the flag of Cortés' successor Antonio de Mendoza, Portuguese Juan Cabrillo became the first European to visit the area. The Spanish named their new-found land El Dorado, after a mythical island in an ancient book, and hoped they would find gold there as they had done further south. Though he passed it both on his way north and back again, Cabrillo failed to discover the Bay's large natural harbour.

An Englishman got even closer, yet still managed to miss it. In 1579, during a foraging and spoiling mission in the name of the Virgin Queen, Elizabeth I, the then-unknighted Francis Drake landed in Miwok Indian territory just north of the Bay. With one ship, the *Golden Hind*, and a crew in dire need of rest and recreation, he put in for a six-week berth somewhere along the Marin coastline, probably near Point Reyes. Long before the Pilgrims landed at Plymouth Rock or the English settled Cupid's Cove at Newfoundland, Drake claimed California for Elizabeth I, naming it 'Nova Albion' or 'New Britain'.

It would take another 190 years for a white man to set eyes on the Bay. Spurred on by the pressure of British colonial ambitions in America, the Spanish sent northbound missions to stake out their own territories, intent upon converting the 'bestias' and claiming land for the Spanish crown. In 1769, the 'sacred expedition' of Gaspar de Pórtola, a Spanish aristocrat who would later become the first governor of California, and the Franciscan priest Father Junípero Serra, set off with 300 men on a gruelling march across the Mexican desert to establish a mission at San Diego. The expedition then worked its way north to Monterey, to claim it for Spain, building missions and baptising Indians as they went. During the expedition, an advance party discovered the unexpectedly wide bay 100 miles (161 kilometres) further up the coast. But since the expedition's brief was only to claim Monterey, the party returned to San Diego.

It was not until August 1775 that the *San Carlos*, a Spanish supply vessel, docked inside the Bay. Meanwhile, a mission set off to establish a safer land route to what would eventually become San Francisco.

MISSION ACCOMPLISHED

Roughly concurrent with the signing of the American Declaration of Independence, a Spanish military garrison, or presidio, was built near Fort Point to strengthen Spain's western claims. It was completed on 17 September 1776. The Mission San Francisco de Asis, named after the holy order operating in Upper California but popularly known as Mission Dolores, was established by Father Junípero Serra on 9 October 1776.

Frontiersmen & trappers

Just as elsewhere in Latin America, a combination of favouritism, authoritarianism and religious fervour helped sow the seeds of resentment and resistance in all the territories colonised by Spain. The country's hold on its American empires first began to crumble in Mexico, which declared itself a republic in 1821. The Mexican annexation of California in the same year opened up the area to foreign settlers, among them American pioneers like fur trapper Jedediah Smith, who in 1828 became the first white American to reach California over the Sierra Nevada mountain range. His feat might have been the more impressive, but the sedate arrival by whaler ship of an Englishman had a more lasting impact. Captain William Richardson, who built the first dwelling on the site of the future San Francisco in 1835, is credited with giving San Francisco its first name: Yerba Buena, named after the sweet mint the Spanish used to make tea.

That same year the United States tried unsuccessfully to buy the whole of the Bay Area from the Mexicans. In the long run, however, they got California for free: the Texan declaration of independence and its consequent annexation by the United States triggered the Mexican-American war in June 1846. The resulting Guadalupe-Hidalgo Treaty of 1848 officially granted the Union all the land from Texas to California and the Rio Grande to Oregon. But before the treaty could be nailed down, a few American hotheads decided to 'liberate' the territory from Mexico themselves.

THE BEAR FLAG REVOLT

The short-lived Mexican rule of California coincided with the era of idealistic frontiersmen like Captain John Fremont and Kit Carson. In June 1846, Fremont convinced a motley crew to take over the abandoned presidio to the north of Yerba Buena in Sonoma, proclaiming his new state the

'Bear Flag Republic' after the ragged banner he raised over Sonoma's adobe square (the design was eventually adopted as California's state flag). Fremont also christened the mouth of San Francisco Bay the 'Golden Gate', after Istanbul's Golden Horn, insisting it would one day become glorious. A few weeks after the Bear Flaggers annexed Sonoma, the US Navy captured Yerba Buena's presidio without a struggle and the whole of California became US territory.

At this point, the infant Yerba Buena was just a sleepy trading post of 800 people. On 30 January 1847, the newly appointed mayor, Lieutenant Washington A Bartlett, officially renamed it 'San Francisco'. Unbeknown to its residents, the tiny settlement was about to change beyond all recognition: something was glittering in the hills…

GOLD!

In the early 1840s, the Swiss-born John Sutter was running New Helvetia, a large ranch, where he encouraged American citizens to settle the land. One of his homesteaders was James Marshall, who built a sawmill for his landlord at Coloma, near Sacramento. Returning from the Bear Flaggers' adventure, Marshall discovered gold in the sawmill's water. Sutter and Marshall attempted to keep their findings secret, but word got out. Once the news hit town, 'boosters' – the San Francisco equivalent of town criers – and newspapers quickly spread it around the world. The 1849 Gold Rush was on.

CALIFORNIA OR BUST

The news of riches sent droves of drifters and fortune-seekers to California. Some sailed around Cape Horn in windjammers, sloops and steamships, some trekked across Panama, others crossed prairies from the east in covered wagons. Their fever was fanned by people like Sam Brannan, whose *California Star* newspaper told of men extracting fortunes within an hour and who marched down Market Street with a jar of gold dust, shouting: 'Gold! Gold!' Many potential prospectors never made it: by land, the journey meant months of exposure to blizzards, mountains, deserts and hostile Indians; by sea, they faced disease, starvation or brutal weather.

Those who did make it became known as Forty-Niners. The port town they arrived in was one without structure, government, or even a distinct name – to many it was still 'Yerba Buena'. They found hardship more than gold: on their way through San Francisco to the mines, predatory merchants fleeced them; when they returned, broke, they were left to grub mean existences from the city streets, seeking refuge in brothels, gambling dens and bars. Within a year of the Sutter discovery, 100,000 men had passed through the city, swelling the tiny community into a giant, muddy campsite. A huge fire levelled the settlement on Christmas Eve in 1849, but a new camp quickly rose up to take its place. The population leapt from 800 to 25,000.

Sonoma honours the Bear Flag Revolt.

DUCKS, HOUNDS & HOODLUMS

San Francisco at the time of the Gold Rush was not a place for the faint-hearted. Lawlessness and arson ruled; frontier justice was commonplace. Writers Mark Twain and Bret Harte and, later, visitors Robert Louis Stevenson, Oscar Wilde and Anthony Trollope all reported on its exciting, lurid reputation, describing an anarchic boom town where guns, violence, gambling and prostitution were the norm.

The opening of the post office marked the city's first optimistic stab at improving communications with the rest of the continent and the world. John White Geary, appointed postmaster by President James Knox Polk, rented a room at the corner of Montgomery and Washington Streets, where he marked out a series of squares for each letter of the alphabet and began filing letters. This crude set-up was the first postal system for San Francisco's 10,000 residents. In April 1850 – the year California became the Union's 31st state – San Francisco's city charter was approved and the city elected Geary its first mayor. In order to furnish the city with proper streets, Geary established a council, which later bought the ship *Euphemia* and turned it into San Francisco's first jail. It proved a sound investment.

The council's first concern was to impose law and order on San Francisco's massive squatter town. Gangs of hoodlums controlled certain districts: the Ducks, led by Australian convicts, lived at a spot known as Sydney Town. Together with New York toughs the Hounds, they roamed Telegraph Hill, raping and pillaging among the more orderly community of Chilean merchants who occupied 'Little Chile'. Eventually, their outrages incurred the wrath of right-minded citizens who decided to take the law into their own hands. Whipped into a fury by rabble-rousing newspaperman Sam Brannan, vigilantes lynched their first victim, John Jenkins, at a Portsmouth Square 'necktie party' in June 1851. They strung up three more thieves during the following weeks by way of warning to the other Ducks and Hounds – who wisely cut out for the Sierras.

Though their frontier justice temporarily curbed the area's excesses, Mayor Geary understandably viewed the vigilantes as part of the problem, not the solution. His crusade against lawlessness was hardly helped when riverbed gold started running dry. By 1853, boom had turned to bust and the resulting depression set a cyclical pattern oft-repeated through the city's history. By the mid-1860s, San Francisco was bankrupt.

NOBS & SNOBS

But then came the Silver Rush. Henry Comstock's 1859 discovery of a rich blue vein of silver (the 'Comstock Lode') in western Nevada triggered a second invasion by fortune-seekers. This time, though, the ore's nature demanded more elaborate methods of extraction, with high yields going to a small number of companies and tycoons rather than individual prospectors. Before the supply had been exhausted, silver barons had made enough money to transform San Francisco, establishing a quarter of *nouveaux riches* mansions atop 'Nob' (from the word 'nabob') Hill. By 1870, the city was no longer just a town of sleazy brothels.

If the nabobs on the hill took the moral and geographical high ground, those on the waterfront at the bottom of Telegraph Hill were busy legitimising their reputation as occupants of the 'Barbary Coast'. Naïve newcomers and drunken sailors were viewed as fair game by the gamblers and hoods waiting to 'shanghai' them (like hoodlum, shanghai is a San Francisco expression), as were immigrant women who found themselves trapped into a life of prostitution or slavery. At one low point, the female population numbered just 22; many a brothel madam made fortune enough to buy her way onto Nob Hill.

WIND FROM THE EAST

The seeds of San Francisco's present-day multiculturalism were sown during this period, when a deluge of immigrants providing food, goods and services poured in from all over the world. French immigrants vying with Italians for the 'best bread' vote in North Beach started baking sourdough. A young German garment maker named Levi Strauss started using rivets to strengthen the jeans he made for miners. In Chinatown, the Tong family controlled the opium dens and other rackets; another Chinese immigrant, Wah Lee, opened the city's first laundry.

Chinatown later expanded with the coming of the Transcontinental Railroad, which employed thousands of Chinese labourers at criminally low pay rates. Despite their usefulness as a cheap source of labour, however, the Chinese became the targets of racist anti-immigrant activity. Proscriptive anti-Chinese legislation would persist until 1938.

But it wasn't all work: entertainment was always high on the agenda for San Franciscans. In 1853, the city boasted five theatres and some 600 saloons and taverns serving 42,000 customers. Citizens downed seven bottles of champagne for every bottle swallowed in Boston. When Lola Montez, entertainer to European monarchs and thieves, arrived on a paddle-steamer from Panama in 1853, her 'spider dance' became an instant hit at the American Theater.

GO WEST, YOUNG MAN

San Francisco's relative isolation from the rest of the continent meant the city was hardly affected by the Civil War that devastated the American South in the early 1860s. The rest of the country seemed remote; sometimes mail took six months to arrive. Communications were slowly improving, however. Telegraph wires were gradually being strung across the continent and where the telegraph poles ran out, the Pony Express would pick up messages, relaying up to 75 dispatch riders across the West to the Pacific coast. By the mid-1860s, the telegraph had all but rendered the Pony Express obsolete and the coming of the Transcontinental Railroad provided its *coup de grâce*.

The completion of the Central Pacific Railroad in 1869 was the signal for runaway consumption in the city. The biggest spenders were the 'Big Four', a quartet of millionaires who were the powerful and influential principal investors behind the Central Pacific – Charles Crocker, Collis P Huntington, Mark Hopkins and Leland Stanford. Their eagerness to impress the West with their flamboyantly successful business practices manifested itself in the mansions they built on Nob Hill.

The Big Four were highly adept at making money for themselves and their favoured partners. They were brutally competitive, too. By 1871, 121 businessmen controlled $146 million, according to one newspaper – but others got in on their act. Four legendary Irishmen – James Flood, William O'Brien, James Fair and John W

Fires rage out of control in the devastated city, following the earthquake of 18 April 1906.

Mackay – were rough-hewn miners and barmen who'd chipped their silver fortunes from the Comstock Lode. The 'Bonanza Kings', as they were known, also had money enough to buy their way onto Nob Hill.

A Scottish-Irish banker, Billy Ralston, opened the Bank of California on Sansome Street in 1864. Partnered by a Prussian engineer called Adolph Sutro (later famous for building the first Cliff House and the Sutro Baths), the industrialist was determined to extract every last ounce of silver from Sun Mountain. Unfortunately, the precious ore ran out before he and Sutro had recouped their investment and Ralston's bank collapsed. Smiling to the last in an effort to calm his investors, Ralston was later found drowned. He left behind the luxurious Palace Hotel and a lasting contribution towards San Francisco's new civic pride – Golden Gate Park. Ralston's company provided the water for designer William Hammon Hall's audacious project, which transformed 1,013 acres of city sand dunes into a magnificent expanse of trees, plants, flowers and lakes.

The Great Quake strikes

The city continued to grow, and by 1900 its population had reached more than a third of a million, making it the ninth largest city in the Union. But on 18 April 1906, shortly after 5am, dogs began howling and horses whinnying – noises, along with glasses tinkling and windows rattling, that marked the tense and unnerving moments before an earthquake.

WHOSE FAULT?

The quake hit: a rending in the tectonic plates 25 miles (40 kilometres) beneath the ocean bed that triggered the shifting of billions of tons of rock, generating more energy than all the explosives used in World War II. The rip snaked inland, tearing a gash now known as the San Andreas Fault down the coastline. Cliffs appeared from nowhere, cracks yawned, ancient redwoods toppled and the dome of the 29-year-old City Hall collapsed like a soufflé. Streets began to undulate and church bells pealed crazily. A second tremor struck, ripping the walls out of buildings. A ghastly pause followed, then people ran into the streets, in their nightgowns and pyjamas.

Tragically, one of the earthquake's many victims was a man the city badly needed just then: Fire Chief Dennis Sullivan, who was not long back from fighting a cannery fire when the earthquake struck. He was found in the rubble of the fire-house and died some days later. The fire brigade seemed lost without him. The second tremor had destroyed the city alarms and disrupted the water pipes feeding the fire hydrants, leaving the famous fire-fighters of the West absolutely helpless.

The fire that followed compounded the disaster of the earthquake. It spread until Mayor Eugene Schmitz and General Frederick Funston were forced to carry out a desperate plan to blow up the houses along Van Ness Avenue and create a fire-break. The mansions belonged to rich folk that any politician would be loathe to alienate; in this instance, however, necessity spoke louder than money.

Bridging the Bay in the 1930s.

RISING FROM THE ASHES

The earthquake and 74-hour inferno was initially thought to have accounted for some 700 dead, though military records now reveal that the figure probably ran into several thousand. Those suspected of looting were shot dead in the chaos that followed the quake and fire. Three-quarters of a million people were left homeless and 3,000 acres of buildings were destroyed. On the third day the wind changed direction and brought rain, and by 21 April the fire was out.

Yet even before the ashes had time to cool, the citizens set about rebuilding their city and within ten years San Francisco had risen, phoenix-like, from the ashes. Some claimed that in the rush to rebuild, city planners passed up the chance to replace its grid street system with a more sensible one that followed the area's natural contours. But there's no doubt that San Francisco was reborn as a cleaner, more attractive city – one that, within three years of the fire, could boast half of the United States' concrete and steel buildings. Such statistical pride was not out of keeping with the 'boosterism' that accelerated its post-gold rush growth from tiny settlement to the large, anarchic and exciting city ready to meet the twentieth century.

Building bridges

The San Franciscans set about rebuilding their city with a vengeance. The most potent symbol of their restored civic pride was the new City Hall, whose construction was secured by an $8 million city bond. By the time it was completed in 1915, City Hall rose some five metres (16 feet) higher than its model – the Capitol building in Washington, DC.

Between 1913 and 1915, two new waterways opened which proved crucial to California's economic vitality. In 1913, the Los Angeles aqueduct was completed, beginning the transformation of a sleepy Southern California cowtown into the urban sprawl of modern LA. In 1915, the Panama Canal's opening considerably shortened shipping times between the Atlantic and Pacific coasts; San Francisco celebrated this achievement by hosting the Panama-Pacific Exposition.

Not even the outbreak of World War I in Europe could dampen the city's spirits. On the contrary, the war provided a boost to California's mining and manufacturing industries. But, as elsewhere in America, the good times were quickly swallowed up in the world depression signalled by the Wall Street Crash of 1929.

BLOODY THURSDAY

The Depression brought to an end the economic well-being of the 1920s. It hit San Francisco port especially badly – three-quarters of the workforce was laid off. On 9 May 1934, under the leadership of Harry Bridges, the International Longshoremen's Association declared a coast-wide strike. Other unions, including the powerful Teamsters, came out in sympathy, shutting down work in the Bay for three months. A crew of blackleg workers managed to break the picket on 5 July – Bloody Thursday – but with disastrous results. As violence escalated, police opened fire, killing two strikers and wounding 30. A general strike was called for 14 July, when 150,000 people stopped work and brought San Francisco to a standstill for three days. The strike fizzled out when its leaders couldn't agree on how to end the stalemate, but the action wasn't completely futile: the longshoremen won a wage increase and more control in the hiring halls.

BRIDGING THE BAY

Despite this black chapter in the city's labour relations, San Francisco managed an extraordinary amount of construction. In 1932, the Opera House was completed; in 1933, the island of Alcatraz was transferred from the army to the Federal Bureau of Prisons, which set about building a high-security lock-up for 'incorrigible' convicts.

The decade's two other landmark constructions were the San Francisco-Oakland Bay and Golden Gate bridges. The former, completed in 1936, constituted two back-to-back suspension bridges connected by a tunnel through Yerba Buena Island. Six months after the Bay Bridge was finished, the russet-orange Golden Gate Bridge began to rise from the Bay with its revolutionary suspension design. The bridges' impact on ferry traffic that had served the city and its suburbs so well was devastating and commuter trains also suffered – at least until the completion of the Bay Area Rapid Transit (BART) subway system in 1972.

To celebrate the new era ushered in by the opening of bridges, the city hosted another fair in 1939, on landfill off Yerba Buena Island. The Treasure Island Golden Gate International Exposition was described as a 'pageant of the Pacific'; those who went were dubbed the Thirty-Niners by local wits. It was to be San Francisco's last big celebration for a while: in 1941 the Japanese attacked Pearl Harbor and America entered World War II.

THE FORTUNES OF WAR

World War II changed the city almost as much as the Gold Rush or the Great Quake. More than a million-and-a-half men and thousands of tons of material were shipped out to the Pacific from the Presidio, Travis Air Force Base and Treasure Island. Between 1941 and 1945, almost the entire Pacific war effort passed under the Golden Gate. Oakland's shipyard workers worked overtime and the massed ranks of troops and some half a million wartime civilian workers flooding San Francisco turned the city into a milling party town hell-bent on sending its boys into battle with smiles on their faces.

Towards the end of the war in Europe, in April 1945, representatives of 50 nations met at the San Francisco Opera House to draft the United Nations Charter. It was eventually signed on 26 June 1945 and formally ratified in October at the General Organisation of the United Nations in London. Many people felt – and still do – that San Francisco was the ideal location for its headquarters, but the British and French thought it was too far to travel and – much to the city's disappointment – the UN moved to New York.

From the Beats to the present

Just as San Francisco during the war was characterised by mass troop mobilisation, the immediate post-war period was coloured by the return of the demobilised GIs. One was poet Lawrence Ferlinghetti, who, while studying at the Sorbonne on a GI scholarship in the early 1950s, discovered Penguin paperbacks and was inspired to open his tiny, wedge-shaped bookshop at 261 Columbus Avenue. Called City Lights, it became a mecca for the bohemians later dubbed the Beat Generation, many of whose works he published in the City Lights Pocket Poets series.

BEAT BUT NOT BEATEN

The Beat Generation, so named by novelist Jack Kerouac, reflected the angst and ambition of a post-war generation attempting to escape both the shadow of the Bomb and the rampant consumerism of ultra-conformist 1950s America. In Kerouac's definition, Beat could stand for beatific or being beat – exhausted. The condition is best explained in his novel *On the Road*, which charts the coast-to-coast odysseys of San Francisco-based Beat saint Neal Cassady (thinly disguised as Dean Moriarty), poet Allen Ginsberg and Kerouac himself (named Sal Paradise).

'The emergence of the Beat Generation made North Beach the literary centre of San Francisco and nurtured a new vision that would spread far beyond its bounds,' reflected Lawrence Ferlinghetti, 40 years on. 'The Beats prefigured the New Left evolution and the impulse for change that swept eastward from San Francisco.' The attention of the world might have been on the beret-clad artists and poets populating North Beach cafés (*see chapter* **Literary San Francisco**), but an event in Anaheim, 500 miles (800 kilometres) south was perhaps more truly reflective of mainstream America: Disney's first theme park, Disneyland, opened in 1955.

SUMMER OF LOVE & HAIGHT

Kerouac, Ginsberg and mass media exposure established the Bay Area as a centre for the burgeoning counter-culture, renewing mainstream American suspicions that San Francisco was the fruit and nut capital of the US. Their fears were about to be confirmed by the hippie explosion of the 1960s.

The Beats and the hippies might have shared a love of marijuana and a common distaste for 'the system', but the Beats sometimes mocked their juniors as part-time bohemians. For his part, Kerouac – by now an embittered alcoholic – abhorred what he perceived as the hippies' anti-Americanism. His distaste for these new bohemians was shared by John Steinbeck, winner of the Nobel Prize for Literature in 1964, who shied away from the recognition he was receiving in the streets.

Where the original Beats were never interested in political action, the newer generation were prepared to embrace it full on. A sit-in protest against

You had to be there: 1967's Summer of Love gets going in Golden Gate Park.

a closed session of the House of Representatives Un-American Activities Committee (HUAC) at the City Hall in 1961 drew ranks of protesters from San Francisco State University and the University of California's Berkeley campus. It quickly degenerated into a riot, establishing a pattern of protest and police response to come. In the following years, the civil rights movement and America's involvement in the Vietnam War added urgency to the voices of dissent; Berkeley students were at the forefront of protests on campuses around the country. By the mid-1960s, the counter-culture was split between the politically conscious students behind the free speech movement and the hippies who'd chosen to opt out of the system altogether.

The availability of LSD, its popularity boosted in San Francisco by such events as the Human Be-in organised by Allen Ginsberg in 1967 and the Acid Tests overseen by Owsley Stanley and the Grateful Dead, drew an estimated 8,000 hippies from across America. Some 5,000 stayed, occupying the cheap Victorian houses around the Haight-Ashbury district (later dubbed 'the Hashbury') not far from Golden Gate Park. The combination of San Francisco's *laissez-faire* attitude, sun, drugs and the acid-induced psychedelic music explosion gave rise to the famous Summer of Love that same year. By 1968, however, the spread of hard drugs, notably heroin, had taken much of the shine off the hippie movement.

THE BLACK PANTHERS & THE PUBLISHER'S DAUGHTER

Like its drugs, the city's politics were getting harder, too. Members of the Black Panther movement, a radical black organisation founded across the Bay in Oakland by Huey Newton and Bobby Seale, asked themselves why they should ship out to shoot the Vietnamese when the real enemy was at home. Around Oakland, the Panthers took to exercising the American right to bear arms; gunfights inevitably followed. In April 1968, Panther leader Eldridge Cleaver was wounded and 17-year-old Bobby Hutton was killed in a shoot-out with Oakland police. By the early 1970s, the Black Panther movement had petered out, its leaders either dead, imprisoned or, like Cleaver, on the run. The 1997 release of Panther Elmer 'Geronimo' Pratt heralded a re-examination of some of the Panthers' alleged crimes.

The kidnapping of Patty Hearst, heir to the newspaper fortune, by the Symbionese Liberation Army in 1974 was perhaps the point at which the 1960s revolution turned into deadly farce. When she was eventually captured along with the other members of the tiny radical outfit, Hearst had apparently been brainwashed into joining its cause.

Despite the violence that characterised the student and anti-war protests, black radicalism and failed revolutions, the enduring memory of 1960s' San Francisco is as the host city to the Summer of Love. The psychedelic blasts of the Grateful Dead, Big Brother and the Holding Company, Janis Joplin, Country Joe and the Fish, Jefferson Airplane and Quicksilver Messenger Service defined both the San Francisco sound and counter-cultural attitude. Jann Wenner founded *Rolling Stone* magazine in 1967 to explain and advance the cause, and later document its growth into a multi-million dollar mass entertainment industry, helping to invent New Journalism in the process.

HARVEY MILK & THE RISE OF GAY RADICALISM

San Francisco's radical baton was taken up in the 1970s by the gay liberation movement. Local activists insisted that gay traditions had always existed in San Francisco, first among the Ohlone Indians and later during the 1849 Gold Rush, when women in the West were more scarce than gold. Early homophile groups like the Daughters of Billets, the Matching Society and the Society for Individual Rights (SIR) had paved the way for more radical political movements in the 1970s. In 1977, gay activists made successful forays into mainstream politics: SIR's Jim Foster became the first openly gay delegate at a Democratic Convention and Harvey Milk was elected onto the city's Board of Supervisors.

Then, on 28 November 1978, Dan White entered City Hall and shot and killed Milk and Mayor George Moscone. White was a former policeman from a working-class background, who had run for supervisor as an angry, young, blue-collar populist – and won. But he suffered poor mental health and had to resign under the strain of office. He quickly changed his mind and asked Mayor Moscow to reinstate him. Milk, who held the deciding vote, persuaded the Mayor not to let the unstable White back in – with catastrophic consequences. White turned himself in after the killings; in the poorly prosecuted court case, the jury returned two verdicts of voluntary manslaughter and White was sentenced to seven years.

Just as the killings had stunned San Francisco, so the verdict outraged its gay populace, who responded by storming City Hall and hurling rocks through the windows. The disturbance escalated into a full-blown battle, known as the White Night Riot. White's sentence prompted one journalist to wonder why the jury had not posthumously convicted Harvey Milk of 'unlawful interference with a bullet fired from the gun of a former police officer'. Dan White committed suicide not long after his release from prison.

POSITIVE OUTLOOK

Gay life and politics changed radically and irrevocably with the onset of the HIV virus, which tore the gay community apart and caused controversy when the bath houses (long a symbol of gay liberation and promiscuity) were closed in panic over the disease's spread. Gay radicals branded writer Randy Shilts a 'fascist Nazi, traitor and homophobe' when he ran a story in the *San Francisco Chronicle* criticising bath house owners who refused to post safe sex warnings.

Since its identification, some 18,000 San Franciscans have died of Aids. Although the levelling in the numbers of new cases in the gay community and the dangerous misperception that the epidemic is ebbing have endangered fundraising efforts of late, the city remains home to the most efficient volunteers in the country. Medical preventionists continue to make inroads into all sexually active communities; caretakers have taken charge of housing, food and legal problems for the many thousands of people – about two per cent of the city – diagnosed as HIV-positive. Hospices, support agencies, hotlines, even pet services are available to those living with HIV. As sufferers are living longer thanks to new drug treatments, the city continues to need more resources and money to assist them.

STRIKE TWO

Because of its location on the San Andreas Fault, San Francisco has always lived in anticipation of a major earthquake to rival the 1906 disaster. One came in October 1989, interrupting the first game of the World Series between the Oakland Athletics and the San Francisco Giants baseball teams. The Loma Prieta earthquake (named after the ridge of mountains at its epicentre) registered 7.1 on the Richter Scale. Damage was extensive: a section of the West Oakland Freeway collapsed, crushing drivers beneath; the Marina district and Bay Bridge were hit hard; and buildings in the region suffered billions of dollars worth of damage.

BACK TO THE FUTURE

As it enters the twenty-first century, San Francisco reflects many of the social problems that plague major US cities in the wake of economic cutbacks exercised by the conservative federal administrations of the 1980s. Homelessness is particularly severe in the city. Up to 14,000 destitute men and women sleep without nightly shelter, overwhelming the underfunded agencies set up to help them. Those who have shelter are doubly lucky: available housing is at one per cent – an all-time low – and landlords are raising rents sky-high. Traditionally ethnic neighbourhoods are being gentrified and traffic snarls much of the city much of the time (though plans to rebuild the Central Freeway, torn down after the 1989 quake, remain in the works).

On the whole, however, the city continues to offer the best advantages of a modern municipality. It remains a magnet for the world's migrants: Asian, Hispanic, Western and East European immigrants, as well as countless Americans dreaming of a better life. Silicon Valley's economic boom has rejuvenated the city's business structure and the healthy economy has encouraged several ambitious building projects. And the city maintains its best-of-the-West-Coast reputation for magnificent food, stylish design, charming architecture and a diverse, idea-driven population. Multicultural San Francisco continues to function as a crucible for new trends and influences as it looks forward to another millennium of 'dancing on the brink of the world'.

San Francisco Today

San Francisco is challenging its liberal history as it undergoes the transformation into a whiter, richer city.

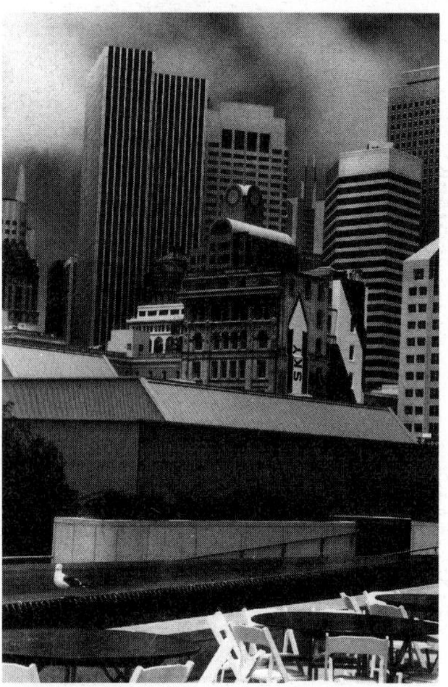

The changing **Yerba Buena** *skyline.*

As it has done now for more than 150 years, San Francisco represents an odd set of contradictions. Savvy and urbane in many ways, it is naïve and unpolished in others. At the dawn of the millennium, liberal politics remain at the heart of City Hall, with each mayor wrestling to establish his or her own legacy. Art Agnos, who succeeded the popular Dianne Feinstein in 1987, found himself saddled with the task of restoring the city's lustre and confidence in the wake of the 1989 earthquake. Frank Jordan is best remembered as the moderate conservative who did little of anything during his term. In 1995 Jordan lost to Willie Brown Jr, a longtime politico squeezed from his machiavellian post as Speaker of the California State Assembly by term limit laws.

NOT-SO-SLICK WILLIE

The city had a lot of hope vested in Brown, a local-boy-made-good who rode into office on promises to fix the ailing transport system, help the homeless and re-instill a sense that City Hall be accountable to locals' needs. Willie won by a landslide, with solid support from the African-American and gay communities and many old-money patrons as well. Brown's old-school political manoeuvring, it was anticipated, would set the city on a clear course into the 2000s.

Suffice it to say, this hasn't happened. It's true that San Francisco has much improved in the years since Brown's election, but little of it has to do with 'Da Mayor'. Rather, the city's renewed sense of optimism has more to do with money (and San Francisco can thank Silicon Valley and a booming national economy for that), than with any improvements to the local infrastructure. Using influence and favouritism, Brown has bullied several expensive pet projects into being – a pair of new sports stadiums and the civilian expansion of Treasure Island are but three – and allowed countless real estate developments, while sloughing off promises to make the existing city infrastructure work better.

Willie's not all bad, however. He's a vocal advocate for students, labourers and the city's gay and lesbian population and, as the city's first African-American mayor, has given minorities a strong voice in local government. He's audacious, obnoxious and snappily-dressed. But to anticipate a groundswell of support for his re-election is optimistic to say the least. As this edition of the guide went to press, no strong candidate had yet emerged to challenge him.

Other members of the Board of Supervisors, the city's legislative body, have career aspirations of their own. Gavin Newsom, a young, savvy businessman with a progressive streak, has his eye on a future national office; Tom Ammiano, a former comedian, has solid support from gay and lesbian constituencies and may one day make his own bid for the Mayor's office.

As we went to press, the Mayoral election had become something of a joke: running against

Recent SoMa developments include the arts and technology museum, **Zeum**.

Mayor Brown was former Mayor Frank Jordan and Clint Reilly, a brassy political consultant who has never before held public office. Neither appear likely to beat King Willie. Barring a massive gaffe on Brown's part in the few weeks before the election, he'll still be on his throne for the next four years of the new millennium.

BUILD IT & THEY WILL COME

Whoever it is, the city's first mayor of the twenty-first century will have his or her hands full. On the one hand, San Francisco is a dream ticket worth inheriting: the city is enjoying its healthiest economy in decades, fed by the booming computer industry nearby and year after year of record tourist spending. Crime is down and scores of new buildings are going up. New projects include expansions in and around the Moscone Convention Center and the Yerba Buena Gardens – the dazzling new Metreon, Zeum and the W Hotel – as well as the renovation of City Hall and the US Court of Appeals building. The opening of the new Pacific Bell Park, relocation of the Jewish, Asian and Mexican museums, a seismic upgrade of the MH de Young Museum, the opening of the resurrected 3Com Park stadium and the expansion of the San Francisco International Airport – all are on the drawing board for the early 2000s (*see chapters* **Sightseeing**, **Shops & Services**, **Accommodation**, **Museums & Galleries** and **Sport & Fitness** for more details). Make no mistake about it: the rumble of the 1989 earthquake has been drowned out, more than a decade later, by a building boom.

Other expansive plans for the future are less coherent. The graceful return of the Presidio – run by the military for the last 200 years – to civilian control continues to stymie local officials. There are indications that George Lucas' Lucasfilm Ltd will soon lease the lion's share of the area; the cinema giant already has the lease of Letterman Hospital, a veterans' facility at the edge of the property. But the rest of the land was, as we went to press, up for grabs. The same is the case for Treasure Island, a prime piece of real estate in the middle of the Bay, over which developers, National Park officials and lobbyists for the homeless are squabbling.

As a result of this, San Francisco real estate is incredibly valuable. Since the early 1990s, housing prices have soared, counterbalanced by a plunge in available residential space. One per cent of city property is vacant, the lowest rate in its history. Although most rents are controlled for those with leases, new renters are beginning to find the price of housing nearly comparable to that in New York City – and frequently a queue of 50 other tenants competing to pay it.

The housing market is unreal: renters line up for bare-minimum flats in shabby neighbourhoods or are forced to share with room-mates, all of whom are professionals. Most home buyers find they have to bid for properties and the sellers often fetch tens of thousands of dollars above their original asking price. Peripheral regions – north in

Marin County and south in San Mateo and Santa Cruz Counties in particular – are no longer forested, inexpensive escapes, but rather bedroom communities for the city and Silicon Valley.

THE LOFT GENERATION

The loft phenomenon goes hand-in-hand with the gentrification taking place in the Mission, Potrero Hill, South of Market and Bernal Heights neighbourhoods. Once solidly working class, these districts are now undergoing rampant development – 'yuppification' is perhaps the kindest word used. Lofts, condominiums and 'live-work' spaces have sprung up overnight like mushrooms and the new homeowners are for the most part young, WASP professionals with jobs in multimedia, high-tech or tech-related commerce. Their arrival, often behind the wheel of a huge sport utility vehicle or late-model sports car, is driving the original residents of the neighbourhoods – artists, ethnic minorities and the poor – further out. Such is gentrification's motif; but in a celebratedly diverse city like San Francisco, the long-term benefits of such up-market homogeneity are questionable.

In the face of such demographic change, other concerns seem minimal. Heavy traffic continues to be a major problem in the city, exacerbated by the earthquake damage-related demolition of several major viaducts. Finding a parking space can still range from frustrating to impossible. A simple hop across town may constitute an hour stuck in traffic. Inconceivably, some major building projects – the Metreon for one – have been approved without providing parking for their patrons, thus contributing to the problem.

MORE MODERN AILMENTS

The public transport alternative, of course, is Muni, incorporating the city's well-worn fleet of buses, trolleys, streetcars and cable cars. Muni has its own problems: vehicles break down, drivers can be surly and service is reliably unreliable. But the combined system goes almost everywhere, and you'll arrive at your destination less stressed and more in touch – sometimes literally – with the city's residents. Stash a few dollar bills in your pocket for the fare and allow plenty of time.

On the Bay itself, the authorities have plans to beef up the ferry service in an attempt to accommodate the 275,000 commuters who arrive daily. Efforts are being hampered, however, by environmental activists who argue that this will add to pollution levels in the already fragile San Francisco Bay, where fish and shellfish populations were recently reported to contain dangerous levels of toxins.

In the city, homelessness also remains a serious problem. For the gay community, the Aids epidemic continues apace and although new drug treatments mean patients are living longer, they also require additional funding at a time when charities are facing budget cuts. Donations have declined, partly because the (misinformed) word on the street is that the Aids crisis is over.

THE CITY THAT KNOWS HOW

But don't think for a minute that San Francisco doesn't have the wherewithal to counter many of its concerns. Like much of the rest of the US, San Francisco is currently enjoying economic flushness – something of an anomaly when one considers its estimated 14,000 homeless residents. Nonetheless, banking and computer industries remain strong and the service industries are basking in the influx of consumer spending. Tourism – the city's number one business, brings about $5.1 billion in spending into the city annually; business conventions large and small are scheduled far into the next century. And dozens of major corporations – BankAmerica, Intel, Apple, Hewlett-Packard, Sun, Gap, Pacific Telesis, Levi Strauss – oversee their trade from headquarters in or near San Francisco.

A 1993 study placed San Francisco as the top-ranked metropolitan area in the US for per capita personal income. Most of its residents are well-educated and many are very wealthy – sometimes ostentatiously so in the face of outlying poverty. But such wealth comes with benefits for the traveller, among them prime accommodation and countless spending opportunities.

For the foodie, the city's 3,000 or so restaurants offer all kinds of culinary adventures and the proximity of the Wine Country means diners can enjoy a wide selection of award-winning varietals at the same time. Many are lured to the city by the arts: the Opera House, Symphony Hall and the museums are always crowded; the Main Library is a showpiece of 1990s architecture and a hospitable public space. Golden Gate Park is safe and quiet and, in its more remote corners, still offers a pastoral escape.

Like the boom times of the Gold Rush era, San Francisco knows how to enjoy itself, a proud city which wears its chequered past and controversial image as a badge of honour. Thousands of people still move to the city every month to start bands, go to school, come out of the closet, follow a dream, start an Internet company or lead a tiny revolution.

The Costanoans were correct in assessing the sheltering peninsula that became San Francisco as a place of natural bounty and dynamic beauty. It's fitting that centuries before a white settler ever dreamed of the region it already had a reputation as a place to dance – a community balanced perpetually on the brink. Of its future, only two things about the city are certain: that its fortunes are cyclical and that sometime soon, literally and metaphorically, the ground beneath San Francisco will shake again.

San Francisco by numbers

Official city population	**789,600**
Population of the nine Bay Area counties	**6.9 million**
Estimated gay and lesbian population of the city	**200,000**
Workforce with college or professional degrees	**54 per cent**
Estimated homeless population	**14,000**
Area of San Francisco	**46.38 square miles**
Number of San Franciscans per square mile (extrapolated), making the city the second densest in the US after New York City	**17,024.6**
Area of shoreline	**29.5 miles**
Approximate number of visitors each year	**16 million**
Number of passengers a year at San Francisco International Airport	**40 million**
Number of licensed taxis	**961**
Annual economic impact of the arts industry in San Francisco	**$150 million**
Cost of renovating City Hall, re-opened in 1999	**$300 million**
Cable car riders a year	**9,600,000**
Different fog signals transmitted around the Bay	**26**
Historical landmarks within the city limits	**215**
Total annual visitors to Alcatraz	**1,200,000**
Number of Victorian houses	**14,000**
Total length of the Golden Gate Bridge, including approaches	**8,981ft**
Gallons of paint used annually to paint the Golden Gate Bridge (the official colour is International Orange)	**5,000**
Earthquakes over magnitude 6.0 in the Bay Area over last 160 years (an average of one every seven years)	**22**
Possibility of the Bay Area experiencing an earthquake of 6.7 before 2020	**67 per cent**

Architecture

Tracing the history of the city's skyline – from painted ladies to pyramids and jukeboxes.

The **Haas-Lilienthal House**. *See page 19.*

Rather than being a handicap, San Francisco's spectacular topography – a series of dramatic hills framed by the Bay's surrounding waterscape – poses challenges that entice architects to it and inspires some of their best designs.

Since they erected its first buildings, San Franciscans have fought to save the city from sand dunes, fires, earthquakes and the visually banal. They struggle on with mixed results. A series of bonds passed by voters recently improved western Market Street and the southern stretch of the Embarcadero, which now boast palm trees and restored Muni trolley tracks. For pedestrians, the completion of the Embarcadero Promenade, which encompasses the city's scenic eastern side with a beautiful, glass brick-framed footpath, was a welcome addition. And by and large, San Francisco's resolute avoidance of 'Manhattanisation' – the unwillingness to build concrete boxes a mile high – is helped by the threat of earthquakes and the diligence of conservation lobbies.

For more information on the major venues mentioned below, *see chapter* **Sightseeing**.

EARLY ARCHITECTURE

The oldest building in the city is the **Mission Dolores** (Dolores Street, at 16th Street), whose thick adobe walls and painted hammer beams represent the early European settlement of Yerba Buena. Founded in 1776, the simple chapel sits north of a cemetery where Indians, outlaws and the city's first Irish and Hispanic mayors are buried. Mission Dolores was one of 21 missions built in California by the Spanish; only two others, at Carmel and Monterey, rival it for authentic atmosphere (*see chapter* **Trips Out of Town**). Together with a portion of the original walls of the Officers' Club in the Presidio, Mission Dolores is the only piece of colonial architecture to have outlived the city's steep progress from hamlet to metropolis.

The town inhabited by the Forty-Niners or 'Argonauts', as the Gold Rush immigrants were called, suffered a series of fires. Tiny **Portsmouth Square** (in present-day Chinatown) marked the heart of the early outpost, but was razed by two blazes; the surrounding streets all perished in the fire that followed the 1906 earthquake. The best examples of buildings surviving from the Gold Rush era are preserved in the **Jackson Square Historical District** (best viewed on Jackson between Mont-gomery and Sansome Streets) and now serve as design showrooms, law offices and antique shops.

THE PAINTED LADIES

A sudden burst of nineteenth-century prosperity quickly filled San Francisco's once-empty sloping streets with what have become its signature Victorian terraced houses. Built by middle-class tradesmen in the Mission and Lower Haight districts and by rich merchants in Presidio Heights and around Alamo Square, these famous 'Painted Ladies' provide San Francisco's most distinctive architectural face. One of the most popular views of the city framed by a row of six painted 'Victorians' is along **Steiner Street** between Hayes and Grove Streets; although these are the most-photographed examples, there are over 14,000 other, equally charming, versions of the city's architectural vernacular to rival them in ornamentation.

Built of wooden frames decorated with mass-produced ornamentation, San Francisco Victorians come in four distinct styles. The earliest Gothic

San Francisco's characteristic wood-framed 'Victorians', each one different to the next.

Revival houses feature pointed arches over their windows and were often painted white, rather than the bright colours of the later styles. The later Italianate style, with tall cornices, neo-classical elements and add-on porches, are best exemplified in the Lower Haight, notably on **Grove Street** near Webster Street. Other examples can be found at **1900 Sacramento Street** (near Lafayette Park) and at the **Lilienthal-Pratt House**, built in 1876 at 1818 California Street.

The Italianate was succeeded by the Stick-Eastlake style, named after furniture designer Charles Eastlake and characterised by square bay windows framed with angular, carved ornamentation. The 'Sticks' are the most common among Victorian houses left in the city; a shining example is the over-the-top extravaganza at **1057 Steiner Street**, on the corner of Golden Gate Avenue.

Finally, with its turrets, towers and curvaceous corner bay windows, the so-called Queen Anne style is amply demonstrated by the **Wormser-Coleman House** in Pacific Heights (1834 California Street, at Franklin Street). Fans of this more ornate Victorian style will find no more extravagant example than the **Haas-Lilienthal House** (2007 Franklin Street, near Washington Street), built in 1886 by Bavarian grocer William Haas. He treated himself to a home with 28 rooms and six bathrooms – one of which features a bidet, a Victorian Gothic shower head and a gas jet used for heating curling tongs. The house has been turned into a museum and is one of the few Victorians open to the public.

HOTELS & MANSIONS

Another example of the ostentation that was part and parcel of San Francisco's booming late nineteenth-century lifestyle can be seen at the **Sheraton Palace Hotel** (at Market and New Montgomery Streets, *see page 104* **Accommodation**), whose guests have included everyone from Rudyard Kipling to visiting European royalty. Opened in 1875, it epitomised local entrepreneur Billy Ralston's dreams – and his inability to resist Italian marble and solid gold dinner services, still on display in the lobby. San Franciscans mourned the original building after it burned down in the Great Fire of 1906, but the city rebuilt it, glassing in the atrium for elegant dining and adding fashionable Art Deco murals in the bar. Painstakingly and splendidly restored, the Sheraton remains a wonderful time-tunnel to the past, combining echoes of Old Vienna and a Prohibition era speakeasy.

Engineer Adolph Sutro was Ralston's friend and equal in ambition, buying a sandy wasteland on San Francisco's westernmost edge in 1881 for his **Sutro Baths**. Annexed by the new Golden Gate Park, Sutro's therapeutic baths were the most elaborate in the western world. Much in need of repair by the 1960s and badly burned in a fire, Sutro Baths were sold to developers for high-rise apartments that were never built. For its part, the adjoining **Cliff House** hotel and saloon burned to the ground twice: the rebuilt eight-storey 'castle' destroyed in 1907 is now open to the public as an unremarkable bar and restaurant (*see chapter*

Bars). It offers spectacular views of Seal Rocks and the Pacific Ocean, however, and plans are underway to restore it to its original grandeur. West of the Cliff House stand a camera obscura and Musée Mécanique, the latter containing a collection of vintage mechanical games. Situated on land earmarked for the Cliff House's restoration, their future remains uncertain.

Closer to the downtown area, San Francisco's 'Big Four' businessmen – Mark Hopkins, Leland Stanford, Collis P Huntington and Charles Crocker – made their architectural mark in the late nineteenth century by building substantial edifices. Their mining investments funded railroads and public transport, banks and businesses, and their baronial mansions on Nob Hill, victims of the 1906 fire, now mark the sites for some of the city's best luxury hotels. These include the **Mark Hopkins Inter-Continental Hotel** (1 Nob Hill, at California and Mason Streets) and the **Stouffer Stanford Court Hotel** (905 California Street).

The Crocker Mansion, a Queen Anne manor built in 1888, filled half the block now occupied by **Grace Cathedral** (between Taylor, Jones, California and Sacramento Streets). One surviving house that has not been turned into a hotel is the **Spreckels Mansion** (2080 Washington Street), an impressive Beaux Arts building occupying an entire block. It was built in 1912 for sugar baron Adolph Spreckels and is now owned by mega-selling novelist Danielle Steel and is not open to the public.

The **Main Library**. *See page 21.*

OODLES OF ODDITIES

The city has more than its share of architectural curiosities, among them the **Columbarium** (1 Loraine Court, off Anza Street). Built in 1898, this neo-classical temple holds the ashes of thousands of San Franciscans and is decorated with mosaic tiling and elaborate urns in imaginatively bedecked niches – a china football and photo of Candlestick Stadium fill one, doll's furniture another.

Oriental promise meets occidental vulgarity at the **Vedanta Temple** (2963 Webster Street), an eccentricity built in 1905 for the Hindu Vedanta Society. Its bizarre mix of architectural styles includes a Russian Orthodox onion-shaped dome, a Hindu cupola, castle-like crenellations and Moorish arches. It is open to the public for Friday night services.

You can also visit the **Octagon House** at 2645 Gough Street, near Union Street. Built in 1861, when the latest craze dictated that an eight-sided building was better for one's health, the house is one of just two octagon-shaped buildings left in the city. Furnished in early colonial style with Chippendale and Hepplewhite furniture, the upper floors have been restored to their original state with a central staircase leading to a domed skylight.

CIVIC STRUCTURES

When the growing city began to burst at its peninsular seams, a ferry network evolved to carry passengers to and from the Bay Area cities. In 1896, the Embarcadero **Ferry Building** was built as a centrepiece, its clock-tower inspired by the Moorish campanile of Seville Cathedral.

After the earthquake, a passion for engineering spurred an interest in Chicago architect Daniel Burnham's City Beautiful project. This proposed a heroic new Civic Center planted below a terraced Telegraph Hill, enlaced with tree-lined boulevards that traced the city's contours. The plan was the result of Burnham's two-year consultations with leading city architects Bernard Maybeck and Willis Polk and countered the city's impractical grid street pattern – but it never came to fruition.

Under Mayor 'Sunny Jim' Rolph, the main thrust of the 1915 **Civic Center** complex came from public contests, many won by Arthur Brown, architect of the mighty-domed **City Hall** (200 Polk Street, at Van Ness Avenue). Other Civic Center buildings erected at this time include the former **Main Library** (soon to be the Asian Art Museum, at 190 Larkin Street at McAllister Street), the **War Memorial Opera House** (301 Van Ness Avenue) and the **Bill Graham Civic Auditorium** (99 Grove Street). All reflect the imperial style named after the Ecole des Beaux Arts in Paris and sometimes described as French Renaissance or Classical Baroque. The buildings were distinguished by their grandiose proportions and their ornamentation, as well as their theatrical halls and stairways.

It was largely Rolph's idea to host the huge Panama-Pacific Exposition in 1915, for which he commissioned Bernard Maybeck to build the **Palace of Fine Arts** and its myriad pavilions. Originally made of wood and plaster, the Palace (3601 Lyon Street, just east of the Presidio) is the only building that remains from the Exposition (it was rebuilt of reinforced concrete in the 1960s). At around the same time, Julia Morgan, another Arts and Crafts architect, was at work on much of the East Bay and on the extravagant Hearst Castle – home of San Francisco newspaper magnate William Randolph Hearst – located 322 kilometres (200 miles) south along the coast at San Simeon.

Passionate rebuilding continued during the Depression, resulting in the opening of the **San Francisco-Oakland Bay Bridge** (1936), **Golden Gate Bridge** (1937) and a slew of Works Project Administration buildings such as the **Coit Tower** and **Alcatraz** island prison. The WPA, introduced as part of President Roosevelt's New Deal job-creation scheme, had a hand in everything from murals by Mexican artist Diego Rivera to the organisation of community archives. The best examples of projects from this period include the 1932 **Herbst Theater** with its murals by Frank Brangwyn (inside the Veteran's Building at 401 Van Ness Avenue), the 1930 **Pacific Coast Stock Exchange** with its Rivera mural (301 Pine Street) and the **Rincon Annex Post Office Building** (now part of the Rincon Center on Spear Street). The Rincon, built in 1940 to include Anton Refregier's murals of Californian history, is a wonderful example of steel-trimmed marble.

The only Frank Lloyd Wright building in the city is the oval-entranced, red brick **Folk Art International** at 140 Maiden Lane, near Union Square. Designed in 1948, this prototype Guggenheim is now a private exhibition space.

RECENT ARCHITECTURE

Pietro Belluschi's **St Mary's Cathedral** (1111 Gough Street at Geary), a 61-metre (200-foot) high concrete structure supporting a cross-shaped, stained-glass ceiling, is a 1970s symbol of anti-quake defiance. So is the 853-foot (260-metre) high **Transamerica Pyramid** (600 Montgomery Street), built in 1972. One of San Francisco's best-known buildings, the Transamerica's $34 million seismic-proofed structure boasts an internal suspension to protect it against tremors. Successfully, it would seem: the 48 storeys and 65-metre (212-foot) spire did not suffer in the 1989 quake. At first unpopular, the tower now has few detractors and features prominently in the *Beach Blanket Babylon* revue – a sure sign of civic affection.

The **Main Library** (100 Larkin Street), designed by Cathy Simon of architects Pei Cobb Freed, is a marriage of Beaux Arts and newer forms. One side links the building to the more contemporary Marshall Plaza while the other echoes the old library to the north with grandiose neo-classical columns. The dramatic interior centres around a five-storey atrium beneath a domed skylight designed to let natural light filter throughout the building. The Asian Art Museum which will occupy the former library space when it relocates from Golden Gate Park in 2001, is to be similarly light-centric.

Recent architectural activity has been centred around the **Moscone Convention Center** and nearby **SFMOMA** (151 Third Street), both part of the Yerba Buena complex. SFMOMA, designed by Mario Botta and opened in 1995, features a series of stepped boxes and a signature squared circle facing west. Immediately to the south of it, the luxurious new **W Hotel** (*see page 107* **Accommodation**) rises 32 storeys above a steel-trimmed central lobby and whimsical oval bar area. West of SFMOMA, Yerba Buena's **Esplanade Gardens** remain the city's most beautiful urban park, framed by museums, theatres and shops, and replete with lush greenery, fountains, sculptures and cafés. Finally, the post-modern 'juke-box' **San Francisco Marriott Hotel** (55 Fourth Street, *see page 101* **Accommodation**) reflects the penchant for suspended glass panels which has dominated buildings erected over the past ten years.

Other projects are in the works, including the opening of a new baseball park (*see chapter* **Sport & Fitness**), the renovation of the de Young Museum and the new Jewish and Mexican Museums (*see chapter* **Museums & Galleries**). With them, San Francisco can continue to lay claim to producing architecture as dramatic as her hilly topography.

The initially unpopular **Transamerica Pyramid**.

Literary San Francisco

The city where Jack London was born, the Beat movement thrived and a slew of new writers now flourishes.

Perhaps it's the hills that rise and fall like the plot of a good story or the fog that seems to foreshadow mystery, but San Francisco has always drawn writers to its streets – poets, novelists and essayists who eke out their living by spinning words. In the mid-nineteenth century, Mark Twain and Bret Harte came to report the weirdness during the Gold Rush; 100 years later, Tom Wolfe arrived to write about hippies, remembering them in his *Electric Kool-Aid Acid Test.* From Dashiell Hammett and Jack London to Alice B Toklas, William Saroyan or Danielle Steel – some of the country's best-known writers have called the city home. And while a few big names have marked the city on the literary map, a number of lesser-known authors are intent on guaranteeing the city's future as a storytellers' haven.

FROM TOM SAWYER TO MCTEAGUE

Journalist and budding fiction writer Mark Twain worked in the city in the 1860s, constructing his literary persona and leaving for New York once *The Celebrated Jumping Frog of Calaveras County* hit the big time in 1867. Like most San Francisco writers, Twain came to create himself and went East when he was ready. Legend has it he took the name Tom Sawyer from a man who owned a bar on Montgomery Street. Twain, Bret Harte and Ambrose Bierce built on a foundation of journalistic irony and muckraking that gave the West an independent literary culture in the 1860s and 1870s – something that didn't happen again in the city until after World War II.

Robert Louis Stevenson arrived in 1879 in pursuit of the strong-willed (but already married) Fanny Osbourne. He lived at 868 Bush Street while Osbourne was in Oakland awaiting her divorce. Stevenson eventually collapsed from tuberculosis and she scooped him up. He wrote about San Francisco in *The Wrecker* and about their Napa Valley honeymoon in *The Silverado Squatters.* Stevenson's house is in Saint Helena and **Robert Louis Stevenson State Park** is nearby (*see chapter* **Trips Out of Town**).

Jack London, one of San Francisco's few native sons to make it as a writer, was born at Third and Brannan Streets, the illegitimate son of a wandering astrologer and a medium. He survived all manner of child labour and after a stop in Berkeley, headed north for the Yukon gold rush. The first great American writer of proletarian origins, London became famous with *The Call of the Wild* and *The Sea Wolf* and spent his later years in Wolf House in Glen Ellen in the Sonoma Valley, north of San Francisco. The rebuilt house is worth a visit, if only to get a chilling sense of the connection between turn-of-the-century US Nietzscheanism and Nazi philosophy. The Jack London Museum, Wolf House and the writer's grave can all be found in the **Jack London State Historic Park** in Glen Ellen, north of the town of Sonoma (*see chapter* **Trips Out of Town**).

Like London, Gertrude Stein was raised in Oakland. Her partner Alice B Toklas was born in San Francisco on O'Farrell Street and raised at 2300 California, among the Jewish haute bourgeoisie. In her autobiography *What is Remembered,* Toklas wrote about it – and about the 1906 earthquake: 'My father was apparently asleep,' Toklas wrote of the quake. 'Do get up, I said to him. The city is on fire. That, said he with his usual calm, will give us a black eye in the East.' Jack London wrote a much more dramatic account of the quake for the *Argonaut.* Both remembrances are published in the excellent collection *San Francisco Stories,* edited by John Miller (Chronicle Books, 1990).

Frank Norris, Jack London's contemporary, represents the left-wing version of the early twentieth-century mixture of romanticism and naturalism. Norris was one of the first American disciples of Zola and a forerunner of the progressive era. His most famous novel, *The Octopus,* is about the railroad barons; *McTeague,* set on Polk Gulch where Norris grew up, was later turned into Eric von Stroheim's silent movie *Greed.*

THE CITY OF SAM SPADE

Dashiell Hammett came to San Francisco in 1921, at the tail end of his career as a Pinkerton operative. Beginning in 1923, Hammett published 11 of his 'Continental Op' stories in *Black Mask*, stories set in the city and written while the tubercular Hammett was living at 620 Eddy Street. In 1926 he went to work for the Albert Samuels jewellery company at 985 Market (the Samuels clock is still standing). Shortly afterwards he collapsed. He went on full disability pay, shipped his family to the countryside and became a full-time writer. Living at 891 Post Street, he wrote the sequence of novels that established the crime novel as *the* American genre, including *Red Harvest* and *The Dain Curse* (1929), *The Maltese Falcon* (1930) and *The Glass Key* (1931).

The Maltese Falcon sent Hammett to Hollywood, where he wrote *The Thin Man* and a string of movie sequels; he was saved from drinking himself to death by the onset of World War II. Blacklisted in the 1950s as a Communist, Hammett was jailed for refusing to testify during the McCarthy trails and disappeared from public life until Lillian Helman rehabilitated him.

America is still uncomfortable with Hammett, which may be why his commemorative plaque (on Burrit Street, off Bush Street) acknowledges Sam Spade, not his creator. 'On approximately this spot,' it reads, 'Miles Archer, partner of Sam Spade, was done in by Brigid O'Shaughnessy'. The plaque's author, Warren Hinckle (a San Francisco journalist famous for bankrupting magazines), published a Dashiell Hammett issue of his *City* magazine in 1975. It lists every known Hammett and Sam Spade location and is required reading for enthusiasts. Hammett's and Spade's intertwined journeys are also detailed in Don Herron's *Literary Guide to San Francisco* (City Lights, 1985). John's Grill (63 Ellis Street, at Market; 986 0069) which appeared in *The Maltese Falcon*, is another shrine for Hammett fans.

THE BEAT GENERATION

Jack Kerouac came to the city in 1947, at the end of the cross-country trip that was to make him famous a decade later with the publication of *On the Road*. Because Neal Cassady was in San Francisco, the city became the western terminus of Kerouac's restless cross-country swings. He cut the original teletype-roll manuscript of *On the Road* into paragraphs in Cassady's flat on Russian Hill in 1952. *San Francisco Blues* was written in the Cameo Hotel in what was then skid row on Third Street, an area that was later bulldozed to make way for the Moscone Center. *The Subterraneans*, written in 1953, is set in North Beach – actually a New York story transposed to protect the characters.

Another novel, *The Dharma Bums*, chronicles the impact of the Beat movement on the West Coast. It also vividly reports the poetry reading of 13 October 1955 at the old Six Gallery on Fillmore Street, when Allen Ginsberg read the first part of his famous poem *Howl*, with Kerouac and the 150-strong crowd shouting 'Go! Go! Go!'. That night, other notable poets Philip Whalen, surrealist Philip Lamantia, Michael McClure and Gary Snyder were also introduced to the wildly enthusiastic audience by literary guru Kenneth Rexroth, the leading figure of post-World War II literary San Francisco. An irascible literary pacifist and Orientalist whose salon at 250 Scott Street was the centre of the post-war poetry renaissance, Rexroth's main contribution to San Francisco literary history – much to his own disgust – became his role as godfather to the Beats.

Ginsberg himself had come to San Francisco to (in his own words) 'find the Whitman self-reliance to indulge a celebration of self'. Here he came to terms with his homosexuality, met his lover Peter Orlovsky, moved into the Hotel Wentley and began writing a poem that would turn into *Howl*. The central image of the poem is the Moloch-face of the Drake Hotel on Powell Street as observed by Ginsberg high on peyote. There is a fine picture of Ginsberg (and of the hotel) in Lawrence Ferlinghetti and Nancy Peters' *Literary San Francisco* (City Lights, 1980). Lawrence Ferlinghetti, owner of the City Lights bookshop, later wrote to Ginsberg: 'I greet you at the beginning of a great career. Where's the manuscript?' *Howl*'s subsequent obscenity charges and the resulting trial catapulted the Beats to public attention and opened the way for the breakdown of the American obscenity laws in the 1960s.

The Beat scene was centred around North Beach – the Coexistence Bagel Store at Grant Avenue and Green Street, the Cellar on Green, the Coffee Gallery and the Place on Upper Grant (home of the 'blabbermouth nights', predecessors of today's poetry slams). Gino and Carlo's bar still stands at 548 Green Street (at Columbus Avenue; 421 0896). Vesuvio (255 Columbus Avenue; 362 3370) is where Kerouac drank away his chance of meeting Henry Miller. The bar is located across Jack Kerouac Alley from **City Lights**, the scene's epicentre and still the best literary bookshop in San Francisco (*see page 162* **Shops & Services**). 'So here comes Snyder with a bottle of wine,' Kerouac wrote, 'and here comes Whalen, and here comes what's-his-name… Rexroth and everybody… and we had the Poetry Renaissance of San Francisco.'

FROM THE HASHBURY TO BARBARY LANE

Compared to North Beach, the Haight-Ashbury scene doesn't seem to have left much of a literary monument – though this is perhaps because (to quote Tom Wolfe) if you can remember it, you weren't really there. Ken Kesey and the reborn Neal Cassady began their trips festivals at the Longshoreman's Hall on Fisherman's Wharf, and the scene moved through the Avalon Ballroom on Polk Street and the Fillmore on Geary, to the Haight itself. Wolfe's *Electric Kool-Aid Acid Test* is the best account of the literary and psychological voyage, along with Emmet Grogan's memoir of the Diggers, *Ringolevio*. Kesey and Robert Stone, who was part of the scene and wrote about the era's psychic fallout in *Dog Soldiers*, were both products of Wallace Stegner's writing programme at Stanford. Stegner, a long-respected Western writer of an older school, must have been horrified to see what his literary progeny made of themselves.

The Castro hasn't produced its literary testament yet. Before his death, Randy Shilts produced a stirring (if somewhat melodramatic) account of the coming of Aids in *And The Band Played On*, a treatise on gays and lesbians in the US military, and also wrote the biography of Harvey Milk. Frances Fitzgerald gives a cooler view in *Cities on a Hill*. Armistead Maupin's popular 'Tales of the City' series is in fact set in Macondray Lane on Russian Hill, not particularly a gay locale.

CONTEMPORARY CURRENTS

The literary tradition remains strong in San Francisco, as writers continue to settle in and write about the city. Readings and book signings are still a popular SF pastime and the advent of 'zine and online publishing has delivered a crop of nouveau printers to the city.

The Bay Area supports a number of women authors, including Amy Tan (*The Joy Luck Club* is set in Chinatown), Alice Walker (who wrote *The Color Purple* from her Alamo Square Victorian), and JoAnn Levy (whose *I Saw the Elephant* and *Daughter of Joy* chronicle the California Gold Rush). Joanne Weir and Joyce Goldstein are perhaps the region's best-known chef/authors and writers Isabel Allende, Terry McMillan and Anne Lamott all regularly sell out their reading and speaking engagements. Molly Giles is another up-and-coming local fiction writer; and novelist and short-story writer Alice Adams was a long-time resident of the city before her death in 1999.

Many other writers have settled in San Francisco: novelist Ethan Canin; Silicon Valley critic Po Bronson; trendspotter David Batstone; and memoir writer Daniel Duane. Michael Lerner edits *Tikkun* magazine and writes about the Jewish-American experience from the city. For a book list of titles relating to San Francisco, *see page 282* **Further Reading**.

Authors incarnate

The American West Coast is something of a mecca for touring authors. The cities are unique, the geography lovely, the plane fares cheap. And while LA has the size and Seattle the hippness, when it comes to planning writerly events San Francisco and the Bay Area has the crowd – a literary society who have supported the authorial canon since Samuel Clemens first chose Mark Twain as the *nom* for his *plume*.

Bookworms fortunate enough to be in town for the **San Francisco Bay Area Book Festival**, held each November (*see chapter* **San Francisco by Season**), may enjoy three days of author's readings and an acreage of book merchants, publishers and distributors. More than 200 poets, novelists, essayists, playwrights and memoir writers turn out, as well as child authors, cyberauthors, cartoonists and illustrators. But whatever season you arrive in, you'll find plenty of literary readings. Pick up either of the two weekly arts papers, the *San Francisco Bay Guardian* or *SF Weekly* and check their listings (the *Bay Guardian*'s 'Lit' section is the best resource, published in the last issue of the month); or phone the bookshops directly for a list of who's currently speaking and signing.

Start with **A Clean Well-Lighted Place for Books**, a big, centrally-located store with quirky, helpful staff and a lengthy roster of events. The late Alice Adams appeared here regularly, as has fiction writer Leslie Marmon Silko, San Francisco's resident Italiophile Frances Mayes, seasoned Beat Gary Snyder and poets Thom Gunn and Jane Hirshfield. Check the shop's series and 'In Conversation' listings, which often create panel discussions or interviews with groups of writers.

In the Haight, **The Booksmith** is the obvious stop, a well-stocked, cutting-edge shop with a good balance of subjects and titles. The store takes bigger risks than most with its live events, promoting writers like cyberauthor Neal Stephenson and statesman-poet Czelaw Milosz; Wendy Weir promoted *Spirit*, her New Age book about Jerry Garcia, here; Nick Hornby pitched *Fever Pitch*; and Michael McClure and Peter Coyote recalled their Beatnik past.

Stacey's has several branches throughout the Bay Area, including ones in Palo Alto and Cupertino to the south. Its downtown San Francisco branch is a large, comfortable store on Market Street and features such American political writers as Michael Isikoff and George Stephanopoulis as well as novelist Molly Giles and poet Nikki Giovanni.

Several smaller shops deal in more specialist readerships: in Noe Valley, **Cover to Cover** featured local writers such as Po Bronson and former baseball broadcaster Hank Greenwald at their grand re-opening; **Get Lost**, in the Castro, schedules travel writers from all over the world. And **Solar Light**, a cosy shop in Cow Hollow, focuses on female writers seeking to better women's lives. Finally, for those addicted to corporate book chains, the **Borders** store has signings featuring children's book authors, non fiction scribes and lots of singer-songwriters strumming guitars.

A Clean Well-Lighted Place for Books
See page 162 **Shops & Services** *for listings.*

The Booksmith
See page 162 **Shops & Services** *for listings.*

Borders Books & Music
Union Square, at corner of Powell & Post Streets (399 1633). BART Powell Street/Muni Metro F, J, K, L, M, N/bus 2, 3, 4, 76/cable car Powell-Mason or Powell-Hyde. **Open** 9am-11pm Mon-Wed; 9am-midnight Thur-Sat; 9am-9pm Sun. **Credit** AmEx, MC, V. **Map G3**
Website: www.borders.com
Branches: 233 Winston Drive, at 19th Avenue (731 0665); 588 Francisco Boulevard West, (off Hwy 101 North), San Raphael (454 1400).

Cover to Cover
3812 24th Street, at Church Street (282 8080). Muni Metro J. **Open** 10am-9pm Mon-Sat; 10am-6pm Sun. **Credit** AmEx, MC, V. **Castro/Mission Map Y2**

Get Lost
1825 Market Street, at Guerrero Street (437 0529/info@getlostbooks.com). Muni Metro F, K, L, M/bus 6, 7, 66, 71. **Open** 10am-7pm Mon-Fri; 10am-6pm Sat; 11am-5pm Sun. **Credit** AmEx, DC, Disc, MC, V. **Map F5**

Solar Light
2068 Union Street, between Webster & Buchanan Streets (567 6082). Bus 22, 45. **Open** 10am-10pm Mon-Thur; 10am-11pm Fri, Sat; 11am-7pm Sun. **Credit** AmEx, Disc, MC, V. **Map E2**

Stacey's
581 Market Street, between 1st & 2nd Streets (421 4687). BART Mongomery Street.
Open 8.30am-7pm Mon-Fri; 10am-7pm Sat; 10am-6pm Sun. **Credit** AmEx, MC, V.
Map H3

San Francisco by Season

From the Exotic Erotic Ball to the Nutcracker, film fests and street parades, there's always something to celebrate in the City by the Bay.

San Francisco may be in California, but its climate, like its politics, is all its own. When planning a trip, don't anticipate the normal seasons, climatically, at least. Spring and autumn are relatively predictable, with warm days and cool nights. During the summer, however, the days are usually chilly and foggy, alleviated by two or three hot days which momentarily lift the city's collective spirit. Conversely – or is it perversely? – the nights are usually mild. In mid-winter, what feels like months of constant rain will suddenly break for a week of brilliant sunshine. Tourists shivering in T-shirts are a never-ending source of amusement for locals: if you don't want to look like one, pack accordingly.

Whatever the climate, San Francisco remains a city that knows how to throw a civic party. In addition to the scheduled national holidays, you'll always find some kind of celebration on the streets. The dates listed below are approximate. For the most up-to-date information on events, consult the **San Francisco Visitor Information Center** (391 2000/www.sfvisitor.org) or check local weekly and daily newspapers.

US holidays

New Year's Day (1 Jan); **Martin Luther King Jr Day** (3rd Mon in Jan); **President's Day** (3rd Mon in Feb); **Memorial Day** (last Mon in May); **Independence Day** (4 July); **Labor Day** (1st Mon in Sept); **Columbus Day** (2nd Mon in Oct); **Veteran's Day** (11 Nov); **Thanksgiving Day** (4th Thur in Nov); **Christmas Day** (25 Dec).

Spring

St Patrick's Day Parade

(Information 661 2700). Parade goes from Fifth & Market Streets to the Embarcadero. BART Powell Street/Muni Metro F, J, K, L, M, N/bus 5, 9, 14, 26, 27, 31. **Date** Sun before 17 Mar.

San Francisco has a large Irish population, so this parade is one of the city's biggest. Most pubs celebrate long into the night.

St Stupid's Day Parade

Starts at Transamerica Pyramid, 600 Montgomery Street, between Clay & Washington Streets. Bus 1, 15, 41. **Date** 1 Apr.

On April Fools' Day for the past two decades, Bishop Joey of the First Church of the Last Laugh has led the St Stupid's Day Parade, a zany, parodic assembly that snakes through San Francisco's Financial District. The parade concludes on the steps of the Pacific Stock Exchange, where sermons are given and everyone removes a sock for the 'Pacific Sock Exchange'. It should come as no surprise to learn that many go home sockless, as the event usually degenerates into a sock fight. The starting point varies, so check the website or the local papers for the latest information.

Website: www.saintstupid.com

Whole Life Expo

(Information 721 2484). Concourse Exhibition Center, Eighth Street, at Brannon Street. Bus 19. **Date** early Apr. **Admission** $15. **Credit** AmEx, Disc, MC, V.

A newly popular weekend gathering for those interested in alternative healing techniques, personal growth methods and environment-friendly products.

Cherry Blossom Festival

(Information 563 2313). Japan Center, Geary Boulevard, between Fillmore & Laguna Streets. Bus 2, 3, 4, 22, 38. **Date** Apr.

Held across two weekends in April, the Cherry Blossom Festival celebrates traditional Japanese arts and crafts and includes a parade, dance, drumming and martial arts demonstrations.

SF International Film Festival

See p190 **Film** *for listings.* **Date** mid Apr-early May.

Featuring two weeks of events, the San Francisco Film Festival may not be the largest, but it definitely screens enough films to make a run at being the world's most eclectic cinematic experience. It is particularly strong on independent documentaries and Third World films rarely shown at other US festivals. Tickets sell out quickly, so book in advance.

Cinco de Mayo

(Information 826 1401). Civic Center Plaza, bordered by McAllister, Grove, Franklin & Hyde Streets. BART Civic Center/Muni Metro F, J, K, L, M, N/bus 5, 19, 26, 42, 47. **Date** Sun before 5 May.

It's not the winning, it's the taking part: the **Examiner Bay to Breakers Foot Race**.

Many San Franciscans join the city's Mexican population to celebrate General Ignacio Zaragoza's defeat of the French army at Puebla in 1862. A weekend of parades, fireworks and music.

Aids Candlelight Memorial March & Vigil

(Information 863 4676). Begins at Castro & Market Streets; finishes at United Nations Plaza, Civic Center. **Date** late May.

The vigil begins with a solemn parade from the Castro to Civic Center and continues with an evening of speeches, awards, celebrations and remembrances. *Website: www.actupgg.org*

Carnaval

(Information 826 1401). **Parade** *Mission Street, from 24th to 14th Streets. BART 16th or 24th Street/ bus 12, 14, 22, 49, 53.* **Festival** *Harrison Street, between 16th & 22nd Streets. BART 24th Street/bus 22, 33, 48, 53.* **Date** Memorial Day weekend.

Carnaval gets better every year: the South American festival features a dazzling parade, excellent cuisine and music that will get even the most staid souls up and dancing. If you like steel drum bands, samba and sangria, catch the party that transforms the Mission into Rio de Janeiro once a year.

Examiner Bay to Breakers Foot Race

(Information 808 5000 ext 2222/breakers@ examiner. com). Starts at corner of Howard & Spear Streets. BART Embarcadero/Muni Metro J, K, L, M, N. **Date** 3rd Sun in May.

The *San Francisco Examiner* and other corporate sponsors encourage 70,000 athletes, weekend warriors, jog-walkers, joggers-for-a-day and just plain freaks to run to Ocean Beach. The course is about 12km (7.6 miles), a perfect length for most to make it without much training. The race is famous for its costumes, nudity (there are always a few running free and bouncy), and a school of runners dressed as salmon who attempt to run the course 'upstream'. On the subject of futility, don't attempt to cross the city from north to south on Bay to Breakers morning. *Website: www.baytobreakers.com*

Haight Street Fair

(Information 661 8025/pabloji@earthlink.net). Haight Street, between Masonic & Stanyan Streets. Muni Metro N/bus 6, 7, 43, 66, 71. **Date** early June.

Compare and contrast: the Haight Street Fair, as opposed to its North Beach counterpart (*see below*), is a sardine-fest with over 200 booths of food, live music stages and plenty of folks tripping on acid, both real and imaginary. Strictly for the courageous thrill-seeker, especially if you arrive late when the crowd is thickest and the drugs are wearing off. *Website: www.haightstreetfair.org*

North Beach Festival

(Information 989 2220/mrg@sirius.com). Grant Avenue, Green Street & Washington Square. Bus 15, 30, 41, 83/cable car Powell-Mason. **Date** June.

North Beach's fair is heavy on art, homemade crafts and great Italian food. It's not as crowded as some of the street fests and loaded with Old World music. *Website: www.sfnorthbeach.com*

San Francisco Pride Parade & Celebration

(Information 864 3733/sfpride@aol.com). Market Street, between Embarcadero & Eighth Street. **Date** 3rd or 4th weekend in June.

One of San Francisco's most famous and popular rituals, the gay parade (held on a Sunday) and the party that follows it are every bit as outlandish as you'd expect. Local pols share the route with drag queens,

The **North Beach Festival**. *See page 27.*

leather daddies, Harley-revving dykes, TVs in platform heels and gay marching bands. It's the wildest, friendliest parade you'll witness, but for all its entertainment value the event really celebrates countless numbers of private lives going public with their desire.
Website: www.sfpride.org

Summer

Summer Solstice

(Information 431 9962). **Date** 21 June.
The impromptu celebration that accompanies the summer solstice used to feature free stages of live music throughout the city. More recently it's gone grassroots, with pagans and their sympathisers meeting on the city's hills and beaches to drum and dance and celebrate. The longest day of the year closes with a drum circle in Justin Herman Plaza at the Embarcadero and bonfires on Baker Beach.

Fourth of July

(Information from San Francisco Visitor Information Center 391 2000). Fireworks on the Bay, between Aquatic Park & Pier 39. **Date** 4 July.
On Independence Day even San Francisco admits it's part of the US. The day is filled with live entertainment, food stalls, shows for children and so on, and culminates in spectacular (and occasionally foggy) firework displays shortly after dark.

Jazz and All That Art on Fillmore

(Information 346 9162). Fillmore Street, between Jackson & Ellis Streets. Bus 1, 2, 3, 4, 12, 22, 24, 38. **Date** early July.
With a long history of great jazz, the Fillmore pays tribute to its legacy with a steadily-growing street fair that mixes the usual crafts and handiwork with booths selling original art and several stages of live performance. Fillmore Street is due to be designated an 'Historic Jazz District' in the early 2000s.

San Francisco Marathon

(Information 1-800 698 8699). **Date** July.
It may not be as well known as the London or New York version yet, but over 5,000 people took part in the city's first-ever marathon in 1999. Destined to become an annual event, the 26.2 mile course starts in the heart of Golden Gate Park and crosses the entire city, taking in some of its best sites en route.

Stern Grove Festival

(Information 252 6252). Stern Grove, 19th Avenue, between Sloat Boulevard & Wawona Street. Muni Metro K, M/bus 17, 23, 28. **Date** early June-late Aug.
A series of free jazz, classical and world music concerts set in a 33-acre, idyllic grove of eucalyptus trees in the Sunset district. This amphitheatrical festival is a pleasant summer reprieve – as long as the fog doesn't roll in. Bring a picnic lunch, something to lie or sit on and an extra sweater just in case. Parking is limited; use public transport.
Website: www.sterngrove.org

Mime Troupe in the Park

(Information 285 1717). First show held at Dolores Park, 18th & Dolores Streets. Muni Metro J/bus 33. **Date** early July-early Sept.
For 40 years, the San Francisco Mime Troupe has developed and performed free shows in the parks of San Francisco during the summer. Between the satire, the warm sun, the cool grass, the happy dogs and the views of the city, the festival goes a long way toward restoring one's sanity.
Website: www.sfmt.org

Comedy Celebration Day

(Information 777 7120). Sharon Meadow, between Kezar Drive & John F Kennedy Drive, Golden Gate Park. Muni Metro N/bus 5, 7, 21, 71. **Date** mid-late Aug.
There's no better way to round out the summer than lying on a blanket in the park, drinking, eating and laughing at local and national stand-up comedians. Watch out for cameos by famous figures from San Francisco's comedy history.

Stoli A La Carte, A La Park

(Information 458 1988/eventswest@aol.com). JFK & Kezar Drives, Golden Gate Park. Muni Metro N/bus 5, 7, 21, 71. **Date** early Sept. **Admission** $10; $8 concessions; under-12s free. **No credit cards**.
At this huge outdoor food fair, you can sample an impressive array of cooking from over 40 restaurants in the San Francisco and Bay Area in just three days. Dozens of Californian wines and local microbrews provide plenty of lubrication.

Autumn

San Francisco Fringe Festival

(Information 673 3847/mail@sffringe.org). **Date** early Sept. **Admission** $8. **No credit cards**.
This dramatic marathon, now almost a decade old, features 260 performances by some 50 local, national and international theatre companies – a broad spectrum of comedy, classic theatre and performance art. It's held at various locations throughout the city.
Website: www.sffringe.org

San Francisco Shakespeare Festival

(Information 422 2222/recorded information 422 2221). Golden Gate Park. Muni Metro N/bus 5, 7, 21, 71. **Date** Sept.

The Bard knows no chronological or geographical limits, especially in Northern California. No less than five theatre companies produce Shakespeare plays during the summer, but the event closest to home is the San Francisco Shakespeare Festival, performed free to the public on outdoor stages in Golden Gate Park at various weekends throughout the month of September.

Website: www.sfshakes.org

San Francisco Blues Festival

(Information 979 5588/sfblues@earthlink.net/tickets from BASS 478 2277). Great Meadow, Fort Mason Center, Marina Boulevard, at Buchanan Street. Bus 28. **Date** 3rd or 4th weekend in Sept. **Admission** from $20. **Credit** AmEx, Disc, DC, MC, V.

Traditionally kicking off at noon on a Friday, this weekend-long shindig blurs into one eternal afternoon, exposing blues fans to the elements and set after set of broken-hearted chords. Expect plenty of guest stars; wear your shades and bring a blanket and a cooler full of refreshments.

Website: www.sfblues.com

Folsom Street Fair

(Information 861 3247). Folsom & Harrison Streets, between Seventh & 12th Streets. Muni Metro F, J, K, L, M, N/bus 12, 14, 16, 27, 42. **Date** last Sun in Sept.

The Queen Mother of all leather street fairs, the Folsom Fair has become an out-of-towner's gawkfest, but is still plenty of fun. Like Chinese New Year, Lombard Street and the Golden Gate Bridge, it's a San Francisco institution. Parental discretion is advised.

Artists' Open Studios

(Information 861 9838/artspan@dnai.com). **Date** Oct.

Local Bay Area artists invite the public to visit their studios during selected weekends in October. A free map and the *Directory of San Francisco Artists*

Weather report

While Southern California is basking in summer sun, San Franciscans are often bundled up in sweaters – damp, chilly and surrounded by the familiar foggy 'marine layer'. Yet when some of San Francisco's northern counterparts are freezing in late autumn or early spring, the city is often basking in the radiant stretches of clear, warm days locals refer to as 'earthquake weather'. The rainy season generally lasts from February to April, yet it has been known to snow in December. The only thing consistent about San Francisco's weather is that, cold or hot, it's windy most of the time.

What makes San Francisco's weather so unique? Part of the explanation comes from the city's geography, located as it is at the north end of a peninsula and surrounded on three sides by icy water – the Pacific on one side, San Francisco Bay on two. If you've dipped a toe into the regional tides you'll know just how cold they are, due to the Gulf Stream which travels along the West Coast from the Arctic to the Equator. Add to this combination steady prevailing winds which buffet the coastal range that runs parallel to the Northern California coastline, blowing chilly air off the water and across the maze of city hills, and you'll realise you're not in Kansas anymore.

In the summer, California's wide, hot Central Valley (the agricultural region spanning the coastal ranges and the Sierras on the state's eastern border) creates pressure differences that draw fog off the Pacific and over the city itself. Afternoon and evening winds exacerbate the condition, shooting fog across the city and the Bay into Berkeley and Oakland, catching many a tourist in shorts and T-shirt shivering in the cable car queue or on the deck of a ferry.

Even on the foggiest days, however, you can generally track down a more temperate region: the further south and east you go in the city, the more likely you are to find sun. The **Mission** district is famously warmer than other neighbourhoods, as are **South Park**, **SoMa** and **South Beach**. On the other hand, **Bernal Heights** is usually pretty windy and even **Noe Valley** can disappear under a blanket of fog on most afternoons. The new San Francisco Giants' Pacific Bell Park stadium in **China Basin** is specially designed to block out the wind, though preliminary tests have found it to be just about as windy, overall, as 3Com Park.

The way to cope with the climate is to dress in layers, peeling them off when the sun shows and pulling them back on again when the wind starts whipping. Often a cold afternoon will be followed by a gorgeous, warm night; a chilly, grey beach might clear by noon. Temperatures rarely rise above 21°C (70°F) or fall below 40°F (5°C). And don't forget that the wind blows away the fog – so you'll have a terrific city view anywhere you look. For daily weather information, phone the **National Weather Service Forecast Office** on 1-650 364 7974 or check the San Francisco screen of weather.yahoo.com/forecast.

($12.95) are available from bookshops; a map is also published in the *San Francisco Examiner & Chronicle* on the last Sunday in September. Bring your chequebook.
Website: www.artspan.org

San Francisco International Art Exposition

(Information 1-877 278 3247). Fort Mason Center, Marina Boulevard, at Buchanan Street. Bus 28. **Date** late Sept-early Oct. **Admission** $10; $7 concessions; under-10s free.
A recent addition to the city's fine art scene, this gala event includes 100 art galleries representing the work of over 1,500 artists in all the major media. Prices are considerably higher than those at **Artists' Open Studios** (*see p29*). Bring your credit card.
Website: www.sfiae.com

Reggae in the Park

(Information 459 1988/eventswest@aol.com). Sharon Meadow, between Kezar Drive & John F Kennedy Drive, Golden Gate Park. Muni Metro N/ bus 5, 7, 21, 71. **Date** early Oct.
You'll hear it from blocks away and smell the smoke long before you get there: RITP is quickly becoming one of the city's best-attended music festivals, mainly because it always seems to take place during the best autumn weather. A two-day event, it attracts artists and fans from all over the world.

Fleet Week

(Information 705 5000). Between Fisherman's Wharf & Pier 30-32. **Date** Oct (Columbus Day weekend).
Frightening pets and setting off car alarms throughout the city, the US Navy's Blue Angels tear up the heavens in a *Top Gun* display of speed, daring and taxpayer-baiting – though to watch them fly beneath the Golden Gate Bridge is an undeniable thrill. If you prefer your fleet aqueous (or just love a man in uniform), you can take free tours of various US and international ships.
Website: www.fleetweek.com

San Francisco Jazz Festival

(Information 788 7353). **Date** 3rd & 4th weeks in Oct. **Tickets** $3-$50. **Credit** DC, Disc, MC, TC, V.
In competition with the well-known fest held in Monterey each summer, the San Francisco Jazz Festival has angled itself to attract some of the biggest names in the jazz biz. The festival's popularity is growing and the arrival in 2001 of a Blue Note jazz club on Fillmore Street will increase its chances of surviving in the long term.
Website: www.sfjazzfest.org

Exotic Erotic Ball

(Information 1-888 396 8426). Cow Palace, 2600 Geneva Avenue, at Santos Street. Bus 9, 15, 43. **Date** last Sun in Oct. **Tickets** $50. **Credit** MC, TC, V.
It's obnoxious! It's exploitative! It's 20 years old now and the bridge-and-tunnel crowd's annual excuse to pull on the latex and fishnets and party with other sex kittens at the world's largest indoor masquerade ball. Strippers, sideshows and a costume competition are among the tamer perks.
Website: www.exoticerotic.com

Hallowe'en

(Information from San Francisco Visitor Information Center 391 2000). **Date** 31 Oct.
It used to be that Hallowe'en meant joining the claustrophobic fray in the Castro, where crazy costumes, cameras and cops were *de rigeur*. But the scene became infiltrated with obstreperous out-of-towners, so the SFPD banned assembly there. The Castro is still crowded with drag queens (and half-naked pagans celebrating their own version), but the city has yet to adopt an official locale for its favourite transformative holiday. Keep an eye on the local papers to see whether the masked masses are convening in Civic Center, at the Embarcadero or elsewhere. And don't forget to shop early for your get-up.

Día de los Muertos

(Information 826 8009). Evening procession starts from Mission Cultural Center, 2868 Mission Street, between 24th & 25th Streets. BART 24th Street/ bus 14, 48, 49, 67. **Date** 2 Nov.
A celebration of the Mexican the Day of the Dead – a traditional holiday for welcoming departed spirits with a feast and a slow-moving night-time procession.

Winter

San Francisco Bay Area Book Festival

(Information 487 4550/festival@sfbook.org). Fort Mason Center, Marina Boulevard, at Buchanan Street. Bus 28. **Date** late Oct or early Nov. **Admission** $3-$5; under-17s free. **No credit cards**.
The biggest book fair of the year features acres of retail sales, remainders and new release racks from big-name houses and independent publishers alike. One of the best-kept secrets in the city, the Book Fair draws hundreds of up-and-coming authors to its readings. A great place to shop for the holidays.
Website: www.sfbook.org

Great San Francisco Snow Party

(Information 705 5500). Pier 39, Embarcadero. Bus 15, 30, 32, 39, 42/cable car Powell-Hyde or Powell-Mason. **Date** Nov.
Though snow in the Bay Area is rare, a whole blizzard of it is trucked and blown into Pier 39 for a month-long celebration of skiing, snowboarding and ice-skating. For once, San Francisco's quirky weather is an advantage – imagine frolicking in snowdrifts without wearing a winter coat.

Holiday Tree Lighting Ceremonies

(Information 705 5500). At Pier 39, Embarcadero, & Ghirardelli Square, 900 North Point Street, at Polk Street. **Date** late Nov.

A ring-side view of the action at the **Burning Man** *festival, held near the Black Rock Desert in Nevada. See page 32.*

Your chance to get into the holiday spirit. Check the local press for precise starting times and places.

Run to the Far Side

(Information 759 2690). Golden Gate Park. Bus 5, 7, 21, 33, 66, 71. **Date** weekend after Thanksgiving.

This fund-raiser for the California Academy of Sciences constitutes a 5-km (3-mile) walk and 10-km (6-mile) run through Golden Gate Park, where many participants dress as their favourite characters from Gary Larson's cartoons. Runners get a free T-shirt and a free museum entry ticket.

The Nutcracker

War Memorial Opera House, 301 Van Ness Avenue, at Grove Street (865 2000). BART Civic Center/ Muni Metro F, J, K, L, M, N/bus 21, 42, 47, 49. **Date** Dec. **Admission** $9-$120. **Credit** AmEx, MC, TC, V.

America's oldest ballet company presents dozens of performances of Tchaikovsky's beloved classic ballet for every holiday season. *See also chapter* **Performing Arts**.

Website: www.sfballet.org

New Year

(Information from San Francisco Visitor Information Center 391 2000). **Date** 31 Dec.

The city celebrated the arrival of the millennium with a huge party, one that featured the temporary shutting down of the Golden Gate Bridge for a phalanx of fireworks. It also saw the arrival of a new tradition outside the St Francis Hotel in Union Square: taking its cue from the Times Square midnight ball drop – but with an inimitably San Francisco slant – a huge, illuminated olive dropped seven storeys into the world's largest martini glass.

Martin Luther King Jr Birthday Celebration

(Information 771 6300). Parade ends with rally at Yerba Buena Gardens, Fourth & Mission Streets. BART Powell Street/Muni Metro F, J, K, L, M, N/ bus 14, 26, 30, 45. **Date** Mon after 15 Jan (King's birthday).

In honour of the great civil rights leader, the US takes a day off and holds birthday parades. The start of the route varies, so phone to check.

Tet Festival

(Information 885 2743). Larkin Street, between Eddy & O'Farrell Streets. Bus 19, 31, 38. **Date** Jan-Feb.

San Francisco has a sizeable population of Vietnamese-Americans who, together with Cambodian-, Latino- and African-American families, transform the Civic Center and Tenderloin areas into a multicultural carnival.

San Francisco Tribal, Folk and Textile Arts Show

(Information 267 4895 ext 310). Fort Mason Center, Marina Boulevard, at Buchanan Street. Bus 28. **Date** early Feb. **Admission** $10; under-16s free. **No credit cards**.

Over 100 folk and ethnic art dealers converge at Fort Mason to sell pottery baskets, textiles, jewellery and the like.

Chinese New Year

(Information 982 3000). Parade starts from Market Street, at 2nd Street, ends at Union Square. **Date** Feb.

With beauty pageants, drumming, martial-arts displays, mountains of food, endless strings of fireworks and a huge parade through Chinatown, Chinese New Year turns San Francisco jubilant and upside-down. If you're in town, don't miss it.

Out of town

Gilroy Garlic Festival

(Information 1-408 842 1625). South of San Jose on US 101. **Date** last weekend in July.

A food and wine fest that features the 'stinking rose' of Gilroy – the lowly garlic clove, made into every edible concoction you can imagine. Over 100 craft booths, puppetry, magicians, singing and live music round out the event.

Burning Man

(Information 863 5263). Near Black Rock Desert, Nevada. **Date** Labor Day weekend.

Thousands of San Franciscans ride in convoy out to Nevada for a long weekend of bizarre fun in a scorching, featureless desert. A camp forms for parties, fashion shows, neo-pagan rituals, live music, pirate radio stations, drive-by shooting ranges and just about any game you'd care to invent. The climax is the immolation of a monstrous figure, laced with neon and packed with explosives. After it collapses in flames, circle dances begin. Originally a ceremony held with a few friends, Burning Man has grown huge in recent years; for some, it has replaced Hallowe'en as the main ritual of the year. Get your tickets ($75-$100) well in advance.

Website: www.burningman.com

Renaissance Pleasure Faire

(Information 1-800 523 2473). **Date** late Aug to early Oct.

For 20 years, the Renaissance Faire was held in the incomparable Black Point Forest near Novato, transforming the ancient grove into an Elizabethan festival complete with jousting, jesting and plenty of meat and mead. After a long battle, development won over, and the medieval lords and ladies have moved across the Bay to Vacaville. Huzzah!

Website: www.renfair.com/nocali.cfm

Sightseeing

Sightseeing

Your 'hood by 'hood guide to going native.

Bounded by the Pacific Ocean on one side and the Bay on two more, San Francisco is a city whose blueprint is as unique as its history. Geographical restrictions mean the city is squeezed into a relatively small area, a blessing for the visitor keen on exploring the many sights. Tramping the streets is the best way to do this, but if the shockingly steep hills become too much, you can always turn to public transport and hop on a bus or cable car. We've listed a selection of scenic routes that can be taken by bus or Muni Metro at the end of this chapter: *see page 78*.

Unlike most major municipalities, San Francisco doesn't have a true centre, but is more a collection of neighbourhoods, each with its own distinct character and style. Most tourists will find themselves led in the direction of Union Square and the Wharf, but the savvy traveller will quickly realise that these allow only the barest of introductions to the city. Our recommendation? Head where the locals go: into the Haight, the Mission, North Beach or the other central neighbourhoods; sample the funky shopping districts of Hayes Valley, the splendid views of Russian Hill, the start-up energy of South Park or the magnificent urban vistas of the resurrected Embarcadero.

Arranged by neighbourhood, our sightseeing chapter begins at Union Square, where tourists are most likely to have procured a hotel or come to shop. From here, we explore the rest of 'downtown' – the Financial District, the Tenderloin, North Beach and Chinatown – neighbourhoods that make up the north-eastern corner of the city. This region is bounded by the Embarcadero, Van Ness Avenue and Market Street and marks the centre of activities for much of San Francisco.

From downtown we move south and, after covering South of Market and the Mission district, head progressively west, touring the central neighbourhoods. These include Civic Center, Hayes Valley, the Castro, the Haight, the Western Addition and Japantown, Pacific Heights and the Marina district. Finally, we investigate the areas tucked up against the Pacific – the outlying Presidio, Richmond and Sunset neighbourhoods, as well as Golden Gate Park.

We cover beaches, bridges and islands in separate sections, together with a list of our recommended organised tours (*see page 77*) for those who want to get city-savvy in a short space of time.

A few things remain constant about San Francisco: the city is remarkably safe (for danger zones *see* **Safety** *in chapter* **Directory**) and it is consistently topographically challenging. Stretch those quads and calves, lace up your walking shoes and hit the streets.

The tourist heart of the city – downtown's **Union Square**.

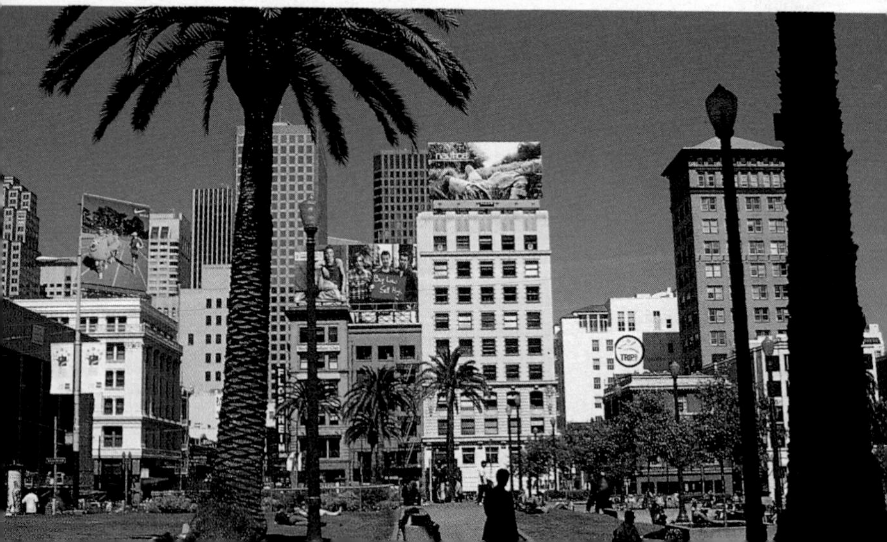

Downtown

Bounded by the Embarcadero, Van Ness Avenue and Market Street, San Francisco's downtown is a bustling triangle of activity, where smartly-dressed salespeople and office workers on their lunch hour mix with rubbernecking tourists, blue-collar workers waiting for buses and the homeless looking for a spare buck. The region contains the city's most varied demographic cross-section and its busiest streets – the best time to navigate them is early on a weekday morning. Camera-toting out-of-towners queuing for the cable car brush shoulders with street-corner evangelists, kids on skateboards whizz past cops mounted on horses and everyone seems to be carrying a bag from Macy's or the Gap.

Hemmed in by the gleaming towers of the Financial District to the east and the affluent hotels of Nob Hill to the west, Chinatown is one of the oldest ethnic neighbourhoods in America, while North Beach, San Francisco's predominantly Italian neighbourhood, is famous for its Beat heritage of the 1950s and 1960s; nowadays it's an odd mixture of Italian, bohemian, touristy and sleazy, with strip joints and clubs doing business alongside some of the city's best restaurants and coffee shops.

The Tenderloin represents just about every nationality on the globe and some of the city's poorest residents. At the northernmost tip of downtown, Fisherman's Wharf, Ghirardelli Square and Aquatic Park remain the tourist hubs, for no other reason than their reputation as – well, tourist hubs.

Don't miss

Angel Island
For hiking and biking with great views of the Bay. *See p73.*

City Hall
After a stunning $300 million face-lift. *See p57.*

The Embarcadero
The freeway's gone and the walkin' is easy. *See p46.*

Golden Gate Bridge
The city's ubiquitous symbol. *See p75.*

The Haas-Lilienthal House
The height of Victorian grandeur. *See p63.*

Yerba Buena Gardens
San Francisco's single most entertaining square block. *See p48.*

Around Union Square

With Post and Geary Streets to the north and south, Stockton and Powell to the east and west, **Union Square** (*see below for listings*) takes its name from the pro-Union rallies held here on the eve of the Civil War. Though a little bedraggled nowadays, it stands at the heart of downtown's concentration of hotels and upmarket shops and so is usually packed with tourists. Palm trees shelter the buskers, mime artists and a determined army of panhandlers who congregate on the grass and benches. Kerbside flower stalls add an exotic touch; double-decker tour buses crowd the streets.

At the centre of the square stands the **Dewey Monument**, a 30-metre (97-foot) Corinthian column commemorating Admiral Dewey's 1898 naval victory at Manila during the Spanish-American war. A few years later – following the great quake of 1906 – Union Square became a tent refuge for the VIPs who had been staying in nearby hotels. The square is where much of Francis Ford Coppola's movie *The Conversation* was shot.

Nowadays, plans are underway to redesign the square: suggestions have included building a landscaped urban mall or expanding its much-needed parking capacity. On the easternmost side, the **TIX Bay Area** booth (*see chapter* **Shops & Services**) sells half-priced tickets to theatre and other performances; **Niketown** (278 Post Street; 392 6453) is on the north-east corner; the elegant 1928 **Sir Francis Drake Hotel** (450 Powell Street; 395 7755/1-800 227 5480) with its Disney-like Beefeater doormen, is to the west; the monstrous, newly-renovated **Macy's** store (*see chapter* **Shops & Services**) fills the southern side.

A two-block walk south on Powell from Union Square delivers you to Market Street and the **San Francisco Center** – a nine-storey vertical mall that includes **Nordstrom** and other clothing stores, boutiques, shoe shops, a food court in the basement and a graceful exterior escalator (*see chapter* **Shops & Services**). Though you can't see them, the mammoth centre houses two 60,000-pound freight elevators, each big enough to hold a semi-trailer truck.

For even more upmarket shopping, head east from Union Square to the **Crocker Galleria** complex on Post Street where top-flight stores compete for tourist dollars. Other retail opportunities in the neighbourhood include the **FAO Schwarz** toy shop at 48 Stockton Street (hard to pass up if you have a child in tow) and myriad clothing stores – **Banana Republic**, **Diesel**, **Urban Outfitters**, **Georgiou**, and the holy trinity of **Tiffany**, **Hermès** and **Chanel** – surely enough to satisfy

Cable cars

If the cable cars are a legendary part of the city, so is the hassle of getting a ticket to board one at the Powell Street turnaround, located opposite the San Francisco Center on the other side of Market Street. You may be tempted, lemming-like, to join the long queue of tourists waiting to embark here or to buy your ticket from some shady character. Resist these urges: instead, do what the locals do – walk up the hill a few blocks and board the car en route. You can pay cash for your ticket once you're rolling.

Out of the original 30 cable car lines, only three survive: the Powell-Mason and Powell-Hyde, both of which depart from the Powell Street turnaround, and the California line, which runs between Market Street and Van Ness Avenue in a long, straight path up and down California Street. This line is the least crowded, while the tourist-jammed Powell-Hyde line (to Fisherman's Wharf) and the Powell-Mason line (to Ghirardelli Square) afford the best views.

The story of how Scotsman Andrew Hallidie got the idea for a cable car – supposedly after watching a hapless horse-drawn vehicle being dragged backwards down a steep hill – is probably fictitious. As it happened, he owned the patent on a wire cable grip developed by his father and wanted a market for it. Hallidie originally intended to take passengers to the top of Nob Hill and his invention was first tested along five steep blocks of Clay Street in 1873. An amusing photograph of this maiden voyage, along with other cable car memorabilia and an insight into how the system works, can be seen at the **Cable Car Barn Museum** (*see chapter* **Museums & Galleries**).

For more information on travelling by cable car and other modes of public transport, *see page 268* **Directory**.

even the most hardened shopaholic. For more details, *see chapter* **Shops & Services**.

On Market Street, several local buildings are worth seeking out. It's hard to miss the **Phelan Building**, built in 1908 by Mayor James Phelan as part of his famous post-quake reconstruction programme. It is San Francisco's largest 'flatiron' structure (so-called because of its triangular shape) and takes up most of the block on Market Street between Third and Fourth Streets. A more modern counterpart lies towards the Financial District – the teardrop-shaped **388 Market**, an office building erected in 1986, is an addition of noteworthy design.

The nondescript building at **49 Geary** houses more than a dozen fine art galleries, including **Jennjoy**, **Robert Koch** and **Catharine Clark** (*see chapter* **Museums & Galleries** for all three). The rest of the neighbourhood is chock-a-block with galleries as well, particularly on Sutter, Geary, and Post Streets. Not far away, linking Stockton and Kearny Streets, lies **Maiden Lane**. Once a dangerous and seedy alleyway (famous early in the last century for having the cheapest prostitutes), the cul-de-sac has since been transformed into a posh shopping street, the centrepiece of which is the exquisite **Folk Art International** at No.140 (392 9999), a circular brick building designed by Frank Lloyd Wright in 1948.

Hungry? **Café de la Presse** on Grant Avenue has a simple café menu and a broad selection of international magazines and newspapers to browse through; it's a perfect place to sit outside on a sunny morning and watch passers-by. Bustling **Café Claude**, tucked away in an alley, feels like a French backstreet bistro, with chairs and tables outside and live jazz on some evenings. For both *see chapter* **Restaurants & Cafés**.

At the end of the day pay a visit to **Club 36**, which is on the 36th floor of the Grand Hyatt Hotel on Union Square (*see chapter* **Accommodation**). A jazz venue with fabulous views over the city, it has also been called 'one of the best places to kiss in California'.

Union Square

Bounded by Geary, Powell, Post & Stockton Streets. Bus 2, 3, 4, 30, 38, 45, 76/cable car Powell-Hyde or Powell-Mason. **Map G3/4**

The Financial District

East of Union Square, the Financial District comprises the triangle bounded by Market Street from Kearny Street to the Embarcadero and north to Jackson Street, and has marked the commercial centre of San Francisco for over a century. Nowadays it's dominated by the **Transamerica Pyramid** on Montgomery Street (*see below for listings*). William Pereira's 260-metre (853-foot) building – the tallest in San Francisco – provoked public outrage when it opened in 1972, but has since become an accepted (if not particularly loved) part of the city skyline. Built to be earthquake-proof, the building is covered with panels that move laterally and sits on giant rollers that allow it to rock safely; it must work, since the building wasn't damaged by the 1989 Loma Prieta quake. The lobby is open to the public during business hours.

Other notable buildings abound. One of the most interesting structures is the **Merchant's Exchange** (*see below for listings*), rebuilt in 1906 after the Great Fire and home to an impressive collection of William Coulter seascapes. The architecturally creative high-rise at **456 Montgomery** straddles two turn-of-the-century banks: the Italian-American and the Anton Borel, both built in 1908. The West Coast home of the stock market can be found inside the **Federal Reserve Bank Building** (101 Market Street). To catch the fever of the Gold Rush days, visit the free **Wells Fargo Museum** (420 Montgomery Street; 396 2619). Mementos of the Wild West include paintings, photographs, gold nuggets and a stage coach; it's only open during the week.

Every 18 April, a select few centenarians who survived the 1906 earthquake gather at **Lotta's Fountain** at the intersection of Market, Kearny and Third Streets. The ornate, lion-headed granite fountain – recently restored – served as a message centre for families separated by the quake, an 8.0 trembler which led to a four-day fire and killed hundreds (and probably thousands) of San Franciscans (*see chapter* **History**).

The area also has some non-financial landmarks, including the **Transamerica Redwood Park**, next to the Transamerica Pyramid, notable for its free jazz and blues concerts, and the **Pacific Heritage Museum** on Commercial Street (*see below for listings*), which traces the city's artistic, cultural and financial links to the Far East. The **American Indian Contemporary Arts Gallery** (685 Market Street; 989 7003) has a gift shop upstairs.

Geographically within the bounds of the Financial District, the area known as the **Jackson Square Historical District** marks all that remains of the once-notorious Barbary Coast – a few blocks of low-rise brick buildings dating from the 1850s which marked the city's original shoreline. Built on foundations made from the hulls of ships abandoned during the Gold Rush, the area was once one of the city's most notorious red-light districts. In the 1930s Jackson Square (bounded by Washington, Kearny and Sansome Streets and Pacific Avenue) became popular among artists and writers, including John Steinbeck and William Saroyan, who used to drink at the long-vanished Black Cat Café. Socialist painter Diego Rivera had a studio on nearby Gold Street. Much of the area

A flavour of the Financial District: the high-rises of **Montgomery Street**.

perished in the 1906 Great Fire, but today it's lined with lovingly restored offices and an individual collection of antique, furniture and bookshops.

Local establishments popular with after-work drinkers include the **Cypress Club** (500 Jackson Street, *see chapter* **Restaurants & Cafés**), where a bizarre, 1940s-inspired interior might make you wonder if your appetisers have been spiked with hallucinogens, and **Bix** (56 Gold Street, *see chapter* **Bars**), which enjoys a well-founded reputation for brilliant martinis. There are several excellent restaurants in the area: *see chapter* **Restaurants & Cafés** for details.

Merchant's Exchange

465 California Street, at Sansome Street. Bus 3, 15, 45. **Open** 8am-6pm daily. **Map H3**
Website: www.merchants_exchange.com

Pacific Heritage Museum

608 Commercial Street, at Montgomery Street (399 1124). Bus 1/cable car California. **Open** 10am-4pm Tue-Sat. **Admission** free. **Map H3**

Transamerica Pyramid

600 Montgomery Street, between Clay & Washington Streets (983 4100). Bus 1, 15, 41, 42. **Open** *lobby only* 8.30am-4.30pm Mon-Fri. **Map H3**

The Tenderloin

By contrast to the Financial District, the downtown area west of Union Square is San Francisco's poorest and a red-light district. Its name is variously attributed to the ladies' legs on display there, and to its long, narrow shape. During the daytime, Cambodian grandmothers forage the vegetable markets, while their grandchildren blend in among the homeless and the occasional drug dealer. At night, transvestites, hookers and hustlers take to the streets and the aroma of Asian and Indian cooking mixes with the smell of cheap perfume. In the hours after dark, it's sensible to know where you're going in this neighbourhood: take a cab if necessary.

But while much is made of the Tenderloin's potential for danger, there are many reasons to explore the area, whose generally disenfranchised citizens are also among the most politically organised in the city. Deep into the Tenderloin are a pair of churches that share a long and compassionate history. **St Boniface Catholic Church** at 133 Golden Gate Avenue (*see below for listings*) offers Mass in English, Spanish, Tagalog and Vietnamese, and hosts dozens of benefit programmes, including a dining room that serves more than 2,000 daily meals to the needy. Unremarkable from the street, St Boniface's Romanesque interior, restored in the 1980s, includes some impeccable stencilling. A magnificent organ counterbalances the beautifully gilded apse which is topped by a four-storey cupola painted with Latin text and decorated with scenes from the life of Saint Francis. Martyrs depicted in the stained glass include Saints Anthony and Emydius – protector against earthquakes. Four blocks away, the walls and murals of **Glide Memorial United Methodist Church** on Ellis

Entertainment in the 'Loin

The Tenderloin is where the city's major theatres are to be found. The central theatre district is based around Geary Boulevard just west of Union Square, where the **American Conservatory Theater** or **ACT** (also known as the Geary) is located, as well as **Marine's Memorial Theatre** (on Sutter Street), the **Theatre on the Square** (on Post Street), the **Curran** and **Alcazar Theaters** (both on Geary). Further south, near the intersection of Market Street and Golden Gate Avenue, lies the **Golden Gate Theater** (on Taylor Street) and the **Orpheum** (on Market). All these spaces can feature nationally- or internationally-touring performances; several smaller theatres catering more to local companies can be found in both areas and there are more in the Mission district. *See chapter* **Performing Arts**.

If you're an aficionado of live music, **Biscuits and Blues** on Mason Street features blues bands, and the **Blue Lamp** on Geary Street is a shoebox-sized hangout for jazz and R&B (*see chapter* **Nightlife** for both); the **Edinburgh Castle**, at 950 Geary (885 4074) is a Scottish pub that serves fish and chips wrapped in newspaper, books Gaelic or alternative rock bands and an occasional Scottish poet.

For destination bars in the region, don't miss **Backflip** at 601 Eddy Street (*see chapter* **Bars**), a trendy cantina which shares ground with the **Phoenix** hotel (*see chapter* **Accommodation**), preferred lodging for alt-rock stars playing at the nearby Warfield Theater on Market Street. Clubbers will love **Polly Esther's** at 181 Eddy Street (*see chapter* **Nightlife**), a favourite dance venue with a 1970s motif. If you're up late, the **Grub Stake** at 525 Pine Street (673 8268), where exotic dancers, punk singers, cops and off-duty prostitutes mingle with tourists and late-night clubbers, serves greasy-spoon fare until 4am.

The only way is up

Although many of them are overgrown with foliage and often unmarked, San Francisco's stairways provide a network of some of the city's most untravelled paths and views both broad and intimate. Nearly 400 different stairways connect the city's 42 hills, treacherous topography that not even a Roman army would have joined with a road. If you don't spend much time on foot, you could visit the city without even noticing their existence – but once you discover one hidden stairway, uncovering others becomes compulsive. Park your car, lace up your favourite pair of comfortable climbers and discover another side of San Francisco.

The best stairways are those that replace road or pavement altogether. Just such a stairway street is leafy **Macondray Lane** (off Leavenworth Street, between Union and Green Streets), inspiration for Armistead Maupin's Barbary Lane and miraculously secluded. Idiosyncratic houses line one side, through which you can catch tantalising glimpses of the Bay beyond. As with many of the better stairways, the signpost is hard to spot (look for the name imprinted in the concrete of the kerb).

Novice stairway spotters should look for the yellow diamond-shaped signs on hilly routes that say 'Not a Through Street' and assume that a staircase lies beyond. You won't walk many before you become a stairway snob; soon you'll be discriminating between those that are just a small set of stairs ending a street (such as you'll find descending the seven steps at the corner of **Clifford Terrace** and **Roosevelt Way** in Twin Peaks), those that are just pavements with stairs in them (**Filbert Street**, between Leavenworth and Hyde Streets, on Russian Hill) and those that offer architect-designed steps, breathtaking views and arum lilies growing in the adjacent flower beds (**Vallejo Street**, between Jones and Mason Streets, and several other stairways on Russian Hill).

Some walks are best combined with several stairways. Try walking east from **Jones** and **Vallejo Streets** (uphill) for a block, admiring the collision of architecture at the peak of Nob Hill. Take the stairs to the right of the overlook (made famous in a scene during the 1978 remake of *Invasion of the Body Snatchers*) and, winding past landscaped backyards and friendly cats, descend slowly to **Coolbrith Park** a block down. Continue down another long block of stairs, enjoying the view of the Bay Bridge, the piers and Treasure Island, until you reach **Mason Street** – where you'll find the Mason Street cable car line at the periphery of Chinatown and North Beach.

From there, walk diagonally through **Washington Square Park**, and catch Greenwich east until it winds up **Telegraph Hill**. Walk up the hill – it's a long one, take your time – and spiral up the walk to **Coit Tower**, where a drinking fountain awaits you. After you've caught your breath, take the **Filbert Street** steps that wind away from Coit on the east side. These will drop you, slowly at first and then quickly and abruptly, onto **Levi Plaza** and, eventually, the **Embarcadero**. Consider taking a cab home.

Stairway-walking is not for the faint-hearted or cardiac-challenged. But for those who persevere, there is usually a parapet or seat at the top to rest on while admiring the city view. Try the climb along **Broadway** between **Taylor and Jones Streets**, where you can rest on a bench and take in the view of the Bay Bridge with the Transamerica Pyramid and the Financial District spread out below. At the **Pemberton** stairway

in Twin Peaks, a seat is perfectly positioned for the waverers in your party – at the bottom.

For more detailed guidance, consult Adah Bakalinsky's exhaustive (and exhausting) *Stairway Walks in San Francisco*, which offers 27 graded and tested stairway walks.

Other stairways to explore include:

Culebra Terrace

Chestnut Street, between Larkin & Polk Streets. Bus 19/cable car Powell-Hyde. **Map F2**

A climb shaded by Monterey pines, which offers a great view of the Golden Gate Bridge.

Lyon Street Steps

Between Green Street & Broadway. Bus 3, 24, 43. **Map D3**

Begin at Green Street, where you'll climb the edge of the Presidio into Pacific Heights. There are great views of Alcatraz, the Palace of Fine Arts and the Golden Gate Bridge. At the top you're just a stone's throw from the entrance to the Presidio.

Macondray Lane

Leavenworth & Jones Streets, between Union & Green Streets. Bus 41, 45/cable car Powell-Hyde. **Map F2**

A great climb for *Tales of the City* nostalgia and leafy views from Russian Hill.

Ord Court Feline Appreciation Walk

Off Levant Street, between States & Lower Stairway Terrace Streets. Bus 33, 37. **Map D6**

A shady, intimate walk in the heart of Buena Vista overlooking the Upper Haight. More cats than people will be visible on your descent.

Sanchez Street

Between Liberty & 21st Streets. Muni Metro J/ bus 24, 35. **Castro/Mission Map X2**

Descend the wide stairway in Dolores Heights, the hilly region of the Mission district. With views of downtown and sloping Dolores Park, this climb is one of the best in the city.

20th Street Bun-Buster

20th Street, between Douglas & Tennessee Streets. Bus 22, 48.

A little-known fact is that 20th Street, from Potrero Hill to the base of Twin Peaks, is fully walkable. Start at either end and enjoy a series of freeway crossovers, park views – and stairs.

23rd Street Urban Hike

Begin at 23rd & Diamond Streets. Bus 24, 53, 48. **Castro/Mission Map X2**

Climb west (towards Eureka – the streets are laid out in alphabetical order). At Grand View, take the pedestrian overpass across Portola Street, then follow the series of stairways that climb to the base of Twin Peaks. A trail to the right will lead you to the top of the southernmost peak, a full 278 metres (910 feet) above the city's skyline. Pack a camera.

Vallejo Street

Between Jones & Taylor Streets. Bus 41, 45/cable car Powell-Mason. **Map G2**

More views, with houses and steps designed by Willis Polk (1867-1924). Don't miss 1045 Vallejo, the top floor of which was remodelled by Polk to allow views in all directions. Laura Ingalls Wilder stayed with her daughter Rose at 1019 in 1915.

Street (*see below for listings*) which serves food to some 3,000 homeless a day, are decorated with eye-catching art nearly as interesting as the characters who gather there.

Good art can be found throughout the Tenderloin. The **Tenderloin Recreation Center** on Ellis Street (*see below for listings*) offers an amazing panorama of children's works and the courtyard of the **Phoenix** hotel at 601 Eddy Street (*see chapter* **Accommodation**) features a sculpture garden, an artfully-tiled swimming pool and several large murals.

Tenderloin Recreation Center

570 Ellis Street, between Leavenworth & Hyde Streets (292 2162). BART Powell Street/Muni Metro F, J, K, L, M, N/bus 27, 31, 38. **Open** 10am-8.30pm Mon-Fri; 9am-6pm Sat; noon-5pm Sun. **Map F/G4**

Glide Memorial United Methodist Church

330 Ellis Street, at Taylor Street (771 6300). BART Powell Street/Muni Metro F, J, K, L, M, N/bus 27, 31, 38. **Map G4**

St Boniface Catholic Church

133 Golden Gate Avenue, at Leavenworth Street (863 7515). Bus 5. **Map G4**

Russian & Nob Hills

Overlooking the Tenderloin and Union Square to the north, Nob Hill was named after the wealthy 'nabobs' who built their mansions in the area and was described by Robert Louis Stevenson as 'the hill of palaces'. A short but incredibly steep walk (or cable car ride) up from Union Square, the hill stands 103 metres (338 feet) above the Bay. It wasn't until after the opening of the cable car line in the 1870s that its steep slopes began to attract wealthy residents, namely the 'Big Four' boom era spenders – Charles Crocker, Leland Stanford, Mark Hopkins and Collis P Huntington (*see chapter* **History**). Their palatial mansions perished in the fire that razed the city after the 1906 earthquake and the sole survivor was James C Flood's mansion, built in 1886. It was later remodelled by Willis Polk and is now the site of the exclusive 'gentlemen's' **Pacific-Union Club** (1000 California Street, at Mason Street).

Stevenson's 'palaces' were replaced by what are now the city's most elite hotels, including the **Fairmont** (950 Mason Street, at California Street; 772 5000), with its plush marble lobby and infamous ersatz-islander **Tonga Room**, complete with simulated tropical rainstorm; the **Huntington** (1075 California Street, between Taylor and Mason Streets; 474 5400) with its Big Four bar; and the **Mark Hopkins Inter-Continental** (999 California Street, at Mason Street; 392 3434), where the **Top of the Mark** bar offers fabulous views over the city and live jazz every night of the week. *See also chapter* **Bars**.

Nearby, on the corner of California and Taylor Streets is **Grace Cathedral** (*see below for listings*), an Episcopalian church built on the site of the former Crocker mansion and begun in 1928. With a façade modelled on Notre Dame, a fine rose window, gilded bronze doors made from casts of the Doors of Paradise in Florence's Baptistry and a magnificent organ, the cathedral is an architectural extravaganza. Midnight mass here, intoned by the celebrated boys' choir, is a Christmas ritual. Sung Eucharist is heavily attended and there's always plenty of action in between – from concerts, weddings and funerals to appeals by visiting dignitaries. Grace took 54 years to build and sports a recent $13.3 million retrofit. The cathedral also houses an indoor and outdoor **Labyrinth Walk** – a meditative path copied from the one laid in the floor of the cathedral at Chartres. A free guided tour starts at 1pm daily; you can explore yourself any time between 7am and 6pm. Across California Street from Grace sits the classy white marble **Masonic Auditorium** (1111 California, *see chapter* **Performing Arts**), scene of jazz festivals, authors' readings and pop concerts.

Named after a group of Russian sailors thought to have been buried here, Russian Hill is the quiet, residential neighbourhood roughly bordered by Van Ness Avenue, Broadway, Powell and Chestnut Streets. It's most famous for containing the 'crookedest' (and surely most photographed) street in the world, **Lombard Street**, which snakes steeply down from Hyde Street, packing nine hairpin bends into one brick-paved and over-landscaped block. In the summer, tourists queue up for the thrill of driving down its hazardous 27 per cent gradient at 5mph – arrive early or late if you want to avoid them and their cameras. For further thrills, try negotiating the steepest street in the city: Filbert Street between Hyde and Leavenworth descends at a whopping 31.5 per cent gradient.

Also on Russian Hill is the **San Francisco Art Institute** (*see below for listings*), housed in a 1920s Spanish Revival building on Chestnut Street and containing a wonderful Diego Rivera mural. Take a stroll up Vallejo Street to **Ina Coolbrith Park** at Taylor Street and have a secluded picnic; if you arrive early, you'll catch the Chinese elders practising tai chi. Walk back down via the **Vallejo Street Stairway**, designed by Willis Polk and surrounded on each side by landscaped gardens (*see page 40* **The only way is up**). Landmark addresses include **29 Russell Street**, where Jack Kerouac lived with Neal and Carolyn Cassady in the 1950s and the octagon-shaped house at **1067 Green Street**, one of San Francisco's oldest dwellings.

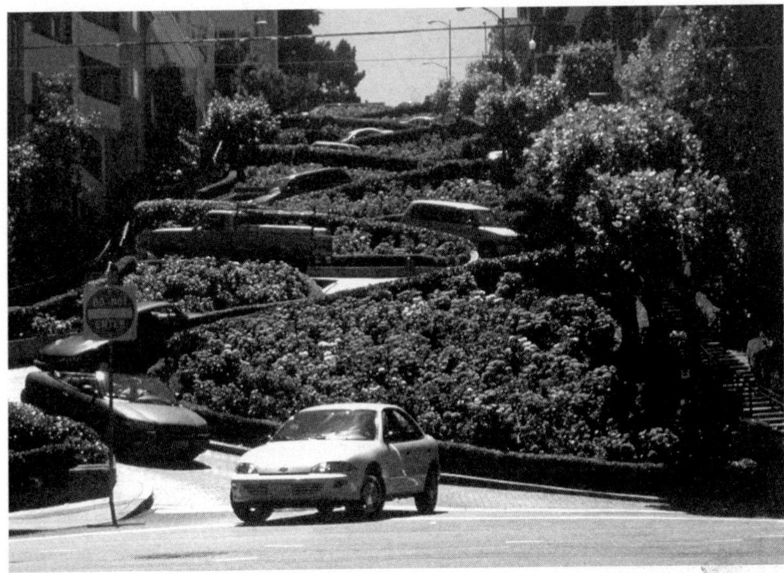

Lombard Street: *nine landscaped hairpin bends and a 27 per cent gradient.*

Grace Cathedral

1100 California Street, at Taylor Street (749 6300). Bus 1, 27/cable car California. **Open** 7am-6pm daily. **Map G3**

San Francisco Art Institute

800 Chestnut Street, at Columbus Avenue. (749 4510). Cable car Powell-Hyde/bus 30, 45. **Map G2**

See also chapter **Directory**.

Chinatown

The influx of Cantonese into San Francisco began in the late 1840s, fuelled by the dream of striking it rich and the need to escape the Opium Wars and famine at home, and later by the prospect of work on America's transcontinental railway. The area the Chinese had settled was completely destroyed by the 1906 earthquake and fire, yet, despite attempts by city politicians to confiscate what had become premium land, the community managed to rebuild on it. The new Chinatown was as cramped as the old and today the crowded streets are thronged with tourists and shoppers lured by the scent of herbal shops, markets and hundreds of restaurants offering regional Chinese food. Before the discovery of gold in the Sierra foothills, there were only a few hundred people living here. Today, it has nearly 10,000 residents and forms part of the largest Asian community outside Asia.

A few blocks from Union Square on Bush Street, the dragon-topped **Chinatown gateway** that marks the southern entrance to Chinatown was a gift from Taiwan in 1970. The ornate, three-arched design is based on the ceremonial entrances traditional in Chinese villages. Its green-tiled roofs are topped by various good-luck symbols, including two dragons and two large carp. The gateway leads onto **Grant Avenue**, Chinatown's main – and usually most tourist-thronged – thoroughfare.

Once called Dupont Street and a notorious hub of gambling and opium dens, Grant Avenue was patrolled by *tongs*, the secret groups formed in the late 1870s and 1880s to combat racial attacks, but which quickly developed into Mafia-style gangs fighting to control gambling and prostitution rackets. Today the street is clogged with souvenir shops peddling T-shirts, sweatshirts, cameras, Chinese 'art', ceramics and toys.

On California Street, a block north of the Chinatown gateway, is the city's first-ever Catholic cathedral, built in 1854. At the time, what is now known as **Old St Mary's Cathedral** (*see below for listings*) represented the most solid structure yet built on the West Coast and, although its bell and altars melted, it survived the 1906 earthquake and fire. Constructed of granite imported from China, the church offered the city's first English language school for its Chinese community. The clock tower reads: 'Son, observe the time and fly from evil' – probably a reference to what was at the time the particularly seedy neighbourhood in which it was built.

One block east of Grant, **Portsmouth Square** marks the historical centre and pulse of Chinatown. Bounded by Washington Street to the north and Clay to the south, the square has been unprepossessingly rebuilt over an underground car park. It was here that the small village of Yerba Buena was first claimed for the United States (from Mexico) in 1846, and where Sam Brannan, owner of the city's first newspaper, the *California Star*, announced the discovery of gold two years later. The surrounding streets were the first to be settled by the Chinese in the 1840s and 1850s. Locals gather in the square to practise tai chi each morning and, later, Chinese men congregate on the east side to play Russian poker or Chinese chess. Robert Louis Stevenson spent some time in San Francisco in 1879 and a monument on the northwest side of the square – the galleon *Hispaniola* – stands in his honour.

Across the square on the third floor of the Holiday Inn at 750 Kearny Street is the **Chinese Culture Center** (*see below for listings*), linked to Portsmouth Square by a concrete footbridge. The centre sponsors art exhibitions and cultural events and stocks a useful collection of books in its gift shop. Two blocks south, on Commercial Street, the **Chinese Historical Society Museum** (*see chapter* **Museums & Galleries**) traces the history of the Chinese people in America in pictures and documents and also houses the original – handwritten – Chinatown telephone directory.

It's worth exploring the surrounding network of side streets and alleyways. In the days when Chinatown was confined to a five-block area, you didn't need a map to get around – a good nose was enough. The street now called **Wentworth Alley**, off Washington Street, was known as 'Salted Fish Alley' and was the place to buy fresh and preserved fish. Refrigerators were a rarity in the cramped conditions where several families had to share one tiny kitchen and fish was salted and 'sun-dried' on the rooftops. Eggs were preserved in brine for 40 days or more.

Walk back along Washington Street and follow the scent of the **Golden Gate Fortune Cookie Factory** (56 Ross Alley; 781 3956) to watch the cookies being made by hand. On the south side of Washington Street is 'Fifteen Cent Street', named after the price of a haircut in the 1930s and officially called **Waverly Place**. It's a wide, picturesque street that stretches between Washington and Sacramento Streets, parallel to Grant and Stockton. On the fourth floor of brightly painted 125 Washington is the **Tien Hau Temple**, dedicated to the Queen of the Heavens and Goddess of the Seven Seas. Opening times vary, but if you're lucky you'll be able to peep into the incense-filled sanctuary.

The **Bank of Canton** (743 Washington Street), almost directly across the street from Waverly Place, is one of the most photographed buildings in the Chinatown. The *California Star*'s offices originally occupied the site, but the present pagoda-like creation was built for the Chinatown Telephone Exchange.

The small alley to the west of Ross Alley, off Washington Street, is called **Old Chinatown Lane**. Once known as the 'Street of Gamblers', it was where Donaldina Cameron, the determined New Zealander who devoted her life to saving young Chinese girls from slavery and prostitution, once lived. **Cameron House** at 920 Sacramento Street – a youth centre that also offers social services to immigrants in Chinatown – is her legacy to the neighbourhood.

Chinese herbalists are one of the neighbourhood's pleasures. There's a string of them on Jackson and Clay Streets, with entire walls filled with hundreds of drawers containing various herbs, intended not just to cure ills but also to maintain good health. Look in at the famous **Li Po** bar (916 Grant Avenue; 982 0072), decorated with Asian kitsch and one of San Francisco's more outlandish spots. At 949 Grant Avenue is the **Ten Ren Tea Company** (*see chapter* **Shops & Services**), the largest tea shop in San Francisco, where you can choose from 40 different types of Chinese tea.

To the west of Grant Avenue, running the length of Chinatown, is **Stockton Street**, where the locals shop. It is lined with Chinese fish markets, supermarkets, grocery stores, windows displaying roast pigs and dim sum restaurants. If you're in a hurry, duck into one of the many takeaway restaurants to pick up an order of chow mein or a cha sil bow (steamed barbecued pork bun). Otherwise, for our recommended list of restaurants and dim sum houses in Chinatown, *see chapter* **Restaurants & Cafés**.

Chinese Culture Center

750 Kearny Street, at Portsmouth Square (986 1822). Bus 1, 15, 30, 45/cable car California
Open *gift shop* 10am-4pm Tue-Sun. **Credit** MC, V.
Map G2

Old St Mary's Cathedral

660 California Street, at Grant Avenue (288 3800). Bus 1, 15, 30, 45/cable car California. **Open** 7am-7pm Mon-Fri; 10am-7pm Sat; 7am-4pm Sun.
Map G3

North Beach

Despite being a popular tourist attraction as much for its literary heritage as for its thriving Italian cafés and restaurants, North Beach retains a sense of authenticity. Bordered by Bay, Washington, Montgomery and Leavenworth Streets, it is San

Francisco's oldest Italian community, where the Beats, jazz musicians and free sex advocates put down roots in the 1950s. Now, with Chinatown only a block away, tai chi practitioners and Chinese businessmen mix with young parents and their kids, elderly gents chatting in Italian, would-be poets drifting from one café to another, and the lawyers and accountants who've moved into the increasingly upmarket neighbourhood. Most of the people on the streets and in the cafés and bars live and work in the area, among them movie director Francis Ford Coppola, who has an office in **Columbus Tower** – the turreted green building on the corner of Columbus Avenue and Kearny Street. On the building's ground floor is the new café/shop, **Café Niebaum-Coppola**, which sells Coppola's own brand of pasta alongside wines from his vineyard.

A quick tour of **Columbus Avenue** and the nearby streets will unearth North Beach's treasures and much of its history: **City Lights** shop at 261 Columbus (*see chapter* **Shops & Services**) is still owned by Beat poet Lawrence Ferlinghetti and is open until midnight every day. **Vesuvio**, at 255 Columbus, was once frequented by literary drunks Jack Kerouac and Dylan Thomas.

Two hotels sum up the different sides of North Beach. The aptly named **Hotel Bohème** at 444 Columbus Avenue celebrates its Beat heritage with framed photographs of bohemian North Beach scenes from the 1950s and 1960s, while the *pension*-like **San Remo Hotel**, a pretty Italianate Victorian at 2337 Mason Street, is more ideal for soaking up the area's Italian ambience. For both, *see chapter* **Accommodation**.

The neighbourhood's array of excellent coffee shops is truly dazzling. Particular landmarks include **Caffè Trieste** at Vallejo Street and Grant Avenue – the oldest coffee shop in San Francisco, where Coppola is supposed to have discussed the script of *The Godfather* with Mario Puzo and where there are mini concerts on Saturday afternoons. At **Caffè Roma** (526 Columbus Avenue; 296 7942), the coffee is roasted on the premises and John Lee Hooker is an occasional customer. **Mario's Bohemian Cigar Store** (566 Columbus), sells delicious focaccia sandwiches and great cappuccinos but no cigars. *See chapter* **Restaurant & Cafés**.

Across the street, **Washington Square** marks the heart of North Beach. The 1879 statue in its centre is of **Benjamin Franklin**, who stands atop a granite-encased time capsule scheduled for re-opening in 2079. Any number of public art fairs fill the park during the weekends in summer and it's a lovely place to sit and watch people walk their dogs, play Frisbee or practise juggling. The square is overlooked by the white stucco Romanesque **Church of Sts Peter and Paul**, where Marilyn Monroe and Joe DiMaggio had their wedding photos taken (since both were divorcees, they had to get married at City Hall).

The North Beach end of **Grant Avenue** (*see* **San Francisco's Nolita** *in chapter* **Shops & Services**) is packed with idiosyncratic shops. **Figoni Hardware** (1351 Grant; 392 4765) has

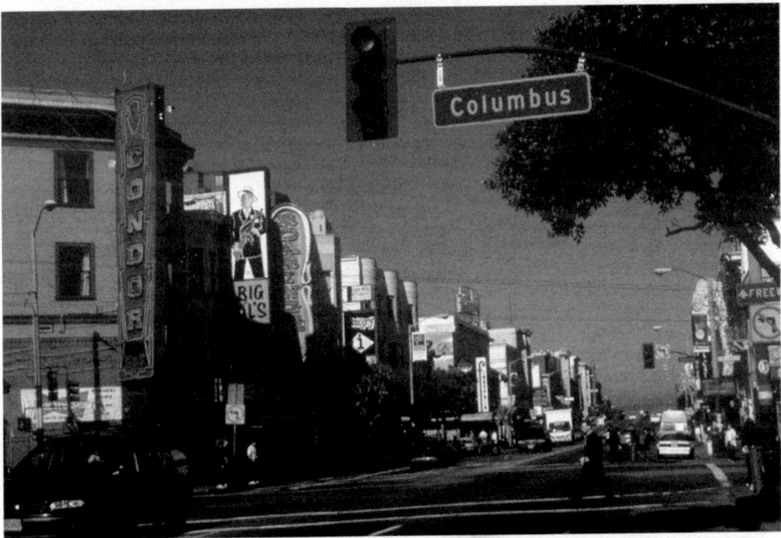

Stroll along **Columbus Avenue** *to get a sense of North Beach's history.*

been run by Mel Figoni since 1924 and is the only place in San Francisco to sell bocce balls. The game is still played at the North Beach Playground, two blocks north-east of Washington Square. Continuing along Grant Avenue, **Prudente & Company** at Union Street is the oldest butcher in the city and a good place to get exotic picnic ingredients such as own-cured cheeses and home-made sausages. There are also several good music bars on the street, including **Grant and Green** blues club at 1371 Green Street (*see chapter* **Nightlife**). Don't miss the rustic Spanish restaurant **La Bodega** (1337 Grant Avenue; 433 0439); the food is average but the flamenco dancing is great.

Telegraph Hill

Telegraph Hill was the site of the West Coast's first telegraph, one that tapped out bulletins from ships arriving from across the Pacific. Bordered by Grant Avenue, Green, Bay and Sansome Streets, Telegraph Hill's best feature is **Coit Tower** (*see below for listings*), which is shaped like the nozzle of a fire hose. This 64-metre (210-foot) high concrete turret, built by City Hall architect Arthur Brown in 1933, was a gift to the city from the eccentric Lillie Hitchcock Coit, who was snatched as a child from a blaze and subsequently became a lifelong fan of firemen.

Before you take the lift to the top of the tower (which provides spectacular vistas of the city and Bay), spend some time inspecting the murals inside the base of the column, artworks supervised by Diego Rivera for the WPA (Works Project Administration) set up by Roosevelt to create employment during the Depression. The Socialist Realist images of muscle-bound Californian workers were deemed subversive at the time of their completion in 1934; a hammer and sickle were erased from one and nervous authorities delayed the tower's opening.

Descend the hill east from Coit Tower via the steep wooden **Filbert Steps** (*see page 40* **The only way is up**), which run from Montgomery to Sansome Streets, past flower bedecked paths and cottages and the eccentric Julius Castle restaurant perched at the crest of Montgomery Street. At the bottom, head a block east to Levi Plaza, where you can follow a path through a fountain designed by Lawrence Halprin. In their current corporate offices, some of the first jeans ever stitched by Levi Strauss are on display. (The factory, which you can tour, is in an insalubrious block at 250 Valencia near 13th Street in the Mission. Phone 565 9153 for a tour appointment.)

Coit Tower

Telegraph Hill (362 0808). Bus 39. **Open** 10am-7pm daily. **Admission** *elevator* $3.75.
Map G2

The Embarcadero

Before the San Francisco-Oakland Bay and Golden Gate Bridges were built in the 1930s, the Embarcadero, which stretches along the waterfront from Market Street in both directions from the Bay Bridge, used to be the landing point for more than 50,000 daily commuters from Marin and the East Bay. Subsequently overshadowed by an ugly freeway, the area went from being one of San Francisco's busiest places to one of its emptiest. Things improved considerably after the 1989 earthquake damaged the freeway beyond repair and it was demolished. The rediscovered area crowns the downtown region and connects Fisherman's Wharf with South Beach in a graceful, palm tree-lined boulevard.

At its centre is the stately **Ferry Building**, which divides even-numbered piers (to the south) from odd (to the north). Opposite the Ferry Building stands **Justin Herman Plaza** and a huge sculpture and fountain by French-Canadian artist Armand Vaillancourt. A section of the Embarcadero has been christened **Herb Caen Boulevard…** in honour of the *Chronicle*'s longtime daily columnist (and devotee of the three point ellipsis), who died in 1997. He attended the renaming ceremony before he died and there's a statue of him next to the Ferry Building. The clock on the Ferry Building's tower – an 1894 replica of Seville cathedral's campanile – stopped at the precise minute the 1906 and 1989 earthquakes struck, but, although the building's spire leaned precariously, on neither occasion did it fall.

A perfect place for a long walk on a balmy autumn evening, San Francisco's most spectacular promenade has been refurbished, dotted with public art, fortified with historical markers and benches and highlighted with a path of glass bricks that glow at night. The Embarcadero remains pleasantly uncrowded except for the area immediately parallel to the **Embarcadero Center** – a huge complex of hotels, offices, restaurants and shops that spans four city blocks, between Battery, Drumm, Clay and Washington Streets (*see chapter* **Shops & Services**).

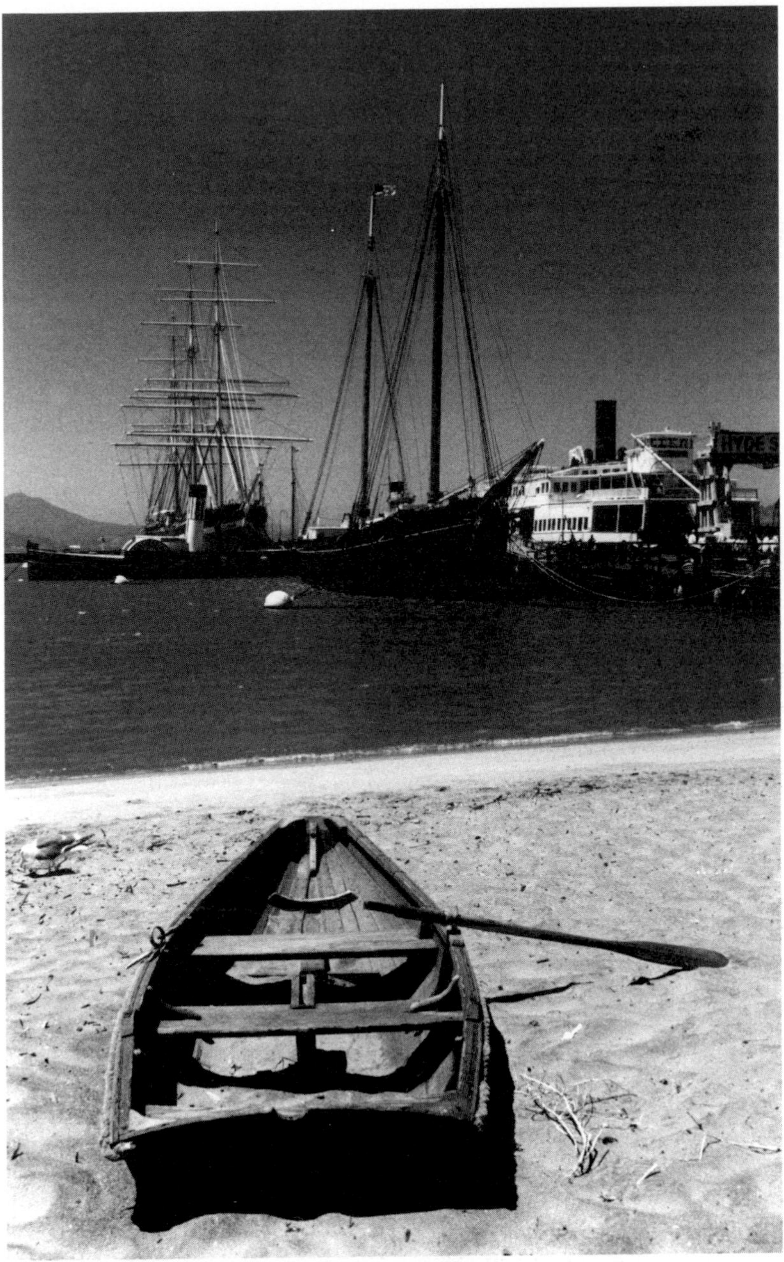

Hyde Street Pier and the man-made shores of **Aquatic Park**. *See page 48.*

Fisherman's Wharf, Aquatic Park & the Waterfront

At the north-western end of the Embarcadero, San Francisco's port was once the soul of the city, but as the commercial shipping and fishing moved out, **Fisherman's Wharf** (*see below for listings*) was converted into a garish and inexplicably popular tourist site. Except as a departure point for day trips by ferry to **Alcatraz Island** (*see page 73*), the Wharf doesn't have a great deal to recommend it unless you're a fan of the sort of 'souvenirs' on sale all over the world that all seem to be made in Hong Kong anyway. The magic of the Wharf's history survives only in the early hours when the few fishermen still working unload their catch for buyers from the city's restaurants.

If you have a taste for the kitsch or the macabre, however, you won't want to miss the newly rebuilt **Wax Museum** (145 Jefferson Street; 1-800 439 4305/885 4975/www.waxmuseum.com), or **Ripley's Believe It Or Not** (175 Jefferson Street; 771 6188). Further east is **Pier 39** (*see chapter* **Shops & Services**), a 45-acre amusement arcade/shopping complex where you can get anything from fast food and souvenir T-shirts to giant chocolate teddy bears. The best entertainment here (both fun and free) is provided by the barking, belching sea lions that congregate on the pontoons nearby.

Further west, the nineteenth century red-brick **Ghirardelli Square** (*see chapter* **Shops & Services**) housed a famous chocolate factory until the 1960s, when it was turned into a complex of shops and restaurants. You can sort through your swag in the central plaza, where the lovely Mermaid Fountain was designed by local artist Ruth Asawa. Another reminder of the area's former industrial life is **The Cannery** on Leavenworth Street (*see chapter* **Shops & Services**). Built in 1909 as a Del Monte fruit-canning factory, it's now yet another twee shopping mall modelled along the lines of London's Covent Garden, complete with street performers. The Cannery also houses **Cobb's Comedy Club** (*see chapter* **Nightlife**) which showcases some of the top comedians in the country; on open mike night, you might even witness the career baby-steps of the next Robin Williams.

The shores of **Aquatic Park** (*see below for listings*) offer one of the best strolls in the city, providing a panorama of the Golden Gate Bridge, Alcatraz, windsurfers, sailing boats, wildly coloured kites and dogs catching Frisbees. If it's a stormy day, opt for a (free) tour of the **National Maritime Museum** (*see chapter* **Museums & Galleries**), a curved white Art Deco building that looks like an ocean liner. Along the Municipal Pier, accessible from the northern end of Van Ness Avenue, fishermen try their luck; historic ships are moored at the Hyde Street Pier, to the east, including the **Eureka**, an 1890 steam-powered ferry. It's here that the 21.7-kilometre (32-mile) Golden Gate Promenade begins, continuing along the Bay past the defunct gun emplacements of **Fort Point** (*see page 65*) to Crissy Field where open-air concerts are often held and the Golden Gate Bridge.

The entire waterfront as far west as Ocean Beach was incorporated into the Golden Gate National Recreation Area in 1972, when the authorities barred the tourist kitsch of Fisherman's Wharf from spreading further into the world's largest urban park. Only hardy regulars from the nearby **Dolphin Club** (502 Jefferson Street, at Hyde Street; 441 9329) wearing matching Speedos, risk a plunge into the choppy sea.

Aquatic Park

Between Hyde Street & Van Ness Avenue. Bus 19, 30, 32, 42/cable car Powell-Hyde. **Map F1**

Fisherman's Wharf

Jefferson & Beach Streets, between Kearny & Hyde Streets. Bus 15, 30, 32, 39, 42/cable car Powell-Hyde or Powell-Mason. **Map F1**

SoMa, South Beach & the Mission

Formerly known as South-of-the-Slot, the area south of Market Street is also called **SoMa**, which, like New York's Soho, was for many years a neglected area occupied predominantly by warehouses and sweatshops. The current moniker was first adopted to help overcome the district's sketchy reputation, and it worked: SoMa is now a hub for multimedia businesses, visual arts, good restaurants and all-night parties. It contains two huge arts centres, a world-class convention hall, reconditioned warehouses with loft spaces that double as residences and offices, and a new waterfront plaza made possible by the removal of the earthquake-damaged freeway.

Yerba Buena Gardens

If you're discovering SoMa for the first time, you might as well start with the best it has to offer: the **Yerba Buena Gardens Complex**, the 87-acre compound bounded by Mission, Third, Folsom and Fourth Streets. If you can't find something to occupy yourself here, there's no hope for you. Start with the **San Francisco Museum of Modern Art (SFMOMA)** on Yerba Buena's north-eastern side: the $60 million red-brick landmark with the huge cylindrical skylight was designed by Mario Botta and opened in 1995. Under current director David Ross, SFMOMA has begun to amass an essential permanent collection, including works by Jasper Johns, Imogen Cunningham, Roy Lichtenstein and many others (*see chapter* **Museums & Galleries**). Across Third Street from SFMOMA, **Esplanade Gardens** are made up of a large urban park with sculptured walks, an outdoor stage, benches, fountains and cafés.

Surrounding them are the **Center for the Arts**, which contains the **Galleries and Forum**, and, at the corner of Third and Howard Streets, the **Theater at Yerba Buena Center of the Arts**, an architectural beauty of an auditorium.

Ingeniously covering the top of the Moscone Convention Center, the newly developed **Rooftop at Yerba Buena Gardens** contains several new child-friendly attractions: **Zeum** (*see chapter* **Children**), an arts and technology museum; the brand new **Yerba Buena Bowling Center** (*see chapter* **Sport & Fitness**), the **Yerba Buena Ice Skating Center** (1750 Folsom Street; 777 3727); and a lovely, refurbished **carousel** – all within a half-block walk of Yerba Buena.

Continuing clockwise, the huge new Sony **Metreon** (*see chapters* **Shops & Services** *and* **Film**) fills an entire block on Fourth Street from Howard to Mission. This over-the-top entertainment mall holds no less than 15 cinemas, several shops, restaurants, game rooms and a 86-metre (270-foot) long public lobby that exits into Yerba Buena Esplanade Gardens. Developers are hoping that despite the current parking nightmare – unbelievably, the Metreon was built without providing additional parking – San Franciscans and other Bay Area residents will opt to spend their cash on the many diversions inside. Only time will tell.

The true economic engine of this section of SoMa, however, is the vast **Moscone Convention Center** (*see below for listings*) on Howard Street, a two-block hive of exhibition halls named after former Mayor George Moscone. Hundreds of thousands of members of the world's business community have passed through its doors, which frame Howard Street between Third and Fourth Streets. The real centre is a world away from the rest of Yerba Buena: **Moscone North** is built entirely underground, beneath the Esplanade Gardens; **Moscone South** is a windowless box, girded and soulless and open only to paid-up conventioneers. The two buildings are connected by a walkway that runs under Howard Street. Since it was first begun in 1978, the centre has been under a constant process of enlargement, with plans to build an additional free-standing space in 2000 on the northwest corner of Howard and Fourth Streets.

Moscone Convention Center

Howard Street, between Third & Fourth Streets (974 4000). Bus 12, 15, 30, 45, 76.
Map H4
Website: www.moscone.com

Yerba Buena Gardens Complex

Third & Fourth Streets, between Mission & Folsom Streets (information 541 0312). Bus 12, 15, 30, 45, 76. **Map H4**
For **SFMOMA** and the **Yerba Buena Center for the Arts** *see chapter* **Museums & Galleries**; for the **Theater at Yerba Buena Center for the Arts** *see chapter* **Performing Arts**.

Around SoMa

In addition to the Yerba Buena Center, SFMOMA and Moscone, there are countless other places to explore in the neighbourhood. The unmissable **Ansel Adams Center for Photography** at 250 Fourth Street (*see chapter* **Museums & Galleries**) features exhibitions of the work of masters of photography, old and new. Fans of public art (and local artists) will appreciate the two huge works that sit either side of SFMOMA: a two-part mural, 'SKY/GROUND', by local artist Rigo is painted onto the unmodernised building at Third and Mission; and a dramatic, nine-metre (30-foot) figure by sculptor MD Stutz reclines on the upper atrium of the newly-opened **W Hotel** at Third and Howard (*see chapter* **Accommodation**). Based on Fourth Street, members of the **Society of California Pioneers** (*see below for listings*) are descendants of the state's first settlers. The SCP maintains a research library, museum and gallery and also organises educational and social activities. Access is by appointment only: consult their website for more information.

If you're hungry in this part of SoMa, you're in luck. In addition to dozens of cafés, there's **LuLu** at 816 Folsom Street, a noisy and popular eatery in a warehouse space, and the stylish new **XYZ** at 181 Third Street which offers elegant, minimalist dining inside the swanky W Hotel (*see chapter* **Restaurants & Cafés** for details of both).

Society of California Pioneers

300 Fourth Street, at Folsom Street (957 1849/ pioneers@wenet.net). Bus 12, 15, 30, 45, 76.
Open *by appointment* 9am-5pm Mon-Fri.
Map H4
Website: www.wenet.net/~pioneers

11th & Folsom Streets

Although it has diversified and gentrified somewhat and many of its new loft-living residents are grumbling about the noise, SoMa still remains high on the list of nightlife destinations. Several corners of the area are axes for multiple businesses: the junction of 11th and Folsom Streets remains a good area for both clubs and restaurants. If you like live music, try the **Paradise Lounge** (1501 Folsom Street) or **Slim's** (333 11th Street). *See chapter* **Nightlife** for both.

For dance clubs near 11th and Folsom, around the corner in one direction looms the **Holy Cow**

(1531 Folsom Street) and a three-block walk towards Eighth Street will land you at the **Cat Club** (1190 Folsom Street), which has different music on different nights. The same applies to the cavernous **Ten15 Folsom** (1015 Folsom Street; *see chapter* **Nightlife** for all three) – also currently under attack by yuppie condowners. For a laundry stop and a cappuccino during the day or a decent selection of beers on tap in the evening, drop into **Brainwash** (1122 Folsom Street; *see chapter* **Shops & Services**), a full-service bar, café and Laundromat. The late-night crowds convene, as they always have, at **Hamburger Mary's** (1582 Folsom Street) for a post-partying bite (*see chapter* **Restaurants & Cafés**).

South Park & South Beach

To the south of Moscone, South Park offers a pastoral escape from the snarled three-lane boulevards surrounding it. A pioneer residential development designed by an Englishman during the Gold Rush, the neighbourhood surrounding this charming, oval-shaped park became an African-American enclave in the years following World War II. Undervalued for decades, South Park's potential was not lost on the private sector, which began renovating the garages, workshops and houses in the area in the early 1980s. The developers have since been rewarded handsomely for their efforts.

Investors saw South Park initially as a perfect spot for new restaurant ventures. First to open was the **South Park Café** (108 South Park Avenue). Other more casual venues such as **Caffè Centro** (102 South Park) weren't far behind (*see chapter* **Restaurants & Cafés** for both).

The more recent and headline-grabbing element of the South Park story, however, is the explosion of digital technology and Internet commerce. The area marks the centre of the so-called 'Multimedia Gulch'. Though there isn't much of a gulch, the Wild West-sounding name has stuck and come to represent the area and the industry as a whole, just as Madison Avenue stands for the advertising world or Hollywood the movies. Many of the customers cramming South Park's cafés and picnic tables are employed by telecommunications firms, Internet ventures or other related media. Other than Silicon Valley, perhaps, this is the best place to observe the starry-eyed youth plugged into America's latest cultural fantasy/profit motive.

Further east from South Park, **South Beach** comprises a gentrifying area from the **Rincon Center** at the corner of Mission and Spear Streets (*see below for listings*) along the Bay to **Pacific Bell Park** near Pier 40. Rincon is a huge residential tower and shopping mall which contains a pair of huge WPA murals and one of San Francisco's most impressive fountains, a 26-metre (85-foot) atrium with a cascade of water. Pacific Bell Park is better known as the San Francisco Giants' new baseball stadium, scheduled to open on April Fool's Day of 2000 (*see chapter* **Sport & Fitness**). The edges of the neighbourhood are connected by the E, Muni's latest Metro line. Should you decide to hoof it, you'll be rewarded with a gorgeous stroll along this section of the Embarcadero promenade, replete with palm trees and a stunning view of the **Ferry Building** (*see page 46*), the **Financial District** (*see page 37*) and city hills behind, and the underside of the **San Francisco-Oakland Bay Bridge** (*see page 73*).

If its views are diverse, South Beach's citizenry isn't. A demographic cross between young Financial District investors and South Park geeks, the neighbourhood is yuppie central. Expect to see lots of mobiles, BMWs, women with *Friends* hairstyles and groups of overdressed white guys high-fiving each other. Among the waterfront attractions are the **Gordon Biersch** brewpub at 2 Harrison Street (*see chapter* **Bars**) and the five-star **Boulevard** on Mission Street. The design-heavy **Entros** at 270 Brannan Street rides the coat-tails of Asian-Caribbean fusion; and **MoMo's San Franciscan Grill**, at 760 Second Street serves hearty, rustic fare to healthy, wealthy young patrons in the shade of the new ballpark (*see chapter* **Restaurant & Cafés**).

Rincon Center

Spear & Mission Streets (243 0473).
BART Embarcadero. **Open** 24 hours daily.
Map J3

The Mission

Further south, the city's oldest neighbourhood is the embodiment of change in San Francisco. Inhabited by the Spanish early in the city's history, the district has seen influxes of Irish, German, Italian, Latin and, most recently, Asian immigrants, all of whom brush shoulders today with the 'New Bohemians' who populate the region's cafés, bars and music venues. The Mission is like no other area: the weather is warmer, the streets more crowded – even the smells are different: a mix of chilli, garlic, onion, tomatoes, coriander and seared meat permeates the air.

Often the first port of call for a steady influx of newcomers waiting to enter the American mainstream, the Mission's history is one of tolerance. It is home to a dazzling array of political and spiritual art: there are more than 200 murals in the district alone, painted on the walls of banks, schools and restaurants, many celebrating the struggles and achievements of its Latino residents. Though the *barrio* also has more than its fair share of prostitutes, drug addicts and gangs, it definitely invites exploration beyond the Mission Dolores, the only stop on the tourist bus routes.

Escape from the busy boulevards into **South Park**, *centre of 'Multimedia Gulch'.*

Recently, the area – or at least a wide swath at its eastern edge, in the region dubbed 'Silicon Alley' – has begun to gentrify, its individual, blue-collar funkiness giving way to loft conversions, condominiums and a wealthier, whiter demographic. Though such changes open up the area to new possibilities, the yuppie arrival has also meant the skyrocketing of real estate prices, the exodus of blue-collar families and an inevitable loss of local diversity and vital culture. If the trend continues, in ten years the Mission will have transformed into another Marina district, with chain restaurants on every corner and SUVs (sport utility vehicles) double-parked on every street.

Mission Street

Mission Street is the district's economic lifeline, a river of commercialism catering to the area's middle-to-low-income residents with cheque-cashing operations, banks and shops crammed with cheap clothes, kitchen appliances and second-hand goods. It also offers some of the best people-watching in the city. Locals still report seeing the Red Man and the White Lady, two residents who for years have strolled the local streets, their skin painted a flaming red and pallid white respectively.

Despite Mission Street's overt dedication to trade, it contains some noteworthy sights. Don't miss **Ritmo Latino** (2401 Mission Street), with its huge selection of Latin music (*see chapter* **Shops & Services**). Inside the **Bank of America** (2701 Mission Street), a powerful mural depicts the area's history. Near 24th Street, the **Kings Bakery Café** (2846 Mission Street; 282 4550) exemplifies how different cultures have met and melded in this area: the trilingual Korean owner sells Mexican pastries to a stream of Anglo, Asian and Central American customers. **La Traviata** (2854 Mission Street; 282 0500), an upmarket Italian restaurant once favoured by visiting opera singers, offers a cosy, quiet retreat from the crowds. And **Rockapulco** (3140 Mission Street) is the place to catch a big brass salsa band (*see chapter* **Nightlife**).

Valencia Street

The Mission is perpetually sunny, even on the foggiest days and a walk in most directions is an easy one. On Valencia Street, you can measure your stroll by checking out the two **Muddy Waters** cafés, set nearly a mile apart on 24th and 17th streets (521 Valencia Street, 863 8006 and 1304 Valencia Street, 647 7994). In between, the curious

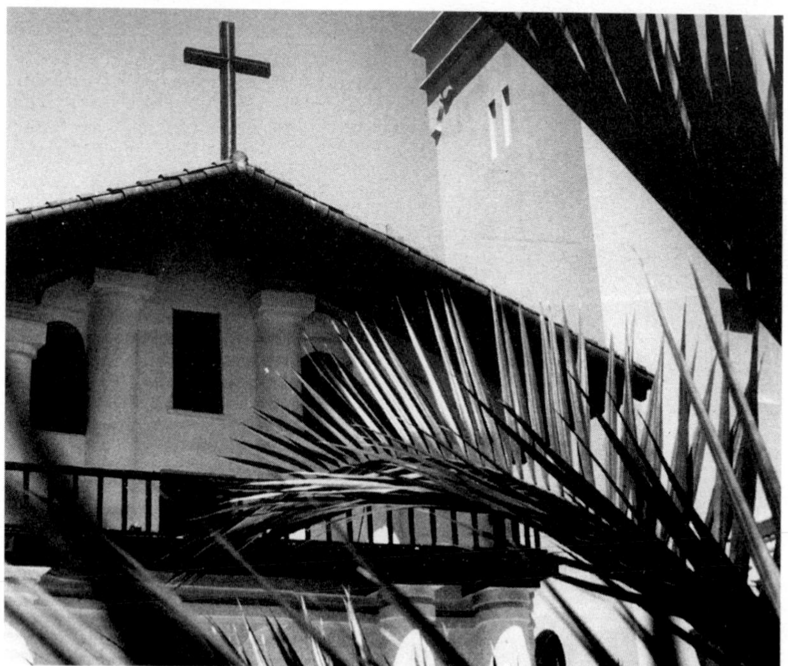

The oldest standing structure in the city, **Mission Dolores**.

will find off-beat bookshops such as **Books on Wings** (La Casa de Libros) near 20th Street (973 Valencia Street; 285 1399/285 1145) and the long-standing women's sex shop **Good Vibrations** at 23rd Street (*see chapter* **Shops & Services**).

There are dozens of eateries in this section of the neighbourhood, serving a nightly influx of insatiable San Franciscans in search of good food. Just try to get a table at the **Slanted Door** at 584 Valencia, the hot new **Delfina** at 3621 18th Street (*see chapter* **Restaurants & Cafés**) or **Esperpento**'s Spanish hideaway (3295 22nd Street; 282 8867), and you'll get a sense of the district's culinary reputation.

16th Street

The stretch of 16th Street between Mission and Dolores Streets constitutes only three blocks, but is packed with goodies. Crowded restaurants dispense everything from French crêpes (**Ti Couz Crêperie**, 3108 16th Street; *see chapter* **Restaurants & Cafés**) to Spanish tapas and sangria (**Picaro**, 3120 16th Street). At Rondel Alley, just past the cool **Skylark** pub (3089 16th Street; *see chapter* **Bars**), **Pancho Villa Taqueria** (3071 16th Street) is one of the district's most visited taquerias, where the machine-gun rat-tat-tat of cleavers bouncing on butcher blocks is matched with the smell of seared onion and chillis (*see chapter* **Restaurants & Cafés**). Across Valencia Street, the **Roxie** cinema (3117 16th Street) screens an eclectic playbill of avant-garde films (*see chapter* **Film**).

A walk west to **Dolores Street** takes you to San Francisco's oldest building, the 200-year-old **Mission Dolores** (*see below for listings*), founded when a zealous *conquistador* planted a simple white cross on the edge of what was once a lake. Small wonder that the cool, dim interior of the Mission San Francisco de Assisi looks authentic. The oldest standing structure in the city, its thick adobe walls have withstood the test of time (and earthquakes). Dedicated on 2 August 1791, Mission Dolores was the sixth of 21 Franciscan missions built by Spanish settlers and was named after the nearby Laguna de los Dolores (Lake of Our Lady of Sorrows). Now it's attached to a basilica (rebuilt in 1918) where most of the religious services take place, including the traditional midnight mass at Christmas. There's a tiny museum and a flower-filled cemetery containing the remains of the city's first mayor as well as Spanish settlers and the mass grave of thousands of Indians who died in their service.

Two blocks south is **Mission Dolores Park** (*see below for listings*), worth visiting during daylight hours for the view of San Francisco and the Bay from the apex at 20th and Church Streets and for the mélange of people who frequent the park. At the same intersection, notice the small, bronze-painted fire plug, which in 1906 provided firefighters with the only working water source after the earthquake. The little hydrant did its job, keeping the flames away from homes in the Noe Valley district. A couple of blocks east on 18th Street is the **Women's Building** (*see below for listings*), which houses a refuge, recreation centre and theatre workshop. The outside of the building is adorned with one of the grandest of the Mission's murals, a larger-than-life retelling of woman's history in the New World, topped with a portrait of Guatemalan Nobel Laureate Rigoberta Menchu.

Around 24th Street

At the neighbourhood's southern end, 24th Street offers a variety of tastes from different Latin American countries: there's the Caribbean-spiced **El Nuevo Frutilandia** (3077 24th Street, *see chapter* **Restaurants & Cafés**); **El Farolito** (2950 24th Street, at Alabama; 641 0758), which serves simple but good Mexican food; **La Palma Mexicatessen** (2884 24th Street, at Bryant; 647 1500), which sells the only authentic, handmade corn tortillas in the district, and nearby on Folsom, **El Pollo Supremo** (2801 Folsom Street, at 25th; 550 1193), whose fruit-juice-and-garlic-marinated chicken draws Financial District business types as well as local families. Another local favourite is the **St Francis Fountain and Candy Store** (2801 24th Street; 826 4200), birthplace of the city's beloved 49ers football team.

Near the intersection of 18th and Bryant, a media community has sprung up. Dubbed 'Silicon Alley' by the locals, the conglomerate includes local public radio and television station KQED-FM and KQED-TV, offices of the *San Francisco Bay Guardian* and a host of tiny multimedia start-ups – animation studios, publishers and pioneers in online electronic commerce, game developers – who leapt into the neighbourhood while rents were still cheap. The social hubs for this 'hood-within-a-'hood seem to be the **Slow Club** at 2501 Mariposa Street (*see chapter* **Bars**) for drinks, and the sunny **Universal Café** at 2814 19th Street (*see chapter* **Restaurants & Cafés**) for lunch and dinner. But other restaurants – notably **Blowfish Sushi** at 2170 Bryant Street and **Gordon's** at 500 Florida Street (*see chapter* **Restaurants & Cafés**) have made this neo-hip industrial mecca even more of a destination. The **Atlas Café** at 3049 20th Street (648 1047) sells decent soups and sandwiches and seems to have kept the original spirit of the neighbourhood alive.

Mission Dolores

3321 Dolores Street, at 16th Street (621 8203). BART 16th Street/Muni Metro F, J, K, L, M/ bus 22, 24. **Open** 9am-4pm daily. **Admission** $2; $1 concessions. **Map E6**

Mission Dolores Park

Bordered by 18th, 20th, Church & Dolores Streets. Muni Metro J/bus 33. **Castro/Mission Map Y1**

Mission murals

The Mission district is famous for hundreds of exuberant, brilliantly coloured murals, artworks that decorate everything from restaurants, banks and buildings to garage doors and sidewalks (for details of organised tours, *see page 78*). Subjects range from seasonal celebrations to the building of the BART transport system, covering every political and social preoccupation of the neighbourhood. Originally inhabited by Italian, German and Irish immigrants, the area has since been settled by thousands of Hispanic families (who began emigrating from Central America in the 1960s) as well as Asian immigrants from Vietnam, Cambodia and Laos. 24th Street is the Mission district at its diverse, multicultural best.

Like the area's other main streets, 24th is lined with murals: at South Van Ness Avenue, an illustration of Mexican-American rock star Carlos Santana is surrounded by plumed participants in the Mission's annual carnival. Further east along 24th Street, **Balmy Alley** was once a showplace for some of the best and freshest murals. It's beginning to suffer from neglect – and from homeowners who resent the constant flow of pedestrian traffic that the urban gallery has inspired. Some works have been replaced by iron fencing, others painted over. Still, there's plenty to see and the small street remains a crucial tableaux of San Francisco's artistic and political history.

Further down 24th Street, on the north wall of St Peter's Catholic Church at Florida Street, a mural describes the catastrophic meeting of the Old and New Worlds. At the intersection of Bryant Street, **Galeria de la Raza** displays ever-changing exhibitions by local artists (*see chapter* **Museums & Galleries**). Its adjoining **Studio 24** (*see chapter* **Shops & Services**) supports the gallery by selling contemporary and traditional Latin American crafts.

Balmy Alley

Off 24th Street, between Treat & Harrison Streets. BART 24th Street/bus 12, 48, 67. **Castro/Mission Map Z2**

Women's Building

3543 18th Street, at Valencia Street (431 1180/1181). Bus 26, 33. **Castro/Mission Map Y1**

Potrero Hill & Noe Valley

To the east of the Mission, **Potrero Hill** is nearly always sunny, even when the rest of the city is shrouded in fog. Newspaper and magazine outlet **Farleys** at 1315 18th Street (*see chapter* **Shops & Services**), is a favourite dessert hangout, as is **Klein's Delicatessen** at 510 Connecticut Street (821 9149), for succulent sandwiches. Just a few blocks away is the **Esprit** factory outlet store, at 499 Illinois Street (*see chapter* **Shops & Services**), for marked-down designs. Across Esprit's parking lot, is **42 Degrees**, an excellent spot for lunch or a reviving cup of coffee after a hard morning's shopping (235 16th Street; 777 5558). The **Bottom of the Hill** at 1233 17th Street (*see chapter* **Nightlife**) has good local bands and an outdoor patio where barbecues are held on Sunday afternoons.

Quaint **Noe Valley**, the area roughly bordered by 20th, Dolores, 30th and Douglass Streets, was once populated by Irish families. Still a predominantly residential area, it is now frequented by young couples pushing strollers who flock to the area because the architecture is pretty, the people friendly and the neighbourhood quiet and sunny. The peaceful residential streets are lined with beautifully restored Victorian houses and gardens and filled with locals walking their dogs or enjoying the sunshine. **Twin Peaks** and **Sutro Tower** overlook the area from the west (*see page 58*) and to the east are great views of East Bay.

Activity in Noe Valley is centred around **24th Street**, between Church and Douglass, which has an excellent selection of clothes shops, book and magazine stores and cafés. Starting at the top of the hill, **Firefly** restaurant serves enormous portions in intimate, romantic surroundings (4288 24th Street, *see chapter* **Restaurants & Cafés**). Heading east down the hill, **Déjà Vu** (4156 24th Street; 642 1122), sells second-hand wedding dresses, vintage clothing, American pottery and dinnerware, as well as small pieces of furniture. The **San Francisco Mystery Bookstore** on the corner of Diamond and 24th Streets (*see chapter* **Shops & Services**) is a tiny gem selling new and second-hand mystery books and magazines.

A relative newcomer to the area is **Lovejoy's English Tea Room** (1195 Church Street; 648 5895), where you can have a traditional English high tea and then buy the cup and saucer you drank it from, as well as the chair you sat on and the paintings on the wall. **La Sirena Botanica** (1509 Church Street; 285 0612), supplies magical herbs, incense and spiritual goods to neighbourhood pagans.

Expect the unexpected in the constantly changing **Mission district**.

24

The central neighbourhoods

If SoMa and parts of the Mission represent gentrification, the central neighbourhoods stand for continuity and the sense that little has changed in many years. Although the inhabitants of the Haight, the Castro, the Marina or Pacific Heights may come and go, they still represent the young, gay, straight or wealthy demographics which are characteristic of their respective 'hoods.

Civic Center

On either side of Van Ness Avenue just north of Market Street, a phalanx of Beaux Arts buildings houses the offices of city government and many of its attending arts and performance centres and auditoria. Standing out among them is the stunning **City Hall** (*see opposite* **Civic centrepiece**), which has recently been retrofitted to protect it against earthquake damage. It was originally built in 1915 under the auspices of Mayor 'Sunny Jim' Rolph to replace the one that collapsed during the 1906 earthquake. Designed by Arthur Brown at an original cost of $3.5 million, it was here that Dan White assassinated Mayor George Moscone and gay Supervisor Harvey Milk in 1978 (*see chapter* **History**).

Civic Center and its surrounding buildings (which extend east to Hyde Street, west to Franklin and north to McAllister) were designed at the turn of the last century on a grand scale that was intended to suggest (ironically enough for San Francisco) balance and order. The **Louise M Davies Symphony Hall**, on the block between Van Ness Avenue and Franklin Streets, Grove and Hayes Streets, is the base of the San Francisco Symphony Orchestra and chorus, and regularly hosts lectures, authors' readings and other special events. North across Grove Street is the **War Memorial Opera House**, which underwent major retrofitting and renovation in 1996. The $86.5 million task included everything from newly gilding the trim on the doors and walls to re-upholstering seats, adding new curtains and hanging a 66,000-watt chandelier. Gaetono Merola founded the San Francisco Opera in 1923 and the company moved into this Beaux Arts gem – designed by Arthur Brown and dedicated to the soldiers of World War I – in 1932. In June 1945 51 nations signed the United Nations charter here and so gave birth to the UN (*see chapter* **Performing Arts** for both).

To the north of the Opera House is the **Veterans' Building**, which until 1995 was home to the San Francisco Museum of Modern Art. During the restoration of City Hall, the building housed the bulk of city services; it still functions primarily as overflow for local government offices. However, the building also contains the delightful **San Francisco Art Commission Gallery** at 401 Van Ness Avenue at McAllister Street (*see chapter* **Museums & Galleries**), a free exhibition space based on the main floor which specialises in politically- or sociologically-driven art.

North of City Hall, the **Civic Center Courthouse** (400 McAllister Street) stands just east of the massive **State of California Building** (300 McAllister Street), distinguished from the building of the same name on Van Ness by being named after former US Supreme Court Chief Justice Earl Warren; both opened in 1999. Just east, on the corner of Larkin and McAllister Streets, the former Main Library building will eventually contain the **Asian Art Museum**, currently in Golden Gate Park, but due to move here in 2002 after the building undergoes a formidable interior redesign (*see chapter* **Museums & Galleries**).

Continuing around the plaza, **San Francisco Main Library** (*see below for listings*) on the southeastern corner of Civic Center re-opened in 1996 in a gorgeous six-storey structure that combines the Beaux Arts style with a healthy dash of modernism. Enter from the Larkin Street side and descend the stairway into the atrium-like lobby, where vaulted floors rise in tiers above you. The **San Francisco History Room** occupies the top floor, and has changing exhibitions, a large photo archive and knowledgeable, friendly staff. The café in the basement sells mediocre, expensive food, good only in a pinch.

Standing back-to-back with the Main Library, is **United Nations Plaza**. Each Wednesday and Sunday morning the Plaza hosts a local **Farmers' Market**, where hundreds of merchants sell the region's freshest produce and other farm-raised edibles.

South and west of the Library, the **Bill Graham Civic Auditorium**, on Grove Street between Polk and Larkin, is named after the city's late favourite concert promoter (Graham was behind the Summer of Love acts and some of San Francisco's first big rock bands). It accommodates up to 5,000 in a boxy, utilitarian space. It's a good – though not ideal – place to hear artists too popular to fill the nearby Warfield Auditorium but not faddish enough for arena shows. It also hosts conferences and conventions that attract fewer attendees than those at the Moscone Center. (*See chapter* **Nightlife**).

For shopping and entertainment in the area, head north on Van Ness one block to Opera Plaza (at McAllister) where you'll find one of the city's best bookshops: **A Clean Well-Lighted Place For Books** (*see chapter* **Shops & Services**)

Civic centrepiece

On 5 January 1999, in a feat of architectural and technological brilliance, San Francisco's City Hall re-opened to the public. The event marked the end of a four-year closure and a $300 million seismic upgrade made necessary by damage the building sustained in the 1989 earthquake. Originally erected in 1915 and designed by Arthur Brown and John Bakewell, City Hall is the epitome of the Beaux-Arts style seen in the rest of Civic Center, with lots of ornamental ironwork, elaborate plasterwork and a giant dome modelled on the one in St Peter's in Rome. Not to be outdone, San Francisco's version stands 4.9 metres (16 feet) higher than the dome of the Capitol in Washington, DC.

Facts and figures, however, cannot convey the grandeur of City Hall's restoration. Step through the doors on Van Ness Avenue or Polk Street and into the central rotunda, a vast, elegant space with sweeping stairway and striking detail. Joe DiMaggio and Marilyn Monroe, like so many other San Franciscans, stepped down this stairway getting hitched here. Above, the magnificent dome overlooks a five-storey-high colonnade, limestone and granite masonry, regal lighting and majestic marble floors. Dubbed 'the most significant interior space in the United States' by a New York architecture critic when it originally opened, the two-block-long, one-block-wide City Hall successfully inspires a sense of municipal awe.

Beneath its classical exterior, City Hall hums with modern technology. Right down to the style used for lettering the directories and room numbers, the place appears as it would have in 1915. But the renovation included installation of sophisticated, up-to-the-minute electronics, computer and security systems – millennial machinery all but invisible to the eye. A system of rubber-and-steel 'base isolators' allows the building to move nearly a metre in any direction, thus protecting it from potential earthquake damage.

San Francisco's first City Hall was an adobe building erected on Portsmouth Square. Later, the site was moved to its current location where the original edifice took 30 years to build, opened in 1899 and was destroyed in the 1906 earthquake. The newest model, built in four years (and renovated, 80 years later, in four more) contains 600 rooms, each allowing in natural light, and houses both the legislative and the executive branches of San Francisco's city and county government.

Free tours are available daily, each offering behind-the-scenes views of the Board of Supervisors' chambers (panelled in hand-carved Manchurian oak) and the mayor's office (only open on weekdays). Visitors can see the mayor's 'International Room', filled with well-wishing gifts from (mostly Pacific Rim) cities and nations. The view of the rotunda from the fourth floor is superb, as are the constantly-changing art and photography exhibitions on view in the basement.

Arrange your guided tour inside the South Light Court, a fascinating mini-museum arrayed with exhibits covering the city's history, neighbourhoods and varied population. Displays include the building's original coin vault; the head from the figure of the Goddess of Progress, who once looked out from the top of the original City Hall; detailed models of the Golden Gate Bridge tower, Italianate architecture and City Hall's dome; and a fire chief's buggy dating from over a century ago.

Equal parts archive, history lesson and architectural masterpiece, City Hall remains a timeless edifice behind which the pulse of civic activity beats. Don't miss it.

City Hall

200 Polk Street, between McAllister & Grove Streets (554 4000). Bus 5, 42, 47, 49.
Open 8am-5pm Mon-Fri. **Map F4/5**

features a great selection and weekly authors' readings. **Stars** restaurant at 555 Golden Gate Avenue (*see chapter* **Restaurants & Cafés**) is the place for celebrity spotting; if it's too pricey for you, then try the dining room of the **California Culinary Academy** on Polk and Turk Streets, where decently priced meals are prepared by tomorrow's chefs.

San Francisco Main Library

Corner of Larkin & Grove Streets (library 557 4400/History Center 557 4567). BART Civic Center/Muni Metro F, J, K, L, M, N/bus 5, 6, 7, 9, 19, 21, 66, 71.
Library **Open** 10am-6pm Mon; 9am-8pm Tue-Thur; 11am-5pm Fri; 9am-5pm Sat; noon-5pm Sun.
Admission free; 3-month visitor's card to check out books $25.
History Center **Open** 10am-6pm Tue-Thur; 11am-5pm Fri; 9am-5pm Sat; noon-5pm Sun.
Both **Map F/G4/5**
Website: http//sfpl.lib.ca.us

Hayes Valley

West of Civic Center, one of San Francisco's fastest developing – and uncharacteristically flat – neighbourhoods used to be one of its least salubrious. In spite of its close proximity to Symphony Hall and the Opera House, few came to Hayes Valley except to visit the prostitutes and drug dealers who did business under cover of an ugly raised freeway. But when damage from the 1989 earthquake brought down the viaduct and, more recently, several blocks of nearby project housing were dismantled, the area started to revive.

Today, the area is one of contrasts and **Hayes Street** is the most typical: older establishments where under-priced treasures can still be unearthed do business alongside stores owned and run by the talented young fashion and furniture designers who have more recently taken over the area. Block parties are held four times a year when shops serve wine and hold fashion shows,

Twin Peaks

The crackerbox apartments that clutter the foreground are ugly and the climate may be windy, cold and foggy, but it's usually worth the gamble driving or walking to the top of Twin Peaks for the city view. Ohlone legend had it that these paired mountains (275 metres/903 feet and 278 metres/913 feet respectively) were twin daughters of an Indian chief, frozen forever by the Great Spirit.

On a clear day you'll get an unobstructed view of the length of Market Street, the Financial District, Civic Center, the Mission district, the San Francisco-Oakland Bay Bridge and the East Bay cities of Oakland and Berkeley. To the south, you can make out Daly City's rikki-tikki houses; nearby, the giant TV and radio aerial **Sutro Tower** looms to the northwest, and beyond it you can catch a bands play, fire-eaters perform and the streets are packed with revellers.

Shops worth a special mention include **Zeitgeist** at 437 Hayes Street for vintage watches; **Bella Donna** (539 Hayes Street; 861 7182) for wonderful clothes and unusual fabrics; and **Worldware** (336 Hayes Street; 487 9030), which sells furniture and body-pampering accoutrements. The **African Outlet** at 524 Octavia Street sells African art; here, too, you can get your body decorated with henna. **Richard Hilkert** (333 Hayes Street; 863 3339) deals in new books, but is probably the best source in the US for valuable, second-hand and out-of-print editions on interior design. *See chapter* **Shops & Services**.

The area's restaurants are similarly idiosyncratic. If you like tarot with your tea, get down to **Mad Magda's Russian Tea Room** at 579 Hayes Street (864 7654). The oldest restaurant in the region is **Powell's Place** (511 Hayes; 863 1404) which serves soul food in the best Southern tradition; the best seafood in the area can be found at the **Hayes Street Grill** at 320 Hayes. Swank new **Absinthe** (398 Hayes) is just down the street from stylish **Suppenküche** (601 Hayes), which is run along the lines of a German *wirtshaus* (for details of the latter three, *see chapter* **Restaurants & Cafés**).

A few blocks away at 66 Page Street, between Franklin and Gough, the oldest Harley Davidson dealership in town, **Dudley Perkins Co** (703 9494), has been selling the noisy beauties since 1914. **Bell'occio** at 8 Brady Street (*see chapter* **Shops & Services**) is worth the minor detour for its stock of European toiletries, antique ribbons and jewellery, as is the clothes shop next door, **Salon de Thé** (6 Brady Street; 863 8391). In the other direction, the **San Francisco Performing Arts Library and Museum** at 399 Grove Street (*see chapter* **Museums & Galleries**) contains a huge collection of performing arts memorabilia.

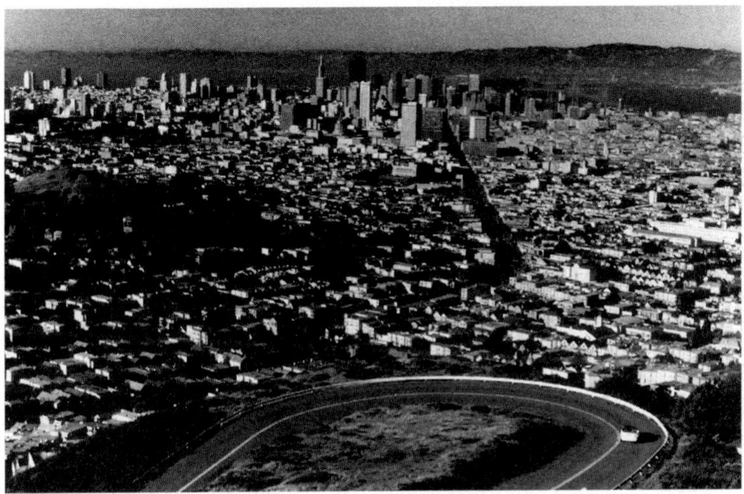

glimpse of the Golden Gate Bridge, as well as most western landmarks (Golden Gate Park and St Ignatius, the cathedral that lords it over the Jesuit University of San Francisco, are but two). Though you're only a couple of hundred feet above the street grid, you'll feel as though you're flying. Further south, **Mount Davidson** (286 metres/938 feet), is the highest spot in San Francisco.

Twin Peaks

Twin Peaks Boulevard, off Portola Drive, between Glenview Drive & Woodside Avenue. Bus 36.

To get there by public transport, take Muni Metro K, L, or M to Forest Hills Station, then bus 36 from the other side of the road. Ask the driver to let you off at Marview, walk up as far as Farview and take the footpath on the right (leaving the reservoirs to your left).

There are also several large, hard-to-miss, antique shops on the up-and-coming section of Market Street that leads you towards Hayes Valley proper. Make time to stop for breakfast or lunch at **Zuni Café** at 1658 Market (*see chapter* **Restaurants & Cafés**). Just across the Rose Street, check out **New Deal** at 1632 Market (552 6208) for one-off, new and second-hand furniture and *objets d'art*. This really is San Francisco's nearest equivalent to New York's Soho, chock-a-block with wonderful shops and restaurants. Don't miss **Flax** at 1699 Market (*see chapter* **Shops & Services**) for incredible art supplies, or the monthly-changing menu at **Carta**, at 1772 Market (*see chapter* **Restaurants & Cafés**).

The Castro

Bordered by 20th, Market, Diamond and Church Streets, the Castro was originally a Mexican ranch. In the 1880s, the land was broken into lots and sold off to mainly working-class Irish families and subsequently became a Catholic stronghold. Rumour has it that the opening of the **Twin Peaks Bar** (401 Castro, at Market Street), the area's first gay bar, caused a mass exodus, and the cheap, picturesque housing left behind was bought and renovated by those who gradually established the area as the capital of gay San Francisco – if not the whole US.

The Castro is one of San Francisco's busiest neighbourhoods. Its geographical marker is the huge neon sign for the beautiful **Castro Theater** at Castro and Market (*see chapter* **Film**), where movies are preceded by entertaining renditions on a Wurlitzer organ. The main thoroughfare is **Castro Street**, between Market and 20th Streets, and **Market**, from Castro to Church Streets.

Sightseeing in the Castro brings home the significance of the city's gay and lesbian scene. Beneath a colossal rainbow flag, **Harvey Milk Plaza**, the Castro Muni stop on the corner of Market and Castro is named after the camera store owner-turned-politician who became San Francisco's (and the nation's) first publicly gay elected official (*see chapter* **History**). Milk's camera store, now occupied by **Skin Zone** at 575 Castro (626 7933), is commemorated by a small sidewalk plaque and a slew of memories, a local counterpart to New York's Stonewall bar and its place in the history of gay politics.

There are plenty of interesting shops and restaurants on Castro Street. Pop into **Cliff's Variety** at 479 (431 5365), which sells fabrics, gifts, toys and general hardware; it gets packed around Hallowe'en when everyone flocks in to buy costume accessories. Just a few doors away, **A Different Light** at 489 (*see chapter* **Shops & Services**) sells books and magazines by, for and about gays and lesbians. On Market Street heading towards downtown, the **Names Project** at 2362 (*see below for listings*) serves as a memorial to all those who have died of Aids. The visitor centre exhibits panels from the Aids quilt, each square created in memory of a lost friend or family member.

Among the many outdoor cafés and restaurants in the neighbourhood, **Fuzio** (469 Castro Street; 863 1400) serves a stylish mix of Asian and Italian dishes at low prices. Down the street, the garden at **Café Flore** at 2298 Market (*see chapter* **Restaurants & Cafés**) is a good people-watching spot and the food is cheap but good. In the other direction is the **Firewood Café** (4248 18th Street; 252 0999), which serves unmissable roast chicken.

The Names Project

2362A Market Street, between Castro & Noe Streets (863 1966/intlquilt@aidsquilt.org). Muni Metro F, K, L, M/bus 24, 35, 37. **Open** noon-5pm Mon-Fri. **Admission** free. **Map E6**
Website: www.aidsquilt.org

The Haight-Ashbury

Along with North Beach, perhaps, no other neighbourhood in the city shares as rich a history as the Haight. Only the fabulous architecture remains as evidence of the district's original incarnation as a late nineteenth-century weekend resort where people came to play in Golden Gate Park or take the steam train to Ocean Beach, and where the wealthy stayed in weekend homes or at the Stanyan Park Hotel.

But if the Victorian era gave the neighbourhood its physical design, 1967's Summer of Love provided an ideology, which, over 30 years later, the Haight-Ashbury has yet to live down. Nowadays, the young panhandlers who jokingly ask for 'spare change for drugs and alcohol?' are mimicking the ethos of the 1960s when many of the shops gave away clothes and food and several restaurants went bust because they let so many people eat without paying.

Upper Haight

To 1960s pop (and dope) aficionados, the historical value of the Upper Haight, or 'Hashbury' is high. The **Grateful Dead** lived at 710 Ashbury Street; **Janis Joplin** at 122 Lyon Street, and **Jefferson Airplane** at 2400 Fulton Street. The address of the 'Red House' referred to in the Jimi Hendrix song is now the **Ashbury Tobacco Center** at 1524 Haight Street. Less appealing landmarks include **Charlie Manson's** mid-1960s house at 636 Cole Street. Wandering the length of Haight Street from Stanyan Street (the entrance to Golden Gate Park) to around Central Avenue will give you a true feel for the area.

To stay in the thick of things you can't do better than the **Red Victorian** at 1665 Haight Street (*see chapter* **Accommodation**). The rooms are decorated in hippie style and everyone has breakfast together in the morning. Work the meal off rollerblading in the park – blades can be rented from **Skates on Haight** at 1818 Haight (*see chapter* **Sport & Fitness**). The **Booksmith** at 1644 Haight (863 8688) is an excellent bookshop that also sells international newspapers and magazines and organises readings. In the evening, you can catch an independent movie at the **Red Vic** cinema at 1727 Haight (*see chapter* **Film**), which has church pew seating (with cushions) and serves homemade snacks and popcorn in big wooden bowls. Up the street, **Cha Cha Cha** (1801 Haight, *see chapter* **Restaurants & Cafés**) is the place to go for Caribbean food and atmosphere; the tapas are cheap, the place is always packed and the sangria is excellent – guaranteed to break the ice on even the chilliest first date.

In line with its gentrification, the neighbourhood sports a swathe of celebrities, including Danny Glover and Bobby McFerrin, both of whom live nearby. Take Rachel Heller's Flower Power tour (*see page 78*) for the lowdown.

Lower Haight

A mile east, the Lower Haight is the name given to the area at the once-seedier eastern end of Haight Street. Here a tattooed, skateboarding crowd mixes with street vendors selling junk from rugs on the pavement. The demolition of nearby project housing indicates an almost certain gentrification for the neighbourhood, but it's a young and hip area, with myriad gems to be found. Don't miss the **Mad Dog in the Fog** pub (530 Haight Street; 626 7279), where you can buy British as well as American beer, eat bangers and mash and shepherd's pie and play darts with the locals. At 557 Haight is the self-consciously hip bar **Noc Noc** (861 5811); a fine breakfast can be scored at **Kate's Kitchen** (471 Haight Street; 626 3984) and across the street, one of the city's best dancing venues is **Nickie's Barbecue** (460 Haight Street; 621 6508) which boasted DJs long before DJs became the latest craze.

Another kind of music can also be found nearby. The incense-scented sanctuary of the **African Orthodox Church of St John Coltrane** on Divisadero Street (*see below for listings*), is a storefront church that shakes to the sound of live music. Located halfway between the Upper and Lower Haight, St John's is dedicated to preserving the musical and spiritual philosophies of its patron saint, the late saxophonist John William Coltrane. And to support this, its leader and founder, Bishop Franzo FW King, plays a mean soprano sax as part of his liturgy.

African Orthodox Church of St John Coltrane

351 Divisadero Street, between Oak & Page Streets (621 4054). Bus 6, 7, 24, 66, 71.
Services 6pm Wed; 10am, 10.30am, 11.45am, Sun.
Map E5

Cole Valley

If the panhandlers and scruffy kids get too much for you, walk south on Cole Street from Haight where you'll find the charming confines of Cole Valley. Nicely situated between **Stanford Medical Center**, **Buena Vista Park** and **Twin Peaks**, the tiny neighbourhood centres on **Cole Valley**, the intersection of Cole and Carl Streets. On the way up Cole, keep an eye out for the local character who sits on the steps outside his house wearing a Viking helmet or a huge golden crown, chatting to passers-by.

For a quintessential San Francisco experience, seek out the **Sword and Rose** (85 Carl Street; 681 5434), the funkiest (and most accurate) place in the city for a Tarot reading. The tiny, stylish **Zazie** (941 Cole Street; 564 5332) is open for breakfast, lunch and dinner, and the **Kezar Bar and Restaurant** (900 Cole; 681 7678) is a friendly local pub that also serves food. If you're feeling more elegant, the **Eos Restaurant and Wine Bar** (*see chapter* **Restaurants & Cafés**) offers sophisticated dining in a bright, airy setting.

If you want some peace and quiet, walk west on Cole, south down Stanyan Street and turn left on Belgrave Avenue to reach **Tank Hill**. This secluded area of grass and rocks is nearly always empty (except for the occasional raccoon exploring the rubbish bins) and offers a romantic view of San Francisco at night.

The Western Addition & Japantown

Bounded approximately by Fell, Arguello, Bush, and Gough Streets, the Western Addition is one of San Francisco's largest neighbourhoods. Once a thriving community of Jewish Americans in the 1920s and 1930s and African Americans after the late 1940s, the area was also home to many Japanese at the onset of World War II. Since that time, the region has suffered more than its share of civic neglect, enduring a brutal series of 'rehabilitations' under the guise of urban renewal. In the 1950s and 1960s, more than a thousand black families' homes were condemned and demolished, and subsequent promises to provide affordable replacements were not kept. Until the construction of the Fillmore Center in the early 1990s, project and ugly subsidised housing were the norm.

The area supports a mix of cultures, young and old, families and single residents. The University of San Francisco sits perched on its western edge;

the 'panhandle' of Golden Gate Park marks its southern boundary; wide, ugly Geary Boulevard, the city's main east-west artery, bisects it. In the 1940s and 1950s, the area was where the original jazz clubs and heart of black culture in the city were to be found. Some elements of this era prevail – in the soul food and barbecue restaurants on Divisadero and the bookshops in the Lower Fillmore – and reflect a culture that's been slowly replaced by demographic change.

The Western Addition is mainly a residential area, with the occasional street corner business and a fine park. **Alamo Square** (bounded by Steiner, Scott, Hayes and Fulton Streets) provides the most photographed view of the city, thanks to the six picture-perfect restored Victorian houses ('**Postcard Row**') that flank its eastern side. The windy square also incorporates a tennis court, picnic area and children's playground.

At the neighbourhood's eastern end, **St Mary's Cathedral** (*see below for listings*), designed by Pietro Belluschi and completed in 1971, is a huge, white, concrete structure that resembles a washing machine (some say a food mixer) and dominates the skyline for miles around. Its soaring, 61-metre (200-foot) stained glass windows look dated, although the interior is light, plain and simple. Local legend has it that Belluschi took some flak for the fact that, on some days, the afternoon sun creates a perfect silhouette of a female breast on the cathedral's side.

Plans are underway to create a **Fillmore Historic Jazz District** that will revitalise the neighbourhood's central avenue between Post and Eddy Streets, and the area is already a destination for live music. At Geary Boulevard, check out the **Boom Boom Room**, a blues club where partner John Lee Hooker has been known to turn up for impromptu gigs. **Rasselas** (1534 Fillmore Street, at Geary Boulevard), a 200-seat jazz club, is anticipating the new jazz boom.

The funky, friendly **Someplace Else** (1795 Geary Boulevard) lies just around the corner from Rasselas and a huge **Blue Note** club is planned to open at Fillmore and Ellis Streets some time in the year 2001. The nearby **Fillmore Auditorium**, at 1805 Geary Boulevard, which booked the likes of Jimi Hendrix and The Doors in the 1960s, continues to feature upcoming new acts as its headliners. A few blocks away, the **Justice League** (628 Divisadero Street) has sought to keep a good club scene thriving on Divisadero, with live acts, turntablists and dance nights. *See chapter* **Nightlife** for more details.

St Mary's Cathedral

1111 Gough Street, at Geary Boulevard (567 2020). Bus 2, 3, 4, 38. **Open** 6.45am-4.30pm Mon-Fri; 6.45am-6.30pm Sat; 7.15am-4.45pm Sun. **Map F**

Japantown

East of Fillmore Street and north of Geary Boulevard, tiny Japantown used to comprise a much larger area covering about 40 blocks, until the internment of World War II combined with aggressive urban renewal forced many Japanese out. In 1968, in a vague spirit of reparation, San Francisco's urban planners created the **Japan Center** (*see below for listings*), a huge shopping, dining and entertainment complex which takes up three blocks between Post Street and Geary Boulevard and one block of Buchanan Street. The area feels a little lacklustre, but its businesses are thriving.

To immerse yourself (literally) in the Japanese experience, indulge in a relaxing massage at the recently re-opened **Kabuki Springs & Spa** (1750 Geary Boulevard, *see chapter* **Shops & Services**), a traditional Japanese bathhouse with communal pools, saunas and steam rooms. Spend a restful half hour or so in the **Buddhist Church of San Francisco** on Pine Street, or just sit in the **Peace Plaza Garden**, overlooked by the five-tiered, concrete **Peace Pagoda**, which was given to the community by Japan. In April, a **Cherry Blossom Festival** (*see chapter* **San Francisco by Season**) marks a month-long celebration of Japanese culture, with flower-arranging demonstrations, martial arts displays, traditional dance performances and a parade on the last day.

Also on Post Street, the eight-screen **Kabuki 8** cinema complex is the venue for most of the events and films shown during the annual San Francisco International Film Festival in April and May, and for the latest movies during the rest of the year (*see chapter* **Film**).

Japan Center

Post Street, between Geary, Laguna & Fillmore Streets (recorded information 922 6776). Bus 2, 3, 4, 38. **Map E4**

Pacific Heights, Cow Hollow & the Marina

The northern neighbourhoods from Bush to the Bay and from Gough to the Presidio are the city's richest, where clean-cut, WASP urbanites dart in and out of hair salons, restaurants and coffee retailers with mobile phone in one hand and briefcase in the other. Though to the uninitiated there may seem no difference between the three, Pacific Heights, Cow Hollow and the Marina are, like their elevations, arranged in order of relative descent.

Pacific Heights

Pacific Heights is San Francisco's high society neighbourhood, as is evident from the wide, mansion-lined streets and well-heeled locals. Socialites Gordon and Ann Getty have a house here, as does rock star Linda Rondstadt and novelist Danielle Steel, who lives in the ornate **Spreckels Mansion** which spans the entire block between Jackson, Gough, Washington and Octavia Streets.

It's possible to spend hours in the area, wandering the streets and marvelling at the opulence. Look out for the **Octagon House** (2645 Gough Street), built as a result of the nineteenth-century answer to feng shui and now restored to its 1861 splendour, and the 28-room 1886 **Haas-Lilienthal House** (2007 Franklin Street); both are open to the public (*see below for listings*). A walk down any lane or avenue offers glimpses of beauty and magnificence, though the stretch of **Broadway** between Divisadero Street and the Presidio affords some of the best architecture. A stroll through either **Alta Plaza Park** (at Jackson and Steiner Streets) or **Lafayette Park** (at Washington and Gough Streets) supplies a great excuse to ogle the surrounding homes and chat with the dog-walking locals. Both also offer great views over the city.

Fillmore Street between Bush and Jackson Streets comprises the region's central shopping hub, with plenty of excellent stores and smart restaurants. **Vivande Porta Via** (2125 Fillmore Street; 346 4430) used to be cookery queen Elizabeth David's favourite restaurant for lunch in San Francisco – quite a recommendation when you consider that she had several thousand others to choose from. Further south, the quirky **Pizza Inferno** (1800 Fillmore Street; 775 1800) is a good place for a quick bite. For designer furniture, decorating accessories and gifts, check out **Fillamento** at 2185 Fillmore Street (*see chapter* **Shops & Services**), though its marvellous selection is notoriously overpriced. Detour a few blocks west, and you'll find the antiques and clothes shops on **Sacramento Street** between Presidio Avenue and Spruce Street are comparatively expensive, but a few second-hand clothes stores offer regular bargains.

Haas-Lilienthal House

2007 Franklin Street, at Washington Street (441 3004). Bus 12, 42, 47, 49. **Open** noon-3pm Wed, 11am-4pm Sun. **Admission** $5; $3 concessions.
Map F3

Octagon House

2645 Gough Street, at Union Street (441 7512). Bus 41, 45. **Open** noon-3pm three days a month; phone for details. **Admission** free.
Map E2

Cow Hollow

From Pacific Heights, it's a few blocks downhill to Cow Hollow, once a dairy pasture and now a trendy shopping area. The crowd here tends to be older and more established than that of the Marina below, reflected in the relative chicness of the bars, shops and restaurants along **Union Street** (between Broderick and Fillmore Streets) which are housed mainly in tastefully renovated Victorians. The Asian-flavoured **Betelnut** (2030 Union Street; 929 8855) and classic American **PlumpJack Cafe** (3127 Fillmore Street; 563 4755) are the neighbourhood's best restaurants (*see chapter* **Restaurants & Cafés**).

Fort Mason Center

At the Marina's eastern edge, **Fort Mason** is a waterfront complex of reconditioned military buildings that served as a command post for the US Army in the 1850s.

Among the museums on site is the delightful **Mexican Museum**, which exhibits Mexican art and sells handcrafted jewellery and embroidery (and is due to relocate in the early 2000s to the Yerba Buena Center). Other museums in the complex include the **African-American Historical & Cultural Society Museum**; the **Museo Italo-Americano**; and the **San Francisco Craft and Folk Art Museum**, which features exhibitions covering anything from book binding to furniture. The **Book Bay Bookstore** (771 1076), run by Friends of the San Francisco Public Library, sells second-hand books for a mere 25¢.

Fort Mason also houses one of the city's favourite restaurants, **Greens** (*see chapter* **Restaurants & Cafés**) and is where the **Magic**, and **Cowell** performance theatres are based (*see chapter* **Performing Arts**). In addition, you'll find a constant array of changing displays at the two pavilions – actually reconstituted shipbuilding bays – at the waters' edge: gardening competitions, dances, concerts and even the Spiral Dance, the major autumn holiday fête for the local pagan community, are held here. When you're in the area, check Fort Mason's scheduled events in the Datebook section of the Sunday *San Francisco Chronicle and Examiner.*

Fort Mason Center

Marina Boulevard at Buchanan Street (information 441 5706). Bus 28.
Map E1

Views

With its plummeting hills and Bay vistas, San Francisco offers an abundance of amazing views. One of the most clichéd is from the 19th-floor bar of the Mark Hopkins Hotel on Nob Hill, where the **Top of the Mark** offers a panorama of the night sky (*see chapter* **Bars**). One of the best cheap thrills to be had downtown is a ride in one of the great glass elevators of the **Westin St Francis Hotel** (335 Powell Street, at Union Square; 397 7000). Framed like a vanity mirror with light bulbs, the transparent lifts shoot up the outside of the hotel's tower, providing stunning views and a rollercoaster adrenaline rush.

During the day, take the lift to the top of the **Coit Tower** (*see page 46*) on Telegraph Hill for another favourite view, where you can see piers and jetties poking out into the Bay.

From **Aquatic Park** (*see page 48*), stroll along the Golden Gate Promenade, past Marina Green and Crissy Field for more Bay- and bridge-scapes, and continue round the coastal path in the **Presidio** (*see opposite*) for more of the same.

Fort Point (*see opposite*) provides an underside view of the magnificent Golden Gate Bridge, while further to the west, the **Cliff House** (*see page 69*) is a tourist-packed spot, but nonetheless a good one for gazing out over the Seal Rocks below at sunset.

The **Marin Headlands** (*see chapter* **Trips Out of Town**), just north of the Golden Gate Bridge off US 101, provide another much-loved perspective. The usual stop for tourists is Vista Point, just across the bridge. Another option is to cross underneath the highway to the Marin Headlands and then take the winding, windswept road that climbs past gun emplacements to a number of parking areas that allow you to gaze east over the city. The view of the city in the early morning fog from across the bay at **Sausalito** (*see chapter* **Trips Out of Town**) also takes some beating.

Finally, nothing beats the view you get of the Financial District – by day or night – when you enter the city along the top deck of the suspended **San Francisco-Oakland Bay Bridge** (*see page 73*).

The Marina

The pastel-painted Marina district, between Fort Mason and the Presidio, is known as the neighbourhood of yuppie singles. Unashamedly heterosexual, the local bars are full of young and trendy, bare-midriffed, twentysomethings drinking and making eye contact. Even the local **Safeway** grocery at 15 Marina Boulevard is a famous pick-up joint. Built on the rubble of the 1906 earthquake, the Marina was the worst hit of San Francisco's neighbourhoods in the 1989 Loma Prieta quake. Over a decade later, evidence of the disaster only remains in the renovated pavements and several suspiciously new-looking buildings.

Interesting bars, restaurants and shops are to be found along the main drag, **Chestnut Street** from Fillmore to Divisadero, including the charming **Presidio** cinema (*see chapter* **Film**) on the western end, the **Grove** café (*see chapter* **Restaurants & Cafés**) and **Chadwicks of London** (*see chapter* **Shops & Services**), a sophisticated lingerie shop. If you're not in the mood to shop, head for the **Marina Green** (Marina Boulevard, at Fillmore Street), where you can fly kites, jog or picnic and which offers grand views of the **Golden Gate Bridge** and San Francisco Bay. At the end of the yacht harbour jetty to the north of Marina Green, the amazing **Wave Organ**, a bizarre structure of underwater pipes and benches built from the remains of an old cemetery, produces 'music' with the ebb and flow of the Bay current.

West of here, set in a small park at the foot of the Marina, is the only surviving piece of finery left from the 1915 Panama-Pacific Exposition. The **Palace of Fine Arts** at Baker and Beach Streets (*see below for listings*) was once the centrepiece of a mile-long swathe of temporary buildings that stretched as far as Fort Mason. Builder Bernard Maybeck's *pièce de résistance* is a neo-classical domed rotunda supported by a curved colonnade topped with friezes and statues of weeping women, and is one of the most atmospheric spots in the city. Its lifespan was intended to be short, and the original plaster structure was mortal indeed. It was expensively replaced by a permanent concrete version in the 1960s, finished in time for the 1969 opening of the famous **Exploratorium**, a hands-on science museum which lies behind the Palace (*see chapter* **Museums & Galleries**). The Palace is flanked by a lagoon full of lily pads, ducks and swans.

Palace of Fine Arts

3601 Lyon Street, between Jefferson & Bay Streets (information & tours 563 6504). Bus 28, 30, 43, 76. **Map C2**

The outer neighbourhoods

The outer neighbourhoods of the city are as individual as the central, from the memory-soaked lanes that criss-cross the Presidio and the verdant paths of the Golden Gate Park to the bustling shops of the Richmond and Sunset districts. From this vantage, the city feels less noisy, more cathartic – almost lazy at times. Perhaps it's the Pacific's lull that slows the pace of life here.

The Presidio

With a long and colourful history, the Presidio (*see below for listings*) covers 1,500-acres of green parkland that is still undergoing the laborious process of turning from an army base into a National Park.

The area stretches from the northern tip of the Richmond district to the Golden Gate Bridge, and eastward as far as the edge of Marina district. Before it became part of the Golden Gate National Recreation Area in 1993, the Presidio was a military outpost, established in 1776 when Captain Juan Bautista de Anza planted the Spanish flag here. The land includes some 18 kilometres (11 miles) of hiking trails, 22.5 kilometres (14 miles) of bicycle routes and five kilometres (three miles) of windswept beaches. During **Fleet Week** in October (*see chapter* **San Francisco by Season**) there's no better vantage point from which to watch the Blue Angels' air show – the pilots fly *under* the Golden Gate Bridge – than from the National Cemetery on Lincoln Boulevard.

The gate at Pacific Heights on Presidio Boulevard and Jackson Street leads you through fairytale woods. Points of interest include a creepy **Pet Cemetery** on McDowell Avenue, the more cheerful **Mountain Lake Park** (reached most easily from Lake Street in the Richmond between Eighth and 12th Avenues) and the long **Lovers' Walk** that runs parallel to Presidio Boulevard just north of the Broadway gate and marks the original path from the Presidio to the (then much smaller) city.

A spectacular brick fortress with a melodramatic setting beneath the southern edge of the Golden Gate Bridge, **Fort Point** (*see below for listings*) resembles a vast outdoor stage crying out for some good open-air theatre. Interestingly, the performances here are historic re-enactments of the Civil War, performed by and for children. The fort was built between 1853 and 1861 to protect the city from a sea attack that never came, and its 126 cannons remained idle until the fort was closed in 1900. The four-storey vaulted building houses a giant ten-inch Rodman gun as well as various military exhibitions. Guided tours are available. The pier is famous as the spot where

Golden Gate Park

One of the world's largest urban green havens – its 1,013 acres range from the Haight to the Pacific Ocean – Golden Gate Park forms an oasis of lakes, landscaped vistas, flower beds, meadows, trails and forest, much of it seemingly completely removed from the city. Over the years, the park has hosted everything from encampments for earthquake victims and the homeless, to rock concerts, performances of Shakespeare and opera, the annual Bay to Breakers race, a funeral for Grateful Dead icon Jerry Garcia attended by 10,000 fans, and food festivals serving up every imaginable type of cuisine. There are days' worth of activities to be discovered in this magnificent reserve.

In 1871, landscape architect William Hammond Hall took up the challenge of turning a barren stretch of sand dunes into a park respecting the land's natural contours. A million trees were planted over the years under the tutelage of gardener John McLaren and, as the park's fame spread, horticulturists from all over the world sent in seeds and cuttings. The result is a treat. It's quite a trek from end to end of the long, narrow park, but bicycles can be rented (from **Golden Gate Park Cyclery** at 1749 Waller Street; 221 3777/751 7368) as well as rollerblades (from **Golden Gate Park Skate and Bike** at 3038 Fulton Street, *see chapter* **Sport & Fitness**) to speed the time between sights. In any case, **John F Kennedy Drive** runs the distance from end to end and yields the best viewing points.

Entering the park from the Panhandle (between Fell and Oak Streets), **McLaren Lodge** (*see below*) on the immediate right was the original residence of the park's first gardener. It now houses the headquarters of the park's offices and a small visitor center. The **Conservatory of Flowers** (currently under restoration after suffering storm damage) at Middle Drive is modelled on the Palm House in Kew Gardens; it displays award-winning flowers inside and out, all year round.

Further along John F Kennedy Drive, past the **rhododendron dell** and **rose garden**, a left turn into the Music Concourse brings you to the **MH de Young Memorial Museum**, which houses art from the Americas, and the **Asian Art Museum**, which has the largest collection of Asian art outside Asia (*see chapter* **Museums & Galleries** for both). The Asian is due to move to Civic Center within the next couple of years. Continuing along the Drive, the **Japanese Tea Garden** is an oasis of peace with delightful bridges, flowering trees, relaxing paths, a huge bronze Buddha and an outdoor tearoom with waitresses dressed in kimonos; entry is free on the first Wednesday of the month.

You can circle the Concourse, which has pollarded trees and a band shell where free concerts are held each summer; opposite the de Young and Asian museums is the **California Academy of Sciences**, the oldest scientific institution in the western US (*see chapter* **Museums & Galleries**). It houses the fabulous **Steinhart Aquarium** (*see below*), the Morrison Planetarium and Laserium, as well as wonderful, changing, natural history displays and an earthquake exhibition.

Back on John F Kennedy Drive, follow the signs left to **Stow Lake**, which provides a tiny, charming detour where you can rent paddle-boats or canoes, feed ducks, or hike a short, steep path to the top of Strawberry Hill – the latter affording some fine views.

Kim Novak's character attempts suicide in *Vertigo*. On your way back, dodge the runners and bicyclists who populate **Crissy Field**, a large open space and occasional home to concerts or sports events.

Among the 500 or so buildings from the former military base, ranging from Civil War mansions to simple barracks of the 1890s, the old-fashioned **Presidio Museum** (*see below for listings*), on Lincoln Boulevard at Funston Avenue, is the most interesting. Built in 1864, the museum is based in the old station hospital and serves as a repository of documents and artifacts from the city's military and political past.

The Presidio's clumsy return to civilian management finds its future in question: opinion vacillates between returning the land to natural uses, reclaiming part of the vacated housing for the homeless or allowing its takeover by prestigious social and cultural bodies.

Recently, the **Letterman Hospital** near the East Gate of the Presidio was leased to Lucasfilm Inc, George Lucas's moviemaking company and there are plans in the pipeline to turn the site into a huge film production campus. Meanwhile, commercial developers continue to clamour for the rest of the Presidio's $2 billion-worth of prime real estate potential.

Further west, the **Golden Gate Park Stables** at 36th Avenue offers horse riding lessons (*see chapter* **Sport & Fitness**). **Spreckels Lake** is a haven for model yacht racers, while the **Buffalo Paddock** always has a small herd of bison conveniently clustered near its fence for easy viewing. At the western edge of the park, the **Wilhelmina Tulip Garden** surrounds the **Dutch Windmill** next to 48th Avenue – both garden and mill were gifts to the city from the Dutch Queen.

Overlooking the Pacific Ocean at the western edge of the park, the **Beach Chalet** (*see below for listings*) originally opened in 1925 as a restaurant and bathhouse. Designed by local architect Willis Polk, the building's interior was chosen in 1936 as the site for one of the city's most magnificent murals. Painted by Lucien Labaudt, a French-born artist, the murals depict San Francisco life during the Depression. In the 1940s, the Beach Chalet was recommissioned for use by the Army Corps of Engineers and later closed; preservationists reopened the place in 1996. Its frescoes restored to their original state, the main floor of the building now serves as a visitor centre for the park. Upstairs, the restaurant serves basic pub fare and its own selection of house-brewed beers.

Golden Gate Park has plenty more to offer (and many other lanes to explore). Botanical enthusiasts will love the **Strybing Arboretum**, planted with 6,000 species of plants, trees and shrubs from different countries, while literary gardeners should head for the **Shakespeare Garden** to the west of the Academy of Sciences, which is stocked with plants mentioned in the Bard's plays and poetry. Kids can ride the beautifully restored **carousel**, next to the **children's playground** just off Kezar Drive and enjoy pony rides at the **Golden Gate Park Stables**. A **fly casting pool** and dozens of other lakes and dells can also be found.

Beach Chalet

1000 Great Highway, between Fulton Street & Lincoln Avenue (visitor centre 751 2766). Bus 5, 18.
Open 9am-6pm daily.
See chapter **Restaurant & Cafés** for details of restaurant opening times.

Golden Gate Park

Park *Between Fulton & Stanyan Streets, Lincoln Way & the Great Highway.* **Open** dawn to dusk daily. **McLaren Lodge Visitor Center** *John F Kennedy Drive, at Stanyan Street (666 7200).* **Open** 9am-5pm daily. **Both** *Muni Metro N/bus 5, 7, 18, 21, 28, 29, 33, 44, 66, 71.*
Admission free. **Map A-C/5/6**

Steinhart Aquarium

Golden Gate Park, inside the Academy of Sciences (750 7145). Muni Metro N/bus 5, 21, 44, 71. **Open** *summer* 9am-6pm daily; *winter* 9am-5pm daily. **Admission** $8.50; $2-$5.50 concessions. **Credit** AmEx, MC, TC, V.
Map B6

For further information on the aquarium and other kid-friendly activities, *see chapter* **Children**.
Website: www.calacademy.org

Fort Point

Marine Drive (556 1693). Bus 28, 29.
Open 10am-5pm Wed-Sun. **Admission** free.
Map A1

The Presidio

Main entrances at Lombard Street (at Lyon Street), Presidio Boulevard (at Broadway), Arguello Boulevard (at Jackson Street), Lincoln Boulevard (at 25th Avenue) & Golden Gate Bridge Toll Plaza (information 561 4323). Bus 3, 29, 43. **Map A1-C3**

Presidio Museum

Lincoln Boulevard, at Funston Avenue (561 4331). Bus 3, 29, 43. **Open** noon to 4pm Wed-Sun.
Admission free. **Map C2**

Richmond

The Richmond district borders the northern edge of Golden Gate Park, from Arguello Boulevard to the ocean and from Fulton Street to the Presidio. Once a sandy wasteland, the region was developed as a residential area following the 1906 construction of the Geary Boulevard tramway. Settled by Russian and Eastern European Jews after World War I, it's now a mixed neighbourhood, dominated by Russian, Irish and, increasingly, Chinese immigrants.

Clement Street, from Fourth to 20th Avenues, is the district's main commercial centre and viewed by many as the city's 'real' Chinatown. Huge shops

The Presidio. *See page 65.*

sell cheap kitchenware and enamel crockery; acupuncture clinics and small Chinese medicine shops can be found on every block. Hundreds of Asian restaurants are here too: notable ones include the busy **Fountain Court** (354 Clement, at Fifth Avenue; 668 1100); **Minh's Garden** (208 Clement Street; 751 8211), where you can get a meal for under $5; the more upmarket Vietnamese **Le Soleil**, on the next block (133 Clement Street; 668 4848); and the vegetarian **Red Crane** (115 Clement, at 12th Avenue; 751 7726).

At the Ocean Beach end of the Richmond, **Sutro Heights Park** is a tiny idyll, virtually empty except for a few Russians walking their dogs or playing chess. By the park entrance at Geary Boulevard, a statue of the goddess Diana is often decorated with flowers by local pagans. In the nearby walled garden you can enjoy a secluded picnic and marvel at the spectacular panoramic view of the ocean – fog permitting.

Nearby, perched on the very edge of the city and also overlooking the ocean, is the **Cliff House** (*see below for listings*). Tobacco magnate Adolph Sutro built the first house on this spot (1090 Point Lobos Avenue) in the 1860s; after a fire in 1894 he replaced it with a magnificent, eight-storey Victorian turreted palace. When this also burned down, a year after surviving the great quake, the building was replaced by the present architectural muddle, which serves as a touristy bar, restaurant and gift shop. The Cliff House is due to undergo some major restoration, which means that the **Musée Mécanique** and **Camera Obscura** that are part of the complex may be displaced. As we went to press, no concrete plan was in place for these local attractions, the former an arcade of antique coin-operated games and the latter a nineteenth century wireless curio. The National Park Service still maintains a **visitor centre** for the Golden Gate National Recreation Area beside the Cliff House (556 8642).

Below the Cliff House, and to the north, are the ruins of **Sutro Baths.** Built by Sutro in 1896, these were once the world's biggest swimming baths, with seven heated pools under a magnificent glass roof, all sadly destroyed by fire in 1966. You can walk a dicey three-mile windswept coastal path from the Cliff House to the Golden Gate Bridge.

North of Sutro Heights Park, in **Lincoln Park**, the **California Palace of the Legion of Honor** is architect George Applegarth's homage to the Palais de la Légion d'Honneur in Paris (*see chapter* **Museums & Galleries**). Built in the 1920s on a promontory overlooking the Golden Gate Bridge, it was donated to the city as a memorial to Californians who died in World War I. The museum originally only displayed French works of art, but today contains a wide-ranging permanent collection. Of these, the **Rodin Collection** is the second-finest outside the Musée Rodin in Paris (the Stanford Art Museum now has more works by the sculptor) and includes a cast of 'Le Penseur', as well as some fine works by Camille Claudel. The vast **Achenbach Foundation** is devoted to works of graphic art. Just north of the Palace's car park is the haunting **Jewish Holocaust Memorial** sculpted by George Segal. The surrounding wooded and hilly park houses an 18-hole golf course and offers picturesque glimpses of the Golden Gate Bridge and Marin Headlands.

Don't leave the Richmond without visiting the **Columbarium** (*see below for listings*). This beautiful Victorian building and miniature 'museum' of funeral architecture is set in two acres of gardens and is the only such burial site in the city.

Cliff House

1090 Point Lobos Avenue, at the Great Highway (386 3330). Bus 18, 31, 38. **Open** 11am-2am daily.

Columbarium

1 Loraine Court, off Anza Street (752 7891). Bus 18, 31, 38. **Open** 9am-5pm Mon-Fri; 10am-2pm Sat, Sun.

Sunset

The Sunset district is a large and mainly residential area stretching along the southern length of Golden Gate Park to the ocean and south to Rivera Street. Like the Richmond district, it can be foggy between June and September; on clear days, however, there are spectacular sunsets over the ocean. Start your tour on **Irving Street**: the main shopping area stretches from Fifth to Tenth Avenues. **Le Video** (1239 Ninth Avenue; 242 2120/566 5606/www.levideo.com) is arguably the best video store in San Francisco, with a broad selection of films ranging from mainstream to the downright obscure. Anyone with photo ID, a credit card and a San Francisco address is welcome to rent a film.

The neighbourhood is a haven for interesting restaurants, including seafood specialist **PJ's Oyster Bed** (737 Irving Street; 566 7775); **Ebisu** (1283 Ninth Avenue; 566 1770), which serves some of San Francisco's best sushi; **Organica** (1224 Ninth Avenue; 665 6519), and the Asian-flavoured **House** (1269 Ninth Avenue; 682 3898). *See chapter* **Restaurants & Cafés** for more details.

At the northern end of the Sunset, **Ocean Beach** (*see page 77*), the city's biggest, is good for a blustery walk and for watching surfers. Take a break at the **Java Beach Café** (139 La Playa, at 47th Avenue; 665 5282), where the coffee is famously good. The best restaurant in the immediate vicinity is the Vietnamese **Thanh Long** (4101 Judah Street; 665 1146), famous for its garlic crab.

At the southwest corner of the neighbourhood – nearly at the county line – the **San Francisco Zoo** (*see below for listings*) is small but exotic, with a well-stocked insect house and a special children's section. It houses more than 1,000 different species of mammals and birds and features the Koala Crossing (it's one of the few zoos in the US that has koalas), Musk Ox Meadows, Gorilla World (inhabited by two young and five adult gorillas), Tuxedo Junction for penguins and Wolf Woods, among other delights. Beyond it, **Harding Park** (Harding Road, near Skyline Boulevard) is a municipal golf course cradled by the huge **Lake Merced**, which has biking and jogging trails and boats to rent (Lake Merced Boating & Fishing Co; 753 1101). **Stern Grove** (19th Avenue and Sloat Boulevard), a 63-acre oasis of eucalyptus, redwood and fir trees, is popular in the summer when San Franciscans brave the fog to attend the free Sunday afternoon concerts (*see chapter* **San Francisco by Season**). **Stonestown Galleria** shopping mall, on 19th Avenue at Winston Drive, a block north of San Francisco State University, satisfies most consumers in the area (*see chapter* **Shops & Services**).

Finally, **Fort Funston Reservation** is a large greensward at the city's southwest corner, an acreage hatched with hiking trails, dramatic promontories and jagged beaches. It's mostly a place to get out and walk your dog, but many Sunset residents steal a few hours here to run, walk, fish or meditate.

San Francisco Zoo

Sloat Boulevard, near 45th Avenue (753 7080). Muni Metro L/bus 18, 23. **Open** *Main Zoo* 10am-5pm daily; *Children's Zoo* winter 11am-4pm Mon-Fri, 10.30am-2.40pm Sat, Sun; summer 10.30am-4.30pm daily. **Admission** $9; $3-$6 concessions; free first Wed of the month. **Credit** AmEx, MC, V.
Website: www.sfzoo.org

Islands & bridges

Though San Francisco Bay contains 14 islands, only four are of major interest to the visitor. **Treasure Island**, built on the shoals of neighbouring Yerba Buena Island, marks the midpoint of the San Francisco-Oakland Bay Bridge. It's an artificial island, constructed of bay sand in 1936-7 and the site of the Golden Gate International Exposition of 1939-1940 which celebrated the ascendancy of California and San Francisco as

That unmistakable symbol of the city, the **Golden Gate Bridge**. *See page 75.*

SHEAR MADNESS
San Francisco's Hilarious Whodunit
"Screamingly funny! Makes you laugh wildly and uncontrollably."
-Contra Costa Times
America's longest-running play ever!
Tue-Fri 8; Sat 6:30 & 9:30; Sun 3 & 7:30
Mason St. Theatre • 340 Mason St.
Tickets 415•982•5463
www. shearmadness.com

THE CITY STORE
SAN FRANCISCO MEMORABILIA
UNIQUE SOUVENIRS AND AUTHENTIC PIECES OF SAN FRANCISCO HISTORY
HAIGHT 1500
600 ASHBURY
CLOTHING OPTIONAL BEYOND THIS POINT
CITY OF SAN FRANCISCO
ONE HOUR TIME LIMIT
TIME EXPIRED
STREET SIGNS
BOOKS & PRINTS
LOMBARD ST. BRICKS
GIFTS BY BAY AREA ARTISANS
FIRE & POLICE DEPARTMENT APPAREL
PIER 39, SECOND FLOOR 788-5322
THE BEACH CHALET 831-4758
CITY HALL 431-2747
MOSCONE CENTER - EXHIBIT LEVEL

STEVE SILVER'S
BEACH BLANKET
BABYLON®
CLUB FUGAZI
SAN FRANCISCO, CALIFORNIA
415-421-4222
©SSPI 1995

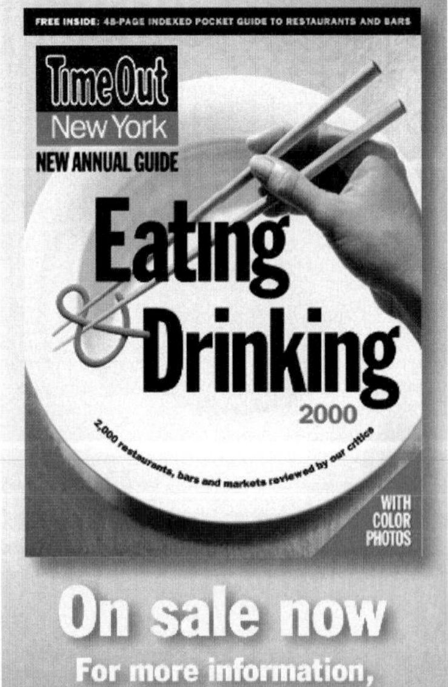
FREE INSIDE: 48-PAGE INDEXED POCKET GUIDE TO RESTAURANTS AND BARS
Time Out New York
NEW ANNUAL GUIDE
Eating & Drinking 2000
2,000 restaurants, bars and markets reviewed by our critics
WITH COLOR PHOTOS
On sale now
For more information, call 212-539-4444.

economic, political and cultural forces in the increasingly important Pacific region; the island has been a US Naval station since 1941. Recently, Treasure Island has opened to the public for occasional special events. The **Treasure Island Museum** (*see chapter* **Museums & Galleries**) tells the story behind the building of the bridges and the island's naval history.

Much more famous than its military counterpart to the east is **Alcatraz** (*see below for listings*). The name means 'pelican' in Spanish, after the birds that nest here, but to Al Capone, Machine Gun Kelly and Robert 'the Birdman' Stroud, the tiny island was 'the Rock'. The first lighthouse on the West Coast was built here in 1854; Alcatraz first became a prison in the 1870s. It housed quarantined soldiers after the Spanish-American War, then prisoners from city jails that crumbled after the 1906 earthquake. Now the craggy outcrop lures 4,000 willing visitors a day – well over a million each year – and is San Francisco's single biggest tourist attraction.

Every November, Native Americans land to commemorate their 1969 occupation with an Unthanksgiving ceremony, and Hollywood still favours it as a place to shoot motion pictures – though 1996's *The Rock* was consummately more forgettable than Clint Eastwood's 1979 *Escape From Alcatraz.* The island also boasts one of the only deep-pitched foghorns left in the Bay Area. Admission includes a walking tour of the facility, with audio narration by former inmates. Visit the semi-derelict concrete cell blocks where incorrigible lifers were sent between 1934 and 1963, after which the cost of supporting an island jail without its own water supply forced its closure. Book your visit far in advance and come prepared for crowds and chilly weather.

If you're seeking a forested getaway that's close to the city, a ramble and bicycle ride around **Angel Island** – the Bay's largest – is only a 20-minute ferry ride away (*see below for listings*). Boats arrive at Ayala Cove, where you can rent bikes and claim a picnic table. The eight-kilometre (five-mile) Perimeter Trail brings you to the deserted Camp Reynolds, with its picturesque Civil War barracks – the only remaining garrison of its type. The top of Mount Livermore (238 metres/781 feet) affords a great view.

A bus takes you across the island to Quarry Beach – a sheltered, sandy, sunbathing strip popular with kayakers. The island also offers nine campsites with stunning views of the Bay and city skyline.

San Francisco's bridges are among the most famous anywhere. The two-part **San Francisco-Oakland Bay Bridge** (*see below for listings*) is distinguished by being the longest high-level steel bridge in the world (13.52 kilometres/8.5 miles) and marks the city's most dramatic entrance by highway. Designed by Charles H Purcell and opened in 1936, the bridge and its piers are bigger than the highest pyramid and built of more concrete than New York's Empire

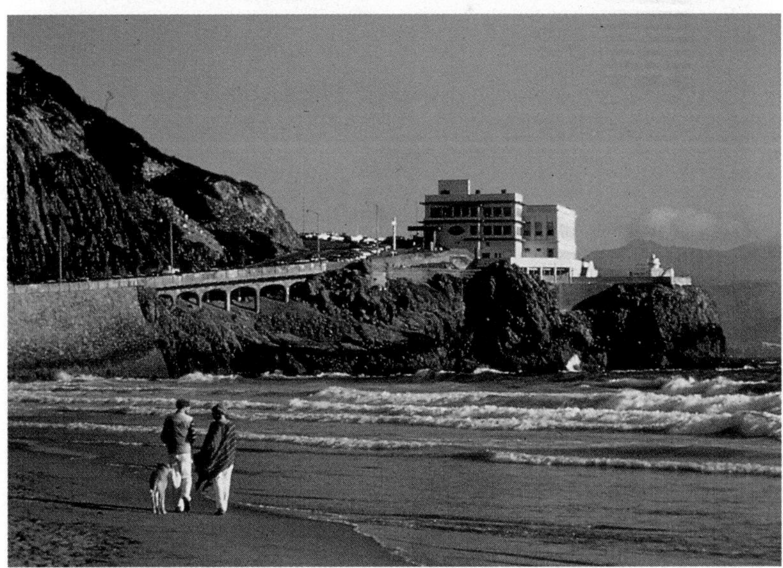

The **Cliff House** *overlooks Ocean Beach and the Pacific beyond.* *See page 69.*

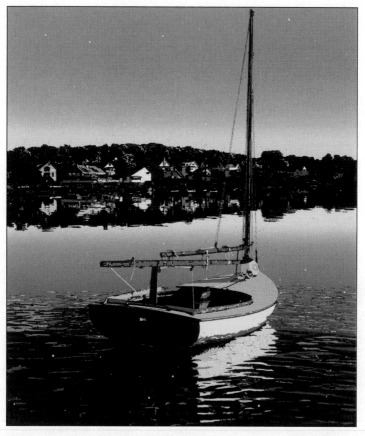

State Building. Two levels and five lanes of traffic tunnel through **Yerba Buena Island**, where drivers can stop off for the spectacular views of the West Bay section. For a brief moment in October 1989, the Bay Bridge became more famous than the Golden Gate Bridge, when part of the upper storey collapsed during the Loma Prieta quake. Since then, engineers have advocated rebuilding the eastern span.

Luminous symbol of San Francisco and star of countless films, the **Golden Gate Bridge** (*see below for listings*) remains the city's ultimate icon. Taking its name from the mile-wide span of bay christened by Captain John Fremont in the 1840s, the Golden Gate took 13 years to plan, five to build and had claimed 11 lives by its completion in 1937. It incorporates 129,000 kilometres (80,000 miles) of cable into its 27,572 pencil-thick strands. The span is continuously repainted with rust-proof paint (5,000 gallons of 'International Orange' each year), rendering it fiery at sunset and surreally suspended when foggy. Walk across it for the best views of how the unique metal gussets allow flexibility in high winds.

Over 1,000 people have jumped from the bridge in suicide attempts, a statistic the police understandably aren't keen on publicising. A film on its construction can be seen at Fort Point, located beneath the south tower (11.30pm, 3.30pm Wed-Sun).

Alcatraz Island

Blue & Gold ferry from Pier 41, Embarcadero (tickets 705 5555/recorded information 773 1188). Bus 32, 42/cable car Powell-Mason. **Return tickets** *with audio tour* $12.25; $7-$10.50 concessions; *without audio tour* $8.75; $5-$7 concessions. **Credit** AmEx, Disc, MC, V.

Ferries leave every half hour from 9.30am during the week. Advanced booking is essential.

Angel Island

San Francisco Bay, off Tiburon (campsite reservations 1-800 444 7275/tour information 897 0715). Blue & Gold ferry from Pier 41, Embarcadero (tickets 705 5555/recorded information 773 1188). **Return tickets** $11; $6-$10 concessions. **Credit** AmEx, Disc, MC, V.

There are three departures daily.

Website: www.angelisland.com

Golden Gate Bridge

Linking the Toll Plaza near the Presidio with Marin County (921 5858). Bus 28, 29, 76 to the bridge/Golden Gate Transit bus 10, 20, 30, 50, 60, 70, 80, 90 across the bridge. **Bridge toll** $3 city bound. **Map A1**

San Francisco-Oakland Bay Bridge

Linking the East Bay & Oakland with downtown, near Rincon Annex (1-510 286 1148). Bus 32, 42 to the bridge/AC Transit bus F, O, N across the bridge. **Bridge toll** $2 eastbound. **Map J3**

Beaches

If you've arrived in San Francisco with little more than your beach towel and bathing suit then you're in for a disappointment. Going to the beach is a relatively rare activity in the city, mostly because of the regularly cool weather and the prevailing coastal winds, which can cool off even the loveliest day and draw the euphemistically-titled 'marine layer' – the accursed fog – off the Pacific and over the beach. Most San Franciscans go to the beach only a few times a year, usually during the rare spate of hot days that come in late spring or early autumn.

Because of cold currents and rare great white shark sightings, it's the wetsuited few who enjoy beach culture (in the Southern Californian sense), paddling into the chilly waves to boogie-board, surf or occasionally snorkel and dive. This doesn't mean that the beaches aren't spectacular, however. Running for almost a mile along the craggy shoreline, **Baker Beach** is the former hiding place of a huge cannon, camouflaged here by the army in 1905 to protect the Bay, although it never saw active service. A replica of the original 95,000-pounder has been installed for the curious. Picnic tables, sunbathing and fishing are the real lure now, since cold water, occasional water pollution and strong currents deter swimmers. A northern section of the beach (towards the Golden Gate Bridge) is predominantly gay and nudist. Behind the beach are the exclusive Sea Cliff houses that sit perched above the water, many of them bringing new meaning to the phrase 'every man's home is his castle'. Walk along El Camino del Mar for the full movie set effect.

Part of the fun of Baker Beach is getting there by car. If you're driving from the north, take Lincoln Boulevard through the Presidio to Bowley Street and turn right; from the south, take 25th Avenue to Lincoln Boulevard, then turn left at Bowley. You can also cycle or walk the Coastal Trail from the Golden Gate Bridge, a beautiful path flanked by the Presidio and providing some breathtaking views of the Pacific.

Further south, slotted between Baker Beach and Lincoln Park in the exclusive Sea Cliff neighbourhood, is the beautifully sheltered and windproof James D Phelan Beach, better known as **China Beach**, which takes its nickname from the settlement of Chinese fishermen who camped here in the last century. It's the nicest of all the beaches, small and sheltered from the wind, and local residents

would prefer to keep it for themselves. Public demand prevails, however, and it's still open to all. It has a free sundeck, showers and changing rooms. Pacific Heights nannies, students and unmolested sunbathers all favour the beach, which has plenty of parking and a pleasant hike down to the sand. China Beach is also a popular spot for barbecues and weddings.

Stretching from the Cliff House south past the city limits, **Ocean Beach** (*pictured opposite*) is San Francisco's biggest beach – a five-kilometre (three-mile) sandy strip that stretches along the Pacific coast. Widening into magnificent dunes and plateaus at the end of the fog-bound Sunset district, Ocean Beach is the place to stroll, walk dogs, paddle and have illicit midnight revels. It's also a haven for the homeless (when the weather is nice) and local pagans, who hold rituals on it several times a year. There are also local surfing competitions and the recent exhibition of 'extreme' sporting events, the X-Games, took place here (*see* **The X-philes** *in chapter* **Sport & Fitness**).

If nature had its way, the sand dunes of Ocean Beach would advance inland as far as Twin Peaks, but the movement of the beach is prevented by a large wall (built in the 1920s) that runs parallel to the Great Highway. A cycle and pedestrian path passes along Ocean Beach as far as Sloat Avenue and the **San Francisco Zoo** (*see page 70*), from where you can stroll to **Fort Funston** (*see page 70*) and Mussel Rocks, headquarters of daredevil hang-gliders and windsurfers. However, it's worth pointing out that the currents are strong, especially at Point Lobos, where a number of experienced surfers drown every year, and swimming is not advised.

To the south and north of the city, along Hwy 1 (SR 1), lies a glorious string of beaches, each a protected pearl guarded by conservationists and sinfully under-used. To the north are several with nudist corners, including **Kirby Cove**, **Black Sand**, **Red Rock**, **Bonita**, **Bolinas**, **Rodeo** and **Muir** beaches. To the south unfold endless miles of ravishing sands, including **Devil's Slide** (constantly battling storm damage) and **Gray Whale Cove**, continuing past **Pomponio** and **San Gregorio** to **Santa Cruz** and **Monterey**. *See chapter* **Trips Out of Town** for more on the coast beyond San Francisco.

For **Aquatic Park**, San Francisco's man-made harbour beach, *see page 48*.

Baker Beach

Gibson Road, off Bowley Street. Bus 1, 29.

China Beach (James D Phelan Beach)

Seacliff Avenue, off 26th Avenue. Bus 18, 29.

Ocean Beach

Great Highway, between Balboa Street & Sloat Boulevard. Muni Metro N/bus 18, 31, 38.

Organised tours

For those who prefer an escort, San Francisco offers a suitably wide-ranging variety of tours. There are excursions that cover specific regions, such as Chinatown, the Mission, the Castro or North Beach; and those that focus on themes – architecture, film locations, views or crime scenes, real (the Patty Hearst bank robbery) or fictitious (the murder of Miles Archer in *The Maltese Falcon*). A rough selection of what's on offer appears below; for more suggestions, visit the **Visitor Information Center**, at the corner of Market and Powell Streets under Hallidie Plaza (*see 279* **Directory**), or consult the pink Datebook section of the Sunday *San Francisco Chronicle and Examiner*.

Walking tours

Architectural Tours

Heritage Tours Foundation for San Francisco's Architectural Heritage (441 3004).
Victorian Home Walks (252 9485).
The Heritage Foundation, a preservation group, offers a weekly guided tour of Pacific Heights mansions, homes and architecture. Jay Gifford of Victorian Home Walks conducts daily, laid-back, custom-designed tours of the city's Victorian architecture.

Chinatown

All About Chinatown Tours (982 8839).
Wok Wiz Chinatown Tours & Cooking Co (1-800 281 9255).
Glorious Food Culinary Tours (441 5637).
Each of the many tours of the 24-block enclave offers a varied menu of stops both historical and culinary. Led by television chef and writer Shirley Fong-Torres, the Wok Wiz tour covers historical alleyways, Chinese herbalists and groceries, dim sum restaurants and fortune cookie factories, among other things. Glorious Food also offers a North Beach tour.

The Castro

Crusin' the Castro (550 8110).
Trevor Hailey still runs the Castro's best and most informative tour, pointing out the historic landmarks and tracing the origins of San Francisco's gay community.

Dashiell Hammett Walking Tour

(1-510 287 9540).
Follow writer-guide Don Herron around the Tenderloin in the footsteps of his hero, Dashiell Hammett. The four-hour tour (on Saturdays in May and June only) starts at the northwest corner of the

Main Library: look for the guy in the hat and trench-coat. Finish the tour at Hammett's regular hangout, John's Grill at 63 Ellis Street.

Golden Gate Park

Friends of Recreation and Parks (recorded information 263 0991).
Free walking tours (offered between May and October) of the green giant are led by the Friends of Recreation and Parks, who cover the major stops such as the Strybing Arboretum and Botanical Gardens, and create specialty walks for various levels of exertion.

The Haight-Ashbury

Flower Power Walking Tours (221 8442).
This two-hour walk relives the Summer of Love, with pointers to the history and locations of the Haight's most famous subcultural movement. See where the Dead shacked up, where Janis died and where hippies and the 1960s will live forever.

Mural Tours

Precita Eyes Mural Arts Center Tours (285 2287).
Choose among half a dozen weekend public art tours made available by Precita Eyes, the experts with 15 years' experience in local mural painting and preservation. Led by volunteers, the most popular tour is a Mission mural walk that includes over 75 works of art in an eight-block stroll. Other tours are given on bikes, aboard a Mexican bus (with refreshments) and in various customised groups. Tours in Spanish are also available.

Neighbourhood Walks

The City Guides, Friends of the San Francisco Public Library, Main Library, San Francisco, CA 94102 (557 4266).
Voluntary guides steer visitors around town, shedding light on some unusual corners of the city. Most popular are the tours of North Beach, Victorian San Francisco, Pacific Heights, the Mission and Japantown; others cover the Beaux Arts Buildings and City Hall, Chinatown, Cityscapes and the Roof Gardens. All tours are free and extra ones are organised from May to October; for a brochure, send an SAE to the above address.

By public transport

Pick the right routes, allow plenty of time and you can explore the city for the price of a Muni ticket. Here are some of our favourites.

J-Church Muni Metro

The J starts at the Embarcadero, heads underground along Market Street and then turns south at Church Street. You can jump off to explore the Mission district or continue overground through Dolores Heights and Noe Valley.

L-Taraval & N-Judah Muni Metro

If you're heading for San Francisco Zoo or Ocean Beach, take the L. It runs underground as far as West Portal station and then heads west along Taraval Street towards the sea. The N-Judah ends up near the beach south of Golden Gate Park.

The **N-Judah Muni Metro** *passes through the Sunset district on its way towards the ocean.*

Tours of the city: of Victorian architecture, or by boat or bicycle.

Bus 29

This north-south bus route starts in the Presidio on Lombard Street and takes you across Golden Gate Park near Stow Lake, through the Sunset district to the shores of Lake Merced. Enjoy views of the Golden Gate Bridge and the ocean en route.

Bus 38

Long and not pretty, the 38 takes you via Union Square and much of downtown before travelling east along Geary Boulevard, through the Western Addition and Richmond, ending up at Lincoln Park, near the Cliff House and the ocean.

Other tours

49-Mile Scenic Drive

The city's basic driving tour, signposted by blue-and-white seagull markers, is a good one, designed to take tourists through the most scenic or historic parts of the city. The **Visitor Information Center** (*see 279* **Directory**) provides a map of the tour, which will lead you to all the city's standard attractions. If this is your first visit to San Francisco, the 49-Mile Drive is worth exploring.

Bus Tours

Gray Line (558 7300) offers six bus tours daily that pick up passengers at central hotels; its Cable Car Tours send motorised cable cars from Union Square to Fisherman's Wharf, or to the Golden Gate Bridge, the Presidio and Japantown. Other tour companies include **Golden Gate Tours** (788 5775) and **Super Sightseeing Tours** (362 7808).

Cycling Tours

The San Francisco Department of Parking & Traffic has designated a grid of major bicycle routes that criss-cross the city. Although they're not organised tours per se, the routes will give you a particular view on the city – and improve your quads at the same time. *See page 270* **Directory** for more details, or phone 585 2453; *see chapter* **Sport & Fitness** for bike hire.

Seaplane Tours

San Francisco Seaplane Tours (332 4843).
Tickets $89; $59 children.
Fly the old-fashioned way on a seven-seater de Havilland seaplane, taking off from the water just outside Pier 39 for a 30-minute trip over the Bay, the Golden Gate Bridge and downtown. There are also flights from Sausalito.

Out of town

For a tour of the beauty spots outside the city, try the **Great Pacific Tour**, which offers trips that cover the Bay Area and Wine Country (626 4499). For more information on exploring the countryside beyond the bounds of the city, *see chapter* **Trips Out of Town**.

Museums & Galleries

San Francisco's gallery scene is as dynamic as some of the art to be found within.

From the sleek marble corridors of the **San Francisco Museum of Modern Art** (SFMOMA) and the **California Palace of the Legion of Honor** to the **Exploratorium**'s funky, curving confines, San Francisco's museums offer a fine range of reference. A few museums are in transition: the **MH de Young Memorial Museum** open in Golden Gate Park will soon be restored, better to gird it against earthquakes and the **Asian Art Museum** next door is due to relocate to Civic Center. The **Jewish** and **Mexican Museums** will also move within the next couple of years, to new buildings in Yerba Buena Gardens south of Market Street.

For a city that prides itself on its provocative and diverse culture, however, San Francisco's civic galleries are relatively conservative. Perhaps it's the old money that pours into these institutions; or that – like other American arts organisations – they are toeing the line since government funding is slim. But with a new crop of galleries, curators and artists, and with a museum-going public more willing to take risks, things may not stay conservative for long.

The gallery scene, on the other hand, continues to be dynamic, invigorated by a new generation of young (and, thanks to the booming Internet economy, frequently flush) collectors. The rapidly gentrifying Mission district is the location for most new spaces, although the majority of the city's galleries can still be found within a few blocks of Union Square. If you're searching for interesting art to see or buy don't forget that three major art schools – the **San Francisco Art Institute** on Chestnut Street (*see page 43* **Sightseeing**), the **Academy of Art College**, with campuses in SoMa and on Nob Hill, and the **California College of Arts and Crafts** near Potrero Hill (*see page 280* **Directory**) – lie within the city's bounds, each offering student and faculty shows as well as independently-curated exhibitions. **San Francisco State University** out near Lake Merced has also opened a new gallery for exhibiting work (*see page 280* **Directory**).

Another of the city's strengths is its plethora of public art: murals by Diego Rivera or Rigo, sculptures by Keith Haring – fill spaces with compelling, controversial visuals. One of the newest of these works is the stunning **Bikeway Mural** that graces Duboce Avenue, on the back of the Safeway building between Church and Market Streets. The block-long mural, designed by Mona Caron and commissioned by the City of San Francisco Bike Program, is an integrated homage to two-wheeled transportation. For details of the Mission's famous Balmy Alley murals, *see page 54* **Sightseeing**.

Detail from Mona Caron's **Bikeway Mural**.

INFORMATION

For the best of the city's art scene pick up a copy of the *SF Bay Area Gallery Guide*, published bi-monthly and available at virtually every gallery in town. The handy brochure is a bible for addresses, individual shows and out-of-town museum listings; it also mentions special events which can include art walks, emerging artists' tours or various auctions. If you'd like a copy before you arrive, write to 1369 Fulton Street, San Francisco, CA 94117, or phone 921 1601.

For museums of special interest to kids, including the new **Zeum**, *see chapter* **Children**.

Museums

Major museums

Asian Art Museum

Music Concourse, Golden Gate Park (668 8921). Muni Metro N/bus 5, 21, 44, 71. **Open** 9.30am-5pm Tue-Sun (9.30am-8.45pm first Wed of the month). **Admission** $7; $4-$5 concessions; free first Wed of the month. **Credit** MC, V. **Map B5**

Adjacent to the **MH de Young Memorial Museum** (*see p83*), and next door to the Japanese Tea Garden, the Asian makes the most of San Francisco's enviable position on the Pacific Rim. Its Avery Brundage Collection is one of the biggest and best of its kind in the Western world, so large that only 5% of its holdings is on display at any one time. These displays put European history in perspective: some Chinese works date from 70 centuries ago. There are jade pieces, bronzes, ceramics, fans, albums, scrolls – all in the first-floor galleries devoted to Chinese and Korean art. Works from 40 other countries, including India, Tibet, Japan and parts of South-east Asia and the Middle East are displayed upstairs. The gallery's pending relocation to Civic Center hasn't dampened its spirits: a recent exhibition of contemporary Chinese art was as well-attended as it was controversial. Admission includes entry to the de Young.

Website: www.asianart.org

California Academy of Sciences

Music Concourse, Golden Gate Park (recorded information 750 7145/Morrison Planetarium 750 7141). Muni Metro N/bus 5, 21, 44, 71. **Open** *summer* 9am-6pm daily; *winter* 10am-5pm daily. **Admission** $8.50; $2-$5.50 concessions; *Planetarium* $2.50; $1.25 concessions. **Credit** AmEx, MC, V. **Map B6**

This science museum, which faces the de Young across the Music Concourse in Golden Gate Park, is a perennial favourite. More than 1.5 million visitors come here each year to see the displays mounted by the oldest scientific institution in the western US. The big attraction is the **Steinhart Aquarium** (*see p67* **Sightseeing**), but there's much more, including a simulated earthquake exhibit that recreates the seismic lurches of the 1906 and 1989 tremblers and a brilliant display of

Don't miss

Ansel Adams Center for Photography

Historical displays from photography's biggest names. *See p89.*

California Palace of the Legion of Honor

For Rodin, for Sunday concerts and for the city's most regal museum. *See p82.*

Cartoon Art Museum

For archives of all your old newspaper and magazine favourites. *See p84.*

Exploratorium

Hands-on science for kids of all ages. *See p82.*

Jennjoy

The best of the 49 Geary Street 'art mall'. *See p88.*

New Langton Arts and 111 Minna Street Gallery

For young collectors, the hottest spots in town. *See p87.*

SFMOMA

For its stunning new building and Thursday evening jazz. *See p83.*

Yerba Buena Center for the Arts

Taking the biggest risks in the city's modern art galleries. *See p84.*

California Palace of the Legion of Honor.

the flora and fauna of California's numerous climates and varied terrain. The Academy includes a permanent exhibition of works by 'Far Side' cartoonist/science freak Gary Larson; its changing displays have included everything from dinosaurs to spiders. Also within the complex is the **Morrison Planetarium**, which presents educational and amusing sky shows as well as laser-guided music spectaculars.
Website: www.calacademy.org

California Palace of the Legion of Honor

Lincoln Park, Legion of Honor Drive, at 34th Avenue & Clement Street (750 3600). Bus 1, 2, 18, 38. **Open** 9.30am-5pm Tue-Sun. **Admission** $8; $5-$6 concessions; free second Wed of the month. **Credit** AmEx, MC, V.

San Francisco's prettiest museum was founded in 1894 by Alma de Bretteville Spreckels and reopened in the autumn of 1995 after a three-year hiatus for expansion and seismic upgrading. Located in a wooded spot near the Pacific, the Legion's original neo-classical façade has not been altered. A cast of Rodin's 'Le Penseur' still dominates the entrance, which has now been enhanced by a glass pyramid. The Legion's famous collections include more than 87,000 paintings, sculptures, decorative arts, works on paper, tapestries and other objects, spanning 4,000 years. The entrance level is dedicated to the permanent collection; an expanded garden level houses temporary exhibition galleries, as well as the Achenbach Foundation for Graphic Arts and the Bowles Porcelain Gallery and study centre. In 1999, the museum co-curated a huge Picasso exhibition; more recently, works by Francis Bacon made for a grim and fascinating show. A Palace ticket stub will also get you into the de Young on the same day.
Website: www.thinker.org

Exploratorium

3601 Lyon Street, at Marina Boulevard (563 7337/recorded information 561 0360/Tactile Dome 561 0362). Bus 28, 29, 30, 43, 76. **Open** *summer* 10am-6pm Mon, Tue, Thur-Sun; 10am-9pm Wed; *winter* 10am-5pm Tue, Thur-Sun; 10am-9pm Wed. **Admission** $9; $2.50-$7 concessions; free first Wed of the month. **Credit** MC, V. **Map C2**

Conceived by physicist Frank Oppenheimer and opened in 1969, the extraordinary Exploratorium reveals the secrets of heat, light, electricity, electronics, temperature, touch, vision, waves, patterns, motion, language and colour through clever, mostly hands-on displays. A series of charts on the history of language, for example, traces hundreds of dialects according to their family trees; additional exhibits impart theories on balance, perspective and other concepts that kids often grasp more quickly than adults. A recent exhibition on memory included old newsreels, juke-boxes and artefacts from eons past. While much of the space resembles a post-space age video arcade, there are also more passive displays (and a library where you can search for explanations the old-fashioned way). The

A different perspective at the **Exploratorium**.

museum offers a smorgasbord of seminars devoted to such offbeat topics as bubble blowing and car-horn symphonies. To a background cacophony of blinking lights and whizzing machines, you can grab a bite in the café, or pick up an espresso or Spanish *churros* as you go along. There's also a gift shop that sells scientific toys and educational baubles. The Exploratorium's artist-in-residence series is not to be missed.
Website: www.exploratorium.edu

MH de Young Memorial Museum

Music Concourse, Golden Gate Park (750 3600). Muni Metro N/bus 5, 21, 38, 44, 71. **Open** 9.30am-5pm Tue-Sun; 9.30am-8.45pm first Wed of the month. **Admission** $7; $4-$5 concessions; free first Wed of the month. **Credit** MC, V. **Map B5**

The MH de Young Memorial Museum houses collections of the art of the Americas, which date from colonial times to the present day and include sculpture, paintings, textiles and decorative arts. American masters such as Thomas Eakins, John Singer Sargent and George Caleb Bingham are represented, as well as works by contemporary Bay Area artists. Because of damage sustained in the 1989 quake, the de Young (named after the local family who launched the *San Francisco Chronicle*) is due to be rebuilt, expanding its galleries and adding a rooftop conservatory. In the meantime, insurance concerns have meant that major exhibitions scheduled for the de Young have been moved to the **Palace of the Legion of Honor** (*p82*) or the **Yerba Buena Center for the Arts** (*see p84*). Admission includes entry to the adjacent Asian Arts Museum and your ticket stub will also get you into the Palace of the Legion of Honor on the same day.
Website: www.thinker.org

San Francisco Museum of Modern Art

151 Third Street, between Mission & Howard Streets (357 4035). BART Montgomery Street/Muni Metro F, J, K, L, M, N. **Open** 11am-6pm Mon, Tue, Fri-Sun; 11am-9pm Thur. **Admission** $9; $5-$6 concessions; free first Tue of month, children under 12 accompanied by adult; half price 6-9pm Thur. **Credit** *café & bookstore* AmEx, MC, V. **Map H4**

This 20,925sq m (225,000sq ft) building, designed by Swiss architect Mario Botta, looms above Yerba Buena Gardens with its distinctive red brick edifice and huge circular skylight, making it a handsome Cyclops from the outside. The second-largest museum in the US devoted to modern art, SFMOMA opened with a flourish in 1995, culling enthusiastic approval as much for its modernist design as for any improvement over its predecessor. It still feels brand new. Four floors of galleries rise from a stark and stunning black marble lobby, an awe-inspiring reception area that holds a café and splendid bookshop. The permanent collection of over 15,000 works includes paintings, sculptures and works on paper, as well as thousands of photographs and a growing collection of works related to the media arts. Its range is formidable – Katharina Fritsch, Dorothea Lange, Matisse, Diebenkorn, Klee; from Alexander Calder to Tibor Kalman, there's a smattering of everything, though not in any number. With an evident fondness for electronic and digital mediaists, San Francisco Museum of Modern Art director David Ross has made efforts to regularly include Bay Area artists in most group shows; its SECA (Society for the Encouragement of Contemporary Art) award shows nod to such local luminaries as Gay Outlaw and Katherine Spence. As in the museum's previous quarters, a lot of stair-climbing is required to reach the fifth-floor galleries (there are lifts, but they're slow). Once you've reached the top, however, don't miss the spectacular catwalk just beneath the skylight – though not recommended for those who suffer from vertigo. Note that the museum is closed on Wednesdays.
Website: www.sfmoma.org

San Francisco Museum of Modern Art.

Wheels roll at the **Cable Car Barn Museum**.

Yerba Buena Center for the Arts

701 Mission Street, at Third Street (978 2787). BART Powell Street/Muni Metro F, J, K, L, M, N/ bus 15, 30, 45, 76. **Open** 11am-6pm Tue, Wed, Sat, Sun; 11am-9pm Thur, Fri. **Admission** $5; $3 concessions; free 5-8pm first Thur of the month. **Credit** AmEx, MC, V. **Map H4**

Last in the alphabet but first in the hearts of many, the Yerba Buena Center for the Arts lurks in SFMOMA's shadow, yet seems unintimidated, tugging at the modern art scene's shirt-tails with a scrappy itinerary and a great attitude. Housed in a futuristic-looking building designed by Japanese architect Fumihiko Maki, it contains four changing galleries and a 96-seat theatre. The museum's focus is on the new and innovative – installation and video art, outsider art, art that challenges the existing canon – and has included such diverse names as Henry Darger, Fred Thomaselli and Kumi Yamashita.

Website: www.yerbabuenaarts.org

Specialist museums

African American Historical & Cultural Society Museum

Building C, Fort Mason Center, at Buchanan Street (441 0640). Bus 28. **Open** noon-5pm Wed-Sun; noon-7pm first Wed of the month. **Admission** $2; $1 concessions; free first Wed of the month. **Credit** *gift shop* AmEx, MC, V. **Map E1**

One of two facilities managed by the society (the other, with a library and listening room for historical tapes, is on Fulton Street), this museum/gallery combines a permanent collection with changing exhibitions. Its archival materials relate to African-American life and culture from the nineteenth century to the present day, including photos and related items that shed light on little-known aspects of American history, while the gallery's emphasis is on new and master artists of African descent. The gift shop sells African and African-American arts and crafts.

Cable Car Barn Museum

1201 Mason Street, at Washington Street (474 1887). Bus 1, 12, 83/cable car Powell-Mason or Powell-Hyde. **Open** *summer* 10am-6pm daily; *winter* 10am-5pm daily. **Admission** free. **Map G3**

After the mooing foghorn, the single sound most often associated with San Francisco is the clanging bells of the cable cars. The best way to study them is, of course, to ride one of the three lines that operate nowadays; second best is to tour the Cable Car Barn, where an underground excavation area allows visitors to see the system as it has been operating for more than 120 years. The cables, wheels and engines keep everything moving; you'll learn about emergency procedures, bell-ringing competitions and workmanship. Vintage cable cars, associated artifacts and dozens of old photographs complete the display.

Website: www.sfcablecar.com

Cartoon Art Museum

814 Mission Street, between Fourth & Fifth Streets (227 8666). BART Powell Street/Muni Metro F, J, K, L, M, N/bus 6, 7, 14, 15, 26, 27, 30, 45, 66, 71, 76/cable car Powell-Hyde or Powell-Mason. **Open** 11am-5pm Wed-Fri; 10am-5pm Sat; 1-5pm Sun. **Admission** $5; $2-$3 concessions. **Credit** MC, V. **Map G4**

A treat for artists and 'toonphiles, the Cartoon Art Museum consists of four rooms of exceedingly well-arranged exhibits. The sources are myriad – individual artists, sketchbooks, the *New Yorker* magazine – and add up to an informative lesson on the artistic, cultural and historic merits of this original art form. Displays cover artists from Edward Gorey to Hanna-Barbera, Charlie Brown to Art Spiegelman. Currently the only museum west of the Mississippi dedicated to the preservation, collection and exhibition of original cartoon art, the sizeable space also includes a children's museum, an interactive CD-ROM gallery and a nifty gift shop with books, cards and related cartoon-ery.

Chinese Historical Society Museum

644 Broadway, between Stockton & Grant Streets (391 1188). Bus 12, 15, 30, 45, 83, 15. **Open** 1-4pm Mon; 10.30am-4pm Tue-Fri. **Admission** free. **Map G2**

Bilingual displays at this subterranean space trace the presence and contributions of California's Chinese population, from the frontier years to the Gold Rush, the building of the railroads (which would have taken another 100 years were it not for low-paid Chinese labour) and the days of opium dens on the Barbary Coast. Lovingly kept displays include a small nineteenth century Chinese Buddhist altar; a 4m (14ft) Californian sampan for fishing, and a Chinese dragon head made in 1911 for use in ceremonies and parades – one of the first to incorporate electric lights. A must for unravelling California's complex historical tapestry.

Jewish Museum of San Francisco

121 Steuart Street, between Mission & Howard Streets (543 8880). BART Embarcadero/Muni Metro F, J, K, L, M, N/bus 1, 2, 7, 9, 14, 21, 31, 32, 66, 71. **Map J3**

San Francisco now has its own museum devoted to linking the Jewish community with the community at large. More a gallery than a stodgy exhibition hall, the museum features displays and educational programmes and shows works by established artists and students, many of which are political or controversial in nature. Its future location, across Mission Street from the Yerba Buena Gardens complex, opens in 2002. In the meantime, phone for details and opening times of the latest exhibition.

Website: www.jewishmuseumsf.org

Levi Strauss Museum

250 Valencia Street, between 14th Street & Duboce Avenue (565 9159). Bus 14, 26. **Open** *by tour only* 9am, 11am, 1.30pm, Tue, Wed. **Admission** free. **Map F6**

Of all the inventions emanating from the West Coast, perhaps the most ubiquitous is blue jeans. The history of this all-American icon is displayed at this museum, housed in a 1906 commercial Victorian building. Trace the birth of jeans during the Gold Rush, when a resourceful German immigrant fashioned a pair of trousers from the heavyweight canvas normally used for gold miners' tents. Follow it to the present day, where middle America – and the world – has made them indispensable. The tour includes a video and a visit to the factory's cutting and sewing rooms. Book in advance.

Mexican Museum

Building D, Fort Mason Center, at Buchanan Street (441 0404). Bus 28. **Open** 11am-5pm Wed-Sun; 11am-7pm first Wed of the month. **Admission** $4; $3 concessions; free first Wed of the month. **Credit** *gift shop* AmEx, MC, V. **Map E1**

The Mexican Museum, the first museum in the United States dedicated to the work of Mexican and other Latino artists is cramped – and delightful. Over the years, the curators have acquired some 9,000 objects reflecting a spectrum of Mexican art ranging from traditional to experimental, decorative to functional, ancient to contemporary. The museum curates shows on Mexican surrealism and also mounts travelling exhibits, including a major Frida Kahlo retrospective and a superb spraycan artists' workshop; there is also a sizeable gift shop. In late 2001, the museum will relocate to a new address on Mission Street just north of the Yerba Buena Gardens complex.

Musée Mécanique

Cliff House, 1090 Point Lobos Avenue, at the Great Highway (386 1170). Bus 18, 31, 38. **Open** *summer* 10am-8pm daily; *winter* 11am-7pm Mon-Fri; 10am-8pm Sat, Sun. **Admission** free.

Pack a pocketful of quarters and visit this wonderful – endangered – cliffside museum, actually an arcade housing dozens of old-fashioned mechanical gizmos ranging from fortune-telling machines to player pianos. Best of all is the Unbelievable Mechanical Farm, with 150 moving objects and figures. Like the Victorian camera obscura next door (which projects an image of the world outside onto a giant parabolic screen) the Musée Méchanique's fate awaits the restoration of the Cliff House, on whose land it sits. *See also chapter* **Sightseeing**.

National Maritime Museum *or ocean liner?*

Museo Italo-Americano

Building C, Fort Mason Center, at Buchanan Street (673 2200). Bus 28. **Open** noon-5pm Wed-Sun; noon-7pm first Wed of the month. **Admission** $3; $2 concessions; free under-12s; free first Wed of the month. **Credit** MC, V. **Map E1**

One of three ethnic museums housed in the unprepossessing Fort Mason complex (the others are the **African-American** and **Mexican Museums**, *see p84 and p85*), the Museo Italo-Americano functions as a gallery and community centre, offering classes in Italian language, art, architecture and related subjects. Along with a few historical exhibits, the museum displays works by Italian and Italian-American artists. It also has a nice little gift shop.

Website: www.well.com/museo

National Maritime Museum

Beach Street, at Polk Street (556 3002). Bus 19, 30, 32, 42, 47, 49/cable car Powell-Hyde. **Open** 10am-5pm daily. **Admission** free. **Map F1**

Based in a curvaceous 1930s building that looks like an ocean liner, the National Maritime Museum documents maritime history with the aid of photographs and ship models, including miniatures of passenger liners and US Navy ships. It's a little dated, but still offers interactive exhibits that children will enjoy and enough sea lore to fill a few hours. It's just across the street from the Ghirardelli Square shopping centre (*see p158* **Shops & Services**).

Website: www.maritime.org

San Francisco Performing Arts Library & Museum

Fourth floor, 401 Van Ness Avenue, at McAllister Street (255 4800). Muni Metro F, J, K, L, M, N/ bus 21, 42, 47, 49. **Open** 1-7pm Wed; 11am-5pm Thur, Fri; noon-5pm Sat. **Admission** free. **Map F5**

With exhibitions relating to the performing arts, be it a puppet show or an opera, this museum is worth a visit if you're in the Civic Center area. Of most interest to fine arts scholars is the prodigious amount of resource material: thousands of books on design, fashion, music, theatre, opera and other art forms augment a focus on local arts groups.

Website: www.sfpalm.org

Tattoo Studio and Museum

841 Columbus Avenue, at Greenwich Street (775 4991). Bus 15, 30/cable car Powell-Mason. **Open** noon-9pm Mon-Thur, Sun; noon-10pm Fri, Sat. **Map G2**

The arrival of tattoos in the Western world supposedly occurred after the English privateer William Dampier returned from the South Pacific to shock and titillate London with the sight of Giolo, a native 'painted prince'. Now, it seems, everyone has one. Trust San Francisco to have a museum dedicated to them. Master tattoo artist Lyle Tuttle has gathered what may be the world's largest assortment of skin art paraphernalia – designs, articles, photographs and even an old set of hand needles. If you like what you see, you can get one yourself: Tuttle is one of the best skin artists in the world (*see p178* **Shops & Services**).

Treasure Island Museum

Building 1, Treasure Island, San Francisco-Oakland Bay Bridge (652 2772). Bus T Transbay Terminal. **Open** times vary; phone for details.

A stone's throw (or a quick drive) from downtown San Francisco, the Treasure Island Museum, located on a man-made island, traces the island's history as a location for the 1939 World's Fair and use thereafter as a naval station. A rich resource for information about the Bay and Golden Gate Bridges and historical shipbuilding and aviation.

Galleries

Not-for-profit galleries

Galeria de la Raza/Studio 24

2857 24th Street, at Bryant Street (826 8009). BART 16th Street/bus 27, 48. **Open** noon-6pm Wed-Sun. **Credit** AmEx, MC, V. **Castro/Mission Map Z2**

This tiny gallery in the heart of the Mission collects and curates the most vibrant artefacts from contemporary Latino culture into bi-monthly changing displays. From cartoonists and performance artists to mural-makers, magazine editors and photographers, the talent pool of selected artists is superb. With an archive of protest and political art, the gallery inclines towards left-of-centre; its exhibits chronicling workers' movements and various religious holidays are quintessentially Hispanic-American.

Intersection for the Arts

446 Valencia Street, between 15th & 16th Streets (626 2787). BART 16th Street/bus 14, 22, 26. **Open** noon-5pm Tue-Sat. **No credit cards. Castro/Mission Map Y1**

A venerable SF institution where many up-and-coming artists make their début, in its well-chosen group shows or solo exhibitions. The gallery's nondescript shopfront is at the centre of a new community of spaces that have begun to assemble around the Mission/16th Street area. Intersection also hosts Artists' talks and events that take place outside the gallery. The opening hours are subject to change.

The Lab

2948 16th Street, at Capp Street (864 8855). BART 16th Street/bus 14, 22. **Open** noon-5pm Wed-Sat. **No credit cards. Castro/Mission Map Y1**

A first-floor space on a slightly seedy corner, the Lab favours punk photography, painting and multimedia displays that are often political, subversive or controversial in nature. It holds art auctions several times a year, but can always be counted on as a resource for edgy art at decent prices. Like all not-for-profit venues, the Lab operates on a shoestring budget with mostly volunteer staff; for that reason, the opening times are limited.

New Langton Arts

1246 Folsom Street, between Eighth & Ninth Streets (626 5416). Bus 12, 19, 27, 42. **Open** noon-5pm Wed-Sat. **Credit** MC, V. **Map G5**

In the forefront of the alternative art scene, this second-floor loft is as unprepossessing as some of its SoMa neighbours, at least from the outside. The choice of exhibitions is eclectic, to say the least, but the gallery is best known for its installations and performance pieces. It hosts an annual autumn showcase, the Bay Area Awards show, presenting top regional talent in literature, media arts, music, performance and the visual arts. As the National Endowment for the Arts' (NEA) regional grant-making site for Northern California, it also acts as an unofficial cultural centre for many different artists.

San Francisco Art Commission Gallery

401 Van Ness Avenue, at McAllister Street (554 6080). Muni Metro F, J, K, L, M, N/bus 21, 42, 47, 49. **Open** noon-5.30pm Wed-Sat. **Map F4**

The San Francisco Art Commission maintains this tidy exhibition space inside the Veteran's Memorial building in Civic Center. Drawing from local, Bay Area and national artists, the gallery exhibits all kinds of media in all kinds of contexts. A recent show to commemorate California's 150th anniversary included many works sympathetic to native Americans and other displaced cultures; a photo exhibit by photographer Jim Goldberg provoked thought and discussion about race relations in the region. The SFAC also maintains **Exploration**, a public art space on Grove Street between Van Ness and Polk Streets (two blocks from the gallery) that incorporates shopfront windows and a vacant lot. Don't miss either of these city-funded treasures.

SoMarts Gallery

934 Brannan Street, between Eighth & Ninth Streets (552 2131 ext 8). Bus 19, 42. **Open** noon-4pm Tue-Sat. **No credit cards**. **Map G5**

Tucked under the freeway and nearly overshadowed by a Toys R Us sign, the SoMarts Gallery might be easy to miss. But don't overlook one of the city's long-lived art traditions, housed in an ancient warehouse with a cavern-like series of rooms. Besides being headquarters for ArtSpan, the organisation which runs **Artists' Open Studios** each October (*see p29* **San Francisco by Season**), SoMarts hosts its own group and solo shows, as well as live music performances, dramatic works and events outside the gallery. One of the latter was the Art Car Fair, a parking-lot's worth of uniquely-fashioned automobiles.

Southern Exposure

401 Alabama Street, between Mariposa & 17th Streets (863 2141). BART 16th Street/bus 22, 33. **Open** 11am-5pm Tue-Sat. **Credit** MC, V. **Castro/Mission Map Z1**

Much like **Intersection for the Arts** (*see p86*), Southern Exposure has made its reputation as the place for emerging artists to show – and to be discovered shortly thereafter. If Intersection is small and focused, SoEx is large and inclusive, with a bright, sunny space on the west side of **Theater Artaud** (*see chapter* **Performing Arts**). SoEx's group shows and parties are legendarily packed events; their juried art shows have drawn curators from the nation's art community. If you have one non-profit gallery to visit on your travels, make it this one.

Commercial galleries

Catharine Clark Gallery

Second floor, 49 Geary Street, between Kearny Street & Grant Avenue (399 1439). BART Montgomery Street/bus 9, 30, 38, 45, 81. **Open** 10.30am-5.30pm Tue-Fri; 11am-5.30pm Sat. **Credit** AmEx, MC, V. **Map H3**

Director Catharine Clark has a keen eye for modern art with legs – many of the works by her sculptors, painters and mixed-media artists walk their way into the regional museums and collectors' living rooms. The gallery consists of three rooms of various sizes and the art ranges from dangerous-looking kinetic sculptures to figurative painting. It's all good: an exhibit co-curated in Los Angeles of works by Californian artist Sandow Burke perfectly exemplifies Clark's oeuvre – a series of huge painted canvasses and a model ship portraying one of the vessels which fought in the 'Water Wars', a futuristic battle fought over California's most precious resource. Located in the 49 Geary 'art mall' (*see also p88* **Jennjoy** *and p90* **Robert Koch Gallery**).

ESP

305 Valencia Street, between 14th & 15th Streets (252 8191). BART 16th Street/bus 22, 26. **Open** noon-4pm Thur-Sat. **Credit** MC, V. **Castro/Mission Map Y1**

If there's any justice in the world ESP will, in a short time, alter its obscure reputation and become a well-known gallery lauded for its good taste. Tucked into a funky space at the perimeter of the bohemian Mission, the two-room space shows unknown artists with supreme visions: minimalists, experimental photographers, video curators, eroticists, even sticker (one step removed from graffiti) artists have found their way onto ESP's walls. A recent Tom of Finland archives show was kinky and fun and other displays have proved similarly thoughtful.

Website: www.significantproductions/esp

Four Walls Projects

69A Duboce Avenue, between Valencia & Mission Streets (626 8515). Bus 14, 49, 53. **Open** 3-7pm Wed-Fri; noon-7pm Sat. **Credit** MC, V. **Map F6**

Almost too good to be true – a bright, roomy gallery with a keen curatorial sensibility that steadily fills it with fine work. Recently relocated from its long-standing haunt above an old fire station in the Mission district, the gallery features works on paper, sculpture and installations, but has also been known to host projected, musical and filmed events. The new space is a little more elegant and looks set to feature art of predictably high quality. The 'Post Card' show, featuring small art pieces for $20 or less, is an annual hit.

Gallery scramble

For years, San Francisco's commercial galleries have honoured a tradition of staying open late on the first Thursday of every month – or 'first Thursdays', – to offer food and drink to their patrons. Once merely a little-known freebie-fest enjoyed by art students and their friends, the event now seems to draw most of the art-friendly populace. Admittedly, first Thursdays are as much a social event as they are an excuse to look at art. But if you enjoy being where the action is head for the blocks just east of Union Square.

Start your evening at 6pm at **49 Geary Street**, the 'art mall' where you'll find a dozen galleries spread over four floors. Take the lift to the fifth floor (or take the stairs when it's crowded) and for the pick of the litter head to **871 Fine Arts** which displays interesting works from its 1950s and 1960s pop and abstract expressionist archives (543 5812), the **Haines Gallery** (397 8114) which usually shows provocative sculpture or painting and the superb **Brian Gross Gallery** (788 1050) which never disappoints with its modern work (and the classiest wine selection). A floor down, don't miss the modern contrast of **Jennjoy** (*see above*) and **Toomey-Tourell Gallery** (989 6444), across the hall from each other, nor the **Particia Sweetow Gallery** (788 5126) which features a variety of edgy works. Walk down to the second floor to find **Catharine Clark** (*see above*), whose several rooms are always jammed with provocative art and patrons.

For modern photography, the **Robert Koch** (fifth floor; 421 0122), **Fraenkel** (fourth floor; 982 2661) and **Scott Nichols** (fourth floor; 788 4641) galleries will never lead you astray. Several other galleries feature more traditional painting styles, including the **Ebert** (fourth floor; 296 8405), **Stephen Wirtz** (third; 433 6879) and **Don Soker** (fourth; 291 0966) galleries.

After you've exhausted all possibilities here, walk two blocks north to Sutter Street. (You might want to catch the prestigious **Gallery Paule Anglim** at 14 Geary, 433 2710; or **Rena Bransten Gallery** at 77 Geary, 982 3292 on the way). At 250 Sutter take the lift to the third floor and the recently-opened **Quotidian Gallery** (788 0445) which shows quirky painters, then next door to **Graystone** (956 7693), where fascinating sculpture and works on paper can be seen next to original works by Roy Lichtenstein. Upstairs one floor is the delightful **Hackett-Freedman Gallery** (362 7152) which shows twenty-first-century figurative work.

Nearby Post Street is also lively, with good viewing to be had at the **Olga Dollar Gallery** (210 Post Street; 398 2297), the **Meyerovich** (251 Post Street; 421 7171) and the **John Pence** (750 Post Street; 441 1138). A hot new property is the **Hang Gallery**, at 556 Sutter Street (956 5000), a space devoted to emerging Bay Area artists. And if you've headed this far west you're close to the campus of the **San Francisco Academy of Art** and its satellite college at 740 Taylor Street, between Bush and Sutter Streets, which is bound to have a good show on (*see page 280* **Directory**).

Jennjoy

Suite 410, 49 Geary Street, between Kearny Street & Grant Avenue (398 2040). BART Montgomery Street/bus 9, 30, 38, 45, 81. **Open** 11am-5.30pm Tue-Sat. **Credit** MC, V. **Map H3**

The 49 Geary Street building houses more than a dozen galleries, and Jennjoy, one of the newest, is also making one of the biggest splashes. Exhibitions are changed monthly and are consistently interesting, whether they incorporate a group show of video and minimal works, an installation of tangled webs and wires or a solo show by the likes of Kathleen White, an artist who sculpts with human hair. Friendly and casual, Jennjoy offers a welcome change from the potential snootiness you might feel in other galleries. A few hours can easily be spent perusing the various galleries on other floors. *See also above* **Gallery scramble**.
Website: www.jennjoygallery.com

Modernism

685 Market Street, between Third & New Montgomery Streets (541 0461). BART Montgomery Street/Muni Metro F, L, K, M, N/ bus 7, 9, 14, 15, 71. **Open** 10am-5.30pm Tue-Sat. **No credit cards. Map H3**

The gallery space Modernism, grapples with the age-old contradiction many established galleries face: how to meld fine art that attracts a high price with an atmosphere that is hospitable. Sadly, the latter often suffers – if you're not rich, you might not feel comfortable here. Yet the art on display is amazing, ranging from Mark Stock's and Sheldon Greenberg's moody figures to Cesar Santander's wacky tin toy portraits.

111 Minna Street Gallery

111 Minna Street, at Second Street (974 1713). Bus 9, 12, 14, 71. **Open** 1-4pm Tue-Fri; 4-7pm Sat. **No credit cards. Map H3/4**

Amy Ellingson's 'A great, unexpected, extra-gratuitous good thing' at **Jennjoy**.

A few points to consider while enjoying your first first Thursday: most spaces will be crowded, so if you are a real art aficionado, you'll need to arrive early. The same rule applies for refreshments – arrive before the crowd hits if you're set on procuring your glass of wine and paper plate of crackers and cheese, or you'll be out of luck. First Thursdays often coincide with show openings, so you might be lucky enough to catch the artist meeting the public and occasionally offering up a brief lecture.

Other neighbourhoods have galleries too. Many patrons prefer to stroll south from Market Street past the **SFMOMA** and **Yerba Buena Center for the Arts** (also open late on first Thursdays, *see above*), where they can find several spaces open. The ever-popular **Refusalon** (*see above*) is located in the same building as **Crown Point Press** (974 6273) which specialises in fine art prints. The **111 Minna Street Gallery** (which has the best food) and **SF Camerawork** and the **Ansel Adams Center** (which cater to the shutterbugs) are located within a block or two (*see above*).

If you still have time left (most galleries close at 8pm sharp) or, better yet, if you're in San Francisco for another month – cab it to a couple of other neighbourhoods for more diverse tours. An arrival at 16th and Mission puts you within range of **Intersection for the Arts**, **The Lab**, **Four Walls** and **ESP Galleries** (*see above*), as well as the new **381G Gallery** at 381 Guerrero Street (255 1821). In Hayes Valley, the Hayes-and-Gough intersection puts you near to the galleries for **Boucheon** (540 Hayes Street; 863 2891), **Vorpal** (393 Grove Street; 397 9200) and the **San Francisco Art Commission Gallery** (*see above*), as well as the **San Francisco Women Artists Gallery** (370 Hayes Street; 552 7392).

Much more laid-back is 111 Minna, an artspace-cum-lounge whose bold taste for art has placed it at the top of the city's hot galleries. The shows here are nothing if not successful, from Andre Mirapolsky's post-graffiti splashes to Winston Smith's twisted punk collages. The group shows are also great, including a series called 'Pop Tarts' which features edgy work by female artists. If you like the exhibition you can stay for a drink: Minna serves decent beers on tap and wines by the glass as well as some of the community's best spreads at openings. For the gallery's evening dance club incarnation, *see p217* **Nightlife**.

Website: www.111annex.com/gallery.htm

Refusalon

20 Hawthorne Street, between Second & Third Streets (546 0158). Bus 9, 12, 38.
Open noon-6pm Tue-Sat; noon-8pm first Thur of the month. **Credit** MC, V. **Map H4**

Though its artists might not yet be household names, this charming, austere gallery in the shadow of SFMOMA houses some of the most interesting art in the city. Specialising in 'peripheral' works, Refusalon has hosted shows by Eric Saks, Patrick Tierney, Pip Culbert and her sons Rae and Clay as well as edge-surfers like Gay Outlaw. Recently, the space has taken new chances with sculpture and sound exhibits.

Website: www.refusalon.com

Photography galleries

Ansel Adams Center for Photography

250 Fourth Street, between Folsom & Howard Streets (495 7000). Bus 12, 14, 15, 30, 45.
Open 11am-5pm daily; 11am-8pm first Thur of the month. **Admission** $5; $2-$3 concessions. **Credit** AmEx, MC, V. **Map H4**

In 1989, 22 years after Ansel Adams founded the Friends of Photography along with other prominent

photographers, the group relocated headquarters from Carmel to Fourth Street, just west of Yerba Buena Gardens. Of the Center's five galleries, one is devoted to exploring and preserving Adams' photographic legacy; the rest showcase contemporary and historical photography and have included such seminal collections as a history of the Polaroid and the Summer of Love as seen in pictures. The centre also has an outstanding bookshop.
Website: www.friendsofphotography.org

Robert Koch Gallery

49 Geary Street, between Kearny Street & Grant Avenue (421 0122). BART Montgomery Street/ bus 9, 30, 38, 45, 81. **Open** 10.30am-5.30pm Tue-Sat. **Credit** AmEx, MC, V. **Map H3**
If you're in the Geary Street art mall, make a special trip to catch the photos on display at the Robert Koch Gallery. The curators seem to have honed an environmental edge, favouring such international photographers as Ed Burtynsky and Josef Koudelka; experimental works are also exhibited, by such artists as Shimon Attie, Lynn Hershman Leeson and Robert Parke Harrison. Most works are large format; few are terribly affordable, but the selection is always good.

SF Camerawork

115 Natoma Street, at New Montgomery Street (764 1001). BART Montgomery Street/Muni Metro F, L, K, M, N/bus 14. **Open** noon-5pm Tue-Sat. **Credit** MC, V. **Map H4**
It's a bit of a trek to SF Camerawork's just-south-of-Market studio, up a long stairway from out-of-the-way Natoma Street. But it's worth the trouble for the roster of innovative local, regional and national photographers. The group shows traditionally include more than a dozen shooters at once; the members' shows are more selective – and no less enjoyable. After 25 years in the (non-profit) gallery business, SF Camerawork is a San Francisco fixture.

Out of town

Berkeley Art Museum & Pacific Film Archives

2626 Bancroft Way & 2621 Durant Avenue, between Bowditch & College Streets (1-510 642 0808). BART Downtown Berkeley. **Open** 11am-5pm Wed, Fri-Sun; 11am-9pm Thur. **Admission** $6; $4 concessions; free 11am-noon, 5-9pm, Thur. **Credit** DC, MC, V.
Modernist printer Hans Hofmann provided the impetus for an art museum on the UC Berkeley campus. Opened in 1970, the dramatic exhibition space is arranged in terraces enabling visitors to see the works from various vantage points. The collection's strength is in twentieth-century painting, sculpture, photography and conceptual art, as well as Asian art. Ten galleries and a bookstore occupy the upper level, while the Sculpture Garden and café share the lower level with the Pacific Film Archives, one of the country's most comprehensive academic film programmes. The PFA screens some 650 films and videos a year and has a collection of more than 7,000 titles, including Soviet, US avant-garde and Japanese cinema, among other genres.
Website: www.bampfa.berkeley.edu

Oakland Museum of California

1000 Oak Street, at 10th Street, Oakland (1-510 238 2200). BART Lake Merritt.
Open 10am-5pm Wed-Sat; noon-5pm Sun; 10am-9pm first Fri of the month. **Admission** $6; $4 concessions; free second Sun of the month.
Credit AmEx, DC, MC, V.
The only museum in California devoted exclusively to the art, history and environment of the state, the Oakland Museum was established in 1969. The Gallery of California Art displays paintings, sculpture, prints, illustrations, photos and decorative arts by Californian artists, or by artists addressing related themes and subjects. Exhibited in some 2,790sq m (30,000sq ft) of space, the collection includes sketches by early explorers; genre pictures from the Gold Rush; massive panoramic landscapes; and Bay Area figurative, pop and funk works. The Natural Sciences displays are devoted to the variegated Californian landscape and the Cowell Hall of California History has furniture, machines, tools, costumes, craftwork, clothing, decorations and vehicles prominent in the state's development.
Website: www.museumca.org

San Francisco Bay Model Visitor Center

2100 Bridgeway, Sausalito (332 3870). Golden Gate Transit bus/ferry from Pier 45.
Open *June-Sept* 9am-4pm Tue-Fri; 10am-5pm Sat, Sun; *Oct-May* 9am-4pm Tue-Sat.
Admission free.
A 15-acre (37-hectare) model of the Bay established by the US Army Corps of Engineers shows how navigation, recreation and ecology all interact in this complex water system. Best of all, walkways are strung all over so that visitors can, figuratively at least, walk on water. When the model is in operation, a lunar day is simulated in under 15 minutes, complete with tidal action. Hands-on displays include video games and an introduction to indigenous birds and fish, and there are videos on the Corps' work in hydroelectric power, flood control and construction.
Website: www.spn.usace.army.mil/bmvc

Consumer

Accommodation

San Francisco's lodging logistics.

As one of the most popular tourist destinations in the world, San Francisco goes the distance to cater to every type of visitor – from penny-watching hostel-goers and 1960s throwbacks to wealthy jet setters and gender benders. However, even with over 30,000 rooms available nightly, it's not unusual to find the town sold out during high season and at convention weekends. Make sure you book your accommodation well in advance.

Hotel Metropolis. *See page 101.*

Most hotels are packed into the ultra-touristy Union Square and Nob Hill areas, close to downtown shops, cable cars, Chinatown, North Beach, SoMa and some of the city's best restaurants, clubs and bars. Although downtown may be one of the most convenient areas to stay, it also means high parking expenses and separation from the real San Francisco – that is, from where most residents live and play. The city's geography being what it is, however, you'll have no problem hailing a cab or taking public transport from the downtown area to explore any of the other neighbourhoods.

PRICES & SERVICES

For a basic double bed, private bathroom, phone and TV within the city, expect to pay between $80 and $120 a night during the peak season, which runs roughly between May and October. For anything more luxurious expect to pay considerably more. This price doesn't include a 14 per cent room tax, telephone surcharges and nightly parking fees, which range from negligible to around $20.

When making a hotel reservation, have your credit card handy and be prepared to pay for at least one night in advance. Most hotels hold reservations until about 6pm, unless you've notified them you'll be arriving late. Most hotels will ask for an imprint of your credit card upon arrival for 'incidental expenses' and to prevent walk-outs. Service from the staff at most moderate to expensive hotels in San Francisco is usually superb and you'll be expected to tip accordingly (*see chapter* **Directory** for notes on tipping).

If you would rather hand over the booking process to a reservation service, a number of reputable companies will do the work for you. The best is **San Francisco Reservations** (*see page 97*). At no cost to you, they'll find a hotel, motel or bed and breakfast in your price range and even negotiate for a discounted rate.

All 1-800 numbers can be called free of charge from within the US and most can be accessed from outside the US, though not always free of charge. Be warned that most hotels add a surcharge for use of their phones, whatever number you call. Unless otherwise stated, all rooms listed below have TV and telephone.

See also chapter **Gay & Lesbian San Francisco**.

Hipper than thou: the **Hotel Triton** *on the edge of Chinatown (above and left). See p101.*

Best for...

Old San Francisco splendour:
The Archbishop's Mansion *(p109).*
Small-scale charm in the Big Bad City:
Bed and Breakfast Inn *(p112).*
The English experience:
Edward II Inn & Pub *(p112).*
The melding of art and architecture:
Hotel Monaco *(p99).*
The young, the hip and the restless:
Hotel Triton *(p101).*
Million-mile views:
Mandarin Oriental *(p104).*
Feng shui devotees:
The Metropolis *(p101).*
The hard-core clubber:
The Phoenix *(p109).*
The Flower Power experience:
The Red Victorian *(p110).*
Fat cats:
Ritz-Carlton San Francisco *(p105).*
Penny pinchers with style:
San Remo *(p107)* or **Marina Inn** *(p113).*
Teddy bears and fresh-baked cookies:
White Swan Inn *(p103).*
Sex appeal in the city: **W Hotel** *(p107).*

Golden Gate Hotel. *See page 103.*

Reservation services

Bed-and-Breakfast California

12711 McCartysville Place, Saratoga, CA 95070 (1-800 872 4500/1-408 867 9662/fax 1-408 867 0907/info@bbintl.com).

Provides a selection of B&Bs ranging from budget to moderately priced, with a two-night minimum stay. Accommodation ranges from simple rooms in private homes to luxurious Victorian homes, carriage houses and houseboats.

Website: www.bbintl.com

San Francisco Reservations

22 Second Street, CA 94105 (1-800 677 1500/ 227 1500).

Arranges reservations for more than 300 of San Francisco's hotels, often at discounted rates. Inquire about their events and hotel packages that include VIP or discount admissions to various San Francisco museums. Internet users can make their reservations on-line.

Website: www.hotelres.com

Around Union Square

First-class

Campton Place Hotel

340 Stockton Street, CA 94108, at Post Street (1-800 235 4300/781 5555/fax 955 5536/reserve@campton.com). Bus 2, 3, 4, 30/cable car Powell-Hyde or Powell-Mason. **Rates** *rooms* $295-$435; *suites* $550-$2,100. **Credit** AmEx, DC, MC, $TC, V. **Map G3**

After a hefty $18 million retrofit in 1981, the former Drake-Wiltshire Hotel re-opened as the Campton Place and has attracted a very discreet (and wealthy) following ever since. The hotel neatly packs 110 rooms into a small space, although some guests may still wonder what their money is paying for. Recent renovation should add a little more elbow room. The services here are exceptional and include valet-assisted packing and unpacking and 24-hour room, concierge, maid and valet service. Two additional enticements are the central location (on a corner of Union Square) and the Campton Place Restaurant.

Hotel services *Air-conditioning. Bar. Concierge. Conference facilities. Currency exchange. Disabled: specially adapted rooms. Fax. Laundry. No-smoking rooms. Valet parking. Restaurant. Roof garden. Website: www.camptonplace.com.* **Room services** *Dataport. Hairdryer. Mini-bar. Radio. Room service (24-hour). Safe. VCR.*

Clift Hotel

495 Geary Street, CA 94102, at Taylor Street (1-800 652 5438/775 4700/fax 931 7417). Bus 2, 3, 4, 30, 38, 45/cable car Powell-Hyde or Powell-Mason. **Rates** *rooms* $255-$305; *suites* $360-$905. **Credit** AmEx, DC, JCB, MC, $TC, V. **Map G4**

Since Ian Schrager acquired this 357-room property,

The **Mandarin Oriental**: *first-class prices matched with first-class views.* *See page 104.*

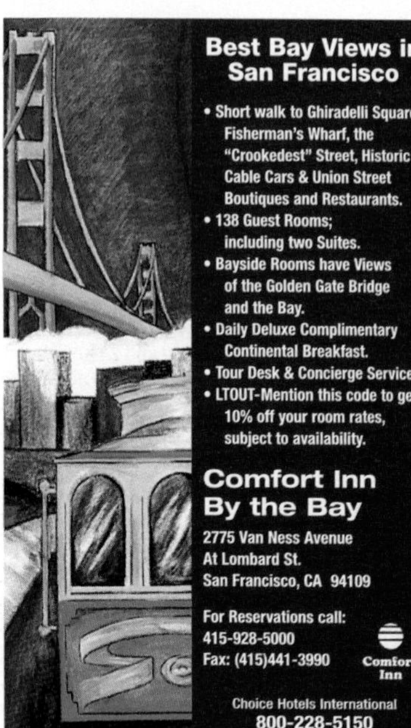

Best Bay Views in San Francisco
• Short walk to Ghiradelli Square, Fisherman's Wharf, the "Crookedest" Street, Historic Cable Cars & Union Street Boutiques and Restaurants.
• 138 Guest Rooms; including two Suites.
• Bayside Rooms have Views of the Golden Gate Bridge and the Bay.
• Daily Deluxe Complimentary Continental Breakfast.
• Tour Desk & Concierge Services.
• LTOUT-Mention this code to get 10% off your room rates, subject to availability.
Comfort Inn By the Bay
2775 Van Ness Avenue
At Lombard St.
San Francisco, CA 94109
For Reservations call:
415-928-5000
Fax: (415)441-3990
Comfort Inn
Choice Hotels International
800-228-5150
http://www.hotelchoice.com

CRS
Central Reservation Service

everyone has been anxious to see what the brains behind New York's Royalton and Los Angeles' Mondrian will do with the space. Three years on and we're still waiting. (And meanwhile, it still costs a small fortune to stay here). One thing is certain: when Schrager gets his act together, this *will* be the hottest hotel in town. Located two blocks from Union Square in the city's theatre district, the Clift is renowned for its pampering staff, palatial lobby and romantic **Redwood Room** lounge (*see chapter* **Bars**). Décor has until now leaned toward old-fashioned, with high ceilings, elaborate mouldings and Georgian reproductions. This is all set to change, when the long-awaited Schrager-treatment is revealed.
Hotel services *Babysitting. Business services. Concierge. Conference facilities. Currency exchange. Fax. Gift shop. Gym. Laundry. Limousine service. No-smoking rooms. Parking. Website: www.clifthotel.com.* **Room services** *Fax & dataport. Hairdryer. Mini-bar. Radio. Refrigerator. Room service. Safe.*

Grand Hyatt

345 Stockton Street, CA 94108, between Post & Sutter Streets (1-800 233 1234/398 1234/fax 391 1780). Bus 2, 3, 4, 30, 45/cable car Powell-Hyde or Powell-Mason. **Rates** *rooms* $189-$280; *suites* $450-$1,500. **Credit** AmEx, DC, Disc, JCB, MC, $TC, V.
Map G3
The 693-room Grand Hyatt offers just about everything the business or pleasure traveller would expect from a four-star hotel. Its location – at the north-east corner of Union Square – couldn't be better, nor the view from most of the 36 floors more spectacular (especially from the roof-top Club 36 jazz club). Room décor is rather corporate, but additional perks include use of a spacious health club, a car service to the Financial District, a fully-equipped business centre and surprisingly good (and reasonably priced) food at the handsome 36th-floor Grandviews Restaurant. Request a larger-than-average 'Regency Room' which includes continental breakfast and evening hors d'oeuvres.
Hotel services *Air-conditioning. Babysitting. Bar. Beauty salon. Business services. Concierge. Conference facilities. Currency exchange. Disabled: specially adapted rooms. Fax. Gym. Interpreting service. Laundry. No-smoking rooms. Parking. Restaurant. Safe.* **Room services** *Dataport. Hairdryer. Mini-bar. Radio. Refrigerator. Room service (6am-midnight daily).*

Hotel Monaco

501 Geary Street, CA 94102, at Taylor Street (1-800 214 4220/292 0100/fax 292 0419). Bus 2, 3, 4, 38. **Rates** *rooms* $249-$269; *suites* $329-$459. **Credit** AmEx, DC, Disc, JCB, MC, $TC, V.
Map G4
Few hotels offer the romantic and larger-than-life ambience of the Monaco. The remodelled Beaux Arts building, built in 1910 and previously known as the Hotel Bellevue, re-opened in June 1995 after a $24-million dollar facelift. Everything about the Monaco is big: from the hand-painted ceiling domes and grandiose common areas where antique knick-knacks contrast with local contemporary art, to the 201 rooms with canopy-draped beds surrounded by a jumble of vibrant patterns (though the less expensive rooms are a tad too small). If you tire of gawking at the details, wander next door to the Grand Café and get a load of the fantastic 1920s and 1930s décor accented by more local art – including a three storey-high bunny sculpture.
Hotel services *Air-conditioning. Bar. Business services. Conference facilities. Disabled: specially adapted rooms. Fax. Laundry. Limousine service. No-smoking rooms. Parking. Restaurant. Safe. Spa.* **Room services** *Fax machine & dataport. Hairdryer. Kitchenette. Mini-bar. Radio. Refrigerator. Room service (6am-11pm daily). Voicemail.*

Pan Pacific

500 Post Street, CA 94102, at Mason Street (1-800 533 6465/771 8600/fax 398 0267). Bus 2, 3, 4, 30, 38, 45/cable car Powell-Hyde or Powell-Mason. **Rates** *rooms* $315-$420; *suites* from $460. **Credit** AmEx, DC, Disc, JCB, MC, V. **Map G3**
Rarely does a hotel get everything right, but the Pan Pacific has hit the bull's-eye. Rooms? Immaculate. Service? Outstanding. Cuisine? Superb. Architecture? Breathtaking. For a hefty room price, guests are supplied with lavish marble bathrooms, personal valet and complimentary Rolls Royce service. Even if you're not staying here, the 330-room hotel is worth visiting just to ride in one of the glimmering glass elevators inside the 18-storey, atrium lobby. Located one block from Union Square.
Hotel services *Air-conditioning. Babysitting. Bar. Business centre. Concierge. Conference facilities. Currency exchange. Health club. Laundry. Restaurant. Secretarial service.* **Room services** *Massage service. Room service (24-hours). Valet.*

The Prescott

545 Post Street, CA 94102, at Taylor Street (1-800 283 7322/563 0303/fax 563 6831/sales@prescotthotel.com). Bus 2, 3, 4/cable car Powell-Hyde or Powell-Mason. **Rates** *rooms* from $265; *suites* $315-$1,200. **Credit** AmEx, DC, Disc, MC, $TC, V.
Map G3/4
There was a time when guests would check into the Prescott solely to get preferential seating at the adjoining **Postrio** (*see chapter* **Restaurants & Cafés**). While the restaurant has lost some of its divine status, the Prescott remains one of San Francisco's finer small hotels. The 164 rooms, including 30 suites, are decorated with custom-made cherry-wood furnishings, silk wallpaper and wonderfully cushy beds. The penthouse is a lavish affair complete with roof-top Jacuzzi, grand piano and twin fireplaces. Highly recommended is the Concierge Level, a private floor where the deal includes free drinks, hors d'oeuvres, continental breakfast and a host of other amenities. Union Square is just a short walk away.
Hotel services *Air-conditioning. Babysitting. Bar. Concierge. Conference facilities. Disabled: specially adapted rooms. Fax. Laundry. Limousine service.*

No-smoking rooms. Parking. Restaurant. Safe. Website: www.prescotthotel.com. **Room services** *CD player. Fax machine & dataport. Hairdryer. Mini-bar. Radio. Refrigerator. Room service (7am-midnight daily).*

San Francisco Marriott Hotel

55 Fourth Street, CA 94103, between Market & Mission Streets (1-800 228 9290/896 1600/fax 1-408 567 0391). BART Powell Street/Muni Metro F, J, K, L, M, N/bus 5, 6, 7, 9, 21, 30, 31, 45, 66, 71. **Rates** *rooms* $265-$285. **Credit** AmEx, DC, Disc, JCB, MC, $TC, V. **Map G/H4**

Completed in 1989, when a storm of controversy arose over its design (critics likened it to a giant jukebox or parking meter), the 39-storey Marriott is, for better or worse, undoubtedly striking: with its numerous arches of tinted glass and steel, one almost expects to see Batman astride the roof. The 1,500 rooms, however, are more down to earth, with huge beds, large bathrooms and wonderful views of the city and Bay (ask for a room overlooking Yerba Beuna Gardens). Free unlimited use of the on-site health club, indoor pool and Jacuzzi make the Marriott worth considering.

Hotel services *Air-conditioning. Bars. Business services. Concierge. Conference facilities. Currency exchange. Disabled: specially adapted rooms. Gym. Laundry. No-smoking rooms. Restaurant. Swimming pool. Website: www.marriott.com.* **Room services** *Dataport. Hairdryer. Mini-bar. Radio. Room service (5.30am-1am daily). Safe.*

Mid-range

Commodore International Hotel

825 Sutter Street, CA 94109, at Jones Street (923 6800/1-800 338 6848/fax 923 6804). Bus 2, 3, 4, 27, 76. **Rates** *rooms* $129-$139. **Credit** AmEx, DC, Disc, MC, $TC, V. **Map G3**

Are you stylish? contemporary? wearing black? If the answer is yes, then you're Commodore material. From the company that raised the legendary **Phoenix** (*see p109*) from its ashes comes the most far out, curvaceous and cool hotel to hit the San Francisco scene since the **Triton** (*see below*). The Commodore's young and chic staff has all the tips for touring the far side of San Francisco and will even take you there by van or on foot. Of the 110 spacious rooms – all with large bathtubs and closets – request one of the 'post-modern deco' rooms with custom furnishings fashioned by local artists. Don't miss the hotel's **Red Room** (*see chapter* **Bars**), a groovy cocktail lounge that reflects no other colour of the spectrum.

Hotel services *Babysitting. Bar. Business services. Coffee shop. Concierge. Conference facilities. Fax. Laundry. No-smoking rooms. Safe.* **Room services** *Dataport. Hairdryer. Radio.*

One of North Beach's finest: the **Hotel Bohème**. *See page 105.*

Hotel Metropolis

25 Mason Street, CA 94102, at Turk Street (1-800 553 1900/775 4600/fax 775 4606). BART Powell Street/Muni Metro F, K, L, M, N/ bus 27, 38, 76. **Rates** *rooms* $110-$225. **Credit** AmEx, DC, Disc, MC, $TC, V. **Map G4**

Decorated in the theme of 'Earth, Wind & Fire' the newly-opened Metropolis is all eco-friendly ying meets yang. Each floor is colour-coded in elemental shades of olive green (earth), taupe (wind), yellow (fire) and aquamarine (water), and the pristine rooms have nicely understated furnishings, with wave-shaped headboards and port holes. Better-than-average toiletries and Nintendo/pay-per-view movies and cable TV complete the picture. The pitfalls of a less-than-salubrious location on the edge of the Tenderloin are skillfully overcome. The management participates in projects to help local homeless families on the one hand, whilst carefully directing residents to turn left, not right, out of the front door, to avoid them. There are splendid views over Potrero Hill and the Oakland hills beyond from the tenth floor, where some rooms also have balconies. Convenient for the Moscone Convention Center and popular with business travellers.

Hotel services *Business centre. Cardio centre. Continental breakfast. Concierge. Holistic well being centre. Laundry. Library. Website: www.hotelmetropolis.com.* **Room services** *Dataport. Hairdryer. Iron & ironing board. Nintendo/cable TV. Mini-bar. No-smoking rooms. Radio. Safe.*

Hotel Triton

342 Grant Avenue, CA 94108, at Bush Street (1-800 433 6611/394 0500/fax 394 0555). Bus 2, 3, 4, 30, 45/cable car Powell-Hyde or Powell-Mason. **Rates** *rooms* $179-$219; *suites* $299-$305. **Credit** AmEx, DC, Disc, JCB, MC, $TC, V. **Map G3**

Everything about the Hotel Triton screams hip, from the lobby's glimmering dervish chairs to the bellmen's eclectic uniforms. Designed by a team of Bay Area artisans, the 147-room hotel is a visual smorgasbord of stylish eccentricities including mythological murals, inverted-pyramid podiums and gilded floor-to-ceiling pillars. Two dozen environmentally sensitive 'eco rooms' – equipped with biodegradable soaps, all-natural linens and filtered water and air – have been added to satisfy the tree-hugger within you. Add a prime location (steps away from the entrance to Chinatown) and the adjoining **Café de la Presse**, a small 'European' coffee house (*see chapter* **Restaurants & Cafés**) and you have the local version of Alice in Wonderland's pad.

Hotel services *Air-conditioning. Babysitting. Café. Concierge. Conference facilities. Fax. Gym. Interpreting service. Laundry. No-smoking rooms. Parking. Website: www.tritonsf.com.* **Room services** *Dataport. Fax. Hairdryer. Mini-bar. Radio. Refrigerator. Room service (7am-10.30pm daily). Voicemail.*

The Maxwell

386 Geary Street, CA 94102, at Mason Street (1-888 734 6299/986 2000/fax 397 2447). Bus 2, 3, 4, 30, 38, 45/cable car Powell-Hyde or Powell-Mason. **Rates** *rooms* $155-$205; *suites* $495-$595. **Credit** AmEx, DC, Disc, MC, TC, V. **Map G4**

Call it chic boutique, or masterfully moody, but don't liken this boldly-designed new hotel to the Rafael, its quirky predecessor. After re-opening in 1997, the only feature to survive the 12-storey, 152-room hotel's metamorphosis is its convenient location a block from Union Square. Now rooms blend colour, texture, patterns and eclectic extras to create a 'deco-Victorian' look. If you have the dough, reserve one of the suites, which are like personalised penthouse apartments.

Hotel services *Air-conditioning. Baby-sitting. Bar. Café. Business services. Concierge. Conference facilities. Fax. Laundry. No-smoking rooms. Parking. Restaurant. Safe.* **Room services** *Dataport. Hairdryer. Radio. Room service (7am-1pm daily). Voicemail.*

Savoy Hotel

580 Geary Street, CA 94102, between Jones & Taylor Streets (1-800 227 4223/441 2700/fax 441 2700/mmsavoy1@aol.com). Bus 38/cable car Powell-Hyde or Powell-Mason. **Rates** *rooms* $129-$265; *suites* $209-$279. **Credit** AmEx, DC, Disc, JCB, MC, $TC, V. **Map G4**

Imported French furnishings, lovely curtains, billowy feather beds and continental breakfast served in the brasserie add sophistication to the 83 individually decorated small rooms that make up this hotel. Built in 1913 for the Panama-Pacific Exposition and since resurrected in a profusion of black marble and mahogany, the Savoy is centrally located in the theatre district – a few blocks from Union Square, but near enough to the Tenderloin to keep its prices relatively low.

Hotel services *Bar. Business services. Concierge. Conference facilities. Disabled: specially adapted rooms. Fax. Laundry. No-smoking rooms. Parking. Restaurant.* **Room services** *Dataport. Hairdryer. Mini-bar. Radio. Safe. Room service (6.30-11am, 5-10pm, daily).*

White Swan Inn

845 Bush Street, CA 94108, between Taylor & Mason Streets (1-800 999 9570/775 1755/fax 775 5717). Cable car Powell-Hyde or Powell-Mason/bus 2, 3, 4, 76. **Rates** *rooms* $165-$180; *suites* $195-$250. **Credit** AmEx, DC, Disc, MC, $TC, V. **Map G3**

If you like the sound of a hotel decorated with teddy bears that serves platters of freshly-baked cookies, read on. The 26-room White Swan Inn likes to think of itself as a cosy 'English inn', right down to the wallpaper, prints, working fireplaces and fresh flower arrangements in each room. Afternoon tea is served in a large parlour decorated with old teapots and yet more teddy bears. Just as sweet as can be, though not to everyone's taste.

Hotel services *Babysitting. Breakfast. Concierge. Fax. Garden. Gym. Laundry. No smoking. Parking.* **Room services** *Hairdryer. Mini-soft-drink bar. Radio. Refrigerator. Voicemail.*

Budget

Adelaide Inn

5 Isadora Duncan Court, CA 94102, off Taylor Street, between Post & Geary Streets (441 2261/fax 441 0161). Bus 2, 3, 4, 38. **Rates** *rooms with shared bath* $45-$64. **Credit** AmEx, MC, V. **Map G4**

It's mostly European tourists who reap the benefits of this old-fashioned pensione tucked into a quiet downtown cul-de-sac. All three levels are bright, cheerful and adorned with the sort of unintentionally funky furniture that reminds you just how old the place is. If you don't mind sharing a bathroom and sleeping on a spongy mattress, the place is cheap and cheerful. Rooms have TVs but no phone.

Hotel services *Concierge. Continental breakfast. Fridge. Internet access. No smoking. Pay phone.*

The Andrews

624 Post Street, CA 94109, between Jones & Taylor Streets (1-800 926 3739/563 6877/fax 928 6919/andrews@flash.net). Bus 2, 3, 4, 27, 38, 76. **Rates** *rooms* $92-$112; *suites* $142-$162. **Credit** AmEx, DC, JCB, MC, $TC, V. **Map G3/4**

Finding a decent hotel room within two blocks of Union Square for under $100 is as hard as finding a taxi when you need one. The seven-storey Andrews offers 48 small, comfortable rooms, each decorated in a pleasant pastel and floral theme with the usual TV, radio and telephone amenities. Free continental breakfast is served in the lobby (with trays available if you want breakfast in bed). The adjoining Fino Bar and Restaurant serves moderately priced Italian dishes.

Hotel services *Air-conditioning. Babysitting. Bar. Concierge. Conference facilities. Continental breakfast. Fax. No smoking. Restaurant. Website: andrewshotel.com.* **Room services** *Hairdryer. Kitchenette. Mini-soft-drink bar. Radio. Room service (5.30-11pm daily). Refrigerator.*

Golden Gate Hotel

775 Bush Street, CA 94108, between Powell & Mason Streets (1-800 835 1118/392 3702/fax 392 6202). Bus 2, 3, 4, 30, 45, 76/cable car California, Powell-Mason or Powell-Hyde. **Rates** *rooms with shared bath* $72; *rooms with private bath* $109. **Credit** AmEx, DC, MC, $TC, V. **Map G3**

The 25-room Golden Gate Hotel is one of San Francisco's best small hotels, particularly given the more-than-reasonable prices. It's a family-run establishment, so expect to be fussed over by John and Renate Kenaston, the affable innkeepers who take obvious pride in their clean, cute establishment. Rooms have antique, turn-of-the century furnishings and fresh flowers. Request one with a claw-foot tub if you enjoy a good soak. The location is good, too: two blocks from Union Square and the crest of Nob Hill, with cable car stops at the corner for easy access to Fisherman's Wharf and Chinatown.

Hotel services *Afternoon tea. Concierge. Continental breakfast. No-smoking rooms. Parking. Website: www.goldengatehotel.com.* **Room services** *Hairdryer.*

ALSO RECOMMENDED IN UNION SQUARE

Touchstone Tulip Inn
480 Geary Street, CA 94102, between Mason & Taylor Streets (1-800 524 1888/771 1600). **Rooms** $109-$169.

Hotel Diva
440 Geary Street, CA 94102, at Mason Street (1-800 553 1900/885 0200). **Rooms** $169-$219.

Hotel Halcyon
649 Jones Street, CA 94102, between Post & Geary Streets (1-800 627 2396/929 8033). **Rooms** $109-$129.

Hotel Rex
562 Sutter Street, CA 94102, between Powell & Mason Streets (1-800 433 4434/433 4434). **Rooms** $155-$245.

Hotel Union Square
114 Powell Street, CA 94102, at Union Square (1-800 553 1900/397 3000). **Rooms** $139-$189.

Kensington Park Hotel
450 Post Street, CA 94102, between Powell & Mason Streets (1-800 433 4434/788 6400). **Rooms** $175-$205.

Nob Hill Inn
1000 Pine Street, CA 94102, at Taylor Street (1-888 982 2632/673 6080). **Rooms** $99-$249.

Stratford Hotel
242 Powell Street, CA 94102, at Geary Street (1-888 554 6835/397 7080). **Rooms** $89-$159.

Financial District

First-class

Mandarin Oriental
222 Sansome Street, CA 94104, between Pine & California Streets (1-800 622 0404/276 9888/ fax 433 0289). Bus 1, 12, 42/cable car California. **Rates** *rooms* $415-$610; *suites* $950-$2,000. **Credit** AmEx, DC, Disc, JCB, MC, TC, V. **Map H3**

Few hotels in the world can boast such an extraordinary view as the Mandarin Oriental. Its lobby is on the ground floor of the 48-storey First Interstate Building and all of its 158 rooms and suites are on the top 11 floors. The view is phenomenal, particularly when the fog settles below you – it's like being in heaven. In keeping with the Japanese décor, the rooms contain a sparse selection of blond-wood furnishings and Asian artwork. Rumour has it that the staff to guest ratio is 1:1. Adjoining the lobby is the hotel's restaurant, Silks.

Hotel services *Air-conditioning. Babysitting. Bar. Business services. Concierge. Conference facilities. Disabled: specially adapted rooms. Fax. Gym. Laundry. No-smoking rooms. Parking. Restaurant. Safe. Video library.* **Room services** *Dataport. Hairdryer. Mini-bar. Radio. Refrigerator. Room service (24-hours).*

Sheraton Palace Hotel
2 New Montgomery Street, CA 94105, at Market Street (1-800 325 3535/512 1111/fax 543 0671). BART Montgomery/Muni Metro J, K, L, M, N. **Rates** *single* $300-$310; *double* $320-$330; *suites* $800-$2,900. **Credit** AmEx, DC, Disc, MC, $TC, V. **Map H4**

It took 27 months and a cool $170 million to restore the Palace Hotel to its original grandeur, but in return the Sheraton boasts one of the most breathtaking dining rooms in the world. The spectacular Garden Court contains 80,000 panes of stained glass; the hotel's glass-domed swimming pool is by far the finest in the city. The 554 rooms, by comparison, are rather modest, but spacious enough, with rich wooden furniture and marble-clad bathrooms. Even if you don't stay here, it's worth a look or – even better – Sunday brunch.

Hotel services *Air-conditioning. Babysitting. Bar. Business services. Conference facilities. Currency exchange (up to $100). Disabled: specially adapted rooms. Fax. Gym. Laundry. No-smoking rooms. Parking. Restaurant. Swimming pool. Website: www.sfpalace.com.* **Room services** *Dataport. Hairdryer. Radio. Refrigerator. Room service (24-hours). Safe.*

ALSO RECOMMENDED IN THE FINANCIAL DISTRICT

Hyatt Regency
5 Embarcadero Center, CA 94111, at California Street (1-800 233 1234/788 1234). **Rooms** $235-$310.

Park Hyatt
333 Battery Street, CA 94111, at Clay Street (1-800 492 8822/392 1234). **Rooms** from $350.

Nob Hill

First-class

Nob Hill Lambourne
725 Pine Street, CA 94108, between Powell & Stockton Streets (1-800 274 8466/433 2287/ fax 433 0975). Bus 1, 2, 3, 4, 30, 45/cable car Powell-Hyde or Powell-Mason. **Rates** *rooms* $210-$230; *suites* $275-$350. **Credit** AmEx, DC, Disc, JCB, MC, $TC, V. **Map G3**

Billed as a 'business-boutique' hotel that caters to the executive traveller, the 20-room Lambourne has found its niche as a healthy haven for well-paid business executives. Mints on the pillow? Hardly: extras here include beta-carotene tablets, aromatherapy gels, body scrubs and yoga lessons, as well as your own personal fax machine, voicemail and laptop computer with Internet access. The expensive handsewn bedcovers and pillows indicate the Lambourne's sense of indulgence (and even the nearby **Ritz-Carlton**, *see p105*, sends guests here when it's overbooked).

Hotel services *Business facilities. Concierge. Conference facilities. Continental breakfast. Fax. Laundry. No smoking. Safe. Spa.* **Room services** *Fax machine & dataport. Hairdryer. Kitchenette. Laptop computer. Mini-bar. Radio. Refrigerator. Room service (11am-11pm daily). VCR. Voicemail.*

Ritz-Carlton San Francisco
600 Stockton Street, CA 94108, at California Street (1-800 241 3333/296 7465/fax 986 1268). Bus 1, 30, 45/cable car California, Powell-Hyde or Powell-Mason. **Rates** *rooms* $335-$450; *suites* $525-$575; *executive suites* $3,000-$3,500. **Credit** AmEx, DC, Disc, JCB, MC, TC, V. **Map G3**
Among the fine hotels at the top of Nob Hill it's the Ritz that gets all the attention, and deservedly so. After a four-year, multi-million dollar renovation, the 336-room Ritz-Carlton opened its doors in 1991 and has continued to wow its guests ever since. Amenities include an indoor spa with swimming pool, whirlpool and sauna; a fully-equipped training room; the award-winning Dining Room restaurant; daily piano performances in the Lobby Lounge and an armada of valets and ushers to assist your every need. The rooms, while regally sumptuous, are a bit of a let-down compared to the fancy façade and lobby, but are quite comfortable and come with all the luxury items you would expect from the Ritz.
Hotel services *Air-conditioning. Babysitting. Bar. Business services. Concierge. Conference facilities. Disabled: specially adapted rooms. Fax. Garden. Gym. Laundry. Limousine service. No-smoking rooms. Parking. Restaurants. Swimming pool. Website: www.ritzcarlton.com.* **Room services** *Fax machine on request. Hairdryer. Mini-bar. Radio. Refrigerator. Room service (24 hours). Safe.*

ALSO RECOMMENDED ON NOB HILL

Fairmont Hotel & Tower
950 Mason Street, CA 94108, at California Street (1-800 527 4727/772 5000). **Rooms** from $249; *suites* from $450.

The chain gang

High-season vacancy is a bitch. When you've given up trying to find a unique place to stay in San Francisco, it's time to try one from the corporate cookie cutter. All the organisations listed below have accommodation in the city or nearby.

Best Western (1-800 528 1234)
Comfort Inn (1-800 228 5150)
Days Inn (1-800 325 2525)
Doubletree Hotels (1-800 222 8733)
Econo Lodges (1-800 553 2666)
Holiday Inn (1-800 465 4329)
Howard Johnson (1-800 654 2000)
La Quinta Motor Inns (1-800 531 5900)
Motel 6 (1-800 466 8356)
Ramada (1-800 272 6232)
Rodeway Inns (1-800 228 2000)
SUPER8 (1-800 800 8000)
Travelodge (1-800 255 3050)
Vagabond Inns (1-800 522 1555)

Huntington Hotel
1075 California Street, CA 94108, at Taylor Street (1-800 227 4683/474 5400). **Rooms** $250-$325.

Mark Hopkins Intercontinental
1 Nob Hill, CA 94108, at Mason Street (1-800 662 4455/392 3434). **Rooms** $290-$380.

Renaissance Stanford Court Hotel
905 California Street, CA 94108, at Powell Street (1-800 227 4736/989 3500). **Rooms** $199-$289.

Chinatown

Budget

Grant Plaza Hotel
465 Grant Avenue, CA 94108, at Pine Street (1-800 472 6899/434 3883/fax 434 3886/grantplaza@wellnet.att.net). Bus 1, 30, 45/cable car California or Powell-Hyde. **Rates** *rooms* $55-$129. **Credit** AmEx, DC, JCB, MC, V. **Map G3**
As long as you don't have a car – the Grant Plaza is located in the middle of Chinatown – you'd be hard pressed to find a better deal anywhere in the city. As little as $62 buys you a night in an immaculately clean (albeit small) room complete with contemporary furnishings, private bath, colour TV and telephone. If you split one of the larger rooms four ways then you'll pay less than hostel rates – definitely a bargain. The corner rooms on higher floors are the largest and brighest.
Hotel services *Business services. Fax. Laundry. Website: www.grantplaza.com.* **Room services** *Dataport. Hairdryer. Voicemail.*

ALSO RECOMMENDED IN CHINATOWN

Temple Hotel
469 Pine Street, CA 94104, at Montgomery Street (781 2565). **Rooms** $50-$55.

North Beach

Mid-range

Hotel Bohème
444 Columbus Avenue, CA 94133, between Vallejo & Green Streets (433 9111/fax 362 6292/info@hotelboheme.com). Bus 15, 30, 41, 45/cable car Powell-Mason. **Rates** *rooms* from $154. **Credit** AmEx, DC, Disc, JCB, MC, V. **Map G2**
If you dislike corporate incubators such as the Hyatt or Marriott, you'll love the Bohème. It's a small, suave and artistic hotel where art, poetry and hospitality collide in one particularly engaging combination. Conveniently located on Columbus Avenue, the lifeline of North Beach, the 15-room hotel is surrounded by dozens of small cafés and boutiques and within walking distance of Chinatown and Fisherman's Wharf. Light sleepers should request a room that doesn't face Columbus Avenue.
Hotel services *Business services. Concierge. Fax. No smoking. Safe. Website: www. hotelboheme. com.* **Room services** *Dataport. Hairdryer. Radio.*

Washington Square Inn

1660 Stockton Street, CA 94133, at Filbert Street (1-800 388 0220/981 4220/fax 397 7242). Bus 39, 41, 45/cable car Powell-Mason. **Rates** *rooms* $120-$185. **Credit** AmEx, DC, Disc, JCB, MC, $TC, V. **Map G2**

You can't ask for a better hotel location in San Francisco: across from Washington Square in the heart of North Beach and within walking distance of Chinatown. This well-run 15-room hotel has a would-be English flavour, right down to the cucumber sandwiches served during afternoon tea. Each room is decorated with French and English antiques and loads of fresh flowers. The overall feeling is of casual, quiet elegance. A continental breakfast and wine and cheese are included in the room price.

Hotel services *Business services. Concierge. Continental breakfast. Laundry. No smoking. Parking.* **Room services** *Hairdryer. Radio. Room service (7.30am-9pm daily). VCR.*

Budget

San Remo Hotel

2337 Mason Street, CA 94133, at Chestnut Street (1-800 352 7366/776 8688/fax 776 2811). Bus 15, 30, 39/cable car Powell-Mason. **Rates** *rooms* $50-$70; *penthouse* $100. **Credit** AmEx, DC, JCB, MC, $TC, V. **Map G2**

Originally a boarding house for dock workers displaced in the Great Fire of 1906, this meticulously restored three-storey Italianate Victorian building is now home to one of San Francisco's best bargains. Though the rooms are small and the spotless bathrooms (showers, actually) shared, you will not find finer accommodation at this price anywhere in the city. All the 63 rooms have brass or cast-iron beds, wicker furniture and antique armoires. Ask for a room on the upper floor facing Mason Street if you can, or if the penthouse is free, book it – you'll never want to leave.

Hotel services *Conference facilities. Fax. Laundry. Parking. Safe.* **Room services** *Hairdryer.*

Fisherman's Wharf

Mid-range

Tuscan Inn

425 Northpoint Street, CA 94133, at Mason Street (1-800 648 4626/561 1100/fax 561 1199). Bus 42, 49/cable car Powell-Mason. **Rates** *rooms* $138-$178; *suites* $198-$218. **Credit** AmEx, DC, Disc, MC, $TC, V. **Map G1**

Part of the Best Western motel chain but still a classy hotel, the 220-room Tuscan Inn is located in the heart of Fisherman's Wharf. The rooms are handsome, spacious and comfortable; the staff are exceedingly helpful and the adjoining Café Pescatore – a gleaming Italian trattoria – is as good as it looks for breakfast, lunch or dinner. If you tire of the touristy Wharf, escape is on hand: the Inn is a block away from the cable car turnaround.

Hotel services *Air-conditioning. Babysitting. Bar. Concierge. Conference facilities. Courtyard. Disabled: specially adapted rooms. Fax. Laundry. Limousine service. No-smoking rooms. Parking. Restaurant. Website: www.tuscaninn.com.* **Room services** *Hairdryer. Mini-bar. Radio. Refrigerator. Room service (7am-10pm daily). VCR.*

The Wharf Inn

2601 Mason Street, CA 94133, at Beach Street (1-800 548 9918/673 7411/fax 776 2181). Bus 15, 30, 32, 42/cable car Powell-Mason. **Rates** $145-$350. **Credit** AmEx, DC, Disc, JCB, MC, $TC, V. **Map G1**

For those who can't resist the garish lure of Fisherman's Wharf, the Wharf Inn represents the best deal in accommodation. It's essentially an old-school motel, but they've done an admirable job refurbishing rooms in handsome tones of forest green, burgundy and pale yellow. Rooms also come with all the standard amenities – TV, telephone, private bath – as well as complimentary coffee and tea. The hotel is right in the middle of the Wharf and a two-block walk from Pier 39 and the cable-car turnaround. The Embarcadero and North Beach are also within easy walking distance. Parking is free – another bonus.

Hotel services *Concierge. Fax. No-smoking rooms. Parking. Website: www.pacificplaza.com.*

SoMa

First-class

W Hotel

181 Third Street, at Howard Street, CA 94103 (1-800 946 8357/777 5300). BART Montgomery Street/Muni Metro F, J, K, L, M, N/bus 6, 7, 9, 15, 21, 30, 38, 45, 71, 76. **Rates** *rooms* $179-$319. **Credit** AmEx, DC, Disc, JCB, MC, $TC, V. **Map H4**

San Francisco may not be as hip as New York, but it's definitely in the running for second best since the W Hotel branched out from the Big Apple in 1999. Fittingly located in the city's hottest slice of real estate, the W is an amalgamation of art, technology, service and sex appeal. The lobby consists of a cocktail lounge with a horseshoe-shaped counter; to the right is an international newsstand and to the left the new waggishly-named **XYZ** restaurant (*see chapter* **Restaurants & Cafés**). Only after a bit of exploration do you find the lobby, where the young and beautiful staff check in the young and beautiful clientele. And the rooms? As artistically sensual as the lobby and loaded with the latest toys such as CD players, 27-inch TVs and cosy goose down duvets. If you have the money and the desire to be with the 'in' crowd, this is where to stay.

Hotel services *Bar. Business services. Conference facilities. Concierge. Currency exchange. Disabled: specially adapted rooms. Fax. Gym. Laundry. No-smoking rooms. Restaurant. Swimming pool. Website: www.whotels.com.* **Room services** *CD player. Dataport. Mini-bar. Hairdryer. Radio. Refrigerator. Room service (24 hours). Safe. VCR.*

Budget

Bay Bridge Inn

966 Harrison Street, CA 94107, between Fifth & Sixth Streets (397 0657/fax 495 5117/dbpatel@pacbell.net). BART Montgomery Street/Muni Metro F, J, K, L, M, N/bus 6, 7, 9, 15, 21, 30, 38, 45, 71, 76. **Rates** *rooms* $37-$105. **Credit** AmEx, DC, MC, $TC, V. **Map H5**

You won't be spending a lot of time in the Bay Bridge Inn's rather ordinary, motel-style rooms though they're clean and in good condition, with firm queen-size beds (or king-size beds for an extra $20). You'll be at nearby Moscone Convention Center attending a business convention, or late-night clubbing at local nightspots. Cheap hotels and free parking are rare south of Market Street, but you'll find both at the Bay Bridge Inn.

Civic Center

Mid-range

The Abigail

246 McAllister Street, CA 94102, between Hyde & Larkin Streets (1 800-243 6510/861 9728/fax 861 5848). BART Civic Center/Muni Metro F, J, K, L, M, N/bus 5, 19. **Rates** *rooms* $125; *suites* $250. **Credit** AmEx, DC, Disc, JCB, MC, $TC, V. **Map F/G4**

Another so-called 'European' hotel – due in part to the continental antiques, quilts and turn-of-the-last-century English lithographs and paintings adorning each room – the 60-room Abigail is located within walking distance of the Opera House and Symphony Hall. It's a safe bet for visitors seeking a clean, comfortable room at a reasonable price. The weekly and monthly rates are a bargain.

Hotel services *Concierge. Continental breakfast. Fax. No-smoking rooms. Restaurant.*
Room services *Dataport. Hairdryer. Radio.*

Archbishop's Mansion

1000 Fulton Street, CA 94117, at Steiner Street (1-800 543 5820/563 7872/fax 885 3193). Bus 5, 22. **Rates** *rooms* $129-$199; *suites* $215-$385. **Credit** AmEx, DC, MC, $TC, V. **Map E5**

The Archbishop's Mansion is one of the most opulent small hotels in San Francisco. What's more, despite the ostentation – elaborate chandeliers, gorgeous antiques, canopied beds – the staff are genuinely friendly. Indulge in splendour in one of the Mansion's 15 wildly elegant rooms, such as the Don Giovanni suite with its hand-carved, cherub-encrusted four-poster bed, two fireplaces and a seven-headed shower. Built in 1904 for the Archbishop of San Francisco – and a fortunate survivor of the earthquake two years later – the Mansion manages to combine romance, history and luxury into a surprisingly affordable package. *De rigueur* for honeymooners.

Hotel services *Concierge. Conference facilities. Continental breakfast. Fax. Laundry. No smoking. Parking.* **Room services** *CD player. Dataport. Hairdryer. Radio. VCR.*

The Phoenix

601 Eddy Street, CA 94109, at Larkin Street (1-800 248 9466/776 1380/fax 885 3109). Bus 19. **Rates** *rooms* $109-$129; *suites* $139-$159. **Credit** AmEx, DC, Disc, JCB, MC, $TC, V. **Map F4**

What do Ziggy Marley, Johnny Depp, the late John F Kennedy Jr and Pearl Jam have in common? They've all stayed at the funky Phoenix, one of San Francisco's hippest hostelries – located, oddly enough, in one of the city's least glamorous neighbourhoods. The 44 bungalow-style rooms equipped with bamboo furniture and tropical plants help to create the feel of an oasis, particularly when guests bask by the pool on a sunny day. The adjoining **Backflip** restaurant and cocktail lounge (*see chapter* **Bars**) provides funky food and music that perfectly accompanies the Phoenix's style.

Hotel services *Babysitting. Bar. Concierge. Conference facilities. Continental breakfast. Fax. Laundry. Limousine service. Parking (free). Restaurant. Swimming pool. Safe.*
Room services *Hairdryer. Radio. VCR.*

ALSO RECOMMENDED IN CIVIC CENTER

The Inn at the Opera
333 Fulton Street, CA 94102, at Franklin Street (1-800 325 2708/863 8400). **Rooms** $140-$195.

The Castro

Mid-range

Dolores Park Inn

3641 17th Street, CA 94103, between Church & Dolores Streets (phone/fax 621 0482). Muni Metro J/bus 22, 33. **Rates** *rooms* $99-$129 *suites* $229. **Credit** MC, $TC, V. **Castro/Mission Map Y1**

Rumour has it that Tom Cruise and Robert Downey Jr, among other celebrities, have stayed at this discreet and beautiful Victorian inn – one of the best lodgings in the Castro district. Rooms are all individually decorated with beautiful antiques and queen-size beds. The two most popular rooms are the Carriage House, which has such luxury amenities as a Jacuzzi, kitchen, heated marble floor, washer/dryer, fireplace and VCR, and a suite with a kitchen and cable TV/VCR, as well as a four-poster bed and large sundeck overlooking Twin Peaks. A two-night minimum stay is required, though you'll probably want to stay longer, since many of San Francisco's best sights and restaurants are within easy walking distance.

Hotel services *Continental breakfast. Fax. No smoking.* **Room services** *Hairdryer. Radio.*

ALSO RECOMMENDED IN THE CASTRO

Beck's Motor Lodge
2222 Market Street, San Francisco, CA 94114 (1-800 227 4360/621 8212). **Rooms** $99-$124.

Castillo Inn
48 Henry Street, CA 94114, at 15th Street (1-800 865 5112/864 5111). **Rooms** $70-$160.

Inn on Castro
321 Castro Street, CA 94114, at Market Street (861 0321). **Rooms** $90-$200. *See also chapter* **Gay & Lesbian San Francisco**.

The Parker House
520 Church Street, CA 94114, at 17th Street (1-888 520 7275/621 3222). **Rooms** $109-$199.

24 Henry
24 Henry Street, CA 94114, at Noe Street (1-800 900 5686/864 5686). **Rooms** $60-$105. *See also chapter* **Gay & Lesbian San Francisco**.

The Willows Bed & Breakfast Inn
710 14th Street, CA 94114, between Church & Market Streets (431 4770). **Rooms** $82-$108. *See also chapter* **Gay & Lesbian San Francisco**.

The Haight-Ashbury

Mid-range

Stanyan Park Hotel

750 Stanyan Street, CA 94127, between Waller & Frederick Streets (751 1000/fax 668 5454/info@stanyanpark.com). Muni Metro N/bus 6, 7, 33, 66, 71. **Rates** *rooms* $110-$160; *suites* $229-$279. **Credit** AmEx, DC, Disc, MC, $TC, V. **Map C6**

If you want to stay in the Haight but you're way beyond the any-old-room-will-do stage, consider the Stanyan Park Hotel, one of the classiest places on this stretch of San Francisco. The stately three-storey Victorian has been accommodating travellers in style since 1904 and is even on the National Register of Historic Places. It's charmingly decorated with Victorian period furnishings, drapes and quilts and bath/shower rooms equipped with massaging shower heads and sweet smelling soaps. The suites have full kitchens, dining rooms and living rooms, and can sleep up to six (something to consider if you're with a family or group). Rates include breakfast and afternoon tea.

Hotel services *Concierge. Continental breakfast. Disabled: specially adapted rooms. Fax. No smoking.. Website: www.stanyanpark.com.* **Room services** *Dataport. Hairdryer. Radio.*

Budget

The Herb'n Inn

525 Ashbury Street, CA 94117, between Haight & Page Streets (553 8541/2/hasf525@aol.com). Bus 6, 7, 33, 43, 66, 71. **Rates** *rooms with shared bath* $70-$75; *rooms with private bath* $80-$85. **Credit** MC, $TC, V. **Map D5**

Sister and brother duo Pam and Bruce Brennan run one of the coolest B&Bs in San Francisco, a big Victorian inn that's a mere half-block from the famous intersection of Haight and Ashbury – the street corner that gave power to the flower. The inn consists of four guest rooms, a huge country-style kitchen, a sunny flower-filled back garden and Bruce's Psychedelic History Museum (formerly the dining room). The most popular guest room is the Cilantro Room, which is the largest and the only room with a private bathroom and a view of the garden. The Tarragon Room is preferred by smokers, who can fire up on the small private deck. A fantastic breakfast ranging from potato pancakes to waffles, popovers and crêpes is included, as are personal city tours given by Bruce, office services (including forwarded e-mail) and unlimited free advice on how to spend your day in the city.

Hotel services *Breakfast. Computer access. Concierge. Fax. Garden. No smoking. Parking. Refrigerator.* **Room services** *Hairdryer. Radio.*

The Red Victorian

1665 Haight Street, CA 94117, at Cole Street (864 1978/fax 863 3293). Muni Metro N/bus 6, 7, 33, 37, 71, 77. **Rates** *rooms* $65-$136; *suite* $200. **Credit** AmEx, MC, $TC, V. **Map C6**

Nothing comes as close to offering the quintessential Haight-Ashbury experience as a night at the Red Vic. Haight Street's only hotel offers 18 wildly decorated rooms, each with its own thematic twist, such as the rainbow-coloured Flower Child room or the tie-dyed Summer of Love double. A continental breakfast is included in the room price, as is free use of the meditation room. Highly recommended for hippie-loving souls. Rooms do not have TVs.

Hotel services *Continental breakfast. Conference facilities. Fax. No smoking. Website: www.redvic.com.*

ALSO RECOMMENDED IN THE HAIGHT-ASHBURY

Metro Hotel
319 Divisadero Street, CA 94117, between Oak & Page Streets (861 5364). **Rooms** $59-$109.

Pacific Heights

First-class

Sherman House

2160 Green Street, CA 94123, between Webster & Fillmore Streets (1-800 424 5777/563 3600/fax 563 1882/tshrez@mhotelgroup.com). Bus 22, 41, 45. **Rates** *rooms* $385-$445; *suites* $650-$850. **Credit** AmEx, DC, MC, $TC, V. **Map E3**

This stately, four-storey Victorian mansion had its ups and downs over the years until the present owners dumped a small fortune into a four-year restoration project. Today its 14 rooms – each furnished in Jacobean, German Biedermeier or French Second Empire style with fireplaces, tapestries and brocaded bed hangings – are good enough for the likes of Shirley MacLaine, Ted Kennedy and Bill Cosby. If you have an equally fat bank account you can afford to stay here too.

Hotel services *Business services. Concierge. Disabled: specially adapted suite. Fax. Garden. Laundry. Limousine service. No smoking. Parking. Restaurant. Website: www.thesherman house.com.* **Room services** *CD player. Computer. Dataport. Hairdryer. Radio. Room service (24-hours daily). VCR.*

The new **W Hotel**: *SoMa gets its own branch of the Big Apple original.* *See page 107.*

Mid-range

Hotel Majestic

1500 Sutter Street, CA 94109, at Gough Street (1-800 869 8966/441 1100/fax 673 7331/ hotelmaj @pacbell.net). Bus 2, 3, 4, 38, 42, 47, 49. **Rates** *rooms* $150-$225; *suites* $425. **Credit** AmEx, DC, Disc, JCB, MC, $TC, V. **Map F4**

The Majestic has long been regarded as one of the city's most romantic hotels. Built in 1902, it was one of the first grand hotels and the owners have obviously spent a fortune keeping it that way. Each of the 51 rooms and nine suites has been renovated in 1999 and features canopied four-poster beds with quilts, a host of English and French Empire antiques and matching custom-made furniture. Many rooms also have fireplaces. The adjoining Café Majestic is also known for its setting and good seasonal dishes. After dinner, adjourn to the mahogany bar for a cognac.

Hotel services *Air-conditioning. Babysitting. Bar. Concierge. Conference facilities. Currency exchange. Disabled: specially adapted rooms. Fax. Interpreting services. Laundry. No-smoking rooms. Parking. Restaurant. Safe.* **Room services** *Dataport. Hairdryer. Radio. Room service (24-hours).*

Jackson Court

2198 Jackson Street, CA 94115, at Buchanan Street (929 7670/fax 929 1405). Bus 12, 24. **Rates** *rooms* $150-$215. **Credit** AmEx, MC, $TC, V. **Map E3**

Not many people know about Jackson Court, a nineteenth-century brownstone mansion that has been converted into a superb ten-room bed-and-breakfast inn. Located on a quiet residential stretch of Pacific Heights – one of San Francisco's more prestigious neighbourhoods – the inn is elegant and as quiet as a church. All the newly renovated rooms have private baths, antiques and contemporary furnishings – and surprisingly reasonable rates. If you don't mind walking five or so blocks to Union Street, you'll find wonderful shops and restaurants there.

Hotel services *Concierge. Continental breakfast. Fax. No smoking.* **Room services** *Dataport. Hairdryer. Radio.*

ALSO RECOMMENDED IN PACIFIC HEIGHTS

El Drisco

2901 Pacific Avenue, CA 94115, at Broderick Street (1-800 634 7277/346 2880). **Rooms** $230-$335.

Queen Anne Hotel

1590 Sutter Street, CA 94109, at Octavia Street (1-800 227 3970/441 2828). **Rooms** $120-$295.

The Marina & Cow Hollow

Mid-range

Bed and Breakfast Inn

4 Charlton Court, CA 94123, at Union Street (921 9784/fax 921 0544/info@1stb-bsf.com). Bus 41, 45. **Rates** *rooms with shared bath* $80-$100; *rooms with private bath* $150; *penthouses* $250-$300. **Credit** $TC. **Map E2**

The Bed and Breakfast Inn is a real charmer. A forerunner of the B&B craze, the small 13-room inn is awash with fresh flowers, antiques and the sort of personal touches that create the American version of an old English hostelry. Tucked into a tiny cul-de-sac off Union Street, the inn consists of three immaculate Victorian houses and one exquisite garden – a good place to enjoy breakfast on sunny mornings. It's in a great location, too, with some of the city's best shops and cafés steps away. Only rooms with a private bathroom have a TV and telephone.

Hotel services *Communal TV room. Concierge. Garden. No smoking. Parking.* **Room services** *Dataport. Hairdryer. Radio. Room service (8am-9.30pm daily).*

Union Street Inn

2229 Union Street, CA 94123, between Fillmore Street & Steiner Street (346 0424/fax 922 8046). Bus 22. 24. **Rates** *rooms* $149-$255. **Credit** AmEx, MC, V. **Map E2/3**

A B&B based in a two-storey Edwardian house that overlooks trendy, bustling Union Street, the Union Street Inn is as quiet as a nunnery inside. The individually decorated rooms are furnished with canopied or brass beds, down duvets, fresh flowers, and all have private bathrooms (some with Jacuzzi tubs). Alternatively, you can opt for the ultimate honeymoon retreat – the private carriage house behind the inn. An extended continental breakfast is served either in the parlour, in your room, or on an outdoor terrace overlooking the lovely garden; evening hors d'oeuvres and drinks are also included in the room price.

Hotel services *Breakfast. Fax. Garden. No-smoking rooms. Website www.unionstreetinn.com.* ***Room services*** *Hairdryer. Radio.*

Budget

Edward II Inn & Pub

3155 Scott Street, CA 94123, at Lombard Street (1-800 473 2846/922 3000). Bus 28, 43, 76. **Rates** *rooms with shared bath* $75-$85; *rooms with private bath* $105; *suites* $175-$235. **Credit** AmEx, MC, $TC, V. **Map D2**

This self-styled 'English country inn' has a wide array of room styles that cater to almost everyone's budget. Its Lombard Street location is a little over congested with traffic, but nearby Chestnut and Union Streets offer a fine choice of shops and restaurants. You can choose from fancy suites and cottages with kitchens, living rooms and whirlpool baths or the more basic rooms with shared baths. Regardless of the rate, all rooms are always clean and comfortably appointed with antique furnishings and lots of fresh flowers. Complimentary breakfast and evening drinks are served in the adjoining pub.

Hotel services *Bar. Continental breakfast. Disabled: specially adapted rooms. Fax. No smoking rooms. Parking.* **Room services** *Hairdryer on request. Radio.*

Marina Inn

3110 Octavia Street, CA 94123, at Lombard Street (1-800 274 1420/928 1000/fax 928 5909). Bus 28, 43, 76, 40. **Rates** *rooms* $65-$125. **Credit** AmEx, MC, V. **Map E2**

Though this 1924 four-storey Victorian inn is located on one of the busiest streets in San Francisco, the rooms are surprisingly quiet and stylishly furnished with pinewood fittings, a four-poster bed, pretty wallpaper and soothing tones of yellow, green and rose. There are even top-dollar touches such as new remote-control televisions, full-size bathtubs with showers and a nightly turndown service with chocolates on your pillow. Rates include continental breakfast and afternoon sherry; the Marina district's shops and restaurants are within easy walking distance.

Hotel services *Beauty salon. Continental breakfast. No smoking. Disabled: specially adapted rooms.*

Motel Capri

2015 Greenwich Street, CA 94123, at Buchanan Street (346 4667/fax 346 3256). Bus 28, 43, 76. **Rates** *room* $58-$70; *suites* $90-$148. **Credit** AmEx, DC, Disc, JCB, MC, $TC, V. **Map E2**

Low-maintenance travellers who need little more than a quiet, inexpensive room will enjoy staying at the funky old Capri. Here the décor is anything but up-to-date (rather, it's unintentionally 1970s retro) but you'll find that the 46 rooms are squeaky clean and the beds comfortable. Added bonuses are free parking (a valuable commodity in this crowded neighbourhood) and its location, a few blocks from Chestnut and Union Streets. The suites, recommended for families, have a kitchenette with refrigerator.

Hotel services *Concierge. Fax. No-smoking rooms. Parking.* **Room services** *Dataport. Refrigerator.*

ALSO RECOMMENDED IN THE MARINA & COW HOLLOW

Art Center Bed & Breakfast

1902 Filbert Street, CA 94123, at Laguna Street (567 1526). **Rooms** $105-$145.

Marina Motel

2576 Lombard Street, CA 94123, at Divisadero Street (1-800 346 6118/921 9406). **Rooms** $79-$149.

Richmond

Budget

Seal Rock Inn

545 Point Lobos Avenue, CA 94127, at 48th Avenue (752 8000/fax 752 6034). Bus 5, 18, 31, 38. **Rates** *rooms* $90-$124. **Credit** AmEx, DC, MC, $TC, V.

One would assume that San Francisco, which is surrounded on three sides by shimmering seas, would have a savvy selection of seaside hotels. Not the case. In fact, the only plausible contender, the Seal Rock Inn, isn't even on the beach. Located at the western edge of the Richmond district and about as far from Union Square and Fisherman's Wharf as you can get, it's ideal for anyone who wants to stay in San Francisco but doesn't want the bustling big-city scene or steep room rates. Most rooms in the boxy brown building have at least partial views of the ocean. They're also large and spotless, though the ageing furnishings in hues of beige, brown and grey won't win any interior decorating awards. Covered parking and free use of the enclosed patio and pool area are standard; you can upgrade to a two-room suite with wood-burning fireplace. When things quieten down at night, you can fall asleep to the sound of the surf and distant foghorns.

Hotel services *No smoking. Parking. Restaurant. Swimming pool. Website: www.sealrockinn.com.*
Room services *Hairdryer. Radio. Refrigerator.*

Hostels

Hostelling International publishes a useful free brochure called *California Hostels* which contains details of affordable accommodation throughout the state, often in spectacular locations. Copies can be picked up at either of the hostels listed below, or by e-mailing hiayh@norcalhostels.org.

Hostel at Union Square (AYH)

312 Mason Street, CA 94102, between Geary & O'Farrell Streets (1-800 909 4776 access code 02/788 5604/fax 788 3023). BART Powell Street/Muni Metro F, J, K, L, M, N/bus 27, 38. **Rates** $17-$18. **Credit** MC, $TC, V. **Map G4**

Make your reservation at least five weeks in advance during the high season (between June and September) to stay at this downtown 260-bed hostel. The popular hostel prides itself on privacy and security. Guests are accommodated in small two-, three-, four- or five-person rooms, with their own lock and key (the larger rooms also have their own bathroom). There are always beds for walk-ins available on a first-come-first-served basis: remember to bring ID or you'll be turned away at the door.

Hotel services *Dining room. Disabled: specially adapted rooms. Free nightly movies. Kitchen. Library. Lockers. Microwave. No smoking. Pay phones. Refrigerator. Website: www.hiayh.org*

Fort Mason Youth Hostel

Fort Mason Building, 240 Fort Mason, CA 94123 (771 7277/fax 771 1468). Bus 28, 42, 47, 49. **Rates** $18. **Credit** MC, JCB, $TC, V. **Map E1**

Many San Franciscans would kill for the Bay view from this affordable vacation spot. One of the most desirable locations in the city is available for under $20 per night, though you must book at least 24 hours in advance. Located on National Park property, the hostel's dorm-style accommodation sleeps 170, in rooms fitting three to four people. Guests have easy access to the Marina's shops and restaurants. Unlike some hostels where, if you're not asleep, you'd rather be elsewhere, here you'll want to enjoy the fireplace, pool table, dining room, coffee bar, complimentary movies and the rarest of San Francisco amenities – free parking. There's no curfew, either.

Hotel services *Continental breakfast. Disabled: specially adapted rooms. Kitchen. Laundry. Parking. No-smoking rooms. Website: www.norcalhostels.com*

Restaurants & Cafés

Fusion? Fish and chips? Fresh focaccia? Whatever you're hungry for...

San Francisco remains one of the best cities in the world for eating well. Its largely immigrant population has brought with it a rich diversity of cooking influences; and the city's proximity to the ocean and a rich local agricultural base means that fresh produce and high quality seafood are available all year round. Add to this the influence of the nearby Napa, Sonoma and Monterey wine regions and a healthy competition among chefs, and the result is a city where fine food is more than just sustenance: it's one of the main reasons to stay.

The Bay Area became a foodie mecca in the 1970s, when California cuisine – the infusing of local seasonal ingredients and traditional recipes with cross-cultural influences – was born. While it continues to permeate almost every aspect of San Francisco's cult of food, California cuisine hasn't stopped more recent trends from having pronounced impacts. The late 1990s, for example, witnessed an explosion in culinary decadence. As the stock market rose, so did the calorie count. In a city known for its liberal vegetarianism, few would have predicted that premium American steak, Asian lamb, quail, rabbit and even veal would stage respective comebacks. Though the 'architectural' or stacked presentation, locally-grown organic vegetables and cheeses of California cuisine still reign supreme, they've recently begun to be paired with obscure and hitherto out-of-fashion companions.

Yet good food isn't just to be found in high-priced restaurants. Great ethnic cooking can be had in any number of smaller eateries – in taquerias in the Mission, Italian bakeries in North Beach, in the stunning array of Thai, Chinese, Vietnamese and Korean restaurants that line the streets of the Sunset district, or the in-and-out noodle shops of Japantown. Whatever you choose, you'll be amazed by the number, variety and quality of restaurants in San Francisco.

The average prices listed below are for a three-course meal without alcohol. For a list of the city's supper clubs – where you can combine good food with live music – *see chapter* **Nightlife**.

Restaurants

Around Union Square

See also page 120 **Farallon** *and page 121* **Postrio**.

Fleur de Lys

777 Sutter Street, between Jones & Taylor Streets (673 7779). Bus 2, 3, 4, 27, 76. **Dinner served** 6-9.30pm Mon-Thur; 5.30-9.30pm Fri, Sat. **Average** $90. **Credit** AmEx, DC, JCB, MC, V. **Map G3**

After a quarter-century, Fleur de Lys has undergone a face-lift, giving the fabric on its grand tent setting a warm makeover in hues of (as they say) 'pomegranate and saffron'. Even better news is that the food has stayed superb. Hubert Keller is an extraordinary chef with a vast culinary repertoire and his menu is lush and extraordinarily expensive. But the quality of the French food and the splendid wine list go a long way towards helping you forget you're about to spend a fortune. Service is attentive without being overbearing. Splash out on the prix-fixe, five-course tasting menu; one is also available for vegetarians.

Scala's Bistro

432 Powell Street, between Post & Sutter Streets (395 8555). Bus 2, 3, 4, 76/cable car Powell-Hyde or Powell-Mason. **Breakfast served** 7-10.30am Mon-Fri; 8-10.30am Sat, Sun. **Lunch served** 11.30am-4.30pm, **dinner served** 5.15pm-midnight, daily. **Average** lunch $26, dinner $32. **Credit** AmEx, DC, MC, V. **Map G3**

Part of the Sir Francis Drake Hotel, this bustling bistro is frequented by tourists staying in Union Square and locals who come for the reasonably priced Italian food. Salads always feature the season's freshest produce and the sweetbreads, when available, are worth every calorie. Enjoy a plate of house-made ravioli with basil and ricotta in a lemon-cream sauce, or seared salmon with mashed potato. If you're here on a Friday night, watch out for the arrival of the elderly twin sisters, dressed alike: the famous San Francisco twosome has dined here once a week for decades.

The Financial District

See also page 120 **Cypress Club** *and page 121* **Rubicon**.

Globe Restaurant

290 Pacific Avenue, at Battery Street (391 4132). Bus 12, 42, 83. **Lunch served** 11.30am-3pm Mon-Fri. **Dinner served** 6pm-1am Mon-Sat; 6-11.30pm Sun. **Average** lunch $20, dinner $30. **Credit** AmEx, MC, V. **Map H2**

Chef Joseph Manzare is a New Yorker and one-time protégé of LA's Wolfgang Puck, which explains both the Globe's late opening hours and its penchant for California cuisine. An exposed-brick dining room adds a Soho touch and from the kitchen standards such as wood-oven pizzas and grilled salmon with buttery pasta and watercress are transformed by the freshness of their ingredients. Side dishes include baked tomatoes, creamed spinach, polenta and roast potatoes. The Globe's 1am closing time means it's a favourite among other food service employees – a high compliment in this restaurant-packed town.

Oritalia

586 Bush Street, at Stockton Street (782 8122). Bus 30, 45. **Dinner served** 5.30-10.45pm daily. **Average** $35. **Credit** AmEx, MC, V. **Map G3**

The idea of combining oriental and Italian influences in a restaurant may sound foolishly outlandish, but at this plush place – recently relocated to the edge of the Financial District – it actually works a treat. The rich interior incorporates fabulous Fortuny lamps, a rich colour scheme and upholstered booths. There's a bar at the front, which is an ideal place to drop in for a couple of appetisers – definitely the high point of the menu. Try the tuna tartare on sticky rice cakes, the nori wrapped crab cakes with lemongrass cream or the wonderful lobster gnocchi – and skip the main courses. While the defection of its founding chef has caused the quality of the food to vary somewhat, Oritalia's clientele remains loyal.

Plouf

40 Belden Place, between Bush, Pine, Kearny & Montgomery Streets (986 6491). Bus 2, 3, 4, 15. **Lunch served** 11.30am-3pm Mon-Fri. **Dinner served** 5.30-10pm Mon-Thur; 5.30pm-midnight Fri, Sat. **Average** lunch $17, dinner $30. **Credit** AmEx, Disc, MC, V. **Map H3**

Flex your mussels: 'Plouf' is French onomatopoeia for the sound of a pebble dropping into water and all dishes at this restaurant come from the sea. Bivalves are prepared at least ten different ways, including the popular standard mussels with parsley and garlic, and oysters on the half-shell. Fish dishes are excellently prepared: try the grilled tuna niçoise with baby greens. Chef Ola Fendert was the originator of the Grand Marnier souffle and Plouf's is a dandy. The staff come dressed in black-and-white-striped, three-quarter-length Gallic shirts and are unusually friendly. Outdoor alley seating adds to the bistro ambience and the spillover from a nearby French bar and dance club can make the atmosphere carnival-like in the evenings.

Don't miss

Blowfish Sushi

A fresh, edgy menu in animated surroundings. *See p127.*

Café Flore

The Castro's quintessential see-and-be scene. *See p145.*

Jardinière

Veggie goodness in an extravagant setting. *See p131.*

Moonshine

Down-home meals in uptown North Beach. *See p122.*

Pintxos

The next-generation Basque incarnation. *See p128.*

PlumpJack Café

San Francisco's high society hangout. *See p139.*

XYZ

Upscale dining on the precipice of the Yerba Buena Center. *See p125.*

Zuni Café

A classic: art-filled walls and a first-rate South-western menu. *See p133.*

Sam's Grill

374 Bush Street, between Montgomery & Kearny Streets (421 0594). BART Montgomery Street/Muni Metro F, J, K, L, M, N/bus 2, 3, 4, 15. **Meals served** 11am-9pm Mon-Fri. **Average** $30. **Credit** AmEx, DC, MC, V. **Map H3**

Granddad number one: established in 1867, Sam's – all wood-panelling and worn lino – is a monument to the old days of leisurely three-martini lunches. The waiters are older and more sincere than elsewhere and the dishes are traditional but none the worse for it: there's no designer lettuce here. Fried zucchini, creamed spinach and fish (prepared any way you'd like it) all hit the spot. By contrast, the wine list is current and Californian.

Tadich Grill

240 California Street, between Battery & Front Streets (391 1849). BART Embarcadero/Muni Metro F, J, K, L, M, N/bus 1, 12, 41, 42/cable car California. **Meals served** 11am-9.30pm Mon-Fri; 11.30am-9.30pm Sat. **Average** $25. **Credit** MC, V. **Map H3**

Granddad number two: since 1849, the Tadich Grill has been revered as the quintessential San Francisco restaurant. Inside you'll find private wooden booths, plenty of counter seating and professional staff, many of whom have worked here for decades. This is the place to come for high-quality seafood: thick clam chowder, cioppino (San Francisco's answer to

Restaurants by cuisine

Afghani
The Helmand *p122.*

American
Butter *p123;* Beach Chalet Brewery & Restaurant *p140;* Black Cat *p121;* Fog City Diner *p117;* Hamburger Mary's *p124;* Harris' *p119;* Indigo *p131;* MoMo's San Francisco Grill *p126;* Moonshine *p122;* Pluto's *p125;* Sam's Grill *p115;* 2223 Market *p135.*

Basque
Fringale *p123;* Pintxos *p128.*

Cafés, Coffeehouses & Delis
Armani Café *p142;* Atlas Café *p145;* Bisou Café *p146;* Brainwash *p144;* Café Abir *p146;* Café Bastille *p142;* Caffé Centro *p145;* Café Claude *p142;* Café Flore *p145;* Caffé Greco *p143;* Caffé Museo *p145;* Café de la Presse *p142;* Caffé Proust *p146;* Cafe De Stijl *p143;* Caffé Trieste *p144;* Chloe's Café *p145;* CoffeeNet *p145;* Daily Dose *p146;* Doidge's Kitchen *p142;* Dottie's True Blue Café *p142;* Ella's *p142;* Food Inc Trattoria *p146;* The Grind Café *p146;* The Grove *p146;* Imperial Tea Court *p144;* Jammin' Java *p146;* Java Beach Cafe *p146;* Kate's Kitchen *p142;* Mama's on Washington Square *p142;* Mario's Bohemian Cigar Store *p144;* Martha & Brothers Coffee Company *p145;* Mel's Drive-In *p143;* Miss Millie's *p143;* Radio Valencia *p145;* Saigon Sandwich Café *p146;* San Francisco Art Institute Café *p144;* Savoy Tivoli *p144;* Seattle Street Coffee *p143;* Sear's Fine Foods *p143;* Steps of Rome *p144.*

Cajun
Elite Café *p135.*

Californian
Bay Wolf *p129;* Boulevard *p117;* Chez Panisse *p129;* Delfina *p127;* Farallon *p120;* Firefly *p129;* Flying Saucer *p127;* French Laundry *p129;* Globe Restaurant *p115;* Hawthorne Lane *p120;* House *p141;* LuLu *p124;* Moose's *p122;* Oliveto *p129;* PlumpJack Café *p139;* Postrio *p121;* Rubicon *p121;* Stars *p121;* Universal Café *p128;* Zuni Café *p133.*

Chinese
Alice's *p129;* House of Nanking *p120;* Kowloon *p119;* Mayflower *p140;* New Fortune *p119;* R & G Lounge *p120;* Ton Kiang *p140;* You's Dim Sum *p119;* Yuet Lee *p120.*

French & Continental
Absinthe *p129;* Fleur de Lys *p114;* Jardinière *p131;* La Folie *p119;* Pastis *p117;* Rivoli *p129;* South Park Café *p126;* Ti Couz Crêperie *p125.*

German
Suppenküche *p131.*

Indian
Maharani *p119.*

Italian, Cal-Ital & Pizza
Antica Trattoria *p119;* Capp's Corner *p121;* Caffe Delle Stelle *p131;* Cypress Club *p120;* Enrico's *p121;* Il Fornaio *p117;* Laghi *p137;* L'Osteria del Forno *p124;* Michelangelo Café *p122;* Pane e Vino *p139;* Pauline's Pizza *p128;* Rose's Café *p125;* Rose Pistola *p123;* Scala's Bistro *p114;* Tommasso *p123;* Vicolo Pizzeria *p133;* Vivande Porta Via *p137;* Zinzino *p140.*

Japanese
Blowfish Sushi *p127;* Ebisu *p140;* Isobune Sushi *p135;* Isuzu *p135;* Kabuto *p140;* Mifune *p135;* Sanppo *p135;* Sushi Groove *p119;* Yoshida Ya *p140.*

Korean
Brothers Restaurant *p140;* Seoul Garden *p135.*

Lebanese
Byblos *p139.*

Mexican & Tex-Mex
La Rondalla *p128;* Roosevelt Tamale Parlor *p128;* Taqueria Cancun *p125.*

Oriental & Fusion
Betelnut *p137;* Eos Restaurant & Wine Bar *p133;* Long Life Noodle Company & Jook Joint *p124;* Oritalia *p115;* Pancho Villa Taqueria *p128;* Shanghai 1930 *p139;* Tin Pan Asian Bistro *p133;* XYZ *p125.*

Seafood
Alioto's *p123;* Franciscan Restaurant *p123;* Hayes Street Grill *p131;* PJ's Oyster Bed *p141;* Plouf *p115;* Swan Oyster Depot *p119;* Tadich Grill *p115.*

South American & Caribbean
Cha Cha Cha *p124;* El Nuevo Frutilandia *p127;* Fina Estampa *p124.*

Spanish
Thirsty Bear Brewing Company *p125;* Zarzuela *p119.*

Thai & Vietnamese
Khan Toke *p140;* Neecha Thai Cuisine *p137;* The Slanted Door *p128;* Thep Phanom *p133.*

Vegetarian
Greens *p139;* Organica *p141. See also* The greens scene *p130.*

World
Carta *p131;* Gordon's House of Fine Eats *p127.*

bouillabaisse), calamari or swordfish steaks, prawns sautéed in Chardonnay or fresh salmon in lobster sauce. Sour is the dough of choice and desserts are simple yet satisfying.

The Embarcadero

See also page 139 **Shanghai 1930**.

Boulevard

1 Mission Street, at Steuart Street (543 6084). BART Embarcadero/Muni Metro F, J, K, L, M, N/ bus 1, 2, 6, 7, 9, 14, 21, 31, 32, 66, 71. **Lunch served** 11.30am-2pm Mon-Fri. **Dinner served** 5.30-10pm Mon-Wed, Sun; 5.30-10.30pm Thur-Sat. **Average** lunch $25, dinner $50. **Credit** AmEx, DC, Disc, MC, V. **Map J3**

Not a recommendation for the budget-conscious, Boulevard attracts with its combination of spectacular setting, enhanced by a view of the Bay Bridge, and the dynamic duo of designer Pat Kuleto and self-taught chef Nancy Oakes. Oakes's stacked, elaborate dishes (perhaps a sautéed Sonoma foie gras, served on corn bread with a wild blackberry sauce and mâche) make local suppliers proud. Signature entrées at dinner include honey-cured pork loin and classic osso buco with garlic mash; wood-roasted dishes are another forte. Service is casual although the prices are not: try the bar at lunchtime as a cheaper option.

Fog City Diner

1300 Battery Street, at Embarcadero (982 2000). Bus 32, 42. **Meals served** 11.30am-11pm Mon-Thur, Sun; 11.30am-midnight Fri, Sat. **Average** $20. **Credit** DC, Disc, MC, V. **Map H2**

Who'd have thought that the oxymoronic 'swanky diner' concept would still succeed a decade and a half later? Fog City's best bets are its small plates – crab cakes, Chinese-style pork burritos, a scallop ceviche – and desserts, which beckon with such specialties as bread pudding and a 'turtle' sundae (a melted-chocolate concoction with walnuts). Around you, the long room is complemented with deep booths and lots of chrome, and a bartender who fixes a mean Margarita. A long walk on the Embarcadero before or after your meal is recommended.

Il Fornaio

Levi Plaza, 1265 Battery Street, at Union Street (986 0100). Bus 12, 42. **Breakfast served** 7.30-10.30am, **brunch served** 9am-2pm, Sat, Sun. **Lunch served** 11.30am-4pm Mon-Fri. **Dinner served** 4-11pm Mon-Thur, Sun; 4pm-midnight Fri, Sat. **Average** lunch $23, dinner $45. **Credit** AmEx, DC, MC, V. **Map H2**

Il Fornaio means 'the baker' in Italian and this successful Californian chain's bread and pastries are award-winning. But while Il Fornaio's goods are sold in gourmet groceries throughout the state, the Italian cooking served in this high-ceilinged, light-filled room overlooking Levi Plaza also holds its own. Enjoy home-made pastas, creamy polenta and just about anything roasted – chicken, veal chops, steak. Arrive early in the day for a sun-dappled breakfast or brunch and don't forget to stock up on bread and other cooking essentials from the shop inside the main door.

Pastis

1015 Battery Street, between Union & Green Streets (391 2555). Bus 42. **Lunch served** 11.30am-2.30pm Mon-Fri. **Dinner served** 5.30-10.30pm Mon-Sat. **Average** lunch $20, dinner $40. **Credit** AmEx, MC, V. **Map H2**

While the anise-flavoured pastis is found all over France, the food at chef Gerald Hirigoyen's 'quiet' place (compare and contrast with **Fringale**, *p123*) is

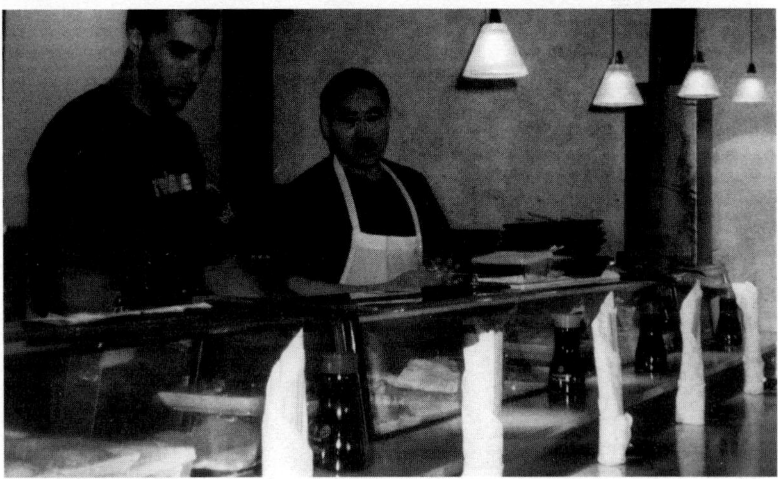

Organic ingredients and sleek design at **Sushi Groove**. *See page 119.*

Outlandish design and down-to-earth cooking at the **Cypress Club**. *See page 120.*

from his native Basque country. Appetisers include seared oxtail, caramelised quail and ravioli escargot; entrées range from a huge plate of steamed mussels or sautéed mahi-mahi with tapenade, to a New York strip steak with Roquefort butter. As always, 'match-stick fries' are $3. Favourites are bouillabaisse with a hint of saffron, an artichoke, tomato and fennel salad, and grilled chicken with a caramelised orange sauce. A caramel and meringue parfait rounds out your dinner – and your waistline. Prices are reasonable.

Russian Hill, Nob Hill & Polk Gulch

Antica Trattoria

2400 Polk Street, at Union Street (928 5797). Bus 19, 41, 45, 76. **Dinner served** 5.30-10pm Tue-Sun. **Average** $25. **Credit** DC, MC, V. **Map F2**

While Italian restaurants are a dime a dozen in San Francisco, this dark-panelled one stands out for its gorgeous simplicity and commitment to culinary quality. Antica is Italian-owned, its surroundings are casual and its food is great. Dishes like stuffed calamari with mozzarella in a tomato-saffron broth, or sliced fennel with blood oranges and red onions pair nicely with more hearty fare. Everything is bargain-priced: for years, no entrée has cost more than $14.

Harris'

2100 Van Ness Avenue, at Pacific Avenue (673 1888). Bus 42, 47, 49. **Dinner served** 5.30-9.30pm Mon-Thur; 5-10pm Fri; 5-10.30pm Sat; 5-9.30pm Sun. **Average** $55. **Credit** AmEx, DC, Disc, JCB, MC, V. **Map F3**

Unchanged for decades, Harris' offers old-style dining, the kind your great-uncle would have loved. Start with a strong cocktail, sink into your booth, then proceed with a Caesar salad (made at your table), steak and a baked potato with all the trimmings and, of course, a hefty dessert. Beef – for which the place is famous – is dry-aged for 21 days and proudly displayed from a windowed refrigerator that faces the street. If red meat from the West Coast isn't your style, go east: try an Atlantic salmon, grilled or poached with champagne sauce or a steamed whole Maine lobster with clams.

La Folie

2316 Polk Street, between Union & Green Streets (776 5577). Bus 19, 41, 45, 47, 49, 76. **Dinner served** 5.30-10pm Mon-Sat. **Average** $75. **Credit** AmEx, DC, Disc, JCB, MC, V. **Map F2**

Chef Roland Passot presides over this delightful French-Californian eatery on Russian Hill, whose prices are steep but whose cooking is exquisite and refined. Opt for the five-course discovery menu ($75, includes soup, appetiser, sorbet, entrée and dessert), which allows you to sample such dishes as Sonoma free-range duck stuffed with Camargue rice or blanquette of sweetbread and lobster. The Provençal décor and attentive staff add to La Folie's charm. The extensive wine list remains under the aegis of Passot's brother, Georges.

Maharani

1122 Post Street, between Polk Street & Van Ness Avenue (775 1988). Bus 2, 3, 4, 19, 42, 47, 49, 76. **Lunch served** 11.30am-2.30pm daily. **Dinner served** 5-10pm Mon-Thur; 5-10.30pm Fri, Sat; 5-10pm Sun. **Average** lunch $9, dinner $20. **Credit** AmEx, Disc, DC, JCB, MC, V. **Map F4**

This under-noticed North Indian restaurant, halfway between a 24-hour gym and a transvestite bar, has a healthy emphasis, with reduced amounts of oil and salt in many of its dishes. House specialties include excellent breads (chapati and the fabulous nan) and several vegetarian main courses; a cheap lunchtime buffet will stretch your culinary dollar. Escape the overly-pink décor of the front room and seek out the fantasy room at the back, a wonderland of lush draperies and cushioned settees.

Sushi Groove

1916 Hyde Street, at Union Street (440 1905). Bus 41, 45/cable car Powell-Hyde. **Dinner served** 5.30-10pm Mon-Thur, Sun; 5.30-10.30pm Fri, Sat. **Average** $10. **Credit** AmEx, MC, V. **Map F2**

This inventive, techno-flavoured sushi restaurant, with a rich post-modern décor of sleek surfaces and natural hues, has inspired a number of imitators since it opened three years ago. None, however, has lived up to the promise of Sushi Groove's booming drum 'n' bass mood music and original rolls and salads. Fresh crab, sea urchin and eel join traditional favourites such as mackerel, tuna and salmon; everything is delicious. All vegetables used are organic and the impressive cold saké selection is itself worth a trip up Hyde Street.

Swan Oyster Depot

1517 Polk Street, between California & Sacramento Streets (673 1101). Bus 1, 19, 42, 47, 49, 76/cable car California. **Meals served** 8am-5.30pm Mon-Sat. **Average** $12. **No credit cards. Map F3**

Half fish market and half counter service hole-in-the-wall, the Swan has served seafood to San Franciscans since 1912. The best time of year to visit is between May and November, when the local Dungeness crab is in season. Classic clam chowder, the smoked salmon plate and an obscenely large variety of oysters are specialties of the house. You can also buy shellfish to take away – a good option if the place is too crowded.

Zarzuela

2000 Hyde Street, at Union Street (346 0800). Bus 41, 45/cable car Powell-Hyde. **Meals served** 5.30-11pm Tue-Sat. **Average** $20. **Credit** Disc, MC, V. **Map F2**

Zarzuela features authentic Spanish cuisine in a cosy restaurant filled with posters of bull fights and maps of Spain. The special tapas are always a treat, but old stand-bys such as grilled eggplant filled with goat's cheese, sautéed shrimps in garlic and olive oil, and fried potatoes with garlic and sherry vinegar never disappoint. Parking is impossible; take a cab or walk over Russian Hill so you don't arrive too stressed for dinner. No bookings are accepted.

Chinatown

A culinary contradiction in San Francisco is that the best Chinese food is generally found outside Chinatown (in the Richmond district, for example). That said, in addition to the places listed below, several low-profile spots offer good selections of dim sum, 'potstickers' or healthy, brothy soups. The food at **You's Dim Sum** (675 Broadway, at Stockton Street; 788 7028) is basic and delicious; **New Fortune** (811 Stockton Street, at Sacramento Street; 399 1511) is a standing-room-only takeaway counter; and **Kowloon** (909 Grant Street, at Washington Street; 362 9888) features a good all-vegetarian menu and ice-cream counter.

House of Nanking

919 Kearny Street, between Jackson Street & Columbus Avenue (421 1429). Bus 12, 15, 41, 83. **Meals served** 11am-10pm Mon-Fri; noon-10pm Sat; 4-10pm Sun. **Average** $12. **Credit** ($20 min) MC, V. **Map G2**

Why would we direct you to a shabby, somewhat less than pristine-looking diner, where you'll queue for an hour only to get perfunctory service, bordering on the rude? Because House of Nanking serves some of the best, freshest Chinese food in town and for that reason can get away with the rest. Have a delicious dinner, then scoot for dessert and coffee elsewhere – the place is handily perched on the edge of North Beach.

R & G Lounge

631 Kearny Street, between Sacramento & Clay Streets (982 7877). Bus 1, 15. **Meals served** 11am-9.30pm daily. **Average** $9. **Credit** AmEx, MC, V. **Map H3**

An excellent choice if you want some Chinese seafood. Choose your lobster – or let him choose you – or prawns from the tank, then sit down to a feast that won't break your budget.

Yuet Lee

1300 Stockton Street, at Broadway (982 6020). Bus 12, 15, 30, 83. **Meals served** 11am-3am Mon, Wed-Sun. **Average** $15. **No credit cards. Map G2**

Chefs and restaurant folk are often spotted at this tiny, bright green Chinese eatery, probably because the seafood is excellent and available until 3am. Also worth trying are the roasted squab with fresh

Gala grub

Is the Boss buying? Is the exchange rate in your favour? Feeling flush? San Francisco offers plenty of opportunities to spend excess cash, but the most enjoyable is to eat your way through it. Come for the food, stay for the service and don't be afraid of the wine list.

Cypress Club

500 Jackson Street, between Montgomery Street & Columbus Avenue (296 8555). Bus 12, 15, 41, 42, 76, 83. **Dinner served** 5.30-9.30pm Mon-Thur, Sun; 5.30-10pm Fri, Sat. **Average** $50-$60. **Credit** AmEx, MC, V. **Map H3**

The Cypress Club's $2 million design, complete with plump banquettes, curvaceous phallic pillars and draped fabrics, evokes either a fantasyland or a drug trip – and little in between. The food is only slightly more down-to-earth, featuring polenta-dusted soft shell crabs, a Moroccan-style stuffed spring chicken or veal scallopine with basil gnocchi. Desserts come as a suitably grand finale – perhaps a chocolate coconut terrine or a warm pineapple napoleon. The bar is stocked with bourbons, single-malts and all manner of spirits.

Farallon

450 Post Street, between Mason & Powell Streets (956 6969). Bus 2, 3, 4, 76/cable car Powell-Hyde or Powell-Mason. **Lunch served** 11.30am-2.30pm, **dinner served** 5.30-10pm, Mon-Sat. **Average** lunch $38, dinner $55. **Credit** AmEx, DC, Disc, MC, V. **Map G3**

One of the city's toniest and most creative restaurants, Farallon is named after the islands visible (on a clear day) from the Golden Gate Bridge. An undersea theme carries the deep, dimly-lit room, where jellyfish light fixtures hang like – well, jellyfish, and barely a right angle is to be seen. Former **Stars** (*opposite*) chef Mark Franz pilots the kitchen, turning out entrées such as sautéed Gulf prawns or seared striped bass with lobster and morels. Fishy appetisers include three kinds of caviar as well as fresh crab with urchin sauce. Everything is top-notch: in this case the bottom of the sea is an apex of culinary achievement.

Hawthorne Lane

22 Hawthorne Street (777 9779). Bus 12, 15, 30, 45, 76. **Lunch served** 11.30am-2pm Mon-Fri. **Dinner served** 5.30-10pm Mon-Fri, Sun; 5.30-10.30pm Sat. **Average** lunch $20, dinner $38. **Credit** MC, V. **Map H4**

This $3 million destination dining room is the creation of Wolfgang Puck protégés David and Anne Gingrass, chefs from Postrio. The food, a selection of sophisticated California-Asian dishes, is outstanding, creative and ultra fresh: a seafood platter features oysters and clams on the half-shell, mussels, jumbo prawns, a lobster tail and claw and several dipping sauces. Hawthorne's clientele have included the President and various rock stars and on any night the crowd-watching is of the best.

cilantro (coriander) and lemon, sautéed clams with black bean sauce and 'eight precious noodle soup', made with eight different kinds of meat. Lighting is fluorescent and service is hospitable without being overly gracious. Cash only.

North Beach

See also page 124 **L'Osteria del Forno**.

Black Cat

501 Broadway, at Kearny Street (981 2233). Bus 12, 15, 30, 41, 83. **Meals served** 5.30pm-1.15am daily. **Average** $50. **Credit** AmEx, Disc, MC, V. **Map G2**

Local celebrity restaurateur Reed Hearon's latest venture infuses his American diner-style eatery with the disparate cultural influences endemic in San Francisco. Wok-seared Bay scallops in a ginger reduction shares menu space with tuna au poivre, Ligurian pizzas and a classic American steak and fries. The open kitchen adds to the lively atmosphere and there's a mellow jazz club in the basement (*see p218* **Nightlife**).

Capp's Corner

1600 Powell Street, at Green Street (989 2589). Bus 15, 30, 41, 45/cable car Powell-Mason. **Lunch served** 11.30am-2.30pm Mon-Fri. **Dinner served** 4.30-10.30pm daily. **Average** lunch $9, dinner $17. **Credit** AmEx, MC, V. **Map G2**

Opened in North Beach in 1960, Capp's Corner has seen food fads and themes come and go, but has continued to rely instead upon Italian home cooking to keep its customers loyal. Decked out in baseball memorabilia and other American kitsch, the interior is nothing special. The hearty menu, too, is basic, but the location – the long-running theatrical spoof *Beach Blanket Babylon* shows next door – and reasonable prices keep it on the list of favourites.

Enrico's

504 Broadway, at Kearny Street (982 6223). Bus 12, 15, 30, 41, 83. **Lunch served** 11.30am-5pm Mon-Sat; 11.30am-4pm Sun. **Dinner served** 5-11pm Mon-Thur; 5pm-midnight Fri, Sat; 4-11pm Sun. **Average** lunch $12, dinner $25. **Credit** AmEx, MC, V. **Map G2**

What's not to love about Enrico's? Pristine location, first-rate food, an outdoor patio for prime people-

Postrio

545 Post Street, between Taylor & Mason Streets (776 7825). Bus 2, 3, 4, 76/cable car Powell-Hyde or Powell-Mason. **Breakfast served** 7-10am, **lunch served** 11.30am-2pm, Mon-Fri. **Dinner served** 5.30-10pm Mon-Wed, Sun; 5.30-10.30pm Thur-Sat. **Brunch served** 9am-2pm Sun. **Average** lunch $25, dinner $55. **Credit** AmEx, DC, Disc, JCB, MC, V. **Map G3/4**

Celebrity chef Wolfgang Puck's entry into the competitive Northern California restaurant market has been a success since day one. Make your entrance down a dramatic staircase into the (invariably packed) restaurant below and tuck into exotic fare such as a sautéed Atlantic skate wing with potatoes, beets and tarragon butter or Sonoma lamb chops with a port wine sauce. Desserts are magnificent: try the dark chocolate tart with Burgundy plums and crème fraîche ice-cream. Reservations are necessary, as is a very flexible credit card.

Rubicon

558 Sacramento Street, between Sansome & Montgomery Streets (434 4100). BART Montgomery Street/Muni Metro F, J, K, L, M, N/bus 1, 12, 15, 41. **Lunch served** 11.30am-2pm Mon-Fri. **Dinner served** 5.30-10pm Mon-Sat. **Average** lunch $30, dinner $50. **Credit** AmEx, DC, MC, V. **Map H3**

Despite backing from Robin Williams, Francis Ford Coppola and Robert DeNiro, Rubicon isn't opulent, leaning instead towards a clubby, masculine atmosphere. It features excellent California cuisine and a superb wine list assembled by one of the country's top sommeliers, Larry Stone. Two tasting menus ($59 for six courses; $79 with wine) will provide an abundance of food; à la carte choices include rich gnocchi, grilled game and fresh fish.

Stars

555 Golden Gate Avenue, between Van Ness Avenue & Polk Street (861 7827). Bus 19, 42, 47, 49. **Lunch served** 11.30am-2.30pm Mon-Fri. **Dinner served** 5.30-10pm daily. **Late dinner served** 10-11pm Mon-Thur, Sun; 10.30pm-midnight Fri, Sat. **Average** lunch $23, dinner $45. **Credit** AmEx, DC, MC, V. **Map F4**

Jeremiah Tower's big, brassy bistro is still a favourite among locals who love to see and be seen; its buzz has died down somewhat, but Stars is still a place where San Francisco's élite come to eat. Portions are large and prices high (although you can eat well and more affordably at the extra-long bar) and feature the best of American food. Menu highlights include a plate of oyster cocktail shooters, duck gumbo, capon breast with lemon sauce, and seafood bisque with mussels, scallops and prawns. Desserts remain some of the best in town and there's a pianist to provide background sounds. Booking is essential.

Life imitates art at the fin de siècle **Absinthe***. See page 129.*

watching, a live jazz band – perhaps the only complaint could be North Beach's lack of parking. Enjoy a wood-fired pizza with porcini mushrooms, or perhaps an ahi tuna fillet with slow-braised beans, crispy polenta and smoked tomato vinaigrette. It's all served in a noisy, friendly environment with a long wood bar at one end. Enjoy dessert as the band starts tuning up, then graduate to a cognac or port as a nightcap. If you're feeling the urge to walk, you can head across the street to the new **Black Cat** (*see p121*), where more music will greet your ears. Solve the parking problem by taking a cab here.

The Helmand

430 Broadway, between Kearny & Montgomery Streets (362 0641). Bus 12, 15, 30, 41, 83. **Dinner served** 5.30-10pm Mon-Thur, Sun; 5.30-11pm Fri, Sat. **Average** $20. **Credit** AmEx, MC, V. **Map G/H2**

The Helmand consistently appears on lists of recommended eateries, partly because the city has so few Afghani restaurants, but also because the food is inexpensive and deliciously aromatic. Its cooking is influenced by India, Asia and the Middle East; marinades and fragrant spices give each dish a unique character. The pumpkin ravioli with a leek sauce, when available, is exquisite, as is koufta challow, a dish of tender lamb meatballs in a cinnamon-spiked tomato sauce. The pleasantly formal dining room belies the reasonable prices on the menu.

Michelangelo Café

579 Columbus Avenue, at Union Street (986 4058). Bus 15, 30, 39, 41, 45. **Dinner served** 5-11pm Mon-Sat; 3-10pm Sun. **Average** $17. **No credit cards. Map G2**

There are dozens of quaint, secluded Italian restaurants in North Beach; Michelangelo isn't one of them. Noisy and bright, the triangular-shaped restaurant is festooned with art – Tiffany lamps, oil paintings, faux-granite sculpture – and the staff move at a lightning pace to deliver hearty pastas, fresh fish and basic salads to a constant stream of diners. The one-page menu is simple, but what will keep you coming back is the staff's unceasing cheerfulness, low prices and the consistency of the food. Split a seafood pasta special between two: it'll be plenty. Desserts consist of communal bowls of amaretto cookies and gummi bears. No reservations are taken, but don't fret – the queue moves quickly.

Moonshine

498 Broadway, at Kearny Street (982 6666). Bus 12, 15, 30, 41, 83. **Lunch served** 11.30am-3pm Mon-Fri. **Dinner served** 6-10.30pm Mon-Thur, Sun; 6pm-midnight Fri, Sat. **Average** $20. **Credit** AmEx, MC, V. **Map G2**

The newest addition to North Beach's burgeoning restaurant strip focuses on the distinctive flavours of the American South. Styled like a New Orleans speakeasy (complete with louvred doors and a resident piano player), Moonshine offers the likes of Texas beef brisket (smokehouse roasted for ten hours), crabmeat-stuffed hush puppies and hickory-grilled salmon. There's a certain Disneyland-like quality to the place and a sense that its authenticity is only paint-deep. Nonetheless, it's a sufficient alternative to the gazillion Italian restaurants of the area and the food's undoubtedly a pleasure. On Fridays and Saturdays, the music continues until 1.30am. Yee-haw!

Moose's

1652 Stockton Street, between Union & Filbert Streets (989 7800). Bus 15, 30, 39, 41, 45. **Brunch served** 10am-2.30pm Sun. **Lunch served** 11.30am-2.30pm Mon-Sat. **Dinner served** 5.30-10pm Mon-Thur; 5.30-11pm Fri, Sat; 5-10pm Sun. **Average** lunch $25, dinner $60. **Credit** AmEx, DC, MC, V. **Map G2**

Long-time restaurateurs Ed and Mary Etta Moose create environments that are uniquely San Franciscan. A full bar, an open kitchen serving consistently good California cuisine and an extensive wine list are the draws here. Chef Brian Whitmer favours hearty fare such as grilled pork chop with braised cabbage or beef fillet on Gorgonzola-stuffed ravioli. Regardless of changes in the menu, the Mooseburger persists. Moose's also serves a society-studded Sunday brunch, replete with such classics as eggs benedict and a great selection of muffins and fruit.

Rose Pistola

532 Columbus Avenue, between Green & Union Streets (399 0499). Bus 15, 30, 39, 41, 45/cable car Powell-Mason. **Lunch served** 11.30am-5.30pm daily. **Dinner served** 5.30-10.30pm Mon-Thur, Sun; 5.30-11.30pm Fri, Sat. **Late-night menu** 10.30pm-midnight Mon-Thur, Sun; 11.30pm-1am Fri, Sat. **Average** lunch $15, dinner $27. **Credit** AmEx, DC, MC, V. **Map G2**

Named after a longtime North Beach resident, Rose Pistola is a large, open-plan restaurant whose food is predominantly from Liguria in the north of Italy. Consultant chef Reed Hearon favours grilled dishes; try the delicious, shareable antipasti plate among the appetisers and roasted rabbit as an entrée. Jazz bands play several nights a week and the staff are amiable but exacting. The wine list is exhaustive, with an emphasis on California and Italian varietals.

Tommasso

1042 Kearny Street, at Broadway (398 9696). Bus 12, 15, 30, 41, 45, 83. **Dinner served** 5-11pm Tue-Sat; 4-10pm Sun. **Average** $25. **Credit** AmEx, DC, MC, V. **Map G2**

Tommasso's cave-like dining room is filled with appetising aromas and a buzz from the hordes of people who frequent its well-known North Beach confines. The wood-oven pizzas and calzones are extremely popular, as is the house red wine which is served in ceramic pitchers. If you're looking for a break from trendy Italian eateries and crave good old-fashioned spaghetti (or ravioli) with meat balls, you'll be happy here. Reservations are not accepted, so queue up and get to know your fellow diners.

Fisherman's Wharf

Alioto's

8 Fisherman's Wharf, at Taylor Street (673 0183). Bus 32, 39, 42/cable car Powell-Mason. **Lunch served** 11am-4pm, **dinner served** 4-11pm, daily. **Average** lunch $14, dinner $25. **Credit** AmEx, DC, Disc, MC, V. **Map F1**

Owned by a prominent San Francisco family, Alioto's began as a sidewalk stand offering crab and shrimp cocktail served in a paper cup. Now, 70 years later, the establishment has an amazing view of the Bay and crowds of tourists fighting their way to get in. The kitchen turns out fine – though expensive – seafood prepared any way you desire and Sicilian specialties for the fish-o-phobic. The wine list is outstanding.

Franciscan Restaurant

Pier 43, Embarcadero (362 7733). Bus 15, 32, 39, 42/cable car Powell-Mason. **Lunch served** 11.30am-4pm daily. **Dinner served** 4-10pm Mon-Thur, Sun; 4-10.30pm Fri, Sat. **Average** lunch $15, dinner $25. **Credit** AmEx, DC, MC, V. **Map G1**

The décor has been remodelled and the menu updated, but the Franciscan's requisite dishes – classic Dungeness crab with lemon mayonnaise, cioppino, prawns, sea scallops, clams and fresh fish – have remained to please the out-of-towners. Every seat in the house has an expansive view of either North Beach or the Bay, while the café downstairs has outdoor seating. Less overpriced than **Alioto's** (*above*), the Franciscan remains your best bet in this touristy area.

SoMa

See also page 120 **Hawthorne Lane** *and page 124* **Hamburger Mary's**.

Butter

354 Eleventh Street, between Folsom & Harrison Streets (431 6545). Bus 9, 12, 42. **Brunch served** 7am-2pm Sat, Sun. **Lunch served** 11am-2pm Wed-Fri. **Dinner served** 5pm-2am Wed-Sat; 5-9pm Sun. **Average** $6. **Credit** MC, V. **Map G5**

Living up to its professed moniker as a 'white trash bistro', Butter only serves meals that can be prepared in a microwave, a menu that's sure to please what one critic called 'the best of six-year olds and the worst of adults'. There's a po-mo edge to it all, of course, with décor including a 1950s travel trailer and a DJ who spins from behind the bar in the evenings. In the midst of all this, patrons down TV dinners, macaroni and cheese, Tater-Tots and anything else associated with America's backwoods, trailer-living denizens, and wash it all down with (what else?) tequila and beer. Open until 2am at the weekends in case you get the munchies. Interesting – if a little scary.

Fringale

570 Fourth Street, between Bryant & Brannan Streets (543 0573). Bus 15, 30, 45, 76. **Lunch served** 11.30am-3pm Mon-Fri. **Dinner served** 5.30-10.30pm Mon-Sat. **Average** lunch $15, dinner $20. **Credit** AmEx, MC, V. **Map H4/5**

In the ten years that Gerald Hirigoyen's first Basque bistro has occupied a nondescript block of SoMa, tens of thousands of diners have enjoyed its simplicity and warmth. Literally translated, the restaurant's name means 'the urge to eat' and you'll find it's easy to do it here. Frisée salads, a beef carpaccio, lamb sweetbread fricassée – the flavours are definitely French, but with a rural air that cuts their elaborateness and their richness. Entrées such as a duck confit or veal medallions with braised leeks are standards. You'll need to book well in advance and come prepared to sit shoulder-to-shoulder (the place has around 50 covers), but every noisy bite will be worth the trouble.

Long Life Noodle Company & Jook Joint

139 Steuart Street, between Mission & Howard Streets (281 3818). BART Embarcadero/Muni Metro F, J, K, L, M, N/bus 1, 2, 6, 7, 9, 14, 21, 31, 32, 66, 71. **Open** 11.30am-10pm Mon-Fri; 5-10pm Sat. **Average** lunch $9, dinner $12. **Credit** MC, V. **Map J3**

Long Life is an anglicised version of the noodle shops that nourish all of Asia. Noodle salads, soups, jooks (porridge), rice dishes, fried noodles and popiahs (wraps) fill the menu and also appear in dishes such as pad thai, Shanghai-style crispy spring rolls with barbecue pork and cabbage, and Ghengis buns – one of the token dishes from China. A seat at the bar gives you a view of the chefs in action. Though not as cheap as its counterparts in Asia, prices are reasonable – most dishes cost less than $8. Long Life has a sister restaurant in the new Metreon complex in SoMa.

Branch: in the Metreon, 221 Fourth Street, at Mission Street (369 6188).

LuLu

816 Folsom Street, between Fourth & Fifth Streets (495 5775). Bus 12, 30, 45, 76. **Lunch served** 11.30am-3.30pm daily. **Dinner served** 5.30-10.30pm Mon-Thur, Sun; 5-11.30pm Fri, Sat. **Average** lunch $20, dinner $33. **Credit** AmEx, DC, JCB, MC, V. **Map H4**

This warehouse space – with a seasonal Provençal menu of wood-fired oven, rôtisserie and grilled specialties, pizzas, pastas, and fresh shellfish – is usually filled to capacity. Chef Jody Denton turns out a delicious duck sausage with grilled polenta or a toasted monkfish bouillabaisse with rouille and Gruyère; don't miss the full array of side dishes including grilled corn with red pepper butter, broccoli rabe with chilli flakes and garlic or pole beans with hazelnut brown butter. Dishes come on large platters and sharing is encouraged. Reserve a table in advance, or risk your chances in the buzzing bar, but be warned: conversation is difficult in the large, noisy and crowded room. Denton's new restaurant **Azie** is due to open soon next door.

Gourmet budget

Luckily, one needn't spend a small fortune to sample some of Northern California's finest cooking. San Franciscans take great pride in all of their meals – whether they be five-star and four-course or simply a cheap and easy night out. Some of our favourites are listed below.

Cha Cha Cha

1801 Haight Street, at Shrader Street (386 5758). Muni Metro N/bus 6, 7, 33, 43, 66, 71. **Lunch served** 11.30am-4pm daily. **Dinner served** 5-11pm Mon-Thur, Sun; 5-11.30pm Fri, Sat. **Average** lunch $15, dinner $20. **Credit** MC, V. **Map C6**

The second chapter of this Caribbean hotspot takes place in a huge corner location just a half-block from its original, phone-booth-sized restaurant. Expect reasonably-priced tapas, including calamari, deep-fried new potatoes, fried plantains, black beans, yellow rice and Cajun-style fish dishes. Although the quality can be inconsistent and the wait ridiculously long, the festive ambience and pitchers of sangria make Cha Cha Cha well worth trying.

Fina Estampa

2374 Mission Street, between 19th & 20th Streets (824 4437). Bus 14, 33, 49. **Lunch served** 11.30am-3.30pm, **dinner served** 5-9pm, Tue-Thur. **Meals served** 11am-9pm Fri-Sun. **Average** lunch $7, dinner $10. **Credit** MC, V. **Castro/Mission Map Y1**

Outstanding and wide-ranging Peruvian food is served in this nondescript space. In addition to reasonably-priced seafood, chillis and grilled chicken, the restaurant serves delicious paellas – rice dishes flavoured with meat and fish. There's a selection of Peruvian beer and Spanish wines to accompany your meal.

Branch: 1100 Van Ness Avenue, at Geary Street (440 6343).

Hamburger Mary's

1582 Folsom Street, at 12th Street (626 1985). Bus 9, 12, 42. **Meals served** 11.30am-12.15am Mon-Thur; 11.30am-1.15am Fri; 10am-1.15am Sat; 10am-12.15am Sun. **Average** $15. **Credit** AmEx, MC, V. **Map G5**

A block from the nightlife bulls-eye at 11th and Folsom Streets, Hamburger Mary's has good (not great) food and knows it can get by with it. It's a late-night place where you can choose between countless mainstay burgers and middling breakfast selections. 'Shit on a shingle' is creamed chipped beef on toast. A warning (or tip): after the clubs close, the place gets packed.

L'Osteria del Forno

519 Columbus Avenue, between Green & Union Streets (982 1124). Bus 15, 30, 41, 45, 83. **Meals served** 11.30am-10pm Mon, Wed, Thur; 11.30am-10.30pm Fri, Sat. **Average** $18. **No credit cards. Map G2**

Some great food can be had at this tiny hole-in-the-wall, where an imaginative and ever-changing menu features thin-crusted pizzas and pastas and, if you're lucky, focaccia and pork braised in milk, a Tuscan and North Beach favourite. L'Osteria's wine list is like Danny DeVito: short and Italian.

Thirsty Bear Brewing Company

661 Howard Street, between Second & Third Streets (974 0905). Bus 9, 12, 14, 15, 30, 45, 76. **Lunch served** 11.30am-2.30pm Mon-Fri; noon-2.30pm Sat. **Tapas served** 2.30-10.30pm Mon-Thur; 2.30-11pm Fri, Sat; 2.30-10pm Sun. **Dinner served** 5.30-10.30pm Mon-Thur; 5.30-11pm Fri, Sat; 5-10pm Sun. **Average** lunch $12, dinner $30. **Credit** AmEx, DC, MC, V. **Map H4**

Gamers, bar flies and diners all enjoy the Thirsty Bear, known for its upstairs pool tables and dart boards, its microbrewed beers and a rotating selection of Spanish tapas. Try the mushrooms and garlic with grilled bread, white beans and fennel sausage, or spicy potatoes. Patrons are often corporate clones from the Financial District, out for an evening beer and a quick meal, but don't let that put you off. This is a casual place, one where anybody can feel at home.

XYZ

181 Third Street, at Howard Street (817 7836). Bus 14, 15, 30, 45. **Breakfast served** 8-11am Mon-Fri. **Brunch served** 8am-2.30pm Sat, Sun. **Lunch served** 11.30am-2.30pm Mon-Fri. **Dinner served** 5.30am-10pm daily. **Average** lunch $20, dinner $45. **Credit** AmEx, DC, Disc, MC, V. **Map H4**

Adjacent to the lobby of the swanky new **W Hotel** (*see p107* **Accommodation**), restaurant XYZ (geddit?) exemplifies trendy dining in San Francisco – this week. The minimalist décor perfectly complements chef Alison Richman's simple food, which favours fresh seafood with a Japanese accent. Try an appetiser of seared scallops with baby greens and toasted nori, or Chilean sea bass braised in mirin (rice wine vinegar) and served in broth. Basics such as a tomato salad with Havarti cheese are also good; desserts are more conservative. An overpriced wine list is leavened with fine selections by the glass and half-bottle; service is perfunctory but pleasant. A stone's throw from the SFMOMA, the Yerba Buena, the Metreon and the Moscone Center, XYZ and its sprawling bar attracts a broad clientele – though you'll feel most comfortable if you're young, dressed in black and employed by an Internet start-up company.

Pluto's

3258 Scott Street, between Lombard & Chestnut Streets (775 8867). Bus 22, 28, 30, 43, 76. **Breakfast served** 9.30am-11.30am Sat; 9.30am-10pm Sun. **Meals served** 11.30am-10pm Mon-Thur, Sun; 11.30am-11pm Fri. **Average** lunch $7, dinner $14. **Credit** MC, V. **Map D2**

When it opened, Pluto's food wasn't that great. Recently, however, the fancy cafeteria's fresh-to-order salads (with dozens of ingredient options) and simple main courses (marinated flank steak with farmer's greens) have begun to hit the spot. The restaurant's space age décor and friendly service are additional plusses; all seem to indicate a stellar effort.

Branch: 627 Irving Street, between Seventh & Eighth Avenues (753 8867).

Rose's Cafe

2298 Union Street, at Steiner Street (775 2200). Bus 22, 41, 45. **Open** 7am-10pm Mon-Thur, Sun; 7am-11pm Fri, Sat. **Credit** AmEx, Disc, DC, MC, V. **Map E2/3**

Tucked away at the hilly end of Union Street, this attractive and sunny café – a former Il Fornaio bakery that's now a mini-version of Reed Hearon's North Beach restaurant **Rose Pistola** (*see p123*) – satisfies weary diners with food that's easy on the wallet. You can choose from a selection of focaccia sandwiches, salads with balsamic vinaigrette, pizzas and more substantial dinner specials. The tuna sandwich is made with fresh yellowfin.

Taqueria Cancun

2288 Mission Street, at 19th Street (252 9560). BART 24th Street/bus 14, 49. **Meals served** 9am-1am daily. **Average** $5. **No credit cards. Castro/Mission Map Y2**

It's almost painful to give away one of the city's best-kept secrets: this chain of taquerias (three of them, currently) that serves some of the best burritos at the best prices in town. Grilled chicken, spicy carne asada and a dangerously delicious mojado (with red and green sauces and sour cream) are particularly good, but you can't go wrong with anything you choose. Opt for the Market Street branch if you're seeking the least dodgy neighbourhood.

Branches: 1003 Market Street, at 6th Street (864-6773); 3211 Mission Street, at Fair Street (550 1414).

Ti Couz Crêperie

3108 16th Street, between Guerrero & Valencia Streets (252 7373). BART 16th Street/bus 14, 22, 26, 33, 49, 53. **Meals served** 11am-11pm Mon-Fri; 10am-11pm Sat; 10am-10pm Sun. **Average** $20. **Credit** MC, V. **Map F6**

Ti Couz's crêpes are made from buckwheat and wheat flour and served as in Brittany – in savoury and sweet versions. An entrée might be a crêpe filled with ratatouille, the dessert version with fresh peaches and topped with ice-cream. A list of big salads and savoury onion soup complete the menu. Ti Couz is immensely popular, so anticipate a long wait for a table.

South Park & South Beach

MoMo's San Francisco Grill

760 Second Street, at King Street (227 8660). Bus 30, 42, 45. **Lunch served** 11.30am-5pm Mon-Fri. **Dinner served** 5-10pm Mon-Thur; 5-11pm Fri; 4.30-11pm Sat; 4.30-10pm Sun. **Average** lunch $12, dinner $17. **Credit** AmEx, MC, V. **Map J4**

Located conveniently close to San Francisco's new Pacific Bell baseball park (*see chapter* **Sport & Fitness**), MoMo's challenges the notion that American sports fans desire nothing more than a beer and a ballpark frank when going to a game. Hearty 'comfort food' with a worldly flair make this restaurant as much of a destination as the arena which it abuts. Sweet pea risotto, seared rare ahi tuna and maple-glazed quail are just a few of the dishes that hit a home run.

South Park Café

108 South Park Avenue, between Second, Third, Bryant & Brannan Streets (495 7275). Bus 15, 30, 42, 45, 76. **Breakfast served** 7.30-11am, **lunch served** 11.30am-2.30pm, **snacks served** 2.30-6pm, Mon-Fri. **Dinner served** 6-10pm Mon-Sat. **Average** lunch $15, dinner $35. **Credit** AmEx, MC, V. **Map H/J4**

A longtime favourite in the heart of 'multimedia gulch', this ever-popular bistro overlooking South Park is as first-rate as ever. Service is unrushed and attentive and the French food satisfies both the local yups and those who arrive from districts far and wide. An appetiser of brandade (salt cod) and potato cakes is good, as is a fillet of salmon poached in lemon and coriander broth or roast chicken with pommes frites. Desserts are classics, including crème brûlée and the best profiteroles in town. An excellent spot for a long, relaxed dinner.

The chain game

Like all American cities, San Francisco has its share of chain restaurants, well-lit corporate establishments one step up from fast food but whose *raison d'être* is to provide quick and simple meals rather than a full-fledged dining experience. Fortunately for the traveller, many of these tend to be quite reliable and often healthy, if a little soulless – perfect for scoring a quick bite out on your way to a movie, concert or other commitment.

The best of the chain gang is the omnipresent **Pasta Pomodoro**, a locally-based franchise that specialises in fresh pasta, sandwiches and salads, prepared individually and served in upmarket, though rather sterile, eateries. There's one in almost every neighbourhood in the city and you can count on leaving happy, usually in less than 30 minutes. A selection of dinner specials varies from location to location (as does the quality of the food), but the 'healthy pasta' selection is reliable and cooking is quite good overall.

Similarly, a pair of 'wrap' chains, **World Wrapps** and **Wrap Works**, serve stuffed tortillas in various flavours – Mexican, Thai, Chinese, American – with various condiments and accompaniments. Except for their décor, the two are essentially indistinguishable. Order your lunch or dinner in line, then wait for it to be delivered to your table. Barbecued shrimp, noodles and rice, and spicy vegetarian wraps are usually delicious; odd combos are more risky, though the overall concept is sound.

Links in a longstanding San Francisco-based chain are the **Boudin Bakeries**, retail venues with a soup/salad/sandwich menu and nearly a dozen locations. While their clam chowder-in-a-bread-bowl is something everyone should eat at least once while visiting the city, the rest of the menu is predictable, middling fare. Their breads, however, are delicious.

La Salsa is a chain of Mexican restaurants, recently opened in some upscale neighbourhoods, that promotes the freshness of its ingredients and features a salsa bar in each location. While undeniably fresh, the food is uniformly boring and tastes as though it was designed to appease 'white people with wimpy palates'. In a town brimming with great taquerias, this is a safe but unadventurous option.

Finally, a few **Boston Markets** still survive, where you can choose from a selection of classic American foods – roast chicken, meat loaf, mashed potato and buttery vegetables – in a cafeteria-line setting. These joints are lowest on the recommendation list, scarcely one-up from fast food. Still, if you're desperate (or off a diet), you can score a decent meal in one.

But since San Francisco has more restaurants per capita than any other city in the world, there's plenty of choice when it comes to eating well. The chains are designed for a rushed clientele who don't want to think about what they're eating and whose sense of culinary adventure is akin to the thrill they feel at finding a parking space out front. Does that sound like you?

Consult the telephone directory for the location of your nearest branch of the chains listed above.

The Mission

See also page 124 **Fina Estampa** *and page 125* **Taqueria Cancun**.

Blowfish Sushi

2170 Bryant Street, between 19th & 20th Streets (285 3848). Bus 27. **Meals served** 11.30am-10.30pm Mon-Thur, Sun; 11.30am-11.30pm Fri, Sat. **Average** $15. **Credit** AmEx, MC, V. **Castro/Mission Map Z1**

An upscale sushi restaurant with raver chic, Blowfish offers visual, aural and oral sensory overload. Highly stylised appetisers (such as deep-fried ritsu roll served around a cocktail glass filled with soy dipping sauce) and inventive fish preparation make this ground zero for urbanites in the know. Though service is still chilly, Blowfish has attempted to soften its original hardcore image with moderate success. The daring order the northern pufferfish (cousin to the poisonous Japanese fugu), giving new meaning to the restaurant's motto 'sushi to die for'. Before you eat, dig the surroundings: Japanese animé, odd sculpture and neo-Tokyo architecture.

Delfina

3621 18th Street, between Dolores & Guerrero Streets (552 4055). Bus 33. **Open** 5.30-10pm Mon-Thur, Sun; 5.30-11pm Fri, Sat. **Credit** MC, V. **Average** $20. **Map Castro/Mission Map Y1**

Culinarily and geographically, Delfina stands apart from the rest of the Mission restaurant ghetto and it has been packed since day one. Inside a warm, art-dotted room not much bigger than a large lobby, cheerful staff serve a fresh selection of intriguing appetisers and hearty entrées. Food manages to be both comforting and trendy: try roasted beets with goat's cheese or a rich salt cod brandade spread on cracker bread; follow this with local halibut roasted in a fig leaf with sweet corn or roast chicken with garlicky mashed potatoes. Desserts include a gooey chocolate cake and a fresh fruit tart; the wine list represents solid contenders from California, Italy and France. Don't risk turning up without a reservation, or you'll find yourself waiting for an hour at Delfina's blue-tiled bar.

Zuni Café. *See page 133.*

El Nuevo Frutilandia

3077 24th Street, between Folsom Street & Treat Avenue (648 2958). BART 24th Street/bus 12, 48, 67. **Lunch served** 11.30am-3pm Tue-Fri. **Dinner served** 5-9pm Tue-Thur; 5-10pm Fri. **Meals served** noon-10pm Sat; noon-9pm Sun. **Average** lunch $8, dinner $12. **Credit** MC, V. **Castro/Mission Map Z2**

Specialising in Cuban and Puerto Rican food, this tiny, noisy eatery near Balmy Alley dishes up appetisers such as dumplings stuffed with chicken, meat-filled plantains and yucca fritters, as well as 'higado a la Frutilandia', a succulent dish of calf's liver cooked with green peppers and onions in a spicy sauce. Vegetarian dishes include yucca with garlic, black beans and rice. Most of the main courses can also be ordered as tapas or small plates.

Flying Saucer

1000 Guerrero Street, at 22nd Street (641 9955). BART 24th Street/bus 14, 26, 49. **Dinner served** 5.30-9.30pm Tue-Sat. **Average** $40. **Credit** AmEx, MC, V. **Castro/Mission Map Y2**

With a healthy style and more than a dollop of pretension, Flying Saucer creates meals it's proud to label 'out of this world'. Granted, most of the fare is delicious – a wafer of tuna sashimi with a red miso 'coulis', crisp noodle 'fence' and bonito flakes or a fan of lamb chops with roasted baby red beets. What's more, the menu reflects a well-travelled chef whose plates are as architecturally styled as Jeremiah Tower's (*see p121* **Stars**). But there's also an unstated snobbishness about Flying Saucer which has, like its fine culinary reputation, preceded it for years.

Gordon's House of Fine Eats

500 Florida Street, at Mariposa Street (861 8900). Bus 27. **Lunch served** 11.30am-4.30pm Mon-Sat. **Dinner served** 5.30-11pm Tue-Wed; 5.30pm-midnight Thur-Sat; 5.30-10pm Mon, Sun. **Average** $15. **Credit** Disc, MC, V. **Castro/Mission Map Z1**

Gordon Drysdale, former chef of downtown staple **Bix** (*see p148* **Bars**), recently opened this Mission joint in an attempt to keep the neighbourhood's diners from culinary ennui. Comfort foods like short-ribs and mashed potato share a menu with asparagus spring rolls, beluga caviar and Provençal-style country terrine. Especially noteworthy are Drysdale's robust 'healthful' plates such as the organic vegetable salad primavera and a zucchini, corn and caper calzone. The minimal design is given a whimsical edge with rotating art installations and an accompaniment of live music.

La Rondalla

901 Valencia Street, at 20th Street (647 7474). Bus 14, 26, 49. **Meals served** 11.30am-2am Tue-Sun. **Average** $10. **No credit cards. Castro/Mission Map Y1**

It's Christmas all year round at this Mexican dive with its tree lights, stuffed birds and other outlandish holiday decorations. Mariachi musicians drown out conversation and pitchers of Margarita drown your taste buds – not necessarily a bad thing, since the food is mediocre. Try the asado: thin, barely-grilled steak smothered with fresh onions, potatoes and tomatoes; you might get a few bites in before the noise level reaches deafening point.

Pancho Villa Taqueria

3071 16th Street, between Mission & Valencia Streets (864 8840). BART 16th Street/bus 14, 22, 26, 49, 53. **Meals served** 10am-midnight daily. **Average** $6. **Credit** AmEx, MC, V. **Map F6**

If you've been over-spending on your meals, here's a place to get back on track. Pancho Villa serves some of the best – and fattest – burritos in the Mission. Be prepared to answer a barrage of questions about the type of burrito you want, the strength of salsa, the type of bean (black or refried) and your desired filling. There's a delicious prawn version and another with fresh red snapper and a squeeze of lime; non-fish eaters can choose among a standard selection of beef, chicken, carne asada (barbecued pork) and vegetarian versions. There's almost always a queue, but the line moves fast thanks to the speediness of the (brusque) staff. Eat in at one of the rough-and-ready tables, or take away.

Pauline's Pizza

260 Valencia Street, at Brosnan Street, between Duboce Avenue & 14th Street (552 2050). Bus 14, 26, 49. **Dinner served** 5-10pm Tue-Sat. **Average** $11. **Credit** MC, V. **Map F6**

Unassuming Pauline's specialises in inventive, thin-crusted pizza made with top-quality produce. This is gourmet pie, where ingredients such as roasted peppers, goat's cheese, edible flowers and countless exotic vegetables make their way to your mouth, and where it's impossible to choose badly. Complement your main course with an organic salad or delicious, home-made soup. The original headquarters of Levi Strauss occupies the yellow, saloon-type building next door (*see chapter* **Museums & Galleries**).

Pintxos

557 Valencia Street, between 16th & 17th Streets (565 0207). BART 16th Street/bus 14, 26, 49, 53. **Lunch served** 11.30am-3pm Tue-Sat. **Dinner served** 5.30-10pm Tue-Thur, Sun; 5.30-10.30pm Fri, Sat. **Average** lunch $15, dinner $20. **Credit** AmEx, MC, V. **Castro/Mission Map Y1**

Pronounced *peen*-chos, this Spanish Basque restaurant offers small plates of savoury appetisers with a heavy emphasis on seafood. The culinary preponderance of anchovies, olives, saffron and anise stands in flavourful contrast to the Latin American slant of the neighbourhood. Try the terrific esqueixada when it's available (a cold salad of salt cod, grated tomato, lemon and garlic oil) or any of the house paellas. The wine list emphasises Spanish reds as well as a number of local vintages.

Roosevelt Tamale Parlor

2817 24th Street, at Bryant Street (550 9213). Bus 27, 48. **Meals served** 10.30am-9.40pm Tue-Sat; 10am-8.40pm Sun. **Average** $7. **No credit cards. Castro/Mission Map Z2**

Since 1922, this establishment has been cranking out huge servings of pork or chicken-filled tamales. They're made fresh on the premises and accompanied by a battery of sauces, including fresh pico di gallo (a hot salsa made with tomatoes, avocado and chillis) and spicy chocolate mole.

Slanted Door

584 Valencia Street, at 17th Street (861 8032). BART 16th Street/bus 22, 26, 53. **Lunch served** 11.30am-3pm, **dinner served** 5.30-10pm, Tue-Sun. **Average** lunch $15, dinner $23. **Credit** MC, V. **Map F6**

Long a favourite before the Mission neighbourhood began its recent yuppification, this Vietnamese restaurant has the flair of a top class California cuisinerie. Served in a sleek, elegant setting, the clay pot-roasted catfish is near-legendary, as is the steamed fillet of sea bass with shiitake mushrooms and ginger. Other favourites include a fresh green papaya salad and a number of the different spicy seafood curries. Make your reservations in advance and enjoy one of the city's most consistently sparkling establishments.

Universal Café

2814 19th Street, between Bryant & Florida Streets (821 4608). Bus 12, 27. **Brunch served** 9am-2.30pm Sat, Sun. **Lunch served** 11.30am-2.30pm Tue-Fri. **Dinner served** 6-10pm Tue-Thur; 6-11pm Fri, Sat. **Average** lunch $8, dinner $18. **Credit** AmEx, DC, MC, V. **Castro/Mission Map Z1**

The Universal Café was among the first of the upmarket spots to open in this area, near what has become the epicentre of the Mission district's techno business-based gentrification. From the same stable as the popular **South Park Café** (*see p126*), the Universal has held its own with an understated industrial-design dining room and fresh, interesting food. It's a great spot for breakfast, when you can enjoy potato pancakes at an outside table in the warm Mission sun; lunch features a selection of focaccia sandwiches, salads and tiny pizzas. Dinner brings higher prices but a decent menu as well – choose from a roster of fresh pastas, oven-roasted meat, grilled fish and various desserts. If you're in the area, don't miss this place.

Noe Valley

Alice's

1599 Sanchez Street, at 29th Street (282 8999). Muni Metro J/bus 24, 26. **Lunch served** 11am-3pm Mon-Sat; noon-3pm Sun. **Dinner served** 3-9pm Mon-Thur, Sun; 3-10pm Fri, Sat. **Average** lunch $5, dinner $10. **Credit** MC, V.

Off the beaten track but worth the trek, Alice's serves spicy Hunan and Mandarin cooking in a clean, airy setting. Asparagus salmon in a black bean sauce or the delicate orange beef are favourite entrées; a plate of spicy fried string beans will sear you in the best possible way. Reasonable prices and punctual (if a little dull) service complete the experience. You'll probably have to wait a while before you're seated.

Firefly

4288 24th Street, between Diamond & Douglass Streets (821 7652). Bus 35, 48. **Dinner served** 5.30-10pm daily. **Average** $25. **Credit** AmEx, MC, V. **Castro/Mission Map X2**

The collision of Asian and Californian culinary influences results in some innovative dishes at Firefly, a close-seated, quirky eatery located at the western edge of Noe Valley. The biweekly-changing menu might feature scallop potstickers with sesame soy dipping sauce or a braised leek and new potato soup with gold chanterelles. The main courses will please vegetarians as well as meat-eaters – the selection ranges from a portobello mushroom Wellington to fillet of beef from Niman-Schell, a local organic ranch. Chef Brad Levy's mother's beef brisket with gravy and mashed potato has also featured on the menu.

Civic Center & Hayes Valley

See also page 121 **Stars**.

Absinthe

398 Hayes Street, at Gough Street (551 1590). Bus 21, 42, 47, 49. **Brunch served** 10.30am-3pm Sat, Sun. **Meals served** 7.30am-1.30am Tue-Fri; 5pm-1.30am Sat; 5-10.30pm Sun. **Average** $15-$25. **Credit** AmEx, DC, MC, V. **Map F5**

Contemporary and classic Absinthe favours fin de (deux) siècles southern French cooking in belle époque style. The sepia-toned bar room serves oysters and appetisers along with first-rate cocktails, while the plush main dining room dishes out decadent servings of rabbit, risotto with langoustines and flatiron steaks. The talented bartenders have done their bit to revive classic, turn-of the-century cocktails and though they don't serve the illicit version of the restaurant's wormwood namesake, they are wonderful with pastis. From Tuesday to Saturday, a late-night bar menu is available until 1.30am.

Bay Area dining

The Bay Area's dining scene is as good as the city's, with a plethora of culinary options in any of the nearby hamlets. In Berkeley, **Chez Panisse**, where chef/owner Alice Waters created California cuisine back in the 1970s, continues to reign supreme, serving a high prix-fixe menu downstairs and a perfectly acceptable menu at the **Chez Panisse Café**. Ingredients are of the very best, and the excellent wine list is French and Californian.

Also in Berkeley, **Rivoli** is a small, French-inspired restaurant run by talented chef Wendy Brucker. How can you miss with a starter of fried portobello mushrooms and a chervil butter sauce or a grilled quail with prosciutto di Parma, hazelnut stuffing, scalloped potatoes and a balsamic black pepper jus? Finally, Chef Paul Bertoli, formerly of Chez Pannise, has brought its savvy reputation to **Oliveto**, his first-floor Mediterranean restaurant. Of these three, Chez Panisse is the most expensive, Rivoli the least.

In Oakland, the **Bay Wolf** has been serving Mediterranean food using the freshest produce available for nearly a quarter-century. Try a Liberty Ranch duck with lavender and prunes, followed by crème brûlée refreshed with a dose of mint.

In the Wine Country, you'll find one of the best restaurants in the country: the **French Laundry**, Thomas Keller's masterpiece in the tiny town of Yountville. A four-, five-, or nine-course tasting meal will set you back a couple of hundred dollars, with wine, but it's worth it – every bite is nothing short of sensational. Book ahead two months to the day you want to eat and call early.

For more on the Bay Area beyond the city, *see chapter* **Trips Out of Town**.

Bay Wolf *3853 Piedmont Avenue, opposite Rio Vista Avenue, Oakland (1-510 655 6004). BART McArthur then short cab ride.*

Chez Panisse *1517 Shattuck Avenue, at Cedar Street, Berkeley (1-510 548 5525/www.chezpanisse. com). BART Berkeley.*

French Laundry *6640 Washington Street, Yountville (1-707 944 2380).*

Oliveto *5655 College Avenue, at Shafter Avenue, Berkeley (1-510 547 5356). BART Rockridge.*

Rivoli *1539 Solano Avenue, at Neilson & Peralta Streets, Berkeley (1-510 526 2542/ www.rivoli restaurant.com). BART Berkeley or El Cerrito, then AC Transit bus 67.*

The greens scene

The days of brown rice, seaweed and tofu dogs are long gone and vegetarians can indulge themselves just as extravagantly – or cheaply – as any one else in this foodie city.

Millennium, in the lobby of the Abigail Hotel, is the best (and one of the most pricey) vegetarian restaurants in Northern California. Its extensive menu is ever-changing and adheres to California cuisine's use of fresh, seasonal ingredients. Portions are generous and while most of the food is vegan – made without eggs, cheese, milk, butter, or any other animal products – it's filling and full of flavour. The menu's only downside is that some newer dishes haven't been completely thought-out. Ask your server for recommendations.

Greens (*see page 139*), with its beautiful views of the Golden Gate, is the grand dame of the local vegetarian scene, having served gourmet vegetarian food since 1979. The restaurant is run by students from the San Francisco Zen Center, so the staff turns over frequently and the cooking has its ups and downs. Dishes can be spectacular or merely passable and lunch often tends to outshine dinner. The menu always includes vegan entrées and Green's goes out of its way to accommodate special dietary needs.

If you can afford the splurge, several of the city's best French bistros serve impressive, prix-fixe vegetarian feasts. **Jardinière** (*see page 131*), a hot hangout for upscale singles, features a six-course tasting menu ($75), although vegetarians should phone ahead to make sure they can be accommodated. **Fleur de Lys** (*see page 114*) doesn't look like much from the street, but its five-course vegetarian meal ($58) will make you see stars. The restaurant was a pioneer of 'vertical food design' so every dish also looks spectacular. At the opposite end of the snob scale is **Organica** (*page 141*), one of the city's oddest veggie places where nothing is cooked – even pizza crusts are sun dried – and everything is ultra-fresh.

The city's large Asian population has spawned countless affordable vegetarian eateries; most have lunch specials that will cost less than $5. For Vietnamese, try both the **Golden Turtle** and the **New Golden Turtle**, along with **Mai's #1**, and **Minh's Garden**. Thai is good at **Thai House #1** and **#2**, **Chaam**, **Thailand Restaurant** and **Marnee Thai**. **Neecha Thai Cuisine** (*see page 137*) has extensive vegetarian entrées and unusual dishes like steamed rice noodle rolls. Of the establishments on Clement Street **Burma Superstar**, marries Indian curries to Thai stir-frying techniques with large portions and low prices.

Finally, San Francisco also sports hundreds of great taquerias. Local favourites include **Azteca**, **Pancho Villa Taqueria** and **Roosevelt Tamale Parlor** (*see page 128*), the outlying **Mom is Cooking** and **El Toreador**, whose eye-popping décor makes it great for kids. Three **Sweet Heat** locations serve healthy, yuppified tacos, burritos and salads and last but not least, don't miss **Taquería El Balazo**, whose $5 tamale plate is one of the best deals in town.

Azteca *235 Church Street, at Market Street (255 7330).* **Open** 11am-11pm daily.

Burma Superstar *309 Clement Street, between 4th & 5th Avenues (387 2147).* **Open** 11am-10pm daily.

Chaam *701 Folsom Street, at 3rd Street (546 9710).* **Open** 11am-10pm daily.

El Toreador *50 West Portal Avenue, near the Twin Peaks Tunnel (566 2673).* **Open** 11am-9pm Mon-Wed; 11am-9.30pm Thur; 11am-10pm Fri-Sun.

Golden Turtle *2211 Van Ness Avenue, between Broadway & Vallejo Street (441 4419).* **Dinner served** 5-11pm Tue-Sun.

Mai's #1 *316 Clement Street, between 4th & 5th Avenues (221 3046).* **Open** 11am-10pm Mon-Thur; 11am-11pm Fri, Sat.

Marnee Thai *2225 Irving Street, at 23rd Avenue (665 9500).* **Open** 11.30am-10pm Mon, Wed-Sun.

Millennium *246 McAllister Street, between Hyde & Larkin Streets (487 9800).* **Open** 5-9pm daily.

Minh's Garden *208 Clement Street, between 3rd & 4th Avenues (751 8211).* **Open** 11am-10pm Mon-Sat; 4-10pm Sun.

Mom is Cooking *1166 Geneva Avenue, between Edinburgh & Naples Streets (586 7000).* **Open** noon-10pm daily.

New Golden Turtle *308 Fifth Avenue, between Clement Street & Geary Boulevard (221 5285).* **Open** 5-10pm Mon; 11am-11pm Tue-Sat; 11am-10pm Sun.

Sweet Heat *1725 Haight Street, at Cole Street, (387 8845).* **Open** 11am-10pm daily.
Branches: 2141 Polk Street, at Broadway (775 1055); 3324 Steiner, between Lombard & Chestnut Streets (474 9191).

Taquería El Balazo *1654 Haight Street, at Belvedere Street (864 8608).* **Open** 10.30am-11pm daily.

Thai House #1 *151 Noe Street, at Henry Street (863 0374).* **Open** 5pm-10pm daily

Thai House #2 *2200 Market Street, at 15th Street. (864 5006).* **Open** 11.30am-3pm, 5.30pm-10.30pm, daily.

Thailand Restaurant *438A Castro Street, between Market & 18th Streets (863 6868).* **Open** 11am-3.30pm Mon, Wed-Sun; 4-10pm Mon, Wed, Thur, Sun; 4-10.30pm Fri, Sat.

Caffe Delle Stelle

395 Hayes Street, at Gough Street (252 1110). Bus 21, 42, 47, 49. **Lunch served** 11.30am-3pm daily. **Dinner served** 5.30-10pm Mon-Thur; 5.30-10.30pm Fri, Sat. **Credit** AmEx, DC, MC, V. **Map F5**

Set on the high-visibility street corner directly across the street from hot new restaurant **Absinthe** (*p129*), well-established Stelle offers rustic Italian fare that ranges from home-made pastas (try the pumpkin manicotti) to braised meat, savoury stews and mouthwatering bruschetta. Reasonable wines by the glass and creamy tiramisu round out the hand-written menu. Service can be variable, but the staff counter their lethargy with plenty of Mediterranean charm.

Carta

1772 Market Street, at Gough Street (863 3516). Muni Metro F, J, K, L, M, N/bus 6, 7, 66, 71. **Brunch served** 10am-3pm Sun. **Lunch served** noon-3pm Tue-Fri. **Dinner served** 5.30-11pm Tue-Sun. **Average** lunch $9, dinner $20. **Credit** AmEx, DC, MC, V. **Map F5**

Every month, this small, airy restaurant features a different cuisine from around the world. A focus on the Pacific Islands offers a shrimp and coconut ceviche from Guam and gado gado, the Indonesian vegetable dish topped with peanut sauce. From the American heartland there are cornmeal-dusted onion rings, pan-fried red trout with bacon and mint or three-cheese macaroni. The restaurant's favourites seem to hail from Tuscany and the Mediterranean. Phone to find out what region it's currently featuring.

Hayes Street Grill

320 Hayes Street, between Franklin & Gough Streets (863 5545). Bus 21, 42, 47, 49. **Lunch served** 11.30am-2pm Mon-Fri. **Dinner served** 5-9.30pm Mon-Thur; 5-10.30pm Fri; 5.30-10.30pm Sat; 5-8.30pm Sun. **Average** lunch $18, dinner $35. **Credit** AmEx, DC, Disc, MC, V. **Map F5**

It would be easy to forget the Hayes Street Grill, given its staid, conservative approach in the face of lavish, twenty-first-century establishments with haute menus. But that would be to deny the restaurant's place as a 20-year-old mainstay of the city's dining scene. Inside the simple room decorated with black-and-white photos, you can dine on the city's freshest fish – Pacific snapper, Hawaiian swordfish and California white sea bass go fin-to-fin with crab cakes, fresh mussels and other shellfish. Select from several different sauces (herb butter, salsa, lemon butter, beurre blanc) and tuck into San Francisco's most perfectly prepared seafood.

Indigo

687 McAllister Street, at Gough Street (673 9353). Bus 21, 42, 47, 49. **Dinner served** 5-11pm daily. **Average** $30. **Credit** AmEx, MC, V. **Map F4**

'New American' cuisine is the culinary catch-phrase of this Hayes Valley restaurant, cooking which does more with less and draws its influences from the bounty of North and South America. In a setting that features a long, open kitchen, graceful draperies and a woodworked bar, enjoy such favourites as grilled asparagus with smoked Virginia ham, Cajun tasso-infused risotto, Littleneck clams and seared Pacific salmon with mango salsa. Vegetarians can enjoy a good selection here as well. For dessert, don't miss the lavender crème brûlée, a house specialty.

Pricey but nice: **Boulevard**. *See page 117.*

Jardinière

300 Grove Street, at Franklin Street (861 5555). Bus 21, 42, 47, 49. **Dinner served** 5.30-10.30pm daily. **Average** $75. **Credit** AmEx, DC, Disc, MC, V. **Map F5**

When celebrity chef Traci des Jardin left her post at **Rubicon** (*p121*) in the late 1990s to open her namesake eatery, she single-handedly revived the city's flagging pre-opera and theatre dining scene. Designed by the renowned Pat Kuleto of **Boulevard** and **Farallon** fame (*see p117 and p120*), the whimsically shaped restaurant serves appetisers such as a stellar ahi tuna carpaccio and a wonderful lobster and chanterelle salad. The cured pork tenderloin entrée is legendary – though for the more decadent, rabbit and quail are seasonally available. Start your meal with a plate of caviar-topped oysters.

Suppenküche

601 Hayes Street, at Laguna Street (252 9289). Bus 21. **Brunch served** 10am-2.30pm Sat, Sun. **Dinner served** 5-10pm daily. **Average** brunch $9, dinner $33. **Credit** AmEx, MC, V. **Map F5**

A respite from California cuisine, Suppenküche's menu is authentically German and features spätzle, schnitzels and dense, dark breads. The fresh

For budget dim sum, potstickers and noodles galore, head to **Chinatown**. *See page 120.*

ingredients can seduce a person into a love affair with sauerkraut and then commit to a relationship with sweetbreads, hearty salads and home-made soups. The bar serves beers from Germany in tall steins, and seating is on benches at bare pine tables.

Vicolo Pizzeria

201 Ivy Street, at Franklin Street (863 2382). BART Van Ness/Muni Metro F, J, K, L, M, N/bus 21, 42, 47, 49. **Meals served** 11.30am-9.30pm Mon-Fri; noon-10.30pm Sat; noon-9.30pm Sun. **Average** $12. **Credit** MC, V. **Map F5**

Handy for a pre-theatre meal, this alleyway pizzeria serves some of the city's best. Vicolo's gourmet crusts are thick and made of cornmeal and its toppings range from roasted garlic and Gorgonzola to standards such as mushroom and a scrumptious four-cheese blend. Salads complement plates of greens with additions like roasted baby beets or a medley of black, white and green beans. A little pricey for what you get, but it tastes dee-lish.

Zuni Café

1658 Market Street, between Franklin & Gough Streets (552 2522). Muni Metro F, J, K, L, M, N/ bus 6, 7, 66, 71. **Lunch served** 11.30am-3pm, **late lunch served** 3-6pm, Tue-Sat. **Dinner served** 6pm-midnight Tue-Sun. **Average** lunch $25, dinner $35. **Credit** AmEx, MC, V. **Map F5**

A quintessential San Francisco experience, Zuni is nearly 20 years old now, yet it feels timeless. The restaurant serves Cal-Ital food in an art-filled setting; its choice of dishes is minimal but its use of the freshest possible ingredients makes them memorable. For some, sourdough bread and oysters served on an iced platter is enough; others can investigate the more substantial dishes – roasted chicken, delicious pizzettas – cooked in a wood-fired oven. High, plate-glass windows overlooking Market Street bring in lots of light and make the place a great one from which to watch the world go by.

The Castro & the Haight

See also page 124 **Cha Cha Cha** *and chapter* **Gay & Lesbian San Francisco**.

Eos Restaurant & Wine Bar

901 Cole Street, at Carl Street (566 3063). Muni Metro N/bus 37, 43. **Dinner served** 5.30-11pm Mon-Sat; 5-11pm Sun. **Average** $33. **Credit** AmEx, MC, V. **Map C6**

This comfortably spare, architecturally designed restaurant presents the best of East-West fusion by the classically trained chef/owner Arnold Eric Wong. Dishes such as trumpet mushrooms on a chow mein noodle cake in a velvety heirloom tomato sauce, or lamb garnished with cherry chutney are backed up by one of the most extensive wine lists in the Bay Area. The same menu – as well as the restaurant's delightful dessert platter – is served in the small wine bar next door.

Thep Phanom

400 Waller Street, at Fillmore Street (431 2526). Bus 6, 7, 22, 66, 71. **Dinner served** 5.30-10.30pm daily. **Average** $8. **Credit** AmEx, DC, Disc, MC, V. **Map E5**

Possibly the best Thai restaurant in San Francisco, Thep Phanom draws rave reviews from around the country, all of which contribute to the inevitable evening queue. If you're smart, you'll make reservations; if you're brilliant, you'll order the tom ka gai (coconut chicken soup) as a starter. An order of 'angel wings' – fried chicken wings stuffed with glass noodles – is universally popular.

Tin Pan Asian Bistro

2251 Market Street, between Noe & Castro Streets (565 0733). Muni Metro F, L, K, M/bus 24, 35, 37. **Meals served** 11am-11pm daily. **Average** $15. **Credit** AmEx, DC, Disc, MC, V. **Castro/Mission Map X1**

As much a social hub as it is a respected restaurant, Tin Pan serves huge portions of inventive and challenging dishes from South-east Asia to mostly gay patrons and the occasional handsome interloper. Anticipate a generous selection of creative appetisers and salads, carefully hand-stuffed potstickers and buns and a wide array of noodle and rice dishes. Mongolian lamb, Chinese pork buns and pad thai are among the pan-Asian selections and (in contrast to much of the rest of the Castro) are both well-priced and well-prepared.

2223 Market

2223 Market Street, between Noe & Sanchez Streets (431 0692). Muni Metro F, K, L, M/bus 24, 37. **Brunch served** 10am-2pm Sun. **Dinner served** 6.30-10pm Mon-Thur, Sun; 6.30-11pm Fri, Sat. **Average** brunch $10, dinner $25. **Credit** AmEx, DC, MC, V. **Map E6**

The Castro's clientele jam 2223 Market for dinner and lunch, enjoying such all-American specials as huge pork chops with red pepper stuffing or pan-roasted chicken with garlic mashed potato and fried onion rings. But it's a great place for brunch as well, when you can choose among a list that includes chorizo scrambled eggs with warm corn tortillas, roasted banana French toast or a portobello mushroom and prosciutto omelette. It's all as good as it sounds and desserts are of the same divine ilk.

Funky feline: North Beach's **Black Cat**, *p121.*

Japantown

Isobune Sushi

Restaurant Mall, Kinetsu Building, 1737 Post Street, at Webster Street (563 1030). Bus 2, 3, 4, 38, 32. **Meals served** 11.30am-10pm daily. **Average** $15. **Credit** JCB, MC, V. **Map E4**

It's occasionally hard to differentiate between Japantown's many sushi restaurants, but this one has a gimmick: orders are delivered on wooden boats which circle around a long oval bar. When your ship comes in, take the little plates from the boats. You'll be charged for the size and number of plates you take. The sushi is good quality and reasonably-priced.

Isuzu

1581 Webster Street, at Post Street (922 2290). Bus 2, 3, 4, 22, 38. **Lunch served** 11.30am-2pm Mon-Fri. **Dinner served** 5-10pm Mon-Fri; noon-10pm Sat; 4-9pm Sun. **Average** lunch $7, dinner $12. **Credit** DC, MC, V. **Map E4**

Isuzu is a noisy, Japanese family-style establishment, specialising in sashimi, sushi and trays of golden tempura. The helpful staff with reliable recommendations are a plus for those new to the place.

Mifune

Japan Center, 1737 Post Street, between Webster & Buchanan Streets (922 0337). Bus 2, 3, 4, 22, 38. **Meals served** 11am-9.30pm daily. **Average** $10. **Credit** AmEx, DC, Disc, JCB, MC, V. **Map E4**

Mifune's speciality is the lowly noodle, prepared in at least 30 different ways. Orders come quickly, inexpensively and deliciously to your table. A good place to take kids and also great for vegetarians who can get their protein from seaweed, egg or miso.

Sanppo

1702 Post Street, opposite Japan Center, at Buchanan Street (346 3486). Bus 2, 3, 4, 22, 38. **Meals served** 11.30am-midnight daily. **Average** lunch $7, dinner $10. **Credit** MC, V. **Map E4**

For nearly 25 years, this small, casual restaurant has been turning out good, rustic Japanese food – soups, lightly battered tempuras, fresh fish and East-West salads – all at the right price. Service is charming.

Seoul Garden

22 Peace Plaza, Japantown (563 7664). Bus 2, 3, 4, 22, 38. **Meals served** 11am-midnight daily. **Average** $12. **Credit** MC, V. **Map E4**

Grill the marinated beef at your table and try the myriad little dishes that typically make up Korean cuisine. A good place to remember when all the Japanese restaurants in the neighbourhood are packed.

Pacific Heights

See also page 125 **Rose's Café**.

Elite Café

2049 Fillmore Street, at California Street (346 8668). Bus 1, 3, 22. **Brunch served** 10am-3pm Sun. **Dinner served** 5-11pm daily. **Average** lunch $12, dinner $25. **Credit** AmEx, DC, Disc, MC, V. **Map E3**

Tokyo comes to the Mission in the form of **Blowfish Sushi**. *See page 127.*

A survivor from the clubby venues of the 1930s and 1940s, the Elite remains one of the city's few Cajun-inspired restaurants. It offers authentic gumbo, the stew made with celery, carrots, onions, sausage and crawdads from New Orleans. All dishes have a pronounced Louisiana accent, except the sourdough bread and those from the oyster bar. There's a great Cajun brunch as well, complete with spicy Bloody Marys.

Laghi

2101 Sutter Street, at Steiner Street (931 3774). Bus 2, 3, 4, 22, 38. **Dinner served** 5-9.30pm Mon-Thur, Sun; 5-10.30pm Fri, Sat. **Average** $25. **Credit** AmEx, DC, MC, V. **Map E4**

Occupying a new location at the edge of Pacific Heights, the formerly outlying Laghi specialises in authentic, rustic Italian cooking of the sort you'd find in a trattoria in Emilia Romagna. Run by a husband-and-wife team, the much-larger new space offers the same Italian-flavoured wine list, home-made pasta with rich sauces and regional versions of classics like risotto with red wine and black truffles.

Neecha Thai Cuisine

2100 Sutter Street, at Steiner Street (922 9419). Bus 2, 3, 4, 22, 38. **Lunch served** 11am-3pm Mon-Fri. **Dinner served** 5-10pm daily. **Average** lunch $6, dinner $12. **Credit** AmEx, MC, V. **Map E4**

A Thai interloper near Japantown, this long-established local restaurant features a menu whose highlights include good salads, appetisers and noodle dishes at remarkably low prices. Like **Laghi** (*see above*), Neecha is within walking distance of Japantown, the new Fillmore Historic Jazz District and the Kabuki 8 cinema.

Vivande Porta Via

2125 Fillmore Street, between Sacramento & California Streets (346 4430). Bus 1, 3, 22, 24. **Lunch served** 11.30am-5pm, **dinner served** 5-10pm, daily. **Average** lunch $12, dinner $30. **Credit** AmEx, DC, Disc, JCB, MC, V. **Map E3**

From the outside, Vivande looks like a kitchen shop selling cookbooks and Italian wine. Inside, however, a long deli counter filled with scrumptious takeaway parallels a tightly-packed dining area. Renowned chef Carlo Middione, who also owns the huge Vivande Ristorante near Civic Center, serves authentic Italian fare with a Sicilian accent. Perfect pastas, fresh salads and seafood are all delivered with panache. Leave room for luscious desserts and, on your way out, stock up on fundamentals like balsamic vinegar and truffle-infused olive oil.

Branch: **Vivande Ristorante** 670 Golden Gate Aveune, between Van Ness Avenue & Franklin Street (673 9245).

The Marina & Cow Hollow

See also page 125 **Pluto's**.

Betelnut

2030 Union Street, between Webster & Buchanan Streets (929 8855). Bus 22, 41, 45. **Meals served** 11.30am-11pm Mon-Thur, Sun; 11am-midnight Fri, Sat. **Average** $20. **Credit** DC, MC, V. **Map E2**

Modelled on a Chinese beer garden, Betelnut – packed with yuppies and foodies – is at the heart of

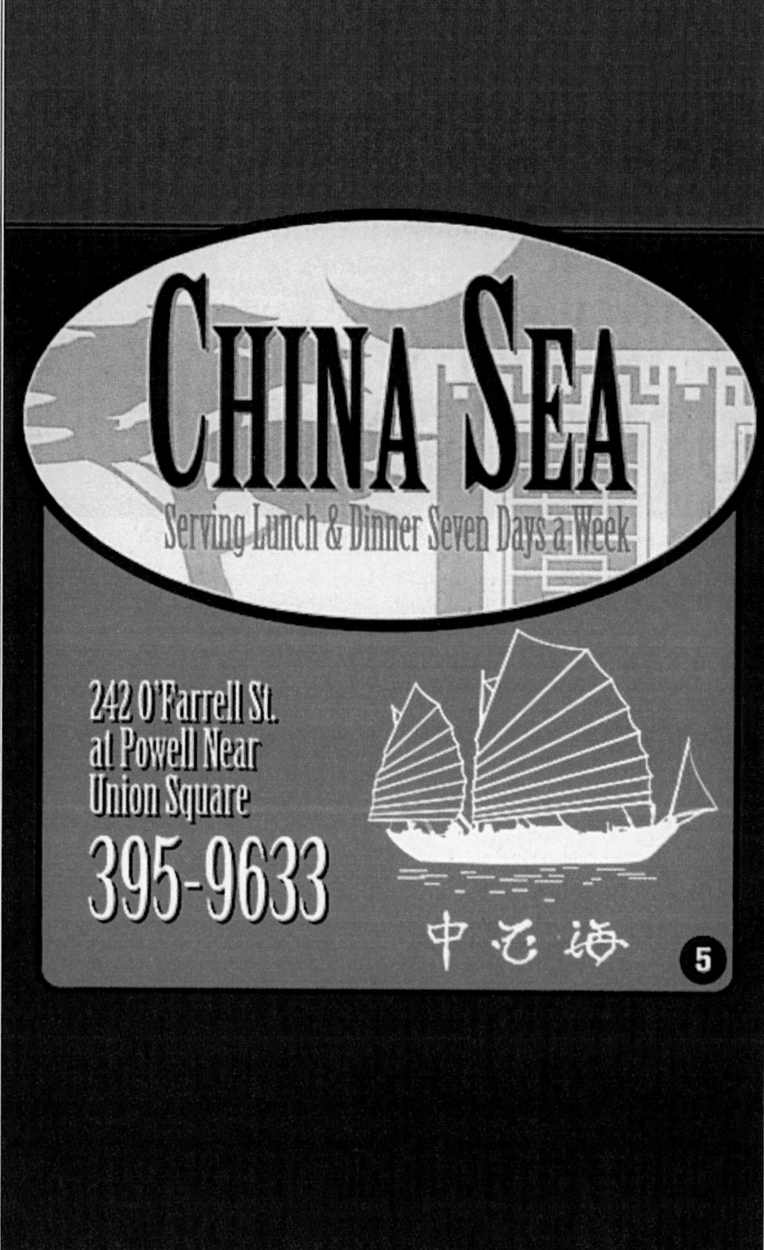
CHINA SEA
Serving Lunch & Dinner Seven Days a Week
242 O'Farrell St.
at Powell Near
Union Square
395-9633
5

the Union Street shopping scene. Decked out in rich red and black, the restaurant offers a consistently magnificent array of contemporary Asian dishes ranging from Singaporean crab to Korean char-broiled pork and Vietnamese barbecued chicken. Every two weeks, the restaurant's chefs highlight a specific country or region for their specials and the result is food that's both traditional and inventive, mixing the best of each culture into a culinary triumph. Don't miss this fusion favourite.

Byblos

1910 Lombard Street, at Buchanan Street (292 5672). Bus 22, 28, 30, 43, 76. **Dinner served** 5-11pm daily. **Average** $14. **Credit** MC, V. **Map E2**

Byblos is one of the few Lebanese restaurants in San Francisco and even its wine list includes a few eastern Mediterranean selections. If you're with a group of six or more (and give 48 hours' notice) you can order the special spit-roasted lamb; otherwise, stick to the mezes – small plates that range from pickled vegetables, dolmas and steak tartare to delicious home-made sausages. There's belly-dancing to entertain on selected nights.

Greens

Building A, Fort Mason Center, Marina Boulevard, at Buchanan Street (771 6222). Bus 28. **Brunch served** 10am-2pm Sun. **Lunch served** 11.30am-2pm Tue-Fri; 11.30am-2.30pm Sat. **Dinner served** 5.30-9.30pm Mon-Thur; 5.30-10pm Fri; 5.30-9pm Sat. **Average** lunch $20, dinner $35. **Credit** DC, MC, V. **Map E1**

With a great view of the Golden Gate Bridge and an award-winning all-vegetarian menu, Greens, despite its dated burlwood interior and spacey service, keeps its reputation sterling. Fresh produce and an extensive wine list complement mesquite-grilled vegetables or wood-fired pizzas topped with wild mushrooms. Pastas, flans and salads are likewise veggie-laden. Greens makes a good stopping-off place between Fisherman's Wharf and the Fort Mason Center; take advantage of the takeaway counter for sandwiches and soups if you don't want to brave the queue for a table.

Pane e Vino

3011 Steiner Street, at Union Street (346 2111). Bus 22, 41, 45. **Lunch served** 11.30am-2.30pm Mon-Sat. **Dinner served** 5-10pm Mon-Thur, Sun; 5-10.30pm Fri, Sat. **Average** lunch $20, dinner $30. **Credit** AmEx, MC, V. **Map E2/3**

This small Italian trattoria, filled with friendly staff and a Pacific Heights clientele, has good, authentic food. Lightly-sauced pasta dishes are excellent, especially the fusilli with eggplant and sausage, as are other simple dishes like the grilled salmon with white beans. The wine list (like the staff) is mostly Italian. Booking is advised.

PlumpJack Café

3127 Fillmore Street, between Greenwich & Filbert Streets (563 4755). Bus 22, 28, 41, 43, 45, 76. **Lunch served** 11.30am-2pm Mon-Fri. **Dinner served** 5.30-10.30pm Mon-Sat. **Average** lunch $25, dinner $50. **Credit** AmEx, MC, V. **Map E2**

Following the success of PlumpJack Wines down the street, this restaurant opened in 1994, a testament to the blending of new ideas and old money. Thirtysomething owner Gavin Newsom is a local society brat turned SF Supervisor, his partner the son of railroad magnate Gordon Getty; their special-occasion eatery is a centrepiece for outstanding California cuisine. Chef Keith Luce has cooked at the White House, but his food is unintimidating and incredibly delicious. Try lamb sirloin with Provençal

Shanghaied!

One of San Francisco's greatest assets has always been its proximity to the Orient and the Far East has never been quite so close as it is in the city's culinary repertoire. The flavours and ingredients of South-east Asia have indelibly marked end-of-the-millennium tastes in San Francisco. One of the best examples of this trend is a new, ultra-popular dining room with pan-Asian flair: **Shanghai 1930**.

Shanghai 1930 basks in the decadent ambience its name suggests, a singular focus on pre-war Shanghai. Rather than the casual rice plates and noodles endemic to most American-Chinese establishments, Shanghai 1930 artfully arranges each dish so that it is as pleasing to eat as to see. 'Fish on the vine' comes in deep-fried 'grapes' of fish reminiscent of a hanging bunch; the dim sum arrives in stacked steamers filled with beautifully wrapped opalescent dumplings.

Elsewhere on the menu, minced duck is mixed with its own skin, celery and water chestnuts and served in hoisin-smeared lettuce cups. The Szechuan crispy chewy beef is braised and wok-fried, served in a pungent peppercorn sauce, with julienned carrots and celery. Don't pass up the wok-roasted cod, smothered in a velvety sauce, and set off with crunchy bamboo shoots, black mushrooms and garlic.

Shanghai 1930 revels in a sense of luxury and exclusivity. Cocktails replace beer and the service is formal but friendly. It's a swanky example of San Francisco's ability to make diners feel that geographical distance becomes negligible when transferred to the palate.

Shanghai 1930

133 Steuart Street, between Mission & Howard Streets (896 5600). BART Embarcadero/Muni Metro E, J, K, L, M, N/bus 6, 7, 14, 21, 66, 71. **Dinner served** 5-10pm Mon-Thur; 5-11pm Fri, Sat. **Average** $42. **Credit** AmEx, Disc, MC, V. **Map J3**

vegetables or an appetiser of fresh tuna tartare with a touch of wasabi; for dessert, the chocolate soufflé is a knockout. Service is flawless. An extensive, inexpensive wine list culls the best from the wine shop. Don't miss this one.

Yoshida Ya

2909 Webster Street, at Union Street (346 3431). Bus 22, 41, 45. **Lunch served** 11.30am-2pm Mon-Fri. **Dinner served** 5-10.30pm Mon-Thur, Sun; 5-11pm Fri, Sat. **Average** lunch $9, dinner $22. **Credit** AmEx, Disc, DC, JCB, MC, V. **Map E2**

This quiet restaurant at the edge of Cow Hollow serves up some of the city's best Japanese food. An extensive sushi list complements teriyakis and yakatoris, and a coastal touch prevails in the California roll with crab and avocado, and the salmon teriyaki. There's a tatami room upstairs for the full, authentic experience.

Zinzino

2355 Chestnut Street, between Scott & Divisadero Streets (346 6623). Bus 28, 30, 43, 76. **Dinner served** 6-9.30pm Mon; 6-10pm Tue-Thur; 5.30-11pm Fri, Sat; 5.30-9.30pm Sun. **Average** $30. **Credit** AmEx, MC,V. **Map D2**

Only a block from hotel-laden Lombard Street, this long restaurant serves Italian food with Californian flair. Seafood and pizzas are best: try the lobster with potatoes and caviar or grilled prawns with white beans and arugula; a grilled steak is also a winner. Eat at the counter in front of the open kitchen or on the outdoor (heated) patio. Portions can be skimpy.

Richmond

Beach Chalet Brewery & Restaurant

1000 Great American Highway, between Fulton Street & Lincoln Avenue (386 8439). Bus 5, 18. **Brunch served** 10am-3pm Sun. **Meals served** 11.30am-10pm Mon-Thur; 11.30am-11pm Fri; 10am-11pm Sat. **Average** $15. **Credit** MC, V.

The Beach Chalet represents something of a dilemma for San Franciscans, who love the restaurant's setting (overlooking the Pacific at the western edge of Golden Gate Park) and the history it represents (its first-floor frescoes, painted by Lucien Labaudt in the 1930s, are among the city's best-preserved). But the restaurant's clientele leans heavily towards tourist, and its menu towards the fried and overly-spicy. Your best bet? Opt for a hearty house-brewed beer and a grilled organic hamburger as you enjoy the view, skip dessert and spend some quality time with the murals downstairs. *See also chapter* **Sightseeing**.

Brothers Restaurant

4128 Geary Boulevard, between Fifth & Sixth Avenues (387 7991). Bus 38. **Meals served** 11am-3am daily. **Average** $15. **Credit** MC, V. **Map B4**

Both the Brothers restaurants look the same, but this one serves the best food. Order the bulgogi (marinated beef), chap chae (vermicelli with beef, spinach and mushrooms) or bi bim bop (vegetables, a fried egg and beef on rice; there's also a vegetarian version). Don't miss the kim chee – pickled cabbage in a light, hot pepper sauce, served in one of the many small dishes that come with the main courses.
Branch: 4014 Geary Boulevard, between Fourth & Fifth Avenues (668 2028).

Kabuto

5116 Geary Boulevard, between 15th & 16th Avenues (752 5652). Bus 28, 38. **Dinner served** 5.30-11pm Tue-Sat. **Average** $25. **Credit** MC, V. **Map A4**

Out on Geary, miles from Japantown, Kabuto's nondescript exterior disguises the excellent raw fish sold within. San Francisco restaurateurs have been spotted at this tiny sushi bar, so you know the fish is fresh. Eschew the few tables and grab a seat at the sushi bar, where the chefs will give you a show – and a meal – you won't forget.

Khan Toke

5937 Geary Boulevard, between 23rd & 24th Avenues (668 6654). Bus 29, 31, 38. **Dinner served** 5-10.30pm daily. **Average** $9. **Credit** AmEx, MC, V.

Take off your shoes and choose a seat on the floor – on a low chair with a padded back support – in one of the city's most attractive (and overlooked) Thai restaurants. Fiery and colourful curries and excellent noodle dishes can be accompanied by a good selection of Sauvignon Blancs and Gewürztraminers.

Mayflower

6255 Geary Boulevard, at 27th Avenue (387 8338). Bus 28, 38. **Lunch served** 11am-2.30pm Mon-Fri; 10am-2.30pm Sat, Sun. **Dinner served** 5-9.30pm daily. **Average** $18. **Credit** MC, V.

This family-oriented Cantonese restaurant is consistently good. Seafood is its speciality, but the kitchen never disappoints with several clay pot dishes, roast chicken or duck; Mongolian beef is another perennial favourite. Arrive after 8pm if you want to avoid the hordes of families.

Ton Kiang

5821 Geary Boulevard, between 22nd & 23rd Avenues (387 8273). Bus 29, 38. **Meals served** 10.30am-10pm Mon-Fri; 10am-10.30pm Sat, Sun. **Average** lunch $10, dinner $16. **Credit** AmEx, MC, V.

This restaurant serves hakka, Chinese gypsy cuisine. For the most authentic entrées, try salt-baked chicken served with a paste made of ground garlic and ginger or fresh cod fillets sautéed with black bean sauce. Around Chinese New Year the restaurant features a delicious special menu of seasonal delicacies.

Sunset

Ebisu

1283 Ninth Avenue, between Irving Street & Lincoln Way (566 1770). Muni Metro N/bus 6, 44, 66. **Lunch served** 11.30am-2pm, **dinner served** 5-10pm, Mon-Wed. **Meals served** 11.30am-midnight Thur-Sat; 11.30am-10pm Sun. **Average** lunch $12, dinner $18. **Credit** AmEx, DC, MC, V. **Map B6**

Considered by many locals to be the best sushi bar in town – some say the best outside Japan – Ebisu might as well mean Japanese for 'long wait'. As soon as you arrive, register your name on the list and have a beer while you await your seat. Once you've sat down, try the selection of house specialties: 'pink Cadillac', albacore tatake, seafood salad, '49er roll': none will let you down. The more conservative can try salmon, tuna or cooked eel instead.

House

1269 Ninth Avenue, between Irving Street & Lincoln Way (682 3898). Muni Metro N/bus 6, 44, 66.
Lunch served 11.30am-3pm Tue-Fri. **Dinner served** 5.30-10pm Tue-Thur; 5.30-11pm Fri; 5-11pm Sat; 5-10pm Sun. **Average** lunch $12, dinner $25. **Credit** AmEx, DC, MC, V. **Map B6**

House's chef Larry Tse is a graduate of the California Culinary Academy and runs two restaurants, each showcasing exemplary fusion food at fantastic prices. Inside a cool, high-ceilinged room, diners may enjoy fillet of grilled sea bass with a miso soy sauce accompanied by mashed potato; buttermilk calamari with chives is served with a side order of bean sprout salad; soft-shell crabs arrive tempura style. Desserts run the gamut from exotic sorbets to flourless chocolate cake.

Branch: 1230 Grant Street, at Columbus Avenue (986 8612).

Organica

1224 Ninth Avenue, at Lincoln Way (665 6519). Muni Metro N/bus 44, 71. **Meals served** 11am-10pm Mon-Thur; 11am-11pm Fri, Sat; 11am-9pm Sun. **Average** $10. **No credit cards**. **Map B6**

Ambient music, potted plants and mellow folks (staff and customers) with plenty of body piercing fill Organica's blue-hued room, where everything is vegan and nothing – that's *nothing* – is cooked. A 'burrito' comprises a purple cabbage leaf coated with pine nut spread, packed with crunchy vegetables and wild rice (which has been soaked for 30 days); carrot cake is made from pulp. There are 'sushi' and ice-cream sundaes, too. It's not for the culinarily timid, but Organica – formerly known as Raw – is an assuredly unique eatery in a city with plenty of competitors.

PJ's Oyster Bed

737 Irving Street, between Eighth & Ninth Avenues (566 7775). Muni Metro N/bus 4, 6, 66.
Lunch served 11.30am-3pm Mon-Sat. **Dinner served** 5-10pm Mon-Thur; 5-11pm Fri; 4-11pm Sat; 4-10pm Sun. **Average** lunch $9, dinner $15. **Credit** AmEx, DC, Disc, MC, V. **Map B6**

A noisy, friendly neighbourhood oyster bar, PJ's dishes out some of the freshest and most authentic Cajun food in San Francisco. Seafood selections are displayed on ice and shucked to order. Portions are generous and the restaurant is always packed. If you're looking for dinner on a budget, enjoy a bowl of PJ's clam chowder and a salad.

Cafés

In San Francisco as elsewhere, the definition of the word 'café' is a hazy one. It can mean anything from a coffee shop, where one can get a fresh-pressed espresso or cup of tea and a pastry to go with it, to somewhere where you can have a full meal.

Most of the city's cafés are informal places to relax – where you can command a table for the duration of a chapter or the time it takes to reacquaint yourself with an old friend. A few, however – particularly those in the Financial District – are designed for executive lunches. If a crowd of people is staring you down during the lunch hour, consider uprooting yourself and returning later. In the evening many coffee houses also offer beer and wine and, occasionally, a happy hour.

Finally, a word about franchise establishments: avoid 'em. Starbucks and Tully's, a pair of competing Seattle-based chains, have extended their tentacles into the heart of the city's unique collection of cafés. This has threatened long-standing local favourites (Peet's, Pasqua, Oh La! La!) and continues to drive independent establishments out of business (RIP Spinelli). Their world-dominating business plans will only succeed if the public gets lazy or apathetic – for which a double espresso from your local independent café remains the best antidote.

Francophiles unite at **Café Bastille**, *p142.*

Around Union Square

See also below **Dottie's True Blue Café** *and* **Sears Fine Foods**.

Armani Café

1 Grant Avenue, between O'Farrell & Market Streets (677 9010). BART Montgomery & Powell Streets/ Muni Metro F, J, K, L, M, N/bus 5, 6, 7, 21, 30, 31, 38, 45, 66, 71. **Open** 10am-7pm Mon-Fri; 10am-6pm Sat; noon-6pm Sun. **Credit** AmEx, DC, Disc, JCB, MC, V. **Map G/H4**

The food at the Armani is as stylishly Italian as the expensive clothes that are sold in the shop – though, thankfully, not in the same price range. Hungry Union Square shoppers can choose from a range of pastas, salads and sandwiches, served until the early evening only. The outdoor seating will give you the best see-and-be-seen scene, although the high surrounding buildings will keep you in perpetual shade.

Café Bastille

22 Belden Lane, between Montgomery & Kearny, Pine & Bush Streets (986 5673). Bus 2, 3, 4, 15/cable car California. **Open** 11am-10.30pm Mon-Sat. **Credit** AmEx, DC, MC, V. **Map H3**

Francophiles and homesick Parisians flock here for pastis, steak frites, pâté with cornichons, croque monsieur (or madame) or just for the feel of a continental café. Bastille has indoor and outdoor seating and the staff are as genuinely French as the food. Belden Lane is also the venue for the city's annual Bastille Day party in July, which spills out into the nearby Financial District.

Café Claude

7 Claude Lane, between Sutter & Bush Streets, Kearny Street & Grant Avenue (392 3505). BART Montgomery Street/Muni Metro F, J, K, L, M, N/ bus 2, 3, 4, 15, 30, 45, 76. **Open** 10am-10.30pm Mon-Sat. **Credit** AmEx, Disc, JCB, MC, V. **Map H3**

The story, of course, is legendary: owner Stephen Decker purchased Le Barbizon café in France and shipped it piecemeal over into this space. The result is a real slice of Paris, from setting to service. Signature dishes such as cassoulet, soups and mousse au chocolat maintain the delightful illusion.

Café de la Presse

352 Grant Avenue, at Bush Street (398 2680). Bus 2, 3, 4, 15, 30, 45, 76. **Open** 7am-11pm daily. **Credit** AmEx, DC, Disc, MC, V. **Map G3**

Best brunches

Doidge's Kitchen

2217 Union Street, between Fillmore & Steiner Streets (921 2149). Bus 22, 41, 45. **Meals served** 8am-1.45pm Mon-Fri; 8am-2.45pm Sat, Sun. **Credit** MC, V. **Map E2**

This unpretentious café is popular for its plethora of brunch offerings, which range from cheese-laden omelettes and home-made granola and steel-cut oats to buttermilk pancakes and traditional eggs florentine. You read it here first: make a reservation.

Dottie's True Blue Café

522 Jones Street, at Geary Street (885 2767). Bus 38. **Open** 7.30am-2pm Mon, Wed-Sun. **Credit** Disc, MC, V. **Map G4**

A tiny and incredibly popular breakfast joint, with checked tablecloths and a tiled floor. Get there early to avoid the inevitable queue (you can't book), especially at the weekends. Breakfast specials and standards such as French toast, pancakes and eggs any which way are supplemented at lunchtime by a short list of sandwiches and burgers. The staff are particularly friendly and cope with the crowds admirably.

Ella's

500 Presidio Avenue, at California Street (441 5669). Bus 1, 3, 4, 43. **Breakfast served** 7-11am, **lunch served** 11.30am-5pm, **dinner served** 5-9pm, Mon-Fri. **Brunch served** 9am-2pm Sat, Sun. **Credit** AmEx, MC, V. **Map D4**

The queue is long, but weekend brunches are stellar at this Pacific Heights institution. Try a plate of delicious turkey hash or an omelette with sausage, roasted pepper, pesto and Provolone.

Kate's Kitchen

471 Haight Street, between Fillmore & Webster Streets (626 3984). Bus 6, 7, 22, 66, 71. **Meals served** 9am-2.45pm Mon; 8am-2.45pm Tue-Fri; 9am-3.45pm Sat, Sun. **No credit cards. Map E5**

Kate's customers range from healthy types getting a good breakfast before a hike, to less salubrious characters hung-over in the Lower Haight. Huge portions of granola may appeal to the calorie conscious, but Kate's wins most admirers with its fried hushpuppies, mammoth omelettes and signature bacon-cheddar pancakes.

Mama's on Washington Square

1701 Stockton Street, at Filbert Street (362 6421). Bus 15, 30, 39, 41, 45. **Meals served** 8am-3pm Tue-Sun. **No credit cards. Map E2**

The weekend wait is infamous at this friendly brunch spot at the base of Telegraph Hill, but even after an hour of queuing, most devotees still can't decide on what to order. Club sandwiches thick with bacon, chicken breast and avocado compete with quiche, omelettes and cranberry-orange French toast.

Troisième in the French café trinity is Café de la Presse, where you'll find a variety of international newspapers and magazines to read, outdoor seating, postcards and plenty of attitude. Celebs filming in San Francisco (and there are many) tend to find their way here, as do fashion industry mavens staying at the swanky **Hotel Triton** next door (*see p101* **Accommodation**). Once you've recharged your batteries, you can head out into the streets of Chinatown – the entrance is directly across the road.

Seattle Street Coffee

456 Geary Street, between Mason & Taylor Streets (922 4566). Muni Metro F, J, K, L, M, N/bus 38, 76/cable car Powell-Hyde or Powell-Mason. **Open** 6am-10pm Mon-Sat; 7am-9pm Sun. **No credit cards.** **Map G4**

Opened a couple of years ago as a cybercafé, Seattle Street is conveniently located a block and a half from the shops and hotels of Union Square. Walk all the way to the back to find the screens and to the counter to find fantastic coffee and hearty snacks. The café has two terminals for internet surfing, at $2.50 an hour.

The Embarcadero

Cafe De Stijl

1 Union Street, at Front Street (291 0808). Bus 32, 42. **Open** 7am-5pm Mon-Sat. **No credit cards. Map G2**

Named after the early twentieth-century Dutch art movement, De Stijl is a rarity: it offers easy parking, sidewalk seating and hearty food with a Middle Eastern accent. Try the chicken sandwich with tahini or a mixed platter complete with kibbeh (ground lamb patty), baba ganoush (eggplant purée) and tabouleh (bulghur with mint, tomatoes and cucumber). A sunny downtown setting and a variety of breakfast pastries round out the selection at what could fast become your favourite neighbourhood café.

North Beach & Russian Hill

See also below **Mama's on Washington Square**.

Caffè Greco

423 Columbus Avenue, between Green & Vallejo Streets (397 6261). Bus 15, 30, 39, 41, 45. **Open** 7am-11.30pm Mon-Thur, Sun; 7am-1am Fri, Sat. **No credit cards. Map G2**

Mel's Drive-In

2165 Lombard Street, between Steiner & Fillmore Streets (921 3039). Bus 22, 41, 45. **Meals served** 6am-2am Mon-Thur, Sun; 24 hours Fri, Sat. **No credit cards. Map E2**

Tourist-laden and overflowing with kids, the diner made famous by *American Graffiti* is now famous for its breakfasts. Service is quick and the offerings are plentiful: eggs every which way, pancakes, oatmeal and fruit – even a grilled steak. **Branch**: 3355 Geary Boulevard, between Parker & Stanyan Streets (387 2244).

Miss Millie's

4123 24th Street, between Diamond & Castro Streets (285 5598). Bus 24, 35, 48. **Brunch served** 9am-2pm Sat, Sun. **Dinner served** 6-10pm Tue-Sun. **Credit** MC, V. **Castro/Mission Map X2**

Lemon ricotta pancakes are served with a generous slather of blueberries, baguette French toast with bananas, and omelettes with a side of roasted root vegetables, at this popular Castro district weekend brunch spot. Arrive around 12.30pm if you want to miss the crowds and hope for one of the coveted seats on the small patio outside.

Sears Fine Foods

439 Powell Street, between Sutter & Post Streets (986 1160). Bus 2, 3, 4, 38, 76/cable car Powell-Hyde or Powell-Mason. **Meals served** 6.30am-3pm daily. **No credit cards. Map G3**

Breakfast at **Mama's.**

Once you've found that coveted parking spot and braved the crowds of Union Square, try Sears' 'world-famous 18 Swedish pancakes' or perhaps a Denver omelette filled with bell pepper, onion and ham. Afterwards you can catch a cable car from directly outside.

Slip between the Greeks. **Caffè Greco**, *p143.*

In a neighbourhood known for its cafés, Caffè Greco stands out for its mixed crowd and friendly vibe – Grecos, Italianos, Americanos, all hanging out in an airy, open space with large sliding windows and a prime view along Columbus Avenue. Sip a cappuccino or indulge in some creamy tiramisu, or perhaps one of the focaccia sandwiches or Italian antipasti.

Caffè Trieste

601 Vallejo Street, at Grant Avenue (392 6739). Bus 12, 15, 30, 41, 45, 83. **Open** 6.30am-11pm Mon-Thur, Sun; 6.30am-midnight Fri, Sat. **No credit cards. Map G2**

A North Beach survivor from the Beat era, the espresso bar of choice for Jack Kerouac and Allen Ginsberg remains within walking distance of the famous **City Lights** bookstore (*see p162* **Shops & Services**). Trieste's dark walls are plastered with photos of opera singers and other famous regulars. There are muffins, pastries and sandwiches to eat and wonderfully potent lattes to drink.

Imperial Tea Court

1411 Powell Street, between Broadway & Vallejo Street (788 6080). Bus 12, 83/cable car Powell-Mason. **Open** 11am-6.30pm daily. **Credit** AmEx, MC, V. **Map G2**

This teahouse marks a quiet respite from the bustle of Chinatown. Take a break and sip some exotic blends like Silver Needle or chrysanthemum.

Mario's Bohemian Cigar Store

566 Columbus Avenue, at Union Street (362 0536). Bus 15, 30, 39, 41, 45/cable car Powell-Mason. **Open** 10am-midnight Mon-Sat; 10am-11pm Sun. **No credit cards. Map G2**

Located across Union Street from Washington Square Park, Mario's offers a light menu of focaccia sandwiches and salads, with beer and coffee drinks to accompany them. It's always packed and lunch may be slow in coming, but you'll find no more essential North Beach café. Despite its name, you won't find a cigar in sight, nor be allowed to smoke one.

Branch: 2209 Polk Street, between Vallejo & Green Streets (776 8226).

San Francisco Art Institute Café

800 Chestnut Street, at Jones Street (749 4567). Bus 30/cable car Powell-Mason or Powell-Hyde. **Open** *early Sept-mid May* 8am-9pm Mon-Thur; 8am-5pm Fri; 9am-2pm Sat; *end May-Aug* 9am-2pm Mon-Fri. **No credit cards. Map F2**

Despite a steep walk up to SFAI's campus, the advantages of this place are multiple: a view of the Bay, three art galleries (and many more displays of student works-in-progress), a Diego Rivera mural on the way in – and the café is rarely busy. For your money, you'll get medium-quality but filling food, strong coffee and interesting conversation.

Savoy Tivoli

1434 Grant Avenue, between Union & Green Streets (362 7023). Bus 15, 30, 39, 41, 45. **Open** 5pm-2am Mon-Sat. **No credit cards. Map G2**

Nearly every twentysomething goes through a brief Savoy Tivoli phase when they first hit town: it's *the* place to pick up (or get picked up by) the (straight) person of your choice. A Continental-style, open-air café, it's also a great venue to drink imported beers and shoot pool. Not surprisingly, the Savoy is packed cheek-by-jowl on weekend nights.

Steps of Rome

348 Columbus Avenue, between Green & Vallejo Streets (397 0435). Bus 12, 15, 30, 41, 45, 83/ cable car Powell-Mason. **Open** 8am-2am Mon-Thur, Sun; 8am-3am Fri, Sat. **No credit cards. Map G2**

Steps of Rome's huge windows are usually open, providing excellent seats for people-watching. With closing at 3am on Friday and Saturday, the café is often filled with party-goers staving off the next day's hangover, or making a pit stop before heading South of Market to an after-hours club. Ideal for a caffeine break and a quick bite of dessert.

SoMa & South Park

Brainwash

1122 Folsom Street, between Seventh & Eighth Streets (café 861 3663/laundry 431 9274). Bus 12, 27, 42. **Open** 7.30am-11pm Mon-Thur, Sun; 7.30am-midnight Fri, Sat. **Credit** AmEx, MC, V. **Map G5**

The city's original launderette-cum-café is by now an institution. Its simple menu ranges from soups, salads and burgers to sandwiches and specials, with beer, wine and coffee served in a funky and friendly environment. The addition of a performance schedule only adds to the sense that Brainwash is equal parts SoMa industrial Laundromat with post-apocalyptic amusement park.

Caffé Centro

102 South Park, between Bryant & Brannan, Second & Third Streets (882 1500). Bus 15, 30, 42, 45, 76. **Open** 7.30am-7pm Mon-Fri; 9am-4pm Sat. **Credit** (min $10) AmEx, MC, V. **Map H/J4**

Given the ceaseless stream of young business-people in its neighbourhood, this South Park café could easily stint on food and service and still stay in business. But it hasn't, continuing to serve gratifying soups, fresh salads and interesting sandwiches to the yuppies who slave near South Park. Large windows open onto the park itself and the addition of nearby shops makes Centro even more of a destination.

Caffè Museo

In SFMOMA, 151 Third Street, between Mission & Howard Streets (357 4500). Bus 9, 12, 15, 30, 45, 76. **Open** 10am-6pm Mon-Wed, Fri-Sun; 10am-9pm Thur. **Credit** AmEx, MC, V. **Map H4**

You don't have to patronise the beautiful SFMOMA to enjoy this café, though it does make the day complete. Food is high-quality, slightly-higher-priced café fare, but the chic surroundings (and that stunning art book you've just bought at the gift shop next door) will distract your attention. Order from the counter and claim a window table. *See also chapter* **Museums & Galleries**.

CoffeeNet

744 Harrison Street, between Third & Fourth Streets (495 7447). Bus 30. **Open** 7am-6pm Mon-Fri; times vary Sat, Sun. **Credit** Disc, MC, V. **Map H4**

Purple surfaces, modern art and pleasant staff greet you upon entering this cybercafé from Lapu Lapu alley, off Harrison in the heart of SoMa. CoffeeNet has recently upgraded its internet service to include T1 lines and free e-mail accounts; you'll receive complimentary online time with a minimum food purchase.

The Mission & Noe Valley

See also page 125 **Ti Couz Crêperie** *and* **Farley's** *page 176* **Shops & Services**.

Atlas Café

3049 20th Street, at Alabama Street (648 1047). Bus 27. **Open** 7am-10pm Mon-Sat; 8am-8pm Sun. **No credit cards. Castro/Mission Map Z1**

You won't find the Atlas without looking, and its customers like it that way. Their favourite Mission haunt is untouched by yuppiness, coloured instead with the comfy funk that defines the neighbourhood at its best. A daily list of grilled sandwiches and fresh soups and salads is chalked on the wall; order yours and grab a sunny seat in the patio at the back. Inside, walls are filled with monthly art displays; a hand-picked rack of magazines are for sale. Perfect.

Chloe's Café

1399 Church Street, at 26th Street (648 4116). Muni Metro J. **Open** 8am-3pm Mon-Fri; 8am-4pm Sat, Sun. **No credit cards.**

Long known only to Noe Valley residents, Chloe's serves great brunch on Saturdays and Sundays and is always packed. The three outdoor tables remain the most popular, but inside is a friendly hubbub of community and great food.

Martha & Brothers Coffee Company

3868 24th Street, at Sanchez Street (641 4433). Muni Metro J/bus 24, 48. **Open** 5.30am-8pm Mon-Sat; 7am-7pm Sun. **Credit** MC, V. **Map F6**

There's a new chain of cafés in town: the oddly-named Martha & Brothers, who have opened a half-dozen venues, primarily in south-city locations. They're clean, friendly establishments, with a limited menu of pastries and snacks and have pleasant, competent staff. Seek them out and remember: friends don't let friends drink at Starbucks.

Branches: 2800 California Street (931 2281); 1548 Church Street (648 1166); 745 Cortland Avenue (642 7585); 2475 Mission Street (824 7717).

Radio Valencia

1199 Valencia Street, at 23rd Street (826 1199). Bus 14, 26, 49. **Open** 5pm-midnight Mon, Tue; noon-midnight Wed-Sun. **Credit** MC, V. **Castro/Mission Map Y2**

Recently re-opened following a collision with a San Francisco fire truck, Radio Valencia remains a Mission district favourite. Named after the quirky playlist that pumps from its speakers (a superb mix of world, jazz and other divergent genres), it's a great place to linger over a cup of coffee and enjoy a healthy, light menu. Chipper staff and a diverse clientele are additional plusses.

Civic Center, the Haight-Ashbury & the Castro

See also page 142 **Kate's Kitchen** *and page 143* **Miss Millie's**.

Café Flore

2298 Market Street, at Noe Street (621 8579). Muni Metro F, K, L, M/bus 24, 35, 37. **Open** 7am-11.30pm Mon-Thur, Sun; 7.30am-midnight Fri, Sat. **No credit cards. Map E6**

What can be said about Flore except that it's the perfect San Francisco café? A big, funky room and a wrap-around outdoor patio mean you'll always find a free table, where you can enjoy a limited menu and some of the finest people-watching in the city. It's as gay as the day is long, of course, but its central location and constant eye candy make it second to none. Food is limited to desserts and basic sandwiches, but the coffee and hospitality are first-rate. *See also p199* **Gay & Lesbian San Francisco**.

Grind Café

783 Haight Street, at Scott Street (864 0955). Bus 6, 7, 66, 71. **Open** 7am-10pm daily. **No credit cards. Map E5**

Casual but classic, the Grind is populated with chic and ratty denizens of the lower Haight, who are as likely to be spending the morning leafing through Sartre as they are to be sweating off a hangover. The café's open-air patio hosts smokers and dog lovers. Don't miss the vegetable-packed omelettes and tall stacks of pancakes.

Jammin' Java

701 Cole Street, at Waller Street (668 5282). Muni Metro N/bus 6, 7, 37, 43, 66, 71. **Open** 7am-11pm daily. **No credit cards. Map C6**

Located a block off Haight Street, this popular (if slightly worn) café offers a respite from the noisier locals in the neighbourhood, its comfortable décor a mix of grungy and groovy. There are poetry readings, assorted newspapers and want ads on the bulletin board. Quiet during the day, it's still packed at night. **Branch:** 1398 Judah Street, at Ninth Avenue (566 5282).

Saigon Sandwich Café

560 Larkin Street, at Eddy Street (474 5698). Bus 19, 31. **Open** 7am-4.45pm daily. **No credit cards. Map F4**

This friendly café caters to library patrons and local law students who populate the area north of Civic Center. The speciality is a baguette filled with five-spice chicken or roast pork and topped with a sweet-and-sour sauce of exotic chillis and cilantro.

Pacific Heights & the Western Addition

See also page 142 **Ella's** *and page 143* **Mel's Drive-in.**

Café Abir

1300 Fulton Street, at Divisadero Street (567 7654). Bus 5, 24. **Open** 6am-12.30am daily. **No credit cards. Map D5**

Abir continues to grow and now consists of a large café, organic grocery store, coffee roastery and international newsstand. Choose from freshly-made sandwiches, deli salads and mountains of bagels, and complete your meal with a latte and a copy of *The Times* (London or New York). Friendly staff and well-chosen house music make for a great atmosphere.

Caffè Proust

1801 McAllister Street, at Baker Street (345 9560). Bus 5. **Brunch served** 9am-3pm Sat, Sun. **Lunch served** 11am-4pm Mon-Fri. **Dinner served** 5-10pm Mon-Fri. **Credit** MC, V. **Map D5**

Truly a remembrance of things past, this new café in the heart of the Western Addition is filled with comfy couches, a long bar and menus for breakfast, lunch and dinner. Service is kind and relaxed and the food – simple pastas, sandwiches and an occasional roast chicken – not bad. In this era of corporate cafés, it's nice to see an anachronism like the Proust.

Food Inc Trattoria

2800 California Street, at Divisadero Street (928 3728). Bus 1, 4, 24. **Open** 9am-9pm Mon-Sat. **Credit** AmEx, MC, V. **Map D3/4**

This deli-with-a-few-seats remains an outpost for top-quality food at the edge of Pacific Heights. A 'neo BLT' is composed of bacon, mixed greens and tomato on toasted onion focaccia; a 'salad caprese' of sliced tomatoes, fresh mozzarella and basil leaves. Join the nannies and double-parked urbanites in the queue, then carry your lunch to nearby Alta Plaza park.

The Marina & Cow Hollow

See also page 142 **Doidge's Kitchen.**

Bisou Café

3001 Webster Street, at Filbert Street (441 7790). Bus 22, 41, 45. **Open** 7am-3am daily. **No credit cards. Map E2**

Tucked inside a residential area just a block from Union Street, French-flavoured Bisou is a quiet, classy café with marble-topped tables, comfy chairs and a brief menu of pastries, sandwiches and bagels. A few tables of outdoor seating allow you to take advantage of Cow Hollow's perpetually pleasant weather.

The Grove

2250 Chestnut Street, at Avila Street (474 4843). Bus 28, 30, 43, 76. **Open** 7am-11pm Mon, Tue, Sun; 7am-midnight Wed-Sat. **Credit** MC, V. **Map D2**

The Grove could pass for a fraternity house filled with sweatshirt-sporting alumni, but the corner café is the most happening spot in the Marina. Apart from coffee, beer, wine and comfort entrées such as chicken pot pie or lasagna, the restaurant also provides gaming tables for its patrons. It's so popular that a recent 90-minute limit has been imposed on occupying tables: an SF first.

Sunset

Daily Dose

401 Irving Street, at 4th Avenue (564 5074). Muni Metro N/Bus 6, 66, 43. **Open** 7am-11pm daily. **No credit cards. Map B6**

This sunny spot perched at the edge of the Sunset serves a full array of coffees, in addition to freshly-made wraps, beer, wine and sandwiches. It's a zoo in the morning, when UCSF interns jockey for their morning joe; catch it in late morning or mid-afternoon for a little peace and quiet.

Java Beach Cafe

1396 La Playa Boulevard, at Judah Street (665 5282). Muni Metro N/bus 18. **Open** 6am-10pm Mon-Fri; 7am-10pm Sat, Sun. **No credit cards.**

Java Beach is a hangout for surfers, cyclists and passers-by on their way to the oceanfront. With a basic sandwich, soup and pastry menu, it's both funky, civilised and – because of its wetsuit-wearing clientele and its view of the Pacific – unlike most other cafés in San Francisco.

Bars

Hip haunts, yuppie pubs, classy lounges or noisy sports bars – the city that invented the cocktail has them covered.

Tirelessly working to maintain its reputation as a cosmopolitan city, San Francisco beckons with an impressive repertoire of watering holes. These fall into several rough categories: pubs and brewpubs which feature a wide range of beers on tap and generally a limited menu; upscale dives, which gain points among the locals for character and longevity, though their ambience is often more important than the service, drinks or food; the omnipresent sports bars cater to the football, baseball or basketball fan (some San Franciscans would consider it sacrilege to miss a 49ers game); finally, a select group of historical treasures harken back to San Francisco's more decadent era and are often attached to a fine restaurant.

The Mission district has recently become ground zero for hot new bars (*see page 152* **Hipper than thou**). Cheap food parlours and easy access by public transport have made the area popular with hip and on-the-move young San Franciscans who have begun to bar hop the length of Valencia and Mission Streets each night.

Some nightclubs, such as **111 Minna** in SoMa and **Liquid** in the Mission (*see page 217* **Nightlife**), have thriving bar scenes as well as packed dance floors; there are yet more watering holes listed in the **Gay & Lesbian San Francisco** chapter. It's also worth noting that many of the places listed in the **Restaurants & Cafés** chapter have a bar area where you can drink a cocktail before or after your meal.

Around Union Square

Garden Court

Sheraton Palace Hotel, 2 New Montgomery Street, at Market Street (512 1111). BART Montgomery Street/Muni Metro F, J, K, L, M, N/bus 2, 3, 4, 5, 31, 66, 71. **Open** 11.30am-12.45am Mon-Fri; 10.30am-12.45am Sat, Sun. **Credit** AmEx, DC, MC, V. **Map H3**

The other Art Deco bar that gives the **Redwood Room** (*see below*) a run for its money, the Garden Court, in the Sheraton Palace Hotel, was built after the 1906 earthquake. It's a living testament to post-Gold Rush prosperity with its glass-domed roof and dozens of crystal chandeliers.

Red Room

827 Sutter Street, between Jones & Leavenworth Streets (346 7666). Bus 2, 3, 4, 27. **Open** 5pm-2am daily. **Credit** MC, V. **Map G3**

A local favourite, the Red Room has a prohibitively long queue on most nights to prove it. Everything inside the bar is red – the lighting, the décor, the walls – and looks swanky in a horror-flick sort of way. You can expect lots of attitude from the bartenders and a clientele who are trying to out-cool each other. Sip your $10 martini and dig the beautiful people.

Redwood Room

The Clift Hotel, 495 Geary Street, at Taylor Street (775 4700). Bus 27, 38. **Open** 10am-midnight Mon-Thur, Sun; 10am-1am Fri, Sat. **Credit** AmEx, DC, Disc, JCB, MC, V. **Map G4**

While others may emulate old-school class, this lounge is the genuine article: a high-ceilinged 1930s Art Deco hotel lounge with city atmosphere and the scent of a long and colourful history. True to its moniker, the room's mantelpieces are carved from a single piece of redwood, the mascot of Northern Californian flora. Aside from some classic jazz played on the grand piano, you won't have to compete with much other noise to enjoy a quiet conversation here.

Don't miss

Bubble Lounge
For caviar and champagne. *See p148.*

Club Deluxe
Rockabilly style in the heart of the Haight. *See p151.*

Orbit Room
Amid the Mods and their Vespas. *See p151.*

Red Room
Crimson hues and a cool crowd. *See below.*

The Tonga Room
The underground bar with its own indoor rainshowers. *See p148.*

Top of the Mark
Get a bird's eye view with martini in hand. *See p148.*

Toronado
For the Bay Area's most diverse beer list. *See p154.*

Tonga Room

950 Mason Street, at California Street (772 5278). Bus 1/cable car California. **Open** 5pm-midnight Mon-Thur, Sun; 6pm-1am Fri, Sat. **Credit** AmEx, Disc, MC, V. **Map G3**

This cheeky Polynesian bar in the basement of the historic Fairmont Hotel comes complete with happy hour dim sum, waitresses in sarongs and huge glasses of blended booze. The real attraction, however, is the house musicians performing off-key covers while afloat a raft on the Tonga's indoor 'lake'. Add to this periodic man-made thunderstorms that interrupt the music and you've found a kitsch (and touristy) venue.

Top of the Mark

Mark Hopkins Hotel, 1 Nob Hill, between California & Mason Streets (392 3434). Cable car Mason-Powell or California. **Open** 3pm-12.30am Mon-Sat; 4.30pm-12.30am Sun. **Admission** *after 8.30pm* $6 Mon-Thur, Sun; $10 Fri, Sat. **Credit** AmEx, DC, Disc, JCB, MC, V. **Map G3**

This exclusive bar was the first rooftop cocktail lounge to offer a panoramic view of the city when it opened in 1939. At the top of Nob Hill, one of San Francisco's wealthiest neighbourhoods, Top of the Mark is still considered exclusive. If you can part with $6 to get in after 8.30pm, it's definitely worth a visit for the extravagant view.

Civic Center & the Tenderloin

Backflip

601 Eddy Street, at Larkin Street (771 3547). Bus 19, 31. **Open** 5pm-2am Tue-Sun. **Credit** AmEx, MC, V. **Map F4**

Crazy, sexy and blue, the décor at Backflip is by Fun Display designers Craig Walters and Charles Doll, who were also the sartorial minds behind the **Red Room** (*see p147*). One wall shimmers with blue lighting, creating the illusion of sunshine reflecting from the surface above; a faux window is actually a wall of water. Down the hall from the main room and the round bar sit rows of cabanas and a strip of mirrors that lead to a dining room, where tapas and appetisers are served. At the back is a lounge room covered in white shag carpeting. With a setting this cool, who cares if the drinks aren't quite strong enough?

Bohemia

1624 California Street, at Polk Street (474 6968). Bus 1, 19, 42, 47/cable car California. **Open** 2pm-2am daily. **Credit** AmEx, MC, V. **Map F3**

Although the living-room vibe you get from the couches and fireplace might seem to signal a relaxed atmosphere, twentysomethings with an appetite for loud music dominate here. The young Hollywood set spend hours playing pool and gyrating to alt-rock sounds. Winona Ryder has been spotted dancing with her friends from Green Day.

Hayes & Vine

377 Hayes Street, between Franklin & Gough Streets (626 5301). Bus 21, 42, 47, 49. **Open** 5pm-midnight Mon-Thur; 5pm-1am Fri, Sat; 4-10pm Sun. **Credit** MC, V. **Map F5**

This classy room caters to symphony patrons as well as the well-heeled merchants and shoppers in Hayes Valley – lesbian, gay, straight or otherwise. Enjoy a glass of wine or champagne from a lengthy list (500 available by the bottle, 21 by the glass) and complement it with pâté, cheeses, caviar or biscotti.

Place Pigalle

520 Hayes Street, between Laguna & Octavia Streets (552 2671). Bus 21. **Open** 4pm-2am Thur-Sat; 4pm-midnight Mon-Wed, Sun. **Credit** AmEx, MC, V. **Map F5**

How very San Franciscan to pair an upmarket wine bar with thrift store couches and a trip hop DJ, and have the casual cool populace fighting to get in. Handsome bartenders with tribal tattoos decant Cabernet Sauvignon and taste-test Sancerre to guarantee you the most palatable sip south of the Napa Valley. Don't miss the monthly-changing art gallery at the back.

North Beach & Russian Hill

Bix

56 Gold Street, between Montgomery & Sansome Streets (433 6300). Bus 15, 30, 41. **Open** 11.30am-1am Mon-Fri; 5.30pm-2am Sat; 6-11pm Sun. **Credit** AmEx, DC, Disc, MC, V. **Map H2**

Proposing marriage? Celebrating a business deal? With its three-storey ceilings, secretive locale on Gold Street and stunning supper-club menu, Bix is the kind of place where James Bond would take one of his double-agent lady friends for more than just a little information. The clubby joint combines the glamour of Harlem's 1930s Cotton Club and the splendour of a dining room on a first-class cruise liner. A jazz pianist and singer in an evening gown provide the music for this martini-soaked cinematic fantasy.

Bubble Lounge

714 Montgomery Street, between Washington & Jackson Streets (434 4204). Bus 15, 30, 41. **Open** 4.30pm-2am Mon-Sat. **Credit** MC, V. **Map H3**

After the market closes, stockbrokers and short-skirted executives tickle their noses with an incredible selection of sparkling wines, champagnes and spumantis. These are paired with pâtés, salads and caviars for a top-drawer taste of the Wall Street of the West. Dress is conservative, label-heavy and cut on the bias; credit cards with an open limit *de rigueur*.

Hi-Ball Lounge

473 Broadway, between Kearny & Montgomery Streets (397 9464). Bus 15, 30, 41, 83. **Open** 6.30pm-2am Mon, Sun; 6pm-2am Tue-Thur; 5pm-2am Fri; 8pm-2am Sat. **Credit** MC, V. **Map H3**

Heaven for swingers who give the phrase 'to cut a rug' new depth, the Hi-Ball Lounge is a born-again San Francisco legend stuck between strip joints. Hep cats and urban professionals pack the narrow bar and postage stamp-sized dancefloor, jittering and hopping until the wee small hours. Affordable dance lessons are held twice a week, phone for details. *See also chapter* **Nightlife**.

San Francisco Brewing Co

155 Columbus Avenue, at Pacific Avenue (434 3344). Bus 12, 15, 41, 83. **Open** 11.30am-1am Mon-Fri; noon-1.30am Sat, Sun. **Credit** AmEx, Disc, MC, V. **Map G2**

Housed in a gorgeous turn-of-the-century saloon (once the hub of Barbary Coast nightlife), this brewpub, at the south-eastern tip of North Beach, offers six draught home-brews and live music four nights a week. If you ask, staff will give you a tour of the brewery.

Website: www.sfbrewing.com

Spec's

12 Jack Kerouac Alley, at Broadway (421 4112). Bus 15, 30, 41, 83. **Open** 4.30pm-2am Mon-Fri; 5pm-2am Sat, Sun. **No credit cards. Map G2**

Spec's stands as the quintessential old-school San Francisco bar – smoky and noisy, packed with a variety of drinkers of all ages and consummately friendly employees. You'll hear live music at the weekends and witness an occasional heated discussion – political or literary – among friends, but you'll get the sense that Spec's will remain unchanged. From time to time, William Saroyan's San Francisco play *The Time of Your Life* gets staged here, and aptly so.

Tosca

242 Columbus Avenue, at Broadway (986 9651). Bus 15, 30, 41, 83. **Open** 5pm-1.45am daily. **No credit cards. Map G2**

San Francisco nightspots seldom boast a high concentration of celebrities (even when the celebs are in attendance, they generally get ignored). Tosca is the exception. Its old-fashioned, classy ambience regularly draws a star-studded crowd: Bono, Mayor Willie Brown Jr, Francis Ford Coppola, Tom Waits and Sam Shepard have all been spotted among Tosca's red vinyl booths and high brass lamps. It's one of the city's oldest bars.

SoMa

Café Mars

798 Brannan Street, at Seventh Street (621 6277). Bus 9, 27, 42. **Open** 11.30am-2am Mon-Fri; 6pm-2am Sat. **Credit** AmEx, MC, V. **Map H5**

A bit of a pick-up scene this – and while the pot-stickers are good, Mars isn't an overly popular bar in which to spend a whole evening. The hip hop tunes tend to be too loud for conversation and while the out-of-town contingent is minimal, the stylish set seems to be just passing through.

Caribbean Zone

55 Natoma Street, between First & Second Streets (541 9465). Bus 12, 15. **Open** 11.30am-10pm Mon-Fri; 5pm-2am Sat. **Credit** AmEx, MC, V. **Map H4**

The corrugated tin walls of this bar under the freeway make the Zone look like a dance hall in a Kingston shanty town; inside, the room has been decorated with an honest-to-goodness DC3 jet plane. Though it's all a little turbulent, the Carib serves decent drinks to a mix of down- and up-towners and usually employs a DJ to do a little spinning.

Gordon Biersch

2 Harrison Street, at Steuart Street & Embarcadero (243 8246). Bus, 1, 32, 41. **Open** 11.30am-11pm Mon, Tue, Sun; 11am-midnight Wed, Thur; 11.30am-1am Fri, Sat. **Credit** AmEx, DC, MC, V. **Map J3**

When it first opened, Gordon Biersch was all the rage with the downtown crowd, who crammed the minimalist brewpub after business hours in the hope of getting laid. The highly-charged atmosphere has died down a bit and that's a good thing. Now you can enjoy quality in-house beers, a

Booze, smoking & the law

All bars are subject to California's alcohol laws: you have to be over 21 to buy and consume the stuff (take ID even if you look older) and it can be sold between the hours of 6am and 2am. Last orders vary between 1.15am and 1.30am and, technically, staff are obliged to confiscate unconsumed alcoholic drinks after 2am.

Smokers searching for a place to light up will be hard pressed in San Francisco. Citing the health of those employed in bars, taverns and restaurants, California state law has prohibited smoking in all – and we mean *all* – public indoor places. This means you'll find smokers lurking just outside the door, puffing away and usually feeling rather put out about it. Though some proprietors and bartenders may look the other way, most comply with the new regulations. The only way to know for sure is to look for ashtrays or lit cigarettes. Be forewarned, however, that should the SFPD drop by, they'll fine the patrons as well as the venue.

delectable bar menu and an unimpeded view of the Bay without worrying about the marital status of the person next to you. Here's to conversation and a good hamburger.

Twenty Tank Brewery

316 11th Street, between Harrison & Folsom Streets (255 9455). Bus 9, 12, 42. **Open** 11.30am-1.30am daily. **Credit** AmEx, MC, V. **Map G5**

A noisy landmark among the wealth of nightlife options at 11th and Folsom (*see chapter* **Sightseeing**), Twenty Tank Brewery is the kind of place that feels like home after one visit. Stocked with a dozen good beers, it offers a decent jukebox, shuffleboard, big tables for large parties, a massive upstairs area, sandwiches, soups and table service during dinner hours. The vegetarian chilli is excellent and the home-brews are the best in town. A reliable choice for a good night out.

The Mission & Potrero Hill

See also page 152 **Hipper than thou.**

The Attic Club

3336 24th Street, at Mission Street (643 3376). BART 24th Street/bus 14, 49, 67. **Open** 5pm-2am Mon-Fri; 6.30pm-2am Sat, Sun. **Credit** MC, V. **Castro/Mission Map Y2**

The Attic's black walls and ceiling are decorated with cast-offs that usually end up in dark storage areas – an old tricycle, boxing gloves, a rocking horse. Locals come to wind down over a glass of wine or a pint of Anchor Steam beer. The presence of a mirror ball hints at the occasional wild night when local DJs spin a gamut of rockin' beats.

Lilo Lounge

1469 18th Street, at Connecticut Street (643 5678). Bus 22, 53. **Open** 5pm-2am daily. **Credit** MC, V. **Map H6**

Billed as a tropical oasis in hip Potrero Hill, this lively bar has a miniature Easter Island head watching over the proceedings – which can get ribald pretty quickly. Order the $18 Scorpion – a concoction designed for four drinkers or one brave soldier, which includes a 'volcano' of 151 rum – and you'll be hailing a cab sooner rather than later. Thai appetisers are served in the bar.

The Rite Spot

2099 Folsom Street, at 17th Street (552 6066). Bus 12, 22, 33, 53. **Open** 4pm-2am Mon-Thur; 2pm-2am Fri; 7pm-2am Sat; 6pm-midnight Sun. **No credit cards. Map G6**

The Rite Spot has a jazz pianist playing in the corner while locals throw back pints of Hefeweissen and assorted spirits. With swinging doors marking the entrance and jukes that range from old country and western to new wave, the place has a noirish feel on a foggy night. A humble setting made respectable by candlelight and white tablecloths, it's usually fairly quiet, except when Friday night happy hour fills the bar.

Skylark

3089 16th Street, at Valencia Street (621 9294). BART 16th Street/bus 22, 26, 53. **Open** 4pm-2am Fri; 6pm-2am Mon-Thur, Sat, Sun. **No credit cards. Map F6**

With low light and high class, the Skylark continues to bridge the gap between dance club and bar, with a DJ spinning most nights but little space to bust a move. Fedoras and poodle skirts have given way to fresh-pressed corduroys and urban stylings – all worn in a highly-conscious effort to relax fashionably.

Slow Club

2501 Mariposa Street, between Hampshire and York Streets (241 9390). Bus 9, 27, 33. **Open** 11am-3pm Mon; 11am-11pm Tue-Fri; 6pm-midnight Sat. **Credit** MC, V. **Castro/Mission Map Z1**

Located on the yup-and-coming border between the Mission district and Potrero Hill, this converted garage sports an industrial design – and plenty of venture capitalists and start-up CEOs who've recently moved into the neighbourhood. The Slow is known mostly for its great meals, but also serves up mean martinis, Margaritas and single-malt scotches at the back bar.

The Castro

For more bars in this area, *see chapter* **Gay & Lesbian San Francisco.**

Expansion Bar

2124 Market Street, at Church Street (863 4041). Muni Metro F, J, K, L, M/bus 22, 37. **Open** 10am-2am daily. **No credit cards. Map E6**

Just about the biggest 49er fans in the city own this no-frills saloon, a sports bar in the middle of a sports town. With TVs at each end of the room, it's a place for serious devotees. On Saturday nights, the young city dwellers who don't want to fight the crowds at swankier joints can find the elbow room to settle in for a few games of pool or pinball.

Lucky 13

2140 Market Street, at Church Street (487 1313). Muni Metro F, J, K, L, M/bus 22, 37. **Open** 4pm-2am Mon-Thur; 2pm-2am Fri-Sun. **No credit cards. Map E6**

The stereotype of the laid-back Californian is easily put to rest at Lucky 13, the city's number one punk and alternative bar. 'Umleitung' (detour) reads the arrow pointing to the entrance and once inside you're sure to find a gaggle of San Francisco bicycle messengers on a pitstop drinking pints of beer or cider. The dark décor is enhanced by Iggy Pop posters and a stellar jukebox which includes contributions from the Cure, the Ramones and the Sex Pistols, and adds to the bar's grotto aura. The tattooed and pierced patrons tend to be on the young and hip side.

Devotees are beating a path to the modish **Mecca**.

Martuni's

4 Valencia Street, at Market Street (241 0205). Muni Metro F, J, K, L, M/bus 26. **Open** 4pm-2am daily. **Credit** MC, V. **Map F5**

The back room is where it's really happening at this nouveau martini and piano bar. The piano player and his musical entourage keep the tipsy crowd swaying in their seats, while friendly, slightly harried waiters bearing trays of drinks weave through the crowd. What with the drag queens and single, middle-aged women, the tableau of humanity is straight out of a film – John Cassavetes would have loved it.

Mecca

2029 Market Street, at Duboce Avenue (621 7000). Muni Metro F, J, K, L, M, N/bus 22. **Open** 5pm-1.30am daily. **Credit** AmEx, DC, MC, V. **Map E/F6**

Armani's best customers hold holy congregation at Mecca. Inside frosted-glass front doors, the urban warehouse look is melded successfully with baroque red velvet and chiffon drapery. A floor-to-ceiling marble column in the centre of the bar is encircled with glass trays holding dozens of grappa bottles. If this is your first trip to Mecca, the lounge area is an excellent place to get used to the finery. Once you've tried one of the $6 'Stoli-tinis', you'll understand why everyone's face seems to gleam here.

Orbit Room

1900 Market Street, at Laguna Street (252 9525). Muni Metro F, J, K, L, M/bus 37. **Open** 7.30am-1am Mon-Thur, Sun; 7.30am-2am Fri, Sat. **No credit cards. Map F5**

With its hammered tin ceiling and cool fixtures, the Orbit Room feels timeless; a humming, friendly, neighbourhood hangout with a great jukebox and stoic, efficient bartenders. The Vespa set usually commands the outdoor tables, but there's plenty of room inside as well. If you don't fancy a martini, try a Lemon Drop – a lemon vodka and triple sec substitute served in a chilled, sugared glass. In the morning, when your hangover subsides, you can return for an excellent espresso and one of the selection of pastries and bagels served during the day.

The Haight

Club Deluxe

1511 Haight Street, at Ashbury Street (552 6949). Bus 6, 7, 33, 37, 43, 66, 71. **Open** 4pm-2am Mon-Fri; 3pm-2am Sat; 2pm-2am Sun. **No credit cards. Map D5/6**

Decked out with a deco motif, this classic retro bar hops, particularly at weekends, when the patrons are also dressed to the nines in sharp, vintage garb. The more relaxed weekdays find it a little less serious about style (although Club Deluxe is always serious about its martinis and Bloody Marys). On some nights, small combos perform on a tiny stage in the east room while swing dancers take over the dancefloor. On other nights, the spot-lit centre pedestal is occupied by the bar's owner, Jay, who does a turn as a 1930s-style crooner. Sit at a chrome stool looking on to Haight Street or belly up to the bar.

Hipper than thou

San Francisco is dripping in multimedia money, and the Mission district is no exception. The growing number of new chic bars in the area reflects the pace of local gentrification – nearly a dozen have opened in the past two years and more are on the way. As we went to press, the just-opened **26Mix** (*see page 218* **Nightlife**) was promising to be the chicest roost of them all. Many worry that the influx of white money will eventually squelch the Mission's spicy Latin character and turn it into another bland Marina district. But many of the new establishments have bumped out grim dives and their unsavoury patrons and, for the time being, have only resulted in making the humble Mission safer to roam at night.

Bar

2695 Mission Street, at 23rd Street (647 2300). BART 24th Street/bus 14, 26, 49. **Open** 10am-2am daily. **No credit cards. Castro/Mission Map Y2**

Bar is little more than its name implies – Noir Bar or Dark Bar might be better monikers. Except for a few hints of colour emanating from checkered floors, red pool table, back-lit bar and jukebox, Bar is basic black, the kind of venue to hit if you've got a hot date and need to ignite the libidinous engines. Bar's crowd is unpredictable: midday sees the craggy neighbourhood regulars; at around 8pm, hipsters start filling the booths and sliding quarters into the jukebox which plays everything from Elvis to the Brand New Heavies.

Beauty Bar San Francisco

2299 Mission Street, at 19th Street (285 0323). Bus 14, 49. **Open** 5pm-2am Mon-Fri; 7pm-2am Sat, Sun. **No credit cards. Castro/Mission Map Y1**

This tiny establishment, modelled after the Beauty Bar in New York, is packed with bric-à-brac salvaged from a Long Island hair salon. Most patrons come well-gussied – you'll see lots of leather and vinyl and even the odd boa from time to time. On some nights, a manicurist is on call for those in need of a little cuticle attention (for around $10). If a pink motif makes you think of Pepto-Bismol, take your business elsewhere.

Cha Cha Cha at Original McCarthy's

2327 Mission Street, between 19th & 20th Streets (648 0504). Bus 14, 26, 49. **Open** 5-11pm Mon-Thur, Sun; 5pm-midnight Fri, Sat. **Credit** MC, V. **Castro/Mission Map Y1**

Leave it to the owners of San Francisco's favourite tapas spot, **Cha Cha Cha** (*see chapter* **Restaurants & Cafés**), to transform a sagging Irish pub into the city's most atmospheric new watering hole. Garlic marinated mushrooms, fried potatoes with red-pepper aioli and other big, cheap tapas will lure you in, but the joint's atmosphere will hold you rapt. Prada-clad yuppies sit next to stevedores at the beautiful wooden bar and the red brick walls are decorated with black and white photos of old San Francisco.

Cosmos

2730 21st Street, at Bryant Street (282 9926). Bus 27. **Open** 4pm-2am daily. **No credit cards. Casto/Mission Map Z2**

Nothing good was happening on the corner of 21st and Bryant Street until owner Gus Murad opened Cosmos. Now, well-heeled patrons rolling out of **Gordon's** and **Blowfish Sushi** (*see chapter* **Restaurants & Cafés** for both) are only two blocks from an after-dinner refuge. The blend of patrons is Cosmos's trump card: half of them are talking Internet IPOs, sipping 7-and-7s (7-Up and Segram's Seven) and the other half are rubbing dimes together to afford their second beer. Once the music starts it's too noisy to talk, so if you can't dance, find a seat on one of the *Star Trek*-style bar stools and check out the lovely murals.

Hush Hush

496 14th Street, at Guerrero Street (241 9944). Muni Metro F. **Open** 6pm-2am Mon, Tue, Sun; 4pm-2am Wed-Sat. **No credit cards. Map F6**

In a way, Hush Hush's neighbour, a forbidding housing project, fits the motif of this moody lounge. Owner Kimberly Jordan wanted to create a place that felt illicit yet cosy and she's done it – right down to the flickering blue candles that send shadows skittering across the cement floor. Wool-capped kids huddle in the ostrich-skin booths, trading screenplay ideas while their laundry dries next door. There's a pool table and a jukebox filled with early jazz and blues, old country, exotica, lounge and cabaret. Try the White Russian made with soy milk.

The Liberties

998 Guerrero Street, at 22nd Street (282 6789). Bus 26, 48. **Open** 10am-2am daily. **Credit** AmEx, Disc, MC, V. **Castro/Mission Map Y2**

Mission denizens were still mourning the loss of Café Babar when the Liberties moved into Babar's old space recently. Would the new establishment be as neighbourly, as unpretentious? Almost. The Liberties is certainly more upmarket: everything shines – the brass on the bar, the new hardwood floors, the glass in the big new windows. The Irish undercurrent keeps the place real, with Uillean ballads on the soundtrack and Irish lads pulling

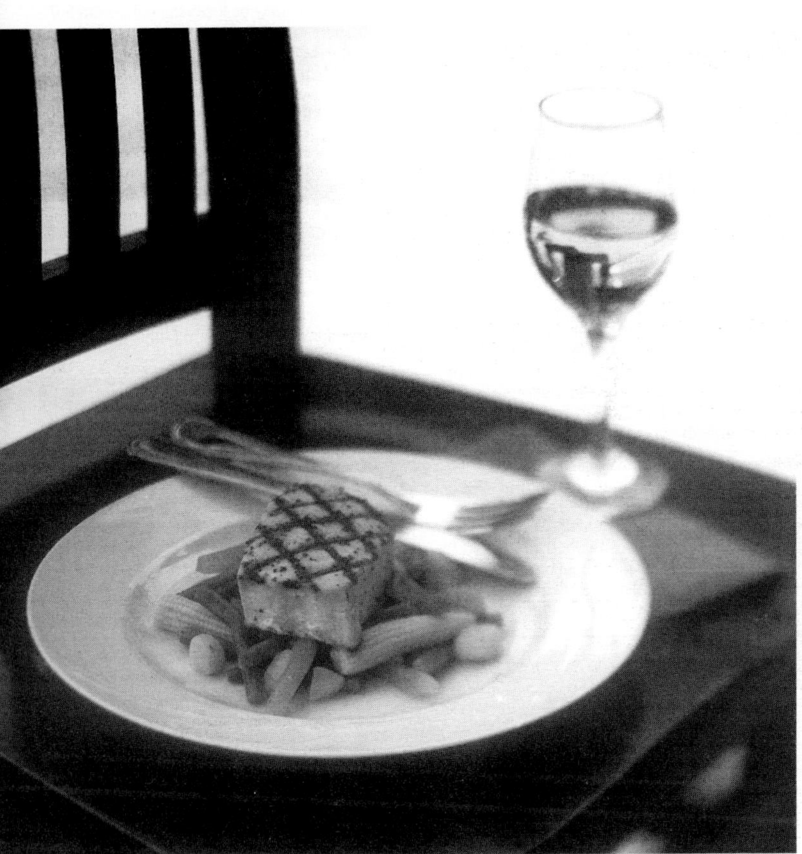

Taking **Liberties**: *Californian grub with a Celtic slant and Guinness on tap.*

Guinness behind the bar. The menu is a hybrid of classic Celtic and trendy Californian.

Sacrifice

800 South Van Ness Avenue, at 19th Street (641 0990). Bus 14, 33, 49. **Open** 5pm-2am daily. **Credit** AmEx, Disc, MC, V. **Castro/Mission Map Y1**

Even on the foggiest day, Sacrifice's bamboo furniture and bright murals can warm you up, as can its cheap-and-spicy New Orleans/Caribbean fare. If you beat the 11pm rush, you can grab a seat on the couch in the bamboo nook and watch silent movies on the TVs above the bar. Alternatively you can study the sphinx mural, Polynesian headdresses, 'Twister' pinball game or sparkling disco ball. When you run out of objects to look at, check out the twentysomethings who dress to fit the environs. A great spot.

Treat Street Cocktails

3050 24th Street, at Treat Avenue (824 5954). BART 24th Street/bus 12, 67. **Open** 4pm-2am daily. **No credit cards**. **Castro/Mission Map Z2**

If you've ever watched the TV programme *Northern Exposure*, you'll appreciate Treat Street's sense of style. Decorative effects include stuffed deer heads and fish trophies, a pool table and poor lighting – all quite an anomaly for a venue located on the most Hispanic corner of the city. Maybe that's why the erudite-looking thirtysomethings come here to escape: Treat Street is a fluke, a groovy hideaway several blocks from the Mission's gentrifying heart.

Molotov's

582 Haight Street, between Steiner & Fillmore Streets (558 8019). Bus 6, 7, 22, 66, 71.
Open noon-2am daily. **No credit cards**. **Map E5**
Molotov's clientele makes a conscious effort to eschew the trappings of the recently trendy and rapidly gentrifying neighbourhood of lower Haight Street. Peanuts are consumed by flannel shirted rockers in an atmosphere reminiscent of a roadside honky-tonk saloon. Beer and whisky remain the drinks with which to listen to the hard country/death rock music blasting from the speakers.

Noc Noc

557 Haight Street, between Fillmore & Steiner Streets (861 5811). Bus 6, 7, 22, 66, 71.
Open 5pm-2am daily. **Credit** MC, V. **Map E5**
An institution and worth a trip just to check out the décor. The bar, stools and pillowed alcoves carved out of synthetic rock turn drinkers into happy troglodytes inside a dark post-modern cave. The great deals on saki and pints at happy hour make this a favourite dive.

Persian Aub Zam Zam

1633 Haight Street, between Clayton & Belvedere Streets (861 2545). Bus 6, 7, 33, 37, 43, 66, 71.
Open times vary. **No credit cards**. **Map C6**
This place allegedly serves the best martini in the city, though few have had the honour of trying one: proprietor Bruno, a gentleman with a reputation for idiosyncratic treatment of his customers and for keeping completely random hours, tends to thwart your efforts. You may be lucky enough to catch the bar open, only to be faced with the greater challenge of charming the owner into bringing out a tray of his legendary libations. He's a purist: order vodka here (or beer) and you'll find yourself out on the street.

Toronado

547 Haight Street, at Fillmore Street (863 2276). Bus 6, 7, 22, 66, 71. **Open** 11.30am-2am daily.
No credit cards. **Map E5**
With perhaps the most diverse selection of beer in the Bay Area, ordering a pint at Toronado may seem a little daunting at first. Luckily, the barstaff are well versed in the language of hops and will readily recommend a brew suited to your taste. Best of all, you can sample each one before you buy it, so you never leave with a bad taste in your mouth.

The Marina & Pacific Heights

Balboa Café

3199 Fillmore Street, at Greenwich Street (921 3944). Bus 22, 43. **Open** 11.30am-2am daily.
Credit AmEx, MC, V. **Map E2**
We never thought we'd recommend it, but the city's most famous pick-up (and original 1930s fern) bar is back on the list. Why? A recent renovation and new ownership have resurrected the Balboa's classic style, from the dark-panelled walls to the bathtub-sized urinal in the men's room. The bar clientele is

Out of town

If you're heading out of the city, there are some great bars to while away a few hours. It's no surprise that most of the nightlife to the east of San Francisco revolves around the University of California at Berkeley. Two favourite student hangouts in the East Bay are **Blake's** (*see page 221* **Nightlife**) and **Jupiter** (2181 Shattuck Avenue, Berkeley; 1-510 843 8277). One of the hippest record stores in Berkeley, Mod Lang, holds occasional appearances by rock musicians at Jupiter, and Berkeley band Papa's Culture plays weekly gigs. Also worth the trip over the Bay Bridge are the **Pyramid Brewery & Alehouse** (901 Gilman Street, Berkeley; 1-510 528 9880) and the **Bison Brewery** (2598 Telegraph Avenue, Berkeley; 1-510 841 7734) both of which offer tours, dining and free samples of their best suds. Bison also has live music several nights a week.

North of the Golden Gate Bridge, the family-friendly **Marin Brewing Company** (1809 Larkspur Landing, Larkspur; 461 4677), set inside Larkspur's ultra-civilised shopping centre, has burgers, pizza, veggie food and a patio – and the beers win medals by the bucketful. In nearby Mill Valley, **Sweetwater** (153 Throckmorton Avenue, Mill Valley; 388 2820) is the quintessential Californian hangout, with six microbrews and a full cocktail bar. Marin County is home to many well-known rock stars and the club has developed a reputation as the venue for 'secret' shows, by everyone from Pearl Jam to Bob Weir's band Rat Dog Revue.

If you're heading south from the city down Highway 1 (SR 1), stop in at the **Moss Beach Distillery** (Beachway, at Ocean Boulevard; 728 5595), an old, renovated Victorian in the town of Moss Beach, overlooking the Pacific Ocean seven miles north of Half Moon Bay. Most Bay Area residents have heard of the Distillery because of its resident ghosts: the TV show *Unsolved Mysteries* reported that at least one, perhaps three, apparitions live here and employees will confirm it. If you get spooked, take a walk in the nearby Marine Reserve to bring you back to earth.

Toronado: *a beer for every punter. Or is it the other way around? See page 154.*

still the same – obnoxious yuppies trying desperately to get laid – but the drinks are strong, the kitchen good and the history long. Go on a week night.

Harry's on Fillmore

2020 Fillmore Street, between Pine & California Streets (921 1000). Bus 1, 3, 22. **Open** 3.30pm-2am daily. **Credit** AmEx, MC, V. **Map E3**

Local socialite Harry Denton opened this bar years ago as his fledgling pub; the place became hugely popular and catapulted the ex-bartender into legendary status. It features a gorgeous walnut bar and live music several nights a week. The crowd is a mix of Pacific Heights locals, yuppies and regulars. *See also* **Harry Denton's Starlite Room** *in chapter* **Nightlife**.

Horseshoe Tavern

2024 Chestnut Street, at Fillmore Street (346 1430). Bus 22, 30. **Open** 10am-2am daily. **No credit cards. Map E2**

More of a neighbourhood hangout than a roadside attraction, the Tavern is a friendly locals' bar for Marina residents with a penchant for pool and a strong taste for sports. It shows recent sporting events on cable TV.

Richmond & Sunset

Cliff House

1090 Point Lobos Avenue, at the Great Highway (386 3330). Bus 18, 38. **Open** 11am-2am daily. **Credit** AmEx, MC, V.

Once strictly a tourist hangout with weak drinks, the Cliff House has gone a long way recently in wooing back some local business. A fistful of good beers on tap and a menu of single-malt scotches can be consumed in a slightly-beleaguered, high-windowed lounge overlooking the restless sea. Service is patchy – the waitresses don't expect to see many of the out-of-towners again – but the overall ambience is comfortable. Future plans to restore the building may close the bar temporarily, but can only improve its conditions in the long run.

Pig and Whistle

2801 Geary Boulevard, at Wood Street (885 4779). Bus 38, 43. **Open** 11.30am-2am daily. **Credit** MC, V. **Map C4**

San Francisco's Irish community is concentrated in various areas of the city, but most visibly in the inner Richmond, where a passel of pubs fill with Celts and their friends. The Pig and Whistle is the cosiest of the neighbourhood's bars, with dart boards, a pool table and a generally good sense of camaraderie; eccentrically, it even has a cricket team. There's good food too – shepherds' pie, 'ploughman's platter' and bangers and mash.

Trad'r Sam's

6150 Geary Boulevard, at 26th Avenue (221 0773). Bus 29, 38. **Open** 10am-2am daily. **No credit cards.**

A San Francisco favourite since 1939, this unabashedly traditional tiki bar serves the kind of cocktails that can only be described as dangerous. Planter's Punch, Mai Tais, Singapore Slings – there's a guaranteed hangover lurking beneath the cheesy umbrellas spinning in Sam's drinks. At the weekend, the place fills with undergraduates bearing fake IDs, but during the week it's a quiet, friendly place to meet old friends or new ones.

Shops & Services

Thrilling ways to get separated from your hard-earned cash.

Union Square *is ground zero for department stores and temples of fashion.*

While San Francisco may not be the über shopping mecca that is New York or Los Angeles, many consumers prefer its less hysterical size and pace – and are pleasantly surprised by the many objects of desire that beckon from its charming streets.

From serious designer names to funky threads that won't break the bank or collectibles with real character (that paint-by-numbers Annunciation you've been searching for) – it can all be found in spades. And because real life in San Francisco takes place in its puzzle of intersecting neighbourhoods (like nation states, each bearing a unique flavour, character and even ethnicity), your quest for goods has the happy result of guiding you into the very heart and soul of the city. And finally: though San Francisco is endowed with all the requisite chain- and department stores, our advice is to head off the beaten path to score the cool stuff you can't find back home. Isn't that why you came here after all?

SHOPPING AREAS

Some shoppers never make it out of **Union Square**, a downtown galaxy of department stores and chains as well as the gods and goddesses of fashion (Gucci, Armani, Chanel, Jil Sander). This is also the place to head in case of a make-up crisis, as premium brands are sold only in department stores and that wondrous temple of beauty, **Sephora** (*see page 177*). Nestled in and around the more recognisable venues are some destination clothing boutiques with character.

From Union Square, a short stroll up Grant Avenue and through the arching pagoda takes you into another world. Not just a tourist magnet but a thriving community, the streets of **Chinatown** are thronged with locals on their daily expeditions to the overflowing vegetable markets, fish shops and herbal apothecaries. A haven for knick-knacks, porcelain, paper lanterns, embroidered silk jackets and other types of chinoiserie, here too are restaurants and dim sum houses that cater to locals and visitors.

Keep walking along Grant Avenue and you'll end up in the Italo-American neighbourhood of **North Beach**, ground zero for the West Coast Beat movement of the 1960s and home to the city's best European cafés and Italian groceries (great for impromptu picnics in nearby Washington Square). Now a fashionably quirky shopping destination, Upper Grant has evolved into a paradise regained for hipsters with a few dollars to drop (*see page 170* **San Francisco's Nolita**), while on Columbus Avenue the legendary **City Lights** bookshop (*see page 162*) draws serious readers, poets and dreamers.

Across the city to the south is the sunny **Mission** district, where there's a new or antiquarian bookshop and second-hand furniture store on almost every block, not to mention a plethora of late-night taquerias and burrito joints as befits its Mexican-American populace. A reflection of the Mission's changing face is the burgeoning number of more upmarket eateries and boutiques. Valencia, Mission and 16th Streets are also packed with the city's cooler clubs and bars, many of which feature live music and local DJs (while quietly ignoring the city's strict anti-smoking ordinance).

Light years away from the Mission is the squeaky clean **Marina** district, where the young and beautiful roam in pursuit of their *après*-work-out, decaff, non-fat lattes. Union and Chestnut Streets offer myriad retail opportunities, albeit with a sanitised sense of adventure. Running off Union Street up and over a sizable hill, Fillmore Street in **Pacific Heights** (sometimes dubbed Pacific Whites), has managed to retain more of its neighbourhood feeling and offers a grab bag of shops filled with clothing, housewares and vintage threads, as well as an arts movie theatre and good, old-fashioned bookshop. Continuing down Fillmore Street leads you to the **Japan Center**, a sort of covered mall housing Japanese-language bookshops, sushi bars, noodle joints, antique and houseware shops and the **Kabuki Springs & Spa** Japanese bath house – an ancient antidote for shopper's fatigue (*see page 177*).

Continuing south, **Hayes Valley**, a scant three blocks of Hayes Street running between Laguna Street and the Civic Center, is a magnet for the pierced-and-tattooed crowd, although rising property prices may have taken some of the shine off its original alternative lustre. Still, trolling the street yields up treasures as diverse as Miu Miu mules (**Gimme Shoes**, *page 169*), a fabulously rusted finial (**Zonal**, *page 159*) and antique watches (**Zeitgeist**, *page 178*) – all interspersed with cafés to slake your shopping-induced thirst. Stroll down Gough to Market Street and you'll find funky antique stores in droves, then cross Market to Brady Street, a tiny alley with even more eye-opening curiosity shops.

More than 30 years after its heyday, **Haight Street** pays homage to its hippie past while courting a newer, more well-heeled following. Second-hand clothing stores, record shops and piercing- and tattoo parlours sit cheek-by-jowl with recherché clothing stores, along the street that ends at Golden Gate Park. And the **Castro** district, with rainbow flags wafting in the breeze, is the epicentre of gay pride – with shops on both Market and Castro Streets catering to the youngish and trendy.

TAX & DUTY

Most shops accept traveller's cheques, but don't forget that local sales tax (currently 8.5 per cent) will be added to all purchases. You can avoid paying this if you live out of state and arrange for the shop to ship your purchase; or you can arrange shipment yourself via the US mail or a courier service (*see chapter* **Directory**). If you are taking goods out of the country, remember that you will be liable for duty and tax on goods worth more than a certain amount (£145 in the UK).

Department stores

All the following shops are located in the Union Square area.

Gumps

135 Post Street, between Grant Avenue & Kearny Street (984 9439). BART Montgomery Street/ Muni Metro F, J, K, L, M, N/bus 2, 3, 4, 15, 30, 45. **Open** 10am-6pm Mon-Sat. **Credit** AmEx, DC, MC, $TC, V. **Map H3**

Presided over by a large Golden Buddha, this is where old moneyed-San Franciscans shop for wedding presents and precious baubles – including oriental wares, jade, antiques and pearls, pearls, pearls.

Macy's

170 O'Farrell Street, at Union Square (397 3333). BART Montgomery Street/Muni Metro F, J, K, L, M, N/bus 2, 3, 4, 38, 45/cable car Powell-Mason or Powell-Hyde. **Open** 10am-8pm Mon-Sat; 11am-7pm Sun. **Credit** AmEx, JCB, MC, TC, V. **Map G3**

Recently renovated, this mother of all department stores (actually three stores, including a home furnishings outpost on Market Street) offers miles and miles of aisles and goods at all price points in an ambience mostly devoid of charm or personal service.

Neiman Marcus

150 Stockton Street, at Geary Street (362 3900). Muni Metro F, J, K, L, M, N/bus 2, 3, 4, 38, 45, 76/cable car Powell-Mason or Powell-Hyde. **Open** 10am-7pm Mon-Wed, Fri, Sat; 10am-8pm Thur; noon-6pm Sun. **Credit** AmEx, $TC. **Map G3/4**

Designer names and labels abound (from Prada to Kate Spade), with a well-edited selection and a somewhat rarefied atmosphere. The cosmetics department stocks many of the newer make-up artist lines.

Nordstrom

San Francisco Shopping Center, 865 Market Street, at Fifth Street (243 8500). BART Powell Street/Muni Metro F, J, K, L, M, N/bus 6, 7, 27, 31, 66, 71/cable car Powell-Mason or Powell-Hyde. **Open** 9.30am-9pm Mon-Sat; 10am-7pm Sun. **Credit** AmEx, MC, $TC, V. **Map G4**

Known for offering exemplary customer service, Nordstrom's five-floor attractions include a shoe department the size of the Ritz and live piano music.

Saks Fifth Avenue

384 Post Street, at Union Square (986 4300). Muni Metro F, J, K, L, M, N/bus 2, 3, 3, 38, 45, 76/cable car Powell-Mason or Powell-Hyde. **Open** 10am-7pm Mon-Wed, Sat; 10am-8pm Thur, Fri; noon-6pm Sun. **Credit** AmEx, Disc, MC, V. **Map G3**

The San Francisco branch of this venerable chain gets better and better. Second-floor designers include Dries Von Notten and Ann Demeulemeester and many newer names (ask for the ever-charming Scott to assist). Two floors up are more accessible (and affordable) creators such as Katyoni Adeli, Helmut Lang and Miu Miu. While service is generally warm, the men's store exudes a touch more attitude.

Shopping centres

The Cannery

2801 Leavenworth Street, between Beach & Jefferson Streets (771 3112). Bus 19, 30, 32, 42/cable car Powell-Hyde or Powell-Mason. **Open** *summer* 10am-6pm Mon-Wed; 10am-8.30pm Thur-Sat; 11am-6pm Sun; *winter* 10am-6pm Mon-Sat; 11am-6pm Sun. **Map F1**

Formerly the site of the Del Monte fruit-canning factory, the upper levels here are a warren of uninspiring stores, with more of the same to be found at The Anchorage across the street.

Crocker Galleria

50 Post Street, at Kearny Street (393 1505). BART Montgomery Street/Muni Metro F, J, K, L, M, N/bus 2, 4, 5, 15, 30, 38/cable car Powell-Mason. **Open** 10am-6pm Mon-Sat. **Map H3**

In this open-ended arcade, the outlets of European and American designers (such as Ralph Lauren) mix with individually owned shops, cafés and restaurants a couple of blocks off Union Square.

Embarcadero Center

Sacramento Street, between Battery & Drumm Streets (772 0550). BART Embarcadero/Muni Metro F, J, K, L, M/bus 1, 31, 41, 42. **Open** 7am-midnight daily. **Map H3**

The shopping areas housed on the first and second floors of four downtown office towers here represent most of the major chains – Banana Republic, Gap, The Limited, Pottery Barn, Williams Sonoma, Nine West, et al. There's also a well-stocked international newsstand and an excellent multi-screen cinema. *See also chapter* **Film**.

Fisherman's Wharf

Jefferson Street, between Hyde & Powell Streets (no phone). Bus 15, 30, 32, 39, 42/cable car Powell-Hyde or Powell-Mason. **Open** times vary. **Map F1**

With scarcely a fisherman – nor a local – in sight, the mystery is why so many tourists continue to flock here. Don't they sell T-shirts back home?

Ghirardelli Square

900 North Point Street, at Beach, Larkin & Polk Streets (775 5500). Bus 19, 30, 32, 42/cable car Powell-Hyde. **Open** 10am-9pm Mon-Sat; 10am-6pm Sun. **Map F1/2**

At this home of the Ghirardelli chocolate factory, you can still watch the stuff being made and consume it as you wander through the mostly souvenir-themed shops.

Metreon

221 Fourth Street, at Mission Street (369 6000). BART Powell Street/Muni Metro F, J, K, L, M/bus 9, 14, 30, 45/cable car Powell-Mason or Powell-Hyde. **Open** 10am-8pm daily. **Map H4**

Sony's new $87 million sensory-overloaded addition to San Francisco's bursting downtown area includes the interactive Discovery Channel Store; Sony Style, a fetish shop for technophiles; the Hear Music CD store, a Microsoft store and a host of activities for kids. No less than 15 cinemas include a monolithic Sony IMAX® screen. An array of kiosks on the ground floor represents local merchants with a (techno) flair for the original. Though chock-full of digital gadgetry, it's all a bit overwhelming and represents, unfortunately, a sort of soulless benchmark for 21st-century consumerism. *See also chapter* **Film**.
Website: www.metreon.com

Pier 39

Beach Street & Embarcadero (705 5500). Bus 15, 32, 42/cable car Powell-Mason. **Open** *Sept-June* 10.30am-8.30pm daily; *July, Aug* 10.30am-10pm daily. **Map G1**

A tourist magnet with a handful of individually-owned stores and the added attractions of wonderful views and noisy (sometimes smelly) seals.

San Francisco Center

865 Market Street, at Fifth Street (495 5656). BART Powell Street/Muni Metro F, J, K, L, M, N/bus 6, 7, 27, 31, 66, 71/cable car Powell-Mason or Powell-Hyde. **Open** 9.30am-8pm Mon-Sat; 11am-6pm Sun. **Map G4**

Like lifeboats bobbing around the mother ship, a flotilla of mid-range chains loop around Nordstrom – including the Body Shop, J. Crew, Z-Gallerie, Ann Taylor and Express.

Stonestown Galleria

Winston Drive, at 19th Avenue (759 2626). Muni Metro M/bus 17, 18, 28, 29. **Open** 10am-9pm Mon-Sat; 11am-6pm Sun.

The city's most traditional-style mall is located in an outlying, fog-shrouded area where residents mostly shop for familiar brand names.

Old curiosity shops

An unabashedly arbitrary listing of favourite places to go hunting for oddities and objects of beauty and originality. Many of these shops mingle the old with the new and all have an original vision – making the browsing process surprising, unpredictable and an adventure in itself.

Bell'occio

8 Brady Street, at Market Street (864 4048). Muni Metro F, J, K, L, M, N/bus 6, 7, 8, 9, 47, 66, 71. **Open** 11am-5pm Tue-Sat. **Credit** AmEx, MC, V. **Map F5**

Located in a tiny alley off Market Street, this shop is stocked with the fruits of the owners' travels: perfumes (one based on Marie Antoinette's), antique linens from Alsace, silky face powders from Paris, seasonal specialty boxes (lumps of coal for Christmas, apples, oysters), and old French athletic prizes and ribbons in every conceivable pattern and colour.

Kitty Katty's

3804 17th Street, at Sanchez Street (864 6543). Muni Metro J/bus 33. **Open** 10am-6pm Sat. **Credit** MC, V. **Castro/Mission Map X1**

Bardot… Baguettes… Berets… *Breathless*… all are evoked at this hot pink shrine to Kitty Katty, a globe-trotting, Gitane-smoking 1960s beatnik *à la française*. Katty's motorcycle and her hot-rod lovin' mates are all lovingly drawn by proprietor/artist Flower Frankenstein, who emblazons T-shirts, stationery, surreal comic/colouring books and other limited-edition stuff with their likenesses.

Maison d'être

92 South Park Avenue, between Third Street & Center Place (357 1747). Bus 9, 30, 45. **Open** 11am-6pm Mon-Sat. **Credit** MC, V. **Map H/J4**

Rococo chandeliers dripping with coloured crystals provide eye-candy above, while gorgeous bottles of Italian ink, grapefruit-vanilla scented candles, old photographs, baroque mirrors and twirly wire picture frames hold court down below.

Nest

2300 Fillmore Street, at Clay Street (292 6199). Bus 22, 24, 83. **Open** 10.30am-6.30pm Mon-Sat; noon-6pm Sun. **Credit** AmEx, MC, V. **Map E3**

Nest sells gauzy Chinese lanterns in rose garden colours (that fold for packing), Shabby Chic bed linens, beaded lamps, reproduction tin motorcycle wind-up toys, Moroccan stemware, Mariage Frère tea pots – they all call your name.

Paxton Gate

1204 Stevenson Street, at Brady Street (255 5955). Muni Metro F, J, K, L, M, N/bus 6, 7, 8, 9, 47, 66, 71. **Open** 11am-6pm Tue-Sat; noon-5pm Sun. **Credit** AmEx, MC, V. **Map F5**

A cross between an entomologist's study and the home of an eccentric botanist, Paxton Gate is a source of treasures and oddities inspired by the garden and the natural sciences. You'll find dried and mounted exotic insects (such as a bird-eating tarantula), hand-forged gardening tools, antique and new watering cans, bird houses, old apothecary jars and flower arranging tools. The original shop on Stevenson Street is decorated with trompe l'oeil monkeys and parrots. At the larger space on Valencia, owner Sean Quigley has added furniture and a peaceful garden complete with pond.

Branch: 824 Valencia Street, at 20th Street (824 1872).

Zonal

568 Hayes Street, at Laguna Street (255 9307). Muni Metro F/bus 21. **Open** 11am-6pm daily. **Credit** AmEx, Disc, MC, $TC, V. **Map E/F5**

With the motto 'always repair, never restore', owner Russell Pritchard collects objects, architectural details, naturally distressed wood furniture and rust-kissed artifacts. A cleanly designed line of chairs and couches covered in comfortable, clubby leather (very reasonable and deliverable) and Bella Notte chenille and cotton linens, softly coloured with non-toxic dyes, complete the mix.

Branches: 2139 Polk Street, at Vallejo Street (563 2220); 1942 Fillmore Street, at Pine Street (255 9307).

Antiques & collectibles

For all its fascination with newness, San Francisco is relatively well-stocked with antique shops. In the streets surrounding the **Design Center** in Potrero Hill (Kansas, Henry Adams, 16th and Brannan), you'll find the upmarket places that cater to interior designers and decorators. **Butterfield and Butterfield** (220 San Bruno Avenue, at 16th Street; 861 7500) auctions off serious furniture, art, rugs, antiques, jewellery and wine, while nearby **Butterfield West** (164 Utah Street, at 15th; 861 7500) attracts a more eclectic crowd with lower-priced estate auctions of generally funkier goods. Several tony shops are clustered in the narrow lanes in the **Jackson Square Historical District** between North Beach and the Financial District, on Jackson, Washington, Sansome and Montgomery Streets (phone 296 8150 for the Jackson Square Art and Antique Dealers Association).

Many of the antique and novelty shops skirting the **Hayes Valley** intersection of Gough and Market Streets are a haven for the city's stylists and photographers, who find examples of every era and aesthetic utterance behind their doors. Our favourite haunts are those that bridge the maw between antique shops and garage sales – where you might find a vintage Schiaparelli perfume bottle one day, a 1960s Ducati poster the next. The following is a short-but-sweet list of a few such places; you'll discover many more if you explore the area on foot.

Beaver Brothers

1637 Market Street, at Franklin Street (863 4344). Muni Metro J, K, L, M, N/bus 6, 7, 26, 71. **Open** 10am-6pm Mon-Sat; noon-6pm Sun. **Credit** MC, $TC, V. **Map F5**

Offering 'junk for sale', this favourite spot for photo-stylists is a time capsule of the great (and not-so-great) eras of design, filled as it is with Art Deco telephones and mirrors, Louis XVI armoires, Depression-era glass and other bygone collectibles. *Website: www.beaverbrosprop.com*

Dishes Delmar

(By appointment only 558 8882).

Inside this Haight-Ashbury Victorian, Burt Tessler and his partner have assembled a pristine collection of the most-sought-after patterns of mid-20th- century American dishware: Fiesta, Harlequin, Lu-Ray and the like, as well as Manhattan glassware. Although visits are only by appointment, it is often possible to stop by the same day – the proprietors' enthusiasm and knowledge more than justifies the extra effort.

Great American Collective

1736 Lombard Street, between Octavia & Laguna Streets (922 2650). Bus 28, 30. **Open** 11am-6pm Mon-Sat; noon-6pm Sun. **Credit** AmEx, Disc, MC, V. **Map E2**

In a warehouse-sized space along the Lombard hotel strip, more than three dozen vendors offer Victoriana, 1960s mod and everything in between. Occasionally you'll even find the same item at two different booths – at wildly different prices.

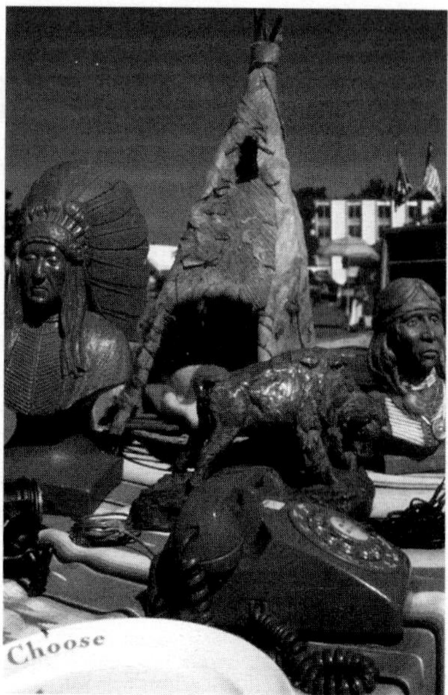

Treasure Island Flea Market. *See page 161.*

One-Eyed Jacks

1645 Market Street, at Gough Street (621 4390). Muni Metro F, J, K, L, M, N/bus 6, 7, 8, 9, 47, 66, 71. **Open** 11am-6pm Mon-Sat; noon-5pm Sun. **Credit** AmEx, Disc, MC, V. **Map F5**

Sporting Americana with a country-and-western twang, Jack's is just the place to round up a set of dishes decorated with steer heads and branding motifs and a pair of spurs to accompany them.

Therapy

545 Valencia Street, between 16th & 17th Streets (861 6213). BART 16th Street/bus 14, 26, 53. **Open** noon-7pm daily. **Credit** AmEx, MC, V. **Castro/Mission Map Y1**

Furniture, fashion, fun gifts and a flea market feeling make Therapy and its branch prime browsing spots in the Mission. A mix of old and new, where kidney shaped tables rest on fluffy Flucatti rugs and vintage tin occasionally gives way to Tiffany.

Branch: Therapy Too 1051 Valencia Street, between 21st & 22nd Streets (648 7565).

Flea markets

Alemany Flea Market

100 Alemany Street, at intersection of US 101 & I-280 (647 2043). Bus 9, 14, 23. **Open** 8am-3pm Sun. **Credit** varies. **Castro/Mission Map Y1**

A favourite Sunday ritual is to roam this open-air flea in the fringes of Bernal Heights and then head for brunch in Bernal, Potrero Hill or the Mission with treasures (and a newspaper) in tow. Often a good selection of old photographs and magazines can be found among the mélange of world-weary goods. As with all such markets, early birds get the juiciest worms.

Treasure Island Flea Market

Treasure Island (255 1923). Bus 108 from Transbay Terminal (see chapter **Directory**). **Open** 6am-4pm Sun. **Credit** varies.

This upstart market is quickly finding its feet and starting to attract vendors from other fleas. With a covered space in the event of inclement weather, Treasure Island offers spectacular views of Bay and city along with a crazy quilt of handicrafts, collectibles and found objects.

Arts & crafts

The African Outlet

524 Octavia Street, between Hayes & Grove Streets (864 3576). Bus 21. **Open** 10am-7pm daily. **Credit** AmEx, MC, $TC, V. **Map F5**

You'll find brilliantly coloured textiles, exotic beads and jewellery, Kenyan masks and authentic African clothes for men, women and children.

Global Exchange Fair Trade Craft Center

4018 24th Street, between Noe & Castro Streets (648 8068). Bus 24, 48. **Open** 11am-7pm daily. **Credit** AmEx, MC, V. **Castro/Mission Map X2**

The Global Exchange sells imported crafts from Mexico, Guatemala, Haiti, Chile and Africa including weavings, jewellery, paintings, carvings, books, international CDs and children's gifts. All craftspeople represented are paid a fair rate for their labours and profits go to support a local crafts co-operative.

Japonesque

824 Montgomery Street, between Jackson & Pacific Streets (391 8860). Bus 12, 15, 41, 30, 83. **Open** 10.30am-5.30pm Tue-Fri; 11am-5pm Sat. **Credit** AmEx, MC, $TC, V. **Map H2/3**

The owner's frequent travels to Japan yield antique and contemporary pieces wrought from stone, wood, glass, ceramic and lacquer, in addition to paintings and sculpture. Unlike many of Japantown's mass-made goods, objects here are singular and precious.

Studio 24

2857 24th Street, at Bryant Street (826 8009). BART 24th Street/bus 24, 27. **Open** noon-6pm Wed-Sun. **Credit** AmEx, MC, $TC, V. **Castro/Mission Map Z2**

Part of the acclaimed **Galeria de la Raza** (*see chapter* **Museums & Galleries**), Studio 24 embraces everything from kitsch to crafts – with Latin American folk art and gifts as well as more serious works by contemporary artists.

Tibet Shop

4100 19th Street, at Castro Street (982 0326). Bus 24, 33, 35. **Open** 10am-6pm Mon-Sat; noon-5pm Sun. **Credit** AmEx, MC, $TC, V. **Castro/Mission Map X1**

Bells, incense, singing bowls, carved skulls, prayer beads, lapis lazuli, turquoise, silver, coral necklaces and the clothing and crafts of Tibet come together in a shop run by a disciple of the Dalai Lama.

A Touch of Asia

1784 Union Street, at Octavia Street (474 3115). Bus 41, 45. **Open** 11am-5.30pm daily. **Credit** AmEx, MC, V. **Map E3**

Come here for 19th- and 20th-century antiques from Korea and Japan, including moderately priced Kyoto tansu chests, vases and a panoply of Asian sculptures, prints and paintings.

Art supplies, stationery & postcards

Arch

407 Jackson Street, at Sansome Street (433 2724). Bus 42. **Open** 9am-6pm Mon-Fri; noon-5pm Sat. **Credit** AmEx, MC, $TC, V. **Map H2/3**

Specialising in drafting and architectural supplies, including an extensive model-making department, Arch also stocks interesting papers, acrylics, watercolours and a potpourri of off-the-wall gifts, candles and delicious bath potions.

Brown Bag

2000 Fillmore Street, at Pine Street (922 0390). Bus 3, 22. **Open** 10am-6pm Mon-Sat; noon-5.30pm Sun. **Credit** AmEx, MC, $TC, V. **Map E3**

Brown Bag represents is an old-fashioned general stationers', with a good vibe and wonderful selection of postcards and rubber stamps in the thick of the Fillmore.

Flax

1699 Market Street, at Valencia Street (552 2355). Muni Metro F, J, K, L, M, N/bus 6, 7, 26, 66, 71. **Open** 9.30am-6pm Mon-Sat. **Credit** AmEx, Disc, MC, $TC, V. **Map F5**

The premier source for art supplies, Flax offers a spellbinding range of stationery, pens, papers, inks, paints, brushes, wrapping paper and handmade specialty papers as well as portfolios. Offerings have grown to include unusual gifts with quirky appeal. The staff tend to be sullen, but you'll find whatever you want.

Kozo Art

1969 Union Street, at Buchanan Street (351 2114). Bus 41, 45. **Open** 11am-6pm Mon-Fri, Sun; 11am-7pm Sat. **Credit** AmEx, MC, $TC, V. **Map E2**

Kozo sells handmade paper wrought from the likes of bark, papyrus and birds' nests; hand silk-screened papers from Japan and Italy; and hand-bound photo albums and journals that share space with luscious wall-hangings and books of stationery. Kozo also offers custom bookbinding services.

Quantity Postcards

1441 Grant Avenue, at Vallejo Street (986 8866). Bus 15, 41. **Open** 11am-11pm daily. **Credit** Disc, MC, $TC, V. **Map G2**

A veritable postcard museum with a funhouse atmosphere, QPC's walls are crammed with new and vintage examples of the art: quaint Victorian flowery tributes, domestic scenes from the 1950s, old snapshots of San Francisco and tinted landscapes of faraway places. There's also a good selection of Frank Kozik's psychedelic music posters – and a real life earthquake machine.

Bookshops

San Francisco is a literary town, where every other waiter is a writer and reading groups proliferate like mushrooms after warm rain. Here, as elsewhere, independent bookshops are under threat from the behemoth chains – a good reason to head for one of the spots listed below. Serious antiquarian booksellers also abound: many of them are congregated near Union Square and in the Mission district. For newsagents, *see chapter* **Media**. *See also* **Authors incarnate** *in chapter* **Literary San Francisco**.

Acorn Books

1436 Polk Street, at California Street (563 1736). Bus 19/cable car California. **Open** 10.30am-8pm Mon-Sat; noon-7pm Sun. **Credit** MC, V. **Credit** AmEx, Disc, $TC. **Map F3**

With a large selection of fiction and non-fiction antiquarian books at prices generally higher than those found in the Mission district haunts, Acorn also offers a stellar collection of vintage science fiction magazines. For many, the real attraction is found in the drawers and drawers filled with old and recent postcards – from Kansas to Kathmandu.

Alexander Book Company

50 Second Street, between Market & Mission Streets (495 2992). BART Montgomery Street/Muni Metro F, J, K, L, M/bus 5, 6, 14, 38. **Open** 9am-6pm Mon-Fri. **Credit** AmEx, Disc, MC, V. **Map H3**

An old-fashioned, full-service independent bookshop in downtown San Francisco offering three floors of browsing fun and monthly lunchtime author's readings.

The Booksmith

1644 Haight Street, between Clayton & Cole Streets (863 8688). Bus 6, 7, 43, 66, 71. **Open** 10am-9pm Mon-Sat; 10am-6pm Sun. **Credit** AmEx, Disc, MC, $TC, V. **Map C6**

The Haight's best-stocked bookshop hosts many author's readings and events and stocks a decent selection of literary (and other) magazines.
Website: www.booksmith.com

Browser Books

2195 Fillmore Street, at Sacramento Street (567 8027). Bus 1, 3, 22. **Open** 10am-10pm Mon-Sat; 9am-10pm Sun. **Credit** MC, $TC, V. **Map E3**

The devoted staff, late hours and cosy armchairs make this a great place to linger during a foggy San Francisco day or after strolling along Fillmore Street.

City Lights

261 Columbus Avenue, between Broadway & Pacific Avenue (362 8193). Bus 12, 15, 41, 83. **Open** 10am-midnight daily. **Credit** AmEx, MC, $TC, V. **Map G2**

The legacy of anti-authoritarian and insurgent thinking lives on in this publishing company and bookshop founded by poet Lawrence Ferlinghetti in the days when the Beats ruled North Beach. The literature selection is especially strong, particularly European works in translation, and poetry. *See also chapter* **Literary San Francisco**.
Website: www.citylights.com

A Clean Well-Lighted Place for Books

Opera Plaza, 601 Van Ness Avenue, between Golden Gate Avenue & Turk Street (441 6670). Bus 42, 47, 49. **Open** 10am-11pm Mon-Thur, Sun; 10am-midnight Fri, Sat. **Credit** AmEx, MC, V. **Map F4**

Centrally located at Civic Center, this well-stocked, general interest bookshop hosts frequent and popular readings and author's events (recent appearances have been made by Will Self and David Foster Wallace) and offers employee recommendations that are often worth following up.

A Different Light

489 Castro Street, at 18th Street (431 0891). Muni Metro F, K, L, M/bus 8, 24, 33, 35. **Open** 10am-midnight daily. **Credit** AmEx, Disc, MC, V. **Castro/Mission Map XI**

Located in the heart of the Castro, A Different Light sells books for and about the gay community as well as gay, lesbian and transgender literature. Check the calendar of in-store events.

European Book Company

925 Larkin Street, at Geary Boulevard (474 0626). Bus 19, 38. **Open** 11am-6pm Mon-Fri; 10am-5pm Sat. **Credit** MC, V. **Map F4**

If your first language is French, German or Spanish, come to the European Book Company for literature, magazines, kids' books and dictionaries.

Get Lost Travel Book, Maps and Gear

1825 Market Street, at Guerrero Street (437 0529). Muni Metro F/bus 26. **Open** 10am-7pm Mon-Fri; 10am-6pm Sat; noon-5pm Sun. **Credit** AmEx, DC, MC, $TC, V. **Map F5**

The theme at this postage-stamp-sized shop is travel and there's a compelling assortment of hands-on guides and literature, plus maps, travel accessories, slide shows and readings.

Green Apple Books & Music

506 Clement Street, at Sixth Avenue (387 2272). Bus 2, 38. **Open** 9.30am-11pm Mon-Thur, Sun; 9.30am-midnight Fri, Sat. **Credit** MC, V. **Map B4**

A destination for bibliophiles from all over, this shop offers a staggering mix of new and second-hand titles. Nirvana for the dedicated browser who doesn't mind a bit of disarray.

Kayo Books

814 Post Street, between Hyde & Leavenworth Streets (749 0554). Bus 27, 38, 76. **Open** 11am-6pm Wed-Sun. **Credit** Disc, MC, $TC, V. **Map F/G4**

This emporium of pulp specialises in vintage paperbacks and dime store novels with fabulous cover art from the 1940s to the 1970s. Many rare and out-of-print books – from Ed Wood to Raymond Chandler – as well as delicious exploitation ephemera. With lots of titles in the $5 range, Kayo paperbacks make great, packable gifts for the folks back home.

Limelight Film & Theater Bookstore

1803 Market Street, at Octavia Street (864 2265). Muni Metro F/bus 26. **Open** 10am-6pm Mon; 10am-8pm Tue; 10am-6pm Wed-Sat; noon-5pm Sun. **Credit** MC, $TC, V. **Map F5**

As the name suggests, the shop is dedicated to the thespian arts.

Marcus Book Stores

1712 Fillmore Street, between Post & Sutter Streets (346 4222). Bus 2, 3, 4, 22. **Open** 10am-7pm Mon-Sat; noon-5pm Sun. **Credit** AmEx, MC, $TC, V. **Map E4**

Marcus specialises in books by African and African-American writers and on related topics.

Modern Times Bookstore

888 Valencia Street, between 19th & 20th Streets (282 9246). Bus 14, 26, 33. **Open** 10am-10pm Mon-Sat; 11am-6pm Sun. **Credit** AmEx, MC, V. **Castro/Mission Map Y1**

Originally a source of left-wing political tracts, Modern Times is now a community centre for the Mission district where political readings and forums take place amidst the good selection of new and second-hand literature, non-fiction books, alternative 'zines and journals.

Rand McNally Map and Travel Store

595 Market Street, at 2nd Street (777 3131). BART Montgomery Street/Metro Muni F, J, K, L, M, N/bus 6, 7, 9, 21, 31, 66, 71, 76. **Open** *summer* 9am-7pm Mon-Fri; *winter* 9am-6.30pm Mon-Fri; 10am-6.30pm Sat, Sun. **Credit** AmEx, Disc, MC, $TC, V. **Map H3**

Downtown San Francisco's source for international guidebooks, globes, folded and wall maps, and all kinds of travel accessories.

Richard Hilkert Bookseller

333 Hayes Street, between Franklin & Gough Streets (863 3339). Bus 21. **Open** 9am-5pm Mon-Fri; 11am-5pm Sat. **Credit** AmEx, MC, V. **Map F5**

A labour of love in this age of mega-chains, this Hayes Valley jewel of a shop is overseen by a literate eccentric who maintains a carefully culled selection of new and second-hand books on interior design and architecture as well as gems of fiction, *belles lettres*, travel and children's books.

SFMOMA Bookshop

151 Third Street, between Mission & Howard Streets (357 4035). BART Montgomery Street/Muni Metro F, J, K, L, M, N. **Open** 10am-6.30pm Mon, Tue, Fri-Sun; 11am-9.30pm Thur. **Credit** AmEx, MC, V. **Map H4**

Art and photography books, catalogues and monographs mix with a typical quirky museum assortment of cards, posters, videos, jewellery, and hyper-designed gifts.

Website: www.sfmoma.org

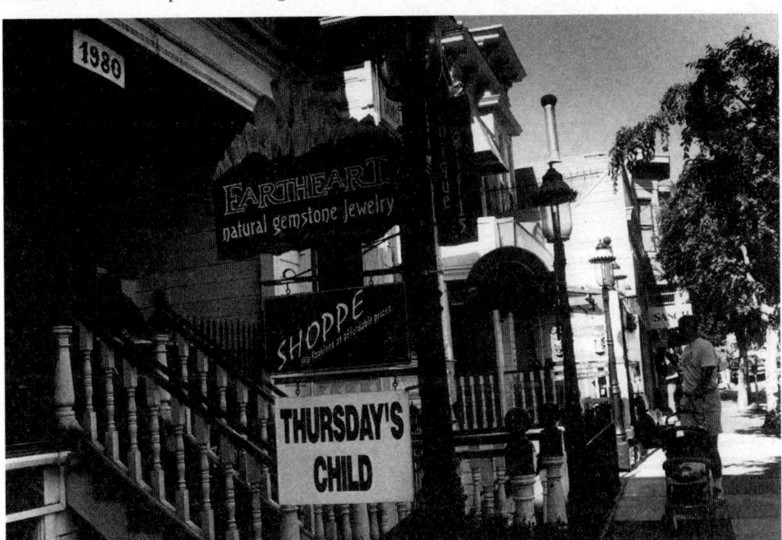

One of the city's many shopping meccas, **Union Street**.

San Francisco Mystery Bookstore

4175 24th Street, between Castro & Diamond Streets (282 7444). Bus 24, 35, 48. **Open** 11.30am-5.30pm Tue-Sun. **Credit** Disc, MC, V. **Mission/Castro Map X2**

With shelves stacked with mystery and detective fiction (in and out of print) and a large selection of Sherlockiana, this Noe Valley novelty is a mystery lover's tonic.

Sierra Club Bookstore

85 Second Street, at Mission Street (977 5600). BART Montgomery Street/Muni Metro F, J, K, L, M/bus 5, 6, 14, 38. **Open** 11am-5.30pm Mon-Fri. **Credit** MC, V. **Map H3**

The Sierra Club Bookstore is dedicated to books about the environment and ecological resources, and includes loads of maps for hiking trails and California wilderness areas.

The chains

For those that think that size is all that matters, there's a branch of **Borders Books & Music** at Union Square (*see chapter* **Literary San Francisco**) and a **Barnes & Nobel** outlet in Fisherman's Wharf (2552 Taylor Street; 292 6762).

Foreign-language bookshops

On Valencia Street, in the predominantly Latin-American Mission district, the following bookshops sell Spanish-language newspapers and *libros en Español*: **Dog Eared Books** (1173 Valencia Street; 282 1901), **Books On Wings** (La Casa de Libros, 973 Valencia; 285 1145) and **Modern Times Bookstore** (*see page 163*). The magnificent **Books on Japan** (1581 Webster Street in Japantown; 567 7625) stocks Japanese language publications. Italians can pick up the latest installment of *Diabolik* at **Cavalli Italian Bookstore** (1441 Stockton Street; 421 4219); and the **European Book Company** (925 Larkin Street; 474 0626) stocks various language publications from the Continent. *See also page 204* **Media**.

Cameras & electronics

The geographical proximity of Silicon Valley means that new computer technologies are often available in the Bay Area three or four months before they're seen in other parts of the world. What's more, laptop or notebook computers in the US often cost half European prices. Whatever you buy, make sure that your item will work in the country in which you want to use it. TVs in the US and Japan use the NTSC system while those in the UK and most of Europe use the PAL system; so American TVs, VCRs, camcorders, laser discs and videotapes will only work in the UK if you have a NTSC-compatible VCR. However, the American-made cartridge-based video games (such as Super Nintendo) are playable, provided you have a converter. Check that the equipment has a built-in voltage selector: transformers and voltage converters are available, but are bulky and fairly costly.

A word of warning about buying e-goods: many of the downtown stores that advertise cheap cameras and electronics are fly-by-night. If a deal seems too good to be true, it probably is. Most locals buy their consumer electronics at **Good Guys** (1400 Van Ness Avenue, at Bush Street; 775 9323) or **Circuit City** (1200 Van Ness Avenue, at Post Street; 441 1300). Both sell everything at guaranteed low prices, offer installation services and deliver larger items. *See page 157* for information on tax and duty.

Adolph Gasser

181 Second Street, between Mission & Howard Streets (495 3852). Bus 5, 6, 12, 38. **Open** 9am-6pm Mon-Sat. **Credit** AmEx, Disc, MC, V. **Map H4**

This justly-famous photographic shop has the largest inventory of photo and video equipment in Northern California. It stocks SLR cameras by Canon and Nikon, priced far cheaper than in the UK; all sorts of lenses; point-and-shoot cameras; and, according to one staff member, 'every kind of photographic doohickey you can imagine'.

Branch: 5733 Geary Boulevard, between 21st & 22nd Avenues (751 0145).

Discount Camera

33 Kearny Street, between Post & Market Streets (392 1100). BART Montgomery Street/Muni Metro F, J, K, L, M, N/bus 2, 3, 4, 6, 7, 8, 9, 15, 21, 31, 66, 71. **Open** 8.30am-6.30pm Mon-Sat; 9.30am-6pm Sun. **Credit** AmEx, Disc, JCB, MC, V. **Map H3**

Concierges at major downtown hotels direct their guests here in the hope that they'll avoid the unscrupulous tourist traps that lie in wait by the Powell Street cable car turnaround. Discount carries a full line of all major brands and stocks PAL system camcorders.

Website: www.discountcamera.com

Franklin Covey

50 California Street, at Davis Street (397 1776). BART Embarcadero/Muni Metro F, J, K, L, M, N/bus 2, 3, 4, 6, 7, 8, 9, 15, 21, 30, 31, 45, 66, 71. **Open** 9.30am-7pm Mon-Fri; 10am-5pm Sat. **Credit** AmEx, DC, Disc, MC, $TC, V. **Map H3**

If you want to take home a Palm Pilot (the *fin-de-siècle* Filofax) or accessorise or empower an existing one, this is the friendliest place for modems, cables, the Cross DigitalWriter combo stylus and ball-point pen – and carrying cases for schlepping it all around.

International Electronics

1161 Mission Street, between Seventh & Eighth Streets (626 6382/1-800 962 4715). BART Civic Center/Muni Metro F, J, K, L, M, N/bus 14, 19, 26. **Open** 10am-6pm Mon-Sat. **Credit** AmEx, Disc, MC, V. **Map G5**

IE sells Walkmans, portable CD players, mini-stereos that work in the UK and voltage converters and transformers for computers. Transformers range from $50 to $400. IE also specialises in kitchen appliances.

Computer repair

If your laptop suddenly freezes and can't be coaxed into recovery, help is just around the corner. As its name suggests, **MacAdam** (1062 Folsom Street; 863 6222) is a Macintosh-oriented store specialising in all things Apple. PC folks should head to **Computown** (710 Market Street, between Third and Fourth Streets; 956 8696), which offers on-site diagnosis and treatment of most major brands. Both stores are open seven days a week.

Duty-free

Duty-Free Shops (DFS)

88 Grant Street, at Geary Street (296 3620). Bus 9, 30, 38. **Open** 10am-7pm daily. **Credit** AmEx, Disc, DC, MC, $TC, V. **Map G3/4**

Cosmetics, perfume, clothing, liquor, tobacco, food and a small selection of cameras are on sale here. At the airport branch, you will have to show your airline ticket to the sales staff; at the downtown shop they will check your ticket and give you a shopping pass. Whatever you purchase will be waiting for you at the boarding gate of your return flight home.
Branch: San Francisco International Airport (1-650 827 8726).

Fabrics

Britex Fabrics

146 Geary Street, between Stockton Street & Grant Avenue (392 2910). Bus 30, 38, 45/cable car Powell-Mason or Powell-Hyde. **Open** 9.30am-6pm Mon-Wed, Sat; 9.30am-7pm Thur, Fri. **Credit** AmEx, MC, $TC, V. **Map G/H3**

With four overwhelming floors of fashion and home textiles and an awesome collection of buttons, Britex is best for those who know exactly what they want: service can range from crisp to cool.

Satin Moon

32 Clement Street, at Arguello Boulevard (668 1623). Bus 2, 33, 38. **Open** 11am-7pm Tue-Thur; 11am-6pm Fri, Sat. **Credit** MC, $TC, V. **Map C4**

Not the biggest but the best collection of fashion-forward fabrics. This shop is owned by seamstress sisters with taste and vision. Shimmery solids and passionate patterns come in silk, linen, cotton and velvet – even if you don't sew you'll want to leave with something.

Fashion

If it's the mega-chains with multiple doorways you're looking for – **Gap**, **Banana Republic**, **Old Navy** – you'll stumble across them almost anywhere you go, including the big shopping centres (*see page 158*). Check the phone book for a complete list of branches. Listed below are the places that sell threads you probably won't see on everybody else (and is khaki really the new black?).

Agnès B

33 Grant Avenue, at O'Farrell Street (722 9995). BART Powell Street or Montgomery Street/Muni Metro F, J, K, L, M, N/bus 6, 7, 9, 21, 31, 38, 66, 71. **Open** 11am-7pm Mon-Sat; noon-6pm Sun. **Credit** AmEx, MC, $TC, V. **Map H4**

Pronounced the French way by the cognoscenti, this downtown boutique bears mention for the relentlessly pretty pieces for women (little cropped cardigans in multiple colours, rose-patterned crisp cotton shirts that defy trendiness) and the upstairs boutique of stretchy, stripy tops for men.

Behind the Post Office

1510 Haight Street, at Ashbury Street (861 2507). Bus 6, 7, 43, 66, 71. **Open** 11am-7pm daily. **Credit** AmEx, Disc, DC, MC, $TC, V. **Map D5/6**

This cool little shop on Haight Street sells hip-hop gear galore – phat, baggy pants and tank tops in every colour.

Betsey Johnson

2031 Fillmore Street, between California & Pine Streets (567 2726). Bus 1, 2, 3, 4, 22. **Open** 11am-7pm Mon-Sat; noon-6pm Sun. **Credit** AmEx, MC, $TC, V. **Map E3**

When you've just got to have a fix of something fresh, girly or vampy, Betsey is always there for you. Slip dresses, stretchy velvets, feathered boas – all at digestible prices. And the shops' neo-bordello sex 'n' roses décor is simply delicious.
Branch: 160 Geary Street, between Stockton & Grant Streets (398 2516).

Dema

1038 Valencia Street, between 21st & 22nd Streets (206 0500). Bus 26. **Open** 11am-7pm Tue-Sat; 11am-5pm Sun. **Credit** MC, $TC, V. **Castro/Mission Map Y2**

Dema Grim is an unabashed mod and her clothing shows it, with geometric shapes, groovy prints and Audreyesque flair, and her Mission district boutique is all the buzz.

Diana Slavin

3 Claude Lane, at Bush Street (677 9939). Bus 2, 3, 4, 15, 30. **Open** 11am-6pm Tue-Fri; noon-5pm Sat. **Credit** AmEx, MC, $TC, V. **Map H3**

In this womenswear emporium, Diana Slavin designs and displays her trademark fashions: menswear-inspired clothing in subtle colours and rich fabrics. She also sells Cutler & Gross sunglasses and Robert Clergerie shoes.

Diesel

101 Post Street, at Kearny Street (982 7077). Muni Metro F, J, K, L, M, N/bus 2, 15, 30, 45. **Open** 10am-8pm Mon-Fri; 10am-7pm Sat; noon-6pm Sun. **Credit** AmEx, Disc, JCB, MC, $TC, V. **Map H3**

Three tragically hip floors of Italian street fashion,

with a zillion styles of jeans and cargoed *everything*. You know you've arrived when your sales assistant's name tag reads 'Denim Manager'.

Duchess

1429 Haight Street, between Masonic & Ashbury Streets (255 1214). Bus 6, 7, 37, 43, 66, 71. **Open** 11.30am-7pm daily. **Credit** MC, V. **Map D 5/6**
Pedro Olmo and Keri White resent being dubbed couturiers for the club kids; when you see their designs, you'll know why. Sweet frocks, rose-scattered shirts, wrap-around skirts that actually stay closed during a San Francisco zephyr – all at prices that won't break the bank.

MAC

Menswear *5 Claude Lane, off Bush Street, at Kearny Street (837 0615). Bus, 2, 3, 4, 15, 76.*
Womenswear *1543 Grant Street, at Union Street (837 1604). Bus 30, 39.* Both **Open** 11am-6pm Mon-Sat; noon-5pm Sun. **Credit** AmEx, MC, V. **Map H3**
At Modern Appealing Clothing, designer labels take a back seat to fit, fabric and fun. The men's store serves up everything from laid back to natty suits, with the best tie selection in the city (Paul Smith, Kenzo). You'll find wonderful vintage items from France and elsewhere for sale among the clothing. The women's store is the flagship of the Upper Grant Avenue retail renaissance (*see page 170* **San Francisco's Nolita**).

Martha Egan

1 Columbus Avenue, at Montgomery & Washington Streets (397 5451). Bus 15, 41, 42. **Open** 11am-6pm Tue-Sat. **Credit** AmEx, MC, £TC, V. **Map H3**
On the fringes of North Beach, Martha Egan designs contemporary women's clothes with vintage styling and retro-looking fabrics.

Métier

355 Sutter Street, between Stockton Street & Grant Avenue (989 5395). BART Montgomery Street/ Muni Metro F, J, K, L, M, N/bus 2, 3, 4, 30, 45, 76.
Open 10am-6pm Mon-Sat. **Credit** AmEx, MC, $TC, V.
Contemporary without being chilly, Shari Evans' store is a welcoming oasis in Union Square, reflecting the care with which she selects and displays her offerings. You'll covet the softest hand-knit sweaters from Souchi in shades of wisteria and tangerine; Katayone Adeli's mythic line of hip-chick separates; Anna Molinari's goddess-wear and separates by Paul & Joe and Trina Turk. Vintage and contemporary jewellery embraces all price points and there's an excellent selection of scarves and embroidered shawls as well as Il Bisonte bags in leather and nylon. Personal, gracious and friendly service is the norm.

Rolo

450 Castro Street, between Market & 18th Streets (626 7171). Muni Metro F/bus 8, 24, 33, 35, 37.
Open 10am-9pm Mon-Sat; 11am-7pm Sun. **Credit** AmEx, MC, Disc, DC, JCB, $TC, V. **Castro/Mission Map X1**
Each store in the Rolo armada caters to a slightly different group, but the common denominator is trendy and fashion forward. On Castro Street the selection is focused on T-shirts, jeans and men's shoes. Market Street has more flamboyant and edgy menswear. Howard Street stocks womenswear, sales goods and shoes. And downtown Stockton Street is the smorgasbord where they all come together.
Branches: 25 Stockton Street, between Ellis & O'Farrell Streets (989 7656); 2351 Market Street, between Castro & Noe Streets (431 4545); 1301 Howard Street, at 9th Street (861 1999).

Get your hip-chick separates at **Métier**.

Six Brady

6 Brady Street, at Market Street (626 6678). Muni Metro F/bus 26. **Open** 11am-6pm Tue, Wed; 11am-6.30pm Thur-Sat; noon-5pm Sun. **Credit** AmEx, MC, $TC, V. **Map F5**
Sporty separates and pretty little dresses hang on either side of this sunny shop. But the big draw are the sweet cashmere sweaters and piles of Michael Stars' wonderful, stretchy, wash-and-wear T-shirts in cotton candy pink, indigo and melon and interpreted in boat-neck, camisole and v-neck styles.

Susan

3685 Sacramento Street, between Locust & Spruce Streets (922 3685). Bus 1, 4. **Open** 10.30am-6.30pm Mon-Fri; 10.30am-6pm Sat, Sun. **Credit** AmEx, MC, $TC, V. **Map B3**
Where the ladies splurge on the big boys: Yohji Yamamoto, Comme des Garçons, Dolce & Gabbana,

Helmut Lang, Marni, Martin Margiela and Lacroix (…darling!), at stratospheric prices. Check out the **Grocery Store**, the sister shop down the street (3615 Sacramento; 928 3615), for re-entry to our solar system.

Urban Outfitters

80 Powell Street, at Market Street (989 1515). BART Powell Street/Muni Metro F, J, K, L, M, N/bus 5, 6, 7, 9, 21, 31, 66, 71/cable car Powell-Hyde or Powell-Mason. **Open** 10am-10pm Mon-Sat; 10.30am-9pm Sun. **Credit** AmEx, Disc, MC, V. **Map G4**

Where young and budget-minded boys and girls find the latest looks interpreted at very easy prices, from rave-wear to baggy cords, knee-scraping capris, baby Ts and fake fur jackets. There is also a bevy of expressive housewares for those setting up digs: lamps, candles, bedspreads, picture frames and pillows.

Villains

1672 Haight Street, between Clayton & Cole Streets (626 5939). Bus 7, 33, 37, 43. **Open** 11am-7pm daily. **Credit** AmEx, Disc, DC, JCB, MC, $TC, V. **Map C6**

Get outfitted from head to toe for the next X-Games: cropped pants, cargo pockets, space-age fabrics – and distracted staff. At **Villains Vault** across the street (1653 Haight Street; 864 7727) the look and prices are more yupscale.

Children's clothes

Kids Only

1608 Haight Street, at Clayton Street (552 5445). Bus 6, 7, 33, 37, 43, 66, 71. **Open** 10am-6pm Mon-Sat; 11am-5pm Sun. **Credit** AmEx, DC, Disc, JCB, MC, $TC, V. **Map C/D5/6**

Kids Only sells black clothing for baby goths, leopard-print blankets and hats, handmade grape and strawberry caps and tie-dyed duds for tiny Deadheads.

Mudpie

1694 Union Street, at Gough Street (771 9262). Bus 41, 45. **Open** 10am-6pm Mon-Sat; 11am-5pm Sun. **Credit** AmEx, MC, V. **Map E2**

An utterly charming shop for clothes and toys, unique handmade accessories and pricey gifts for privileged tots.

Peek-a-Boutique

1306 Castro Street, at 24th Street (641 6192). Bus 24, 48. **Open** 10.30am-6pm Mon-Sat; noon-5pm Sun. **Credit** MC, $TC, V. **Castro/Mission Map X2**

The place to come for second-hand kid's clothing.

Discount fashion

Esprit Factory Outlet

499 Illinois Street, at 16th Street (957 2540). Bus 15, 22, 48. **Open** 10am-8pm Mon-Fri; 10am-7pm Sat; 11am-5pm Sun. **Credit** AmEx, Disc, MC, $TC, V. **Map J6**

The apex of adolescent fashion at rock bottom prices – 30-70% off department store prices. For super bargains, head for the back.

Jeremy's

2 South Park, at Second Street (882 4929). Bus 15, 42, 80. **Open** 11am-7pm Mon-Fri; 11am-6pm Sat; 11am-5pm Sun. **Credit** AmEx, MC, V. **Map J4**

For off-price clothing with panache, fashionistas march to Jeremy's and forget the mostly desultory SoMa outlet stores. Labels? Prada, Jil Sander, Marc Jacobs, Richard Tyler, Sigerson Morrison, TSE, Chanel, Armani, Alberta Ferretti, Missoni, Margiela. Show up during one of the seasonal sales and you've hit the jackpot.

Loehmann's

222 Sutter Street, at Kearny Street (982 3215). BART Montgomery Street/Muni Metro F, J, K, L, M, N/bus 2, 3, 4, 15, 76. **Open** 9am-8pm Mon-Fri; 9.30am-8pm Sat; 11am-6pm Sun. **Credit** MC, V. **Map H3**

Women who would rather be caught *in flagrante* than pay full retail for cut-price designer fashions shop at Loehmann's, a New York institution now found around the country.

Vintage & second-hand clothes

The most fertile hunting grounds for previously worn clothing are on Haight Street, Fillmore Street or in the Mission. Some shops specialise in contemporary looks – pieces cast-off by clothes-horses and sold after a season for a song. Others stock up on vintage looks suitable for evening wear and reflective of eras gone past (Deco, 1940s, or Swing). When on Haight Street, also check out **Aardvark's Odd Ark** (1501 Haight Street, at Ashbury Street; 621 3141) to find diamonds in the rough; **Martini Men's Shop** (1773 Haight Street, between Shrader & Cole Streets; 668 3746) for vintage men's suits, shoes and hats and custom-made zoot suits; and **La Rosa** (1711 Haight Street, between Shrader & Cole Streets; 668 3744) which has fine clothing and estate pieces suitable for proms, parties, fancy dress and weddings. Wherever you look, patience is a virtue: many an unassuming and wrinkled shirt has turned out to be Romeo Gigli gold. Go to it!

American Rag

1305 Van Ness Avenue, between Bush & Sutter Streets (474 5214). Bus 47, 49, 76. **Open** 10am-9pm Mon-Sat; noon-7pm Sun. **Credit** AmEx, MC, $TC, V. **Map F3/4**

The ultra-hip mix of new and recycled clothing is intriguing, with a seemingly endless supply of beaded cardigans, argyle-patterned pullovers and previously-worn jeans with holes in all the right places. The once-supreme shoe selection has taken a tumble, however.

Buffalo Exchange

1555 Haight Street, between Clayton & Ashbury Streets (431 7733). Bus 6, 7, 33, 43, 66, 71. **Open** 11am-7pm Mon-Sat; noon-7pm Sun. **Credit** AmEx, MC, V. **Map D6**

Alla Prima. *See page 169.*

Don't know what to do with that Christmas sweater that's been taking up space in your wardrobe? Trade it in for cash or clothing at this well-known second-hand recycler, one of the city's best thrifts and consistently cheap.

Captain Jacks

866 Valencia Street, between 19th & 20th Streets (648 1065). Bus 26, 33. **Open** 11am-7pm daily. **Credit** AmEx, MC, $TC, V. **Castro/Mission Map Y1**

Where to find greats – and mistakes – from the swinging 1960s and 1970s, including kelly green double-knits.

Clothes Contact

473 Valencia Street, at 16th Street (621 3212). BART 16th Street/bus 22, 26. **Open** 11am-7pm Mon-Sat; noon-7pm Sun. **Credit** Disc, MC, $TC, V. **Castro/Mission Map Y1**

Clothing by the pound – for $8 as we went to press – which is hard to beat unless you're in the market for a lead suit. The fake furs come in at quite a bargain.

Crossroads Trading Company

2231 Market Street, between Sanchez & Noe Streets (626 8989). Muni Metro K, L, M/bus 24, 33, 35, 37. **Open** 11am-7pm Mon-Sat; noon-6pm Sun. **Credit** MC, $TC, V. **Map E6**

The Market Street branch of this favourite local trading shop houses mostly 1980s wear, while the Fillmore Street shop is better for jeans, dresses and classic vintage wear. As we went to press, a new branch had just opened on Haight Street.

Branches: 1901 Fillmore Street, at Bush Street (775 8885); 1519 Haight Street, at Clayton Street (355 0554).

GoodByes

Menswear *3464 Sacramento Street, at Laurel Street (346 6388).* Womenswear *3483 Sacramento Street, at Locust Street (674 0151).* Both *Bus 1, 4.*

Open 10am-6pm Mon-Sat; 10am-8pm Thur; 11am-5pm Sun. **Credit** Disc, MC, $TC, V.

Map C4

Light years from the Haight/Mission scene in pristine Laurel Heights, GoodByes is a consignment shop where you might stumble across a barely-worn Gaultier sweater, last season's Prada coat or a little Chanel number some socialite got tired of. Reap the rewards.

Held Over

1543 Haight Street, at Ashbury Street (864 0818). Bus 6, 7, 33, 43, 71. **Open** 11am-7pm daily. **Credit** Disc, MC, £TC, V. **Map D5/6**

Held Over is as famous for its window displays as for its previously enjoyed threads.

Schauplatz

791 Valencia Street, between 18th & 19th Streets (864 5665). Bus 26, 33. **Open** noon-7pm Tue-Sun. **Credit** DC, MC, $TC, V. **Castro/Mission Map Y1**

German for 'happening place', Schauplatz's offerings are a little more curated here than at other Mission haunts, which makes it easier to spot the Italian glasses frames and intricately beaded Moroccan mules.

Wasteland

1660 Haight Street, at Belvedere Street (863 3150). Bus 6, 7, 43, 66, 71. **Open** 11am-7pm daily. **Credit** AmEx, JCB, MC, $TC, V. **Map C6**

Wasteland sells trendy and sometimes outrageous second-hand clothing-with-a-history. It's possibly the most popular second-hand clothier in the city, with a good supply of vintage costume jewellery and fancy gowns.

Fashion accessories

Leather goods & luggage

Edward's Luggage

3 Embarcadero Center, between Davis & Drumm Streets (981 7047). BART Embarcadero/bus 1, 31, 41, 80, 82/cable car California. **Open** 10am-7pm Mon-Fri; 10am-6pm Sat; noon-5pm Sun. **Credit** AmEx, Disc, MC, $TC, V. **Map H3**

Edward's offers everything you need for travelling, including the full range of easy-to-roll, ultra-sturdy Tumi luggage. It's also an excellent source for leather desk planners.

Johnson Leather Corporation
1833 Polk Street, between Jackson & Washington Streets (775 7392). Bus 12, 27, 30, 42, 47, 49, 83. **Open** 10.30am-6.30pm Mon-Sat; noon-5pm Sun. **Credit** AmEx, DC, Disc, JCB, MC, $TC, V. **Map F3**
A favourite of local motorcyclists, Johnson's is both a factory and a shop, which means good buys on lambskin unisex jackets and alterations done while you wait. You can also find custom-made jackets at laughably low prices.

Kenneth Cole
166 Grant Avenue, between Post & Geary Streets (981 2653). BART Powell/cable car Powell-Mason or Powell-Hyde/bus 2, 3, 4, 38. **Open** 10am-8pm Mon-Sat; noon-6pm Sat. **Credit** AmEx, JCB, MC, V. **Map G/H3**
The socially conscious shoe tsar sells a whole lot more than shoes at his Grant Avenue flagship store. There's also a nicely culled selection of men's and women's leather outerwear, briefcases, wallets, agendas and purses at very decent prices.
Branches: 865 Market Street, at Grant Avenue (227 4536); 2078 Union Street, between Webster & Buchanan Streets (346 2161).

True
1472 Haight Street, at Masonic Avenue (626 2882). Bus 6, 7, 43, 66, 71. **Open** 11am-7pm daily. **Credit** Disc, MC, $TC, V. **Map D5**
Top-notch messenger bags in every conceivable shape and style are sold here.

Lingerie

When it comes to dressing close to the skin, why not eschew the tacky slingers of Lycra and indulge in the tastier fluff?

Alla Prima
1420 Grant Avenue, at Green Street (397 4077). Bus 15, 30, 45. **Open** 11am-7pm Mon-Sat; noon-5pm Sun. **Credit** AmEx, MC, $TC, V. **Map G2**
From ribbed and slinky chemises by local designers such as Underwriters, to La Perla, the undisputed underwear doyenne, Alla Prima stocks it all, in sizes ranging from gamine to well-rounded.

Chadwick's of London
2068 Chestnut Street, at Steiner Street (775 3423). Bus 28, 30, 43, 76. **Open** 11am-7pm Mon-Fri; 10.30am-6pm Sat; noon-6pm Sun. **Credit** AmEx, Disc, MC, $TC, V. **Map D2**
Chock full of feminine mystique, with lacy teddies, stretchy Only Hearts gowns and so much more.

Scarves & shawls

N Peal
110 Geary Street, at Grant Avenue (421 2713). BART Montgomery Street/Muni Metro F, J, K, L, M, N/bus 2, 3, 4, 30, 38. **Open** 10am-6pm Mon-Sat. **Credit** AmEx, DC, JCB, MC, $TC, V. **Map G/H3**
Pashmina is precious cashmere, combed from the neck of the Capra Hircus goat in the remote regions of India and Tibet. If thoughts of a pashmina stole have been burning a hole in your soul, there is no better place to succumb to the craving than N Peal, who offer it in dozens of saturated colours. Whisper-light, warm and packable, it's the ideal wrap for San Francisco's capricious weather.

Shoes

Gimme Shoes
416 Hayes Street, at Gough Street (864 0691). Bus 21. **Open** 11am-6.30pm Mon-Sat; 11am-6pm Sun. **Credit** AmEx, Disc, MC, V, $TC. **Map F5**
Now that there are three branches of Gimme Shoes – one downtown, one on Fillmore Street and the original in Hayes Valley – there's almost no need to look anywhere else. Owner Jerry Warwick creams off the best of each season and offers coveted looks at most price points. The best include Ann Demeulemeester, Dirk Bikkemberg, Martin Margiela and Miu Miu. There's also a cache of hard-to-find trainers by Adidas.
Branches 2358 Fillmore Street, at Washington Street (441 3040); 50 Grant Avenue, at O'Farrell & Geary Streets (434 9242).

Coveted footwear at **Gimme Shoes**.

Nine West

250 Stockton Street, at Post Street (772 1924). Bus 2, 3, 4, 30, 45. **Open** 10am-7pm Mon-Sat; 11am-6pm Sun. **Credit** AmEx, Disc, JCB, MC, $TC, V. **Map G3**

Nine West sells knock-offs of current hot trends at a fraction of the price – thrilling to some, anathema to others.

Shoe Biz

1446 Haight Street, between Ashbury & Masonic Streets (864 0990). Bus 6, 7, 33, 37, 43, 66, 77. **Open** 11am-7pm daily. **Credit** AmEx, MC, $TC, V. **Map D5**

Towering, pointy, chunky, clunky – the emphasis is on trendy and fun for men and women. Pumas are stocked at Shoe Biz II, a block away.

Branch: **Shoe Biz II** 1553 Haight Street, between Ashbury & Clayton Streets (861 3933).

Shoe repair

Anthony's Shoe Service

30 Geary Street, between Grant Avenue & Kearny Street (781 1338). BART Montgomery Street/Muni Metro F, J, K, L, M, N/bus 2, 3, 4, 5, 6, 7, 15, 21, 30, 31, 38, 45, 66, 71. **Open** 8am-5.30pm Mon-Fri; 9am-5pm Sat. **Credit** DC, Disc, JCB, MC, V. **Map G/H3**

A well-known cobbler and convenient to downtown. You name it, they mend it – they'll even put taps on your tap shoes.

Florists

Ixia

2331 Market Street, between Castro & Noe Streets (431 3134). Muni Metro F, K, L, M, N/bus 8, 24, 35, 37. **Open** 9am-6.30pm Mon-Fri; 11am-6pm Sat.

San Francisco's Nolita

In the last couple of years, a tiny stretch of Grant Avenue has seceded and declared itself **Upper Grant Avenue**. Like the few streets that comprise New York's Nolita, North Beach's Upper Grant is small but pithy – with more interesting shops per square foot than many a loftier neighbourhood. Here's a taste of what awaits in the few blocks between Green and Filbert Streets.

MAC stands for Modern Appealing Clothing (*see page 166*) and that's exactly what you'll find in this pretty, salon-like store complete with leopard-print sofa (a good place for companions to peruse magazines while you shop). Across the road, **Lilith** (1528 Grant Avenue; 781 6171) is chock full of natural-fibre separates that can be layered to create full-on outfits (and are designed to fit and flatter women of all shapes). **Fife** (1415 Grant Avenue, at Union Street; 677 9744) is where street waifs and club gals shop for their day clothes, seduced by Andrew Linton's amazing way with stretch fabrics and bold use of colour.

If it's jeans you're after, get down to **AB Fits** (1519 Grant Avenue, between Union & Filbert Streets; 982 5726) where the selection would be overwhelming if not for the patient service and helpful advice that accompanies all that denim. **Martini Merchantile** (1453 Grant Avenue; 362 1944) is a magnet for the swing set, with vintage- and vintage-looking clothing mixed together and lots of pretty, glittery barrettes, retro ties and accessories to go with the skirts, frocks and suits.

Men's and women's dancing feet get shod at **InSolent** (1418 Grant Avenue; 788 3334), which describes itself as 'excessive, immoderate, haughty, arrogant'. Luckily that doesn't refer to the sales staff, who are more than happy to pull out whatever strikes your fancy, from strappy Sigerson Morrison sandals to more earthbound Paraboots. A few doors down, **Alla Prima** (*see page 169*), dishes up the best lingerie in town and takes pride in accommodating even hard-to-fit gals. Party girls and soon-to-be-blushing brides should dive into **Ristarose** (1422 Grant Avenue; 781-8559) for dresses cut and fitted with couture precision and artistry.

Once you've satisfied your clothing jones, **Columbine Design** (1541 Grant Avenue; 434 3016) mixes fresh flowers with Gothic taxidermy: picture a chipmunk clad in tiny golden crown and velvet cloak. **Slips** (1534 Grant Avenue; 362 5652) is where locals take their tired furniture for sprucing up with custom-made slipcovers, but there's also a pristine gathering of 'eclectic collectibles', including old French tins and pillows. For more finds, **Aria** (1522 Grant Avenue; 433 0219) is the ultimate curiosity shop where everything is coated with just the right amount of dust. Paperweights, trophies, typographer's letters, old glass lanterns, anonymous paintings and ornaments imported from Italy sit among refurbished stainless steel office furniture from the 1940's. By now you must be starving: sink your teeth into a real Italian sandwich at **Prudente & Company** (1462 Grant Avenue; 421 0757) while Tony Bennett gazes down from the walls.

Credit AmEx, MC, $TC, V. **Map E6**
You should at least window shop at this Castro district merchant to appreciate the living plant and flower sculptures. Kinky arrangements with an Asian flavour.

Rayon Vert

3187 16th Street, at Guerrero Street (861 3516). Bus 22, 26. **Open** noon-6pm Tue-Sat. **Credit** MC, $TC, V. **Castro/Mission Map Y1**
Florist Kelly Kornegay's shop seduces with buckets of blooms which she transforms unto chic, unfussy arrangements that can be delivered. In amongst the flora is anything that happens to catch her eye – from refurbished old stainless-steel medical furniture to new and vintage housewares, a motley of vases, funky Japanese stationery and lunch boxes, old silver julep cups and striped sake bowls.

San Francisco Flower Market

640 Brannan Street, at 6th Street (392 7944). Bus 9, 27, 42. **Open** 10am-3pm Mon-Sat. **Credit** varies **Map H5**
Where the florists come to pick up their day's offerings, many of the Flower Mart's stores sell to the public as well. The range of varieties and colours is truly staggering, and prices are the best in town.

Food & drink

Bakeries & pâtisseries

Bombay Ice Creamery

522 Valencia Street, at 18th Street (431 1103). Bus 18, 26. **Open** 11am-10pm Tue-Sat; 11am-9pm Sun. **Credit** MC, $TC, V. **Castro/Mission Map Y1**

Grant Avenue's **Columbine Design**: *an eclectic mix.*

Rayon Vert: *for flowers and the occasional bath tub.* *See page 171.*

Vanilla seems so…*vanilla* when you could be lapping up such flavours as chai, ginger, rose, saffron, pistachio and cardamom.

Boulangerie

2325 Pine Street, at Fillmore Street (1-800 833 8869). Bus 22. **Open** 8am-6pm Tue-Sun. **No credit cards. Map E3**

Comparing a croissant or brioche from Boulangerie with the usual doughy fare is like contrasting poetry with the phone book. This authentically French baker also sells savoury tarts and sweets.

Citizen Cake

399 Grove Street, at Gough Street (861 2228). Bus 21. **Open** 7am-7pm Mon-Fri; 9am-7pm Sat, Sun. **Credit** AmEx, Disc, MC, V. **Map F5**

Citizen Cake's pastry chef-owner Elizabeth Falkner has won international raves for her amazing breads, sticky buns, cinnamon rolls, scones, pies, tarts, cakes, wood-oven pizzas and savoury sandwiches. Now located in the heart of Hayes Valley, a stop at this new-wave pâtisserie is a hard habit to break.

Stella Pastry & Caffe

446 Columbus Avenue, between Green & Vallejo Streets (986 2914). Bus 15, 41. **Open** *summer* 7.30am-10pm, *winter* 7.30am-6pm, daily. **Credit** AmEx, $TC, MC, V. **Map G2**

Famous for its St Honoré cake, a gooey, rum-soaked delight, Stella Pastry also makes and sells a perfect espresso with which to accompany it.

Beer & wine

Cost Plus World Market

2552 Taylor Street, at Bay Street (928 6200). Bus 30, 32, 39/cable car Powell-Mason. **Open** 9am-9pm daily. **Credit** AmEx Disc, MC, $TC, V. **Map G2**

In addition to wines and local microbrews, this chain keeps a respectable stock of liqueurs and spirits and loads of furniture and household wares.

Jug Shop

1567 Pacific Avenue, at Polk Street (885 2922). Bus 12, 19, 27, 83. **Open** 9am-9pm Mon-Sat; 9.30am-7pm

Farleys.
See page 176.

Sun. **Credit** MC, $TC, V. **Map F3**
The knowledgeable staff will help you make your selection from a variety of French, Australian, Italian, Spanish, Chilean and Californian wines. There are scheduled tastings from visiting vineyards; staff will deliver cases of wine and kegs of beer for large parties.

Napa Valley Winery Exchange

415 Taylor Street, between Geary & O'Farrell Streets (771 2887/1-800 653 9463). Bus 2, 3, 4, 27, 38, 76. **Open** 10am-7pm Mon-Sat. **Credit** AmEx, JCB, MC, V. **Map G4**
Specialising in Californian wines, including unusual and hard-to-find varietals, the Napa Valley Winery Exchange has over 500 wines in stock and will ship anywhere in the world.

The Wine Club

953 Harrison Street, between Fifth & Sixth Streets (512 9086/1-800-966-7835). Bus 30, 37, 42, 45, 76. **Open** 9am-7pm Mon-Sat; 11am-6pm Sun. **Credit** MC, TC, V. **Map H5**
Some of the best wine bargains around are found in this warehouse of a shop, with prices on very drinkable varietals starting at $5 and going as high as you like. The Club's enthusiastic staff will guide you through the 1,200-plus options and host several tastings each month. Beer and well-priced caviar are also on sale.

Food delivery

Many of the city's smaller restaurants offer delivery services for a minimum food order; it's worth checking those near your hotel. A 15 per cent tip is customary.

Dine One One

(278 3300). **Open** 10am-10pm Mon-Thur, Sun; 10am-11pm Fri, Sat. **Credit** AmEx, DC, MC, $TC, V.
This upmarket restaurant delivery service brings dishes from nearly 100 restaurants to your doorstep. Open daily for lunch and dinner, serving any silver-walleted soul within the city limits.
Website: www.dine11.com

Waiters on Wheels

425 Divisadero Street, at Oak Street (252 1470). Bus 6, 7, 66, 71. **Open** 11am-11pm daily. **Credit** AmEx, DC, Disc, MC, V. **Map D/E3**
Like Dine One One, this service delivers restaurant fare to your home – for a price. Choose from 50 restaurants, serving anything from American to Thai cuisine and nearly everything in between. Phone for a menu.
Website: www.waitersonwheels.com

Gourmet groceries

Bi-Rite Market

3639 18th Street, at Dolores Street (241 9773). Muni Metro J/bus 33. **Open** 10am-9pm Mon-Fri; 9am-8pm Sat; 9am-7pm Sun. **Credit** MC, V. **Castro/Mission Map Y1**

Citizen Cake. *See page 173.*

First opened in 1940 and recently renovated to its original pre-war lustre (even down to the original Art Deco neon sign), this speciality grocery in the Mission sells house-smoked lox (salmon), homemade sausages, fresh-baked cakes, salads, Middle Eastern dips and pasta sauces; it also has an olive bar and more than 100 different cheeses to choose from. Salvaged farm carts overflow with organic produce and fresh Gus pickles are flown in from New York's Lower East Side.

Ferry Plaza Farmer's Market

The Embarcadero, at Green Street (1-510 528 6987). Bus 32, 42. **Open** 8am-1.30pm Sat. **Map H2/H3**
This weekly market is where the foodies flock on Saturdays to find organic lettuces, baby pak choy and dozens of varieties of fruit and veg you've probably never heard of. There are always a couple of fresh flower stalls, and two local restaurants (the **Hayes Street Grill** and **Rose Pistola** *see chapter* **Restaurants & Cafés** for both) sell savoury fare to ravenous shoppers. The market is also open on Tuesdays, from April to November, at the nearby Justin Herman Plaza by the Embarcadero.

Molinari Delicatessen

373 Columbus Avenue, at Vallejo Street (421 2337). Bus 15, 41. **Open** 8am-6pm Mon-Fri; 7.30am-5.30pm Sat. **Credit** MC, V. **Map G2**
Molinari was dishing out home-made gnocchi and pesto alla genovese long before the yupsters ever heard of the stuff. It's still a great place to stop for an al fresco repast.

Molinari Delicatessen. *See page 175.*

Trader Joe's

3 Masonic Avenue, at Geary Boulevard (346 9964). Bus 38, 43. **Open** 9am-9pm daily. **Credit** Disc, MC, V. **Map F3**

Organic goods, healthy fast food, exotic niblets and a selection of inexpensive wines and beers. Try to avoid the weekend crowds.

Branch: 555 Ninth Street, at Bryant Street (863 1292).

Whole Foods

1765 California Street, at Franklin Street (674 0500). Bus 1, 42, 47, 49. **Open** 9am-10pm Mon-Fri; 8am-10pm Sat, Sun. **Credit** AmEx, Disc, MC, $TC, V. **Map F3**

One-stop shopping for the foodie: the challenge is to leave Whole Foods with anything left in your wallet. There's a bakery, gourmet deli and outstanding cheese, fish, sushi and meat counters – the choice of bread alone may cause you panic. Most produce is grown organically and all items are clearly marked to indicate their origins.

Tea & coffee

Known as 'the espresso pioneers of the West', **Caffè Trieste** on Vallejo Street in North Beach sells coffee beans blended and roasted to your specification as well as coffee making equipment, as does **Peet's Coffee & Tea**, the company that started the dark-roasted phenomenon in California. For the nearest **Starbucks** and **Tully's** Mcbranch, consult your telephone directory. *See also chapter* **Restaurants & Cafés**.

Farleys

1315 18th Street, at Texas & Missouri Streets (648 1545). Bus 22, 53. **Open** 6.30am-10pm Mon-Fri; 8am-10pm Sat, Sun. **Credit** $TC. **Map H6**

This Potrero Hill hangout always has a number of interesting (and often noisy) motorcycles parked outside; inside it serves tea, coffee and drinks and sells freshly roasted coffee by the pound. Also an excellent newsstand, there are generally more browsers than buyers in Farleys and nobody seems to mind.

Freed Teller & Freed

1326 Polk Street, at Pine & Bush Streets (673 0922). Bus 19. **Open** 9.30am-5.30pm Mon-Fri. **Credit** MC, $TC, V. **Map F3**

There is a whiff of the Dickensian at Freed's, a speciality coffee roaster and tea blender since 1899. The array of black and green teas is intoxicating. Don't leave without a bag of their signature Bourbon Vanilla.

Graffeo Coffee Roasting Company

735 Columbus Avenue, at Filbert Street (986 2429/1-800 222 6250). Bus 15, 30, 41/ cable car Powell-Mason. **Open** 9am-6pm Mon-Fri; 9am-5pm Sat. **Credit** MC, $TC, V. **Map G2**

A long-standing North Beach shop – practically a San Franciscan institution.

Tea & Company

2207 Fillmore Street, at Sacramento Street (929 8327). Bus 1, 3, 22. **Open** 9am-10.30pm Mon-Thur; 9am-11pm Fri, Sat; 10am-9.30pm Sun. **Credit** AmEx, MC, V. **Map E3**

Teas by the cup, pot and pound, with dozens of exotic-sounding varieties, two daily iced teas (one black, one herbal) and many variations on chai, the current California darling.

Ten Ren Tea Company of San Francisco

949 Grant Avenue, between Washington & Jackon Streets (362 0656). Bus 1, 9, 30, 83. **Open** 9am-9pm daily. **Credit** AmEx, MC, V. **Map G3**

Ten Ren stocks 40 different types of Chinese tea, from the leaves recommended for an ordinary cuppa to expensive infusions for special occasions. Taste before you buy.

Health & beauty

Chinese herbalists

Vinh Khang Herbs & Ginsengs

512 Clement Street, between Sixth & Seventh Avenues (752 8336). Bus 2, 44. **Open** 9.30am-7pm Fri-Sun, Mon-Wed; noon-7pm Thur. **No credit cards. Map B4**

Chinese herbalism is one of alternative medicine's hottest trends and this shop stays open seven days a week to serve local devotees' needs. Inspect their splendid array of roots and remedies while herbal specialists create a customised concoction for you.

Cosmetics & beauty products

The largest collection of make-up and body elixirs can be found in Union Square department stores (*see page 157*). Neiman Marcus stocks the complete line of balms, creams, moisturisers and scented oils from Kiehls, the venerable New York apothecary. Yet most smaller shops, whether they hawk housewares or clothing, now also stock an impressive array of 'natural' products for bath and skin.

Mac Cosmetics

1833 Union Street, between Laguna & Octavia Streets (771 6113). Bus 41, 45. **Open** *summer* 11am-8pm Mon-Fri; 11am-7pm Sat; 11am-6pm Sun; *winter* 11am-7pm Mon-Sat; 11am-6pm Sun. **Credit** AmEx, DC, JCB, MC, $TC, V. **Map E3**

The brand popularised by RuPaul has a stand-alone store in the Marina, where you can make the transformation from virgin to vamp in no time at all.

Sephora

1 Stockton Street, at Ellis Street (392 1545). BART Powell Street/Muni Metro F, J, K, L, M, N/bus 6, 7, 9, 21, 30, 31, 45, 66, 71. **Open** 10am-8pm Mon-Sat; 11am-7pm Sun. **Credit** AmEx, Disc, MC, $TC, V. **Map H4**

France's largest cosmetics retailer has opened a temple of beauty here, a kind of interactive boutique where you can touch, smell and experience most of the premier perfume and make-up brands on the market. Unless you request assistance, the expert staff are happy to let you roam and test at will. Artists are also available if a makeover is on your agenda.

Hair salons

Although most upmarket salons require advance booking to reshape your straggly locks, it's always worth a phone call to see if there's a cancellation or even a bargain cut with a trainee to be had at short notice. Medium-heeled fashionistas swear by **Zip Zap** (245 Fillmore, at Haight Street; 621 1671). Others, for whom no price is too high when it comes to their head, cite **Architects and Heroes** (580 Bush Street, between Grant Avenue & Stockton Street; 391 8833 or 2239 Fillmore Street, between Sacramento & Clay Streets; 921 8383); **Cowboys & Angels** (Suite 400, 207 Powell Street, at O'Farrell Street; 362 8516) or **Louie** (4 Brady Street, at Market Street; 864 3012). All sell the wonderful Bumble & Bumble line of hair-care products.

Spas, saunas & bath houses

See also chapter **Trips Out of Town**.

Family Sauna

2308 Clement Street, at 24th Avenue (221 2208). Bus 1, 2, 29, 38. **Open** noon-10pm daily. **Admission** $9; *massage* $40-$70. **Credit** Disc, MC, $TC, V.

This mellow neighbourhood retreat offers dry-heat Finnish saunas, two therapeutic whirlpool spas (the redwood tub retains heat better but the fibreglass option has more leg room), massage, facials and waxing. Unlike most of the city's day spas, there's neither pretension nor high prices – only a casual, clean and comfortable environment where all types come to cleanse body and soul in a private hot tub.

Kabuki Springs & Spa

Japan Center, 1750 Geary Boulevard, at Fillmore Street (922 6002). Bus 22, 38. **Open** 10am-10pm daily. **Admission** *day pass without massage* $10; *day pass with 25-minute massage* $45; *evening pass* $15. **Credit** AmEx, MC, V, $TC. **Map E4**

Recently revamped, this traditional Japanese bath house has deep ceramic communal tubs, a steam room, sit-down showers, saunas, a cold plunge pool and even a restful tatami room. Shiatsu, Swedish and deep tissue massages are also available by appointment. Women-only days are Wednesday, Friday and Sunday; it's men-only the rest of the week. Spend an hour here and you'll come out feeling revived and pampered.

Osento

955 Valencia Street, at 21st Street (282 6333). BART 24th Street/bus 14, 26, 49. **Open** 1pm-1am daily (last admission midnight). **Admission** $9-$13. **No credit cards. Castro/Mission Map Y2**

A bath house for women only. Walk in to the peaceful surroundings, leave your clothes in a locker, shower off and relax in the whirlpool. After a cold plunge you can choose between wet and dry saunas. An outdoor deck offers the chance to cool down or enjoy the weather on a sunny day. Massages are available by appointment.

77 Maiden Lane Salon & Spa

Second floor, 77 Maiden Lane, between Grant Avenue & Kearny Street (391 7777). Bus 12, 15, 30, 30X, 41, 45. **Open** 9am-6pm Mon; 9am-7pm Tue-Wed, Fri; 9am-8pm Thur; 9am-6pm Sat; 10am-6pm Sun. **Credit** MC, V, $TC. **Map H3**

This full-service salon runs the pampering gamut, including makeovers, hair styling, colouring and facials. Treat yourself to an hour-long pedicure.

Spa Nordstrom

San Francisco Shopping Center, 865 Market Street, at Fifth Street (977 5102). BART Powell Street/Muni Metro F, J, K, L, M, N/bus 6, 7, 27, 31, 66, 71/cable car Powell-Mason or Powell-Hyde. **Open** 9am-7pm Mon-Sat; 10.15am-5.45pm Sun. **Credit** AmEx, Disc, JCB, MC, TC, V. **Map G4**

As you're struggling for air amidst the swarm of shoppers at the San Francisco Center, remember that rejuvenation is within walking distance. Soak your feet in a warm tub before indulging in one of the many restorative services which include aromatherapy, massage and skin care spa packages, eyebrow or bikini wax, manicure or pedicure.

Tattoos & body piercing

Body Manipulations

3234 16th Street, between Guerrero & Dolores Streets (621 0408). Bus 6, 7, 22, 66, 71.

Open noon-7pm daily. **Credit** AmEx, MC, $TC, V. **Map F6**
Specialises in custom body piercing, scarring, branding and just about anything else that can be done to the human figure (except tattooing). Check out BM's catalogues – you can pierce just about anything these days.

Lyle Tuttle Tattooing

841 Columbus Avenue, at Greenwich Street (775 4991). Bus 15, 30/cable car Powell-Mason. **Open** noon-9pm Mon-Thur; noon-10pm Fri, Sat; noon-8pm Sun. **Credit** MC, $TC, V. **Map G2**
Tuttle is one of the world's most respected tattoo artists and for those in the know, this parlour is an essential stop-off point. For the adjoining museum, *see chapter* **Museums & Galleries**.

Household

Pottery Barn, the chain store and catalogue company that makes high design concepts available (and affordable) to the masses has several outlets in San Francisco, where the company's corporate headquarters reside. Check the phone book for your nearest branch.

Bauerware

3886 17th Street, at Noe Street (864 3886). Muni Metro F/bus 8, 24, 35, 37. **Open** 10am-6pm Mon-Sat. **Credit** MC, V. **Castro/Mission Map X1**
Probably the only store that sells drawer handles exclusively, from retro to other-worldly.

Cliff's Variety

479 Castro Street, at Market Street (431 5365). Muni Metro K, L, M/bus 24, 33. **Open** 9.30am-8pm Mon-Sat. **Credit** AmEx, DC, Disc, JCB, $TC, MC, V. **Castro/Mission Map X1**
So much more than just a hardware store, Cliff's is stuffed with all kinds of knobs, vases, bath accessories, fabric, appliances, kitchen gadgets, toys, crafts, paint, rainbow pride gew-gaws – and hardware, too, of course.

Fillamento

2185 Fillmore Street, at Sacramento Street (931 2224). Bus 1, 3, 22. **Open** 10am-7pm Mon-Sat; noon-6pm Sun. **Credit** AmEx, DC, Disc, MC, $TC, V. **Map E3**
Elegant dishes, stylish glassware, distinctive lamps, edgy home furnishings and cool office accessories are sold on the first floor, with an exceptional array of smelly soaps, lotions and bath salts; towels and linens are on the second.

Kamei Restaurant Supply

507 Clement Street, at Sixth Avenue (666 3699). Bus 2, 4, 44. **Open** 9am-7pm daily. **Credit** Disc, MC, $TC, V. **Map B4**
Kamei sells stacks and stacks of delicious Asian tableware, from tiny bowls that open like flowers, to crackled celadon glaze soup bowls, sake sets and bamboo-painted bowls that cry out for noodles.

Jewellery & watches

de Vera

29 Maiden Lane, at Grant Avenue & Kearny Street (788 0828). BART Montgomery Street/Muni Metro F, J, K, L, M, N/bus 2, 3, 4, 30, 45, 76. **Open** 10am-6pm Tue-Sat. **Credit** AmEx, MC, $TC, V. **Map H3**
At Federico de Vera's gorgeous little shop wondrous necklaces, bracelets and earrings made from unusual stones, many an intriguing mix of old and new elements, beckon like lost treasures. Surrounding de Vera's jewellery designs is his notable collection of new and antique art glass from Austria, Italy and the US.
Branch: 580 Sutter Street, at Mason Street (989 0988).

Lang

323 Sutter Street, between Stockton Street & Grant Avenue (982 2213). BART Montgomery Street/Muni Metro F, J, K, L, M, N/bus 2, 3, 4, 76. **Open** 10.30am-5.30pm Mon-Sat. **Credit** AmEx, Disc, DC, JCB, MC, V. **Map G3**
Lang maintains a large inventory of antique and estate jewellery and timepieces, including lots of silver flatware.

Zeitgeist

437B Hayes Street, between Gough & Octavia Street (864 0185). Muni Metro F, J, K, L, M, N/bus 21, 42, 47, 49. **Open** noon-6pm Tue-Sat. **Credit** AmEx, MC, $TC, V. **Map F5**
The city's best-known source for second-hand watches, from quite reasonable lesser-known names to major players such as Philippe Patek and Rolex.

Laundrettes

Brainwash

1122 Folsom Street, between Seventh & Eighth Streets (café 861 3663/Laundromat 431 9274). Bus 12, 27, 42. **Open** 7am-11pm Mon-Thur, Sun; 7am-1am Fri, Sat. **Credit** AmEx, Disc, MC, $TC, V. **Map G5**
San Francisco's original café/Laundromat continues to succeed as a trendy neighbourhood gathering spot and there's live music at the weekend. Enjoy an espresso, glass of wine or bowl of pasta while your clothes are spinning.

Star Wash

392 Dolores Street, at 17th Street (431 2443). Bus 22, 33. **Open** 7.30am-9.30pm Mon-Fri; 8am-8pm Sat, Sun. **No credit cards. Castro/Mission Map Y1**
Another hip gathering place for the suds set, Star Wash shows old and new movies as you sort your socks under the watchful eyes of Fred and Ginger, Marlene, Sophia and Clark, whose images stare down from the walls.

Musical instruments

Clarion Music

816 Sacramento Street, at Waverly Place (391 1317). Bus 30, 45/cable car California. **Open** 11am-6pm Mon-Fri; 9am-5pm Sat. **Credit** AmEx, Disc, MC, $TC, V. **Map G3**

Pre-gig jams and a huge collection of CDs and vinyl at **Amoeba Music** *in the Haight.*

World music central: didgeridoos, sitars, Tibetan singing bowls, African drums, Native American flutes, Chinese stringed instruments and other non-Western noise makers are all stocked. Don't miss the regular Friday night world music concerts.

Drum World

5016 Mission Street, at Geneva Avenue (334 7559). Bus 9AX, 14, 15, 29, 43. **Open** 10am-6pm Mon-Sat. **Credit** AmEx, Disc, MC, $TC, V.

This well-stocked speciality store buys and sells used and vintage drums and keeps a library of videos and books on the subject.

Haight-Ashbury Music Center

1540 Haight Street, at Ashbury Street (863 7327). Bus 7, 43, 66, 71. **Open** 10am-5pm Mon; 10am-6pm Tue-Thur; 10am-5.30pm Fri, Sat; noon-6pm Sun. **Credit** AmEx, DC, Disc, JCB, MC, $TC, V. **Map D5/6**

A stop-off point for local musicians and rockers in town for a gig. Recently expanded after a fire, the shop sells new and second-hand instruments, mikes, mixers, amps and sheet music and keeps hundreds of acoustic and electric guitars. If you're a musician in search of a band, check out the posted notices. *Website: www.haight-ashbury-music.com*

Opticians

City Optix

2154 Chestnut Street, between Pierce & Steiner Streets (921 1188). Bus 22, 28, 43, 76. **Open** 10am-6pm Mon-Sat; 10am-8pm Thur; noon-5pm Sun. **Credit** AmEx, MC, V, $TC. **Map D2**

The most comprehensive collection of great frames in most price ranges, City Optix is staffed by helpful salespeople. Look for Matsuda, Oliver Peeples, LA Eyeworks and a bunch of brands you've probably never heard of. They'll also cheerfully adjust glasses you clearly didn't purchase there.

Eyedare

3199 16th Street, at Guerrero Street (241 0240). Bus 22, 26. **Open** noon-7pm Mon; 11am-7pm Tue-Thur; 9am-5pm Fri, Sat. **Credit** AmEx, Disc, MC, V. **Map F6**

A small but interesting collection of frames in a shop in the heart of the Mission, including Magli, Gaultier, Ferre and even a few American designers.

Pets

George

2411 California Street, at Fillmore Street (441 0564). Bus 1, 3, 22. **Open** 11am-6pm Mon-Fri; 10am-6pm Sat; noon-6pm Sun. **Credit** AmEx, MC, $TC, V. **Map E3**

Founded by a pair of Fox Terrier owners, George sells eye-catching accessories for pets to wear, eat and play with. Baked-from-scratch treats, organic catnip, 'Good Dog' bath towels, natty jackets and sweaters, lucky charms, laurel wreath chew toys and patterned ceramic bowls complement an enticing array of T-shirts, sweatshirts and caps for bipeds.

Records, tapes & CDs

Amoeba Music

1855 Haight Street, between Shrader & Stanyan Streets (831 1200). Bus 7, 33, 37, 43. **Open** 10am-10.30pm Mon-Sat; 11am-9pm Sun. **Credit** Disc, DC, MC, $TC, V. **Map C6**

In a converted bowling alley in the Haight-Ashbury, a community of music lovers converges to sell, buy, trade and bask in the vibes. Amoeba offers a huge collection of CDs, tapes, DVD and vinyl, including many hard-to-find releases and tons of recycled music and videos, dirt cheap. You'll find indie rock,

electronica, DJ mixes, drum 'n' bass, techno, house, jazz and classical. Two or three times weekly, performers such as Luscious Jackson or Jon Spencer Blues Explosion show up for record release parties or free pre-gig jams.
Website: www.amoebamusic.com

Aquarius Records

1055 Valencia Street, at 21st Street (647 2272). Bus 14, 26, 49. **Open** 10am-9pm Mon-Wed; 10am-10pm Thur-Sun. **Credit** AmEx, Disc, MC, $TC, V. **Castro/Mission Map Y2**
Aquarius sells alternative and underground music in a friendly setting. Staff often contribute pithy and highly personal descriptions of their favourite music – and why you'll like it too.

BPM Music Factory

573 Hayes Street, at Laguna Street (487 8680). Bus 21. **Open** 11am-8pm Mon-Fri; noon-8pm Sat; noon-7pm Sun. **Credit** MC, V. **Map E/F5**
BPM is where local DJs gather to gossip and shop for 12-inch house, techno and acid jazz sounds.

Grooves Vinyl Attractions

1797 Market Street, between Guerrero & Valencia Streets (436 9933). Muni Metro F/bus 26. **Open** 11am-7pm daily. **Credit** AmEx, MC, $TC, V. **Map F5**
Dive into Grooves' $1 bin for vintage 1970s crooners (remember Dan Fogelberg?) and vintage vinyl from years gone by. An excellent source for out-of-print soundtracks.

Jazz Quarter

1267 20th Avenue, at Irving Street (661 2331). Muni Metro N/bus 71. **Open** 1-6pm Tue-Sat. **No credit cards. Map A6**
Cool cats come here to score Mingus, Miles, Chet and Charlie; Coltrane, too.

Reckless Records of London

1401 Haight Street, at Masonic Avenue (431 3434). Bus 6, 7, 37, 43, 71. **Open** 11am-9pm Mon-Thur, Sun; 11am-10pm Fri, Sat. **Credit** AmEx, Disc, JCB, MC, $TC, V. **Map D5**
While on Haight Street, pop in for second-hand indie, hip hop and soul on CD, tape and vinyl.

Reggae Runnins Village Store

505 Divisadero Street, at Fell Street (922 2442). Bus 21, 24. **Open** 11am-7pm daily. **Credit** AmEx, MC, $TC, V. **Map D/E5**
If reggae is your jive, this is your hive. There's also a juice bar, Jamaican food and other delights.

Ritmo Latino

2401 Mission Street, at 20th Street (824 8556). BART 24th Street/bus 14, 49. **Open** 10am-9.30pm Mon-Fri; 10am-9.30pm Sat, Sun. **Credit** Disc, MC, V. **Castro/Mission Map Y1**
Indulge your Latin fantasies with ranchera, mariachi, salsa, Tex-Mex, merengue and more.

Tower Records

2525 Jones Street, at Columbus Avenue (885 0500). Bus 15, 30, 41, 42/cable car Powell-Mason.

Out of town

Whichever way you head out of San Francisco, shopping opportunities await. In Oakland in the East Bay, boutiques and antique shops abound in **Rockridge** on Piedmont and College Avenues.

Berkeley's **Telegraph Avenue** is a classic university main drag serving up every kind of store imaginable. For new books, it's hard to beat **Cody's Bookstore** (2454 Telegraph Avenue, at Haste Street; 1-510 845 7852 and 1730 Fourth Street, between Gilman Street & University Avenue; 1-510 559 9500). For rare or used tomes, immerse yourself in the multi-storied **Moe's Books** (2476 Telegraph Avenue, at Dwight Avenue; 1-510 849 2087). Although the cigar-chomping Moe is no longer alive, his spirit lives on. For CDs and vinyl, the original **Amoeba Music** (2455 Telegraph Avenue, at Dwight Avenue; 1-510 549 1125) and **Rasputin's** (2350 Telegraph Avenue; 1-510 848 9004) are still going strong.

Finally, Berkeley's **Fourth Street** started out with a couple of restaurants and a few shops years ago and has evolved into something of an outdoor shopping mall, attracting Bay Area denizens en masse on sunny weekends. Among the highlights are **Erica Tanov**, for pretty hand-knit sweaters and girly frocks (1827 Fourth Street; 1-510 849 3331); the East Bay **George**, simply the best pet store in the world (1829 Fourth Street; 1-510 644 1033); **Hear Music**, with a small but selective collection of folk, blues, ambient, country and classical music, and multiple listening stations (1809 Fourth Street; Suite B; 1-510 204 9595); **Summer House**, filled with new and antique furnishings (1833 Fourth Street; 1-510 549 9914); **The Gardener**, a collection of books, ceramics, furniture, bulbs and botanicals (1836 Fourth Street; 1-510 548 4545); and **Builder's Booksource**, a resource for architects, interior designers, landscapers and contractors (1871 Fourth Street; 1-510 845 6874).

There is also a **Crate & Barrel Outlet**, for discounted and discontinued glassware and other household items (1785 Fourth Street; 1-510

Open 9am-midnight daily. **Credit** AmEx, Disc, MC, JCB, $TC, V. **Map F2**
Although the service is erratic and impersonal, this is a browser's delight, especially with the addition of wall-to-wall listening stations stocked with the latest sounds. The **Classical Annex** (2568 Jones Street, at Columbus Avenue; 441 4880) is an oasis of calm and offers a comprehensive selection and conversant staff.
Branches: **Tower Records and Video** 2280 Market Street, between Noe & 16th Streets (621 0588); **Tower Records and Video** Stonestown Galleria, Winston Drive (681 2001); **Tower Outlet** 660 Third Street, at Brannan Street (957 9660).

Virgin Megastore

2 Stockton Street, at Market Street (397 4525). BART Powell Street/Muni Metro F, J, K, L, M, N/bus 6, 7, 8, 9, 21, 30, 38, 45, 66. **Open** 9am-11pm Mon-Thur; 9am-midnight Fri, Sat; 10am-10pm Sun. **Credit** AmEx, Disc, MC, $TC, V. **Map G4**
Monolithic – with 60 listening stations, an in-house DJ and on-site café in a sterile downtown setting.

Sex shops

Good Vibrations

1210 Valencia Street, at 23rd Street (550 7399). BART 24th Street/bus 14, 26, 49. **Open** 11am-7pm Mon-Thur, Sun; 11am-8pm Fri, Sat. **Credit** AmEx, Disc, MC, V. **Castro/Mission Map Y1**
At this woman-owned and operated co-operative, the art of self- and mutual lovin' is celebrated loudly and proudly. The friendly staff are happy to walk you through the large collection of sex toys, reading matter and videos (many available to rent).
Website: www.goodvibe.com

Stormy Leather

1158 Howard Street, at Seventh Street (626 1672). Bus 12, 19. **Open** noon-7pm daily. **Credit** AmEx, DC, MC, $TC, V. **Map G5**
Somehow more titillating than Good Vibrations is the less clinical atmosphere at the naughtier Stormy Leather. You can get fitted for a leather bustier, buy a rubber nurse or French maid outfit, peruse the edgier collection of books and magazines for as long as you like – and when you have a question about whips, for example, the friendly female staff are right there for you.

Smoking

Ashbury Tobacco Center

1524 Haight Street, at Ashbury Street (552 5556). Bus 6, 7, 43, 71. **Open** 10am-9.30pm daily. **Credit** AmEx, Disc, DC, JCB, MC, $TC, V. **Map D5/6**
This Haight shop will take you back to the days when the area was known as the 'Hashbury'. It offers the full array of psychedelic sundries (maintaining the pretence, of course, that the products are intended for legal substances). In addition to the hookahs, blown-glass pipes and honeybear bongs is a vast offering of tobacco products, from the exotic to the prosaic.

528 5500). A few streets away, **Urban Ore** (1333 Sixth Street, at Gilman Street; 1-510 559 4450), attracts second-hand junkies for the collection of architectural salvage and recycled oddities.

An outlet odyssey awaits you north of the city, at the **Napa Factory Outlets** (1-707 226 9876; SR 29, exit First Street) located about 90 minutes from the Golden Gate Bridge. Some 45 designers, including **Ann Taylor**, **Esprit**, **Nine West** and **Tommy Hilfiger** offer discounts of 25 to 65 per cent. Twenty minutes north of Napa on SR 29, you'll find reduced prices on **Brooks Brothers**, **Joan & David**, **Donna Karan** and **Coach** at the **St Helena Premier Outlets** (1-707 226 9876).

Collectibles hounds should take a field trip to downtown **Petaluma** (about 35 minutes' from the Golden Gate Bridge off Hwy 101; Washington Blvd exit), where there are antique shops every few feet. If you only have time for one stop, make sure it's **Zeppelin** (226 Petaluma Blvd North; 1-707 789 0600) which houses a clean, modern collection of old paintings, glassware, period and mid-century furniture and beautiful objects. The **Gravenstein Highway** (Hwy 116 West, between Cotati and Sebastopol) is a long and winding road chock full of antique and collectibles shops, such as wonderful **Ray's Trading Co** (3570 Gravenstein Hwy South; 1-707 829 9726) identifiable by the old garden ornament at the front. A house-made ice-cream or tangerine mango sorbet at **Screaming Mimi's** in Sebastopol (6902 Sebastopol Avenue; 1-707 823 5902) is a suitable reward for your efforts.

The peninsula and South Bay are mostly suburban residential areas with the same strip malls, one partial exception being the **Stanford Shopping Center** (Embarcadero Road West, off Hwy 101; 1-650 617 8585), an open-air collection of department stores and slightly less generic shops. San Jose's **Capitol Flea Market** (3630 Hillcap Avenue; 1-408 225 5800) and the **Flea Market Inc** (1590 Berryessa Road, between Lundy and Commercial Streets; 1-408 453 1110) are great places for cut-price pickings.

Grant's Tobacconists

562 Market Street, between Sansome & Montgomery Streets (981 1000). BART Montgomery Street/Muni Metro F, J, K, L, M, N/bus 9, 45, 84. **Open** 9am-5.30pm Mon-Fri; 10am-5.30pm Sat. **Credit** AmEx, Disc, MC, V. **Map H3**

Grant's sells pipes, cigars, humidors, tobacco and tony accessories. The walk-in humidor is reportedly stocked with 100,000 cigars.

Ticket agencies

For movie tickets, telephone the cinema where the movie is showing (*see chapter* **Film**). For tickets to live events at smaller venues, telephone the venue. Some theatres and clubs have box offices open on the day of a show. For additional information about seating and ticketing, consult the front section of the *Yellow Pages*.

BASS (Bay Area Seating Service)

165 Kearny Street, at Sutter Street (information & credit card bookings 478 2277/1-510 762 2277/1-650 478 2277/performing arts information 776 1999). **Open** *telephone service* 9am-7pm Mon-Fri; 10am-7pm Sat, Sun; *Kearny Street location* 9am-8pm Mon-Fri; 10am-7pm Sat. **Credit** MC, V. **Map H3**

If you need a ticket for a performance musical or theatrical, BASS can probably sell it to you, either over the phone (be armed with a credit card) or from one of its many outlets throughout the city (check the phone book for your nearest).

Website: www.basstickets.com

TIX Bay Area

Union Square, at Stockton Street, between Post & Geary Streets (433 7827). BART Montgomery Street/Muni Metro F, J, K, L, M, N/bus 2, 3, 4, 38, 45/cable car Powell-Mason or Powell-Hyde. **Open** 11am-6pm Tue-Thur; 11am-7pm Fri, Sat. **Credit** $TC. **Map G3**

San Francisco's only outlet for half-price tickets on selected theatre, dance, opera and performance events. Standard price tickets are also available.

Website: www.theaterbayarea.org

Toys

Chinatown Kite Shop

717 Grant Avenue, at Sacramento Street (989 5182). Bus 1, 15, 30, 45. **Open** 10am-8.30pm daily. **Credit** AmEx, Disc, MC, $TC, V. **Map G3**

Stocks hundreds of different kites, for flying or decoration. Other kite shops in the city include **Air Time of San Francisco** (759 1177) for stunt kites, **Kite Flite** (956 3181) in the touristy Pier 39 arcade, and, in the East Bay, **Highline Kites** (1-510 525 2755).

FAO Schwarz

48 Stockton Street, at O'Farrell Street (394 8700). BART Powell Street/Muni Metro F, J, K, L, M, N/bus 6, 7, 9, 21, 30, 31, 71. **Open** 10am-7pm Mon-Sat; 11am-6pm Sun. **Credit** AmEx, Disc, DC, MC, $TC, V. **Map G4**

Toys from around the world, many of them larger-than-life, can be found at this giant branch of the celebrated New York play palace.

Imaginarium

Laurel Shopping Center, 3535 California Street, at Spruce Street (387 9885). Bus 1, 12. **Open** 9.30am-6.30pm Mon-Fri; 9.30am-6pm Sat; 11am-6pm Sun. **Credit** AmEx, Disc, MC, V. **Map C4**

Imaginarium selects toys for their ability to stimulate developing minds rather than numb them. Many hard-to-find European imports are stocked and playful weapons of destruction are noticeably absent.

Sanrio

39 Stockton Street, between Ellis & O'Farrell Streets (981 5568). BART Powell Street/Muni Metro F, J, K, L, M/bus 9, 30, 45/cable car Powell-Mason or Powell-Hyde. **Open** 10am-8pm Mon-Sat; 10am-6pm Sun. **Credit** AmEx, Disc, MC, V. **Map G4**

All things cute from the Japanese people behind Hello Kitty.

Toys R Us

2400 O'Farrell Boulevard, at Masonic Avenue (931 8896). Bus 38, 43. **Open** 9.30am-7pm Mon-Sat; 9.30am-7pm Sun. **Credit** AmEx, Disc, MC, V. **Map D4**

The biggest toy stores in the US, TRUs are everywhere. This one is the most centrally located in the city. Shop till you drop – your kids certainly won't.

Video rental

There are, of course, countless big-name videodromes in the city; consult the phone book for your nearest branch.

Leather Tongue

714 Valencia Street, at 18th Street (552 2900). Bus 14, 26, 33. **Open** noon-11pm daily. **Credit** AmEx, Disc, MC, V. **Map F6**

Blockbuster, not. Instead, a sizable portion of indie filmmakers as well as local talents, with a heaping helping of sci-fi and film noir.

Le Video

1231 & 1239 Ninth Avenue, between Lincoln Way & Irving Street (566 3606). Muni Metro N/bus 44, 71. **Open** 10am-11pm daily. **Credit** AmEx, MC, V. **Map B6**

Locals head here for foreign features they just can't find anywhere else, as well as more mainstream Hollywood releases. Recently remodelled, Le Vid stocks more than 30,000 titles in all genres, many of them for sale.

Website: www.levideo.com

Naked Eye News and Video

533 Haight Street, between Fillmore & Steiner Streets (864 2985). Bus 6, 7, 22, 66, 71. **Open** 10am-10pm daily. **Credit** AmEx, MC, $TC, V. **Map E5**

Cult classics, alternative comics, trading cards, local 'zines – all can be found under one roof in the heart of the Lower Haight.

Val Diamond in Steve Silver's 'Beach Blanket Babylon'

Entertainment

Children

Got kids? Want to act like one? Here's how and where.

If you thought San Francisco was only for grown-ups, you're in for a pleasant surprise. It's a child-friendly city where under-fives travel free on public transport, many hotels provide babysitting and kids get a great fuss made of them in the Latin and Asian neighbourhoods.

If you're looking for fun excursions with children, start by walking (or driving) down Lombard Street, the 'crookedest street in the world', riding a cable car and taking the lift up Coit Tower. The Bay Area – and Northern California in general – is also a terrific place for those interested in animals and marine mammals, especially sea lions, whales, otters and seals. As well as trying out the suggestions listed below, read the pink Datebook section of the Sunday *Examiner and Chronicle* and check the listings under Children's Events.

For more ideas, *see also chapters* **Sightseeing**, **Sport & Fitness** *and* **Trips Out of Town**.

Creatures, circuses & carousels

For an enjoyable family outing, there's plenty going on at the **San Francisco Zoo** (*see below*), as the 1.2 million visitors a year attest. Travelling further afield, the **Oakland Zoo** (1-510 632 9523) is also worth visiting. Circuses come to San Francisco all year round: watch out for the beautiful French-Canadian **Cirque du Soleil**, which arrives every second summer leaving swarms of fans in its wake. The local **New Pickle Circus** (544 9344) usually performs in San Francisco in December and sometimes has other performances in the Bay Area; look out for their advertisements or phone to find out their schedule. **Make-A-Circus** (242 1414), based at Fort Mason, performs in the Bay Area during the summer months.

If your child has the urge to whirl, San Francisco has several delightful **carousels**: there's one at the Zoo, one in Golden Gate Park, a two-storey Venetian carousel on Pier 39 and a new, 65-figure go-round (the original from Playland-at-the-Beach, San Francisco's first amusement park) installed on the rooftop above the Moscone Convention Center near the **Zeum** (*see page 187*).

The Jungle, Fun and Adventure

555 Ninth Street, between Bryant & Brannan Streets (552 4386). Bus 19, 27, 42. **Open** 10am-8pm Mon-Thur, Sun; 10am-9pm Fri; 9am-9pm Sat. **Admission** *unlimited play until 5pm* $3.95-$5.95 Mon-Fri; *after 5pm* $2.95 Mon-Thur, $3.95 Fri; *2 hours play* $3.95-$6.95 Sat, Sun. **Credit** MC, V. **Map G5**

The Junge is a vast indoor play centre for children from six months to 12 years old, aimed at helping weary shoppers. There's a tangled macaroni maze of colourful tubes to slide and crawl through, nets to climb and tanks full of coloured balls. Parents can grab a cappuccino in the adult rooms while the employees wear your kids out for you.

San Francisco School of Circus Arts

755 Frederick Street, at Arguello Boulevard (759 8123/fax 759 8644/sfsca@sfcircus.org). Muni Metro N/bus 6, 43, 66, 71. **Open** *summer camps* late June-early Aug; *courses* throughout the year. **Credit** MC, V. **Map C6**

The SFSCA organises 'clown classes' for 5-12s throughout the year and week-long summer camps for 7-15 year-olds (9am-3pm, Mon-Fri) where they

Come rain or shine

Foggy days

Visit the **California Academy of Sciences**, which houses the Steinhart Aquarium, Morrison Planetarium and the Natural History Museum. Commandeer a space at **Zeum**, followed by an IMAX movie at the **Metreon** or, if your kid is over the high-tech stuff, snoop about the **Musée Mécanique** or Camera Obscura at the Cliff House. Or resort to bribery at **FAO Schwarz**, the mother of all toy shops.

Blue skies

Take a ferry across the Bay – to **Alcatraz Island**, **Angel Island** or **Sausalito**. Or take the train to **Santa Cruz** and ride the rollercoaster on the Beach Boardwalk (*see chapter* **Trips Out of Town**). Command a rowing boat on Stow Lake or a horse ride in **Golden Gate Park** or join the throng and hire some rollerblades (*see chapter* **Sport & Fitness**). Head for the waterfront and explore the ships at the **Hyde Street Pier**.

Pucker up to a resident of the **Steinhart Aquarium** *in Golden Gate Park.*

learn acrobatics, juggling, stilt-walking and clowning. A one-week course costs about $150.
Website: www.sfcircus.org

San Francisco Zoo

See chapter **Sightseeing** *for listings.*
With more than 1,000 different species of mammals and birds, the SF Zoo offers a lot to see. Kids will love Koala Crossing (the SF is one of the few zoos in the US that has koalas), Musk Ox Meadows, Wolf Woods and Gorilla World (inhabited by three families of gorillas). Recently, the zoo has added a section of South American animals, including a giant anteater, a Baird's tapir, capybaras and an Andean condor. New zoo babies include lion cubs, gorillas and baby rhinos. Other child-oriented features include feeding times at 2pm daily (3pm for the penguins); the Zebra Zephyr train; a wonderfully creepy Insect Zoo; and a great choice of creatures to touch in the Petting Zoo ($1 separate admission).

Steinhart Aquarium

See chapter **Sightseeing** *for listings.*
Kids love the Steinhart's dark confines, which hold more than 14,000 different sea creatures – some of them incredibly weird – from all over the globe. Check out the grumpy eels, fluorescent-gilled sailfish and harmless-looking piranhas. A recently remodelled Fish Roundabout is a delightfully disorienting spiral with schools of finned creatures zig-zagging in one direction or another; try to arrive at feeding time for the most active panorama. There's a tidepool where kids can touch a variety of slimy creatures and the requisite parcel of goofy penguins. The place gets crowded and noisy at the weekend, so go during the week.

Babysitting/childcare

American Child Care Service

(285 2300).
An upmarket childcare agency serving the downtown hotels, which will also take children on excursions to the Zoo, Exploratorium and other places. Rates charged are $12.50 an hour per family, for a minimum of four hours.
Website: www.americanchildcare.com

Bay Area Childcare Agency

(1-650 991 7474).
In business for more than 50 years, this independent agency serves all the major hotels, screens sitters very carefully and won't employ anyone under the age of 35. The rates are $9 an hour plus transport (minimum four hours), which probably means $40-$50 for a child-free evening.

Historical sites

Alcatraz Island

See chapter **Sightseeing** *for listings.*
The world-famous maximum-security prison remains one tourist attraction even locals grudgingly admit is pretty fascinating. Kids love 'the Rock' for its gritty ambience and undercurrent of malevolence; adults love the views. Rangers lead walking tours of the grounds and the multilingual audio cellblock tour, narrated by former prisoners and played though headphones, is well worth the additional $3.25 per person. Dress warmly – the Rock is as chilly as it is chilling.

The rooftop carousel near Zeum.

Jeremiah O'Brien Liberty Ship

(441 3101). May-Oct *At Pier 45 Embarcadero. Bus 19, 30, 32/cable car Powell-Hyde.* **Open** 10am-7pm daily. **Map F1**
Nov-Apr *At Pier 32 Embarcadero. Muni Metro E/bus 42.* **Open** 10am-4pm daily. **Map J4**
All year **Admission** $5; $3-$4 concessions; children under six free. **No credit cards.**
On board this faithfully-restored Liberty Ship, you and your kids can explore the engine room and officers' bunkrooms, and operate the foghorn but not the three-inch 50-calibre gun. The ship is moored near the USS *Pampanito* during the summer months.
Website: www.crl.com/~wefald/obrien.html

USS Pampanito

Pier 45, Embarcadero (775 1943). Bus 19, 30, 32/cable car Powell-Hyde. **Open** *summer* 9am-8pm daily; *winter* 9am-6pm Mon-Thur, Sun; 9am-8pm Fri, Sat. **Admission** $6; $4 concessions. **No credit cards. Map F1**
The only tourable fleet submarine from World War II, the *USS Pampanito* opens your eyes to what it was like to spend the war years underwater in cramped quarters.
Website: www.maritime.org/pamphome.shtml

Libraries

The Bay Area is a haven for storytellers and many local library branches offer story hours where storytellers of all ages and styles will entertain your children with a yarn. Especially recommended are the multilingual **Mission** (695 5090) and **Chinatown** (274 0275) branches.

San Francisco Main Library

See chapter **Sightseeing** *for listings.*
San Francisco's gorgeous new Main Library boasts half an entire floor for children, with a circular story-telling room and more than a dozen computer and Internet terminals; videos, audio tapes and books in 40 languages; a children's multimedia and electronic discovery computer unit; a fairytale and folk collection; a 'creative centre' for live performances and crafts; and a teenagers' drop-in section. Children's art exhibitions change periodically.

Museums

There's no shortage of museums in San Francisco, but those listed below are particularly good for children, with plenty of hands-on displays. The **Cable Car Barn Museum, Cartoon Art Museum** and **National Maritime Museum** and the soon-to-be-relocated **Musée Mécanique** in the Cliff House are also worth a visit; for details of these and other spaces, *see chapter* **Museums & Galleries**.

Exploratorium

See chapter **Museums & Galleries** *for listings.*
If you and your kids are looking for something uniquely San Franciscan, put the Exploratorium at the top of your list. This science museum is perfect for kids: everything is designed to be touched. With over 700 hands-on experiments, your family can learn about sensory perceptions, weather, botany, mechanics, health issues and the physics of sound and light. The favourite attraction is the Tactile Dome, a geodesic hemisphere of total blackness where you fumble around in the dark touching different objects. It's so popular that it attracts noisy crowds, so book in advance. The gift shop is full of educational and interesting scientific toys.

Mission Science Workshop

City College of San Francisco, Mission Campus, 106 Bartlett Street, at 22nd Street (550 4419). BART 24th Street/bus 14, 49, 67. **Castro/Mission Map Y2**
This Mission district children's workshop is the antidote to the super-tech **Zeum** (*see p187*), a collection of countless gadgets and geegaws – microscopes, electronic parts, magnets and more – all designed for kids. Summer hours differ from those during the school year, so phone the college to check details.

Museum of the City of San Francisco

Third floor, the Cannery, 2801 Leavenworth Street, at Beach Street (928 0289). Bus 19, 30, 32, 42/cable car Powell-Hyde. **Open** 10am-4pm Wed-Sun. **Admission** free. **Map F1**
Features include a special earthquake display, artifacts from the city's architectural history and regular storytelling sessions. Curator Gladys Hansen is usually on hand to show you her great-aunt's sewing machine (saved from the flames of the Great Fire) and to tell tales about the survivors.
Website: www.sfmuseum.org

Randall Museum

199 Museum Street, off Roosevelt Way (554 9600). Bus 24, 37. **Open** 10am-5pm Tue-Sat. **Admission** free. **Map D/E6**

This small, friendly museum is scenically located above the city in Corona Heights Park and features a petting zoo with lambs, raccoons, hawks and a lovely pair of San Francisco garter snakes. There are art workshops, storytellers and an elaborate model railway that enthusiasts run occasionally. Perfect for small children.

Zeum

221 Fourth Street, at Howard Street (777 2800). BART Powell Street/Muni Metro J, K, L, M, N/bus 9X, 30, 45. **Open** noon-6pm Wed-Fri; 11am-5pm Sat, Sun. **Admission** $7; $5-$6 concessions. **Map H4**

San Francisco's newest art and technology centre for those aged 8-18, Zeum is the kind of place that children love and that threatens adults with a headache. Exhibits are interactive, which means kids can direct their own video production, create sculptures in the 'Artists' Studio' or experiment with computer-aided design. Nearby is a bowling alley (with gutter bumpers so no kids strike out), a children's garden and play circle, a child-sized labyrinth and an ice-skating rink. With so many distractions, Zeum is the perfect place to entertain your kids while you tackle the **SFMOMA** or the **Yerba Buena Center**, just across the pedestrian bridge. Afterwards, you can watch a movie or grab dinner at the **Metreon** – all without having to repark that rental car. *See also chapters* **Museums & Galleries**, **Shops & Services** *and* **Film**.

Website: www.zeum.org

Park amusements

As well as the attractions of **Golden Gate Park**, you can go cycling in the rambling **Presidio** or take a picnic and watch the kite-flyers on **Marina Green**. At the **Seal Rocks**, below the Cliff House, and at nearby **Point Lobos**, seals gather day and night: the ones with little ears are California seals; the shiny graceful ones are Harbour seals.

Out of town

Bay Area Discovery Museum

557 McReynolds Road, Fort Baker, near north end of Golden Gate Bridge, Sausalito (487 4398). Golden Gate Transit bus 63 (Sat, Sun)/north on US 101 to Alexander Avenue exit, then follow signs. **Open** *summer* 10am-5pm Tue-Sun; *winter* 9am-4pm Tue-Thur; 10am-5pm Fri-Sun. **Admission** $7; $6 concessions. **No credit cards**.

This collection of historic army barracks has been carefully and imaginatively transformed into a place aimed at one- to ten-year-olds and includes an art room where toddlers learn how to paint and model and a series of distorting mirrors and light shows. There's also a pleasant café and outside picnic tables.

Website: www.badm.org

Lawrence Hall of Science

Centennial Drive, near Grizzly Park Boulevard, Berkeley (1-510 642 5132/lhsinfo@uclink.berkeley.edu). BART to Berkeley, then AC Transit bus 8, 65. **Open** 10am-4pm daily. **Admission** $6; $2-$4 concessions. **Credit** Disc, MC, $TC, V.

Perched on the hills facing San Francisco and the Bay, this fascinating science museum in Berkeley offers a replica of the Challenger spacecraft's nose cone, a Wizard's Lab and a huge DNA model to scramble over. Check out the giant telescope and the wind-driven organ pipes at the back.

Website: www.lhs.berkeley.edu

Marine Mammal Center

Marin Headlands, Golden Gate National Recreation Area, Sausalito (289 7325/shop 289 7355). Bus 76/north off US 101. **Open** 10am-4pm daily. **Admission** free.

Just across the Golden Gate Bridge, the Marine Mammal Center in Sausalito is a sanctuary where sick or injured seals and sea lions are fed and nursed back to health by young volunteers. A second centre has recently opened at Pier 39 in San Francisco, just above where the sea lions congregate. Kids can see a sea lion skin and skeleton, learn about marine mammals and try out interactive computer activities.

Website: www.tmmc.org

Paramount's Great America

Great America Parkway, Santa Clara (1-408 988 1776). BART Fremont, then County Transit bus to Santa Clara. **Open** *Mar-June* 10am-9pm Sat, Sun; *June-Aug* 10am-9pm Mon-Thur, Sun; 10am-11pm Fri, Sat; *Aug-Oct* 10am-8pm Sat, Sun. **Admission** $34.99; $11.99-$24.99 concessions. **Credit** AmEx, MC, $TC, V.

About 65km (40 miles) south of the city in Santa Clara, Great America is the closest amusement park to San Francisco. Check out the Nickelodeon Splat City Slime Zone, The Drop Zone, which is the equivalent of throwing yourself off a skyscraper (but only lasts a few seconds and, fortunately, isn't followed by carnage) and the latest ride, Xtreme Skyflier, which simulates skydiving. There are also gentler jaunts and a carousel for smaller kids plus countless booths with soft toys as prizes. Admission includes all rides.

Website: www.pgathrills.com

Golden Gate Park

See chapter **Sightseeing** *for listings.*

If you've got just one day, spend it in Golden Gate Park. It's full of organised fun – rollerskating, horseriding, boating, hothouse palm forests and museums. Older kids will appreciate the **California Academy of Sciences** (*see chapter* **Museums & Galleries**), which houses the **Steinhart Aquarium** (*see p185*), and the Morrison Planetarium. Experience the SafeQuake and visit the Discovery Room for Children, with its hands-on nature exhibits. There's an alligator pit, hundreds of slithery reptiles in cages and a decent cafeteria in the basement. The planetarium has shows such as the Birth of Black Holes or Star Death, and there's rock music in the evening at the Laserium.

At the south-eastern corner of the park, opposite Kezar Stadium, you'll find an old-fashioned carousel, a tree house and swings in the children's playground, with summertime Punch and Judy shows. At Stow Lake you can hire rowing boats, paddle boats and bicycles. Near the west end of the park, opposite Spreckels Lake at JFK Drive, are the **Golden Gate Park Stables** (*see chapter* **Sport & Fitness**), which offer horse trail rides through the park for kids over eight. There are also windmills, a buffalo herd and the beautiful **Japanese Tea Garden** (admission $1-$2.50), where you can enjoy a pick-me-up cup of jasmine tea by the goldfish ponds after a hard day's play.

Shopping

Chinatown is ideal for children, with its baskets full of small toys and trinkets on display on the pavements. The **San Francisco Centre** and **Embarcadero Center** also do well by kids; the older ones will probably prefer the high-wired **Metreon**; **FAO Schwarz** will deplete your wallet but make your kids happy. For these and details of other children's shops and shopping areas, *see chapter* **Shops & Services**.

The waterfront & islands

San Francisco's waterfront isn't all overpriced kitsch. At **Pier 39** you can see – and hear, and certainly smell – a pride of gallumphing great sea lions, who've taken up residence at one of the docks. For human entertainment, you'll find dozens of street performers here and at **Fisherman's Wharf**, the **Cannery** and the **Anchorage** (*see chapter* **Shops & Services**).

Trips to the islands in the Bay are a great diversion. Visit the prison on **Alcatraz** (*see page 185*) or take a ferry to **Angel Island**, the largest island in the Bay, where you can bicycle around the old barracks at Camp Reynolds (you can hire bikes on the island). In December, take a boat to look for whales around the **Farallon Islands**.

The Balclutha, *docked at* **Hyde Street Pier**.

For more on Angel Island, *see chapters* **Sightseeing** *and* **Trips Out of Town**; for bike hire, *see chapter* **Sport & Fitness**.

Hyde Street Pier

End of Hyde Street, at Jefferson Street, at the west side of Fisherman's Wharf (556 2904). Bus 19, 30, 32, 42/cable car Powell-Hyde. **Open** *summer* 9.30am-5.30pm daily; *winter* 9.30am-5pm daily. **Admission** $5; free first Tue of the month. **No credit cards. Map F1**

This is somewhere that adults will enjoy as much as kids. Several ships are docked along the pier, including the *Balclutha*, a three-masted square-rigger built in 1886. Next door is the *CA Thayer*, a schooner built in 1895, and on the other side, the *Eureka*, a paddle-wheel ferryboat used by commuters across the Bay in the 1920s. There's also the *Hercules*, the US's last operable steam-powered tug boat.

Underwater World

Pier 39, Embarcadero (623 5300). Bus 32, 42. **Open** 9am-9pm daily. **Admission** $12.95; $6.50-$9.95 concessions; children under three free. **Credit** AmEx, Disc, MC, $TC, V. **Map G1**

The latest addition to San Francisco's aquatic theme parks, Underwater World gives you a 'diver's-eye view' of the Bay through clear plastic underwater tunnels. Though admission prices are a bit steep, it's still a great place to spy on crabs and sharks, stare in wonderment at the benign-looking jellyfish and watch the slow, gentle combat of giant octopuses. Like any tourist attraction, this place gets mobbed at the weekends and around midday, so get there early.

Film

Though its commercial theatres are battling multiplexification, the city's independent film spirit continues to thrive.

Close enough to (but far enough from) Hollywood and Los Angeles, San Francisco and the Bay Area provide a base for several mainstream directors, notably Francis Ford Coppola and George Lucas, whose Marin-based LucasFilm studio is noted for its special effects abilities (and who has recently relocated some offices to the Presidio). A few major stars also live here: Robin Williams, Danny Glover, Sharon Stone and Nicholas Cage among them.

But the city's major claim to fame is that – except for one small town in Kentucky that's home to a film-making foundation – San Francisco has more film-makers per capita than any other city in the world, many of them avant-garde film- and documentary-makers. From Terry Zwiegoff, who made 1994's *Crumb*, and Iara Lee, director of *Modulations* in 1998, to *Art Car* documentographer Harrod Blank and film-making pair Rob Epstein and Jeffrey Friedman, who won Academy Awards for *The Life and Times of Harvey Milk* and *Common Threads*, the city is home to the genre's better-known directors and producers.

Its residents aside, the city is also a favourite place to locate a film. Whether for Hitchcock's *Vertigo, The Conversation*, *Star Trek IV*, *Mrs Doubtfire* or *Dirty Harry*, the city's hills have set the stage for hundreds of film features and television series.

SCHOOLS & CLASSES

San Francisco State University, UC Berkeley, the San Francisco Art Institute and City College all have thriving film study or film-making programmes, each encouraging and developing new and established film and video artists (*see chapter* **Directory**). In addition, two San Francisco institutions – the **Film Arts Foundation** (*see page 192*) and the **Bay Area Video Coalition** (558 2100) – provide services and continuing education and networking for film-makers and videographers in the area. Phone the **San Francisco Film Commission** (recorded information 554 4004) to find out casting and production details of current films being made in the Bay Area.

> For the fastest film information, including showtimes, cinema locations and ticket purchases (there's a $1 service charge per ticket), phone **Movie Phone** on 777 3456.

TICKETS & INFORMATION

Advance tickets for some cinemas and festivals are available by credit card from Movie Phone (*see below*). Otherwise, you should purchase tickets from festival organisers or at cinema box offices. Check the newspapers for listings and film times at all of the cinemas (the *San Francisco Examiner*, *San Francisco Chronicle* and *Bay Guardian* have up-to-date listings and reviews), and expect opening nights to be popular. Most cinemas run bargain-price matinées – check the venue for its policy.

The cinemas

San Franciscans have a sizeable appetite for foreign and art house movies and the city contains more than a few cinemas that specialise in screening those films. Several of these are run by the Landmark chain, whose cinemas include the **Lumière** (1572 California Street, between Polk and Larkin Streets), **Bridge** (3010 Geary Boulevard, at Blake Street), **Opera Plaza** (601 Van Ness Avenue, between Turk Street and Golden Gate Avenue), **Clay** (2261 Fillmore Street, at Clay Street), and **Embarcadero Center Cinemas** (1 Embarcadero Center, on Battery Street, between Sacramento and Clay Streets). You can get information on all five cinemas from one telephone number: 352 0810. Landmark will often pick up audience favourites from one of the frequent San Francisco film festivals. The **San Francisco Cinematheque** (*see page 193*) provides a prime venue for avant-garde screenings.

A few old, restored movie theatres remain, though they're quickly getting displaced by huge multiplexes (*see page 191* **Invasion of the multiplexes!**). The recently-restored **United Artists Metro** (Union Street, at Webster Street; 931 1685) is a pleasure to visit, as is the colossal **United Artists Coronet** (3575 Geary Boulevard, at Arguello Street; 752 4400), which hosts the biggest cinematic blockbusters. The well-run **AMC Kabuki 8** (1181 Post Street, at Fillmore Street; 931 9800), **Galaxy** (1285 Sutter Street, at Van Ness Avenue; 474 8700) and funky **Presidio** (2141 Chestnut Street, at Scott Street; 921 6720) are good, centrally-located houses.

Most interesting, however, are the independent cinemas housed in unique buildings. Including the **Castro**, **Roxie**, and **Red Vic** theatres, most schedule repertory programmes (*see page 193*).

Film festivals

That the Bay Area appreciates film is obvious: almost every month of the year there's a festival of some sort taking place, many of them drawing directors from around the world. The works of local movie-making and video artists feature prominently in every San Francisco festival, where films can vary from extremely high quality to dire. Some events are tiny and roving, among them the digital **RESFEST** (267 4848/www.resfest.com) and super-cool **Short Attention Span Film & Video Festival** (*see page 192* **Artists' Tele-vision Access**) as well as the **Cin(E)-Poetry Festival** (552 9261/www.slip.net/~ gamuse). For the most complete film fest information, check the SF Film Commission website (www.filmdependent.com/sffests.html).

¡Festival Cine Latino!

(Information 553 8140). **Venues** vary; phone for details. **Date** Sept.

Cine Acción's festival has come into its own as the premier showcase for films from South and Central America, Mexico and those by US Latino film-makers – works that are surprisingly under-distributed in the US. The festival is almost a decade old (though relatively young by comparison with the other Bay Area sprees) and includes films, videos and appearances by the film-makers. It also has great food and music at the opening ceremonies.

Film Arts Foundation Festival

(Information 552 8760). **Venues** Castro Theater; The Roxie; UC Theater, Berkeley. **Date** first week of Nov.

This six-day festival provides the essential venue for a real snapshot of film-making in Northern California. All programming is drawn from Bay Area independent work and features documentary, experimental and traditional narrative pieces.

Website: www.filmarts.org

Jewish Film Festival

(Information 621 0556). **Venues** Castro Theater; UC Theater, Berkeley & peninsula theatres. **Date** late July-early Aug.

This festival, launched in 1981, is intended to showcase contemporary films from around the world on Jewish subjects and to strengthen awareness of Jewish secular culture. Most of the programming is contemporary, but there is also some retrospective and archival work.

Website: www.sfjff.org

MadCat Film Festival

(Information 436 9523/alionbear@earthlink.net). **Venue** phone for details. **Date** late Sept.

The *alternative* alternative women's film festival, tiny MadCat features short films, panel discussions and pioneering features that range from earnest feminist polemics to raunchy sexploitation. A recent programme included a tribute to Doris Wishman, director of notorious 1960s B-movies and soft-core porn.

SF International Asian-American Film Festival

(Information 252 4800). **Venues** Kabuki 8 Cinema; Pacific Film Archive, Berkeley. **Date** Mar.

Nearly 20 years old, the AAFF features film by and/or about Asian Pacific people. Recent hits have included a sneak preview of *The Wedding Banquet* and *Citizen Hong Kong*, San Francisco film director Ruby Yang's cinematic treatment of the British-Chinese transfer of power. An eight-day event, the festival draws huge audiences.

Website: www.naatanet.org/festival/

SF International Film Festival

(Information 929 5000/SF Film Society 931 3456). **Venues** Kabuki 8 Cinema; other cinemas around town. **Date** mid Apr-early May.

Produced by the San Francisco Film Society, this more than 40-year-old festival is North America's longest-running and considered one of its best. Over the course of a few weeks, the society presents multiple screenings of more than 200 films and videos, from dozens of countries and in dozens of languages and it's usually hard to find a loser in the bunch. A variety of cinematic glitterati show up – director Wim Winders, playwright David Mamet and Warner Herzog all attended recently. Some 80,000 tickets sell like hotcakes. Most films are screened at the Kabuki 8 Cinema in Japantown, with related screenings at other venues around town. Tickets go on sale, in advance, at the Kabuki a few weeks before the festival opens.

Website: www.sfiff.org

SF International Lesbian & Gay Film Festival

(Information 703 8650). **Venues** Castro, Victoria & Roxie Theaters. **Date** last two weeks of June; ends with Freedom Day parade.

The Lesbian & Gay Film Festival, which celebrates its 25th anniversary in 2001, is another in a series of events for San Francisco's month-long celebration of Gay Pride. Recent years have seen a rise in gay-themed films produced in Hollywood and the festival often premières such mainstream fare. The rest of the programming runs the gamut from high-quality independent shorts and full-length features, to avant-garde film with a queer sensibility, to high- and low-quality shorts from new and old film-makers. Sponsored by Frameline, the event is the world's oldest and largest of its kind. A programme is available a month in advance from bookshops and cafés and in the *San Francisco Bay Guardian*.

Website: www.frameline.org

Invasion of the multiplexes!

One the best San Francisco experiences used to be seeing a film in one of the city's old, grand movie houses. Armed with popcorn and a sweating soda, movie-goers could enjoy their favourite flicks inside a beautifully-decorated, regal cinema. Every neighbourhood had one: the Regency I near Civic Center, the Alhambra and Royal on either end of Polk Gulch, the Mission in the heart of the Mission district. With few exceptions – the **Coronet**, **Metro** and **Castro** (*see page 189 and page 193*) – the grande dames of cinema have shut down, and signs that once advertised the latest Hollywood sensation now read 'FOR SALE OR RENT'.

The culprit, of course, is the multiplex – the many-screened, single box-office cinemas that define America's shopping malls and, by proxy, America. For years they remained at bay in San Francisco, lurking in the cities and suburbs south of the city. Yet their omnipresence has become undeniable of late and any likelihood of the trend's reversal is as slim as the chance of a new Stanley Kubrick film.

No one was surprised by the arrival of **Stonestown**'s two-screener, tucked into the Stonestown mall (Winston Drive, at 19th Avenue; 759 2626) and the glass edifice that marked the **Galaxy** on Van Ness was interesting enough to disguise the three cinemas within (*see page 189*). When the **AMC Kabuki 8** opened in Japantown (*see page 189*), it was something of a phenomenon, an eight-screen complex with a stunning, three-floor architectural design; similarly, no one begrudged the **Embarcadero Center Cinema**'s graceful incorporation into Embarcadero One because it screened (and still does) the best of the imported films (*see page 189*).

But in 1999, the twin arrival of AMC's **1000 Van Ness** (1000 Van Ness Avenue, at O'Farrell Street; 922 4262) and the Sony **Metreon** (221 Fourth Street, at Mission Street; 369 6000) threw the balance heavily towards mall-ification. Housed in a former car dealership, 1000 Van Ness boasts 14 cinemas; one purchases tickets what feels like blocks away, then rides several long, slow escalators to reach your chosen screen. Not to be outdone, the Metreon features 15 screens, aligned down a frighteningly long hall (it's a bit like departing from the airport) on the super-mall's top floor (*see also chapter* **Shops & Services**).

To their credit, the screens in both are state-of-the-art, with comfortable, high-backed seats and excellent sound systems; yet one has to wonder if a few years from now, they'll remain as well-maintained as their art house counterparts. And, regretfully, the multiplexes are likely to favour a repertoire of blockbusters over the art or foreign fare that plays on most single screens.

The future promises more of the same: plans are underway for Blue Note, the venerable New York jazz venue, to open a combination night club/multiplex in the Fillmore District in 2001, a move that will surely endanger other nearby cinemas. A representative from Landmark, the chain which maintains the **Lumière**, **Bridge**, **Opera Plaza** and **Clay**, put it succinctly: 'It used to be that people from San Francisco would venture to the suburbs if they wanted to attend a mall theatre,' she said with a note of sadness. 'Now it seems like the suburbs have come to us.'

On location: Steve McQueen is the honest cop in Peter Yates' San Francisco-filmed Bullitt.

Spike and Mike's Festival of Animation

(Information 621 6120). **Venues** Castro & Palace of Fine Arts cinemas in the city, and elsewhere in Berkeley & San Jose. **Date** Apr & Nov.

The kings of the cartoon carnivals are Spike and Mike, whose 50-city, biannual Festival of Animation has for nearly a quarter of a century reigned supreme in Bay Area movie houses. Both their spring and autumn festivals have become springboards for local artists' success – Pixar producer John Lasseter (who stunned cinemagoers with his *Toy Story* films) got his start on a Spike and Mike fest; a work by San Francisco film-maker Timothy Hittle was recently nominated for an Oscar. The Sick and Twisted special, added ten years ago, is a must-see for non-fragile minds.

Website: www.spikeandmike.com

Classic, new & experimental

Alliance Française

1345 Bush Street, between Polk & Larkin Streets (775 7755). Bus 2, 3, 4, 19, 76. **Admission** free members; $5 non-members. **Credit** MC, V. **Map F3**

French films are screened on Tuesday evenings.

Website: www.afsf.com

Artists' Television Access

992 Valencia Street, at 21st Street (824 3890). BART 24th Street/bus 14, 26, 49. **Open** 10am-10pm daily. **Admission** from $5. **No credit cards.** **Castro/Mission Map Y2**

Artists' Television Access often has experimental and unusual programming with a do-it-yourself motif, usually from Thursday to Saturday. It supported the first Short Attention Span Film & Video Festival in 1992 – a two-hour programme of *very* short film shorts (each offering is under two minutes); more information on the festival can be found at www.bandaland.com/shortfilm/text/main.htm.

Website: www.atasite.org

Film Arts Foundation

Second floor, 346 Ninth Street, at Folsom Street (552 8760). BART Civic Center/Muni Metro F, J, K, L, M, N/bus 12, 19, 27, 42. **Admission** varies. **Map G5**

The Foundation screens works-in-progress (there's no regular schedule) and hosts lectures and classes by and for film-makers.

Website: www.filmarts.org

Goethe Institute

530 Bush Street, between Stockton Street & Grant Avenue (263 8760). Bus 30, 45. **Admission** free. **Map G3**

Both contemporary and classic German films are screened at the Goethe Institute – telephone for information on the latest schedule.

Istituto Italiano di Cultura

425 Bush Street, between Kearny Street & Grant Avenue (788 7142). Bus 30, 45. **Admission** free

members; $2 non-members. **No credit cards.**
Map G/H3
The Italian Institute shows both contemporary and classic Italian films. Screenings are held on Tuesdays – phone for the latest schedule.
Website: www.sfiic.org

San Francisco Cinematheque

(Information 558 8129). **Venue** Yerba Buena Center for the Arts & San Francisco Art Institute.
Admission $7; $4 students. **No credit cards.**
Cinematheque is at the epicentre of avant-garde film in the Bay Area, offering programmes from late September until early June. It's a place to gather information and inspiration and to see experimental works – from documentaries to features and animated films.
Website: www.sirius.com/~sstark/org/ctek/ctek.html

San Francisco Museum of Modern Art

See chapter **Museums & Galleries** *for listings.*
There's a large 278-seat cinema in the museum, which usually hosts screenings in the spring and autumn (mostly on Thursdays and Sundays), often in conjunction with SFMOMA exhibitions.

Yerba Buena Center for the Arts

See chapter **Museums & Galleries** *for listings.*
Located on the second floor of the Arts building, Yerba Buena's 96-seat media screening room is often used for contemporary and experimental offerings connected with the exhibitions in the Center's galleries.

Repertory

Castro Theater

429 Castro Street, off Market Street (621 6120). Muni Metro F, K, L, M/bus 24, 33, 35, 37.
Admission $7. **No credit cards. Map E6**
Go on a weekend night for the full experience. The popcorn-munching audience is entertained before the screening by an organist playing a battery of favourites on a Wurlitzer; painted murals line the Art Deco ceilings. The film might be anything from an old Bette Davis picture (where everyone knows and recites the best lines) to a director's cut of *Blade Runner* or a world première by an independent queer film-maker.

The Red Vic

1727 Haight Street, at Cole Street (668 3994). Bus 6, 7, 43, 61, 77. **Admission** $4.50-$6.
No credit cards. Map C6
Where else can you sprawl on an old sofa, eat popcorn out of wooden bowls and watch revivals or a current funky flick with a wildly eclectic crowd?

The Roxie

3117 16th Street, at Valencia Street (863 1087). BART 16th Street/bus 22, 26, 53. **Admission** $6.50. **No credit cards. Map F6**
Revivals of film noir classics, Fassbinder festivals and horror movies cover the range of the Roxie's roster. The seats are hard and the sound system is second-rate, but go for the atmosphere.

Out of town

If you're headed out of town and want to see a movie, your best bet is to check the cinema listings in Oakland or Berkeley. The East Bay has a superb selection of film resources and festivals, as well as some of the best cinemas in the Bay Area.

In Berkeley, the programme at the **UC Theater** (2036 University Avenue, at Shattuck Avenue; 1-510 843 3456) is always worth investigating. The **Pacific Film Archive**, located in the same complex as the Berkeley Art Museum (2626 Bancroft Way, between Bowditch and College Streets; 1-510 642 5249/1124/www.uampfa.berkeley.edu/pfa), keeps the reels rolling almost every evening with classic films and a programme of Bay Area-based independent documentaries.

Finally, the **Paramount** in Oakland (2025 Broadway, between 20th and 21st Streets; 1-510 465 6400) is a wonderful, cavernous theatre in which to a rep film or an old classic.

Black Filmworks Festival of Film & Video

(Information 1-510 465 0804). **Venues** The Paramount, Laney College, Oakland Museum, all in Oakland. **Date** late Sept-early Oct.
Presented by the Black Filmmakers Hall of Fame, this competitive fest features films by, for and about Africans and African-Americans. The festival has included tributes to US director Spike Lee and the late Marlon Riggs, whose groundbreaking experimental documentary *Tongues Untied* explored the experiences of African-American gay men.

Mill Valley Film Festival & Videofest

(Information 383 5256). **Venues** Sequoia Twin Theater in Mill Valley & the Rafael Film Center in San Rafael. **Date** Oct.
US and international independent films and videos are the focus of this Marin County festival, which screens dozens of feature films.
It also includes a six-day 'Videofest', interactive media exhibitions, seminars, special events and children's programmes, among other projects.
Website: www.finc.org

Gay & Lesbian San Francisco

Ubiquitous and stylish, San Francisco's queer community remains a central, vital part of the city's character.

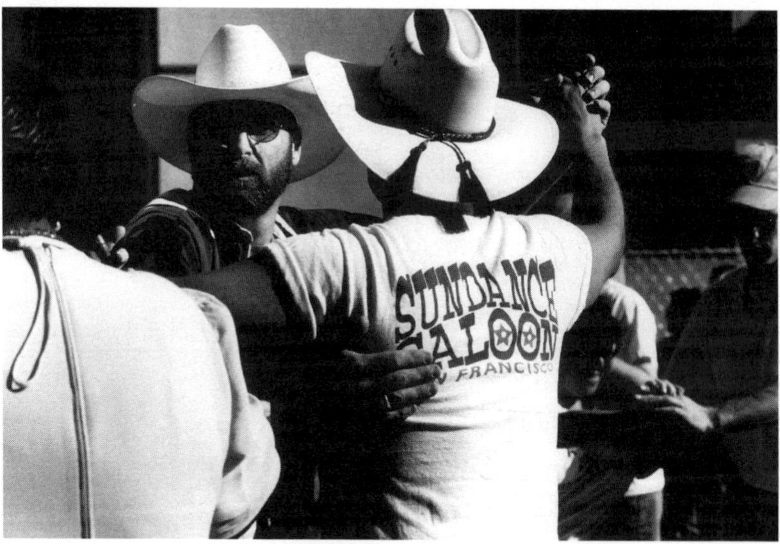

The city's well-attended Gay Pride celebration is held every June.

San Francisco's reputation as the West Coast's mecca for gay pride is rooted in a long history of struggle for equality, rights and freedom that date back to Barbary Coast days. The 1978 assassination of Harvey Milk, the country's first openly gay elected official, marked a turning point for local gay politics, and vitalised the population's sense of civic and social responsibility (*see chapter* **History**). Though it wasn't voiced until years later, the gay mantra – 'We're here, we're queer; get used to it!' – was born in spirit decades ago.

The month of June is dedicated to Gay Pride, which culminates in San Francisco's Freedom Day Parade, commemorating the 1969 Stonewall Riots in New York and the beginning of the modern American gay liberation movement. The city's best-attended street pageant, the parade comprises a noisy party where gays, straights and plenty of gawking onlookers celebrate regional diversity (*see chapter* **San Francisco by Season**). A pair of marches – the Harvey Milk Memorial in November and the Aids Candlelight March in May – mark more solemn events that reverberate just as deeply within the community.

To the first-time observer, what might appear to be blatant ghettoisation of gays and lesbians within certain neighbourhoods is actually a function of convenience and preference. For both genders, to be seen is the thing, but don't be fooled: though they're most visible in the Castro or Bernal Heights (the preferred hangouts for gay men and lesbian women, respectively), friends of Dorothy are omnipresent in the city.

Not all San Francisco's gay scene is flamboyant. The city also offers a welcome refuge for gay people from all over the world in search of lives, not lifestyles. You can connect with lesbian mums at PTA meetings or make new gay friends at church suppers just as easily as you can flirt with a babetoy at a some trendy club. You'll find a guide to all kinds of community activities – from a support group for deaf Latina lesbians to a prom for queer teens – in free papers such as the *Bay Times* and *Bay Area Reporter* (*BAR*).

For a more reflective look at San Francisco's gay past and present, explore the Gay and Lesbian Center at the **Main Library**, or join a walking tour – either one organised by the Gay and Lesbian Historical Society of Northern California (777 5455) or Trevor Hailey's **Cruisin' the Castro** (*see page 77* **Sightseeing**).

NEIGHBOURHOODS

The **Castro** flaunts its reputation as the centre of the known queer universe and even a brief stroll through its busy streets gives a sense of the riches gay San Francisco has to offer. Start at the magnificently restored **Castro Theater**, base for the International Lesbian and Gay Film Festival each June (*see chapter* **Film**). Down the block you'll find **Cliff's Variety**, the fabulously eclectic hardware store whose camp window displays are a show in themselves and, also in the neighbourhood, **A Different Light**, which sells books by and about gays and lesbians (*see page 178 and page 162* **Shops & Services**). Make sure you wind up on the patio of **Café Flore**, the see-and-be-seen spot locals dub 'Café Hairdo', sipping a latte as the fog rolls in (*see page 199*).

Gay life in San Francisco extends beyond the Castro to lesser-known but equally interesting neighbourhoods. **Polk Street** is poorer, rougher and draggier: check out the transgender divas at bars such as the **1100 Club** (*see page 197*). **SoMa**, setting of the infamous leather **Folsom Street Fair** (*see chapter* **San Francisco by Season**), has bars, trendy restaurants, sex clubs and gay dance venues packed with hot, muscled men. Although women patronise the Castro and Hayes Valley bars, cafés and restaurants, the more affordable **Mission** area – particularly Valencia Street from 16th to 22nd Streets – provides a scene for many lesbians, especially younger ones. A perennial favourite is **Osento** (*see page 177* **Shops & Services**), a women-only spa where you can soak in a hot tub or eucalyptus-scented sauna, and then lie outside on the deck beneath the stars.

Don't leave the city without discovering the charms of **Bernal Heights**, a quietly romantic neighbourhood way off the tourist map that's become a hub for gay and lesbian homeowners. Walk up its winding streets past cottages covered in flowering vines to the top of Bernal Hill. On a sunny day you'll be rewarded with a spectacular Bay view – and beautiful Bernal residents walking their dogs.

Main drag: the heart of the Castro district.

INFORMATION

The best sources for up-to-the-minute information on new clubs, shows, films, events and general gay news are the free newspapers, which can be found in almost every café or in boxes on street corners. Look for the *Bay Times,* the *Bay Area Reporter* (*BAR*) and, to a lesser extent, the *San Francisco Bay Guardian* and *SF Weekly*. The **Names Project** at 2362A Market Street (*see page 60* **Sightseeing**) has a visitor's centre and next-door shop benefiting the Aids Memorial Quilt, which is made up of more than 44,000 panels, each commemorating a person who has died from Aids.

The **Women's Building** at 3543 18th Street in the Mission (*see page 54* **Sightseeing**) shelters various women's organisations and is also a central place for newspapers, bulletin board postings, events and information. The rich colours of the mural that covers the outside of the building have made the centre a landmark.

For Aids helplines, gay counselling and medical services, *see page 274* **Directory**.

Accommodation

It's not as necessary in San Francisco as in some cities to make sure that your lodgings are gay-friendly, since most hoteliers are either welcoming or indifferent. Some establishments, however, cater specifically to gay clients. For a complete list of lodgings in the city, *see chapter* **Accommodation**.

The unmissable see-and-be-scene, **Café Flore**. *See page 199.*

Alamo Square Inn
719 Scott Street, CA 94117, at Fulton Street (922 2055/fax 931 1304). Bus 5, 24. **Rates** *single* $85-$125; *suite* $195-$295. **Credit** AmEx, MC, V. **Map E5**

One of the most charming and comfortable guesthouses in the city, located across from the famous row of painted Victorians on Alamo Square. All rooms are non-smoking, breakfast is included and there is free parking – a premium in the area.
Website: www.alamoinn.com

Beck's Motor Lodge
2222 Market Street, CA 94114 , at 15th Street (621 8212/fax 421 0435). Muni Metro F, K, L, M/bus 37. **Rates** *single* $86; *double* $109-$114. **Credit** AmEx, MC, V. **Map E6**

Even after its recent renovation Beck's Motor Lodge remains a quintessential American motel, down to its tacky carpets and glasses sealed in plastic. The relatively cheap rates and prime Castro location keep it popular, however. The management frowns on cruising from the balconies overlooking the parking lot, so behave yourself. There are some non-smoking rooms, free parking and the rates are cheaper in winter.

Hayes Valley Inn
417 Gough Street, CA 94102, at Hayes Street (431 9131). Bus 21. **Rates** *single* $55; *double* $65. **Credit** AmEx, MC, V. **Map F5**

On the edge of Hayes Valley and near to the Opera House and Symphony Hall, this is a pleasant, gay-run little pension. There's a friendly bar downstairs and car parking is available nearby for $3.50 a day.

House O' Chicks Guesthouse
(861 9849). **Rates** *single* $75 per night, $500 per week; *double* $100 per night, $600 per week. **Credit** AmEx, MC, V.

Two rooms in this seven-room flat are available for female visitors to the city; phone for details of its location. It caters to a mostly European clientele and has a shared bathroom, and continental breakfast is included in the price. It's not a stuffy B&B – you'll find notes and scrapbooks compiled by past guests, as well as guidebooks and current lesbian listings for around the city.

Inn on Castro
321 Castro Street, CA 94114, at Market Street (861 0321). Muni Metro F, K, L, M/bus 24, 35, 37. **Rates** *single* $90; *double* $100; *suite* $150-$200. **Credit** AmEx, MC, V. **Map E6**

This beautifully restored Edwardian building has served as San Francisco's premier gay and lesbian hotel for two decades. It has eight rooms, each with a private bath, original modern art and elaborate flower arrangements. The highlight of the stay is the breakfast, including homemade muffins and piles of fresh fruit. The hotel is non-smoking (it's allowed on the back patio) and there are rooms for disabled visitors. Treat yourself like a queen.

Nancy's Bed
(239 5692). **Rates** $25-$35. **No credit cards**.

There are two rooms available in this private home, which is close to the Castro area and public transport.

Ruth's House
(641-8898). **Rates** *single* $40, *double* $45. **No credit cards**.

Another of several small residences in the Castro area with rooms available for women only.

The Willows Bed & Breakfast Inn
710 14th Street, CA 94114, between Sanchez & Church Streets (431 4770/fax 431 5295). Muni Metro F, K, L, M/bus 22, 37. **Rates** *single* $82-$100; *double* $90-$108; *suite* $120-$140. **Credit** AmEx, Disc, MC, V. **Map E6**

The Willows offers 11 nice rooms in a 1904 Edwardian building, breakfast in bed and a location just outside the craziness of the Castro. All rooms have shared bath facilities and there's limited off-street parking ($8 per night).

24 Henry

24 Henry Street, CA 94114, between Sanchez and Noe Streets (864 5686/1-800 900 5686/fax 864 0406). Muni Metro F, K, L, M/bus 24, 37.
Rates *single* $60-$95; *double* $80-$95; *apartment suite* from $105. **Credit** AmEx, MC, V. **Map E6**
Geared towards gay vacationers but welcoming everyone, 24 Henry offers traditional San Francisco charm in the heart of the Castro at a very reasonable rate. Each of the five guest rooms within the Victorian has a private phone line with voicemail and a shared or private bath.

Bars

The **End-up** is a long-standing gay men's bar with a girl-friendly club on Saturday nights, though the venue was under threat of closure as we went to press; the popular **Badlands** (626 9320) was closed for reconstruction. For a drink in classy surroundings, try **Martuni's**, which stands on the edge of the Mission, Castro and Hayes Valley neighbourhoods. And for the ultimate San Francisco Sunday afternoon experience, **El Rio** shouldn't be missed. *See also chapter* **Bars**.

Blondie's Bar & No Grill

540 Valencia Street, between 16th & 17th Streets (864 2419). BART 16th Street/bus 22, 26, 53.
Open 2pm-2am daily. **No credit cards.**
Map F6
On Tuesdays and Sundays, Blondie's is filled with hip young women ready to dance, cruise and watch each other. During off-peak hours you can try out the bar's low-key pool tables. On weekend nights you'll often find a mixed clientele watching a good jazz or blues band.

Club Q

177 Townsend Street, at Third Street (974 6020). Bus 15, 30, 42, 45, 76. **Open** 9pm-3am, first Fri of month. **No credit cards. Map J4/5**
If you're in town while it's happening, catch one of the longest-running women's clubs in San Francisco. Club Q has fun music, girls galore and a hard-dancing, culturally varied crowd.

The CoCo Club

139 Eighth Street, between Mission & Howard Streets (626 2337). Bus 12, 14, 19, 26.
Open 8.30pm-2am Wed-Sun. **No credit cards.**
Map G5
The hottest new lesbian venue features a mix of live and DJ-spun dance music. Known for booking great girl groups, the club often presents showcases of local bands that complement the sweaty dance nights, all in an intimate setting with a low cover charge. There are happy hour specials during the week.

Detour

2348 Market Street, at Castro Street (861 6053). Muni Metro F, K, L, M/bus 24, 35, 37. **Open** 2pm-2am daily. **No credit cards. Castro/Mission Map X1**
High-decibel music, a chain link fence and angst-ridden Gen-X boys with piercings galore – this is a place to look rougher than you feel and get away with it. Pool and pinball are sidelines to the ferocious cruising here.

El Rio

3158 Mission Street, at Army Street (282 3325). Bus 12, 14, 27, 49. **Open** 3pm-midnight Mon; 3pm-2am Tue-Sun. **No credit cards.**
Though it's not strictly a gay bar, El Rio makes the list for its one-of-a-kind live salsa parties, held on Sunday afternoons when the weather is good. The mostly-lesbian crowd shoulders past the pool and shuffleboard tables in the front of the narrow bar to the back, where a garden straight out of Brazil blooms with bougainvillea and beautiful women, all tangoing to the sound of live Latin jazz. *See also p214* **Nightlife**.

1100 Club

1100 Polk Street, at Post Street (771 2022). Bus 19, 47, 76. **Open** 6pm-2am Mon-Thur, Sun; noon-2am Fri, Sat. **Credit** AmEx, Disc, DC, MC, V. **Map F4**
Formerly the Polk Gulch Saloon, the 1100 Club now serves mostly young gay professionals who go for the bar scene and club kids who go for the DJs later in the night. With the recent closing of the Motherlode a block away, a few transient, transgendered divas straggle in.

Esta Noche

3079 16th Street, at Mission Street (861 5757). BART 16th Street/bus 14, 22, 26, 49, 53.
Open 2pm-2am daily. **No credit cards.**
Map F6
Unpretentious and easily overlooked, Esta Noche is one of the city's hottest Latin bars – particularly on Friday nights when it hosts an evening of Latino striptease. Fabulous.

Giraffe Video Lounge

1131 Polk Street, at Post Street (474 1702). Bus 2, 3, 4, 19, 76. **Open** 8am-2am daily. **No credit cards. Map F4**
Perhaps the most popular of the trashy Polk Street bars, the Giraffe is low-key and friendly – a good place for pool or pinball. Rather dead during the week, the place is usually hopping at the weekend.

Hole in the Wall

289 Eighth Street, between Howard & Folsom Streets (431 4695). Bus 12, 19. **Open** noon-2am Tue-Thur; 6am-2am Mon, Fri-Sun. **No credit cards. Map G5**
This is rapidly becoming one of the most popular hangouts of the Gen-X queers who are turning their backs on the clone scene of the Castro. Drop in to compare tattoos with hot boys in torn clothing – a real San Francisco experience.

Lexington Club

3464 19th Street, at Lexington Street (863 2052). Bus 14, 26, 33, 49. **Open** 3pm-2am daily. **No credit cards. Castro/Mission Map Y1**

A funky, street-level hideaway which just might be San Francisco's sole lesbian-only bar, replacing Amelia's (may it rest in peace) in the Mission. Cosy, inviting booths and dim lights set the scene, with women of all kinds smoking, talking and cruising. There's also a great jukebox with a choice that ranges from the Cure to Johnny Cash.

The Lion Pub

2062 Divisadero Street, at Sacramento Street (567 6565). Bus 1, 24. **Open** 3pm-2am daily. **No credit cards. Map D3**

With the recent closing of the Alta Plaza, the Lion is now the only chi-chi (or is it she-she?) gay bar in Pacific Heights. Largely frequented by sweatered professionals, the well-fireplaced Lion also catches some of the younger crowd on their way to the clubs – or with their sugar daddy. It's an odd combination of Victorian chic and Gen-X soundtrack, and the clients range in age from minors to seniors, but it seems to work.

Loading Dock

1525 Mission Street, between Market Street & South Van Ness Avenue (864 1525). Muni Metro F, J, K, L, M/bus 42, 47, 49. **Open** 9pm-1am Thur; 9pm-2am Fri, Sat; 4pm-1am Sun. **No credit cards. Map F5**

With the taming of the **San Francisco Eagle** (*see below*), there is really only one true leather/fetish bar left in the city – this nondescript spot on Mission. The Loading Dock's dress policy (leather, latex, Levi's with boots and uniforms only) and a serious attitude is sure to weed out the Andy-boys and drag queens.

Lone Star Saloon

1354 Harrison Street, between Ninth & Tenth Streets (863 9999). Bus 19, 27, 42. **Open** noon-2am Mon-Fri; 9am-2am Sat, Sun. **No credit cards. Map G5**

A western/leather bar, as the name suggests, Lone Star has a big following and is an important centre for San Francisco's leather scene. If your taste runs toward large men with facial hair, this is your spot.

Martuni's

See p151 **Bars** *for listings.*

Martuni's opened quietly in the mid-1990s and has just hit its stride. Its location is perfect – near but not in the Castro, Hayes Valley and Mission districts – and its ambience is warm and welcoming. Great drinks and a phalanx of friendly staff make it worth going once; the tinkly piano jazz (and an occasional drunken torch song) make it worth returning often.

The Metro

3600 16th Street, at Market Street (703 9750). Muni Metro K, L, M/bus 37. **Open** 4pm-2am Mon-Thur; 3pm-2am Fri; 1pm-2am Sat, Sun. **No credit cards. Map E6**

Perched above the busy intersection at 16th and Market in the Castro, the Metro's balcony is a great place to have a drink and watch the crowds heading out for the night. It has friendly bartenders, great Margaritas and a karaoke machine. The place can get very crowded on weekend nights – the weekday happy hour is more sedate. The attached Chinese restaurant is also worth investigating.

The Midnight Sun

4067 18th Street, between Castro & Noe Streets (861 4186). Muni Metro F, K, L, M/bus 33, 35. **Open** noon-2am daily. **No credit cards. Castro/Mission Map X1**

A popular video bar and a good cruising spot, the Midnight Sun is generally packed for the after-work happy hour (3-7pm weekdays) and crammed full at the weekends. Frequented by a fairly young crowd which enjoys chanting along with their favourite movie or TV clips.

Moby Dick's

4049 18th Street, at Hartford Street (no phone). Muni Metro F, K, L, M/bus 24, 33, 35. **Open** noon-2am daily. **No credit cards. Castro/Mission Map X1**

A cross between a neighbourhood pub and a gay bar, Moby Dick's is popular with pool players (although there's only one table) and pinball addicts (four machines at the back). Big windows and a prime Castro location make street cruising easy.

Powerhouse

1347 Folsom Street, between 9th & 10th Streets (552 8689). Bus 12, 14, 26. **Open** 4pm-2am daily. **No credit cards. Map G5**

Hard and hot, the Powerhouse remains one of the most popular (male) gay bars in the city. Underwear night, uniform night… you get the idea. With sexy bartenders and sexy customers, if you can't meet Mister Right here, he may not exist.

QT

1312 Polk Street, at Bush Street (885 1114). Bus 2, 3, 4, 19, 42, 47, 49, 76. **Open** noon-2am daily. **No credit cards. Map F3**

Two words: Rice Queens. Like its neighbours, QT is slow during the week and packed at the weekend. Check your wallet.

San Francisco Eagle

398 12th Street, at Harrison Street (626 0880). Bus 9, 12, 42. **Open** noon-2am daily. **No credit cards. Map G5**

The row of motorcycles always parked outside signifies that the Eagle was once the centre of San Francisco's leather community. It's tamed a bit but the Sunday afternoon beer bash is still legendary for its consumption and blatant cruising. Some regulars claim the place has gone downhill with the new ownership, but decide for yourself.

Wild Side West

424 Cortland Avenue, at Wool Street (647 3099). Muni Metro J/bus 9, 14, then 24. **Open** 1pm-2am daily. **No credit cards.**

This place has been around forever (although it used to be located in North Beach) and the story goes that

Janis Joplin would hang out and pick up girls at the very same wooden bar that now graces this Bernal Heights location. The walls are a shifting art installation, the pool table a cherry red and the clientele mixed. There's also a fabulous jukebox of classics – you can count on hearing Joplin, Patsy Cline and, of course, Lou Reed's *Walk on the Wild Side*.

Restaurants & cafés

San Francisco doesn't have gay restaurants *per se*: gay and lesbian diners are welcome everywhere. That said, most queer diners congregate in the Castro, Hayes Valley, Bernal Heights and SoMa neighbourhoods, because they live nearby and feel more comfortable than in the Marina, Pacific Heights or North Beach. Many cafés offer a limited menu of sandwiches and soups, but it's also common to have a beer in one venue, dinner in another and dessert at another down the street. *See also chapter* **Restaurants & Cafés**.

Bagdad Café

2295 Market Street, at Noe Street (621 4434). Muni Metro F, K, L, M/bus 22, 35, 37. **Open** 24 hours daily. **Average** $6-$13. **No credit cards**. **Map E6**

Diner-type food and generous portions can be found here (try the 'desert fries'). This sort of I-don't-care-if-it's-bad-for-me-fare is perfect for a late-night snack after a hard evening in the bars.

Café Flore

See p145 **Restaurants & Cafés** *for listings.*

The one café where the patrons spend more time studying each another than their books. Always popular and always crowded, Flore and its garden is the see-and-be-seen centre of the Castro. The food (from salads to burgers) is basic but the coffee excellent. Get a table outside for maximum viewing potential.

Chow

215 Church Street, at Market Street (552 2469). Muni F, J, K, L, M/bus 22. **Open** 11am-11pm Mon-Thur, Sun; 11am-midnight Fri, Sat. **Average** $12. **Credit** MC, V. **Map E6**

Chow has become a favourite for the Castro's eastern flank, a noisy, friendly place with a menu that ranges from basic pastas to hearty dishes such as grilled fish and roasted meat. Service is casual and adept – and most diners seem to be regulars.

Da Flora

701 Columbus Avenue, at Filbert Street (981 4664). Bus 15, 30, 41/cable car Powell-Mason. **Open** 6.30-9.30pm Tue-Sun. **Average** $25-$30. **Credit** MC, V. **Map G2**

This delightful osteria marks a first for San Francisco: a decent, lesbian- and gay-friendly Italian restaurant

Red Dora's Bearded Lady: *café by day, performance space by night. See page 200.*

in North Beach. The place is tiny, with kitsch décor and excellent food. Try the baccala on fresh polenta, the sardines with balsamic onions, or any number of fresh, seasonal pasta dishes cooked to order. There's great vegetarian fare, too. The gracious and gregarious Flora will make you feel welcome.

Firewood Café

4248 18th Street, between Castro & Diamond Streets (252 0999). Muni Metro F, K, L, M/bus 24, 35, 37. **Open** 11am-11pm Mon-Sat; 11am-10pm Sun. **Average** $10. **Credit** MC, V. **Castro/Mission Map X1**

This hip, high-ceilinged bistro has a queue most nights – but don't let that stop you from joining it. Order before you sit down from the large overhead menu and your food will arrive just before you're seated. The roast chicken is moist and succulent and the individual-sized pizzas consistently delicious. Head down the street for coffee and dessert so someone else can have your table.

Fuzio

469 Castro Street, between Market & 18th Streets (863 1400). Muni Metro F, K, L, M/bus 24, 35, 37. **Open** 11.30am-10pm Mon-Thur, Sun; 11.30am-11pm Fri, Sat. **Average** $10. **Credit** AmEx, Disc, MC, V. **Castro/Mission Map X1**

If it wasn't for the great food, Fuzio would be accused of trying to do too much. Asian, Italian and American influences favour the large menu, but the best dishes are the most basic. Thai noodles, angel hair pasta with tomato sauce, decent salads – you can't really go wrong. A nice alternative to the branch of the Pasta Pomodoro chain on every corner.

Hot 'N' Hunky

4039 18th Street, between Hartford & Noe Streets (621 6365). Muni Metro F, K, L, M/bus 33, 35. **Open** 11am-midnight Mon-Thur, Sun; 11am-1am Fri, Sat. **Average** $10. **No credit cards. Castro/Mission Map X1**

An exception to the normal ho-hum Castro dining, the Hot 'N' Hunky burger joint is a perennial favourite. Ignore the 1980s décor and sink your teeth into one of the best burgers in town – this is a place for carnivores to revel in their blood-lust. **Hot 'N' Chunky** (1946 Market Street, at Duboce Avenue; 621 3622), which used to have the same owners, is also worth a try.

Just for You

1453 18th Street, at Connecticut Street (647 3033). Bus 22, 53. **Open** 7am-2.30pm Mon-Fri; 8.30am-3pm Sat, Sun. **Average** $7. **No credit cards.**

A bit off the beaten track, but worth the trip, this tiny dyke-run restaurant serves a hearty New Orleans-style breakfast and lunch with superb grits and great pancakes. Most of the seating is at the counter overlooking the cooking area, where muscled women prepare your meal.

Mad Magda's Russia Tea Room

579 Hayes Street, at Laguna Street (864 7654). Bus 21. **Open** 11am-9pm Mon-Fri; 9am-11pm Sat; 9am-7pm Sun. **Average** $7. **No credit cards. Map F5**

A uniquely San Franciscan spot, Mad Magda's combines all the artsy funk of Hayes Valley with a queer, in-your-face twist. Go for Russian pastries and tea in the garden or have your Tarot read by the psychic. A perfect end to an afternoon's browsing in the surrounding shops and galleries, Magda's also hosts a range of evening 'events', many of which defy description; phone for details.

Muddy Waters

260 Church Street, between Market & 15th Streets (621 2233). Muni Metro F, J, K, L, M/bus 22. **Open** 6.30am-11pm Mon-Thur; 6.30am-midnight Fri; 7am-midnight Sat; 7am-11pm Sun. **No credit cards. Map E6**

A café that takes its name from its unusually strong coffee (the staff will gladly water it down for the faint of heart). Expect lots of students and people reading the free newspapers, as well as interesting rotating exhibitions by local artists.

Patio Café

531 Castro Street, between 18th & 19th Streets (621 4640). Muni Metro F, K, L, M/bus 24, 35. **Open** 9am-10pm Mon-Fri; 9am-10.30pm Sat, Sun. **Average** $10. **Credit** AmEx, MC, V. **Castro/Mission Map X1**

The Patio is the most popular brunch spot in the area, so be prepared to queue. Seating is in a greenhouse-like structure off the street, a soothing place to recover from a hangover. The food is mediocre, though standard breakfast dishes (pancakes, omelettes) pass muster. The entrance is tricky to find: look for the passageway that leads behind the shops.

Red Dora's Bearded Lady

485 14th Street, at Guerrero Street (626 2805). Muni Metro F, K, L, M/26 bus. **Open** 7am-7pm Mon-Fri; 9am-7pm Sat, Sun. **No credit cards. Map F6**

The Bearded Lady is a café by day and, often, a performance space by night. The walls are hung with work by lesbian artists and at the counter you can order anything from espresso to pesto eggs or breakfast cereal favourites.

Sparky's

242 Church Street, at Market Street (626 8666). Muni Metro F, K, L, M/bus 22, 35, 37. **Open** 24 hours daily. **Average** $12. **Credit** DC, Disc, MC, V. **Map E6**

Open 24 hours and particularly popular late at night, Sparky's is the place to come if you're craving hash browns at 4am. There's a large menu and relatively low prices; the food is lousy, but after a long night of drinking and dancing, who cares?

Clubs

Dancing is a San Franciscan passion and the scene is always on the move as new clubs appear and old ones fade away. The places listed below are likely to be around for some time to come, but it is wise to check first: pick up a copy of *Odyssey*, the club scene magazine, to find out the latest on what's in and who's wearing what to go where. For the long-running S&M fetish club **Bondage A Go- Go**, now at the **Cat Club** – and others – *see chapter* **Nightlife**.

The Box

(Information 206 1652).
One of the city's longest-lived free-agent dance clubs was, as we went to press, without a home, having recently vacated its Thursday night slot at the **Justice League** (*see page 212* **Nightlife**). Have no fear, however – legendary DJ Mistress Page Hodel and her promotional minions are bound to land a new venue for their diverse, unpretentious dance scene.

The Café

2367 Market Street, at Castro Street (861 3846). Muni Metro F, K, L, M/bus 35, 37. **Open** 2pm-2am Mon-Fri; 12.30pm-2am Sat, Sun. **No credit cards. Map E6**
Once the neglected Café San Marcos and bitchily dubbed the 'lesbian airport lounge', the Café is now the Castro's most popular dance club. It has two bars, a dance floor and a patio as well as pool and pinball – plus some of the hottest young things (male and female) in town. Expect to queue on Friday and Saturday and wear something lightweight (and revealing): the temperature soars as the night gets going.

Club Universe

177 Townsend Street, at Third Street (974 6020). Bus 30, 42, 45, 76. **Open** 9.30pm-7am Sat. **No credit cards. Map J4/5**
A big warehouse-type club with an emphasis on house sounds, which operates on Saturday nights only. Popular with gay and straight clubbers, it's a good place to go with a mixed group of people.

The End-up

401 Sixth Street, at Harrison Street (357 0827). Bus 12, 27, 42. **Open** 10.30pm-4am Thur; 9pm-3pm Fri, Sat; 5pm-2am Sun. **No credit cards. Map H5**
If Saturday night has turned into Sunday morning and you're still going strong, the party continues at the End-up, starting at 6am. There's a great dance floor in a large space and the Sunday Tea Dance (better even than its Fag Friday) is always popular. Though the club's future is uncertain, if you don't go, you can't really say you've seen gay San Francisco.

Pleasuredome

177 Townsend Street, at Third Street (974 6020). Bus 30, 42, 45, 76. **Open** 9pm-6am Sun. **No credit cards. Map J4/5**
The Pleasuredome is the longest-running gay club in the city. You'll see more bare pectoral muscles than you can shake a stick at – if you've been faithful in your gym attendance, here's the pay-off.

Rawhide II

280 Seventh Street, at Folsom Street (621 1197). Bus 12. **Open** 4pm-2am Mon-Thur; noon-2am Fri-Sun. **No credit cards. Map G5**
A truly authentic country and western bar full of – almost – authentic cowboys and cowgirls. There are $2 Western dance lessons in the early evenings (makes for a good date).

The Stud

399 Ninth Street, at Harrison Street (863 6623). Bus 19, 27, 42. **Open** 5pm-2am daily. **No credit cards. Map G5**
A San Francisco institution buried in SoMa (take a cab both ways), the Stud has one of the most varied crowds: from college students out for an exploratory evening to hardcore muscle boys posing in the corners. Sunday night is 1980s retro, but Wednesday night is the customary time to drop in. Trannyshack, held on Thursday night, is a cross-dressers' delight.

Entertainment

If the men and women don't provide sufficient diversion, gay San Francisco offers other equally theatrical alternatives. You'll be told to see *Beach Blanket Babylon* (do it) and probably the drag show at the Finocchio Club (don't – it's really aimed at trying to shock Midwestern tourists), but do check out the venues listed below as well. For further venues, *see also chapters* **Film** *and* **Performing Arts**.

Brava! for Women in the Arts

Theatre Center, 2789 24th Street, between York & Hampshire Streets (Brava! office 641 7657). Bus 9, 27, 48. **Credit** MC, V. **Castro/Mission Map Z2**
The results of women's performance and writing workshops are featured at this small theatre space. Brava! has encouraged the work of women playwrights and writers for years, and although it can be hit or miss, you may get a sneak preview of great work to come.

Castro Theater

429 Castro Street, off Market Street (621 6120). Muni Metro F, K, L, M/bus 24, 33, 35, 37. **Admission** $7. **No credit cards. Map E6**
A queen of a movie palace, the recently renovated Castro Theater – and the mighty Wurlitzer organ that is played before all features – is one of the city's finest repertory houses. It really comes into its own for the great gay and camp classics: until you've seen *Mommie Dearest*, *Valley of the Dolls* or *All About Eve* in a queer-packed theatre with full audience participation, you haven't really lived. Phone for titles and times, or drop by the cinema to pick up a three-month schedule.

Josie's Cabaret and Juice Joint

See p219 **Nightlife** *for listings.*
The best place in town to catch gay comics, one-man and one-woman shows or performance pieces. The house is small so get tickets in advance. The garden at the back is also a favourite weekend brunch spot.

LunaSea Women's Performance Project

2940 16th Street, between Capp Street & South Van Ness Avenue (863 2989). BART 16th Street/bus 33, 53. **No credit cards. Map F6**

Here you'll find experimental and sometimes cutting-edge work by local lesbian performance artists and writers, as well as a supportive, interested and creative audience. Shows are usually held every Friday and Saturday.

Theatre Rhinoceros

2926 16th Street, between Mission Street & South Van Ness Avenue (861 5079). BART 16th Street/bus 14, 22, 33, 49, 53. **Credit** MC, V. **Map F6**

Many other venues offer queer plays, but Theatre Rhino is the city's only truly gay theatre. A wide variety of shows are performed, many of them original plays. Check the listings in any of the free weeklies for what's on.

Shops

See also chapter **Shops & Services**.

Does Your Mother Know?

4079 18th Street, between Castro & Noe Streets (864 3160). Bus 24, 33, 35. **Open** 9.30am-10pm Mon-Thur; 9.30am-11pm Fri, Sat; 10am-9pm Sun. **Credit** AmEx, Disc, MC, V. **Castro/Mission Map X1**

Though it's still mourning the loss of the queer institution known as Headlines, the Castro has plenty of other places to buy greetings cards. DYMK, around the corner from the area's main drag, remains the favourite with many. It also sells magazines, books and gifts.

Good Vibrations

See p181 **Shops & Services** *for listings.*

You've seen the ads in nearly every progressive publication in the world; now it's time to check out the venue. Good Vibes, as this women's erotica shop is known, features a vibrator museum, all sorts of sex toys and a video collection, and sponsors readings and sexual workshops.

Scarlett Sage Herb Company

1173 Valencia Street, between 22nd & 23rd Streets (821 0997). BART 24th Street/bus 14, 26, 49. **Open** 11am-6.30pm Mon-Sat; noon-6pm Sun. **Credit** AmEx, MC, V. **Castro/Mission Map Y2**

Drop in to experience the comfortable and soothing atmosphere of this lesbian-run store. Wares include organic bulk herbs, herbal extracts, flower essences, bodycare products and a wide selection of books on herbs and homeopathy.

Stormy Leather

See p181 **Shops & Services** *for listings.*

A woman-owned leather, fetish and sexual fantasy shop with everything from leather and latex bustiers to finely crafted whips and paddles. Staff are friendly and helpful.

Worn Out West

582 Castro Street, between 18th & 19th Streets (431 6020). Bus 24, 33, 35. **Open** noon-7pm Mon-Thur, Sun; 12.30-8pm Fri; 11am-6.30pm Sat. **Credit** Disc, MC, V. **Castro/Mission Map X1**

WOW appears at first sight to be a second-hand Western clothing store, but it has lots of new duds, too, plus sexier paraphernalia and fashion accessories. If you're craving full leather, a California State Patrol officer's uniform or just a great-fitting cowboy hat, this is the place to come.

BOOKSHOPS

Almost any good San Francisco bookshop – of which there are droves – has an adequate gay and lesbian section, with both new and second-hand tomes. The best gay bookshop by far, however, is **A Different Light** (*see page 162* **Shops & Services**), the SF branch of the national gay chain. If it doesn't stock what you're looking for, it probably isn't available. Around the corner is the more esoteric (and well-chosen) **Books Inc** (2275 Market Street, at 16th Street; 864 6777); **Jaguar Adult Books** (4057 18th Street, at Hartford Street; 863 4777) offers a wide selection of the 'other' gay literature: pornography. The **Modern Times Bookstore** (*see page 163* **Shops & Services**), is a collectively-owned progressive bookshop with an excellent women's and lesbian section, featuring writers from all over the world.

Working out

The fitness craze has hit San Francisco as much as any other city and the question is no longer 'Do you work out?' but 'Where?'. The city abounds with gyms, but some are more gay-friendly than others. Below are some of the most popular, which also offer day or short-term passes. *See also chapter* **Sport & Fitness**.

Market Street Gym

2301 Market Street, at Noe Street (626 4488). Muni Metro F, K, L, M/bus 37. **Open** 5.30am-10pm Mon-Fri; 7am-9pm Sat; 7am-8pm Sun. **Admission** $10 per day; $38 per week. **Credit** AmEx, MC, V. **Mixed. Map E6**

Muscle System

2275 Market Street, between Sanchez and Noe Streets (863 4700). Muni Metro F, K, L, M/ bus 37. **Open** 5.30am-10pm Mon-Fri; 8am-8pm Sat, Sun. **Admission** $8 per day; $27 per week. **Credit** MC, V. **Men only. Map E6**

Branch: 364 Hayes Street, between Franklin & Gough Streets (863 4701).

Women's Training Center

2164 Market Street, at Sanchez Street (864 6835). Muni Metro F, K, L, M/bus 37. **Open** 5.30am-10pm Mon-Fri; 8am-8pm Sat, Sun. **Admission** $8 per day; $27 per week. **Credit** ($15 min) MC, V. **Women only. Map E6**

Media

What's in the daily news?

San Francisco media evidently exists not only to report and reflect what's going on, but to confirm its readers' and viewers' collective belief that they're living in the most trend-setting quadrant of the globe. Oddly, media here isn't a highly competitive realm – the city supports two mediocre newspapers, a handful of arts tabloids and several indistinguishable TV stations – and lacks the cut-throat rivalry found in cities such as New York or Chicago. In general, San Francisco mainstream media is bland in comparison to the political, technological and social edges that are cut here. It's the San Jose daily paper that remains the best read; and Oakland's KTVU continues to receive the best ratings for news.

San Francisco's media niche seems to be in specialised publications – 'dead tree' and other forms – that celebrate the city's diversity. Excellent business, arts and political journals are published here, as well as a slew of magazines aimed at readers of various races and sexual orientations. The maturing of the Internet has nourished several original web magazines and the city's proximity to Silicon Valley has resulted in the launch of media aimed at technology's attending economic and demographic shifts.

In general, San Francisco seems to view media's role as something just short of what it could be. The city appears content to navel-gaze, to convince itself that just as its weather is pleasant and its populace conciliatory and easygoing, so should its media be.

Café de la Presse. *See page 205.*

Newspapers & magazines

Dailies

Grousing about the quality of the *San Francisco Chronicle* (50¢) has become something of a cliché; at least it's not as bad (so the argument goes) as the *San Francisco Examiner*. The region's largest circulation paper is the best for local news and a number of good columnists – Jon Carroll, CW Nevius, Joan Ryan, Adair Lara – rescue the 'Chron' from utter mediocrity. Different editions of the paper are delivered to the suburbs.

In August 1999, the Hearst corporation, which owns the city's afternoon paper, the *San Francisco Examiner* (25¢), announced it was purchasing the Chron for $660 million, a move met with much grumbling: ineffectual as they are, the two newspapers necessitate at least a modicum of rivalry; with only one daily – and that one potentially owned by a huge newspaper conglomerate – locals fear the end of competition and the heavy editorial hand of a monopoly. To complicate matters, Hearst announced that the Examiner is up for sale, though pundits believe this is merely a ruse to make Hearst appear willing to bust their trust. The US Justice Department has final authority over the Chron's sale and is likely to be slow in determining its legality.

On Sundays, the Chron combines with the Examiner to produce the fat *San Francisco Examiner and Chronicle* ($1.50). It contains a lively mix of articles culled from the major newswires. Its 'Sporting Green' section is decent; coverage of national and international news, however, continues to suck for air. There is also a thick 'Datebook', or what locals call the 'pink' section – a tabloid entertainment and arts supplement published on pink paper, which includes listings, concert reviews, capsule movie reviews and suchlike. For visitors, the pink is probably the single most valuable section of any local newspaper. Both papers maintain websites inside the SF Gate server: www.sfgate.com (*see p205* **Online publications**).

If you're thirsting for news outside San Francisco, the *San Jose Mercury News* (50¢) remains the Bay Area's best overall paper for news reporting, business and sport; its business coverage of Silicon Valley and Internet commerce is first-rate. Otherwise, the regional edition of the *New York Times* ($1) or national edition of the *Los Angeles Times* (50¢) are your best bet. The *Wall Street Journal* ($1) has an excellent news brief on the front page and some of the best feature writing in the country – though its op-ed page is dominated by reactionary and tiresome conservatives who blame the country's ills on the 1960s. The vapid *USA Today* (50¢) works well as fishwrap – you'll soon learn why it's distributed free in hotels.

Weekly & bi-weeklys

Like the dailies, a pair of weekly arts tabloids battle for supremacy in San Francisco. The *San Francisco Bay Guardian* is a thick, lively rag that mixes an unapologetically progressive stance with dedication to a full range of arts listings. Exhaustive and opinionated, it's definitely the better of the two weeklies: executive editor Ron Curran regularly shakes down greedy utility companies, the mayor, the governor and just about anyone else who's thrusting or hypocritical. The Guardian eagerly pisses off the conservative local establishment by exposing cronyism, graft, fraud or double standards. Many writers cover their beats with pith and wit, from alternative political writers and e-culture columnists to the latest punk-rock journalists. The paper's monthly 'Lit' book review is a great read; likewise, its yearly fiction contest. It maintains a good online site, www.sfbg.com, of archived and original material.

Though everyone loves the Guardian, it would benefit from some real competition – and the *SF Weekly* certainly isn't it. With the exception of 'Savage Love', Seattle-based syndicated columnist Dan Savage's brutally frank sex advice column and an occasional hit by Jack Boulware, the Weekly has been reduced to a set of wearisome tirades and surface-level arts coverage. This could reflect the fact that it's owned by a corporation – New Times, of Phoenix, AZ, which runs several other American weeklies; another part of the problem could be regular turnover. The Weekly also has a website, www.sfweekly.com. Both the *San Francisco Bay Guardian* and the *SF Weekly* are distributed free every Wednesday at myriad newspaper boxes and cafés throughout the city.

Up-and-coming is the recently-launched free *SF Metropolitan*, a well-designed bi-weekly tabloid that aims at a younger, more-hip readership. Its features on city style, neighbourhood issues and travel are good, as are its restaurant and book reviews. The Met seems to have a keen feel for nightlife as well, opting to be selective (as opposed to comprehensive, like the Guardian) in its coverage.

There is a host of free papers targeted at gay and lesbian readers, including the *Bay Times* (a tabloid) and *BAR* (Bay Area Reporter), available from coffee shops and bookstores in the Castro and the Mission. Both carry listings of events for gay audiences as well as personal ads and social and political commentary.

Speciality magazines

In San Francisco, magazines are like screenplays in Los Angeles – everyone's working on one. Concurrent with the region's technological boom, several good business publications have come into being: they include the well-established *Red Herring* ($4.99), the fast-rising *Business 2.0* ($4.99), and the trend-setting *Wired* ($4.95) – all monthlies. The hot new *Industry Standard* ($2.95), a weekly devoted to the Internet economy, shanghaied several original *Wired* staff members for its masthead and has gone from a lightweight to a thick publication in just under a year. The longserving *MacWorld* ($7.99) caters to Macintosh users.

Other publications are more arts- and sport-centric: *Speak* ($4.50), a 'fictionmusicfashionfilm' quarterly remains artful and interesting; quarterly *Juxtapoz* ($4.95) preaches to the alternative art crowd; *Schwing!* ($3.95) and *Thrasher* ($3.95) cover golf and skateboarding, respectively (and respectfully). Published by the largest public television station in the Bay Area, *San Francisco Focus* has morphed into *San Francisco Magazine* ($2.95) and remains, unfortunately, light in content. The literary *Zzyzzyva* ($7) publishes short stories, poetry, creative non-fiction and original art. *Dwell* ($4.95) is a new slick devoted to modern homes and architecture.

Political magazines and those designed for a more clannish audience seem to thrive, given the region's diverse demographics. *Mother Jones* ($3.95) still pounds out the heartbeat of the liberal agenda with its left-lurching stance, regularly taking on the Christian Coalition, the Republican Party and any number of anti-environmental groups. The *Jewish Bulletin of Northern California* (75¢) and *Asian Week* ($1 in Chinatown, free elsewhere) sell to their niche markets. In addition, you'll find countless 'zines devoted to alternative music, religion, arts, film and lifestyles. **Naked Eye** on Haight Street is a great place to find them (*see below*).

Foreign-language publications

San Francisco hosts more than 70 resident nationalities, almost all of whom have an own-language paper serving their respective community's local needs and desire for news from 'home'. The *Tenderloin Times*, for instance, is a weekly paper published in Cambodian, Vietnamese, Cantonese and English. For a list of bookshops that stock foreign-language books and newspapers, *see chapter* **Shops & Services**.

Outlets

The very well-read **Harold's International Newsstand** at 524 Geary Boulevard, between Jones and Taylor Streets (441 2665) offers as complete a selection of periodicals as you'll find in the city; **Farleys** at 1315 18th Street (*see chapter* **Shops & Services**), is a decent coffee retailer and café with magazines; and **Juicy News** at 2453 Fillmore Street, between Jackson and Washington Streets (441 3051), is a deceptively small shop given the number of titles it carries.

Those on the hunt for art and poetry publications should try **City Lights** (*see chapter* **Shops & Services**). Collectors will want to visit the

Magazine at 920 Larkin Street, between Geary Boulevard and Post Street (441 7737), a store that sells vintage publications. Those wishing to see a great selection of 'zines (self- and desktop-published volumes often written with a very personal perspective) should visit **Naked Eye News & Video** on Haight Street, or, for an excellent selection of gay and lesbian publications, try **A Different Light** (*see chapter* **Shops & Services** for both).

Tower Records (*see chapter* **Shops & Services**) can be counted on for the latest pop culture and music rags. Homesick Euros needn't miss a beat at **Café de la Presse** (352 Grant Avenue), an ultra-modern café, which has an espresso bar and sells all the major European dailies and glossies (*see chapter* **Restaurants & Cafés**).

Online publications

With the pulse of Silicon Valley beating nearby, San Francisco not surprisingly has its share of online publications. The best of the bunch, *Salon* (www.salon1999.com), is a diverse and literate paean to good writing and reading. It features daily columns, features and interviews, as well as well-wrought discussions in a variety of sections.

Several other online magazines are created in San Francisco: the early-adapting *HotWired* (www.hotwired.com), a trendy cultural critic until recently under the Wired (magazine) Ventures umbrella; the snarky *Suck* (www.suck.com), also a Wired spinoff; and *Addicted to Noise* (www.addict.com), editor Michael Goldberg's anti-*Rolling Stone* venture (which, ironically, is a lot like *Rolling Stone*) and that's now part of the SonicNet server.

Television

Those unaccustomed to American television should be prepared for a blaring deluge of food and car ads and a surprising lack of resistance to them from regular viewers. The fact, for instance, that programming in the US is driven by advertising has moved from the evident to the obvious, the result being that few give this troubling relationship a second thought. What's more, many of television's greatest talents are employed part- or full-time by advertisers to direct or star in their spots. Consequently, for pure entertainment value, advertisements often outshine programming.

The best printed resource for what's on the air remains the *TV Guide* ($1.79). Daily newspapers have 24-hour TV listings and a stapled booklet for the week is included in the combined Sunday *San Francisco Examiner and Chronicle*.

The Networks

The Bay Area has affiliates of all three major networks: ABC (local station is **KGO**, found on channel 7), NBC (**KRON**, channel 4) and CBS (**KPIX**, channel 5). The long-lasting independent station, **KTVU** (channel 2) is now part of the Fox TV network. Reflecting their dependence on advertising, there's little difference, politically or ideologically, between these four – their primary concern is the size of their audience, not any social tendency within it. Their daily fare is almost identical, with variations on a theme.

The morning brings chatty news reports; mid-morning, the confessional and celebrity-driven talk shows begin, yielding to soap operas at midday. After lunch, the soaps wrap up and it's back to more talk shows. As early as 4pm you can catch national network news taped on the East Coast or broadcast live from its 7pm slot in New York and Washington. Early evenings are dominated by news programmes, game shows and re-runs of sitcoms. Melodramas and movies edited for commercial breaks dominate 'prime time' and then it's on to the late-night talk shows where celebrity hosts (David Letterman, Jay Leno, Conan O'Brien and others) interview stars, introduce hit-making bands and work for laughs.

Weekly highlights on the networks include *60 Minutes* (CBS, Sundays at 7pm), the ever-popular *Saturday Night Live* (NBC, Saturdays at 12.30am) and the spooky *X-Files* (Fox, Sundays at 9pm). Most stations run programming around the clock; thus are American insomniacs never without distraction.

Cable TV

To improve their choice of small-screen entertainment, many people in the Bay Area pay monthly fees for cable TV (and most hotels worth their nightly rates offer cable as a standard feature). In addition to the 24-hour music videos of **MTV** and round-the-clock sport on **ESPN**, cable provides access to a number of stations that specialise in news (**CNN**), classic movies (**AMC** and the **Movie Channel**) or recently released movies (**HBO** and **Showtime**). Furthermore, some hit movies and sporting events are available on a pay-as-you-view basis. Some sports bars will pay these fees to attract customers.

If you're searching for more esoteric programming, note that **MSNBC** and **ZDTV** broadcast news about technology; the **Discovery Channel** features shows about animals and natural curiosities; **Disney** programmes family entertainment; and **C-SPAN** broadcasts events happening in the US Senate and House of Representatives. For local cable programmes, **Bay TV** features locally-produced shows and magazine programmes.

For the most up-to-date cable TV guide, check the Sunday Examiner and Chronicle pull-out section or go to www.tvguide.com, click 'TV Listings' and enter a generic San Francisco zip code (94100).

Public TV

The alternative to the relentless advertising of commercial stations is **PBS**, the Public Broadcasting Service, which has stations in San Francisco (**KQED**, on channel 9), San Jose (**KTEH**, channel 54) and San Mateo (**KCSM**, channel 60). These stations receive a meagre subsidy from the federal government and solicit funds from viewers. Criticised for being short on local programming, KQED has an unenviable reputation as one of the fattest of the subsidised stations, with much of the money going into executives' salaries. It broadcasts the *News Hour with Jim Lehrer* every weekday at 6pm. While PBS may be a respite from the advertised life, it trades off its 'prestige' reputation a touch too smugly. The system might appeal to homesick Brits pining for 'quality' TV or re-runs of ancient sitcoms but it hardly represents an authentic American TV-watching experience.

Radio

San Francisco's constantly changing radio profile reflects several difficulties: that of attracting elusive listeners in a competitive market and of outsmarting weather and geography, which combine to undermine reliable radio signals. But don't think for a minute that San Francisco Bay Area radio isn't spectacular. The weaker, non-commercial stations lie to the left of the FM dial; the powerhouses with the loudest ads cluster on the right. AM is mostly reserved for talk and news shows with a few foreign-language, oldie and Christian stations peppering the mix. Between both FM and AM bands, however, the range of programming is nothing short of amazing – from right-wing talk show hosts to hour-long devotions to indigenous music, covering obscure jazz or the latest in hip hop, college rock and urban soul.

News & talk

For the latest news, **KGO** (810 AM), **KQED** (88.5 FM) and its competitor, **KALW** (91.7 FM), remain your best bets. Beyond that, Berkeley-based **KPFA** (94.1 FM) is also determined to give KQED a run for its money, and **KCBS** (740 AM), the local CBS affiliate, has likewise proved itself a station devoted to quality news (and priceless traffic reports, every ten minutes). **KSFO** (740 AM), meanwhile, boasts reactionary talk radio programmes in the morning and broadcasts Oakland A's baseball games in the afternoon. **KNBR** (680 AM) is the voice for Giants' baseball games and the place to tune in later for well-informed sporting debate.

Classical

Advertised as a 'radio concert hall', **KDFC** (102.1 FM, 1220 AM), remains a bit on the stuffy side, interrupting its conservative classical repertoire to run hyperactive ads for cars, wine and singles clubs. As a result, many listeners have defected to **KKHI** (100.7 FM), where the programming is more diverse and the ads more mellow.

Jazz

Following the demise of KJAZ in the mid-1990s, San Francisco and the region have been hurting for a good jazz station. The adventurous **KCSM** (97.7 FM), a public radio station broadcast from a college in San Mateo, has taken up much of the slack, though its signal is relatively weak. Local **KKSF** (103.7 FM) bills itself as a 'soft jazz' station, but all too often sounds more like Muzak than anything worth an extended listening – don't tune in while operating any heavy machinery.

Dance, hip hop, soul

Rarely can one find more energy than on **KMEL** (106 FM), the Bay Area's foremost station for pop and hip-hop. **KYLD** (94.9 FM) is something of a contender and definitely gets partygoers in the mood on weekend nights. For something different, tune in to tiny **KPOO** (89.5 FM), where innovative hip hop and hardcore rap alternate with cool blues shows on weekend nights and a Tuesday afternoon slot featuring four hours of the music of John Coltrane.

Rock & pop

The hot new station for rockers is **KLLC** (97.3 FM), which seems to have stolen listeners from the weakening **KITS** ('Live 105', 105 FM). KITS seems to focus too often on bands that made it big in the 1980s – U2 and Depeche Mode meet Nirvana and Alanis Morissette. **KFOG** (104.5 FM) has a loyal following, providing an above-average mix of classic rock with new material, much of it local. **KOME** (98.5 FM) has staked out the newest and youngest rock/pop territory and is a hit with teenagers. **KRQR** (97.3 FM) leans towards heavy metal; **KSAN** (107.7 FM) recently displaced 'Wild 107' and plays generic rock classics – more Steve Miller Band, anyone?

College & community radio stations

Those in search of more eclectic listening should listen to **KALX** (90.7 FM), **KUSF** (90.3 FM), **KFJC** (89.7 FM) or **KPOO** (89.5 FM). These are the channels where you'll find diversity and innovative sounds, including acid jazz, Irish music, kids' shows, African and Latin music programmes and the latest trip-hop remix. The best aural blend in the region, the indie stations represent the diverse, non-commercial musical bouillabaisse for which San Francisco Bay Area is known.

Country & western

Several country stations have popped up of late, most notably 'Young Country' **KYCY** (93.3 FM and 1550 AM), who plays a range from Garth Brooks and Wynona Judd to some of the genre's early innovators like Johnny Cash and Hank Williams.

Websites & online locations

Away from the broadcast and print media, the Internet offers a wide range of interesting information sites. The *San Francisco Bay Guardian* operates the best newspaper link to the Net from its site at www.sfbg.com, where you'll find the current issue as well as additional articles and columns. The Chronicle and Examiner share an online link, called the **SF Gate** (www.sfgate. com), where you can search the archives of both papers and read the current edition.

The **WELL** (www.well.com), standing for

Whole Earth 'Lectronic Link, was founded on April Fool's Day 1984 and was one of the first virtual communities to attract public use. It's an ideal source of information for exploring 'overground' San Francisco. **C | Net** (www.cnet.com) is an indispensable source for what's happening in computers and multimedia. It combines a computer network, the largest original content on the World Wide Web and several television programmes – C|Net Central, the Web, and the New Edge – which air on the USA Network, the Sci-Fi Channel and on the local KPIX (channel 5).

For what's happening in and around San Francisco, try **SF Station** (www.sfstation.com), an arts hub and listings resource; or **CitySearch** (www.citysearch7.com), another excellent source for arts listings. **Yahoo!** also maintains a good regional site at www.sfbay. yahoo.com. Useful travel and hotel information can be found at the **San Francisco Hotel Reservations** (www.hotelres.com) and **Bay Area Transit Information** (www.transitinfo.org). For the latest earthquake info, go to http://quake.wr.usgs.gov. For a list of useful local websites, *see chapter* **Directory**.

Wired hired, fired; tired?

When it first hit newsstands in 1993, few knew what to make of it: *Wired* magazine's neon colours, eye-searing design, offset print style and bold editorial stance represented the most visible magazine launch from San Francisco since *Rolling Stone*. Its first covers featured Bruce Sterling and Peter Gabriel, as well as net privacy advocates the Electronic Frontier Foundation; interview subjects included futurist and musician Jaron Lanier and futurist and economist Peter Drucker. Created by a group of forethinkers, rebels and nerds working in a tiny South Park office, *Wired* had its finger on the world's technological pulse. It just took a while for everyone to realise it.

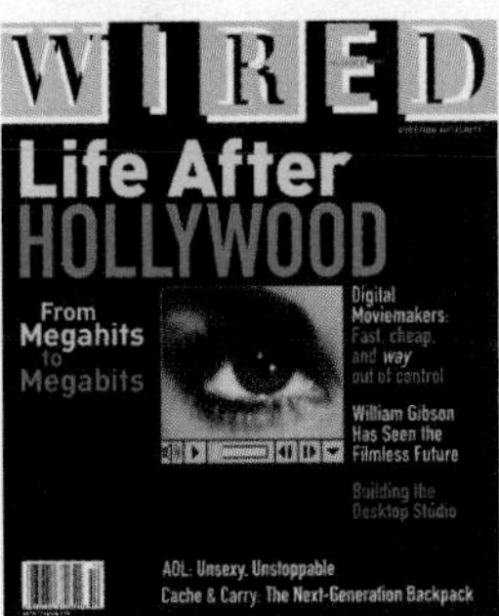

To those who didn't play video games, surf the Net or think much about the digital future, *Wired* was an enigma, one in which it was often difficult to distinguish the product reviews from the products themselves. But the brassy libertarian rag caught on quickly among the digerati and those who believed in the technological xanadu the magazine envisioned. By the end of its second year, *Wired*'s readership had nearly reached 100,000.

Founding publisher Louis Rossetto had initially imagined a lifestyle and culture magazine and *Wired* was that to some degree. But it quickly also became the bible about the money that was attaching itself to the silicon boom. Stories about e-progressives were displaced by those about wealthy young Internet tycoons; futurists like William Gibson and Alvin Toffler gave way to Yahoo! founders and Bill Gates on the magazine's covers. For his part, Rossetto began to envision a media empire. *Wired Japan* was launched and *Wired UK*; a *Wired Germany* was on the cards. HotWired, the venture's edgy online site, represented the first of its kind 'Internet station'. Soon HardWired, a book imprint, and *The Netizen*, a Wired TV programme, all had budgets and staff. The dozen-person startup now occupied two floors of two industrial buildings in SoMa; plans were made to take the venture public.

But the boom went bust. Two IPOs failed, advertising shrank, the magazine cut staff and eliminated departments; HardWired and *The Netizen* were slashed. After five years of ascension, *Wired* found its image and reputation were all too often 'vaporware' – a phrase it loved to bandy in relation to products and software that promised much but delivered little. The magazine suffered frequent advertising/content conflicts of interest, and management was losing staff at a record pace.

In 1998, Condé Nast, owners of the *New Yorker*, *Vogue*, *Traveller*, *GQ*, and other high-profile magazines, bought *Wired* (separate from the other ventures) and injected cash into it. A drastic re-design and editorial coup d'état shuffled the upper decks; the result has been a smarter, somewhat humbler journal with only an echo of the self-righteousness that permeated earlier issues. *Wired* remains a Multimedia Gulch mainstay, but a quick flip through its pages reveals a softer touch; its red-striped cover and neon colours seem more muted. Perhaps the magazine has moved out of its noisy adolescence and into quieter adulthood; or perhaps the world is finally wired enough to catch up with it.

111 Minna *(p217)*.

Nightlife

The moon rises on a diversity of urban activities.

San Francisco offers a diverse nightlife menu ranging from the mainstream to the fetishistic. As with any scene, it's the fledgling and underground spaces that cut the sharpest edge: one-off clubs, edgy comedy venues, tiny stages. But several long-time, reliable clubs and live music venues keep their doors open, a noteable feat in a city where growing gentrification has resulted in the closing of more than a few major establishments.

Just as their customers are varied, so are the clubs' genres: most present a mixture of recorded and live entertainment. While a few are known strictly as dance and others as live music clubs, the creeping American trend to eschew nightlife altogether and curl up at home with a warm VCR has forced clubs of all colours to promote themselves as diversely as possible. For that reason, you'll find DJ nights at live venues and an occasional ensemble playing at a club known for dancing. In short, everyone is trying everything.

Many clubs serve food as a way to lure in revellers (it's also, by law, the only way they are allowed to admit 18- to- 21-year-olds in certain venues) and although the supper club trend has faded somewhat, there are still a handful of places where you can dine first and dance afterwards (*see page 218*).

INFORMATION

Your best overall source for nightlife details is the *San Francisco Bay Guardian*, whose categorical listings of live music, dance clubs, spoken word, comedy and special events are updated every Wednesday. For rock listings, also check out the free bi-weekly *BAM* and phone the weekly-updated, pre-recorded 'Alternative Music and Entertain-ment Newsline' on 221 AMEN (2636), maintained by radio station KUSF. Many younger clubbers prefer the *SF Metropolitan*, a slick-covered tabloid published every other Monday, which boasts a sharper focus on the quickly-changing DJ dance scene. You can also find information in the *SF Weekly* or the Sunday *San Francisco Chronicle and Examiner*'s Datebook section – though the former is geared to the more alternative crowd and the latter is better for upmarket and large events.

For the latest clubbing information, the tried-and-true **Be-At Line** (626 4087) continues to list daily details of where to be and when: phone (with a pen in hand and a supple wrist) after 2pm. Online venues such as www.sfstation.com and www.city-

Don't miss

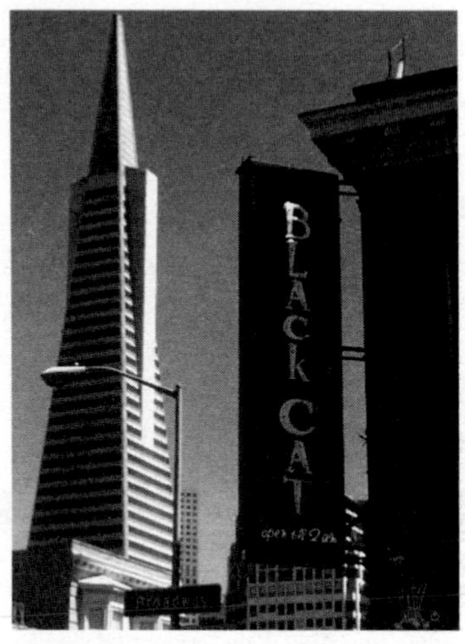

Black Cat
North Beach's hot new supper club. *See p218.*

Boom Boom Room
Is John Lee sitting in tonight? *See p213.*

Bottom of the Hill
For top alternative acts. *See p211.*

Fillmore Auditorium
A piece of San Francisco history. *See p210.*

Great American Music Hall
True to its name. *See p212.*

Josie's Cabaret and Juice Joint
For straight-friendly gay comedy. *See p219.*

Nikki's BBQ
World beats and sweaty dancing. *See p217.*

111 Minna
Art gallery turns dance club in the PM. *See p217.*

26Mix
Turntablist culture at its best. *See p218.*

search7.com also provide reliable, regularly-updated club listings. For classical music, theatre, opera and dance, *see chapter* **Performing Arts**.

TICKETS & ADMISSION

Where possible, buy tickets from the box offices of the major venues (all of which accept most credit cards), where you won't have to pay the mark-up charged by **BASS** (1-510 762 2277) for certain events. Most of the smaller clubs provide a recorded phone message with up-to-date information on where and when tickets go on sale. The smallest clubs just collect a door charge or enforce a drink minimum.

Admission prices for the clubs listed below depend on the night, but usually vary between free entry and $25. Although many dance venues remain open well past last orders, by law they cannot serve alcohol between 2am and 6am, nor to anyone under 21.

TRANSPORT

The Muni Owl Service operates on the L and N Muni Metro lines from 12.30am until 5.30am and on the 5, 14, 22, 24, 38, 90 and 91 bus lines from 1am until 5am. All other lines stop at 12.30am. BART runs roughly until midnight, although it's always best to check the time of the last train to your destination. For information about Muni, BART and a list of taxi companies, *see chapter* **Directory**.

Rock, blues & jazz

Within San Francisco's 46 square miles, dozens of venues and stages compete for your entertainment dollar and hundreds more beckon from the surrounding Bay Area. Fans, critics and musicians themselves have always made the scene, one that balances challenging new acts with touring artists for whom the city remains a favourite stop. Many major headliners, who fill all types of top-40 lists and genres, are based in the San Francisco Bay Area, among them Tracy Chapman, Metallica, Primus, Counting Crows, Green Day and Bobby McFerrin. The city is also home to some of the freshest developments in innovative new music.

San Francisco's musical history has always been vibrant and ground-breaking. The rich jazz scene that thrived in the Fillmore and Western Addition neighbourhoods in the 1950s is being revitalised (*see chapter* **Sightseeing**). Janis Joplin, Jimi Hendrix and Jefferson Airplane all played the **Fillmore Auditorium**, which has survived quakes small and large to remain a crucial venue.

The city's major concert promoter, Bill Graham Presents, began by producing Grateful Dead shows and now has a hand in nearly everything that comes to town. However, the Haight-Ashbury scene that exploded onto the national consciousness in the late 1960s and early 1970s seemed to let out its final gasp with the death of Grateful Dead lead guitarist Jerry Garcia in the summer of 1995. The seminal hardcore band Dead Kennedys put the city's punk parameters on the map in the early 1980s, the full aftershocks of which have yet to be felt. And in the early 1990s, acid jazz bloomed in spots such as the **Up & Down Club** and the **Elbo Room**. More recently, the arrival of turntablist culture has ushered in a new era of DJs-as-performers, jamming in the clubs between bands or, sometimes, as featured artists themselves.

Today, the live music scene offers a mix of sounds and styles, as well as a steady stream of musicians who wheel their gear in and out of clubs such as **Storyville**, **Bottom of the Hill**, **Rasselas** and the **Great American Music Hall**. Testament to both the city's diverse population and its cosmopolitan aspirations, Cuban jazz and Brazilian-inspired salsa artists regularly top the bill at **El Rio** and **Rockapulco**. The scene's main worry is the growing threat by a few homeowners with new lofts in the SoMa warehouse district, who have begun complaining about late-night noise that existed long before they bought into the neighbourhood.

Major live music venues

Two of the Bay Area's largest venues – the **Greek Theater** and **Oakland Coliseum** – are outside the city limits, as is the **Cow Palace** in Daly City (*see page 221* **Out of town**).

Bill Graham Civic Auditorium

99 Grove Street, between Polk & Larkin Streets (974 4000). BART Civic Center/Muni Metro F, J, K, L, M, N/bus 9, 19, 21, 26. **Map F5**

The San Francisco Opera was born in this 5,000-seat, broad-staged auditorium on 26 September 1923. Later renamed after the city's famous rock impresario, the auditorium handled productions during the renovation of the Opera House and now hosts a variety of affairs, from not-quite-stadium-sized rock shows to conferences, multimedia presentations and special events.

Fillmore Auditorium

1805 Geary Boulevard, at Fillmore Street (346 6000/24-hour hotline 346 0600). Bus 22, 38. **Map E4**

The Fillmore is a classic dance hall with a ballroom and mezzanine upstairs, a carpeted lounge and a long history of traditions, including the pail of free apples by the front entrance and the rotating gallery of photographs that line its walls. One of the true institutions of the 1960s, it was here that the late promoter Bill Graham began building his music empire, purveying psychedelic rock to San Francisco and the world. At the heart of the renovated Fillmore Historic Jazz District, it's a great venue for live tunes, with plenty of room to shake it or stand back and soak up the vibes. Book well in advance through BASS.
Website: www.thefillmore.com

The Vince Welwick Band plays that 1960s institution, the **Fillmore Auditorium**. *Page 210.*

Warfield

982 Market Street, between Fifth & Sixth Streets (775 7722). BART Powell Street/Muni Metro F, J, K, L, M, N/bus 7, 27, 31, 66, 71. **Map G4**

A favourite venue for rock fans, the Warfield was built in 1922 and boasts an ornate interior with superb balcony views, three bars and some VIP booths at the back. With its high ceiling and massive public address system, the Warfield feels like a box cavern and fills easily with a decent sound. High energy acts here often prove the most memorable of a concert-goer's career. You can get tickets from the box office at the **Fillmore Auditorium** (*see p210*) or book in advance through BASS.

Rock clubs

Rock 'n' roll aficionados in San Francisco are beginning to panic: a number of venues have closed (Chameleon, Trocadero, Epicenter Zone), banned all bands (Kilowatt) or changed hands. While the sum total of clubs has stayed about the same, some sea change is afoot; the next few years will determine the direction live music takes in the city.

Rock venues are notoriously grungy, smoky and crowded. What follows are the best of the bunch – patronise them and ensure their survival.

Blue Lamp

561 Geary Street, between Taylor & Jones Streets (885 1464). Bus 2, 3, 4, 27, 38. **Open** 11am-2am daily. **No credit cards. Map G3**

Once merely known as a Tenderloin dive bar, the Blue Lamp has begun to attract queues because of its musical reputation. Once in, you'll find the setting – a nondescript bar along one wall, a stage at the back and not much else – jibes with the comfortable vibe and contrasts nicely with the music, mostly local rock or blues acts on their way up. If you're staying in Union Square, the Blue Lamp is an easy, safe walk away.

Boomerang

1840 Haight Street, at Stanyan Street (387 2996). Bus 6, 7, 66, 71. **Open** 2pm-2am daily. **No credit cards. Map C6**

With the closure of the I-Beam and Nightbreak (may they rest in peace) down the street, the Boomerang remains the last live music venue in the heart of the Haight. Long and narrow, it's a dive where local bands and occasional indie touring acts crowd the tiny stage. The 'Bloody Mary Sundays' feature live bands from 5pm to midnight. Bring ear protection.

Bottom of the Hill

1233 17th Street, at Missouri Street (box office 621 4455/advance tickets 1-510 601 8932). Bus 22, 53. **Open** 3pm-2am Mon-Thur; 2pm-2am Fri; 8pm-2am Sat; 3-10pm Sun. **Credit** MC, V. **Map H6**

Hiding discreetly at the foot of Potrero Hill, Bottom of the Hill has become a San Francisco institution. From the quirky, post-earthquake décor to the myriad rock posters that line its walls, it feels utterly unique; the line-up of up-and-coming rock acts verifies that feeling. If you want to catch a new alternative bands a year or two before they hit the commercial big-time, head for the Bottom. A redesigned stage makes for good acoustics (and you can finally see!) and the patio/beer garden offers a cool, quiet(er) reprieve from the sweaty, cramped scene inside. A couple of pool tables at the back and a decent menu make for a perfect alt.evening.

Cocodrie

1024 Kearny Street, between Broadway & Pacific Avenue (986 6678). Bus 12, 15, 83. **Open** 4.30pm-2am Mon-Fri; 6pm-2am Sat, Sun. **Credit** MC, V. **Map G2**

The Cocodrie has successfully filled the void left by the closing of the Chameleon and Kilowatt as live venues. Too bad it's in North Beach, where parking is a nightmare and the sidewalks overflow with fraternity brothers at the weekends. Cocodrie favours small-time touring and local bands – none of whose names you'll recognise – in an intimate space.

Covered Wagon Saloon

917 Folsom Street, at Fifth Street (974 1585). Bus 12, 27. **Open** 4.30pm-2am Mon-Fri; 7.30pm-2am Sat. **No credit cards. Map H4**

Two rooms and a bar that can feel cramped, the CW is no place to go if you can't stand to sweat. The interior and live music run towards grunge and most of the club's nights are dedicated to live music. 'Stinky's Peep Show' features bands and a rotating line-up of chubby go-go dancers.

Great American Music Hall

859 O'Farrell Street, between Polk & Larkin Streets (885 0750). Bus 19, 38, 42, 47, 49. **Open** *box office* 10am-4pm Mon, Sun; noon-6pm Tue-Sat; until 9.30pm on day of show. **Credit** MC, V. **Map F4**

One of the oldest theatres still in operation, the Great American Music Hall is the grande dame of the city's small venues and well worth tracking down. The club presents an eclectic, virtuoso-studded playbill that includes native and touring musicians in equal measure. The hall was originally a bordello and its lavish décor remains intact, with huge mirrors, Roccoco woodwork and gold leaf trim. Snag a coveted seat in the upper balcony, where you'll get a memorable bird's-eye view of the band and the crowd below. The club is reported to be for sale: here's hoping the new owners change little or nothing about it.

Justice League

628 Divisadero Street, between Grove & Hayes Streets (289 2038). Bus 21, 24. **Open** phone for details. **Credit** MC, V. **Map D/E5**

One of San Francisco's most famous venues, the Justice League – like the Crash Palace, the Kennel Club and the VIS before it – brings a new generation of innovative sounds to the heart of the Western Addition. This incarnation is a beauty, with split-level seating at both sides of the large room and a large square bar in the centre; murals on the walls are by Barry 'Twist' McGee, the city's foremost graffiti artist. Onstage, a variety of acts, from experimental solo players to Moroccan singers or touring major artists, maintain the space's sterling reputation. DJs now take over a couple of nights a week. Unpretentious and comfortable, the Justice League has lived up to its charmed inheritance. Don't miss it.

Make-Out Room

3225 22nd Street, between Mission & Valencia Streets (647 2888). Bus 14, 26. **Open** 6pm-2am daily. **No credit cards. Castro/Mission Map Y2**

What was once a nondescript dive bar in the Mission is – well, still a nondescript dive bar in the Mission, but now one with excellent live and DJ-spun music. The Make-Out is packed to the wallpaper, loud and smoky, and unmistakably marks the centre of a tiny, thriving scene.

Maritime Hall

450 Harrison Street, between Fremont & First Streets (974 0634). Bus 12, 42, 76. **Open** phone for details. **Credit** MC, V. **Map J4**

The Maritime stands as a testament to the fact that few buildings qualify as decent musical venues. The huge hall, on the outer fringes of SoMa, has the worst acoustics in town – a pity, since its playlist is so diverse. You might see an internationally-touring reggae artist, a punk band or rapper KRS-One. Don't

Hadda Brooks at **Biscuits and Blues** *near Union Square. See page 213.*

be alarmed when you see a goth-metal band booked the same night as a Senegalese singer: the club actually has two venues, the smaller one downstairs. It features the same bad acoustics, but is more crowded.

Paradise Lounge

1501 Folson Street, at 11th Street (861 6906). Bus 9, 12, 42. **Open** 6pm-2am daily. **Credit** MC, V. **Map G5**

With three stages, the Paradise accounts for all musical tastes: local bands, touring acts, singer-songwriters and the occasional once-great who's still plucking or crooning. The pool tables and drink specials may not be your idea of paradise, but it's a safe bet you'll find something to like. The upstairs lounge, **Above Paradise**, is reserved for acoustic and folk music or spoken-word events. A slightly larger third performance space, the **Transmission Theatre,** showcases local bands on some nights and DJ dancing on others.

Slim's

333 11th Street, between Folsom & Harrison Streets (522 0333). Bus 9, 42. **Open** phone for details. **Credit** AmEx, MC, V. **Map G5**

Once a powerhouse for live performance, Slim's has grown complacent, opting to book a few safe acts every month rather than fill its stages nightly with higher-risk ones. It could be that the club smells death in the air for the live music scene: their 11th-and-Folsom Street corner marks the epicentre of noise complaints from new SoMa loftominium owners. Still, the big blue warehouse is a decent place to catch live acts, which vary from post-punk singer-songwriters to the soul and blues acts who mark the heart of Slims' history. The crowd is ethnically mixed and multi-generational; the sightlines are somewhat compromised by floor-to-ceiling pillars in the centre of the room.

Blues clubs

Blues clubs are holding their own. **Slim's** has morphed into a rock venue (*see above*) and the **Boom Boom Room** is currently the club to beat.

Biscuits and Blues

401 Mason Street, at Geary Street (292 2583). Bus 2, 3, 4, 38, 76/cable car Powell-Hyde or Powell-Mason. **Open** 5pm-1am Mon-Fri; 6pm-1am Sat, Sun. **Credit** AmEx, DC, MC, V. **Map G4**

This favourite blues club close to Union Square has established a good reputation for quality music and award-winning Southern food. It books a blend of local favourites, acoustic players and roots groups, some of whom have achieved national fame. You'll be in the company of tourists and (when you leave the club late at night) a bevy of hookers, but the neighbourhood is relatively harmless and the music's great.

Boom Boom Room

1601 Fillmore Street, at Geary Boulevard (673 8000). Bus 2, 3, 4, 22, 38. **Open** 2pm-2am daily. **No credit cards. Map E4**

Located opposite the **Fillmore Auditorium** (*see p210*) on one of the city's busier corners, the Boom Boom Room stands on the site of what was Jacks Bar, a San Francisco nightlife fixture for more than 50 years. It's presided over by blues legend John Lee Hooker, a regular performer at Jacks and a Bay Area

Let's hear it for John Lee at the blazingly popular **Boom Boom Room**.

resident. Positioned at the north end of the Fillmore Historic Jazz District, the club's location – not to mention its nightly live music schedule – have made it a blazing success.

Grant and Green

1371 Green Street, at Grant Avenue (693 9565). Bus 15, 30, 39. 41. **Open** 6am-6pm daily. **No credit cards. Map G2**

The venue with the $50 bill painted on its front door is a long-kept secret among North Beach locals. A stage fills the back of the room and crusty old bartenders pull draughts of beer. Go on a weeknight or you'll feel claustrophobic. Admission is free.

Last Day Saloon

406 Clement Street, at Fifth Avenue (387 6343). Bus 2, 38, 44. **Open** 2pm-2am Mon-Fri; noon-2am Sat; 10am-2am Sun. **No credit cards. Map B4**

This longtime favourite venue in the heart of the Richmond district offers blues, rock and country bands in a setting that's noisy and friendly. Utterly nondescript but for the TVs that transform the place into a sports bar on weekend afternoons, the Last Day is the only club in the neighbourhood to feature live music.

Lou's Pier 47

300 Jefferson Street, between Jones & Leavenworth Streets (771 0377). Bus 32. **Open** 4pm-1am Mon-Fri; noon-1am Sat, Sun. **Credit** AmEx, MC, V. **Map F1**

The closer you move towards the water in San Francisco, the less likely you are to find locals – ain't that a contradiction? At Pier 47, you're bound to uncover a few Financial District types, but the bulk of the crowd hails from the suburbs. Blues bands blast a mix of covers and others; salsa bands blare on certain week nights. The crowd is white and straight and drinking heavily; you can bet they'll wake up in the morning at least an hour from the city.

The Saloon

1232 Grant Avenue, at Vallejo Street & Columbus Avenue (989 7666). Bus 15, 30, 41, 45. **Open** noon-2am daily. **No credit cards. Map G2**

A blue-collar bar that showcases many of the city's best local roots musicians, the Saloon is a low-rent joint, a piece of North Beach that predates the upmarket eateries and hints at the district that Tom Wolfe aptly described as 'slums with a view'. The interior is lit up like a pinball machine and you'll be able to hear the music from nearly a block away.

Jazz clubs

If the rock scene is suffering from closure-itis, the city's jazz venues are celebrating a new influx of capital and appreciation. Most of this is due to the revival of Fillmore Street as a Historic Jazz District, but it may also be linked to on-going gentrification which has opened up previously unexplored neighbourhoods to new audiences who now consider them safe, white, territory.

The following are not the city's only jazz clubs: *see page 218* for supper clubs **Bruno's, Café du Nord, 42 Degrees, Piaf's, Storyville** and the **Up & Down Club**; *see chapter* **Restaurants & Cafés** for dining establishments which include live jazz.

Bimbo's 365 Club

1025 Columbus Avenue, at Chestnut Street (474 0365). Bus 30/cable car Powell-Mason. **Open** phone for details. **No credit cards. Map G2**

Named after one of the club's original proprietors, Bimbo's is the perfect place to indulge in time-travel delusion: set your clock for the 1940s, pull on your swing dance duds and don your fedora. From the swanky bar in the south room to the cheesy tinsel curtain and latticework booths in the big room, the club hasn't changed in almost 60 years. It has a ballroom-sized dance floor, main stage and separate cocktail lounge; groups with a full, rich sound (big bands, reggae artists and so on) do best here. The club is only open when it's hosting a show, but they do so four or five nights a week. A classic.

Website: www.bimbos365club.com

Elbo Room

647 Valencia Street, between 17th & 18th Streets (552 7788). BART 16th Street/bus 26, 33. **Open** 5pm-2am daily. **Credit** MC, V. **Map F6**

Although the Elbo has been commandeered by yuppie partyers of late, it continues to hold its own as one of the incubators of acid jazz, performed in the smoky, open-raftered space upstairs. The club has recently started booking some Latin jazz artists, an occasional soul combo and an occasional whacked-out experimentalist; the 'Dub Mission' DJ nights on Sundays are legendary. Come on a week night to avoid the gentrifying element.

Website: www.elbo.com

El Rio

See chapter **Gay & Lesbian San Francisco** *for listings.*

You owe it to yourself to take part in a San Francisco tradition – head to El Rio early on a Sunday afternoon and squeeze past the shuffleboard and pool tables to the sunny garden at the back, where you'll find the city's most diverse and lively Latin jazz party. An outdoor barbecue, decent Margaritas, a friendly (primarily lesbian) crowd and great live music greet you; you'll think you've gone to heaven – or at least to Rio – for the afternoon.

Hotel Utah

500 Fourth Street, at Bryant Street (421 8308). Bus 30, 45, 76. **Open** noon-2am daily. **Credit** MC, V. **Map H4**

It's hard to put the historic Utah in any neat category – rock, jazz or experimental – but easy to rave about its central attraction: a tiny stage with even tinier space from which to see it, which showcases a regular roster of fine music. Add a superb beer list, decent food from the tiny kitchen and a low cover charge and it quickly becomes clear why the space is a local institution.

Mick's Lounge

2513 Van Ness Avenue, at Union Street (928 0404). Bus 41, 42, 45, 49, 76. **Open** 6pm-2am daily. **Credit** AmEx, MC, V. **Map F2**

In the great void that is San Francisco's west-of-Van Ness-and-north-of-California clubland, Mick's Lounge stands as an outpost of hope. Without being a major contender, its programme is a sound one, featuring a mix of edge-cutting artists (Greyboy Allstars) with classic ones (Rebirth Brass Band) all piling onto the cramped stage. If you're trapped in the Marina with only a few bucks to spare, hoof it over to Mick's and pray for a long, inspired set.

Pier 23

Pier 23, at Embarcadero (362 5125). Bus 32, 42. **Open** 11.30am-2am Mon-Sat; 11am-10pm Sun. **Credit** Disc, MC, V. **Map H2**

For those rare sunny afternoons in San Francisco, Pier 23 can't be beaten — especially as an appetiser for the live music that plays inside in the evenings. The crowd here is primarily an after-work business one, though on Friday and Saturday nights the place overflows with non-locals. Jazz, reggae and an occasional blues band commandeer the stage.

Rasselas

1534 Fillmore Street, at Geary Boulevard (346 8696). Bus 1, 24, 22, 38. **Open** 5pm-midnight Mon-Thur, Sun; 5pm-1am Fri, Sat. **Credit** MC, V. **Map E4**

The new Rasselas on Fillmore is a beauty: a lavish, 200-seat nightclub with a long, curved bar and restaurant in the outer half and a beautiful, high-ceilinged jazz club further inside. Everything – from the décor to the sound system – is state-of-the-art, bankrolled by Agonafer Shiferaw, owner of this and the original branch on California. If all goes according

After hours

So you and your kittens are leaving the Cat Club, piling into a cab to head to the after-hours underground rave you just got the tip on. Or you're sick of dancing and just want to get a bite of breakfast to ward off the hangover you're certain you're courting. Or you have a sudden urge to go bowling, or settle an argument over a game of pool. Whatever the scenario, you're in luck. Though San Francisco is no New York (much to its chagrin) and many of the city's establishments close relatively early, after-hours felines still have plenty of options when they stumble from the clubs still bright-eyed and bushy-tailed.

If you're hungry for a Chinese meal or some seafood, try **Yuet Lee** (1300 Stockton Street, at Broadway; 982 6020). For Middle Eastern fare, **Kan Zaman** (1793 Haight Street, at Cole; 751 9656) is open until 2am at the weekends. For authentic Mexican food, head for **La Rondalla** (901 Valencia Street, at 20th Street; 647 7474). And **Brother's Korean Restaurant** (4128 Geary Boulevard, at Sixth Avenue; 387 7991) serves food until 3am daily.

Numerous diners are open 24 hours, including **Orphan Andy's** (3991 17th Street, at Castro; 864 9795), the **Grubstake** (1525 Pine Street, at Polk Street; 673 8268) and the ever-famous **Bagdad Café** (2295 Market Street, at 16th Street; 621 4434). The **Brazen Head** (3166 Buchanan Street, at Greenwich Street; 921 7600) is a wonderfully cosy pub that feels British and serves dinner till 1am. Finally, all three locations for **North Beach Pizza** – North Beach (433 2444), Sunset (242 9100) and Haight (751 2300) – will deliver their pies to late-night customers. For pies of a different kind, try **Bepples Pies** (1934 Union Street, at Laguna Street; 931 6225) or the delectables at **Tart to Tart** (641 Irving Street, at Eighth Avenue; 753 0643).

Several other businesses are open late to vie for your dusk-to-dawn dollar: **City Lights** (261 Columbus Avenue, at Broadway; 362 8193) sells books till midnight; **Hollywood Billiards** (61 Golden Gate Street, at Market; 252 9643) is open until 2am or 3am – though it's in the heart of one of the city's least safe neighbourhoods at night – and **Great Entertainer** (975 Bryant Street, at Eighth Street; 861 8833) lets you shoot pool till 2am Mon-Thur, Sun and until 3am Fri, Sat. If you have a craving to soak in a Jacuzzi, head for the **Grand Central Sauna and Hot Tub** (15 Fell Street, at Van Ness Avenue; 431 1370), where they'll accommodate you until midnight most nights and until 2am on Friday and Saturday. For the bowler, **Japantown Bowl** is open without pause, with reduced prices in the dead of night, as are several gyms (*see chapter* **Sport & Fitness**).

Finally, the **Four Star** (2200 Clement Street, at 23rd Avenue; 666 3488) and **Kabuki 8** (1881 Post Street, at Fillmore; 931 9800) regularly screen midnight movies on Friday and Saturday nights. If you'd rather rent them, **Into Video** (1439 Haight Street, at Ashbury; 864 2346) offers a good selection and is open until 1am. Don't cats sleep during the day anyway?

to plan, Rasselas will be the new Fillmore Historic Jazz District's showplace club. With a reputation for attracting both high-ranking local as well as national and international players to his original club, Shiferaw has gambled $1.2 million to bet that it will work; here's hoping it does.
Branch: 2801 California Street, at Divisadero Street (567 5010).

Rockapulco

3140 Mission Street, at Army Street (648 6611). BART 24th Street/Muni Metro J/bus 12, 14, 26, 27, 49, 67. **Open** Fri-Sun; phone for times. **No credit cards**.
The former home of Caesar's Latin Palace, the city's biggest and longest-lived Latin club, Rockapulco is *the* place to catch a big brass salsa band, as well as the major touring artists from Mexico, Colombia, Panama and elsewhere in Latin America and Brazil. At the weekend, Rockapulco is open late for after-hours dancing, usually until sunrise.

Someplace Else

1795 Geary Boulevard, at Fillmore Street (440 2180). Bus 22, 38. **Open** 6pm-2am daily. **Credit** MC, V. **Map E4**
Not to be forgotten in the hubbub over the new Jazz District in the Fillmore is this tiny, family-run organisation, which carves out a niche scheduling smaller artists in the wake of the larger venues. With a full restaurant menu, Someplace Else can potentially satisfy all your needs in one sitting. Admission is free.

Dance clubs

Only the hardened clubgoer can pontificate on the minute differences between house and deep house, jungle and drum 'n' bass, hip hop and old school. Whether you're well-versed or not, the following selection of clubs will provide you with the best overall guide to dancing in the city. Obviously, micro-scenes come and go like twinkling stars in the night sky: for the tip on them, poke your head into any reputable record shop (*see chapter* **Shops & Services**) and watch that ever-reliable word-passing media, the promotional flier. As we went to press, several clubs – namely the **End-up** (*see chapter* **Gay & Lesbian San Francisco**) and **Ten15 Folsom** – were being threatened with closure. Did anyone say gentrification?

The following 'gay' clubs have the best music for dancing: the **Box**, the **Café**, the **End-up**, the **Stud** (*see chapter* **Gay & Lesbian San Francisco** for listings). Finally, many venues known for live music – **Rockapulco** (*see above*), **El Rio** and the **Elbo Room** (*see page 214*), **Storyville** (*see page 220*) and **Boomerang** (*see page 211*) – have DJs spinning dance music on certain nights.

Bahia Cabana

1600 Market Street, at Franklin Street (626 3306). Muni Metro F, J, K, L, M, N/bus 6, 7, 66, 71. **Open** *restaurant* 5-10pm daily; *club* 10pm-2am daily. **Credit** AmEx, Disc, MC, V. **Map F5**
The city's Brazilian community continues to jam this Latin dance club, which offers salsa and merengue on most nights and an occasional live show with flamenco dancers. On Tuesdays, the Bahia rocks with the sounds of Brazilian karaoke – for those who've always wanted to know the *real* words to 'Girl from Ipanema'.

Big Heart City

836 Mission Street, between Fourth & Fifth Streets (777 0666). BART Powell Street/bus 12, 14, 27, 30, 45. **Open** phone for details. **Credit** AmEx, MC, V. **Map G/H4**
Big Heart City continues to hang on, despite constant ownership change and a shabbily-maintained venue. Saturday night seems to be its only regular gig, with DJs spinning house and deep soul. Watch the space for an occasional special event.

Cat Club

1190 Folsom Street, at Eighth Street (431 3332). Bus 12, 19. **Open** phone for details. **Credit** AmEx, MC, V. **Map G5**
The former Cat's Grill and Alley has reinvented itself as another popular club. Locals jam the space on weeknights – especially after the Cat scored Bondage A Go-Go on Wednesdays when the Trocadero closed – for a variety of scenes, including 1980s music, salsa, funk and glam rock. All the clubs go until 3am. Yeah, baby, yeah!

Club X

715 Harrison Street, between Third & Fourth Streets (339 8686). Bus 15, 30, 45, 76. **Open** 10pm-4am Fri. **No credit cards**. **Map H4**
You won't find a local here on Friday nights, when the place becomes a mecca for the 18-to-21ers who've driven up from the suburbs to commandeer the cavernous club's five go-go cages, three bars and multiple dancefloors.

DNA Lounge

375 11th Street, at Harrison Street (626 1409). Bus 9, 12, 19, 42. **Open** 9am-4am Tue-Sat. **No credit cards**. **Map G5**
Like foggy weather, the DNA is a San Francisco tradition, though the club feels a bit like a dungeon inside. One large dance floor is set below the main stage (which is open for show-offs when there isn't a band), flanked by stairs that lead to a mezzanine with corner booths for drinking and necking. The DNA represents a solid, if uninspired choice for a night's entertainment.

Holy Cow

1535 Folsom Street, between 11th & 12th Streets (621 6087). Bus 9, 42. **Open** 8pm-2am daily. **Credit** MC, V. **Map G5**
Seven nights a week, 52 weeks a year, the Holy Cow is open for dancing, a good generic place to work up a sweat. A mix of DJs spin a mix of styles, from breakbeat to trip hop. From the corner of 11th and

Folsom Streets, look south for the life-sized cow with a neon halo. Admission is always free.
Website: www.theholycow.com

Liquid

2925 16th Street, between South Van Ness Avenue & Capp Street (289 6833). BART 16th Street/ bus 14, 22, 26, 53. **Open** 10pm-2am Fri. **No credit cards. Map F6**

Liquid is a late-night club for fans of turntable culture: while some bars have DJs occasionally spinning records, Liquid has a different one every night. Sometimes it's Latin music, sometimes house, sometimes a cut-up of several performers. The décor is pleasant, though the dark blue lighting makes it difficult to see and the music is consistently provocative.

Metronome Ballroom

1830 17th Street, at De Haro Street (252 9000). Bus 19, 22. **Open** phone for details. **Credit** AmEx, MC, V. **Map H6**

If you love to dance but bars ain't your thing, the spacious, airy Metronome Ballroom may come to your rescue. Tucked into the shadow of Potrero Hill, the long-established venue offers dance lessons and general jigging most nights of the week. Come for a lesson, stay for a dance – whether lindy hop, jitterbug, cha-cha, rhumba, swing, salsa or other Latin dance styles, you'll come away with a new set of skills and more than a few potential dance partners.

Nikki's BBQ

460 Haight Street, between Webster & Fillmore Streets (621 6508). Bus 6, 7, 22, 66, 71. **Open** 9pm-2am daily. **No credit cards. Map E5**

One of the city's favourite clubs for more than a decade, Nikki's is an intimate space. Although no one will hold it against you that you're a tourist, they'd just as soon you didn't tell all your travelling friends about it – it gets full enough as it is. The musical selection is fluid – lots of soul, funk, hip-hop, jungle – and the crowd predominantly straight. Don't miss DJ Cheb i Sabbah's Tuesday night world music gig.

111 Minna

111 Minna Street, at Second Street (974 1719). BART Montgomery/Muni Metro F, J, K, L, M, K/bus 5, 14, 15, 38. **Open** 7pm-2am Tue-Fri; 7pm-2am Sat. **No credit cards. Map H4**

Shoebox-sized 111 Minna is an art gallery by day and dance club by night and is consistently packed. From the taps, a selection of microbrewed beers; from the speakers, a mixture of turntablist styles guarantees you'll find a night when your feet can move – since your shoulders won't be able to. *See also chapter* **Museums & Galleries**.

Polly Esther's

181 Eddy Street, at Taylor Street (885 1977). BART Powell/Muni Metro F, J, K, L, M, N/bus 27, 31. **Open** 9pm-2am Thur; 9pm-3am Fri, Sat. **Credit** AmEx, MC, V. **Map G4**

This San Francisco version of the New York-based club chain is lavishly decorated in prime 1970s and

Gallery-cum-dance club, **111 Minna.**

1980s style. That may or may not be a good thing, but the crowds fill the place – two full levels including the Purple Rain Dance Floor downstairs and a disco palace up.
Website: www.pollyesthers.com

Sound Factory

525 Harrison Street, at First Street (339 8686). Bus 12, 42, 76. **Open** 9.30pm-4am Sat. **No credit cards. Map J4**

In a colossal warehouse space, the Sound Factory boasts two floors and multiple rooms., attracting waves of new, mostly young partygoers coming into the city. Like its twin in New York, the Sound Factory is as close to an institution as one can get for a dance club. Plenty of house, funk, the latest imports and pop. Admission is free until 10pm.

Ten15 Folsom

1015 Folsom Street, between Sixth & Seventh Streets (431 7444/recorded information 431 1200). Bus 12, 27, 42. **Open** 10pm-6am Thur, Fri; 10pm-9am Sat. **No credit cards. Map G5**

Like the **DNA Lounge** (*see p216*), the Ten15 is always a safe bet for dancing, before-, during-, or after-hours. With three rooms, each with its own vibe, you

can move through space and time without changing venues. The downstairs speakeasy offers a cool-down groove. The club is several blocks east of the 11th-and-Folsom Street clubland; spring a couple of bucks for the cab ride.
Website: www.1015.com

26Mix

3024 Mission Street, at 26th Street (248 1319). BART 24th Street/bus 14, 26, 49. **Open** 9pm-2am daily. **No credit cards**.
The newest and grooviest spot for turntablist culture. DJs spin and crossfade seven nights a week. Look for special guests and events related to electronica and a low cover charge – never higher than $5. Posh and stylish, 26Mix is a self-described 'soundbar', designed to sound good wherever you're sitting. It's one of several new bars in the Mission that are successfully changing the area's image as a rough-hewn, blue-collar neighbourhood.
Website: www.26mix.com

Supper clubs

Back in their heyday, supper clubs were elegant, exciting nightspots – warm and smoky dining rooms full of atmosphere and the sounds of a 15-piece orchestra. These days, the term fills an array of niches, from fine dining destinations to singles stomping grounds to tourist traps. Most of the supper clubs found in San Francisco fall into the sensible centre. You're apt to get a good meal, hear decent music and feel you are, to all intents and purposes, steppin' out.

The clubs that follow are establishments that emphasise dinner and a show as part of a whole package. Many restaurants and bars feature live music (such as **Bix**, *see chapter* **Bars**, the **Cypress Club** and **Rose Pistola**, *see chapter* **Restaurants & Cafés**); and many clubs offer a menu of some kind. The venues listed below, however, are those which have carefully prepared your tuna to go with their tunes.

Black Cat

501 Broadway, at Kearny Street (981 2233). Bus 12, 15, 30, 41, 83. **Open** 5.30pm-1.15am daily. **Credit** AmEx, Disc, MC, V. **Map G/H2**
Named after one of the oldest jazz establishments in the city, the Black Cat is the chic new downtown club to beat, with live music, a full restaurant with eclectic menu, dancing most nights of the week and a prime location in the centre of North Beach. On the ground floor, the kitchen is open until after 1am. The basement **Blue Bar** has a limited menu – perfect for nibbling as you dig the jazzy tunes. *See also chapter* **Restaurants & Cafés**.

Bruno's

2389 Mission Street, between 19th & 20th Streets (550 7455). Bus 14, 26, 49. **Open** 6pm-2am Mon-Sat. **Credit** MC, V. **Castro/Mission Map Y1**

The last laugh?

For years, San Francisco was a mecca for new, alternative comedians. Dana Carvey, Ellen DeGeneres, Robin Williams and Whoopi Goldberg all honed their craft at clubs in the Bay Area. By 1988, the height of its popularity, comedy was everywhere: clubs ran at capacity seven nights a week in San Francisco alone, and there were others in the east and south Bay Area.

Blame it on complacency or cable TV, but by the early 1990s the larger comedy rooms were 'papering' – giving away blocks of tickets. The smaller clubs followed suit, throwing fistfuls of tickets at unsuspecting tourists at Pier 39. This was the beginning of the end for many venues, who couldn't live off bar receipts alone. By 1995, with the suburban clubs gasping their last breath, only three major clubs remained in San Francisco.

The good news is that fewer rooms means better shows and the three have their pick of the best comedians working the US circuit today. Downtown, the **Punchline** caters to a younger, hometown crowd, while near Fisherman's Wharf, **Cobb's Comedy Club** fills with slightly older, sunburned tourists in T-shirts. The queen of comedy, however, is **Josie's Cabaret and Juice Joint**, which opened in the Castro in 1989 – as comedy was beginning to decline. Josie's thrived because it was servicing the needs of a specific community: it was (and still is) the only gay and lesbian performance space. Shows are complemented by a rather arcane vegetarian menu and the 130-seat club was smoke-free years before California laws took effect. Unlike other clubs, Josie's has no two-drink minimum.

Though it has recently pruned its schedule, the club still books stand-up two nights a week. On Mondays, Josie's offers one of the original real open mike nights in San Francisco. Anyone — *anyone* — can toss their shtick: perhaps Liz Taylor's illegitimate son, some 80-year-old guy from Sacramento, or one of the successful comics who started out at Josie's – Marga Gomez, Bob Smith, Scott Capurro – will drop by to torture the crowd. On Saturday, three seasoned gay comics grace the stage for 90 minutes of high camp and low living. As always,

First opened in the late 1930s, Bruno's was a dive, reborn after it was purchased by the owners of the popular **Café du Nord** (*see below*). With its round burgundy leatherette booths, dark wood panelling and flattering lighting, it remains a class act in the world of supper clubs. The food is excellent (a small but elegant menu puts a gourmet spin on comfort food) and the tunes – big band and blues or an occasional free jazz ensemble – remain top-notch.

Café Du Nord

2170 Market Street, between Church & Sanchez Streets (861 5016). Muni Metro F, K, L, M/ bus 22, 37. **Open** 6pm-2am Mon, Tue; 4pm-2am Wed-Sun. **Credit** AmEx, MC, V. **Map E6**

Du Nord offers something musically different every night, including salsa and swing dance lessons and a Wednesday night glam rock scene. In addition, blues bands, DJs, 'classic' jazz, hip hop, funk and soul DJs all perform in the comfortable, clubby setting. Dinner is served nightly; you'll want to stay for the music more than the cooking.

Website: www.cafedunord.com

Cha Cha Cha at McCarthy's

2327 Mission Street, between 19th & 20th Streets (648 0504). Bus 14, 26, 49. **Open** 5-11pm Mon-Thur, Sun; 5pm-midnight Fri, Sat. **Credit** MC, V. **Castro/Mission Map Y1**

Giving Bruno's a run for its money, the successful Cha Cha Cha on Haight has recently taken over this former dive bar, which now serves its low-budget, not-too-greasy tapas and other Caribbean fare. DJs spin after the dinner crowd thins; live ensembles play on Tuesday and Thursday nights. If anyone can make this spot succeed, it's Cha Cha Cha.

42 Degrees

235 16th Street, at Illinois Avenue (777 5559). Bus 15, 22, 48. **Open** 11.30am-3pm Mon, Tue; 11.30am-3pm, 6.30-11.30pm, Wed-Fri; 6.30-11.30pm Sat. **Credit** AmEx, MC, V. **Map J6**

A hip setting, great Californian food, live jazz, outdoor seating – 42 Degrees is the kind of place that thrives in music- and food-obsessed San Francisco. Open for dinner from Wednesday to Saturday, the high-ceilinged, neo-industrial room could be considered the X generation's **Bix** (*see chapter* **Bars**). Since there's not much else to do in this funky neighbourhood at the city's eastern edge, you may want to make a night of it.

Harry Denton's Starlite Room

Sir Francis Drake Hotel, 450 Powell Street, between Post & Sutter Streets (395 8595). Bus 2, 3, 4, 30, 45, 76/cable car Powell-Hyde or Powell-Mason. **Open** 4.30pm-12.30am Mon; 4.30pm-1.30am Tue-Sat. **Credit** AmEx, MC, V. **Map G3**

Harry Denton and his places are a love 'em or leave 'em affair. This one has a stunning 21st-floor view over Union Square, lots of mirrors for askance eye contact, floral carpets and booths filled with social and financial climbers. The music is less innovative

straight people are welcomed with open limbs.

Several cafés host open mike nights, including **Brainwash** (*see page 178* **Shops & Services**) on Thursdays, the **One World Café** (1799 McAllister Street, at Baker Street; 776 9358) on Fridays and **Java Source** (343 Clement Street, at 5th Avenue; 387 8025) on Tuesdays. The **Luggage Store** artspace holds comedy workshops on Tuesdays at 7pm and open mike night an hour later, and the **Mock Café** – stepchild of the **Marsh** performance theatre (*see chapter* **Performing Arts**) – features a rotating mix of local and better-known performers, plenty of female wordsmiths and an open mike night. Check out their 'late-night' comedy series on Saturdays at 10pm. For information about Comedy Celebration Day, an outdoor event held every August in Golden Gate Park, *see chapter* **San Francisco by Season**.

For complete comedy listings, check the weeklies. And keep your fingers crossed: there might still be some life in that ol' gag yet.

Cobb's Comedy Club

2801 Leavenworth Street, at Beach Street (928 4320). Bus 30, 32, 42/cable car Powell-Hyde. **Open** from 8pm daily. **Credit** MC, V. **Map F1**

Josie's Cabaret and Juice Joint

3583 16th Street, between Market & Pond Streets (861 7933). Muni Metro F, K, L, M/bus 37. **Open** phone for details. **No credit cards**. **Map E6**

Luggage Store

1007 Market Street at Sixth Street (255 5971). Muni F/bus 6, 7, 71. **Open** phone for details. **No credit cards**. **Map G4**

Mock Café

1062 Valencia Street, at 22nd Street (826 5750 ext 2). BART 24th Street/bus 14, 26. **Open** phone for details. **No credit cards**. **Castro/Mission Map Y2**

Punchline

444 Battery Street, at Clay Street (397 7573). Bus 1, 12, 41, 42. **Open** *shows* 9pm Tue-Thur, Sun; 9pm, 11pm Fri, Sat. **Credit** AmEx, MC, V. **Map H3**

Storyville: *a classy joint in a nondescript location.*

jazz, more R&B covers: don't come if you can't stand *Mustang Sally*. Frog-voiced Denton is famous in San Francisco as a man who makes his bars a non-stop twenty- and thirtysomething party. The branch, **Harry Denton's**, is a dance club teeming with straight singles.
Branch: Harry Denton's 161 Steuart Street, at the Embarcadero (882 1333).

Piaf's

1686 Market Street, at Franklin Street (864 3700). Muni Metro F, J, K, L, M, N/bus 6, 7, 66, 71.
Open 5.30-10pm Tue-Thur; 5.30-11pm Fri, Sat; 5-9pm Sun. **Credit** AmEx, Disc, MC, V.
Map F5
Set in the tiny French mini-district near the corner of Market and Franklin, Piaf's is a tiny, almost unnoticed French bistro with a few tables and nightly jazz singers. It's a charming place, with just enough authenticity to keep it interesting and enough cheesiness to keep it from being pretentious. Before dinner, walk to **Zuni Café** (*see chapter* **Restaurants & Cafés**) for a glass of champagne.

Storyville

1751 Fulton Street, between Masonic & Central Avenues (441 1751). Bus 5, 43. **Open** 9.30pm-2am Tue-Sat. **Credit** AmEx, MC, V. **Map D5**
Storyville's deep red walls and warm fireplace nod to something that's seriously missing in most of the city's jazz clubs: good, old-fashioned class. Located in a nondescript block in Western Addition, Storyville has a full bar, good Creole food, excellent service and jazz acts that range from headliners to nervous locals testing their pipes. Recently, the club has added a couple of DJ nights during the week.

330 Ritch

330 Ritch Street, between Brannan & Townsend Streets (541 9574/522 9558). Bus 15, 30, 42, 45, 76. **Open** 5pm-2am Wed, Thur; 8pm-2am Fri; 9pm-2am Sat. **Credit** AmEx, MC, V. **Map H/J4/5**
A young crowd seems right at home amid the exposed brick and dark wood of this spacious yet intimate SoMa spot, which also has an attractive bar and a good-sized dance floor. Events range from Latin jazz and 1980s house DJs to an occasional hip hop

headliner; food ranges from grilled fare to barbecued chicken and you can choose from a selection of small-plate entrées.

Up & Down Club

1151 Folsom Street, between Seventh & Eighth Streets (626 2388). Bus 12, 19. **Open** 9pm-2am Mon, Tue; 8pm-2am Wed, Thur; 9.30pm-2am Fri, Sat. **Credit** AmEx, MC, V. **Map G5**

As one of the centres of the early 1990s jazz renaissance in San Francisco, the Up & Down has built a reputation for quality tunes, hosting original bands with a sound that can hold your full attention. Though its popularity has slackened a bit in recent years, the long, narrow club continues to sell to a full house at the weekend. Model Christy Turlington and her sister are co-owners, but don't count on seeing her.

Out of town

Ashkenaz

1317 San Pablo Avenue, at Gilman Street, Berkeley (1-510 525 5054). BART El Cerrito Plaza, then bus 72, 73. **Open** phone for details. **No credit cards**.

Ashkenaz is non-institutionalised multiculturalism in action. Booking 'world beat', Afro-Cuban, jump, swing and reggae acts, the timber-raftered venue is like a Jamaican mountain lodge. Get sweaty on the dance floor with students, travellers and free-thinking locals and then cool off with a Red Stripe.

Blake's

2367 Telegraph Avenue, at Durant Avenue, Berkeley (1-510 848 0886). BART Berkeley, then bus 51, 64 or walk. **Open** 11.30am-2am Mon-Fri; noon-midnight Sat. **Credit** AmEx, Disc, MC, V.

Over 50 years old, Blake's remains a Berkeley institution. Its musical fare has changed considerably over the past few years, from traditional blues to modern rock and acid jazz, with acoustic sets one night a week. The rest of the week is a changing roster of DJs.

Cow Palace

Geneva Avenue, at Santos Street, Daly City (469 6065). Bus 9, 9X, 9AX, 9BX, 15/CalTrain Bayshore, then bus 15. **Open** *office* 10am-5pm Mon-Sat. **Credit** AmEx, Disc, MC, V.

Cow Palace serves as the venue for many other events, including hockey games and rodeos. Its concerts are little better than stadium shows. Book your ticket through BASS.

Greek Theater

Piedmont Avenue & Gayley Road, Berkeley (1-510 642 9988). BART Berkeley, then bus 52 or walk. **Open** *office* May-Sept 10am-5.30pm Mon-Fri; 10am-2pm Sat, Sun. **Credit** MC, V.

The Greek is an open-air stone amphitheatre located just across the Bay at the edge of the UC Berkeley campus, with lawn and reserved seating. At night it provides a gorgeous setting under the sunset and stars with excellent acoustics.

Kimball's East

5800 Shellmound Street, at Christie Street, Emeryville (1-510 658 2555). BART Ashby, then bus 7. **Open** *office* noon-6pm Mon-Thur; noon-10pm Fri-Sun; *doors open* 6.30pm daily. **Credit** MC, V.

Filling in the booking cracks left by the mighty **Yoshi's** in Oakland (*see below*), Kimballs gives the audience a more up-close and personal experience with the musicians, many of whom are at the peak of their careers.

Oakland-Alameda (UMAX) County Coliseum Complex

7000 Coliseum Way, Oakland (1-510 569 2121). BART Coliseum. **Open** *office* 10am-6pm Mon-Fri. **Credit** AmEx, MC, V.

Home to the Golden State Warriors basketball team, the 15,000-seat Oakland Coliseum is an indoor sports arena first and concert hall second – which may be all you need to know. Book through BASS.

Shoreline Amphitheater

1 Amphitheater Parkway, Mountain View (1-650 967 4040). CalTrain Mountain View, then cab/drive south on US 101 to Mountain View. **Open** *office* 10am-5pm Mon-Fri, Sun. **Credit** MC, V.

Offering a diversity of major acts from Cher to Phish to Barry White, the Shoreline has a repuation as a decent large venue, with reserved seating near the stage and a groomed lawn for the rest. Getting back to the city in the evening by public transport is difficult; go by car if you can.

Website: www.shoreline-amd.com

Yoshi's

510 Embarcadero West, at Jack London Square (1-510 238 9200). BART Oakland City Center, then bus 58, 72L, 301. **Open** *club* 6pm-12.30am daily; *shows* at 8pm, 10pm. **Credit** AmEx, DC, Disc, JCB, MC, V.

Yoshi's offers the kind of refined setting that makes for a splendid occasion. Its separate dining room does a good business on the strength of its kitchen, but come for the music – Yoshi's books the hottest touring jazz talent every week and plays host to some of the best local musicians, as well as artists from around the globe. Book in advance.

Website: www.yoshis.com

Performing Arts

Whether your taste runs to 'Riverdance', 'Rent' or the latest in repertory footwork, you'll find something to suit you here.

Theatre & dance

While San Francisco theatre and dance don't comprise the all-encompassing scenes you'll find in New York, they remain vibrant elements of the Bay Area's arts community. Experimentation is encouraged, even savoured, and cutting-edge work isn't instantly sucked up, commercially packaged and hyped the way it is in NYC and LA.

In the theatre, while much attention goes to high-profile shows like Andrew Lloyd Webber's *Phantom of the Opera*, which enjoyed nearly five years of play here, offbeat performers and socially-conscious artists are allowed the space to hone their creative vision: Tony Kushner, the Pulitzer Prize-winning playwright of the Broadway smash *Angels in America*, developed the play and premièred it in San Francisco. There's also room for the lunatic fringe – performers such as Mark Pauline of the rogue robot directors Survival Research Laboratories – to blow themselves apart in the name of art. Other nationally known playwrights and performers such as Anna Deavere Smith and Eric Bogosian have recharged their cultural batteries in the city.

In dance circles, both the high-profile and the experimental exist in polite détente, the two ends of the spectrum both knowing they need each other to survive. Whether you're attending the San Francisco Ballet at the Opera House or an offbeat performance at a Mission district dance studio, you're likely to see the same sets of faces.

If you're planning ahead, the Datebook section of the combined Sunday *San Francisco Examiner and Chronicle*, the free weeklies and *SF Arts Monthly* (www.artsmonthlysf.org) carry up-to-date reviews and listings. On the Internet, San Francisco's CitySearch site (www.citysearch7.com) maintains current box office data.

For the **Theatre Rhinoceros** and **LunaSea**, *see chapter* **Gay & Lesbian San Francisco**.

Festivals

San Francisco's theatre festivals offer something for everyone. Look out for free events like the Golden Gate favourite **San Francisco Shakespeare Festival**, part of the **California Shakespeare Festival** (held in September), and the **Stern Grove Festival** (Sundays in June-August), where the city's finest – including the San Francisco Opera and Ballet – stage productions for afternoon picnickers. The **Solo Mio Festival** (*see p224* **Climate Theatre**), a feisty series of high-quality solo performances, is a high point of Bay Area theatre, as is the annual **Mime Troupe in the Park** (www.sfmt. org), when the 40-year-old San Francisco Mime Troupe brings its unique combination of humour and hard-hitting politics to various park locations around the Bay Area. For more details on these events, *see chapter* **San Francisco by Season**.

Finally, during the ten-day **Annual San Francisco Fringe Festival** (*see page 224* **EXITheater**) in September, you can expect anything from Oscar Wilde to all-female improv troupes and superhero strippers, all performed by local and visiting companies in various venues around town.

TICKETS

Prices range from $5 for an experimental show to $50 or more for an (off-) Broadway extravaganza. Theatre box offices are usually the cheapest bet for tickets (bear in mind there's often a fee for telephone bookings). **TIX Bay Area** in Union Square (433 7827) sells half-price tickets for theatre, dance and opera events on the day of the show (cash only). It also sells full-price tickets in advance (for which you can pay by credit card). Ticket brokers **BASS** has outlets all over the city, but expect to pay a hefty surcharge (performing arts booking line on 776 1999). You can also try the **St Francis Theater Ticket Service** (362 3500), **Mr Ticket** (292 7328/1-800 424 7328/1-888 722 5737) or **City Box Office** (392 4400). You can buy tickets for some venues online through www.ticketweb.com.

Mainstream theatres

Purchase tickets through BASS and, for the Golden Gate and Orpheum theatres, from the central box office at the Orpheum.

Curran Theater
445 Geary Street, between Mason & Taylor Streets (551 2000). BART Powell Street/Muni Metro F, J, K, L, M, N/bus 27, 38/cable car Powell-Hyde or Powell-Mason. **Credit** AmEx, MC, V. **Map G4**
Website: www.bestofbroadway-sf.com

Golden Gate Theater
1 Taylor Street, between Sixth & Market Streets (551 2000). BART Civic Center/Muni Metro F, J, K, L, M, N/bus 5, 6, 7, 9, 21, 26, 66, 71. **Credit** AmEx, MC, V. **Map G4**

Orpheum
1192 Market Street, at Hyde Street (551 2000). BART Civic Center/Muni Metro F, J, K, L, M, N/ bus 6, 5, 7, 9, 21, 31, 66, 71. **Credit** AmEx, MC, V. **Map G4/5**

Regional theatres

The **American Conservatory Theater (ACT)** and **Berkeley Repertory** (*see page 224*) are the Bay Area's two most established theatre companies; both mount a full season of shows each year.

American Conservatory Theater (ACT)
Geary Theater, 415 Geary Street, between Mason & Taylor Streets (834 3200); box office at 405 Geary Street (749 2228). BART Powell Street/Muni Metro F, J, K, L, M, N/bus 27, 38/cable car Powell-Hyde or Powell-Mason. **Credit** AmEx, MC, V. **Map G4**
Economically and ideologically energised after its triumphant return to the retrofitted and restored theatre near Union Square, ACT produces contemporary and traditional shows with a varied programme throughout the season. You'll regularly catch works by Tom Stoppard and David Mamet, as well as Wilder, Williams, Chekov and Shakespeare. ACT's adaptation of *A Christmas Carol* is a yearly tradition.
Website: www.act-sfbay.org

Lamplighters Musical Theater
Theater at Yerba Buena Center for the Arts (see p224) & Ira and Leonore S Gershwin Theatre, 2350 Turk Boulevard, at Masonic Avenue (978 2787). Bus 5, 31, 38, 43. **Credit** MC, V. **Map D5**
San Francisco's Gilbert & Sullivan repertory company has produced operetta and musical theatre since 1952. Lamplighters regularly presents comic operas and musicals from European and American repertoires. Performances are also held in the East Bay at the **Dean Lesher Regional Center for the Arts** (1601 Civic Drive, Walnut Creek; 1-925 943 7469).
Website: www.lamplighters.org

Mid-sized theatres

Asian American Theater Company
(440 5545). **No credit cards**.
The AATC provides venues for Asian- and Pacific Islander-American playwrights and actors to perform premières and classic works.
Website: www.wenet.net/~aatc

Pushing the envelope at the **Magic Theater**.

Eureka Theater Company
215 Jackson Street, at Battery Street (788 7469). Bus 12, 42, 83. **Credit** AmEx, MC, V. **Map H2**
This innovative company, known for helping Tony Kushner develop the Pulitzer prize-winning *Angels in America*, provides a venue for provocative new works – and works new to the Bay Area.
Website: www.eurekatheatre.org

Lorraine Hansberry Theater
620 Sutter Street, between Mason & Powell Streets (474 8800). Bus 2, 3, 4, 30, 45, 76/cable car Powell-Hyde or Powell-Mason. **Credit** AmEx, MC, V. **Map G3**
Recently partnered with a theatre group in Harlem, the Lorraine Hansberry presents plays by America's foremost African-American playwrights, such as Pulitzer prize-winners Charles Fuller and August Wilson. It also stages adaptations of works by Alice Walker and Toni Morrison, among others, and an occasional classical dramatic work.

Magic Theater
Building D, Fort Mason Center, at Laguna & Buchanan Streets (441 8822). Bus 28. **Credit** AmEx, MC, V. **Map E1**
For more than 30 years, the Magic Theater has been dedicated to developing daring new plays, many of which respond to topical political and social events. In general, the theatre premières five new plays per season and produces festivals of new and developing work and a 'Raw Play' script-in-hand series.
Website: www.magictheatre.org

Theater Artaud
450 Florida Street, at 17th Street (621 7797). Bus 27, 33, 53. **Credit** MC, V. **Map G6**

A gracefully renovated warehouse, Theater Artaud is worth the trip for the space alone. Once inside, you'll find high-quality performances of avant-garde theatre, music and dance performances from San Francisco, the US and the world. The 'Twilight Salon' is a series of Friday night art extravaganzas with dance performances, music, visual projection and art.
Website: www.theaterartaud.org

Theater at Yerba Buena Center for the Arts

701 Mission Street, at Third Street; theatre entrance at intersection of Third & Howard Streets (978 2787). BART Powell/Muni Metro F, J, L, K, M, N/bus 14, 15, 30, 45, 76. **Credit** MC, V.
Map H4

Inside this angled, blue-tiled box is housed the city's most striking new performance space. Events range from the AfroSolo Festival (a celebration of African American solo performances), to renditions of the Lamplighters' *My Fair Lady,* shows by Filipino comedy troupes and performances by musical oddballs including the Kronos Quartet and local computer tunesmith Bob Ostertag. Don't miss this fine venue.
Website: www.YerbaBuenaArts.org

Smaller spaces

Dozens of smaller theatres and performance spaces dot San Francisco and the Bay Area. Check out the **Mason Street Theater** (982 5463), the **Theater on the Square** (433 9500), and **Marine's Memorial Theater** (771 6900), among others. Space for local experimental work and festival programming is provided by the **Bayfront** and **Cowell Theaters** (both at Fort Mason; 979 3010), while **Brava! for Women in the Arts** (641 7657) and **Josie's Juice Bar and Cabaret** have done plenty to develop queer performance in the area (*see chapters* **Gay & Lesbian San Francisco** *and* **Nightlife**).

Climate Theater

252 Ninth Street, between Folsom & Howard Streets (392 4400). BART Civic Center/Muni Metro F, J, K, L, M, N/bus 12, 14, 26. **Credit** MC, V.
Map G5

Home to the acclaimed Solo Mio Festival, the Climate nurtures new work by solo performers who have gone on to achieve wider acclaim. It also produces the annual Festival Fantochio, a fantastical puppet event that is definitely not for children only.

EXITheater

156 Eddy Street, between Mason & Taylor Streets (931 1094/festival information 673 3847). BART Powell Street/Muni Metro F, J, K, L, M, N/bus 27, 31. **No credit cards. Map G4**

Home to the annual **San Francisco Fringe Festival** (*see chapter* **San Francisco by Season**), the EXIT otherwise offers a variety of works, from one-act plays to adaptations of the likes of Sam Shepard, Robert Anton Wilson and Tom Stoppard.

New Conservatory Theater

25 Van Ness Avenue, at Fell Street (861 8972). Muni Metro F, J, K, L, M, N/bus 42, 47, 49.
Credit AmEx, MC, V. **Map F5**

This well-designed performing arts complex, houses three fully-equipped theatres (which range in size from 50-132 seats), a video studio, art gallery and

Out of town: theatre & dance

Artship

Oakland Waterfront (1-510 238 5103). BART Oakland City Center.

In August 1999, the historic former naval vessel USS *Crescent City* was modified and moored at the Oakland Waterfront as a floating centre for creative arts and cultural education. Inside is a rotating exhibition of painting and sculpture, as well as a theatre which currently hosts both dance and dramatic performances. The swords-to-ploughshares transformation is inspired, if not yet spectacular.

Berkeley Repertory Theater

2025 Addison Street, between Shattuck Avenue & Milvia Street (1-510 845 4700). BART Berkeley.
Credit MC, V.

Interpreting works from Bertold Brecht to Ben Jonson, this venerable East Bay company divides productions between its main stage, where it presents five plays a year, and a 'parallel season' of experimental and developing work. The productions often reflect the diverse communities and traditions of the Bay Area and California as a whole, making it a great place to catch innovative and insightful work. Half-price tickets are available from the box office on the day of each performance.
Website: www.berkeleyrep.org

Cal Performances

Zellerbach Hall, UC Berkeley campus (1-510 642 9988). BART Berkeley. **Credit** MC, V.

Hosted in conjunction with UC Berkeley at Zellerbach Hall on campus, this series draws the best national dance companies, from Alvin Ailey and Merce Cunningham to Trisha Brown and June Watanabe, as well as such treats as Les Ballets Africains, the Dance Theatre of Harlem and the Mark Morris Dance Group.
Website: www.calperfs.berkeley.edu

classroom studios. The NCT also produces educational programmes for kids.
Website: www.nctcsf.org

Stage Door Theater

420 Mason Street, at Geary Street (834 3200). Bus 2, 3, 4, 76. **Credit** MC, V. **Map G4**
The Samaritan who sheltered the ACT during its homeless years, the old and elegant 550-seat Stage Door continues to put on solid works that draw the second-tier of Union Square's theatre-going society.

Experimental & performance art

San Francisco and the Bay Area have produced more than their fair share of underground hits. Indeed, the region's theatrical reputation is fired by the raw creative energies generated in its alternative performance spaces.

Intersection for the Arts

446 Valencia Street, between 15th & 16th Streets (626 2787). BART 16th Street/bus 14, 22, 26, 49, 53. **No credit cards. Map F6**
One of the city's favourites, an alternative arts centre mixing theatre with poetry, fiction and non-fiction readings, fine art exhibitions and avant-garde music. Reasonably-priced admission prices keep the Mission neighbourhood residents flocking here.
Website: www.wenet.net/~intrsect

The Marsh

1062 Valencia Street, at 22nd Street (826 5750). BART 24th Street/bus 14, 26, 49. **Credit** AmEx, MC, V. **Castro/Mission Map Y2**
With whimsical fashion shows, play premières and dance performances, you never know what you'll find at this long-established and respected venue. The Marsh bills itself as a 'breeding ground for new performance', and offers select writers and performers an open stage to try out whatever they like. *See also* the **Mock Café**, a comedy space, *in chapter* **Nightlife**.
Website: www.themarsh.org

New Langton Arts

1246 Folsom Street, between Eighth & Ninth Streets (626 5416). Bus 19, 27, 42. **Credit** MC, V. **Map G5**
The centre makes space in its programme of experimental art shows for original presentations penned by regional grant winners. Expect political and social commentary, and gender-bending art and performance. Perhaps the best of the city's alternative arts venues.

In a class of their own

Beach Blanket Babylon

Club Fugazi, 678 Green Street, between Columbus Avenue & Powell Street (421 4222). Bus 15, 30, 41, 45. **Credit** MC, V. **Map G2**
This long-running musical revue features a constantly changing array of characters drawn from US popular culture, local legend and the politics of the day. The slapstick humour places heavy emphasis on the formulaic and the visual. Even so, Beach Blanket Babylon is a San Francisco original.

George Coates Performance Works

110 McAllister Street, at Leavenworth Street (863 8520). BART Civic Center/Muni Metro F, J, K, L, M, N/bus 5. **Credit** AmEx, V. **Map G4**
Techno wizard George Coates is a pioneer in 'virtual' theatre, working actors and musicians into dazzling computer-generated environments. The space commissions only one show a year, usually running from November to March, but hosts special events (from Spalding Grey to Chanticleer) throughout the year. Tickets are available from City Box Office (*see p222*).
Website: www.georgecoates.org

Survival Research Laboratories

In vacant lots and public spaces, post-apocalyptic sculptor Mark Pauline and his SRL demonstrate menacing machines that threaten, shoot, careen and combust. Sign a waver that promises you won't sue them and you can attend the riskiest events in the city. Thus far, no one has been killed. Check the SRL website for future events.
Website: www.srl.org

Hairy gags at **Beach Blanket Babylon.**

Dance

For the latest dance information, check the Bay Area dance links at www.baydance.com/baylinks.htm as well as the local papers.

Performance groups & spaces

See also page 224 **Theater Artaud** *and* **Theater at Yerba Buena Center for the Arts**.

Dancers' Group Studio Theater

3221 22nd Street, at Mission Street (824 5044). BART 24th Street/bus 14, 49, 67.
Castro/Mission Map Y2
A cutting-edge group that has been described as featuring 'tattoos, not tutus', Dancers' Group teaches classes and gives performances, all with an athletic, high-movement content. Look for the annual Edge Festival in February and March, the Improvisational Dance Festival in June as well as occasional residencies by troupes such as Asian American Dance Performances and the Joe Goode Performance Group.
Website: www. dancersgroup.org

ODC Performance Gallery

3153 17th Street, between South Van Ness Avenue & Folsom Street (box office 863 9834/administration 626 6745). BART 16th Street/bus 33. **Credit** MC, V. **Map F6**
This austere and elegant space (formerly known as the New Performance Gallery) showcases the work of mostly local dancers and helps develop innovative modern dance performances.

San Francisco Ballet

War Memorial Opera House, 301 Van Ness Avenue, at Grove Street (865 2000). BART Civic Center/ Muni Metro F, J, K, L, M, N/bus 21, 42, 47, 49.
Credit AmEx, MC, V. **Map F5**
Founded in 1933, the San Francisco Ballet is America's oldest professional ballet company. Following its traditional seasonal opening with the *Nutcracker Suite*, SFB features other works choreographed by George Balanchine, Jerome Robbins and its artistic director Helgi Tomasson, among others. One of its most successful shows in recent years was *Billboards*, an uncharacteristically modern ballet with a score by the Artist Formerly Known as Prince.
Website: www.sfballet.org

San Francisco Performances

Suite 710, 500 Sutter Street, between Mason & Powell Streets (398 6449). Bus 2, 3, 4, 30, 45, 76/cable car Powell-Hyde or Powell-Mason.
Map G3
Though also known as a music venue, San Francisco Performances attracts some of the biggest national and international names in dance to its dance series, which runs from November to April. Performances have featured such dancers and companies as Bill T Jones and the Netherlands Dance Theatre. Tickets are available from City Box Office (*see p222*).

The Joe Goode Performance Group's 'Gender Heroes' at the **Dancers' Group Studio Theater**.

Scenes from the annual In the Street festival.

Classical music & opera

San Francisco's reputation for classical music – especially contemporary music, early music and opera – has always been sterling, with more going on today than in any other city on the West Coast. The recently renovated **War Memorial Opera House** has re-opened with a splash, joining the **Louise M Davies Symphony Hall, Bill Graham Civic Auditorium** and **Herbst Theater** to form a four-part civic quartet for musical venues; they attract audiences in increasing numbers.

The arrival in 1995 of Michael Tilson Thomas, hot from the London Symphony Orchestra, has injected new adrenaline into the San Francisco Symphony Orchestra, whose season runs between September and May. The Symphony's guest artists – ranging from Meredith Monk to Metallica – and a tendency towards the American and the contemporary repertoire have brought new excitement to its concerts. The San Francisco Opera attracts visits from performers like Placido Domingo and Luciano Pavarotti, Jessye Norman and Cecilia Bartoli. The opening gala, held on the first Friday night after Labor Day, is a glittering event attended by everyone from the mayor to the latest reigning football champion. The free **Opera in the Park** (Golden Gate Park) follows on the first Sunday after Labor Day and features the biggest names of the season.

NEW MUSIC

True to its roots, San Francisco continues to encourage musical adventure and is the base for many small, experimental musical outfits, such as the post-modern **Kronos Quartet** or the internationally acclaimed *a cappella* group **Chanticleer**, as well as countless choirs, from the San Francisco Bach Choir to the San Francisco Gay Men's Chorus. The **Other Minds** organisation, which routinely attracts the best and brightest stars in contemporary styles, is based in the Bay Area. In an attempt to make it the Lincoln Center of the West, these and other new music groups have favoured the theatre inside the multi-million dollar complex at the **Yerba Buena Center for the Arts** (*see page 229*).

Audium

Behind its bland streetside façade, the 25-year-old Audium remains one of the most interesting ways in San Francisco to occupy your ears. Inside a tiny theatre wired with 169 speakers, composer/sound manipulator Stan Shaff creates multi-dimensional audio sculptures – chirps and burps that ping-pong around the room, atonal passages of synthesiser music that transform into oppressive industrial static, an invisible marching band. Deprived of sight through both halves of the 90-minute programme, you'll find your senses of smell, touch and memory incredibly heightened. A whimsical sculpture lobby and Shaff's post-performance pontifications make this one of the best entertainment deals in town.

1616 Bush Street, at Franklin Street (771 1616). Bus 2, 3, 4, 42, 47, 49, 76. **Admission** $10. **Performance** 8pm Fri, Sat. **No credit cards. Map F3**

RECORDINGS & SHEET MUSIC

No slouch in any musical department, the city has a good selection of shops where you can buy music, recorded or published. At **Byron Hoyt** (431 8055), a venerable sheet music and instrument shop at the top of Lion House at 2525 16th Street, you'll find a stunning view, solicitous and knowledgeable staff, and copies of every possible score you could ever want, from Bach to Irving Berlin. It's also a good place for information on the city's musical events.

There's a superb selection of CDs and tapes in all kinds of stores. The **Tower Outlet**, on Third, at Brannan Street, is a lucky dip of great bargains; Tower also runs a **Classical Annex** in North Beach on Jones Street. If you prefer an independent music seller, **Star Classics** is a wonderful small shop in Hayes Valley (425 Hayes Street; 552 1110) devoted entirely to classical CDs and tapes, and both **Amoeba Music** and the huge **Virgin Megastore** also have a large selection of classical CDs. *See chapter* **Shops & Services** for more details.

Civic Center venues

For the **Bill Graham Civic Auditorium**, *see page 210* **Nightlife**.

Herbst Theater

401 Van Ness Avenue, at McAllister Street (621 6600). BART Civic Center/Muni Metro F, J, K, L, M, N/bus 42, 47, 49. **Map F4**

The Art Deco Herbst Theater is the preferred performance space for the Kronos Quartet. It's a good size for solo recitals, talks and seminars, authors' readings and 'in discussion' series, and small-scale dance and ballet performances – though be warned, the acoustics are atrocious at the back. Herbst shares a roof with the **Green Room**, used by chamber ensembles and quartet recitals. The San Francisco Chamber Symphony is also based here.

Louise M Davies Symphony Hall

201 Van Ness Avenue, at Grove Street (864 6000). BART Civic Center/Muni Metro F, J, K, L, M, N/bus 21, 42, 47, 49. **Map F5**

A circular, multi-tiered, glittering, curved glass edifice with good sightlines, the Louise M Davies Symphony Hall, the home base of the San Francisco Symphony Orchestra, opened in 1980 – to disappointing aural effect. Renovated in the early 1990s, Davies now flaunts expensively improved, hear-every-pin-drop acoustics. Even from the top row of the back balcony you can hear everything, and see it all, too. Ticket prices start at $20, though there are concessions for the elderly, young and students, and other occasional discounts, phone for details.

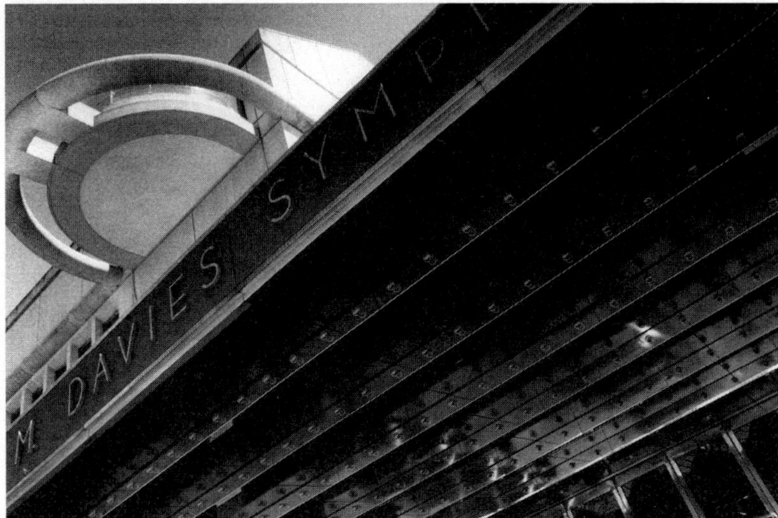

Home of the San Francisco Symphony Orchestra, the **Louise M Davies Symphony Hall**.

Other venues

Masonic Auditorium

1111 California Street, at Taylor Street (776 4917). Cable car California/bus 1. **Map G3**

Built in 1958 with a seating capacity of 3,100, the beautiful white marble Masonic Auditorium is well worth investigating during any visit to the city. A big, luxurious room with dark wooden walls and excellent sightlines, the Masonic hosts a number of events – jazz festivals, authors' readings, conferences and pop concerts by headliners from Gilberto Gil to Van Morrison. The **Henry W Coil Masonic Library Museum** next door (open from 10am to 3pm Monday to Friday; admission free) displays historical artifacts culled from Masonic lodges throughout the world.

Yerba Buena Center for the Arts

See chapter **Museums & Galleries** *for listings.*

Yerba Buena's musical bill has included voicestress/violinist Laurie Anderson, electro-acoustic computer musician Trimpin and toy piano composer/performer Margaret Lang Tan, as well as other brilliantly conceived musical, spoken-word performance and multi media events.

Out of town: classical music

Zellerbach Hall on the UC Berkeley campus is used by the **Berkeley Symphony Orchestra** (1-510 841 2800/www.berkeleysymphony.org), which attracts a roster of distinguished stars under music director Kent Nagano. It is also the venue for concerts, recitals and solo shows organised by **Cal Performances** (*see page 224*); **Berkeley Opera** (1-510 841 1903/www.berkeleyopera.com) also puts on three productions a year there.

Other musical venues worth investigating include the First Congregational Church in Berkeley (1-510 848 3696), and the Paramount Theater in Oakland, where the **Oakland East Bay Symphony** (1-510 444 0801) and the **Oakland Symphony Chorus** (1-510 428 3172) regularly perform. Travelling further afield, the Mountain View Center for the Performing Arts in Mountain View's Civic Center complex (1-650 903 6000) hosts a variety of South Bay performing groups.

Over the Golden Gate Bridge, the **West Marin Music Festival** (663 9650/members.aol.com/wmmfest) presents concerts throughout the year, most of which take place at St Columba's off Sir Francis Drake Boulevard in Inverness, a delightful village near Point Reyes, and an hour north of the city by car.

The **War Memorial Opera House**, *like its neighbour, City Hall, has been splendidly renovated.*

Churches, temples & plazas

Recitals and concerts – often free – are performed in many of San Francisco's churches. They include the **Old First Presbyterian Church** (1751 Sacramento Street, at Van Ness Avenue; 474 1608), where Chanticleer often performs), the **First Unitarian Universalist Church** (1187 Franklin Street, at Geary Boulevard; 776 4580) and **Grace Cathedral** (1100 California Street, at Taylor Street; 749 6310; *see chapter* **Sightseeing**).

The Yerba Buena Center for the Arts organises a **People in Plazas Noontime Concert Series** on Thursdays, that consists of a mélange of blues, jazz, rock and pop performances held on an outdoor stage at Yerba Buena Gardens. In addition, **St Patrick's**, a beautifully-restored Catholic church just across the street, hosts a Noontime Concert Series held every Wednesday (phone 777 3211 for details of these and other concerts). Finally, a great venue for organ recitals or performances by the San Francisco Bach Choir is **St Mary's Cathedral** (1111 Gough Street, at Geary Boulevard; 567 2020; *see also chapter* **Sightseeing**).

Festivals & special events

Check the Visitor Information Center's 24-hour information line (391 2000) or the *SF Arts Monthly* website (www.artsmonthlysf.org) for details of what's on while you're in town. Events to watch out for include the annual **Midsummer Mozart Festival** (954 0850), which celebrates its 30th birthday in 2003, under director George Cleve, with concerts at Berkeley's Congregational Church and in the Davies Symphony Hall. The **Early Music Society** has an annual concert series in May (1-510 528 1725) performing chamber music played on original instruments. Watch out for the **Black and White Ball** (864 6000), held every odd-numbered year in early May, and part in the city's biggest block party, a two-toned extravaganza that fills Civic Center and benefits the San Francisco Symphony.

War Memorial Opera House

Opera was born in San Francisco in 1923, when the city's Grand Opera, founded by Gaetono Merola, inaugurated the Exposition Auditorium (now known as the Bill Graham Civic Auditorium) in Civic Center. The building proved inadequate, however, to both the popularity and quality of the performances. Named for the soldiers who fought in World War I, the War Memorial was completed in 1932 less than two blocks away, a Beaux Arts beauty which opened to gala crowds with a performance of Puccini's *Tosca*. When cracks appeared in its ceiling after the 1989 earthquake, they marked the end of the first chapter in the magnificent building's history.

This temporary darkening of the War Memorial may have been a blessing in disguise, since 55 years of performances had begun to take their toll on the building. Seats were lumpy, curtains musty and structural concerns unaddressed; the few changing rooms were inadequate to the large-scale events the company was producing. Here was an excuse to upgrade – and the city's opera patrons were generally known to be flush with cash.

The resulting $84.5 million makeover, completed in just 18 months, has spared no detail: new curtains hang from the stage and a newly polished 66,000-watt chandelier from the ceiling. The 265 rosettes on the lobby's ceiling have each been re-gilded, as has the trim on the walls. A freshly upholstered seat sits beneath each patron; toilet facilities are new and bigger and wheelchair ramps have been installed. Additional audio, video and lighting systems, as well as a computerised cooling system, have also been put in place. The orchestra stage is raised and lowered using a massive hydraulic lift; a dozen changing rooms ease the company's once-cramped quarters.

The re-opening of the Opera House for the company's 75th anniversary in 1997 marked the beginning of another chapter for the venue. The San Francisco Opera Company is now the second largest in North America, content within a home that matches well its talent and diversity. The 3,176-seat auditorium retains its exquisite acoustics, best appreciated from the back of the uppermost circle. Designed by Arthur Brown, Jr, the architect who also created such San Francisco landmarks as the Coit Tower and City Hall, it stands as one of the city's most well-appointed and richest cultural landmarks.

War Memorial Opera House

301 Van Ness Avenue, at Grove Street (864 3330). BART Civic Center/Muni Metro F, J, K, L, M, N/bus 21, 42, 47, 49. **Map F5**

The winter opera season runs from just after Labor Day (first Monday in September) until mid January; the summer season is usually three weeks in June. Tickets range from $50 to $500. For advance information, phone the **San Francisco Opera Association** box office (864 3330).

Sport & Fitness

San Francisco teems with sports fans who like to work out almost as much as they like to hang out.

Spectator sports

At first glance, San Francisco would seem not to be an athletic town; its citizens are apparently more interested in cafés than contests, in shopping than sporting. But come the weekend (or Monday night, at least), many a businessperson trades in the suit for a sweaty T-shirt, a pair of running shoes or a mountain bike.

Big-money spectator sports are hugely popular, not least because the city's two major teams – the 49ers football and the Giants baseball – have both proved particularly successful in the past decade. Further afield, the San Jose Sharks hockey and the Golden State Warriors basketball teams draw big crowds, while the recent arrival of the Sacramento Monarchs has fans of women's professional basketball momentarily appeased.

In addition, spectators also keep a close eye on their chosen collegiate athletic team; the Bears football team from the University of California at Berkeley and Stanford women's Cardinal basketball team are local favourites. Huge rivalry at the annual Cal-Stanford intercollegiate 'big game' football contest generates enormous press interest.

The biggest news for sports fans is the opening of the new Giants stadium, in the China Basin neighbourhood. **Pacific Bell Park** (972 2000) will seat 42,000 and feature a centre field line of 123 metres (404 feet). The stadium is part of an urban trend among some cities which are trying revitalise downtrodden districts by injecting them with sports money. Pacific Bell Park opens in early 2000; no one knows yet whether it will prove more vital than the old 3Com (or 'Candlestick') Park or whether it's simply the latest monster construction project forced upon the populace.

INFORMATION

The Sporting Green section of the *San Francisco Chronicle* has a calendar of local pro team engagements and broadcasts. Both the *Chronicle* and the *San Francisco Examiner* maintain a free sports information line (808 5000, ext 6000) as does KRON-TV (837 5000, ext 1710). 'Sports talk' radio on KNBR (680 AM) and KCBS (740 AM) remains a popular, if inefficient, source of information and hyperbole.

Newsstands satisfy the nation's passion for sport with weekly and monthly publications; *Sports Illustrated* ($2.95) is one of the best-written.

The new Giants' stadium, **Pacific Bell Park.**

On the web, The Gate's sporting section (www.sfgate.com/sports) is a good bet. Finally, for special events or printed schedules, try the **Visitor Information Center** on Market Street (*see page 279* **Directory**).

TICKETS

The best place to buy tickets is the box office of the team you want to see. This direct approach may save effort and, even if you do end up going to a ticket broker, will give you a better idea of prices. If you get referred to **BASS** (1-510 762 2277/www.basstickets.com), which has several offices and a telephone switchboard, expect to pay 'convenience fees' of $6 or more (*see page 182* **Shops & Services**).

BROKERS & SCALPERS

Money may not buy you love, but it can, on occasion, purchase a seat at a sold-out game. Find ticket brokers in the *Yellow Pages* under Ticket Sales – Entertainment & Sports. If you're stuck with a ticket you can't use, you could sell it for some quick cash. Try **Premier Tickets** (346 7222/www.selltickets.com), **Mr Ticket** (1-800 424 7328/www. mrtix.com), or **Entertainment Ticketfinder** (1-800 523 1515, ext 3/www.ticket finder.com).

Purchasing tickets via a scalper (tout) ought to be a last resort – you might end up buying a fake ticket, purchasing admission for the following evening's game or find yourself with a seat in the third deck where you need binoculars to see the action.

Auto racing

Sears Point Raceway

At the intersection of SRs 37 & 121, Sonoma (1-707 938 8448). US 101 north to SR 37 exit, then ten miles (16km) to SR 121. **Open** *office* 9am-5pm Mon-Fri. **Admission** $5-$85. **Credit** Disc, MC, V.
Hosting just about every kind of motorised race on land, from nostalgic cars to monster truck derbies, this is a loud slice of Americana, only an hour away.

Baseball

The Bay Area supports two major-league baseball teams. As with many West Coast clubs, the **San Francisco Giants** and the **Oakland Athletics** have an East Coast history (in New York and Philadelphia, respectively) prior to their years here. But they're well-loved local franchises: the As won three World Series in a row in the 1970s and the Giants currently have Barry Bonds on their roster, three-time winner of the Most Valuable Player award. The two teams rarely play each other (Giants are in the National League and As in the American): they were set to meet in game one of the World Series in 1989 but were rudely interrupted by the Loma Prieta earthquake. The baseball season runs from April to September; tickets are usually available at the ballparks on the day of the game. If you're heading to Pacific Bell Park, bring a jacket to combat the chilly wind.

Oakland Athletics

Oakland-Alameda County Coliseum Complex/ Network Associates Coliseum (1-510 568 5600). BART Coliseum. **Open** 9am-5pm Mon-Fri; 10am-4pm Sat. **Admission** $6-$28. **Credit** AmEx MC, V.
Website: www.oaklandathletics.com

San Francisco Giants

Information (467 8000).
Currently based at 3Com Park (*see p234* **San Francisco 49ers**), the Giants will move to the new Pacific Bell Park when it opens in 2000.
Website: www.sfgiants.com

Basketball

From fast, trash-talking pick-up games played in the panhandle of Golden Gate Park to college and professional squads, you'll have plenty of good

The X-philes

A brand-new spectator sport has taken root in America in general and in San Francisco in particular. Extreme sports – or 'X' sports – combine death- (or at least injury-) defying skills with thrashing music and unconventional style, and include skateboarding, bicycle stunts, inline skating, snowboarding, aerial skiing, sky surfing and other high-speed, high-risk activities.

X's heroes may be unknown to the rest of the world at the moment, but there's a good chance you'll be hearing more about skateboarder Tony Hawk, sky surfer Viviane Wegreth, bicycle stunt-riders Dennis McCoy and Dave Mirra, inline skaters the Yasutoko Brothers, sports climber Katie Brown or the unforgettably-named street luge-ist Rat Sult. While most X stars are in their mid-20s, some are still teenagers, suddenly caught in the spotlight of fame.

Underwritten by the American all-sports network ESPN, the X-Games, an exhibition of extreme sports, came to San Francisco in 1999, transforming three city neighbourhoods into a media circus of stars, fans and marketing opportunities. Amid plenty of hype, various records were made and broken – Tony Hawk's successful two-and-a-half rotations above the half-pipe marked the first ever '900' in skating history.

What makes X sports unique is their sense of inclusiveness – that any kid can catch air, hang ten or master the vert if given enough practice. It's also a way to sell sports gear, promote a lifestyle and create a gently-rebellious culture that appeals to kids in America and worldwide.

In San Francisco, the best source of information on X sports is a small but growing number of shops and schools keen on the extreme future; those stores on the western edge of Haight-Ashbury are the best. **AcroSports** provides an interdisciplinary athletic/performing arts training and recreation programme to encourage teamwork, build strengths and self-esteem. **FTC Skateboarding** and **SFO Snowboarding** are two side-by-side branches of the same company, dedicated to baiting your riskier senses.

Spend time and trouble to protect yourself against sprains and scrapes by investing in a helmet, knee and elbow pads and gloves, then you're ready for a little learning and a lot of fun. You may not achieve a 900, but you'll be hooked.

AcroSports *639 Frederick Street, at Stanyan Street (665 2276). Muni Metro N/bus 6, 7, 33, 37, 43, 66, 71.* **Open** 9am-6pm Mon-Fri; 10am-6pm Sat, Sun. **Credit** MC, V. **Map C6**
FTC Skateboarding *622 Shrader Street, between Haight & Waller Streets (386 6693)*/**SFO Snowboarding** *618 Shrader Street (386 1666).* **Both** *Muni Metro N/bus 6, 7, 33, 37, 43, 66, 71.* **Open** 10am-6pm Tue-Sun. **Credit** MC, V. **Map C6**

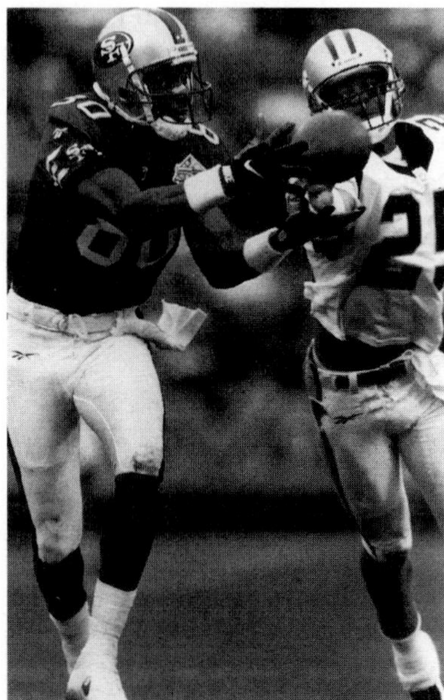

NFL elite, the **San Francisco 49ers***.*

company if you want to watch (or play) roundball while in San Francisco. The Warriors represent the Bay Area in the National Basketball Association (NBA) and play from November to May. For details of the Sacramento Monarchs, a new Women's National Basketball Association (WNBA) team (who play from June to September), *see page 239* **Out of town**.

Golden State Warriors

Oakland-Alameda County Coliseum Complex (Warriors 1-510 986 2222). BART Coliseum. **Open** 8.30am-5.30pm Mon-Fri. **Admission** $13.75-$220. **Credit** AmEx, MC, V.
Website: www.nba.com/warriors

Football

Autumn Sunday and Monday nights in the Bay Area could leave any visitor convinced that football is the new religion. The Raiders' return to Oakland in 1995 brought the league's most notorious winners of yesteryear back into the fold, while the 49ers continue among the National Football League's elite. The season runs through the winter from September to January, but be warned, it gets very cold and getting tickets is almost impossible.

What, you meant *soccer*? The **San Jose Clash** (www.clash.com) is a bush-league team.

Oakland Raiders

Oakland-Alameda County Coliseum Complex (1-510 762 2277). BART Coliseum. **Open** 9am-7pm Mon-Fri; 10am-7pm Sat, Sun. **Admission** *from* $51. **Credit** MC, V.
Website: www.raiders.com

San Francisco 49ers

3Com Park, Giants Drive, at Gilman Avenue (468 2249). Special event Muni bus 47X, at Van Ness Avenue & California Street, 28X at Funston & California Streets. **Open** 9am-5pm Mon-Fri (and weekend if game is on). **Admission** $50. **Credit** AmEx, Disc, DC, MC, V.
Buy tickets in person at the stadium (cash only) or by phone from TicketMaster (421 8497) from the second-to-last week in July. Bring warm clothing.
Website: www.nfl.com/49ers

Horse racing

Bay Meadows Racecourse

2600 South Delaware Street, San Mateo (1-650 574 7223). CalTrain to Bay Meadows or Hillsdale. **Open** phone for details. **Admission** $3-$15. **Credit** AmEx, MC, V.
Website: www.baymeadows.com

Golden Gate Fields

1100 Eastshore Highway, Albany (1-510 559 7300). BART North Berkeley, then AC Transit shuttle bus on race days. **Open** phone for details. **Admission** $2-$10. **Credit** AmEx, MC, V.
Website: www.ggfields.com

Ice hockey

Spectacularly fast-paced and still known for its violence, ice hockey has nevertheless found broad support in the Bay Area. The San Jose Sharks may not be the most accomplished team in the National Hockey League, but they are one of the leading merchandisers – their teal and black colours are worn all over. And their fans are rabid: Sharks games come complete with *Jaws* music and a signature cheer, the 'Shark bite'. The season runs from October to May.

San Jose Sharks

San Jose Arena, at West Santa Clara & Autumn Streets (tickets 1-800 888 2736). CalTrain to San Jose. **Open** 9.30am-5.30pm Mon-Fri; 9.30am-1pm Sat. **Admission** $16-$85. **Credit** AmEx, Disc, DC, MC, V.
Website: www.sjsharks.com

Active sports

To claim that many enjoy the Bay Area's easy access to outdoor adventures is an understatement comparable to 'San Francisco sees its share of fog'. Like arcane healing arts and body piercings, participatory sports come with the territory.

For runners, excellent paths traverse the Marina, Golden Gate Park and the perimeter of

Lake Merced; if you're into aerobics or cross-training, there's a health club on nearly every corner. The city also has numerous superb bike and skate shops as well as those that sell surfing, camping and rollerblading merchandise. New bike paths and a car-free Golden Gate Park on Sundays are further draws.

Some aquatic sports are better served by other parts of the region: the best resources for kayaking and scuba diving can be found in nearby Bay Area cities (*see page 239* **Out of town**); and for skiing and snowboarding, head to the Sierras (*see page 239 and chapter* **Trips Out of Town**).

When hiring equipment, photo ID or a credit card is usually required for a deposit.

GENERAL INFORMATION

The *San Francisco Chronicle* has listings and information on outdoor activities. Every Thursday it publishes Outdoors, a mini-section within the Sporting Green pages, devoted to self-motivated athletic activity. Also useful is *CitySports*, a free national magazine available in many gyms and sports shops.

Boating & sailing

Sailing Education Adventures

Fort Mason, at Laguna & Buchanan Streets (775 8779). Bus 28. **Open** 8am-10pm daily. **No credit cards. Map E1**

This non-profit charity offers instruction for all levels of sailing skill and a summer sailing camp for kids.

Spinnaker Sailing

Pier 40, Embarcadero, at Townsend Street (543 7333). Muni Metro E/bus 32, 42. **Open** 9am-5.30pm daily. **Credit** AmEx, MC, V. **Map J4**

7m to 24m (22ft to 80ft) boats, professional instruction and a great location off the Embarcadero.

Website: www.spinnaker-sailing.com

Stow Lake Boathouse

Stow Lake, Golden Gate Park (752 0347). Bus 5, 28, 29, 71. **Open** *summer* 10am-5pm Mon-Fri; 9am-5pm Sat, Sun; *winter* 9am-4pm daily. **No credit cards. Map A6**

On a clear day, pack a picnic, grab some company and head to Stow Lake in Golden Gate Park, where you can rent a paddleboat or rowing boat.

Bowling

Japantown Bowl

1790 Post Street, at Webster Street (921 6200). Bus 2, 3, 4, 22, 38. **Open** 9am-1am Mon-Thur, Sun; 24 hours Fri, Sat. **Rates** *shoe rental* $1.75; *per game* $2.90-$3.50. **Credit** MC, V. **Map E4**

Presidio Bowling Center

Building 93, corner of Montgomery Street & Moraga Avenue, the Presidio (561 2695). Bus 29, 43. **Open** 9am-midnight Mon-Thur, Sun; 9am-2am Fri, Sat. **No credit cards. Map B2**

Take a hike

Trails with rewarding views and paths through redwood groves await you just 30 minutes from downtown San Francisco. For a short, introductory hike, try the **Morning Sun Trail**, which climbs from a parking lot at the Spencer Avenue exit off US 101 north, just above the Golden Gate Bridge. Look east over the Bay, Angel Island and the urban sprawl or west to the Pacific. A good day-long hike is the **Dipsea Trail** from Mill Valley to Stinson Beach. Reach Mill Valley on Golden Gate Transit bus 10. The **Bootjack Trail**, which leads to the summit of Mount Tamalpais, is also popular. Get trail information for Mount Tam from the Pan Toll Ranger Station (388 2070).

For more information about exploring San Francisco on foot, *see page 40* **Sightseeing** *and page 269* **Directory**. The city's hills should take care of all your quadriceptic exercise needs.

Yerba Buena Bowling Center

750 Folsom Street, between Third & Fourth Streets (777 3726). Bus 9, 15, 30, 45, 81. **Open** 9am-10pm Mon-Thur, Sun; 9am-midnight Fri, Sat. **Admission** $3.50 per game; $2 concessions; *shoe rental* $2. **Credit** MC, V. **Map H4**

Camping

Apart from Kirby Cove, a six-site campground in the shadow of the Golden Gate Bridge, you can't camp anywhere in the city (phone the National Parks department well in advance for reservations; 556 0560). However, you can load up on gear.

Any Mountain

2598 Taylor Street, at North Point Street (345 8080). Bus 30, 32, 42/cable car Powell-Mason. **Open** 9am-9pm daily. **Credit** AmEx, Disc, MC, V. **Map F/G1/2**

A brand new store for this longtime local favourite.

Website: www.anymountaingear.com

Dave Sullivan's Sport Shop

5323 Geary Boulevard, between 17th & 18th Avenues (751 7070). Bus 38. **Open** 8.30am-6.30pm Mon-Fri; 8.30am-6pm Sat; 9am-5pm Sun. **Credit** AmEx, Disc, MC, V. **Map A4**

An institution, with friendly, helpful service and great deals on renting camping and ski equipment.

G&M Sales

1667 Market Street, at Gough Street (863 2855). Muni Metro F, J, K, L, M, N/bus 6, 7, 66, 71. **Open** 10am-7pm Mon-Fri; 10am-5pm Sat; 11am-4pm Sun. **Credit** AmEx, Disc, MC, V. **Map F5**

G&M Sales has sporting gear for every rigorous outing you can think of, including backpacking, skiing and fishing.
Website: www.gmoutdoors.com

Cycling

You can go just about anywhere in San Francisco by bicycle (although you'll need mega-legs for the hills). For more on getting around the city by bike *see page 270* **Directory**. Day trips to Angel Island, over the Golden Gate Bridge to Marin or to Tilden Park in Oakland offer an excellent combination of exercise and sightseeing. Cycle route maps ($2.95) are available in most bike shops, and Ray Hosler's book *Bay Area Bike Rides* ($12.95) is a good investment. Legend has it that mountain biking originated on Mount Tamalpais, an hour (by bike) north of San Francisco. For specific trail information about Mount Tam, call the Golden Gate National Recreation Area Visitor Center (331 1540) or the Pan Toll Ranger Station (388 2070). *See also page 245* **Trips Out of Town**. For cycling tours, *see page 79* **Sightseeing**.

Thanks to bike activists, you can take bikes on BART (992 2278) free of charge, except during commuter hours (7am-9am and 4pm-6pm, weekdays). CalTrain (1-800 660 4287) has limited bike space in designated cars on a first-come-first-served basis, and some Muni buses should be able to handle bikes by the time you read this. Currently, however, the best way to travel with a bike on public transport is by ferry.

American Rentals

2715 Hyde Street, between North Point & Beach Streets (931 0234). Bus 30, 32, 42/cable car Powell-Hyde. **Open** 8am-9pm daily. **Rates** $5 per hour; $25 per day. **Credit** AmEx, MC, V. **Map F1**

From here you can cycle across the Golden Gate Bridge into Sausalito and then return by ferry. Maps, helmet and lock are included in the price; bring a passport or credit card for a deposit. Electric and tandem bikes are also available.
Website: www.americanrental.com

Park Cyclery

1749 Waller Street, at Stanyan Street (221 3777). Muni Metro N/bus 6, 7, 33, 66, 71. **Open** 10am-6pm daily. **Rates** $5 per hour; $25 for 24 hours. **Credit** MC, V. **Map C6**

Conveniently located on the eastern edge of Golden Gate Park.

Start To Finish

672 Stanyan Street, between Haight & Page Streets (750 4760). Bus 7, 33, 37, 43. **Open** 10am-7pm Mon-Fri; 10am-6pm Sat; 10am-5pm Sun. **Rates** from $5 per hour; $25 for 24 hours. **Credit** AmEx, Disc, MC, V. **Map C6**

The city's biggest bike shop, next to Golden Gate Park, sells, services and rents bikes for all budgets.
Website: www.starttofinish.com

Fitness centres & gyms

Just as San Franciscans savour their corner cafés and bars, they love their corner gyms – every neighbourhood seems to have one, offering the usual weight rooms and fitness classes.

You can't fault the views from the 17th hole of **Lincoln Park Golf Course**.

Embarcadero YMCA

169 Steuart Street, at Mission Street (957 9622). BART Embarcadero/Muni Metro F, J, K, L, M, N/bus 2, 6, 7, 9, 14, 21, 31, 32, 66, 71. **Open** 5.30am-10pm Mon-Fri; 8am-8pm Sat; 9am-6pm Sun. **Rates** *day pass* $12. **Credit** MC, V. **Map J3**

One of several YMCAs in the city, the Embarcadero serves downtown San Francisco from a waterfront location. A day pass covers aerobics classes, free weights, Cybex and Nautilus machines, racquetball and basketball courts and an Olympic-sized pool.

24 Hour Fitness Centers

Several locations throughout San Francisco (1-800 249 6756). **Open** 24 hours in most locations; phone to check. **Rates** *day pass* $15. **Credit** AmEx, MC, V.

Cardiovascular and weight machines, and free weights. Most aerobics and fitness classes are held around the workday schedule; in the early morning, at lunchtime or in the early evening.

Golf courses

Harding Park & Golf Course

Harding Road & Skyline Boulevard (664 4690). Bus 18, 29. **Open** 6.30am-7pm daily. **Rates** $26 Mon-Fri; $31 Sat, Sun. **Credit** MC, V.

City-owned and operated, Harding lies by Lake Merced and has a shop and a small bar and café.

Golden Gate Park Course

John F Kennedy Drive, at 47th Avenue, in Golden Gate Park (751 8987). Bus 5, 18, 31, 38. **Open** 6am-8pm Mon-Sat. **Rates** $10 Mon-Fri; $13 Sat, Sun. **No credit cards**.

A nine-hole course sits at the west end of the park, with a pro shop, café and cart rental.

Lincoln Park Golf Course

34th Avenue & Clement Street (221 9911). Bus 2, 18, 38. **Open** sunrise to sunset. **Rates** $9-$23 Mon-Fri; $10-$27 Sat, Sun. **Credit** MC, V.

One of the most photographed courses in the States, with a famous 17th hole view of the Golden Gate Bridge. Prices drop as the light fades. There's also a practice area, putting green, rental shop, pro shop, bar and refreshments.

Golf instruction

Driving Obsession

23 Stevenson Street, between First & Second Streets (357 5970). Bus 12, 42, 76. **Open** 8.30am-5.30pm Mon-Sat. **Credit** AmEx, DC, Disc, MC, V. **Map G3**

Individual and group golf instruction using computers and digital video analysis. Initial one-hour lesson and evaluation costs $110.

Mission Bay Golf Center

1200 Sixth Street, at Channel Street (431 7888). Bus 15. **Open** 7am-11pm daily. **Credit** MC, V. **Map H5**

With a unique view of the freeway, East Bay and the South San Francisco hills, Mission Bay offers a 300-yard, two-tiered driving range, as well as a restaurant and discount golf shop.

Horse riding

Unless you're a mounted police officer, horse riding in San Francisco is limited to Golden Gate Park (*see below* **Golden Gate Stables**). Out of town, horses and tours are available from the **Sea Horse and Friendly Acres Ranch** (726 8550) near Half Moon Bay or the **Chanslor Guest Ranch & Stables** (1-707 875 3520) next to Bodega Bay.

Golden Gate Park Stables

John F Kennedy Drive, at 36th Avenue, in Golden Gate Park (668 7360). Bus 5. **Open** 9am-5pm daily. **Rates** *private lesson* $45; *trail ride* $26. **Credit** MC, V.

Golden Gate Park Stables offers everything from pony rides for small kids to advanced equestrian courses for experienced cowboys and girls.

Indoor rock climbing

Mission Cliffs

2295 Harrison Street, at 19th Street (550 0515). Bus 12, 22, 33. **Open** 6.30am-10pm Mon, Wed, Fri; 11am-10pm Tue, Thur; 10am-6pm Sat, Sun. **Rates** $16 per day. **Credit** AmEx, Disc, MC, V. **Castro/Mission Map Z1**

To enter Mission Cliffs is to penetrate a 3,800sq m (12,000sq ft) kingdom that melts the boundary of 'urban' and 'wilderness' and distills it into a highly polished jungle gym. An X sports HQ (*see p233* **The X-philes**).

Website: www.mission-cliffs.com

Inline hockey

Street hockey made a comeback with the advent of rollerblades. You can often join in a game at the playground on the corner of Scott and North Point Streets. Serious players will want to go to the **Bladium** (*see below*), where any level of play is possible, morning, noon and night.

Bladium

1050 Third Street, at Berry Street (442 5060). Muni Metro E/bus 15, 30, 42, 45, 76. **Open** 8am-midnight daily. **Rate** $5 per person during 'open session'. **Credit** MC, V. **Map J5**

The Bladium provides the in-line hockey enthusiast with a complete environment, including a professional quality rink, locker rooms, showers, warm-up court, slap-shot practice cage, pro shop and sports bar. Leagues include Youth, Adult, Co-ed and Women's.

Website: www.bladium.com

Paragliding

Not to be confused with parasailing, paragliding involves no boat and allows you to fly after less than a day's instruction. The equipment itself weighs only 10lbs and can do just about anything a hang-glider does, except turn upside-down.

No Limits Paragliding

3620 Wawona Street, at 47th Avenue (759 1177). Muni Metro L. **Open** 10am-7pm Thur-Sun, Mon. **Rates** $150. **Credit** MC, V.

A perfect place to learn to paraglide or to take a ten-day course for Class 2 certification.

Website: www.nolimitsparagliding.com

Pool & billards

Pool tables are as common in bars as sofas are in living rooms, but the city also has several purpose-designed pool halls.

Chalkers

1 Rincon Center, at Spear & Mission Streets (512 0450). BART Embarcadero/bus 14. **Open** 11.30am-midnight Mon-Wed; 11.30am-2am Thur-Sat; 3pm-midnight Sun. **Rates** $5-$14 per hour Mon-Thur, Sun; $7-$15 per hour Fri, Sat. **Credit** AmEx, MC, V. **Map J3**

Chalkers has 30 cherrywood tables, a bar and restaurant, and occasionally invites trick-shot experts and pros to dazzle the lunch crowd. Families are allowed from 2-7pm, at the weekend. If you prefer it busy, Friday night happy hour is the time to go.

The Great Entertainer

975 Bryant Street, between Seventh & Eighth Streets (861 8833). Bus 19, 27, 42. **Open** 11am-2am Mon-Thur, Sun; 11am-3am Fri, Sat. **Credit** AmEx, MC, V. **Map G5**

San Francisco's largest indoor gaming facility, with masses of entertainment options, including 40 billiard tables, shuffleboard, snooker, table tennis, darts, football and a video arcade.

Hollywood Billiards

61 Golden Gate Avenue, at Market Street (252 9643). BART Powell/Muni Metro F, J, K, L, M, N/bus 6, 7, 9, 14, 21, 71. **Open** 6pm-2am Mon-Thur, Sun; 5pm-3am Fri, Sat. **Rates** *from* $4-$12 an hour. **Credit** AmEx, MC, V. **Map G4**

A dodgy neighbourhood and infamous 'ladies' nights' make Hollywood a pool room of note. The rates are decent but the equipment isn't of the highest calibre.

Racquetball

Koret Health & Recreation Center

Turk & Parker Streets (422 6820). Bus 31. **Open** *to non-USF students* 6am-2pm Mon-Fri; 8am-2pm Sat, Sun. **Map C5**

This health club is part of the University of San Francisco, but non-students can use the facilities until 2pm on weekdays and at the weekend. There are six racquetball courts and a swimming pool and gym. Bring your own equipment.

Rollerblading

Rollerblading (aka inline skating) has now become a mainstream pursuit. For the novice or veteran, Sunday skating in Golden Gate Park is hard to beat: the beach at one end, plenty of sunny meadows and shady benches along the way, and no auto traffic. A mix of rollerblading and break dancing provides entertainment near Sixth Street on John F Kennedy Drive.

Golden Gate Park Skate and Bike

3038 Fulton Street, at Sixth Avenue (668 1117). Bus 5, 21, 44. **Open** 10am-6pm Mon-Fri; 9am-7pm Sat, Sun. **Rates** $6 per hour; $24 for 24 hours. **Credit** MC, V. **Map B5**

Spending the day in the park? Stop at this friendly, shop for rollerblades, bicycles and roller skates. Fees include a helmet, knee and elbow pads.

Skates on Haight

1818 Haight Street, at Stanyan Street (752 8375). Bus 6, 7, 71. **Open** 10am-6pm Mon-Fri; 11am-7pm Sat, Sun. **Rates** $6 per hour; $24 per day. **Credit** AmEx, Disc, JCB, MC, V. **Map C6**

Skates on Haight was responsible for inspiring the worldwide skateboard craze back in the 1970s and now rents and sells inline skates, roller skates and snowboards. Worth a visit.

Rowing

Rowing opportunities in the Bay Area range from single sculls to whale boat racing. Call **Open Water Rowing** (332 1091/www.owrc.com) in Sausalito or **South End Rowing Club** (776 7372/www.south-end.org) in San Francisco.

Running

Many San Francisco locals will tell you the best place to run, bike or rollerblade is Golden Gate Park – but one of the most stunning alternatives for a jog is the Marina Green. A track encircles the esplanade itself, but a trail extends all the way to Fort Point, just before the Golden Gate Bridge. With the recent expansion of the Embarcadero, many runners prefer the stunning view of the Bay Bridge and piers. *See chapter* **Sightseeing** for more details.

The annual San Francisco **Marathon** is held in mid-July and the **Bay to Breakers Foot Race**, a 12-kilometre (7.5-mile) run from downtown to Ocean Beach, at the end of May (*see chapter* **San Francisco by Season** *for both*).

Skateboarding

No one needs to tell a skate rat where to go. If you're one, you'll find Justin Herman Plaza, a Safeway parking lot or any of a number of downtown concrete ramps on your own.

DLX

1831 Market Street, between Guerrero & Pearl Streets (626 5588). Muni Metro F, J/bus 26, 37. **Open** noon-8pm Mon-Sat; noon-7pm Sun. **Credit** MC, V. **Map F5**

The skateboard merchandiser formerly known as 'Deluxe' is the mother of them all. Make the trip

for a complete line of clothes, boards, accessories and stickers. For an idea of what's on offer, check out the store's slick website.
Website: www.dlxsf.com

Skiing

Although a day trip is possible, it's recommended that you give yourself at least a weekend for skiing in the Sierras. For leading resorts around **Lake Tahoe** (about 3½ hours from San Francisco by car) *see page 261* **Trips Out of Town**. During the season (usually the end of November to early April), most ski shops will have calendars of events and ads for package deals. The **GoSki** server at www. goski.com/calif.htm lists all major Californian resorts.

Soma Ski & Sportz

689 Third Street, at Townsend Street (777 2165). Bus 15, 30, 42, 45, 76. **Open** *Nov-Apr* 10am-7pm Mon-Wed; 10am-8pm Thur, Fri; 10am-6pm Sat; 11am-5pm Sun; *May-Oct* 10am-6pm Mon-Sat. **Credit** AmEx, Disc, MC, V. **Map J5**

Soma Ski & Sportz has downhill skis, poles, boots and bindings, snowboards, cross-country equipment, clothing and car racks. There's a repair and tune-up service, rental prices are competitive, staff are friendly and knowledgeable – and great music is played in the store.
Website: www.somaski.com

Squash

Bay Club

150 Greenwich Street, between Battery & Sansome Streets (433 2200). Bus 42/Bay Club shuttle from BART Embarcadero. **Open** 5.30am-11pm Mon-Fri; 7am-9pm Sat, Sun. **Rates** *guest fee* $15. **No credit cards. Map H2**

The Bay Club tries to make its well-to-do members feel exclusive. Drop-in players must either come with a member or prove they are a member of an IRSA-affiliated squash club. For racquetball courts at the **Embarcadero YMCA** *see p237.*

Surfing

You have to be an experienced surfer to tackle the waves around San Francisco. Currents are strong, sharks frequent and temperatures icy. Whether you're a pro headed to Ocean Beach or Fort Point,

Out of town

The Bay Area and Pacific coastline offer a multitude of water-based activities, with numerous boating, sailing, kayaking and scuba diving outfits that offer equipment, lessons and trips.

In Berkeley, **Cal Adventures** hires out Coronado 15-footers for sporty sailing on the South Sailing Basin; to lease one without recognised certification, you must spend $60 to sail with an instructor who will confirm your ability. Also in Berkeley, **Cal Dive & Travel** arranges trips to Monterey Bay, for the best scuba diving on the California coast. It also offers beginners' classes and hires out scuba equipment for about $60.

California Canoe & Kayak in Oakland is one of the best shops for hiring and buying kayaks and sea-going gear of all sorts. A sea canoe costs $24 for three hours; lessons and day outings are available on the nearby Oakland Estuary.

On the Sausalito waterfront, **Sea Trek** runs summer camps for kids, books expeditions to Alaska and Baja and joins forces with environmentalists to preserve waterways. Beginners' classes in Bay kayaking, guided tours ($50 for three hours) and moonlight paddles are also available. For even more excitement, **Escape Artists Tours** in Half Moon Bay books individual and group adventures ranging from kayaking on the Bay to flying air-combat planes.

If you prefer to watch other people exert themselves, attend a Women's National Basketball Association (WNBA) game. The **Sacramento Monarchs** play from June to September.

Cal Adventures *UC Aquatic Center, Berkeley Marina (1-510 642 4000). BART Berkeley, then bus 51.* **Open** 10am-6pm Mon-Fri.

Cal Dive & Travel *1750 Sixth Street, Berkeley (1-510 524 3248). BART North Berkeley.* **Open** 10am-6pm Mon-Fri; 10am-2pm Sat.

California Canoe & Kayak *409 Water Street, on Jack London Square, at Franklin Street, Oakland (1-510 893 7833). BART 12th Street.* **Open** 10am-7pm Mon-Thur, Sun; 9am-8pm Fri, Sat.

Escape Artist Tours *150 Tiller Court, Half Moon Bay (1-800 728 1384/726 7626/ www.sf-escapes.com).* **Open** 9am-6pm Mon-Fri; 9am-1pm Sat.

Sea Trek Schoonemaker *Point Marina, Libertyship Way, Sausalito (488 1000/beach 332 4465). Bus Golden Gate Transit 10, 50.* **Open** phone for details.

Sacramento Monarchs *ARCO Arena, Sacramento (1-916 928 3650/ www.wnba.com/monarchs).* **Open** 9am-5pm Mon-Sat. **Tickets** $8-$35.

or a newbie boogie-boarding the black sand beaches in Marin County, you'll need the appropriate gear. For most surfers, a wetsuit is a must.

Wise Surfboards

800 Great Highway, 2 miles south of the Cliff House (750 9473). Bus 5, 18, 31, 38.
Open 9am-6pm Mon-Fri; 9am-5pm Sat, Sun.
Credit AmEx, MC, V.
The new store right on Ocean Beach is sure to keep Wise at the top of local surfboard outlets. The shop sells boards, wetsuits and accessories, and maintains a 24-hour information line (273 1618) for surf conditions. Mermen, San Francisco's favourite psychedelic-surf band, live just down the street.

Swimming

The ocean is usually too chilly and turbulent for swimming, but there are plenty of swimming pools in San Francisco. For Olympic-sized swimming pools, try the **Embarcadero YMCA** (*see page 237*), the **Bay Club** (*see page 239*) or the **Koret Center** (*see page 238*). Some health and fitness clubs also have swimming pools. The City of San Francisco maintains eight municipal pools, each with separate times for open swimming. The most central ones are at **Hamilton Recreation Center** at Geary Boulevard and Steiner Street (292 2001) and the **North Beach Pool** at Lombard and Mason Streets (274 0200); adult admission is $3. For your nearest pool, check the *White Pages* under City Government Offices: Recreation and Parks. For information on the best beaches in the city, *see page 75* **Sightseeing**.

Tennis

Indoor tennis in San Francisco is almost exclusively a members-only affair, but much of the best play is outdoors anyway. **Golden Gate Park** has several courts (at the Stanyan Street entrance), and **Dolores Park** in the Mission district is always busy. Both are open from sunrise to sunset and are free. For a complete list of tennis (and other public recreation) facilities, see the Neighbourhood Parks section of the *Pacific Bell Yellow Pages*.

Volleyball

Although it is more popular in Southern California, volleyball is also played in San Francisco. Experienced players should get in contact with the **San Francisco Volleyball Association** (584 2685), which organises leagues. Otherwise, look for pick-up action at the north end of **Marina Green** on weekend mornings. Unfortunately the games held in Lindley Meadow in **Golden Gate Park** are usually family or corporate get-togethers. For further details, look online at www.Volleyball.org/bay_area.

Whale watching

Whale watching primarily occurs further north and south (in Mendocino or Monterey, for example) but can on occasion be as easy as taking a pair of binoculars to the shore and having a look. One recommended location is the tip of **Point Reyes**, an hour's drive north of San Francisco (*see chapter* **Trips Out of Town**). For **Escape Artist Tours** *see page 239* **Out of town**.

Oceanic Society Expeditions

Fort Mason Center (474 3385). Bus 22, 28, 42, 47, 49. **Open** 9am-5pm Mon-Fri. **Rates** $28-$65. **Credit** AmEx, MC, V. **Map E1**
This is a cut above most tourist trips as the staff are experts in natural history and marine life. The full-day trip ($65) heads 42km (26 miles) west to the Farallon Islands, home of the largest sea bird rookery in the continental US, searching for humpback and grey whales, seals and sea lions along the way.
Website: www.oceanic-society.org

Windsurfing (sailboarding)

The Bay Area boasts no less than 32 launch sites for windsurfing, including Coyote Point, 3Com Park and Crissy Field – the site of several international competitions, including windsurfing's World Cup.

SF School of Windsurfing

Candlestick Point Recreation Area (753 3235). Bus 29. **Open** 2-7pm Fri; 8.30am-7pm Sat, Sun. **Rates** *one-day beginner's course* $100. **Credit** MC, V.
The school offers lessons with equipment for all levels on Candlestick Beach, one of the premier training grounds in the US. Gear is available for rent from 2-7pm Tuesday to Friday; and from 10am-7pm Saturday, Sunday.
Website: www.sfwindsurf.com

City Front Boardsports

2936 Lyon Street, between Lombard & Greenwich Streets (929 7873). Bus 28, 41, 43, 45. **Open** 11am-7pm Mon-Fri; 10am-6pm Sat, Sun. **Rates** *complete sailing rig* $50. **Credit** AmEx, Disc, MC, V. **Map D2**
With stores in Berkeley and Marin, City Front is the place to go if you're already a seasoned windsurfer with your own wetsuit and harness.
Website: www.boardsports.com

Yoga

Also try the **Yoga Society of SF** (285 5537).

Yoga College of India

Second floor, 910 Columbus Avenue, at Lombard Street (346 5400). Bus 15, 30, 39, 41/cable car Powell-Mason. **Open** *classes for visitors* 9am, 4.30pm, 6.15pm, Mon-Fri; 9am, 10.45am, Sat, Sun. **Rates** $10 per class. **Credit** MC, V. **Map G2**
The San Francisco branch of the Yoga College of India teaches the techniques of Bikram Choudhury, a yogi who brought his brand of the practice to the US in 1971. Bring a towel.

Trips Out of Town

Trips Out of Town

California dreamin'...

San Francisco is ideally situated for easy getaways. Within an hour's drive, ride or boat trip are beaches, islands, mountains and other delightful distractions. From Marin County to the north, Berkeley and Oakland to the east and San Jose along the peninsula, each area has its own unique identity. Further afield lie the dramatic slopes of the Sierra Nevada mountain range, the celebrated golf links of the Monterey Peninsula, Lake Tahoe's exhilarating ski slopes and the picturesque wineries and spas of the North Bay. For a map of the Bay Area and surrounding coast, *see page 294*.

All telephone numbers listed in this chapter are within the 415 area code unless otherwise stated. For information on car rental and a list of company numbers, *see chapter* **Directory**.

TRANSPORT

Most destinations listed in this chapter are within easy reach of San Francisco and can be covered as a day trip or overnight stay. However, many of the areas are ill-served by public transport. If you can't hire a car, try **BART** (the Bay Area Rapid Transit) rail service, which connects San Francisco with the East Bay (via an underground tunnel) or **Golden Gate Transit**, which has a regular schedule of bus services to and from many Marin County destinations. It also has less frequent services to Sonoma County. You can also use **Greyhound** buses, **Amtrak** (the nearest train station is in Oakland), a charter tour or one of the ferries that run frequently to the North Bay during the day. But if your budget permits it, rent a car – after all, driving is the Californian way.

Amtrak 1-800 872 7245
BART 1-510 464 6000
Golden Gate Transit 455 2000
CalTrain 1-800 660 4287
Greyhound 1-800 231 2222

Heading north

Crossing the **Golden Gate Bridge** is something everyone should do at least once, but unless you're on foot or on a bicycle, it's hard to stop and take in the spectacular view. From **Vista Point**, the first exit north of the bridge, however, the city seems almost close enough to touch.

Marin County

Marin County extends from the Golden Gate Bridge north, along the coast to Bodega Bay and inland to the Wine Country. With some of the most gorgeous scenery in Northern California and a warm climate all year round, Marin lends itself to a very outdoors way of life. It's one of the state's richest counties, as well as one of its most laid-back, embodying a uniquely Californian combination of yuppie wealth and hippie ideals.

In a spectacular setting at the northern foot of the Golden Gate Bridge, is the **Bay Area Discovery Museum**, an imaginative museum for kids (*see page 187* **Children**). Northwest of the bridge, two roads traverse the **Marin Headlands**. The hills here offer amazing views and the valleys are filled with wild flowers. World War II battlements can still be seen dotted about the hilltops, but the vistas are familiar to most Americans from the innumerable automobile ads which use San Francisco and the Golden Gate as a backdrop.

Starting with these headlands, Marin County offers the best hiking and biking – mountain or otherwise – in the Bay Area. Thanks to state and federal legislation, a large percentage of the county is devoted to open space. The most famous parcel of land is **Point Reyes National Seashore** (information 663 1092), part of the vast **Golden Gate National Recreation Area** (331 1540) that extends from San Francisco along most of the Marin coastline.

Marin lacks a real centre: **San Rafael** is its biggest town, but it's also the least interesting to visit (though it's worth making a short detour to see 'Big Pink', the grand **Marin Civic Center** designed by Frank Lloyd Wright). Here, from April to October, you'll find a farmers' market and live entertainment. For more information, call the **San Rafael Chamber of Commerce** (817 Mission Avenue; 454 4163/www.sanrafael.org). For diversity, head to **Mill Valley**, the quintessential Marin town, where the **Mill Valley Film Festival** is held each autumn (383 5256/www.finc.org). The **Buckeye Roadhouse** (15 Shoreline Hwy; 331 2600) is worth a pit stop either on your way out of or back to the city, even if it's just to indulge in oodles of onion rings.

Larkspur is less visited, even though it can be reached by ferry from San Francisco. Stop for a meal at the **Lark Creek Inn** (234 Magnolia Avenue, at Madrone Street; 924 7766), an understated, charming Victorian house that serves great home-made butterscotch pudding. A three-course meal here costs around $25. For the active, water-sports equipment sales, rentals and lessons are available at **Sausalito Sailboards, Inc** (2233 Larkspur Landing Circle; 331 9463). Apart from the **Larkspur Landing** shopping centre and a first-rate pub, the **Marin Brewing Company** (*see page 154* **Bars**), the only other reason to come here is to visit someone in **San Quentin Prison** or to see the prison museum, located about three-quarters of a mile east along Sir Francis Drake Boulevard.

Best day trips

In less than a couple of hours from San Francisco you can be lying on a beach, climbing a mountain, playing golf, lapping it up at a spa, skiing, or wine tasting in the grape capital of California. The following are our recommended day trips from the city.

Angel Island

Take a ferry and pack a picnic for the beach. If you want to camp, phone 1-800 444 7275 to reserve a spot. *See p245.*

Berkeley

Explore the many shops on Telegraph Avenue and Fourth Street and then splash out on a gourmet feast. *See p261 and p180* **Shops & Services**.

Half Moon Bay

Spend the day playing golf, horse riding, biking or hiking – or just vegging out on the beach. *See p253.*

Inverness

Stop in at **Manka's Inverness Lodge & Restaurant** for some barbecued oysters. *See p246.*

Mount Tamalpais

Park at **Stinson Beach** and hike up until you're tired. Finish off with a dip in the Pacific before returning home. *See p245.*

Santa Cruz mountains

Visit the bizarre **Mystery Spot** for some wacky goings on. *See p254.*

Sebastopol

A quirky town in Sonoma County, a little over an hour's drive north of San Francisco. *See p249.*

Sausalito

The southernmost Marin town of Sausalito may not be as quaint as its reputation claims, but it is undeniably picturesque, with a maze of tiny streets stretching from the shoreline up to US 101 far above. Charming bungalows, well-kept gardens and bougainvillea-covered fences characterise the area, one best appreciated on foot. Originally a fishing village, Sausalito is jam-packed with tourists during the summer, but reclaims its waterfront in winter. A population of artists and writers helps support the fair number of coffee shops, waterfront restaurants, galleries and souvenir shops. Some live in the collection of houseboats north of town, where there's also a sizeable marina. Despite its chilly waters, Sausalito is also a centre for Bay kayaking and windsurfing.

Along North Bridgeway, opposite Spring Street, is the turnoff for the **Bay Model Visitor Center** (*see chapter* **Museums & Galleries**), a scale model of the San Francisco and San Pablo Bays.

A fun way to explore the Bay is from the decks of the *Hawaiian Chieftain* (331 3214/www.Hawaiian chieftain.com) a reconstructed 1790s trading vessel which operates out of Sausalito. Between April and October it offers sunset, brunch and adventure sails.

For more information on Sausalito, contact the **Sausalito Visitor Center**, on the fourth floor of

The **Hotel Sausalito** *(above and right) – one of the Bayside town's most picturesque.*

the Village Fair Shopping Center (780 Bridgeway, at Bay Street; 332 0505).

Sausalito's commercial (and tourist) district straddles Bridgeway, though the best cafés and restaurants are along Caledonia Street one block inland, where most of the locals can be found. Try **Fukusuke** for sushi (45 Caledonia Street; 332 2013), the Thai **Arawan** next door (47 Caledonia Street; 332 0882) or **Guernica**, near the marina (2009 Bridgeway; 332 1512).

To get a sense of the old Sausalito, stop for a cocktail or meal at local favourite **Casa Madrona** (801 Bridgeway; 332 0502), a part-Victorian, part-modernised luxurious inn that rambles down a hill. Rooms start at $168. If you want an uninterrupted view across the Bay, try the 30-room **Inn Above Tide** (30 El Portal; 332 9535/fax 332 6714/www.citysearch.com/sfo/innabovetide; rooms from $195). Most rooms have a fireplace, Jacuzzi and panoramic views towards San Francisco. Even prettier is the very chic **Hotel Sausalito** (16 El Portal; 332 0700) run by the Glaswegian Purdie family, where room prices start at $135.

Tiburon

Across Richardson Bay from Sausalito is Tiburon, where a tiny, old-fashioned downtown area brings daytrippers over on the ferry from San Francisco. If you're driving, park your car in any one of the parking lots on Tiburon Boulevard and continue the rest of the way on foot; if you're biking, the bike path brings you directly into town. However, there aren't a lot of tourist attractions and the shops and galleries on Ark Avenue are likely to have a serious impact on your budget.

Most people come to eat lunch and take in the views. Sip a Margarita and admire the vista from **Guaymas** budget-priced Mexican restaurant (5 Main Street; 435 6300). **Sam's Anchor Café** (27 Main Street; 435 4527) is excellent for Sunday brunch: sit out on the waterfront deck, order a Bloody Mary and watch the boats. According to locals, there's a trap door inside the place that was used to access boats bringing in whisky during Prohibition.

If you want to see the lie of the land from above, try an excursion with **San Francisco Seaplane Tours** (332 4843/www.seaplane.com), a great way to get your bearings among the bridges, islands, peninsulas and waterfronts of the Bay Area. The company flies out to the coast, over the Golden Gate Bridge and along the San Francisco waterfront, a trip that's especially good at sunset.

Angel Island

From San Francisco or Tiburon, you can catch a ferry to Angel Island, the largest island in the Bay. The **Angel Island Visitor Center** (435 1915) documents the use of the island from the Civil War to World War II. There are a number of excellent trails and many great picnic spots where you can escape the crowds. Bikes can be hired on the island (*see chapter* **Sightseeing** for more information).

Mount Tamalpais & Muir Woods

Visible from as far away as Sonoma, Mount Tamalpais soars to nearly 800 metres (2,600 feet). Its dramatic rise is so steep it seems to be far taller. The 550-acre park surrounding it contains some of the most majestic groves of redwoods in the world. It dominates and defines recreational life in southern and central Marin County. **Mount Tamalpais State Park** covers some 2,511 hectares (6,200 acres). The roads that snake over Mount Tam, though steep, are great for bicycling; indeed the mountain bike was invented here. For a fully-fledged trip over Mount Tam, take the **Panoramic Highway**, a beautiful two-lane spur with lots of hairpin bends leading through sun-dappled forests to the coast at Stinson Beach. The Panoramic Highway leads past a number of trailheads, some of them near the **Mountain Home Inn** (810 Panoramic Hwy, Mill Valley; 381 9000; rooms from $143), a good stop for coffee, lunch or an overnight stay.

From either Highway 1 or the Panoramic, you can reach the turn-off to Marin's main attraction, **Muir Woods** (admission $2). The coast redwoods growing here are mostly between 500 and 800 years old and as tall as 72 metres (236 feet). Their shade creates excellent hiking on several miles of trails and there's a short path which is accessible to the disabled. Besides the regal *Sequoia sempervirens*, **Redwood creek** is lined with oak, madrone and buckeye trees, wild flowers (even in the winter), ferns and mushrooms. Deer, chipmunks and a variety of birds are frequently sighted in the verdant spaces beneath the redwoods. Complete with gift shop and toilets, Muir Woods' visitor centre is open daily. Park rangers organise walks through the woods: contact the ranger station (388 2595/ www.nps.gov) for a schedule.

From Muir Woods, you can drive or bike to the coast and head on north from Muir Beach. The delightful, Tudorbethan **Pelican Inn** (10 Pacific Way, at Hwy 1; 383 6000) is a good place to refuel and could have been transplanted straight from Surrey. The pub's terrace and lawn make it an attractive lunch spot (average $14) in good weather. Skip the Yorkshire pudding, but order a plate of fish and chips, wash it down with a pint of cider and ask about their overnight rates.

The Panoramic Highway rejoins Hwy 1 at **Stinson Beach**, the closest you'll get in these parts to the famous Californian beach life, popularised by surfers and sun worshippers. If you want to ride the waves, you can rent open-top kayaks at **Off the Beach Boats** (868 9445).

Just 3.3 miles (5.3 kilometres) north of Stinson Beach is the **Audubon Canyon Ranch** (4900 Hwy 1; 868 9244), a 405-hectare (1,000-acre) preserve on the shore of the Bolinas Lagoon. Headquartered in a nineteenth-century white frame house, the ranch houses environmental displays and, in an old milking barn at the back, a natural history bookshop. The ranch is open at weekends from mid-March until mid-July. Donations are welcome. Nearby, the **Alice Kent Trail** leads a short way up to an observation point for viewing egrets and great blue herons nesting in the vicinity.

Point Reyes

North of Stinson Beach along SR 1 at Olema is the turn-off for the **Point Reyes National Seashore**. This vast, protected peninsula is an unforgettable wildlife refuge with fresh sea winds, sea mammals, waterfowl, waterfalls, miles of unspoiled beaches, a highly variegated terrain and campsites. Call the **Visitor Center** (663 1092) for trail maps, camping permits, the latest weather information and tips on fishing, clamming and horse riding. At Point Reyes, head west to **Drakes Beach**. The road ends at the **Point Reyes Lighthouse**, where there are a number of trails, including the popular **Chimney Rock**. The lighthouse sits at the tip of the Point Reyes peninsula and is the perfect spot for whale watching.

If you want to bathe, bypass the beaches of this windswept coast and head along SR 1 to **Tomales Bay**. Tiny beaches such as **Heart's Desire** offer mild tides and water that's not that cold. And if you want to really get to grips with the natural history of the area, **Blue Waters Kayaking** (on Sir Francis Drake Boulevard, beyond Inverness; 669 2600/bwkayak@nbn.com) offers half- or full-day paddle trips or Saturday night full-moon tours, as well as basic kayak hire. Prices start at $25 and the company provides all the gear (including wetsuits); all you need are the biceps.

Nearby **Inverness** is a picturesque town and location of **Manka's Inverness Lodge & Restaurant** (30 Calendar Way; 669 1034), worth stopping off at for some delicious barbecued oysters.

Outside Point Reyes to the other side of SR 1, hikers flock to **Mount Wittenberg**, where miles of hiking and riding trails criss-cross the mountain: here, chaparral, wildlife and fog are facts of life. There are excellent vantage points throughout for sighting migrating Pacific grey whales off the coast during winter, as they pass on their round trip from Alaska to Baja California. A lighthouse stands on a dramatic promontory, and the **Miwok Indian Village** is nearby.

The 1,134-hectare (2,800-acre) **Samuel P Taylor State Park** (488 9897) has 60 campsites and 75 picnic sites, and is located to the east of Olema. Book a campsite in advance through **Reserve America** (1-800 444 7275; 1-619 452 8787 from outside the US).

Getting there

Marin County is dissected from north to south by US 101, which runs the length of California. It's the most popular (and fastest) route for public transport, but isn't very scenic. The other main road is California State Highway 1 (SR 1), also known as the Coast or Shoreline Highway, which leads out of Mill Valley, skirts the lower elevations of Mount Tamalpais and turns north at Muir Beach.

By car

Sausalito is 8 miles (13km) and Muir Woods 15 miles (24km) from San Francisco; Point Reyes is some 32 miles (52km).

By bus

Golden Gate Transit buses link San Francisco to Marin County. For the Marin Headlands, take Golden Gate Transit bus 2, which leaves from Pine and Battery Streets and from the Golden Gate Bridge Toll Plaza Monday to Friday; on Sundays you can take Muni bus 76 from Market and Montgomery Streets.

For Sausalito, Golden Gate Transit bus 10 leaves from the Transbay Terminal, Civic Center and the Toll Plaza (every half-hour Monday to Friday, every hour Saturday, Sunday).

There's no direct public transport to Muir Woods; you'll have to go on a tour or hire a car. Golden Gate Transit bus 63 takes you to trailheads during the weekend. It's a long bike ride to the coast, but if you go around the mountain, via Sir Francis Drake Boulevard, you'll see a lot of fabulous scenery. Bus 63 also stops at Stinson Beach, the Bay Area Discovery Museum, and Audubon Canyon Ranch.

To get to Point Reyes, take Golden Gate Transit bus 24, which leaves from Market and Mission Streets.

By ferry

Golden Gate Transit ferries (923 2000) depart from the Embarcadero Ferry Building and travel north to Sausalito and Larkspur (on separate schedules) daily, with more trips on weekdays than weekends or holidays. The Sausalito ferry takes about 30 minutes to cross the bay and is one of the best cheap thrills in the Bay Area. The lower deck is better in bad weather, but on most days you should ride on the top deck for unsurpassed views of the San Francisco waterfront, the Golden Gate Bridge and Alcatraz Island. The boat docks in downtown Sausalito, close to shops and restaurants.

Blue & Gold Fleet Ferries (705 5555/recorded information 773 1188) runs ferries from Pier 41 near Fisherman's Wharf to Sausalito and Angel Island and from the Ferry Building on the Embarcadero to Tiburon and Vallejo, home of Marine World/Africa USA. The **Angel Island-Tiburon Ferry** (435 2131) runs a ferry from Tiburon to Angel Island.

Inspecting the wildlife on the **Point Reyes National Seashore**.

Wine Country

It's hard to believe that the Wine Country (the general region encompassing Napa, Sonoma and parts of the Medocino County vineyards) is only just over an hour's drive north-east of San Francisco. The region is popular for romantic weekend retreats, but if you can, avoid going during the height of the summer when temperatures soar and tourists arrive in droves. Off-season discounts are available in lush autumn and floral spring, when the area is more peaceful. Most settlers in the area originally came from France, Italy or Germany, bringing with them their family traditions, foodstuffs and winemaking methods, and a European sensibility proliferates. The best way to tackle the area is to take time to enjoy it and be prepared to spend money and accumulate calories.

Sonoma County

At 4,138 square kilometres (1,600 square miles), Sonoma County is larger than the entire state of Rhode Island. The three major areas are the **Sonoma Valley**, which runs about 23 miles (37 kilometres) north from San Pablo Bay; the **Alexander Valley/Dry Creek** area east and north-west of Healdsburg; and the **Russian River Valley**, which stretches west from US 101 along the Russian River towards the ocean. Unlike those in Napa, most of the Sonoma wineries which offer free tastings are off the beaten track. Be prepared to explore.

Besides the wine itself, one of the principal attractions of a Sonoma wine tour is driving along winding roads with sweetly rural views of vineyards and farms. The **SCWA** (Sonoma County Wineries Association, 1-707 586 3795/1-800 939 7666) organises vineyard and winery tours and daily tastings, and is located near US 101 in **Rohnert Park**, one of the few towns with no wineries at all.

The small town of **Sonoma** was founded in 1823 as the Mission San Francisco Solano, the last and northernmost of the Franciscan missions. It developed around a Mexican-style plaza and, in 1846, was where the Bear Flag was raised to proclaim the independent Republic of California (*see page 6* **History**). The plaza is now flanked by adobe and Western-style false-fronted buildings, with restaurants, bookshops, barbershops and plenty of places to grab picnic supplies, including a cheese shop and a bakery. The square contains lots of shady trees as well as a dozen or so picnic tables.

A good stop for children is **Sonoma Train Town** (Broadway, Hwy 12; 1-707 938 3912), about a mile south of the plaza, which offers a 20-minute ride on a miniature steam train past scale models of buildings, a petting zoo and a couple of waterfalls.

The **Sonoma Valley Visitor Bureau** (453 First Street East; 1-707 996 1090) distributes leaflets on walking tours of the downtown area. Among the local landmarks are the whitewashed adobe **Sonoma Mission** on West Spain and First

City hall: one of the centrepieces of **Sonoma** *town square.*

Streets (1-707 938 9560), which served as a Mexican outpost in the seventeenth century. Now restored, it houses a variety of relics. Sonoma State Historic Park includes the Mission building and the town hall, as well as the **Toscano Hotel** and the **Sonoma Barracks** where the troops, under the control of Mexican General Mariano G Vallejo, were stationed.

The history of Sonoma is intertwined with that of the Californian wine industry which began here. Hungarian count Agoston Haraszthy planted the first European grapevines in Sonoma in the 1850s at **Buena Vista Historical Winery** (18000 Old Winery Road, Sonoma; 1-800 926 1266). The winery is open to the public.

Most vineyards offer complimentary tastings of several different wines; for hints on what to take home with you, *see page 251* **Buying wine**. Of the 35 wineries in the Sonoma Valley, many are near Sonoma's plaza. A great picnic choice is **Bartholomew Park Winery** (1000 Vineyard Lane, Sonoma; 1-707 935 9511), which has a museum and a relief map dedicated to the appellation. The **Wine Exchange of Sonoma** (452 First Street East, Sonoma; 1-800 938 1794) offers up to 15 Californian and European wines as well as beers for daily tasting.

The villages of **Kenwood** and **Glen Ellen**, north of Sonoma, would be hard to find were it not for the presence of some of the best wineries and a literary connection. Jack London – adventurer, farmer and one of the most prolific authors of his day – made his home in Glen Ellen (*see chapter* **Literary San Francisco**). A mansion full of memories and the charred remains of Wolf House make **Jack London Historic State Park** (2400 London Ranch Road, Glen Ellen; 1-707 938 5216/1-800 944 7175/www.parks.sonoma.net) one of the valley's top attractions. It's a nice place to stroll in the shade among oak and madrone trees. Near the entrance to the park, the **Sonoma Cattle Company** (1-707 996 8566) leads guided tours of the area on horseback.

One of the most popular stops in Kenwood is the **Kenwood Winery** (at SR 12 and Warm Springs Road, Kenwood; 1-707 833 5891). The site's original barn, now the tasting room and shop, dates from the pre-Prohibition days of the early twentieth century. This friendly, classic Sonoma winery is known for making wine with grapes grown on Jack London's former ranch.

On the other side of US 101 lies the small town of **Sebastopol**. Famous for growing Gravenstein apples, it still retains the feel of an old agricultural town and the roadside fruit stands overflow with produce. Walk along Main Street to explore the scattering of cafés, bookshops and restaurants worth investigating. Try the **East-West Café** (128 Main Street) for tofu omelets and the **Pine Cone Café** (162 Main Street) for pancakes, pancakes and more pancakes.

The **Carneros** district straddles southern Sonoma and Napa. Here you will find establishments such as the **Viansa Winery and Italian Marketplace** (25200 SR 121, Sonoma; 1-707 935 4700/1-800 995 4740/www.viansa.com). A scion of one of the state's oldest wine families, Sam Sebastiani and his wife Vicki built a Tuscan-style winery on a knoll facing the Sonoma Valley. Their spacious tasting room also sells Italian foodstuffs, and the trellis-topped picnic tables outside overlook the valley.

For accommodation, the **Sonoma Hotel** is good value (110 West Spain Street and First Street West, Sonoma; 1-707 996 2996; rooms from $95). The luxurious **El Dorado Inn** (405 First Street, Sonoma; 1-707 996 3030; rooms from $150) is also located directly on the square in Sonoma. If you're looking for peace, the **Gaige House Inn** (13540 Arnold Drive, Glen Ellen; 1-707 935 0237; rooms $215-$355) is worth the extra drive (and cash): sit out by the pool where the creek gurgles, the sun shines and time seems to stop.

For restaurants in Sonoma, the **General's Daughter** (400 West Spain Street; 1-707 938 4004) is good for brunch and based in a beautifully restored Victorian building. **Delle Santina** (133 East Napa Street; 1-707 935 0576) is authentically Italian without any pretence and moderately priced. Picnickers can pick up cheese and crackers at the **Sonoma Cheese Factory** (2 Spain Street; 1-707 996 1000) located on the central plaza.

Napa County

The 25-mile (40-kilometre) long **Napa Valley**, running almost parallel to the Sonoma Valley on the other side of the Mayacamas Mountains, forms the backbone of the Napa wine industry. Originally, Napa was populated by the Nappa Indian tribe; after Europeans had settled the area, Charles Krug introduced grapes into the valley in 1861. SR 29 (also called the St Helena Highway) runs up the middle and is usually crowded with traffic because the largest wineries are found on it. Boutique wineries are mostly to be found on the **Silverado Trail**, or on one of the lanes that criss-cross the valley, or along a winding road up one of the many hillsides.

Wine-tasting is the number one attraction here, with dining a close second. For a complete listing of wineries, pick up a map at any one of the vineyards en route. **Robert Mondavi Winery** (7801 St Helena Highway, Oakville; 1-707 226 1335/1-888 766 6328/www.robertmondaviwinery.com) is a good bet for first-time wine tasters. Also worth investigation is the historic German mansion of the **Beringer Vineyards** (2000 Main Street, St Helena; 1-707 963 7115) and the sparkling wines bottled at **Domaine Chandon** (1 California Drive, Yountville; 1-707 944 2280/www.dchandon.com) which offers one of the best tours, including a stellar Californian interpretation of méthode champenoise. The **V Sattui Winery** (1111 White Lane, at Hwy 29, St. Helena; 1-707 963 7774/www.vsattui.com) is jam-packed in the summer, but does great wine deals sold exclusively at the winery and has a huge, well-stocked deli.

There is more to enjoy in Napa, however, including fishing and boating on remote **Lake Berryessa**, horse riding, bicycling, or hiking. A good way to get an overview is from a hot air balloon, a thrilling pre-dawn experience that demands several rolls of film and a mastery of any fear of heights. For a more down-to-earth method of exploration, several companies offer horse riding tours of the area and the **Napa Valley Wine Train** (1-707 253 2111/www.winetrain.com) runs daily lunch and dinner trips ($59.50-$75 per person) up and down the valley. Cheesy it may be, but at least you don't have to fight the summer traffic.

The town of **Napa** itself has little to offer the traveller, other than a heap of good outlet stores (*see page 181* **Shops & Services**). For more information on the region, phone the **Napa Valley Conference and Visitor Bureau** (1-707 226 7459/www.napavalley.com) or the **Napa Chamber of Commerce** (1-707 226 7455/www.napachamber.org).

For restaurants in the area, the top-rated **French Laundry** (6640 Washington Street, Yountville; 1-707 944 2380) prepares what may be the best meal you'll ever eat for an average of around $70 a head, but make your dinner reservation well ahead: it books three months in advance to the day (*see page 129* **Restaurants & Cafés**). Up the road and at the other end of the spectrum, **Mustards Grill** (7399 St Helena Highway, Napa, 1-707 944 2424) is a popular upmarket diner well worth the wait for a plate of delicious home fries.

St Helena has a number of excellent restaurants, including newcomer, **Pinot Blanc** (641 Main Street, St Helena; 1-707 963 6191) or **Terra** (1345 Railroad Avenue, St Helena; 1-707 963 8931) which is a local favourite. For a picnic, the West Coast installation of New York's **Dean & Deluca** (607 South Street, St Helena; 1-707 967 9980) has an extensive deli section with gourmet delicacies from around the world. Both St Helena's **Cantinetta Tra Vigne** (1050 Charter Oak Avenue, St Helena; 1-707 963 8888) and the **Oakville Grocery** in Oakville (7845 St Helena Highway;

Domaine Chandon: *for a great winery tour and some stellar fizz. See page 249.*

1-707 977 8802) will pack you a picnic hamper if you telephone the day before.

For information on places to stay in Napa, contact **Napa Valley Reservations Unlimited** (1-707 252 1985/1-800 251 6272): rooms get booked up quickly and most options are expensive. A deluxe option in the valley is the **Vintage Inn** (6541 Washington Street, Yountville; 1-707 944 1112/1-800 351 1133/www.vintageinn.com; rooms from $225), which has great looking rooms and is located close to shops and restaurants. Even more expensive is the **Auberge du Soleil** in Rutherford (180 Rutherford Hill Road; 1-707 963 1211; rooms from $350), worth reserving for very special occasions. The **Maison Fleurie Inn** (6529 Yount Street, Yountville; 1-707 944 2056/1-800 788 0369; rooms from $115) is a pretty B&B centrally located within easy reach of wineries.

Calistoga & the Russian River Valley

More than any other town in the wine country, **Calistoga** (home of the hot springs and bottled water) looks Western: it's got saloons and a wide main street often festooned with banners promoting beer tastings, mustard festivals or other celebrations of the California good life. At the end of the avenue is a **glider port** (Crazy Creek Soaring, 18896 Grange Road, Middletown; 1-707 987 9112), from one of whose silent, winged crafts you can see much of the Napa Valley and the forested mountains that flank it.

Dioramas depicting nineteenth-century Calistoga life, along with photos and other artifacts are displayed in the **Sharpsteen Museum** (1311 Washington Street, Calistoga; 1-707 942 5911/www.napanet/vi/sharpsteen). A mile north of town, on Tubbs Lane, **Old Faithful** geyser erupts about every 15 minutes. Water comes from an underground river and heats to around 177°C (350°F) before spewing high into the air. Another quirk of nature is the **Petrified Forest**, five miles (eight kilometres) west on Petrified Forest Road. The **Bale Grist Mill State Historic Park** on SR 29 near Calistoga is a good place to stop for a picnic.

Several wineries are located in and around Calistoga. Take the tram ride up to **Sterling Vineyards** (1111 Dunaweal Lane, Calistoga; 1-707 942 3344). Famous for its Cabernet Sauvignon as well as its white wines, this hilltop winery has commanding views of the countryside and an excellent self-guided tour. **Château Montelena** (1429 Tubbs Lane, Calistoga; 1-707 942 5105) is an 1882 house overlooking a Chinese garden complete with lake, tea houses, bridges and a Chinese junk. A charming example of a small, family-owned winery is **Wermuth** (3942 Silverado Trail, Calistoga; 1-707 942 5924).

Robert Louis Stevenson State Park, named after the writer who honeymooned near here, is seven miles (11 kilometres) north of Calistoga on SR 29 (1490 Library Lane, St Helena; 1-707 963 3757). The **Robert Louis Stevenson Museum** (1490 Library Lane, St Helena; 1-707 963 3757) in nearby St Helena contains memorabilia related to the author (*see chapter* **Literary San Francisco**). And finally, don't leave the area without indulging yourself at one of Calistoga's many famous spas: *see page 258* **Spas & retreats**.

For restaurants in Calistoga, the **Catahoula Restaurant & Saloon** (1457 Lincoln Avenue, Calistoga; 1-707 942 2275) offers part Cajun, part Californian, but mostly American cooking for about $20 for three courses: try the cornmeal fried catfish, seafood gumbo, or Mardi Gras slaw, but save room for dessert. For accommodation, try the **Pink Mansion** (1415 Foothill Boulevard, at Main Street, Calistoga; 1-707 942 0558; rooms from $145), an elegant restored building, offering in-house wine tastings. The **Mountain Home Ranch** (3400 Mountain Home Ranch Road, Calistoga; 1-707 942 6616/www.mtnhomeranch.com) is a secluded resort with all the amenities: swimming pools, tennis and volleyball courts, fishing and hiking trails. Cabins cost from $40-$130 a night. For more information on the area, contact the **Calistoga Chamber of Commerce** (1458 Lincoln Avenue, Calistoga; 1-707 942 6333).

The town of **Healdsburg** is like a miniature Sonoma, with an unusual number of good restaurants and boutiques for its size, and an enviable location at the intersection of three wine valleys – the Alexander, Dry Creek and Russian River. A much cooler wine growing region than Sonoma, the Russian River Valley runs west towards the Pacific. If you want to be on paths less trodden, head to **Bistro Ralph** (109 Plaza Street, Healdsberg; 1-707 433 1380), where you can rub shoulders with the local wine makers. The enchanting **Honor Mansion** (14891 Grove Street, Healdsburg, 1-707 433 4277/1-800 554 4667/www.honormansion.com; rooms from $150) is a romantic getaway with many European touches.

Like Napa, not everything is winecentric in this area. **Guerneville** is popular for river rafting and as a summer resort for San Francisco's gay community; the Russian River itself is also a good bet for fishing. There are bait shops in Guerneville and Healdsburg (you can obtain the licence required to allow you to fish in California from most fishing and camping shops). On the coast, just north of the mouth of the Russian River and the town of Jenner, lies **Fort Ross State Historic Park** (1-707 847 3286), originally settled by Russian colonists in 1812. It has a visitor centre, an extensive park and beach access.

Local vineyards to visit include sparkling wine and brandy maker **Korbel** (13250 River Road, Guerneville; 1-707 887 2294), where there's a micro brewery, picnic grounds, a deli and rose gardens. Family-owned winery **Martinelli** in **Windsor** (3360 River Road, Guerneville; 1-707 525 0570/1-800 346 1627) has a gift shop and art gallery. The **Applewood Inn & Restaurant** (13555 Highway 116, Guerneville; 1-707 869 9093/www.applewoodinn.com) is set among ageing redwoods and apple orchards; it's a great place to unwind and enjoy a beautiful candlelight dinner from around $18 a head. For more information and a further list of places to stay in the area, contact the **Russian River Region Visitor Bureau** (1-707 869 9212/1-800 253 8800).

Mendocino County

Built on a wide bluff that juts out into the ocean, the picturesque town of **Mendocino** has the most dramatic views of any of the northern coastline. The quickest route from San Francisco is via the

Buying wine

Only a tiny selection of California wine labels make it across the Atlantic, so here are some helpful hints on what to look out for on your tour of the Wine Country. The huge volume of fruit and flavour is the hallmark of today's Californian wines; the most common varietals grown in the region include crisp Chardonnays, big Cabernet Sauvignons, soft Merlots, Sauvignon Blancs, Pinot Noirs, Rieslings and the versatile Zinfandel.

Sonoma labels

Cline (Zinfandel); **Dry Creek** (Chardonnay); **Field Stone** (Cabernet and Petite Sirah); **Foppiano** (Petite Sirah and Zinfandel); **Geyser Peak** (Chardonnay); **Gundlach Bundschu** (Merlot, Pinot Noir, Chardonnay, Cabernet and Zinfandel); **Lambert Bridge** (Fumé Blanc, Pinot Noir and Zinfandel); **Matanzas Creek** (Chardonnay); **Pezzi King** (Pinot Noirs, Zinfandel and Cabernet); **Roche** (Chardonnay and Pinot Noir).

Napa labels

Carneros Creek (Pinot Noir); **Chimney Rock** (Chardonnay, Cabernet Sauvignon); **Clos Pegase** (Cabernet Sauvignon, Chardonnay, Merlot and Petite Syrah Port); **Cuvaison** (Cabernet Sauvignon, Chardonnay); **Joseph Phelps** (Chardonnay); **Opus One** (Cabernet Sauvignon); **Pine Ridge** (Chardonnay, Cabernet Sauvignon and Merlot); **Robert Sinskey** (Pinot Noir); **Silver Oak** (Cabernet Sauvignon); **Stag's Leap** (Cabernet Sauvignon, Chardonnay and Sauvignon Blanc).

inland US 101 and connecting state highways (the journey takes about three hours), but the twisting coastal SR 1 with its small towns is more fun: take the detour to **Point Arena Lighthouse** just south of Manchester, for a spectacular view across the ocean.

Mendocino is characterised by New England-style houses and clapboard churches. B&Bs and quaint inns have the monopoly on accommodation. The **Mendocino Hotel** (45080 Main Street; 1-707 937 0511/1-800 548 0513/www.mendocinoinn.com; rooms from $85) is a luxury establishment. Filled with beautiful antiques, the **John Dougherty House** (1-707 937 5266/1-800 486 2104/www.jdhouse.com; rooms from $115) looks as though it has been transplanted straight out of New England. Built in 1882, the **Mendocino Village Inn** (44860 Main Street; 1-707 937 0246/www.mendocinoinn.com; rooms from $75) is more understated and very cosy.

Ten miles (17 kilometres) north is **Fort Bragg**, a larger town with more amenities, offering a range of accommodation at a fraction of the cost. Phone the **Fort Bragg-Mendocino Chamber of Commerce** (1-707 961 6300) for more information on restaurants and accommodation here.

The small **Mendocino Headlands State Park** between Mendocino and the coast (1-707 937 5397) is ideal for hiking, tide-pooling and whale watching. **Van Damme State Park** (1-707 937 4016), just south of Mendocino off Hwy 1, is covered with redwood trees and a popular spot for camping. It contains several hiking trails through fern canyons and pygmy forests. **Russian Gulch State Park** (1-707 937 5804) just north of Mendocino is famous for the **Devil's Punch Bowl**, a blowhole that sends the surf shooting skyward. **Catch a Canoe & Bicycles Too**, half a mile south of Mendocino under the south side of the Big River Bridge (1-707 937 0273), rents mountain bikes, canoes and kayaks. For the hike-weary, well worth the $40-a-head splurge is **Café Beaujolais** (961 Ukiah Street, Mendocino; 1-707 937 5614) – the weekend breakfasts are famous – preceded by a soak in a hot tub next door at **Sweetwater Gardens** (955 Ukiah Street, Mendocino; 1-707 937 4140/www.sweetwaterspa.com).

The Wine Country isn't the only wine growing region in Northern California. The **Santa Cruz** area (*see page 254*) and area around Santa Barbara further south also have numerous varieties. For more information on trips in Southern California and Nevada, consult the *Time Out Los Angeles Guide* and the *Time Out Las Vegas Guide*.

Getting there

By car

The Wine Country is roughly an hour by car from San Francisco (44 miles/71km) over the Golden Gate Bridge along US 101. Turn east at Ignacio to SR 37 and take SR 121 north. Once here, SR 12 points you towards Sonoma, SR 29 towards Napa. Traffic can be hellish, particularly over the Golden Gate Bridge, but by car is still the best way to see the wine country.

To reach Calistoga, continue on SR 29, which turns into SR 128. To reach Healdsburg (74 miles/119km from San Francisco), stay on US 101.

To reach the town of Mendocino (145 miles/233km up the coast from San Francisco), take US 101 north to Cloverdale, then take SR 128 west, which joins up with Hwy 1 at the coast.

By bus

Golden Gate Transit operates buses as far north as Petaluma: bus 80 goes to Petaluma and bus 90 to Sonoma (stopping at San Rafael on the way).

Within the county, **Sonoma County Area Transit** and the **Vine**, Napa's bus service, provide local transport. Several San Francisco operators run Wine Country tours: for more information, contact the **San Francisco Visitor Information Center** (391 2000/www.sfvisitor.org) or a local tourist office.

You can also take **BART** to El Cerrito, then **Vallejo Transit** bus 80 to Vallejo and then bus 10 to Napa. Phone the **Napa Valley Transit Authority** (1-707 255 7631) for more information.

Greyhound runs daily buses from San Francisco to Napa. There are no buses to Healdsburg or Mendocino from San Francisco, but the **Mendocino Transit Authority** (1-800 696 4682) provides a daily service to and from Santa Rosa, where you can connect to or from San Francisco via Golden Gate Transit or Amtrack.

Getting around

By balloon

Several companies offer packages, such as flights for two with champagne, or balloon, brunch and lodging at a local hotel and spa. In Sonoma, **Sonoma Thunder** or **Wine Country Balloon Safaris** are in fact the same company (6984 McKinley Street, Sebastopol; 1-707 829 7695/ 1-707 538 7359/1-800 759 5638/wintour@metro.net).

In Napa, try the **Buonaventura Balloon Company** (1-800 359 6272) or **Balloon Aviation** (1-707 944 4400/ www.nvaloft.com).

By bike

Some wine country tourists prefer to cycle from winery to winery; a few companies provide a gourmet picnic lunch along the way and will carry your purchases in a van for you.
The **Goodtime Bicycle Company** (18503 Hwy 12, Sonoma; 1-888 525 0453/www.bikemantours.com) offers organised excursions and **Getaway Adventures** (620 Washington Street, Petaluma; 1-707 763 3040/getawayadventures.com) offers fully catered packages at various prices that can be tailored to your needs.

Heading south

The San Francisco peninsula stretches 42 miles (68 kilometres) south until it merges with the mainland near San Jose. On the Bay side, there's little of interest to the tourist, the 'burbs melting together into a single blur. **Palo Alto** – or 'shallow Alto', as it's been known – doesn't really have much to offer except Silicon Valley start-ups and is mostly overrun with students from neighbouring Stanford University. The university's internationally acclaimed **Cantor Center for the Arts** (Lomita Drive, at Museum Way, Stanford; 1-650 723 4177/www.stanford.edu/dept/ccva) houses a large sculpture garden full of Rodins, worth visiting at night when the pieces are dramatically lit up. On another note entirely, the **Barbie Doll Hall of Fame** (460 Waverley Street, Palo Alto; 1-650 326 5841) is devoted to one of the most famous popular cult icons of the century.

On the Pacific side of the peninsular, leaving the city behind and heading south, you'll notice a change of scenery as well as a change of pace: from the bustling city to rolling hills full of artichokes, beautiful rugged beaches full of surfers and beach combers, and sleepy towns full of ramshackle barns and country stores. The flat Bay shores contrast with the steep terrain of the Santa Cruz hills. Agriculture has been the economic mainstay of the area since World War II, until the booming 1980s gave way to the technological explosion of Silicon Valley. Inland, instead of orchards of apple trees, there are grids of concrete business parks lined with high tech giants Hewlett-Packard, Intel, Apple and Oracle.

So unless you have a morbid fascination to see the cemeteries of Colma, filled with departed San Franciscans, or aspire to owning a mansion in the exclusive Hillsborough, Los Altos or Woodside neighbourhoods, then weave your way down I-280 and look out for signs to the **Pacific Coast Highway** or **Hwy 1**, where the peninsula's charm can still be found.

Half Moon Bay

Half Moon Bay, just off Hwy 1 and about 30 minutes from San Francisco, is a small, easygoing seaside town with a rural feel, famous for growing Hallowe'en pumpkins and Christmas trees. It contains a couple of golf courses, riding stables, bike paths and beaches. Main Street is filled with bookshops, boutiques, healthfood stores, flower gardens and antique shops. Stay at **San Benito House** (356 Main Street; 1-650 726 3425; rooms from $70), a hotel in a restored building in the heart of town. The **Cypress Inn** (407 Mirada Road; 1-650 726 6002; rooms from $185) is a more expensive romantic hideaway where each room has a fireplace and a private deck that overlooks the ocean. **Two Fools** (408 Main Street; 1-650 712 1222) serves wonderful organic salads and healthy burritos to eat in or take away for a picnic.

May and June are the best months for foraging along the farm trails that dot the surrounding countryside. Worth a visit is the **San Georgio General Store**, just eight miles (13 kilometres) south of Half Moon Bay on SR 84. This funky store has been serving the local farming community since 1889, selling everything from cast-iron pots and pans to second-hand books, antiques and music.

A string of beaches stretches down the coast between Half Moon Bay and Pescadero, including the popular **Half Moon Bay State Beach**. Probably the best of the lot is **San Gregorio State Beach**, a strip of white sand distinguished by sedimentary cliffs and a proximity to a nude beach further north. If you feel like taking horses out for an hour-long trip along the coast, call the **Sea Horse and Friendly Acres Ranch** (at Half Moon Bay and Hwy 1; 1-650 726 8550) which offers beach rides for all levels of ability. The **Costanoa** campground (2001 Rossi Road at Hwy 1, Pescadero; 1-650 879 1100; tents $55; lodge rooms $175) is not your typical campground and even offers room service. It's ideally located for hiking, horse riding, kayaking and windsurfing, and overlooks rugged bluffs and panoramic beaches.

For more information on **Half Moon Bay State Parks**, contact the district office (95 Kelly Avenue, Half Moon Bay; 1-650 726 8819) or the **Half Moon Bay Coastside Chamber of Commerce** (520 Kelly Avenue, Half Moon Bay; 1-650 726 8380).

Just north of Half Moon Bay on Hwy 1, **Princeton** is a lofty name for a tiny town and a great little harbour. It's a place for aimless ambling and perhaps lunch at a casual restaurant. **Barbara's Fishtrap** by the harbour (281 Capistrano Road, Princeton; 1-650 728 7049) has great, reasonably priced local seafood. The **Pillar Point Inn** opposite (1-650 728 7377) is a charming inn with snappy nautical décor and large breakfasts in a building overlooking the harbour.

Further south, you can soak up the atmosphere of **Pescadero** while enjoying a beer at **Duarte's Tavern** (202 Stage Road, Pescadero; 1-650 879 0464), this little town's most celebrated saloon for over a century. The crab sandwiches are famous and the bar is a friendly place for a drink. **Phipps Ranch** (2700 Pescadero Road, Pescadero; 1-650 879 0787) sells berries and other fruit and vegetables throughout the year, which can be eaten on the ranch at picnic tables or packed into your car.

Getting there

By car

Half Moon Bay and Princeton are about a 30-minute drive south of San Francisco on Hwy 1 (roughly 15 miles/24km). Pescadero is a further 15 minutes' south, signposted off Hwy 1.

By bus

SamTrans (1-800 660 4287) buses travel between Half Moon Bay, Pacifica and the Daly City BART Station, among other points.

Santa Cruz

Originally established as a mission and still recovering after extensive damage suffered from the Loma Prieta earthquake in 1989, this quintessentially quirky California beach town is well known for being easygoing and politically progressive. Home of the University of California at Santa Cruz, it has a young population that keeps things lively, as well as plenty of longtime residents who are fiercely protective of the town's liberal heritage.

A hybrid of tacky and nostalgic (but mostly just tacky), the **Santa Cruz Beach Boardwalk** (400 Beach Street, Santa Cruz; 1-831 423 5590/www.beachboardwalk.com) offers 27 different rides, including bumper cars and tilt-a-whirls, a rambling arcade with games, shops and fast food joints. The Giant Dipper, a classic wooden roller coaster, has been proclaimed a National Historic Landmark, along with the nearby 1911 carousel.

The town's popularity as a beach resort dates back to the mid-nineteenth century. The small **Surfing Museum** (1-831 429 3429), located on Lighthouse Point, contains old photographs and vintage boards that tell the story of the sport that has become an entrenched part of the Santa Cruz scene. **Steamer Lane** is right outside the lighthouse and is considered one of the best surfing spots in California. Along with the boardwalk, the **Coconut Grove Ballroom** (400 Beach Street, Santa Cruz; 1-831 423 2053/www.beachboardwalk.com) is another remnant of the town's turn-of-the-century heyday, which still comes into its own at weekends when a mixture of big bands and local rock and pop groups play.

Santa Cruz's **Pacific Garden Mall** (on Pacific Avenue) is slowly recovering from the 1989 quake. All that remains of the **Mission de Exaltacion de la Santa Cruz** (1-831 425 5849) is the current replica, built in the 1930s, though the **Mission Adobe** (off Mission Plaza) is one of California's few original adobes. Built in 1929, the **Santa Cruz Museum of Natural History** (1305 East Cliff Drive, Tyrone Park; 1-831 420 6115/420 6451) contains information on the Ohlone Native Americans who originally populated the area.

For accommodation, the **Babbling Brook Inn** (1025 Laurel Street; 1-831 427 2456/427 2457/1-800 866 1131/www.babblingbrookinn.com; rooms from $155) is a luxurious bed and breakfast set in wooded grounds in the heart of town. If you want a family atmosphere, stay at the **Terrace Court** (125 Beach Street; 1-831 423 3031; rooms from $115), where some of the rooms have kitchenettes. It's opposite the wharf. If you'd rather stay away from the bustle, the **New Davenport Cash Store Bed and Breakfast Inn** (31 Davenport Avenue; 1-831 425 1818; rooms from $78) has beautiful ocean views and access to the beach.

The redwood forests, perched on the hills surrounding Santa Cruz, are ideal for hiking and biking. Explore the **Big Basin State Park** (1-831 338 8860) and **Henry Cowell State Park** (1-831 335 4598), both to the north. Just south of Santa Cruz, you can visit the **Forest of the Nisene Marks** (1-831 763 7063) to see the ruins of a Chinese labour camp, as well as the epicentre of the Loma Prieta earthquake.

In the hills you can also visit the **Mystery Spot** (465 Mystery Spot Road, Santa Cruz; 1-831 423 8897/www.mysteryspot.com), a bizarre plot of land in the woods that apparently defies all known laws of physics without the aid of recreational drugs.

There are two dozen wineries in the Santa Cruz area, without the crowds of Napa. **Bargetto Winery** (3535A North Main Street, Soquel; 1-831 475 2258) is casual and widely known for its fruit wines, including olallieberry and apricot versions. **Boony Doon** (10 Pine Flat Road, Santa Cruz; 1-831 425 3625) grows good Italian-style wines, and the **Storrs Winery** (35 Potrero Street, Santa Cruz; 1-831 458 5030) is run by an award-winning husband and wife wine-making team.

If you need to soak up the alcohol, head to **India Joze** (Art Center, 1001 Center Street, Santa Cruz; 1-831 427 3554) for delicious Middle Eastern and Indian cooking (for around $14 a head) and then move on to the **Santa Cruz Coffee Roasting Company** (1330 Pacific Avenue, Santa Cruz; 1-831 459 0100) for a cup of joe. For more information on Santa Cruz, contact the **Santa Cruz County Conference and Visitor Council** (701 Front Street; 1-831 425 1234).

Capitola & Aptos

Both Santa Cruz and neighbouring **Capitola** to the south, have been overrun – and understandably so. Capitola, which bills itself as the oldest Pacific seaside resort, boasts some good eateries, with very low prices: **Dharma's Natural Foods** (4250 Capitola Road, Capitola; 1-831 462 1717) is possibly the oldest veggie restaurant in the US and **Mr Toot's Coffeehouse** (221 Esplanade, Capitola; 1-831 475 3679) is an earthy hangout full of people slouching around on sofas listening to jazz.

The village of **Aptos**, further down the coast, offers two of the best beaches in the region, **Rio**

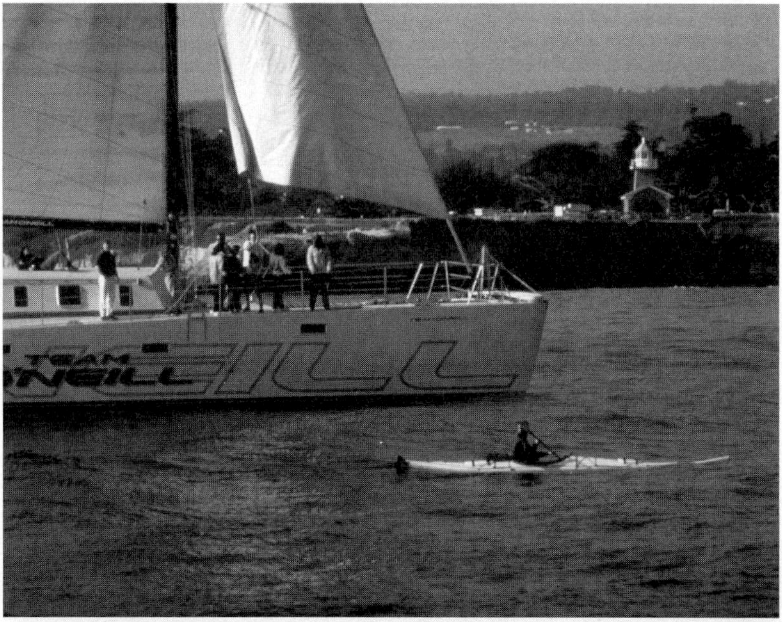

There's more to **Santa Cruz** *than the Beach Boardwalk.*

del Mar and **Seacliff**. It is also a good back-up choice for lodging on popular weekends such as the local **Great Monterey Squid Festival** in late May: the cry of the wild calamari is a siren song for thousands of fans of this delectable treat, which is served in local restaurants during a long weekend of music and entertainment. On a similarly wild note, Aptos is also home to an endangered colony of long-toed salamanders. It also boasts the world's shortest parade, usually held on the weekend closest to 4 July.

Getting there

By car

Santa Cruz is 74 miles (119km) south of San Francisco – about two hours' drive down Hwy 1. Capitola and Aptos are a few miles further south.

By train

CalTrain leaves San Francisco from two stations (Fourth/King Streets and 22nd/Pennsylvania Streets) every half hour. Take the train to San Jose Amtrak station, from where a shuttle bus goes to Santa Cruz.

Monterey peninsula

Jutting into the Pacific between the fun-loving town of Santa Cruz and the dramatic coastline of Big Sur, the **Monterey peninsula** is one of the best attractions on the coast. Writers and artists, including Simone de Beauvoir, Robinson Jeffers, Jack Kerouac and Henry Miller, have been drawn to the area for decades. The **Monterey Jazz Festival** (1-831 373 3366), held each September, and the **Monterey Bay Blues Festival** (1-831 394 2652), held at the end of June, annually draw the top names in jazz and blues. But the area is perhaps best known for its spectacular golf courses, fishing and cycling.

Carmel

The three major towns on the peninsular are Carmel, where Clint Eastwood completed a stint as mayor, Monterey and Pacific Grove. Carmel is a love-it-or-hate-it sort of place. Once a secluded seaside village favoured by the likes of Robert Louis Stevenson and Ansel Adams, it is now an over-popular spot chock-full of mediocre (and expensive) shops. Much of it looks like a particularly picturesque film set, with perfect fake adobe mansions discreetly tucked away in leafy groves leading down to the ocean. The beach is a fantastic white crescent of sand, but not suitable for swimming. **Ocean Avenue** is Carmel's main shopping street, with antique shops, art galleries, boutiques and a tea shop that's straight out of *Snow White and the Seven Dwarfs*. There are several good restaurants, including **Flaherty's** (Sixth Street, between San Carlos and Dolores Streets, Carmel; 1-831 624 0311) which is the best seafood joint in town (expect to wait for a table), and pricey newcomer **Pacific's Edge** (Highlands Inn, at Hwy 1, Carmel; 1-831 622 5445). For breakfast or lunch, try the budget-priced **Katy's Place** (Mission Street, between Fifth and Sixth Avenues, Carmel; 1-831 624 0199).

Highway 1 snakes along the rugged **Big Sur** *coast, from Carmel to San Simeon. See page 259.*

Carmel Mission (3080 Rio Road; 1-831 624 3600), has a baroque church (built in 1797), three museums and beautiful gardens; it shouldn't be missed. For hikers and bikers, visit the **Mission Trail Park** across the street. Just south of Carmel Highlands is one of the most beloved parks in California, **Point Lobos**. It's possible to spend an entire morning or even a whole day exploring its nooks, crannies, beaches and awesome promontories.

Monterey & Pacific Grove

The capital of Alta California during Spanish, Mexican and American governments, Monterey is one of the state's most historic cities. Popular spots include **Colton Hall**, where California's first constitution was written (in 1849) and the **Monterey State Historic Park** (1-831 649 7118), seven acres containing various artefacts relating to the area's architecture and history. **Jacks Regional Park** (1-831 647 7795), just ten miles (16 kilometres) south, provides an escape from the tourists and traffic of downtown Monterey.

The city's best attraction, however, is undoubtedly the **Monterey Bay Aquarium** (886 Cannery Row, Monterey; 1-831 648 4937). Its gorgeous, labyrinthine display of undersea forests, marine life, tide pools and special exhibits are a treat. Even the gift shop deserves some serious browsing. If you can, time your visit to coincide with one of the regularly scheduled feeding times of the sea otters. The aquarium is located on **Cannery Row**, a neighbourhood made famous by native son John Steinbeck. Today the canning factories are gone, abandoned in the 1940s when the commercial sardine population was fished out, to be replaced by tacky shops and disappointing restaurants which occupy their warehouse premises.

Monterey is also a wine-producing region, known for its Chardonnay. Stop in at the **Bargetto Winery** (700 Cannery Row, Monterey; 1-831 373 4053) and take a detour upstairs to the **Paul Masson Museum and Wine Tasting Room** (1-831 646 5446). The **Monterey Vintners Association** (PO Box 1793, Monterey, CA 93942; 1-831 375 9400) provides a free map with information on 25 local wineries.

Spas & retreats

Spas and retreats have become the ultimate Californian experience, an everyday part of the therapeutic lifestyle: fix the body (goes the logic) and you fix the mind. So join 'em and you too can wallow in a hot tub or a mud bath – or simply wallow in self-satisfaction. For opening hours and directions, contact the individual resorts.

Calistoga got its name in the mid-1800s, when San Franciscan Sam Brannan created a resort near St Helena Mountain. Instead of proclaiming that the spa would be 'the Saratoga of California' (referring to the New York resort), Brannan quipped it would be 'the Calistoga of Sariforna'. The volcanic ash from neighbouring St Helena mountain is the magic ingredient in the mud baths that draw the health-conscious as well as the plain curious to Calistoga.

The **Calistoga Village Inn and Spa** (1880 Lincoln Avenue, Calistoga; 1-707 942 0991) offers wonderful herbal wraps, mineral baths, and a mud bath. **Dr Wilkinson's Hot Springs** (*pictured opposite*; 1507 Lincoln Avenue, Calistoga; 1-707 942 4102/6257/ www.drwilkinson.com) is the grand-daddy of the mud bath spas. Old and comfortable, the place has an excellent reputation, drawing indulgent, self-pampering souls from all over the world who come for the ambience, the reasonable rates and simply to mellow out. Packages start at $80 for a two hour mud bath and massage and it's worth every cent.

Roughly half an hour's drive from Calistoga, **Harbin Hot Springs** (18424 Harbin Springs Road; 1-707 987 2477/1-800 622 2477), is a good place to discard inhibitions about public nudity; it's the thing here and while it's not mandatory, you do begin to feel self-conscious in your clothes. Experience a massage in the great outdoors, in the shadow of Mount Harbin.

If you want a spa retreat but don't want a long drive or the high prices of Wine Country getaways, head to the **Claremont Resort and Spa** (41 Tunnel Road, Berkeley; 1-510 549 8566/www. claremontresort.com). In summer, when the city is blanketed in fog, this East Bay haven basks in sunshine and visitors soak up the rays alongside the enormous outdoor pool. Services include mud body wraps, glycolic acid treatments, waxing, a hair salon, tennis, swimming and fitness programmes.

The **Sonoma Mission Inn & Spa** (18140 Highway 12, Boyes Hot Springs; 1-707 938 9000) is considered to be the best spa in the Bay Area: you name the service, they've got it. And you can even get your Tarot cards read while you're having your toes rubbed.

The **Kenwood Inn & Spa** (10400 SR 12, Kenwood; 1-707 833 1293) is refuge to the stars. Perhaps they come for the fabulously over-the-top Ti Amo Togetherness Massage ($280, champagne included, naturally) in which two masseurs give you a 120-minute full-body and foot massage. Not surprisingly, sparing at Kenwood is not about excessive exercising, but pure pampering.

Just a couple of miles west of Monterey is the much prettier small town of **Pacific Grove**, founded in 1875 as a camping retreat for the Methodist Church. Its best-known lodging site, the **Asilomar Conference Center** (800 Asilomar Boulevard; 1-831 372 8016; rooms from $77), has an ascetic ambience that characterises the entire town. **Asilomar State Park** (1-831 372 4076) is a great venue for a picnic; for an evening romantic rendezvous, stop at **Lover's Point Beach**. And as the sun sets, enjoy a to-die-for dessert at the **Old Bath House Restaurant** (620 Ocean View Boulevard; 1-831 375 5195) and take in the spectacular view. If you're in the area during the winter, watch out for the annual phenomenon of thousands of migrating monach butterflies: the **Pacific Grove Museum of Natural History** at Forest and Central Avenues (1-831 648 3116) has all the information.

Pacific Grove provides a good base for exploring the surrounding coast. For accommodation, try the **Gosby House** (643 Lighthouse Avenue, Pacific Grove; 1-831 375 1287; rooms from $100), the **Green Gables Inn** (104 Fifth Street, Pacific Grove; 1-831 375 2095; rooms from $120) or the **Old St Angela Inn** (321 Central Avenue, Pacific Grove; 1-800 748 6306; rooms from $110), all of which are cute B&Bs in great locations.

Pacific Grove's undeveloped shoreline, carpeted with native plants, is a good place to stroll unhampered by throngs of Frisbee players and picnicking families. The **Point Pinos Light Station** (1-831 648 3116), the oldest operating lighthouse on the coast, is one of dozens of older structures still in good repair.

The 17-Mile Drive from Pacific Grove through **Pebble Beach** takes you past some of the most famous and challenging golf courses in the country, although you have to pay for the privilege at strategically placed toll booths, whether on foot or in a car. Walk along the coastal path from Pacific Grove instead: the views are as good and it's free.

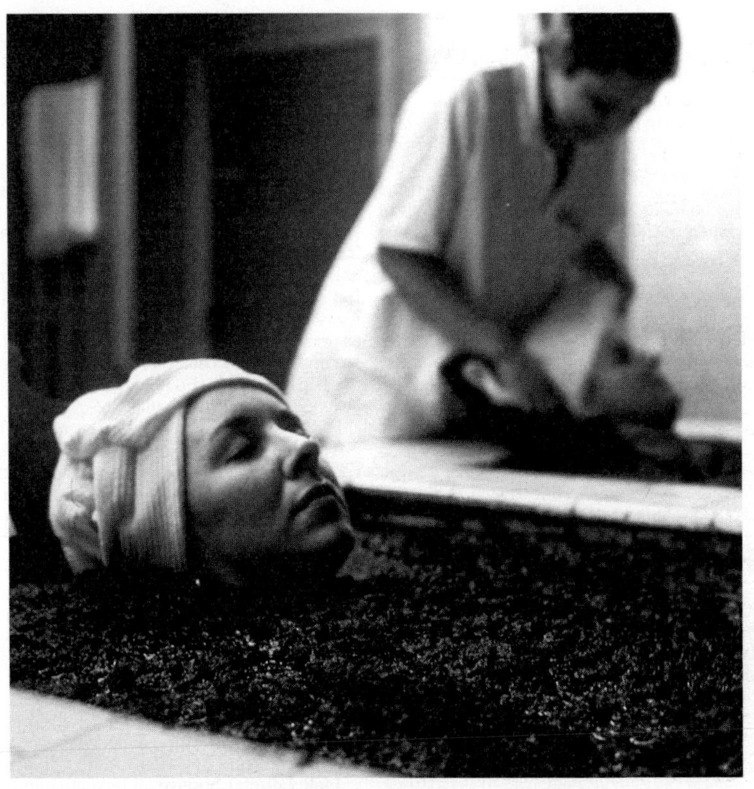

Roy's at Pebble Beach (The Inn at Spanish Bay, 2700 17 Mile Drive; 1-831 647 7423) is a good place to stop for a bite after 18 holes or a few hours behind the wheel.

For more information on the area, contact the **Monterey Peninsula Visitor & Convention Bureau** (1-831 649 1770) or the **Monterey Peninsula Chamber of Commerce** (380 Alvaradeo Street, Monterey; 1-831 648 5360).

Getting there

By car

Monterey is 133 miles (214km) – about 2½ hours by car – from San Francisco on Hwy 1.

By train

Take **CalTrain** to San Jose Amtrak station, where a local bus connects with Monterey. Amtrak runs the **Coast Starlight Train** along the coast, stopping at San Jose, Salinas and Monterey.

By bus

Greyhound buses connect San Francisco with Los Angeles, with regular services to Monterey via Salinas. Although there are local buses, this area is best explored by car.

Big Sur

The majestic coastline from Carmel to San Simeon continues to prove a spectacular journey and there are plenty of pull-outs along the rugged coast on Hwy 1 from which to take in the views.

The **Point Sur Lighthouse** (1-831 625 4419), about 19 miles (31 kilometres) south of Carmel, is an old beacon maintained by the Coast Guard and can only be visited as part of a tour. **Andrew Molera State Park** is a coastal sanctuary for seabirds nearby. **Pfeiffer-Big Sur State Park** (1-831 667 2315) on the eastern side of Hwy 1, is most popular for camping and hiking, especially in the summer. Pfeiffer Ridge and Pfeiffer Falls are worth checking out; Pine Ridge trailhead is also a favourite. The **Julia Pfeiffer Burns Park** (also 1-831 667 2315) offers camping and a large selection of hiking trails. The best trail is to the McWay Creek, which pours 21 metres (70 feet) into the ocean below.

The town of **Big Sur** is about 25 miles (40 kilometres) south from Carmel; stop by the **Big Sur Station** (1-831 667 2423), about half a mile south from Julia Pfeiffer Burns Park, for information and maps on hikes and places to go. The solitude of Big Sur attracted writer Henry Miller to the region in the 1940s. He wrote of the land as a place where 'extremes meet in a region where one is always conscious of the weather, of space, of grandeur, of eloquent silence'. You can visit the **Henry Miller Memorial Library** (1-831 667 2574/www.henrymiller.org) located in the former home of artist Emil White. The **Coast Gallery** (1-831 667 2301), about three miles south, also has a collection of the author's lithographs.

Most people camp in this area (and the hotels tend to be pricey), but the **Big Sur Lodge** (Pfeiffer-Big Sur State Park, Hwy 1; 1-831 667 2171/www.bigsurlodge.com; from $89) is a rustic spot nearby, where many of the cottage-style rooms have kitchens and fireplaces; don't miss their fresh-baked pies. **Deetjen's Big Sur Inn** (Hwy 1, south of Pfeiffer-Big Sur State Park; 1-831 667 2377; rooms from $75) offers a hearty breakfast as well as moderately priced rooms. **Nepenthe Restaurant** (on Hwy 1, Big Sur; 1-831 667 2345; average $22) was once the haunt of Elizabeth Taylor and Richard Burton and has views to die for (the food's not bad, either). **Café Kevah** just below it has similarly good views and is cheaper (1-831 667 2344). The luxurious **Post Ranch Inn** (Hwy 1, 30 miles south of Carmel; 1-831 667 2200; rooms from $395) and the **Ventana Inn** (1-831 667 2331; rooms from $340) across the highway compete for matching views and inflated prices. At Sunday lunchtime, locals head to the **River Inn** (1-831 667 2700) to listen to jazz and the **Big Sur Pub** (1-831 667 2355) sometimes hosts mariachi bands or guitarists.

For more information on Big Sur, call the **Big Sur Chamber of Commerce** (1-831 667 2100). For state park campground reservations, contact **Reserve America** (1-800 444 7275/www.reserveamerica.com).

Heading east

East Bay

The often-underestimated East Bay has many qualities San Francisco lacks, including a world class university, a growing number of unique restaurants, countless good shops, music venues, better weather and a lot more places to park. There's an increasing trend among young professionals fed up with the high rents and overcrowding of San Francisco to migrate to the cities of the East Bay, a region that extends from the **Carquinez Strait** in the north down to **San Jose** in the south.

The East Bay contains a number of notable cities, including the sophisticated bedroom community of **Walnut Creek**, the tiny million-dollar mansion town of **Blackhawk** and the huge warehouses and live/work lofts of **Emeryville**, housing high-tech engineering firms or struggling artists. The cities with the most distinct personalities, however, are **Berkeley** and **Oakland**.

Oakland

Step-sister to San Francisco, Oakland – named after its forests of oaks – originally thrived on the logging industry, but after 1869 the business brought in by the completion of the transcontinental railroad contributed to its growth and established its place on the map. The population expanded again after the 1906 San Francisco earthquake brought in refugees from that city; today, many of its residents commute to and from work in San Francisco, either by BART or across the Bay Bridge.

For information on the best shops and restaurants in Oakland (including the excellent **Bay Wolf**), *see page 180* **Shops & Services** *and page 129* **Restaurants & Cafés**. Centre of the action is **Jack London Square** (at Broadway and the Embarcadero) named after the famous local author, one of whose haunts was **Heinhold's First and Last Chance Saloon** (56 Jack London Square; 1-510 839 6761). You can take a ferry from Fisherman's Wharf in San Francisco to Oakland's waterfront, which has a lively farmers' market on Sundays between 10am and 2pm. Pack a picnic and head to **Lake Merritt Park** which surrounds Lake Merritt and is one of the most beautiful municipal parks in the US. Nearby is **Children's Fairyland USA** (Grand Avenue, Oakland; 1-510 238 6876), a collection of play settings based on classic nursery rhymes that is said to have inspired Walt Disney to create Disneyland. Oakland also hosts superb theatre, dance, ballet and classical music events (*see pages 224 and 229* **Performing Arts**). For jazz and Japanese, **Yoshi's** at Jack London Square is a popular nightspot: *see page 221* **Nightlife** for more details. For more local information phone the **Oakland Convention and Visitor Bureau** (1-510 839 9000/1-800 262 5526).

Getting there

By car

Head across the Bay Bridge and follow signs for Interstate 580 Downtown Oakland.

By BART

There are three **BART** stops that serve Oakland: 19th Street, Lake Merritt and Oakland City Center 12th Street.

Berkeley

The town of Berkeley is a thriving intellectual community rich with the flavours of politics, culture and cuisine. It's dominated by the sprawling campus of the famous **University of California at Berkeley**, whose students were at the forefront of many of the civil rights protests of the 1960s (*see page 12* **History**). On campus, the **University Art Museum**, **Sproul Plaza**, the **Palaeontology Museum**, the **Bancroft Library** and the impressive **Botanical Gardens** are all worth seeking out. For more information, contact the **Berkeley Convention and Visitor Bureau** (1-510 549 7040/www.berkeleycvb.com).

The best way to see Berkeley is to wander down **Telegraph Avenue;** you'll quickly understand how the free speech movement was born here. There are several outstanding bookshops, including **Cody's** and **Moe's** (*see page 180* **Shops & Services**) as well as unusual restaurants that range from dives to world-class gourmet. **Chez Panisse**, **Oliveto** and **Rivoli** are all worth a trip in their own right (*see page 129* **Restaurants & Cafés**). Also explore the many shops along **Fourth Street**, which combine a mixture of East Bay quirkiness and upscale yuppiness.

For more on local arts and entertainment in Berkeley, *see chapters* **Museums & Galleries**, **Film** *and* **Nightlife**.

Getting there

By car

Head across the Bay Bridge and turn north on I 80, following signs for Berkeley exits.

By BART

Berkeley has **BART** stops at North Berkeley and Berkeley.

The Gold Country

The Gold Rush of 1848-9 lured thousands of adventurers to the foothills of the Sierras to seek their fortune. Most of the early pioneers came through Sutter's Point, which grew into **Sacramento**, California's state capital. It was the centre for the Pony Express and the western terminal for the transcontinental railroad, and much of the history is preserved in the city's many museums. To the east of Sacramento lies Gold Country itself, and a string of quirky old mining towns.

The residents in the tiny Gold Rush town of **Downieville** like to hang out and chat, and chairs filled with locals passing the time of day line the sidewalk. The old gallows still stand next to the jail. Back in the old days, **Placerville** was known as Hangtown and the town's staple oyster omelette is still known as the Hangtown Fry. The town also contains the **El Dorado County Historical Museum** (1-530 621 5865; closed Mon, Tue); and you can take a self-guided tour of the tunnels of the old **Goldbug Mine** (1-530 642 5232; for guided tours, call 1-530 642 5238).

The rolling countryside to the south is more refreshing and the town of **Jackson** has a number of reasonable lodgings and is a good base for touring. Mark Twain wrote his famous story *The Celebrated Jumping Frog of Calaveras County* in **Angels Camp** not far away, and you can visit the cabin where he wrote it.

Getting there

By car

I-80 runs east-west through Sacramento, and I-5 runs north-south. SR 49 is the Gold Country backbone, with Placerville dividing the north from the south.

By train

Amtrak serves Sacramento, but to explore the tiny towns spread out along route 49, you'll need to travel by car. Amtrak's **Coast Starlight Train** connects the area with San Francisco.

By bus

Sacramento is the hub for **Greyhound** buses travelling throughout the state; the company serves most of the region, though its schedule to the Gold Country is infrequent.

Lake Tahoe

At the eastern border of California is the beautiful Lake Tahoe, drawing millions of visitors each year. No one knows how deep the lake actually is; locals call it Big Blue. Flanked by snow-capped peaks most of the year, it has become the Californian playground for skiing, waterskiing, fishing, hiking and legal gambling at a number of casinos that line the main drag in **Stateline**, just over the border in Nevada (the state line cuts north-south through the centre of the lake).

The north end of the lake is a three-and-a-half hour drive from San Francisco (longer if there's heavy snow on I-80, in which case you'll need chains). The other route, via US 50 (which branches from I-80 at Sacramento), leads to the south shore, where hotels are usually packed, either with skiers or gamblers. From March to early November, it's easy to drive the 72-mile (116-kilometre) perimeter of the lake and much of it is serviced by public transport. On the California side are attractions such as the **Sugar Pine Point State Park** (1-530 525 7982), near Meeks Bay, and the **Emerald Bay State Park** (1-530 541 3030), a little further south, which overlooks the bay of the same name.

There are plenty of beaches around the lake: **Sand Harbour**, **Zephyr Cove** and **Camp Richardson** are all on the water. Fed by snow and surrounded largely by mountains, the water is only (barely) warm enough for swimming during August and September. An alternative way to get out on the lake is to book a cruise on the *Tahoe Queen* paddlewheeler out of South Lake Tahoe (1-530 541 3364). Daily scenic cruises are available on this and several other tour boats. The **North Lake Tahoe Chamber of Commerce** (245 SR 28, Tahoe City; 1-530 581 6900) has information on guided tours and where to rent canoes and kayaks.

If you want to hit the slopes, **Squaw Valley** (1-530 583 6985), site of the 1960 Winter Olympics, and **Alpine Meadows** (1-530 583 4232/1-800 441 4423/snow conditions recorded message 1-530 581 8374) are two of the most popular ski areas in the West. Alpine is a bit more family-oriented but boasts the best snow-boarding, while Squaw is glitzier and has more exciting runs. Other ski areas include **Boreal** (1-530 426 3666) whose lower prices attract snowboarders; **Northstar at Tahoe** (1-530 562 1010), which offers excellent beginner slopes; and **Sugar Bowl** (1-530 587 7846), where there's a creaky old gondola that takes you to the base lodge. The **Ski Club Hotline** (1-925 827 4303) has information on Bay Area ski clubs. Ski rental is available at the resorts, but if you're driving, it's cheaper to rent your gear in San Francisco and avoid the queues (*see chapter* **Sport & Fitness**). **Heavenly Valley**'s ski lifts operate for sightseeing in summer (1-530 541 7544).

The **North Tahoe Visitor and Convention Bureau** (1-800 824 6348) has information on where to stay in the north, from resorts to country inns, motels and condo referrals. You'll also find an abundance of cheap motels on the South Shore. Try **Camp Richardson** (2100 Jameson Beach Road, South Lake Tahoe; 1-530 541 1801/1-800 544 1801; rooms from $60), whose lakefront cabins and hotel rooms appeal to an active young crowd and where prices are fairly moderate. The **Kirkwood Ski and Summer Resort** (1377 Kirkwood Meadows Drive, off Hwy 88; 1-800 967 7500; rooms from $65) 35 miles (56 kilometres) south of Lake Tahoe, is a family-oriented resort with many amenities and moderate prices. For more information, contact the **South Lake Tahoe Chamber of Commerce** (3066 Lake Tahoe Boulevard, South Lake Tahoe; 1-530 541 5255).

Truckee, an Old West town about 12 miles (19 kilometres) north of the lake, has board sidewalks and wood-frame shopfronts that make it look like a backdrop for a John Wayne film – if it wasn't for

the tourist trade and growing number of bars and restaurants. The **Passage** at the **Truckee Hotel** (1007 Bridge Street, at Donner Pass Road; 1-530 587 7619) offers wonderful Californian food in a pretty, candlelit dining room. The inn itself offers quaint rooms at moderate prices. The **Squeeze Inn** (10060 Commercial Row; 1-530 587 9814) is a very popular local spot, and its omelette breakfasts (about $6) are delicious.

Donner Memorial State Park (1-530 582 7894), a few miles west of Truckee off SR 80, is named after the Donner family, a pioneer party who perished trying to cross the pass in the winter of 1842. The visitor centre has a short movie detailing their grisly fate (they ended up eating each other).

Getting there

By car

It takes 3½ hours to reach Lake Tahoe from San Francisco, traffic permitting. To reach the north shore, follow I-80 over the Bay Bridge, all the way to Truckee; then take SR 89 to Tahoe City. To reach the south shore, take I-80 as far as Sacramento and then turn off onto US 50 to South Tahoe.

By air

Reno Canyon International Airport, 58 miles (93km) north-east of the lake, is served by several airlines. The **Tahoe Casino Express** (1-800 446 6128) offers daily scheduled transport to South Lake Tahoe.

' or camping in the Sierras, by the shores of **Lake Tahoe**. *See page 261.*

By train

There is an **Amtrak** station in Truckee.

By bus

Greyhound buses stop in Truckee, South Lake Tahoe and Reno in Nevada.

Getting around

By balloon

For a bird's-eye view of the area, a trip with **Mountain High Balloons** (locations in Truckee and Tahoe City; 1-530 587 6922/1-888 462 2683) takes you soaring over the Sierras in style and includes a champagne celebration on landing.

Yosemite

It's enchanting, beguiling, intoxicating, stunning, breathtaking – the descriptions of Yosemite are as superlative as they are numerous. The National Park stretches for more than 1,200 square miles (3,108 square kilometres) of lush forests, alpine meadows, sheer granite cliffs, undisturbed wildlife, hiking trails and campsites. Touristy, 20-mile- (32-kilometre-) long **Yosemite Valley** is packed with traffic, especially in the summer, but its views are indisputably spectacular. For non-valley sites, head for **Crane Flat** and **Tuolumne Meadows** (via SR 120), **Glacier Point** (near Badger Pass) and the **Hetch Hetchy Reservoir** (north of Big Oak Flat). These places are most easily accessible from the hiking trails. If you can, avoid visiting the area in high summer; spring finds the wildflowers in bloom and in winter the untamed majesty of the snowcapped peaks is awesome; many have been famously captured by photographer Ansel Adams – but remember that much of the park is inaccessible during the winter months.

Yosemite is all about views: as you drive into the valley, **El Capitan** is the first dramatic sight, a sheer rock wall 914 metres (3,000 feet) high. You'll get a bird's eye view from **Glacier Point** and a spectacular view of the Sierras from **Tunnel View**. **Mist Trail** is the most popular hiking trail: it's a three-mile (five-kilometre) round-trip to Vernal Falls and a seven-mile (11-kilometre) round trip to Nevada Falls. Standing beneath the pounding water of Yosemite Falls is heart-stopping and an ambitious hike is the round-trip to the top (just under seven miles) to **Yosemite Point**. The hike to Glacier Point is just as challenging, but you can also drive there.

The 16-mile (26-kilometre) round-trip **Half Dome** hike is the one to do if you're hard-core, but not for the fainthearted as you have to cling on to cables for the last half mile because the terrain is so steep. Backpacking is the best way to avoid the crowds and get the most out of Yosemite, but the park has a visitor's quota depending on the season, so make sure you plan ahead. If you really want to leave your fear behind, the **Yosemite Mountaineering School** (1-209 372 8344) offers excellent classes for first-time climbers as well as five-day climbs. Alternatively, you can rent a bike from the **Yosemite Lodge** (1-209 372 1274/www.yosemite.com). However you decide to approach Yosemite, remember to hang your food in a tree to keep the bears at bay: everything you've heard about bears eating picnics is true.

For further information on lodging, camping supplies and grocery shops in Yosemite, contact the visitor centres in **Yosemite Valley** (1-209 372 0299) and **Tuolumne Meadows** (1-209 372 0263). If you're planning on hiking, you'll need a free wilderness permit, which can be picked up at either visitor centre. The **Park Information Service** (1-209 372 0265) can answer all questions about Yosemite and the **Yosemite Association** bookstore (1-209 379 2646) has maps, books, suggested hiking routes, and information on bike rental.

Getting there

By car

There are three routes to Yosemite: SR 41 from the south; SR 140 from the west; and SR 120 from the north-west. SR 120 (the Tioga Road) is the only road across the park and is closed in winter (usually between November and May) due to snow. The recommended entrance to the park is SR 140: from San Francisco, take SR I-580 east to I-205, and connect to SR 120 and then SR 140.

In winter, you'll need to have snow chains for your car; allow four hours from San Francisco in summer, five in winter. Once you reach Yosemite, kiosks and park rangers are stationed at each entrance.

By bus

There is no direct public bus service to Yosemite from San Francisco. However, several companies run private tours, including **Gray Line Tours** (558 9400), which offers one-day ($130) and three-day tours, and **Incredible Adventures** (759 7071/1-800 777 8464; $75 one-day, $169 three-day). **Greyhound** runs buses to Merced, from where you can get a **Via Adventures** bus (1-209 722 0366) to Yosemite.

By train

Amtrak leaves from San Francisco each morning to Merced and Fresno, from where you can catch a bus (*see above*).

Getting around

By car

SR 120 runs the entire east-west length (60 miles/97km) of the park, climbing up to 3,031m (9,945ft) at Tioga Pass (the highest automobile pass in California).

By shuttle

Free shuttle buses operate throughout the year. The most popular is the **East Valley Loop**, which runs about every 10 minutes.

Directory

Directory

For information on abbreviations used in this guide, *see page vi* **About the Guide**.

If you're phoning from outside San Francisco, dial 1 and area code 415 before the numbers listed in this guide, unless otherwise stated. All 1-800 and 1-888 numbers can be dialled free of charge within the US.

Getting around

In a nation where the car is king and trains are those things you wait for at railroad crossings, San Francisco is something of an anomaly: it's one of the few cities in the US where driving isn't a necessity. In fact, a car is often more of a hindrance, which is why most locals leave theirs parked for weeks at a time and commute on foot, by taxi, or by public transport, run by the San Francisco Municipal Railway or Muni (*see page 267*).

TravInfo (817 1717) is a very useful information line for all forms of transport in the Bay Area.

Directory

To & from the airports

San Francisco Airport (SFO)

For more information phone the **SFO transportation hotline** on 1-800 736 2008.

By bus

There are three main options for getting to and from the airport. The cheapest method (and least convenient) is via two SamTrans buses; **KX** and **292**, which run every 30 minutes between the airport's upper level and the Transbay Terminal at First and Mission Streets in downtown San Francisco. Bus **292** runs from 5.27am to 1.19am, costs $1.10, takes an hour and has no luggage restrictions. Bus **KX** runs from 6.01am to 12.50am, costs $3 and takes 30 minutes, but you're restricted to only one small carry-on bag.

There are two more complicated but cheap routes. From outside SFO's North and South terminals, catch a **BX** bus to Colma or **193** to Daly City BART stations ($1.10) and then transfer to a BART train. You can also take the free **CalTrain** shuttle from SFO's North and International terminals to Millbrae Station and then a 24-minute train ride ($2) to the CalTrain Depot on Fourth and Townsend Streets in the Mission district. Do not choose this option if you're travelling alone at night.

For more information on any of these options, phone 1-800 660 4287.

By passenger van/shuttle

Shuttles are a definite step up from busing it. Rates range from $10 to $20 per person (tickets can be bought from the driver) and it's a door-to-door service. Companies include **Lorrie's Airport Service** (334 9000), **SuperShuttle** (558 8500), **Bay Shuttle** (564 3400), **American Airporter Shuttle** (202 0733), **Quake City Airport Shuttle** (255 4899) and **SFO Airporter** (major hotel service only; 495 8404). Ask about coupons or discounted rates for two or more travellers. Most passenger vans leave every 10-15 minutes from the upper level of the airport terminal at specially marked kerbs – follow the red signs that read 'passenger vans' outside the baggage claim area.

Vans run throughout the night but are few and far between in the small hours; if your plane arrives late you may be faced with a long wait or an expensive taxi ride. For your return journey to the airport, book the shuttle at least 24 hours in advance.

By taxi or limousine

The most expensive – but most convenient – option for getting into town may be your only recourse if your plane lands in the wee hours. Expect to pay about $35 plus tip for the 14-mile (22.5 kilometres) trip to the city; be sure to haggle for a flat rate. Taxis are found outside the terminal's baggage claim area in a zone marked with yellow columns.

For limousine service, use the toll-free white courtesy phones located in the terminal or phone **Expresso Limousine** (1-800 675 6654).

Oakland International Airport

Many travellers (and San Franciscans) opt to fly into the tiny Oakland Airport across the Bay. To get to San Francisco using public transport, catch the **Air-BART** shuttle from the airport terminal to the Coliseum/Oakland BART station ($2; you'll need exact change for the perpetually-malfunctioning ticket machines). They run every 15 minutes from the central island outside terminals 1 and 2. Then catch the next BART to San Francisco ($2.75); for schedule information phone 989 2278. This is not a safe option for passengers travelling alone at night.

Other options include a shuttle service (**Super-Shuttle**; 558 8500) or a very expensive taxi or limo ride.

San Jose International Airport

Though it's 60 miles (97 kilometres) to the South, San Jose is becoming the destination of choice for many Silicon Valley travellers. It's a tiny, efficient airport, but more than an hour from San Francisco.

To get to the city from SJIA, take **Santa Clara Transit bus 10** to Santa Clara **CalTrain** station (every 20-30 minutes from 5.26am to 11.21pm; $1.25), then board CalTrain to San Francisco (it runs from 4.51am to 10.30pm, takes about 80 minutes and costs $4.75 at peak hours). Disembark at the end of the line, the Fourth & Townsend station (not recommended if you're travelling alone at night). For more information about CalTrain, call 1-800 660 4287.

Don't take a taxi or limo to San Francisco from San Jose unless you're a wealthy multimedia tycoon.

Major international airlines

For domestic and other international airlines, consult the *Yellow Pages*.

American Airlines
(1-800 433 7300)
British Airways
(1-800 247 9297)
Continental Airlines
(1-800 525 0280)
Delta Airlines
(1-800 221 1212)
Northwest Airlines
(domestic 1-800 225 2525/ international 1-800 447 4747)
Southwest Airlines
(1-800 435 9792)
Trans World Airlines (TWA)
(domestic 1-800 221 2000/ international 1-800 892 4141)
USAir
(1-800 428 4322)
United Airlines
(1-800 241 6522)
Virgin Atlantic
(1-800 862 8621)

Public transport

The best plan for finding your way around the city's transport network is to buy a Muni map (available at most bookshops and drugstores or from the **Visitor Information Center** *page 279*). For information on Muni's route schedules, passes and fares, phone **673 6864**.

Travel passes

If you plan to use Muni often, purchase a one-day ($6), three-day ($10) or seven-day ($15) 'passport', which is valid on all Muni vehicles, including the pricey cable cars.

These are available at the **Visitor Information Center** (*see page 279*); Maritime Market (3098 Polk Street, at Bay Street); Muni headquarters (949 Presidio Avenue, at Geary Boulevard); the Muni ticket booth/police kiosk at Powell and Market Streets; the Muni ticket booth at Hyde and Beach Streets; the **Bay Area TIX** booth at Union Square, and various other locations. A Muni passport also entitles you to discounts at 23 of the city's major attractions. For more information and the location of passport vendors, phone 673 6864.

If you're staying for a while, buy a **Fast Pass** ($35), available at shops around town and valid from the first to the last day of the current month.

Buses

The number one mode of public transport is Muni's creaking fleet of orange and white buses. Spewing smog or sparks as they make their perpetually off-schedule rounds, they are at least relatively cheap and can get you within a block or two of almost anywhere you might want to go.

Fares

Fares are $1 for adults (18-64 year-olds), 35¢ for kids, and travel is free for under fives. Exact change is required (paper money is accepted). Place your change or bills in the automatic toll-taker and ask the driver for a free transfer, which is valid for two changes of vehicle in any direction within 90 minutes.

Bus stops

These are marked by one or more of the following: a large white rectangle painted on a street with a red kerb; a yellow marking on a telephone or light pole; a glass-walled bus shelter; a brown and orange sign listing the bus or buses that serve that route.

Route numbers are posted on the front and rear of the bus (so you know which one you've just missed). On busy lines buses run every five to ten minutes during peak hours. Between midnight and 5am a skeleton crew operates the Owl Service – nine lines on which buses run every 30 minutes.

Outside San Francisco

Bus services that connect to the city include:

AC Transit *(817 1717)*. Alameda and Contra Costa counties and Transbay service between those counties and San Francisco.
Golden Gate Transit *(923 2000)*. Marin and Sonoma counties from Sausalito to Santa Rosa.
Greyhound Bus Line *(1-800 231 2222)*. Long-distance bus routes throughout the US.
SamTrans *(1-800 660 4287)*. San Mateo county with a service to downtown San Francisco and the Hayward BART station.

Muni Metro streetcar

A cross between an electric bus and a cable car, the efficient Muni Metro streetcar (or tram) is used surprisingly rarely by

Cable cars

Brought back to life in 1984 at a cost of more than $60 million, San Francisco's beloved cable cars are without question the most enjoyable ride in town, as the lengthy queues at the turnarounds will attest. There are 44 cable cars in all, 27 of them used at peak times, travelling at a steady 9.5mph on three lines: **California**, **Powell-Mason** and **Powell-Hyde**. The Powell-Hyde line has the most thrills, the best scenery and, consequently, the most tourists; board a few stops up from the turnaround if you don't want to queue. Lines run from 6am to 1am. If you don't have a Muni pass, buy a $2 non-transferable one-way ticket from the conductor on board (children under five go free). Cable car stops are marked by pole-mounted signs showing the cable car symbol; their routes are marked on all Muni bus maps. Hold on tight, or you'll get thrown about as the car lurches around a corner and down a precipitous hill.
See also page 36 **Sightseeing**.

tourists. Six lines (E, J, K, L, M and N) run underneath the downtown area and above ground in the outer neighbourhoods; the recently revived F line is made up of restored vintage streetcars that run along Market Street. Heading from east to west on Market, Muni makes the same stops as BART, but past the Civic Center routes branch off in different directions towards outlying districts such as the Mission, Castro and Sunset. Fares are the same as on the buses and the same passports apply. Lines run between 5am and 10pm. For schedule information, phone 673 6864.

BART (Bay Area Rapid Transit)

Looking more like a ride at Disneyland than a form of public transport, BART is a $5-billion network of four interconnected high-speed rail lines that serve San Francisco, Daly City and the East Bay counties. It's one of the most modern, automated and efficient systems in the world, run by computers at the Lake Merritt station in Oakland. Almost everything – trains, ticket dispensers, entry and exit gates, announcements – is automated. Passengers feed money into a vending machine, which dispenses a reusable ticket encoded with the dollar amount entered. When you reach your destination, the cost of the ride (measured by the distance travelled) is deducted from the ticket as you pass through the exit gate, so don't forget to **save your ticket!** Any remaining value on the ticket can be used towards the next trip.

Though BART is of little use for getting around the city – it only stops at five locations within San Francisco – it's a great way to get an inexpensive tour of the Bay Area, as much of the rail is elevated above the streets. Special excursion-ride tickets allow passengers to ride all the lines for up to three hours, but they must enter and exit from the same station, and travelling during peak hours (7am-9am and 4pm-6pm weekdays) isn't recommended.

BART stations close at around midnight and open at 4am on weekdays, 6am on Saturday and 8am on Sunday. Fares range from $1.10 to $4.70. In downtown San Francisco, four boarding stations are located along Market Street; look out for the blue and white '**ba**' signs and the escalators leading down into the station. You can take bicycles on BART free of charge, except between 6.30am and 9am, and 3.30pm and 6.30pm, Monday to Friday, when they are banned. For more information, phone 989 2278 (1-510 839 2220 for the hearing-impaired).

CalTrain

This commuter line connects San Francisco with San Jose and ultimately Gilroy, 'the garlic capital of the world', passing through Burlingame, Redwood City, Palo Alto, Mountain View, Sunnyvale and the other peninsula cities. It's a famously punctual rail system that runs from 5am to midnight. One-way adult fares range from $1.25 to $6.75 ($5.25 from San Francisco to San Jose); senior, disabled, child and off-peak discounts are available, as is a 10-ride ticket at certain trains. Cyclists can bring their bikes onto cars displaying yellow bike symbols and stow them in lockers at the stations at either end of their trip. For more information, phone 1-800 660 4287 (508 6448 for the hearing impaired).

Ferries

The completion of the Golden Gate Bridge in 1937 marked the end of the ferry route between San Francisco and Marin – until 1970, when the service resumed to take a load off commuter traffic. Used mainly by 'suits' during peak commuting hours, ferries double as wonderful and inexpensive excursions across the Bay and into Sausalito or Larkspur.

For more information, phone the **Golden Gate Transit Ferry Service** (923 2000), which serves Sausalito ($4.80 one way) and Larkspur ($2.85 one way). **Blue & Gold** (tickets 705 5555/recorded information 773 1188) runs a service to Sausalito and various cruises to Alcatraz and Angel Island, all of which leave from Pier 41. Its commuter services to Alameda, Oakland (both $4.50 one-way), Tiburon ($6) and Vallejo ($7.50) leave from the Ferry Building on the Embarcadero. *See also chapters* **Sightseeing** *and* **Trips Out of Town**.

Driving

It's not sensible to rent a car to explore San Francisco. There's no street parking and private parking garages charge up to $12 an hour. Locals honk and curse at you for slowing them down. The steep hills fry your nerves and clutch, and you're more than likely to get a parking ticket – the city's favourite source of revenue. The only reason for renting a car is to explore the Bay Area and beyond.

If you must drive in the city, you should know the following. Unless otherwise posted, the speed limit within the city is 25mph and Californian law requires all occupants to wear seatbelts. Cable cars always have the right of way and should be given a wide berth. When parking in residential neighbourhoods, do not block driveways *even slightly*, or you'll get fined and towed away. When parking on hills, set the hand brake and 'kerb' your front wheels (turn them towards the kerb when facing downhill, away from the kerb when facing uphill) or you'll get ticketed. You must always park in the direction of the traffic.

Parking spaces in San Francisco are as rare as they are tightly regulated: always read the information on the meter and/or all the signs on your side of the block. One missed warning could lead to a towed car, in which case you'll have to take a taxi to the municipal garage, pay $135.50 plus your parking ticket and possibly more in storage fees.

But wait – there's more! Don't park at kerbs painted white, which indicate passenger drop-off zones; blue, which are reserved for drivers or passengers with disabilities; yellow, which are for loading and unloading commercial vehicles; or red, in front of bus stops or fire hydrants. Green kerbs signify parking for 10 minutes only; some yellow and white kerbs are only patrolled during business hours. Infringement could net you a $250 ticket.

Most parking meters accept quarters only. For long-term parking, car parks (public garages) are your best bet in the downtown area, particularly if you're there for more than an hour.

And if you should venture across the Golden Gate or Bay Bridges, make sure you have enough cash to pay the toll on the return trip ($3 for the Golden Gate Bridge and $2 for the Bay Bridge).

On foot

Exploring on foot isn't the fastest way to see the city, but it's the most enjoyable and certainly the most complete. Not until you've peeped into a passing Pacific Heights window, hiked the twisting trails in the Presidio, slurped gelato while strolling through Washington Square park or window-shopped the *panaderias* of the Mission have you truly begun to experience the pleasure of pedestrian San Francisco.

The *Sunday San Francisco Examiner and Chronicle*'s pink-paged Datebook supplement lists more than 20 walking tour companies, whose themes range from strolling noshes and urban hikes to waterfront tours and Castro cruises. In a city with more than its share of frustrated drivers, surly cabbies and behind-schedule bus drivers, pedestrians – for the most part – walk unimpeded, often arriving sooner (and in better physical shape) than their petrol-consuming counterparts.

However, walking the streets of San Francisco does come with inherent risks: impatient drivers tend to separate those on foot into the quick and the dead; electric buses sneak up like silent, hulking ghosts; manic, tattooed bike messengers materialise out of the fog. People double-park in crosswalks. Red-light-running is epidemic.
In the Financial District, pedestrian signals work independently of stoplights. Construction crews, house painters, window-washers, ill-mannered dogs – everyone wants to try to slow a pedestrian's progress.

Don't let them. Seeing San Francisco on foot is the best-kept secret in the city. For our list of recommended walking – and other – tours, *see page 77* **Sightseeing**.

Car rental

A credit card and driver's licence is required when renting a car. There are dozens of rental companies within the city and at San Francisco International Airport, and it definitely pays to shop around. Before you rent a car, make sure your own auto insurance or credit card company covers you; otherwise, you'll need to pay an additional surcharge. Most car rental companies stipulate minimum and maximum age requirements. Carrying insurance is mandatory for all drivers in California.

American Automobile Association (AAA)

150 Van Ness Avenue, between Fell & Hayes Streets, CA 94102 (565 2012/touring information 565 2711/ emergency service 1-800 222 4357). **Open** 8.30am-5pm Mon-Fri. **Map F5**
The fabulous Triple A provides excellent – and free – maps, guidebooks, specific travel routes (TripTiks) and towing services to members of the AAA or an affiliated organisation (such as the British AA or RAC).

Rental companies

National companies usually offer the best deals and service. These include:

Alamo (1-800 327 9633)
Avis (1-800 831 2847)
Budget (1-800 527 0700)
Dollar (1-800 800 4000)
Enterprise (1-800 325 8007)
Hertz (1-800 654 3131)
Thrifty (1-800 367 2277)
Rent-A-Wreck (282 6293).

Local car rental companies include:

Ace (771 7711)
Bay Area Rental (621 8989)
A-One (771 3977).

Car services

CalTrans Highway Information Service

(817 1717). **Open** 24 hours daily.
This automated service (which gives information on the latest highway conditions) is accessed by touchtone telephone only. Alternatively, phone 1-916 445 1534 and listen to a recorded message.

Breakdown services

AAA Emergency Road Service

(1-800 222 4357). **Open** 24 hours daily.
Members (including members of affiliated clubs, such as the British AA) receive free towing and roadside service.

Golden Gate Towing Company

(826 8866). **Open** 24 hours daily.
If you don't have a motorclub card, telephone this company for roadside service. It will also recommend repair shops.

Car parks

Although there are some low-cost garages, prices increase dramatically for long-term parking. Check the posted prices before you park and inquire about discounted (or 'validated') rates and times. If you're parking during the day, keep an eye out for a few large city lots where you can plug a parking meter by the hour; keep a pocketful of quarters handy. Here are some useful, late-opening parking garages.

Ellis-O'Farrell Garage

123 O'Farrell Street, between Powell & Stockton Streets (986 4800). **Open** 5.30am-1am daily. **Map G4**

Embarcadero Center Parking

Between Battery, Drumm, Clay & Sacramento Streets, under Embarcadero Center (398 1878). **Open** 24 hours daily. **Map H3**
At certain hours, having your ticket 'validated' at an Embarcadero establishment will decrease the rate.

Fifth & Mission Yerba Buena Gardens Garage

833 Mission Street, between Fourth & Fifth Streets (982 8522). **Open** 24 hours daily. **Map G/H4**

Japan Center Garage

1660 Geary Boulevard, between Webster & Laguna Streets (567 4573). **Open** 6.30am-2.30am Mon-Thur, Sun; 24 hours Fri, Sat. **Map E4**

Lombard Garage

2055 Lombard Street, between Webster & Fillmore Streets (440 1984). **Open** 7am-midnight Mon, Sun; 7am-1am Tue-Wed; 7am-2.30am Thur; 7am-3am Fri, Sat. **Map E2**

New Mission Bartlett Garage

3255 21st Street, between Bartlett & Valencia Streets (821 6715). **Open** 6.30am-midnight Mon-Thur; 6.30am-2am Fri, Sat; 8.30am-midnight Sun. **Castro/Mission Map Y2**

Portsmouth Square Garage

733 Kearny Street, between Clay & Washington Streets (982 6353). **Open** 24 hours daily. **Map H3**

St Mary's Garage

433 Kearny Street, between Pine & California Streets (956 8106). **Open** 24 hours daily. **Map H3**

Sutter-Stockton Garage

444 Stockton Street, between Sutter & Bush Streets (982 8370). **Open** 24 hours daily. **Map G3**

Union Square Garage

333 Post Street, enter on Geary Street between Stockton & Powell Streets (397 0631). **Open** 24 hours daily. **Map G3/4**

Vallejo Street Garage

766 Vallejo Street, between Stockton & Powell Streets (989 4490). **Open** 24 hours daily. **Map G2**

By bicycle

The San Francisco Department of Parking and Traffic recently designated a grid of major cycle routes across the city, indicated by oval-shaped bike-and-bridge markers. North-south routes employ odd numbers; east-west routes even; full-colour signs indicate primary crosstown routes; neighbourhood routes appear in green and white. Look in the *Yellow Pages* for a map or call **585 2453** for more details.

In addition, two scenic cycle routes – one from Golden Gate Park south to Lake Merced, the other from the southern end of Golden Gate Bridge north to Marin County – invite cyclists to share the road with the ubiquitous automobile.

Bicycles can be hired for around $25 per day or $125 per week. Always lock your bike when you're not riding it, or you'll be sacrificing your damage deposit for stolen goods. For rental companies, *see page 236* **Sport & Fitness**.

By motorcycle

Easy riders should head for **Dubbelju Motorcycle Rentals** (271 Clara Street, between Fifth and Sixth Streets; 495 2774), which can set you up with a Harley or BMW of your choice (from $92 a day), as long as you have a valid driver's licence, credit card deposit and plenty of dollars burning a hole in your pocket. **American Scooter and Bicycle Rentals** (2715 Hyde Street, between North Point and Beach Streets; 931 0234) rents scooters from $50 a day; it's open from 9am until 10pm daily.

Taxis & limos

Getting around San Francisco in a taxi is an interesting experience. Because the city is so small, doing so is moderately cheap – fares average $7-$10, with a base fee of $1.70 and $1.50 for each additional mile. But the trick is finding a cab to hire. If you're downtown on a weekday afternoon, you'll have little problem flagging one from a street corner. If you're in an outlying or shabbier neighbourhood, however, or if it's suppertime, or a holiday, or raining, or the commute is heavy that day, forget about it.

There just aren't enough taxis to serve the city. This aberration is due to a quirky local law limiting the number of cab licences, or medallions. In a city with 25 per cent fewer parking spaces than it has cars in business districts, cabs could easily come to San Francisco's snarled transportation rescue – but they don't: repeated attempts to deregulate the medallion monopoly have been thwarted by the cab lobby.

If you're downtown, head for the big hotels, where most have a queue of cabs lurking nearby. If you're out to dinner or shopping, ask the business to call one for you. If you're in an outlying area, phone early and often to request one and ask the dispatcher how long you'll have to wait. If you wait longer, phone again, or call another company and don't apologise if by the grace of god two arrive simultaneously – just hire the one that came when promised. The cabbie you eventually pick will probably drive like a demon anyway. Major companies include:

Luxor (282 4141)
Veteran's (552 1300)
Yellow (626 2345)
National (648 4444)
De Soto (673 1414)
City Wide Dispatch (920 0700).

Limousine services include:

Robertson's (775 6024)
Pure Luxury (485 1764).

Check the phone directory for more local firms.

Resources A-Z

Business

Convention centres

Moscone Convention Center

Howard Street, between Third & Fourth Streets (974 4000). Bus 12, 15, 30, 45, 76. **Map H4**

Courier services

Local messenger and delivery services include the 24-hour **Corporate Express Delivery Service** (1-510 265 8200/1-800 400 7874), which promises under two-hour delivery to locations within the Bay Area; **Quicksilver Messenger Service** (431 2500), famous for its daring bikers; and **Aero Special Delivery** (1-800 443 8333), which specialises in statewide message and parcel delivery. The **US Post Office** (1-800 222 1811) can deliver overnight to most US cities and, in some neighbourhoods, delivers express parcels on Sundays. Check the *Yellow Pages* for more courier services.

DHL

(1-800 225 5345). **Open** 24 hours daily. **Credit** AmEx, DC, Disc, MC, V.
Website: www.dhl.com

Federal Express

(24-hour 1-800 238 5355). **Open** 8.30am-8pm Mon-Sat. **Credit** AmEx, DC, MC, V.
Website: www.federalexpress.com

UPS

(24-hour 1-800 742 5877). **Open** 9am-5pm Mon-Fri. **Credit** (deliveries by air only) AmEx, MC, V.
Website: www.ups.com

Libraries

Law Library

401 Van Ness Avenue, at McAllister Street (554 6821). Bus 5, 42, 47, 49. **Open** 8.30am-5pm Mon-Fri. **Map F4**
Open to the public for research, but only San Francisco-based lawyers can borrow books and materials.

Mechanics Institute Library

57 Post Street, between Montgomery & Kearny Streets (421 1750). BART Montgomery Street/Muni Metro F, J, K, L, M, N/bus 2, 3, 4, 30, 45, 76. **Open** 9am-9pm Mon-Thur; 9am-6pm Fri; 10am-5pm Sat; 1-5pm Sun. **Admission** *research pass* $10; *weekly pass* $25. **Map H3**
This private organisation offers many of the same data sources as the **Main Library** (*see below*), especially CD-ROM-based search tools, but in only a fraction of the space. Its true source of fame, however, lies in its chess room (421 2258; open 11am-10.50pm, Mon-Fri), which has long been considered one of the best places in town for a quiet game.

San Francisco Main Library

See p58 **Sightseeing** *for listings.*
Offers access to annual reports from most major US and Bay Area corporations; Standard & Poors' evaluations of publicly owned companies; the Dunn and Bradstreet Business Database; Securities and Exchange Commission data on US businesses; US Census information; environmental

Business facts

There are, arguably, only one or two other cities in the US that can match San Francisco's simultaneous qualifications as a world-class holiday and business destination. From recent MacWorld conferences to the 50th Anniversary gala held for the United Nations, conventions annually draw 1.4 million participants to the city. Based on a 1993 survey, city Visitor and Convention Bureau officials say that seven million of San Francisco's 16 million yearly visitors perform at least a day or two for their bosses back home. Of that number, some 5.5 million are in town primarily for business meetings or conventions.

BAY AREA INDUSTRIES

The city and its greater Bay Area zone of influence are home to several of the country's biggest companies. Besides banking (the Pacific Stock Exchange, a Federal Reserve Bank and the California State Banking Department are all based in the city, as are the Bank of America, Wells Fargo Bank and Charles Schwab & Co) the region's list of resident corporations covers industries such as telecommunications, bio-medical technology, law, shipping and clothes manufacturing.

High technology is also big business here. Silicon Valley, the name given to the stretch of the Bay Area from Redwood City to San Jose, is where the first working models of personal computers were developed nearly 30 years ago. Apple Computers, Sun Microsystems, Hewlett Packard, Intel and Advanced Micro Devices are all based in Silicon Valley. The city's revived South Park area has been nicknamed Multimedia Gulch because of the ever-growing number of small companies that fuse computers, graphics, information and art.

compliance records; medical news and statistics. You don't need a library card to do in-house print research or read back-dated newspapers and magazines. The research desk staff are among the best in the business and information professionals – journalists, in particular – often seek their help. Phone **557 4488** for their help.

Message services

American Voice Mail

(1-800 347 2861). **Open** 5am-7pm Mon-Fri; 6.30am-4pm Sat. **Credit** (after first payment only) MC, V.
Confidential voicemail service for unlimited messages, 24 hours a day.

Mail Boxes Etc USA

2269 Chestnut Street, at Scott Street (922 4500). Bus 28, 43, 76. **Open** 9am-6pm Mon-Fri; 10am-4pm Sat. **Credit** AmEx, DC, Disc, MC, V. **Map D2**
Passport photos, mailbox rental, mail forwarding, packing and shipping.

Office services

Copy Central

705 Market Street, at Third Street (882 7377). BART Montgomery Street/Muni Metro F, J, K, L, M, N. **Open** 7.30am-10pm Mon-Thur; 7.30am- 7pm Fri; 10am-6pm Sat; noon-6pm Sun. **Credit** AmEx, MC, V. **Map H3**
One of seven franchised shops specialising in photocopying, printing, binding, fax and overnight mail delivery services. Copy Central is trying to compete with the omnipresent Kinko's and though they're not open 24 hours, they're nearly as successful. Many branches have attached desktop publishing centres, and their staff are friendly and helpful.

Kinko's

201 Sacramento Street, at Davis Street (834 0240). BART Embarcadero/ Muni Metro F, J, K, L, M, N/bus 1, 41. **Open** 24 hours daily. **Credit** AmEx, MC, V. **Map H3**
Kinko's numerous outlets offer an array of business machines for temporary hire; phone 1-800 254 6567 for your nearest branch. Services include on-site use of computers, online facilities, printing, photocopying, fax and overnight mail delivery and collection. Be prepared to queue.

Office Depot

855 Harrison Street, between Fourth & Fifth Streets (243 9959). Bus 27, 30, 42, 45, 76. **Open** 7am-8pm Mon-Fri; 9am-6pm Sat; 10am-8pm Sun. **Credit** AmEx, Disc, MC, V. **Map H4**
Photocopying, printing, desktop publishing, custom stamps, engraved signs, fax devices and every office product on the planet.

Consulates

For a complete list, consult the *Yellow Pages*, or phone directory assistance (411).

Australia *362 6160*
Britain *981 3030*
Canada *1-213 346 2700*
EC Delegation (in Washington, DC) *1-202 862 9500*
Republic of Ireland *392 4214*
New Zealand *399 1255*

Consumer information

Better Business Bureau

(243 9999).
Provides information on the reliability of a company or service and a list of companies with good business records. The Bureau also has referral listings for anything from accountants to zipper repair services, plumbers to auto repair, and is the place to call to file a complaint about a company.

California Attorney General's Office Public Inquiry Unit

(1-800 952 5225).
This office reviews consumer complaints. Call to make a complaint about consumer law enforcement or any other agency.

Customs & Immigration

Standard immigration regulations apply to all visitors, which means you may have to wait (up to an hour) when you arrive at Immigration. During your flight, you will be issued with two forms – an immigration and a customs declaration form – to be presented to an official when you land.

You will need to explain the nature of your visit. Expect close questioning if you are planning a long visit and don't have a return ticket or much money with you. You will usually be granted an entry permit to cover the length of your stay. Work permits are hard to get, and you are not permitted to work without one (*see page 280*).

US Customs allow foreigners to bring in $100 worth of gifts ($400 for returning Americans) before paying duty. One carton of 200 cigarettes (or 100 cigars) and one litre of liquor (spirits) is allowed. No plants, fruit, meat or fresh produce can be taken through customs. For more detailed information, contact your nearest US embassy or consulate.

Any questions about US immigration policies or laws can be answered by calling the bi-lingual English/Spanish **Immigrant Assistance Line** (543 6767; open 9.30am-5pm Mon-Fri).

Disabled travellers

Despite its challenging topography, San Francisco has made its mark as a highly accommodating city for disabled travellers. In fact, California is the national leader in providing the disabled with access to facilities and attractions. Privileges include unlimited free parking in designated (blue) parking stalls and free parking at most metered spaces (a visible blue and white disabled 'parking placard' is required for both), and special prices and arrangements for train, bus, air and sightseeing travel.

In addition, all public buildings within the city are required by law to be wheelchair accessible and have disabled-accessible toilets; most city buses can 'kneel' to make access easier and have handgrips and spaces designed for wheelchair users; most city street corners have ramped kerbs and most restaurants and hotels are either designed (or have been redesigned) to accommodate wheelchairs.

Of course, what a building is supposed to have and what it really has can be two different things, so the wheelchair-bound traveller's best bet is to contact the **Independent Living Resource Center** on 543 6222.

Braille Institute of San Francisco

(1-800 272 4553). **Open** 9am-4pm Mon-Fri.
Volunteers at the institute connect anyone who has sight difficulties with services for the blind throughout the US.

Crisis Line for the Handicapped

(1-800 426 4263).
Open 24 hours daily.
A talk line and referral service offering advice on topics ranging from transport to stress.

Electricity

Throughout the United States, electricity voltage is 110-120V 60-cycle AC. Except for dual-voltage, flat-pin plug shavers, you will need to run any European appliances with an adaptor, available at airport shops, pharmacies and department stores.

Earthquakes

It's unlikely that a major quake will strike during your stay, but for those who believe in being prepared, local lore has it that the safest place to be during a quake is on top of Nob Hill. Check the **United States Geological Survey**'s website at **quake.wr.usgs.gov/** for facts and figures, including hourly-updated maps of recent quakes in California and Nevada.

What to do during a quake

- If indoors, stay there. Keep away from windows and, if you can, get under a sturdy piece of furniture, such as a desk. Steer clear of elevators.
- If outdoors, get into an open area away from anything that might shatter or collapse, such as windows, trees, buildings, bridges and power lines.
- If you're driving, pull over to the side of the road and stop. Avoid overpasses and power lines. Stay inside the vehicle until the shaking has stopped.
- After the earthquake, think before you act. Because gas lines may have ruptured, do not use lighters or candles or light a cigarette. Do not turn on lights or use any electrical appliances.

American Red Cross

(427 8000). **Open** 8.30am-5pm Mon-Fri.
Where to find information on earthquake and disaster preparedness.
Website: www.crossnet.org/ disaster/safety/earth.html

Emergencies

Ambulance, fire brigade or police
Dial **911** (toll-free from any phone booth).

Pacific Gas & Electric Company (PG&E)
(Emergency service 1-800 743 5002/ information hotline 1-800 743 5000). **Open** 24 hours daily.

Poison Control Center
(1-800 523 2222). **Open** 24 hours daily.

Water Department City & County of San Francisco
(Emergency service 550 4911). **Open** 24 hours daily.

Gay & lesbian

Gay & Lesbian Medical Association
(255 4547). **Open** 9am-5.30pm Mon-Fri.
Nearly 2,000 gay, lesbian and bisexual physicians and medical students make up this professional organisation, which publishes guides, holds forums, advocates rights of gay and lesbian physicians and offers medical referrals.

Community United Against Violence
(333 4357). **Open** 24 hours daily.
A counselling group assisting gay, lesbian, bisexual and transgendered victims of domestic violence and hate crimes.

Lyon-Martin Women's Health Services
1748 Market Street, at Valencia Street, between Octavia & Gough Streets (565 7667). Muni Metro F, J, K, L, M, N. **Open** 8.30am-5pm Mon, Tue, Thur, Fri; 11am-7pm Wed. **Credit** MC, V. **Map F5**
Named after two of the founders of the modern lesbian movement in the US, the Lyon-Martin clinic offers affordable health care for women in a lesbian-friendly environment. Phone to make an appointment.

New Leaf
(626 7000). **Open** 9am-5pm Mon-Fri.
A counselling service for gay men, transgendered people, lesbians and bisexuals, that deals with issues ranging from substance abuse to HIV.

Parents, Families and Friends of Lesbians and Gays (P-FLAG)
(921 8850). **Open** 24-hour answerphone.
A helpline offering support for families and friends of gay and lesbian teens and adults.

Health & medical

Clinics

Haight Ashbury Free Clinic
558 Clayton Street, at Haight Street (487 5632). Muni Metro N/bus 6, 7, 33, 37, 43, 66, 71. **Open** 1-9pm Mon; 9am-9pm Tue-Thur; 1-5pm Fri; 24-hour answerphone. **Map C6**
Free primary health care is provided to the uninsured. Speciality clinics include podiatry, chiropractics, pediatrics and HIV testing. You will need to make an appointment.

Planned Parenthood Clinics
815 Eddy Street, between Van Ness Avenue & Franklin Street (441 5454). Bus 19, 31, 42, 47, 49. **Open** 9am-5pm Mon, Wed, Fri; 8.30am-4pm Tue; noon-8pm Thur; 9am-2pm Sat. **Credit** MC, V. **Map F4**
In addition to contraception services and the morning-after pill, Planned Parenthood also provides low-cost general health care services, HIV testing and gynaecological exams.

Quan Yin Healing Arts Center
1748 Market Street, at Valencia Street (861 4964). Muni Metro F, J, K, L, M/bus 6, 7, 26, 66, 71. **Open** noon-6pm Mon, Tue, Thur, Fri; 11am-6pm Wed; 10am-2pm Sat. **Credit** MC, V. **Map F5**
The best centre in town for acupuncture; it also offers herbal remedies, massage, reiki and yoga.

St Anthony Free Medical Clinic
105 Golden Gate Avenue, at Jones Street (241 8320). BART Civic Center/Muni Metro J, K, L, M, N. **Open** drop-in clinic 8.30am-noon, 1-4pm, Mon-Fri. **Map G4**
Free medical services for those with or without insurance. Arrive early.

University of the Pacific School of Dentistry
2155 Webster Street, at Sacramento Street (929 6501). Bus 1, 22. **Open** 8.30am-5pm Mon-Fri. **Map E3**
Supervised dentists-in-training provide a low-cost service. Be warned, though: you'll spend little money for a long time in the chair.

Complaints/referrals

Dental Society Referral Service
(421 1435). **Open** 24 hours daily.
Referrals are made by the Society, based on geographic location and the services desired.

Medical Society
(561 0853).
The Society investigates complaints from those who feel they've been overcharged for medical services.

Physicians Complaint Unit
(1-800 633 2322).
Once a complaint is received by the unit, the process takes up to six months to be sent to the medical board for investigation.

SF Medical Society Referral
(561 0853). **Open** 9am-5pm Mon-Fri.
American Medical Association referrals.

Drugstores (24-hour)

Walgreens Drugstore
3201 Divisadero Street, at Lombard Street (931 6417). Bus 28, 43. **Open** 24 hours daily. **Map D2**
Prescriptions and general drugstore purchases.
Branches: 498 Castro Street, at 18th Street (861 6276); 25 Point Lobos Avenue, at 43rd Avenue (387 0706).

Emergency rooms

You will have to pay for emergency treatment. Contact the emergency number on your travel insurance before seeking treatment and you will be directed to a hospital that will deal directly with your insurance company.
Emergency rooms are open 24 hours a day at:

Davies Medical Center
Castro Street, at Duboce Avenue (565 6060). Muni Metro N/bus 24. **Map E6**

Saint Francis Memorial Hospital
900 Hyde Street, between Bush & Pine Streets (353 6300). Bus 1, 27/cable car California. **Map F3**

San Francisco General Hospital
1001 Potrero Avenue, between 22nd & 23rd Streets (206 8111). Bus 9, 33, 48. **Castro/Mission Map Z2**

UCSF Medical Center
505 Parnassus Avenue, between Third & Hillway Avenues (476 1037). Muni Metro N/bus 6, 43, 66. **Map B/C6**

Helplines & agencies

Aids-HIV Nightline
(434 2437). **Open** 5pm-5am daily.
Crisis hotline offering emotional support.

Alcoholics Anonymous
(621 1326). **Open** 24 hours daily.

California AIDS Foundation Hotline
(863 2437/1-800 367 2437).
Open 9am-9pm daily.
A multilingual hotline that offers the most up-to-date information related to the HIV virus, as well as advice on safe sex, taken from an enormous database of Californian services.

Center for Substance Abuse Treatment
(1-800 662 4357). **Open** 8am-4.30pm Mon-Fri.

Drug Crisis Information
(362 3400/hearing-impaired 752 4189). **Open** 24 hours daily.
Call here if you need someone to talk you through a bad drug trip or want to know the effects of a particular drug, an overdose remedy or how to get into a treatment programme.

Lawyers Committee for Civil Rights, Immigrant & Refugee Rights Project
(543 9444). **Open** 9am-5.30pm Mon-Fri.
Legal services are provided on a case-by-case basis for those seeking political asylum.

Lawyer Referral Service
(989 1616). **Open** 9am-5pm Mon-Fri.
Legal interviewers refer callers to experienced attorneys and mediators for all legal problems, including criminal, business and immigration.

Narcotics Anonymous
(621 8600). **Open** 24 hours daily.

SF General Hospital
(206 8125). **Open** 24 hours daily.
Those suffering from a psychiatric breakdown or looking for someone who has been taken by the police or paramedics for acting out of control should contact this hotline.

SF Rape Treatment Center
(821 3222). **Open** 24 hours daily.
Call here within 72 hours of a sex crime and nurses or social workers will provide counselling and guide you through medical and legal procedures. Patients must be residents of San Francisco or victims of a crime occurring within the city.

Suicide Prevention
(781 0500). **Open** 24 hours daily.
Trained community volunteers lend a sympathetic ear.

Talk Line Family Support
(441 5437). **Open** 24 hours daily.
Trained volunteers counsel children suffering from abuse or parents involved in child abuse and provide follow-up services.

Victims of Crime Resource Center
(1-800 842 8467). **Open** 8am-6pm Mon-Fri; 24-hour answerphone Sat, Sun.
Advises victims of their rights and refers them to local resources.

Women Against Rape Crisis Hotline
(647 7273). **Open** 24 hours daily.
This is the place to find counselling, support and legal service for sexual assault victims and their partners.

Insurance

It's advisable to take out comprehensive insurance cover before arriving: it's almost impossible to arrange in the US. Make sure you have adequate health cover, since medical expenses can be high. *See page 274* **Health & medical** for a list of San Francisco hospitals and emergency rooms.

Left luggage

Airport Travel Agency
(1-650 877 0421). **Open** 7am-11pm daily.
Located at the international terminal of San Francisco airport, this company will store anything from a carry-on piece of luggage to a bicycle.

Liquor laws

California has strict drinking laws forbidding any bar, restaurant, nightclub or store from selling alcohol to minors (under-21s). Even if you look 30, bring ID with you (preferably a driver's licence with photo or a passport) – most nightclubs check ID as house policy. Minors are allowed in some clubs that serve alcohol, but it's a good idea to phone first to check.

A major *faux pas* is having any 'open container' in your car or any public area that isn't zoned for alcohol consumption. Cops will give you a ticket on the spot for walking down the street with a beer in your hand, or even having an empty beer can on the back seat of your car. You don't want to know what happens if you're busted for drunk driving, so don't do it.

Lost property

Property Control
850 Bryant Street, between Sixth & Seventh Streets (553 1377). Bus 27, 42. **Open** 8.30am-4.30pm Mon-Fri.
Map H5
Make a police report and cross your fingers, because the chance of someone returning a lost item is often as good as winning the California lottery.

Public transport
If you have left something on **Muni** transport, phone its lost-and-found office on 923 6168. For **BART**, phone 1-510 464 7090, for **AC Transit** 817 1717, **Golden Gate Transit** 923 2000 and **SamTrans** 1-800 660 4287.

Money

The US dollar ($) equals 100 cents (¢). Coins range from copper pennies (1¢) to silver nickels (5¢), dimes (10¢) and quarters (25¢). Half-dollar and dollar coins do exist, but are rarely used (a new $1 coin is scheduled to go into circulation during the year 2000).

In an attempt to clamp down on forgeries, changes have been made to the design of paper money and new $20, $50 and

$100 bills are now in circulation (the redesign of the $5 and $10 is due to be released soon, though the old bills will remain legal tender). Bills are all the same size and colour and come in $1, $5, $10, $20, $50 and $100 denominations, though the $100 bill is not universally accepted.

Banks & bureaux de change

Most banks are open from 9am to 6pm Monday to Friday and on Saturday for limited hours. Identification is required to change travellers' cheques. Many banks do not exchange foreign currency, so arrive with some US dollars. If you're scheduled to arrive in San Francisco after 6pm, change money at the airport or, if you have US dollar travellers' cheques, buy something in order to get some change. If you want to cash travellers' cheques at a shop, ask first – some require a minimum purchase. You can also obtain cash with a credit card from certain banks but be prepared to pay interest rates that vary daily. Most banks and shops accept travellers' cheques in US dollars.

ATMs/Cashpoints

San Francisco is brimming with Automated Teller Machines (ATMs or cashpoints). Most accept Visa, MasterCard and American Express, among other cards. Almost all ATMs charge a usage fee.

Phone the following numbers for ATM locations: **Cirrus** (1-800 424 7787); **Wells Fargo** (1-800 869 3557); **Plus System** (1-800 843 7587). If you don't remember your PIN number or have somehow de-magnetised your card, most banks will dispense cash to card holders. The most omnipresent bank in the city, **Wells Fargo** (1-800 869 3557), offers cash advances at any of its branches.

Credit cards

You are strongly advised to bring at least one major credit card on your trip. They are accepted (and often required) at nearly all hotels, car rental agencies and airlines, as well as most restaurants, shops and petrol stations.

The five major credit cards most accepted in the US are Visa, MasterCard, Discover, Diners Club and American Express.

Lost or stolen cards

American Express
(1-800 992 3404).
Diners Club
(1-800 234 6377).
Discover
(1-800 347 2683).
MasterCard
(1-800 826 2181).
JCB
(1-800 366 4522).
Visa
(1-800 336 8472).

Lost or stolen travellers' cheques

American Express
(1-800 221 7282).
Visa
(1-800 227 6811).

Exchange offices

American Express Travel Services

455 Market Street, at First Street (536 2600). BART Montgomery Street, Embarcadero/Muni Metro F, J, K, L, M, N/bus 2 to 7, 12, 15, 21, 31, 42, 66, 71, 76. **Open** 8.30am-5.30pm Mon-Fri; 9am-2pm Sat.
Map H3
American Express will change money and travellers' cheques, and offers, for AmEx cardholders only, a poste restante service. Call for details of other branches within San Francisco.

Thomas Cook

75 Geary Street, between Grant Avenue & Kearny Street (1-800 287 7362). Muni Metro F, J, K, L, M, N/bus 2, 3, 4, 30, 45, 76. **Open** 9am-5pm Mon-Fri; 10am-4pm Sat.
Map H3
A complete foreign exchange service is offered here, including money transfer by wire.

Western Union

Phone 1-800 325 6000 to find your nearest branch.
The old standby for bailing cash-challenged travellers out of trouble. Expect to pay a whopping 10% or more commission.

Postal services

Most post offices are open from 9am-5.30pm, Monday to Friday, with limited hours on Saturday. Phone **1-800 275 8777** for information on your nearest branch hours and mailing facilities. Stamps can be bought at any post office and also at some hotel receptions, vending machines and ATMs.

Poste Restante (General Delivery)

Civic Center, 101 Hyde Street, San Francisco, CA 94142 (1-800 275 8777). BART Civic Center/Muni Metro J, K, L, M, N/bus 5, 9, 19, 42, 47. **Open** 10am-2pm Mon-Sat.
Map G4
If you need to receive mail in San Francisco and you're not sure where you'll be staying, have it posted to the General Post Office at the above address. Mail is kept for ten days from receipt and you must present some photo ID to retrieve it.

Western Union

(1-800 325 6000). **Open** 24 hours daily.
Telegrams are taken over the phone and charged to your phone bill (not available from pay phones). You can also get advice on how to get money wired to you and where to pick it up at one of a dozen San Francisco locations. You can wire money to anyone outside the state over the phone, using your Visa or MasterCard.

Public toilets/restrooms

These can be found in tourist areas such as Golden Gate Park and Fisherman's Wharf, and in shopping malls. Otherwise, don't hesitate to enter a restaurant or a bar and ask to use its facilities. In keeping with its cosmopolitan standing, San Francisco has installed 20 self-cleaning, French-designed, Decaux lavatories throughout the high-traffic areas of the city. Keep an eye out for the forest-green commodes (they're plastered with high-profile advertising). Admission is 25¢ for 20 minutes; after that, you may be fined for indecent exposure, since the door opens automatically.

Religion

San Francisco is teeming with temples, whether Baptist or Buddhist, Jewish or Jehovah's Witness, Nazarene, New Age or Satanic. For more places of worship, see the *Yellow Pages*.

Calvary Presbyterian

2515 Fillmore Street, at Jackson Street (346 3832). Bus 3, 24. **Map E3**

First Congregational

495 Post Street, at Mason Street (392 7461). Bus 2, 3, 4, 38, 76/ cable car Powell-Hyde, Powell-Mason. **Map G3**

Glide Memorial

330 Ellis Street, at Taylor Street (771 6300). BART Powell Street/ Muni Metro F, J, K, L, M, N/bus 27, 31, 38. **Map G4**

Grace Cathedral

1100 California Street, at Taylor Street (749 6310). Bus 1, 27/cable car California. **Map G3**

San Francisco online

A selection of sites on the world wide web that relate to San Francisco and the Bay Area. For more on multimedia, *see chapter* **Media**.

Bay Area Backcountry
www.kerygma.com/bab/bab.htm
Places to hike and camp in the San Francisco Bay Area.

Bay Area Transit Information
www.transitinfo.org
Instant online access to transit information.

Bay Guardian
sfbayguardian.com
The *Bay Guardian*'s homepage, updated weekly.

Burning Man
www.burningman.com
Online guide, history and photos of the world's wackiest festival.

Cinema Guide
www.movietimes.com
Bay Area movie times, with film clips, previews and photos.

City Camera
www.kpix.com/live
With cameras perched atop the Fairmont Hotel and in the Presidio.

Classified Flea Market
www.cfm.com
Searchable database published on Wednesdays covering the Bay Area.

Concerts
www.sfbayconcerts.com
What's on at which Bay Area venue.

De Young Museum and Palace of the Legion of Honor
www.thinker.org
Covers two museums and an image base.

Earthquakes
quake.wr.usgs.gov
Current San Francisco and Northern California quake information.

Exploratorium
www.exploratorium.edu
An unmissable site from the hands-on science museum.

Film & Video Festivals
www.filmdependent.com/sffests.html
A comprehensive guide to celluloid festivals, small and large, in San Francisco and the Bay Area.

General Information
sfbay.yahoo.com
An excellent online source, including restaurants, classifieds, traffic reports and an events calendar for the city and the Bay Area.
www.citysearch7.com
Exhaustive, well-researched, daily-updated guide to SF and the Bay Area, plus links to other North American city guides.
www.transaction.net/sanfran/ult/index.html
Easy-to-use general guide, with an alternative bent.

Hostels
www.hostels.com/us.ca.sf.html
A complete list of hostels in San Francisco, with prices, addresses and phone numbers.

Hotel reservations
www.hotelres.com/sfr
Where to make your hotel reservations online.

Lesbian and Gay Freedom Day Parade
www.sfpride.org
Info on the annual festival plus gay/lesbian tourist links.

Mexican Museum
www.folkart.com/~latitude/museums/m_mexsf.htm
Arts and cultural institution in the Fort Mason Center.

Museum of the City of San Francisco
www.sfmuseum.org
A scrapbook of the city's past.

Q San Francisco Magazine
www.qsanfrancisco.com
Gay and lesbian publication.

Randall Museum
www.wco.com/~dale/randall.html
A must for kids.

San Francisco Ballet
www.sfballet.org/
Forthcoming productions and ticket information.

San Francisco Bay Area Ski Connection
www.jaws.com/baski/home.html
Online guide to skiing in Northern California.

San Francisco Bicycle Coalition
www.sfbike.org
Bicycling in SF, discussions and membership details.

SF Gate
www.sfgate.com
The combined San Francisco newspapers, the *Chronicle* and *Examiner*.

San Francisco Giants
www.sfgiants.com
The virtual dugout.

San Francisco 49ers
www.nfl.com/49ers
Strictly for fans.

San Francisco Metropolitan Magazine
www.metroactive.com/sfmetro
A new alternative weekly with an online guide to food, films and fun.

San Francisco Opera
www.sfopera.com
Season schedule, history, tickets and lots of photos.

San Francisco Public Library
sfpl.lib.ca.us
With many additional local resources.

San Francisco Symphony
www.sfsymphony.org
Forthcoming concerts, ticket info and musicians' profiles.

Theatre
www.sfstation.com/theatre/index.htm
SF Station arts and entertainment server includes an excellent theatre section.

Time Out
www.timeout.co.uk
What's on in San Francisco and other cities throughout the world.

Weather
www.sfmuseum.org/alm/wx.html
Including an hourly-updated weather map.

Zeum
www.ybgstudio.org/home.html
An eye-popping site devoted to the new kids' technology museum.

Old St Mary's Cathedral
660 California Street, at Grant Avenue (288 3800). Bus 1, 15, 30, 45/cable car California. **Map G3**

St Boniface Catholic Church
133 Golden Gate Avenue, at Leavenworth Street (863 7515). Bus 5. **Map G4**

St Mary's Cathedral
1111 Gough Street, at Geary Boulevard (567 2020). Bus 2, 3, 4, 38. **Map F4**

St Paul's Lutheran Church
930 Gough Street, between Turk & Eddy Streets (673 8088). Bus 31. **Map F4**

St Vincent de Paul
2320 Green Street, at Steiner Street (922 1010). Bus 22, 41, 45. **Map E3**

Temple Emanu-el
2 Lake Street, at Arguello Boulevard (751 2535). Bus 1, 4, 33. **Map B/C4**

Vineyard Christian Fellowship
627 Turk Street, at Van Ness Avenue (558 9900). Bus 31, 42, 47, 49. **Map G5**

Zen Center
300 Page Street, at Laguna Street (863 3136). Bus 6, 7, 71. **Map F5**

Rented accommodation

Look through the Sunday *Examiner and Chronicle* classifieds or the *Yellow Pages* for apartment or house rentals to get an idea of prices.

American Property Exchange
(1-800 747 7784/447 2000/ ampropex@aol.com). **Open** 9am-5pm Mon-Fri.
Luxury accommodation in condos and apartments (studios start at $2,000 a month) and long-term lets.
Website: www.we-rent-sanfran.com

Metro Rent
(563 7368).
For a fee, you'll get daily updates (even by fax or e-mail) on availability in the area and price range of your choice.
Website: www.metrorent.com

Spring Street
(441 2309).
Refers professionals and graduates to apartments, houses, flats, studios and shared rentals.
Website: www.springstreet.com

Safety

Crime is a reality in all big cities, but San Franciscans generally feel secure in their town and follow one basic rule of thumb – use common sense. If a neighbourhood doesn't feel safe to you, it probably isn't.

Only a few areas warrant particular caution during daylight hours and are of particular concern at night. These include the Tenderloin (east of the Civic Center); SoMa (near the Mission/Sixth Street corner); Mission Street from 13th to 22nd Streets; and in the Hunter's Point neighbourhood near 3Com Park. Golden Gate Park and the Haight-Ashbury should be avoided at night.

Many tourist areas are sprinkled with the city's homeless (the Union Square area, for example), who beg for change but for the most part are harmless. Don't flaunt purses, shopping bags or cameras; avoid walking through dark streets and alleys; try not to look too much like a vulnerable tourist. If you drive and park a rental car, lock all valuables out of sight.

If you are unlucky enough to be mugged, your best bet is to give your attacker whatever he wants then call the police from the nearest pay phone by dialling 911. (Don't forget to get the reference number on the claim report for insurance purposes and travellers' cheques refunds). If you are the victim of a sexual assault and wish to make a report, call the police, who will escort you to an Emergency Room for a check-up. For helplines serving crime or rape victims, *see page 275* **Helplines & agencies**.

Bay Area Model Mugging
Mailing address *Suite 104, 629 Bair Island Road, Redwood City, CA 94063 (1-650 366 3631/1-800 773 4448).* **Open** *office* 10am-5pm Mon-Fri. **Credit** MC, V.
Model Mugging offers courses in which women learn effective defence techniques, using full force against padded male 'attackers'. Classes are held in San Francisco, the East Bay and on the peninsula. There are sessions for teenagers and men, too.
Website: www.bamm.org

Smoking

Smokers may rank as the only group of people not particularly welcome in San Francisco, which has some of the stiffest anti-smoking laws in the US (and possibly the world).

Smoking is banned in ALL public places, including lobbies, banks, public buildings, sports arenas, elevators, theatres, restaurants, bars, offices, shops and any form of public transport. Many small hotels and bed-and-breakfast inns don't allow you to light up either (and, boy, do they get cross if you do).

The recent state-wide ban on smoking in bars has resulted in impromptu smoking rooms outside said establishments. A select few bars cheerfully ignore the law altogether.

Students

Visas & ID cards

To study in the Bay Area (or anywhere else in the US), you must apply for either an **F-1 visa** (for exchange students) or a **J-1 visa** (for full-time students enrolled in a degree programme). Both are valid for the duration of your course and for a limited period afterwards.

Foreign students should have an **International Student Identity Card** (ISIC) as proof of student status. This can be brought from your local travel agent or student travel office. In San Francisco, an ISIC costs $20 at **Council Travel** (530 Bush Street, between Grant Avenue and Stockton Street; 421 3473) or **STA** (51 Grant Avenue, between Market and Geary Streets; 391 8407) – you need proof of studenthood, ID and a passport-size photo. Both also offer student discounts.

Accommodation

Cheap short-term accommodation is limited in San Francisco. However, both full- and part-time students at Berkeley can live in dorms or use the useful student housing information service (the **Community Living Office**, 1-510 642 3642) to find off-campus lodgings. *See also chapter* **Accommodation**.

Central YMCA

220 Golden Gate Avenue, CA 94102, at Leavenworth Street (885 0460/ fax 885 5439). BART Civic Center/Muni Metro F, J, K, L, M, N/bus 5, 19, 31. **Rates** *shared room* $27.29; *private room* $48.38. **Credit** MC, V. **Map G4**

A YMCA open to men and women, though the grim Tenderloin environment may be enough to encourage you to look elsewhere.

Telephones

The phone system in San Francisco is reliable and, at least for local calls, cheap. Pay phones only accept nickels, dimes and quarters, but check for dialling tone before you start feeding them your change. Local calls cost 35¢ and the price rises as the distance between callers increases (an operator or recorded message will tell you how much to add).

Long-distance, particularly overseas, calls are best paid with a rechargeable, pre-paid phonecard ($6-$35) available from many stores and vending machines. You can also use your MasterCard with AT&T (1-800 225 5288), MCI (1-800 532 8045) or Sprint (1-800 877 4646).

Telephone directories are divided into *Yellow Pages* (classified) and *White Pages* (business and residential). These directories are available at most public phones and in hotels. Besides phone information, they contain a wealth of information for the traveller, including area codes, event calendars, park facilities, post office addresses and city zip codes. If you can't find one in the phone booth you're using, dial **411** (directory assistance) and ask for your listing by name.

Operator assistance dial 0.
Emergency (police, ambulance, fire) dial 911.
Local directory enquiries dial 411.
Long-distance directory enquiries dial 1 + area code + 555 1212.
Toll-free numbers generally start with 1-800 or 1-888, while pricey **pay-per-call** lines (usually phone-sex numbers) start with 1-900; don't confuse them.

Area codes

San Francisco and Marin 415
Oakland and Berkeley 510
The peninsula cities 650
San Jose 408
Wine Country (Napa, Sonoma and Mendocino counties) 707

International calls

Dial **011** followed by the country code. If you need operator assistance with international calls, dial **00**.

UK 44
Australia 61
New Zealand 64
Germany 49
Japan 81

Direct dial calls

If you are dialling outside your area code, dial 1 + area code + phone number; an operator or recording will tell you how much money to add.

Collect calls

For collect calls or when using a phone card, dial 0 + area code + phone number and listen for the operator or recorded instructions. If you are completely befuddled, just dial 0 and plead your case with the operator.

Time & dates

San Francisco is on **Pacific Standard Time**, which is three hours behind Eastern Standard Time (New York) and eight hours behind Greenwich Mean Time (Britain). Daylight Savings Time (which runs almost concurrent with British Summer Time) runs from the first Sunday in April, when the clocks are rolled ahead one hour, to the last Sunday in October. Going from the west to east coast, Pacific Time is one hour behind Mountain Time (Arizona to Alberta), two hours behind Central Time (Texas to Manitoba) and three hours behind Eastern Time.

In the US, dates are written in the order of month, day, year: therefore 2.5.98 is the fifth of February, not the second of May.

Tipping

Unlike in Europe, tipping is a way of life in the US: many locals in service industries rely on gratuities as part of their income, so you should tip accordingly. In general, tip bellhops and baggage handlers ($1-$2 a bag); cab drivers, waiters and waitresses, hairdressers, and food delivery people (15-20% of the total tab); valets ($2-$3); and counter staff (from 25¢-10% of the order, depending on the size of it). In restaurants you should tip at least 15-20% of the total bill; most will automatically add this to the bill for a table of six or more. If you get good service, leave a good tip; if you get bad service, leave little and tip the management – with words.

Tourist information

Visitor Information Center

Lower level of Hallidie Plaza, corner of Market & Powell Streets (391 2000). BART Powell Street/Muni Metro J, K, L, M, N/bus 6, 7, 8, 9, 21, 26, 27, 31, 66, 71. **Open** 9am-5pm Mon-Fri; 9am-3pm Sat, Sun. **Map G4**

You won't find any parking here, but you will find tons of free maps, brochures, coupons and advice. For a 24-hour recorded message listing daily events and activities or to request free information about hotels, restaurants and shopping, phone the number above. Or send a postcard with your address to PO Box 429097, San Francisco, CA 94102, USA.
Website: www.sfvisitor.org

San Francisco Convention and Visitor Bureau

Suite 900, 201 Third Street, at Howard Street (974 6900). BART Montgomery Street/Muni Metro J, K, L, M, N/bus 12, 15, 30, 45, 76. **Open** 8.30am-5pm Mon-Fri. **Map H4**

Free information on life's essentials: hotels, restaurants and shopping.

Out of town

Marin County Convention and Visitor Bureau

1013 Larkspur Landing Circle, Larkspur (499 5000). **Open** 9am-5pm Mon-Fri.

Oakland Convention and Visitor Bureau

Suite 3214, 550 Tenth Street, at Broadway, Oakland (1-510 839 9000). **Open** 8.30am-5pm Mon-Fri.

San Jose Convention and Visitors Bureau

150 W San Carlos Street, at Market Street, San Jose (1-408 283 8833). **Open** 8am-5.30pm Mon-Fri; 11am-5pm Sat, Sun.

Work permits

It's difficult for foreigners to find work in the US. For you to work legally, a US company must sponsor you for an **H-1 visa**, which enables you to work in the country for five years. For the H-1 to be approved, your employer must convince the Immigration Department that no American is qualified to do the job as well as you.

Students, however, have a much easier time. Your student union should have information on US working holidays. For information on studying over the summer, contact the **Council on International Education Exchange** (CIEE), Work Exchanges Dept,

Where to study

The California higher education system operates as a hierarchy, starting with publicly funded community colleges and city colleges at the lower end of the scale, followed by California State Universities, which cater primarily to undergraduates and do not grant doctorates, and, at the top, the University of California establishments, which tend to be formal, research-oriented universities with rigorous entry requirements. There are also many private – and expensive – universities such as Stanford and USF (University of San Francisco).

In general, US universities are much more flexible about part-time studying than their European counterparts. Each university has a different definition of part-time requirements. Non English-speaking students might have to pass a TOEFL (Test of English as a Foreign Language) exam and most students have to show proof of financial support.

STUDENT ACTIVISM

University life in San Francisco and the Bay Area today reflects a wide mix of students, scenes and schools, and the central tenet seems to be that a once-searing liberal hotbed has cooled. In the 1960s during the civil rights protests, Berkeley was the site of the largest arrest in state history, an 800-student skirmish that resulted in the undergraduate occupation of Sproul Hall. Students at San Francisco State shut their own campus down protesting against the war in Vietnam. Though flashes of this radical mentality have ignited during certain recent events – the wars in Iraq and Kosovo among them – students rarely get up in arms anymore. Instead, they're mostly concerned with procuring a degree that will afford them a comfortable lifestyle.

The colleges

Academy of Art College

79 New Montgomery Street, CA 94105, between Mission & Market Streets (274 2200). BART Montgomery Street/Muni Metro F, J, K, L, M, N/bus 2, 3, 4, 5, 9, 30, 66, 71, 76. **Map H3**

Foreign students flock to this visual arts college, with satellite campuses all over the city, offering practical graduate and post-graduate courses in fine arts, history and graphic design.

Website: www.academyart.edu

California College of Arts and Crafts

450 Irwin Street, CA 94107, between 8th & Wisconsin Streets (703 9523). Bus 19, 22. **Map H6**.

With campuses in Oakland and San Francisco, the CCAC specialises in architectural studies, fine arts and design.

Website: www.ccac-art.edu

City College of San Francisco

50 Phelan Avenue, CA 94112, at Ocean Avenue (main switchboard 239 3000/international students 239 3837). Muni Metro J, K, M/bus 15, 29, 36, 43, 49.

The largest community college in the US, City teaches more than 80 subjects on its eight campuses and 150 satellite sites. It's the most affordable place to study in the city and a good choice for a foreign language or computer class over the summer.

Website: www.ccsf.cc.ca.us

Mills College

5000 MacArthur Boulevard, Oakland, CA 94613 (undergraduate admissions 1-800 876 4557/graduate admissions 1-510 430 3309). BART Coliseum, then AC Transit bus 57, 58 to main entrance at Richards Gate/bus N from Transbay Terminal to Richards Gate.

A beautifully-set, prestigious liberal women's college in Oakland, founded in 1852. Mills offers excellent MFA courses in art and creative writing.

Website: www.mills.edu

205 East 42nd Street, New York, NY10017, USA (www.ciee.org). *See also page 278* **Students**.

Visas

Under the Visa Waiver Scheme, citizens of the UK, Japan and all West European countries (except for Ireland, Portugal, Greece and the Vatican City) do not need a visa for stays in the United States of less than 90 days (business or pleasure). Travellers are required to have a passport that is valid for the full 90-day period and a return or open standby ticket.

Canadians and Mexicans do not need visas but must have legal proof of their citizenship. All other travellers must have visas. Full information and visa application forms can be obtained from your nearest US embassy or consulate. In general, it's a good idea to send in your application at least three weeks before you plan to travel. Visas required more urgently should be applied for via the travel agent booking your ticket.

For further information on visa requirements in the UK, phone the US Embassy Visa Information Line.

US Embassy Visa Information Line

(Recorded information in the UK 0891 200 290).

San Francisco Art Institute

800 Chestnut Street, CA 94133, between Jones & Leavenworth Streets (771 7020/1-800 345 7324). Bus 30, 42/cable car Powell-Hyde or Powell-Mason. **Map F2**

A hip and prestigious art school, offering the spectrum in fine arts including painting, film, photo, sculpture and new genres. Expensive but well-respected, SFAI has a good reputation for fostering one-on-one apprenticeships for its students. Its student exhibitions are legendary.

Website: www.sfai.edu

San Francisco Conservatory of Music

1201 Ortega Street, CA 94122, at 19th Avenue (564 8086). Bus 28.

Full- and part-time students study music at this small, independent conservatory, known for its excellent faculty and high standards.

Website: www.sfcm.edu

San Francisco State University

1600 Holloway Avenue, CA 94132, at 19th Avenue (admissions 338 1113). Muni Metro M/bus 17, 18, 26, 28, 29.

Like all publicly funded California schools, SFSU is trying desperately to do more with less resources. It's the largest in the city, with 27,000 students, and good for creative writing, business, ethnic studies and any number of engineering disciplines. But be patient: undergrad classes are always full and many potential students are turned away at the beginning of each semester. As a result, it can take five or six years to complete a degree.

Website: www.sfsu.edu

Stanford University

Stanford, CA 94305. CalTrain to Palo Alto, then free Marguerite shuttle to campus (graduate admissions 1-650 723 4291/ undergraduate admissions 1-650 723 2091).

A late nineteenth-century campus near Palo Alto, this private college is out of many students' league, with tuition, room and board costing about $31,500 a year. Academically highly competitive, Stanford is known for its business, law and medicine curricula.

Website: www.stanford.edu

UC Berkeley

Office of Undergraduate Admissions, 110 Sproul Hall, UC Berkeley, CA 94720-5800 (graduate admissions 1-510 642 7404/undergraduate admissions 1-510 642 3175 /international students 1-510 642 3246). BART Berkeley.

The oldest in the nine-campus University of California system, Berkeley (called 'Cal' by locals) attracts some 30,000 students, including 9,000 postgrads. Famous for law and engineering, Berkeley also runs a controversial nuclear research lab in Livermore, an East Bay suburb.

Website: www.berkeley.edu

UC Berkeley Extension

English Language Programme, 55 Laguna Street, CA 94102, between Haight & Market Streets (course information & registration 1-510 642 4111). Muni Metro F/bus 6, 7, 66, 71. **Map F5**

Berkeley Extension in San Francisco and other Bay Area sites offers night and weekend courses in such subjects as film, the Internet, writing and women's studies. Classes are offered for working adults for college credits, but not for degrees.

Website: www.unex.berkeley.edu

University of California, San Francisco

400 Parnassus Avenue, CA 94143, at Fourth Avenue (476 9000). Muni Metro N/bus 6, 43, 66. **Map B6**

A top-notch health and sciences university with schools of medicine, dentistry, pharmacy and nursing. UCSF also operates one of the best and least-expensive clinics in the city for good health care. Admission to the school is rigorous but not impossible.

Website: www.ucsf.edu

University of San Francisco

2130 Fulton Street, CA 94117, at Masonic Avenue (admissions 422 6563/financial aid 422 6303). Bus 5, 31, 43. **Map C/D5**

One of 28 Jesuit universities and colleges in the US, with a pleasant campus near the Haight district, USF has reputable business, communication arts and law programmes. The school has around 8,000 students, about half of whom are postgrads. International students make up 10% of the student body and must show proof of financial support.

Website: www.usfca.edu

Further Reading

Fiction & poetry

Alice Adams: *The Last Lovely City: Stories.* Most recent short-fiction collection from this late SF writer.
Francisco X Alarcon: *Body in Flames (Cuerpo en Llamas).* Collection of poetry in English and Spanish from leading Chicano/Latino literary activist.
Ambrose Bierce: *Can Such Things Be?* Tales of horror and the downright horrible.
Marci Blackman, Trebor Healey (eds): *Beyond Definition: New Writing from Gay & Lesbian San Francisco.* Poetry and fiction from a cross-section of queer SF.
Ethan Canin: *For Kings and Planets.* The latest novel by the San Francisco author of *Emperor of the Air* and *The Palace Thief.*
Allen Ginsberg: *Howl and Other Poems.* The rant that caused all the fuss.
Dashiell Hammett: *The Maltese Falcon.* One of the greatest detective novels, in a dark and dangerous San Francisco.
Bret Harte: *Selected Stories and Sketches.* Adventurous tales from the gold-rush era.
Jack Kerouac: *On the Road, Desolation Angels, The Dharma Bums.* Drugs and sex in San Francisco and around the world, from the most famous Beat of them all.
Maxine Hong Kingston: *The Woman Warrior.* Childhood and family history of a Chinese-American.
Jack London: *Tales of the Fish Patrol, John Barleyworn.* Early works, set in London's native city.
Armistead Maupin: *Tales of the City* (6 volumes). Witty soap opera following the lives and loves of a group of San Francisco friends.
Frank Norris: *McTeague.* Cult classic of the 1890s: working-class life and loss set in unromanticised Barbary Coast days.
Thomas Pynchon: *The Crying of Lot 49, Vineland.* Funny, wild novels set in Northern California.
John Steinbeck: *East of Eden, The Grapes of Wrath.* Grim tales of California in the Depression.
Amy Tan: *The Joy Luck Club.* Exploration of the lives of several generations of Chinese and Chinese-American women.
Mark Twain: *The Celebrated Jumping Frog of Calaveras County, Roughing It.* Brilliant tales of San Francisco and early California.
Tom Wolfe: *The Electric Kool-Aid Acid Test, The Pump House Gang.* Alternative life-styles in trippy, hippy, 1960s California.

Non-fiction

Walton Bean: *California: An Interpretive History.* Anecdotal account of California's shady past.
James Brook, Chris Carlsson, Nancy J Peters (eds): *Reclaiming San Francisco History, Politics, Culture.* A recent collection of essays about the city's contrarian spirit.
California Coastal Commission: *California Coastal Access Guide.* Guide to the coastal regions.
Po Bronson: *The Nudist on the Late Shift.* Unblinking treatise on the Silicon Valley scene.
Carolyn Cassady: *Off the Road: My Years with Cassady, Kerouac and Ginsberg.* Not the most enlightened of feminism, but an interesting alternative examination of the Beats.
Randolph Delehanty: *The Ultimate Guide: San Francisco.* Meticulously researched compendium of 13 walking tours through the city.
Joan Didion: *Slouching Towards Bethlehem, The White Album.* Brilliant essays examining California in the past couple of decades.
Timothy W Drescher: *San Francisco Bay Area Murals.* A well-resourced book with plenty of maps and 140 photographs.
Lawrence Ferlinghetti & Nancy J Peters: *Literary San Francisco.* One of the better accounts of the city's literary pedigree.
Robert Greenfield: *Dark Star: An Oral Biography of Jerry Garcia.* The life and (high) times of the Grateful Dead's late frontman.
Don Herron: *The Literary World of San Francisco.* Vital and precise account of the city's literary history.
Peter Lloyd: *San Francisco: A Guide to Recent Architecture.* A miniature guide to the city's newest buildings – perfect for a pocket.
Malcolm Margolin: *The Ohlone Way.* A cultural history of the Bay Area's original inhabitants.
John Miller (ed): *San Francisco Stories: Great Writers on the City.* Contributions by Herb Caen, Anne Lamott, Amy Tan, Ishmael Reed and many others.
John Miller & Tim Smith (eds): *San Francisco Thrillers.* Crimes and local mysteries from Alfred Hitchcock, Jim Thompson and others.
Ray Mungo: *San Francisco Confidential.* A gossipy look behind closed doors.
John Plunkett & Barbara Traub (eds): *Burning Man.* Photo-heavy manual to the po-po-mo festival.
Joel Selvin: *San Francisco: The Magical History.* Tour of the sights and sounds of the city's pop music history by the *Chronicle*'s music critic.
Randy Shilts: *The Mayor of Castro Street.* On Harvey Milk and the development of gay politics.
John Snyder: *San Francisco Secrets: Fascinating Facts About the City by the Bay.* Amusing collection of city trivia, with facts and figures galore.
Sally Socolich: *Bargain Hunting in the Bay Area.* A must for shop-aholics. Now in its 12th edition.
Gertrude Stein: *The Making of Americans.* Autobiographical work that includes an account of her early childhood in Oakland.
Robert Louis Stevenson: *An Inland Voyage, The Silverado Squatters.* Autobiographical narratives describing the journey from Europe to western America.
Ronald Takaki: *Strangers from a Different Shore: A History of Asian Americans.* A hefty survey of Asian-American immigration in North America.

Index

Note: *page numbers in bold refer to key information on the topic; italics indicate illustrations.*

Advertisers' Index

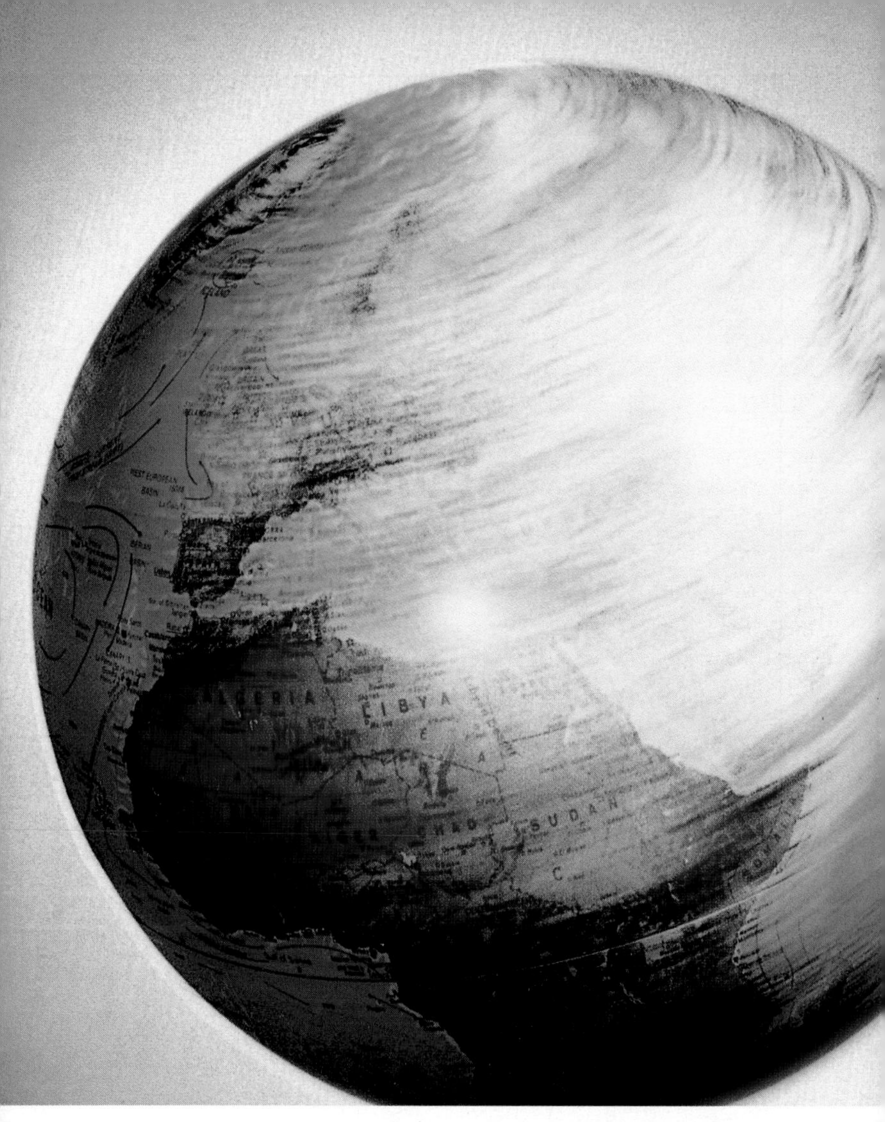

Maps

Downtown San Francisco
PIER 39
Blue & Gold Ferry Terminal
Aquatic Park
Fisherman's Wharf
Passenger Ship Terminal
San Francisco Bay
Fort Mason
National Maritime Museum
The Cannery
Ghirardelli Square
Jefferson
Beach
North Point
Bay
Embarcadero
Francisco
Chestnut
SF Art Institute
Lombard
Greenwich
Filbert
Union
Green
Vallejo
Broadway
Pacific
Jackson
Washington
Clay
Sacramento
California
Columbus
Cable Car
Telegraph Hill
Coit Tower
Washington Square
Russian Hill
North Beach
Hwy 101
Golden Gate Ferries to Marin County
Blue & Gold Ferries to Marin County & Vallejo
Golden Gate Transit to Embarcadero Station & Transbay Terminal
Golden Gate Transit to Civic Center Station & Transbay Terminal
Jackson Square
Chinese Hospital
Chinatown
Cable Car Museum
Chinese Recreation Center
Portsmouth Square
Nob Hill
US Customs
Golden Gateway Center
Drumm
Airporter Airport Express Bus Stop
Justin Herman Plaza
Transbay Tube
Blue & Gold Ferries to the East Bay
Ferry Terminal
Ferry Building
Embarcadero Center
Lafayette Park
Grace Cathedral
Masonic Auditorium
Larkin
Hyde
Powell
Stockton
Grant
Kearny
Montgomery
Sansome
Battery
Front
Davis
Embarcadero
San Francisco Oakland

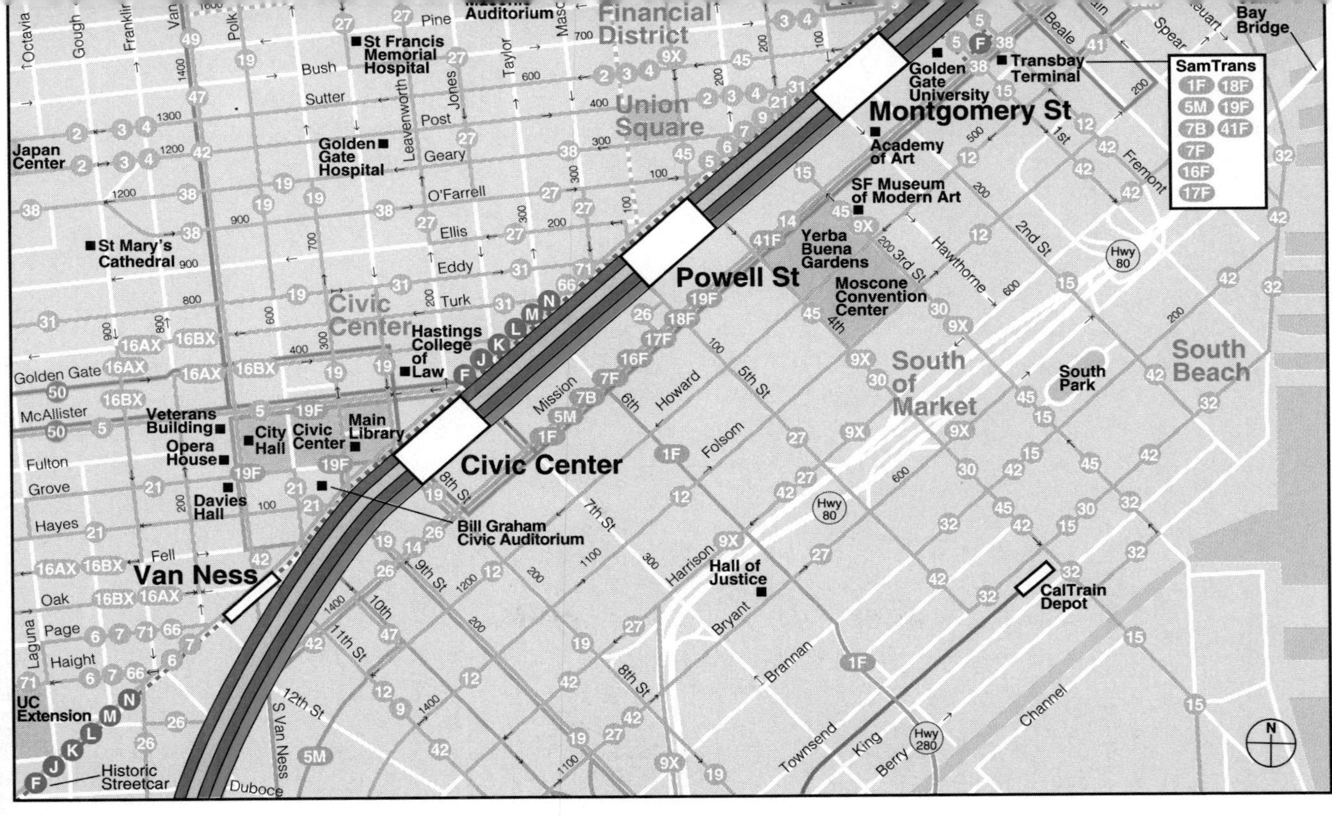
SamTrans
1F 18F
5M 19F
7B 41F
7F
16F
17F
Bay Bridge
Montgomery St
Powell St
Civic Center
Van Ness
Financial District
Union Square
South Beach
South of Market
Civic Center
Transbay Terminal
Golden Gate University
Academy of Art
SF Museum of Modern Art
Yerba Buena Gardens
Moscone Convention Center
South Park
CalTrain Depot
Hall of Justice
Bill Graham Civic Auditorium
Hastings College of Law
Main Library
Civic Center
City Hall
Davies Hall
Opera House
Veterans Building
St Mary's Cathedral
St Francis Memorial Hospital
Golden Gate Hospital
Japan Center
UC Extension
Historic Streetcar
Beale
Spear
Fremont
1st
2nd St
3rd St
4th
5th St
6th
7th St
8th St
9th St
10th
11th St
12th St
Hawthorne
Howard
Folsom
Harrison
Bryant
Brannan
Townsend
King
Berry
Channel
Mission
S Van Ness
Duboce
Pine
Bush
Sutter
Post
Geary
O'Farrell
Ellis
Eddy
Turk
Golden Gate
McAllister
Fulton
Grove
Hayes
Fell
Oak
Page
Haight
Laguna
Octavia
Gough
Polk
Leavenworth
Jones
Taylor
Hwy 80
Hwy 280

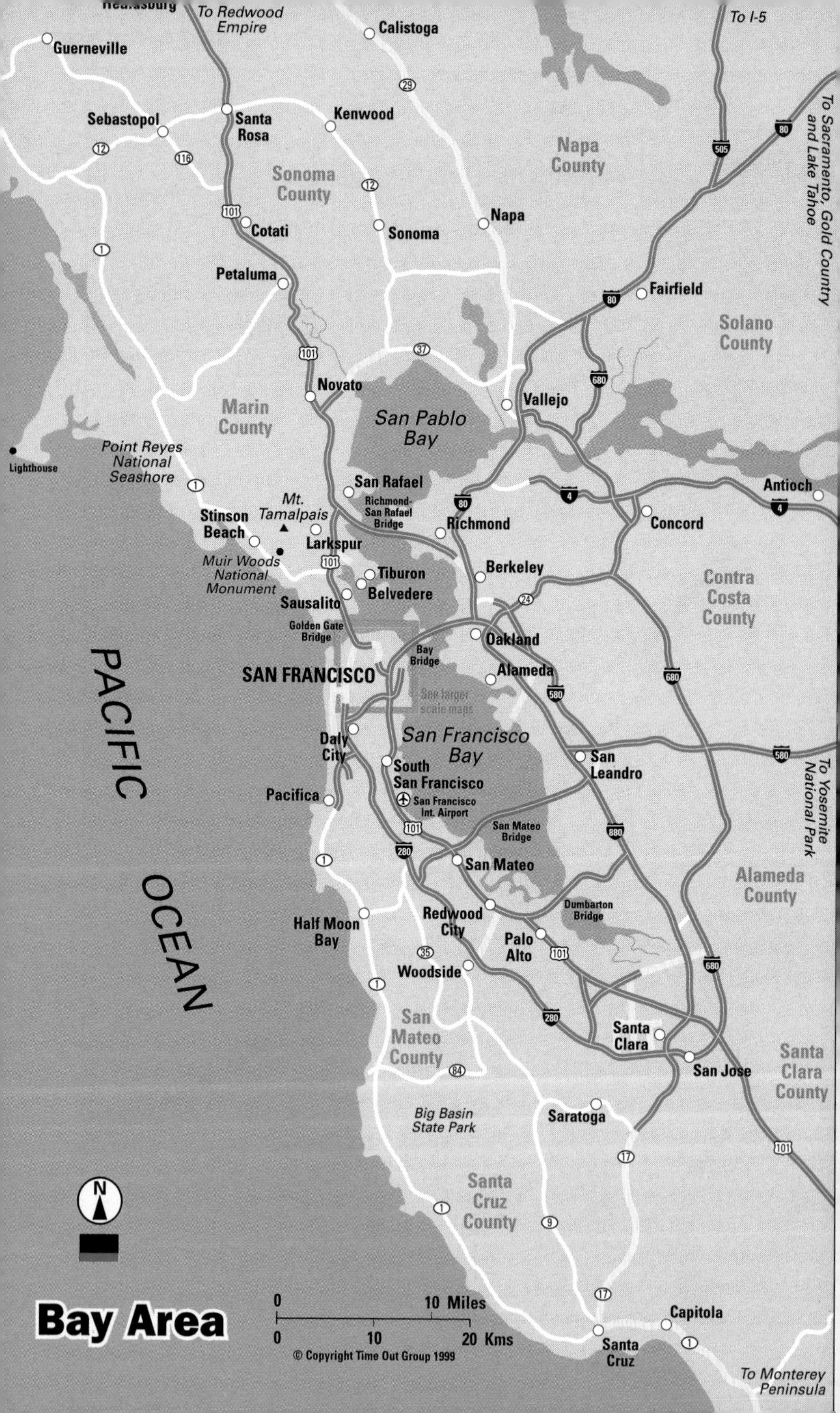

To Redwood Empire
Calistoga
To I-5
Guerneville
To Sacramento, Gold Country and Lake Tahoe
Sebastopol
Santa Rosa
Kenwood
Sonoma County
Napa County
Cotati
Sonoma
Napa
Petaluma
Fairfield
Solano County
Novato
Vallejo
Marin County
San Pablo Bay
Point Reyes National Seashore
Lighthouse
San Rafael
Richmond-San Rafael Bridge
Antioch
Mt. Tamalpais
Stinson Beach
Richmond
Concord
Larkspur
Muir Woods National Monument
Berkeley
Tiburon
Belvedere
Contra Costa County
Sausalito
Golden Gate Bridge
Oakland
Bay Bridge
PACIFIC OCEAN
SAN FRANCISCO
Alameda
See larger scale maps
San Francisco Bay
Daly City
San Leandro
To Yosemite National Park
South San Francisco
Pacifica
San Francisco Int. Airport
San Mateo Bridge
San Mateo
Alameda County
Dumbarton Bridge
Redwood City
Half Moon Bay
Palo Alto
Woodside
San Mateo County
Santa Clara
San Jose
Santa Clara County
Big Basin State Park
Saratoga
Santa Cruz County
Bay Area
0 10 Miles
0 10 20 Kms
© Copyright Time Out Group 1999
Capitola
Santa Cruz
To Monterey Peninsula

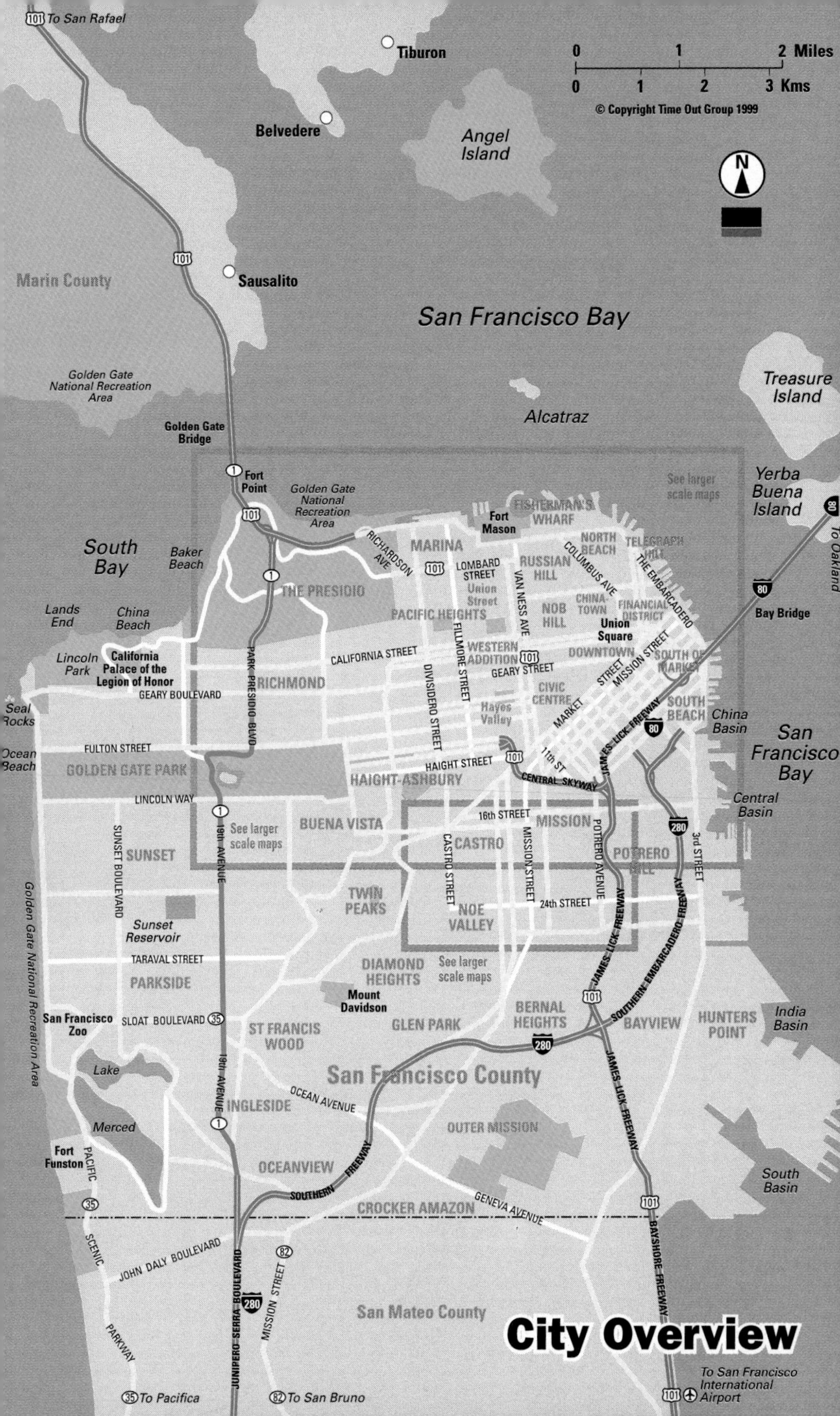

City Overview
To San Rafael
Tiburon
Belvedere
Angel Island
Marin County
Sausalito
San Francisco Bay
Golden Gate National Recreation Area
Golden Gate Bridge
Treasure Island
Alcatraz
Yerba Buena Island
To Oakland
Fort Point
Golden Gate National Recreation Area
South Bay
Baker Beach
Fort Mason
Fisherman's Wharf
Marina
North Beach
Telegraph Hill
Russian Hill
The Presidio
Nob Hill
Chinatown
Financial District
Union Square
Bay Bridge
Pacific Heights
Lands End
China Beach
Lincoln Park
California Palace of the Legion of Honor
Western Addition
Downtown
South of Market
Richmond
Civic Centre
Hayes Valley
South Beach
China Basin
Seal Rocks
Ocean Beach
Golden Gate Park
Haight-Ashbury
Buena Vista
Castro
Mission
Potrero Hill
Central Basin
Sunset
Twin Peaks
Noe Valley
Sunset Reservoir
Parkside
Diamond Heights
Mount Davidson
Glen Park
Bernal Heights
Bayview
Hunters Point
India Basin
San Francisco Zoo
St Francis Wood
San Francisco County
Lake Merced
Ingleside
Outer Mission
Fort Funston
Oceanview
Crocker Amazon
South Basin
San Mateo County
Golden Gate National Recreation Area
See larger scale maps
To Pacifica
To San Bruno
To San Francisco International Airport
0 1 2 Miles
0 1 2 3 Kms
N

Street Index

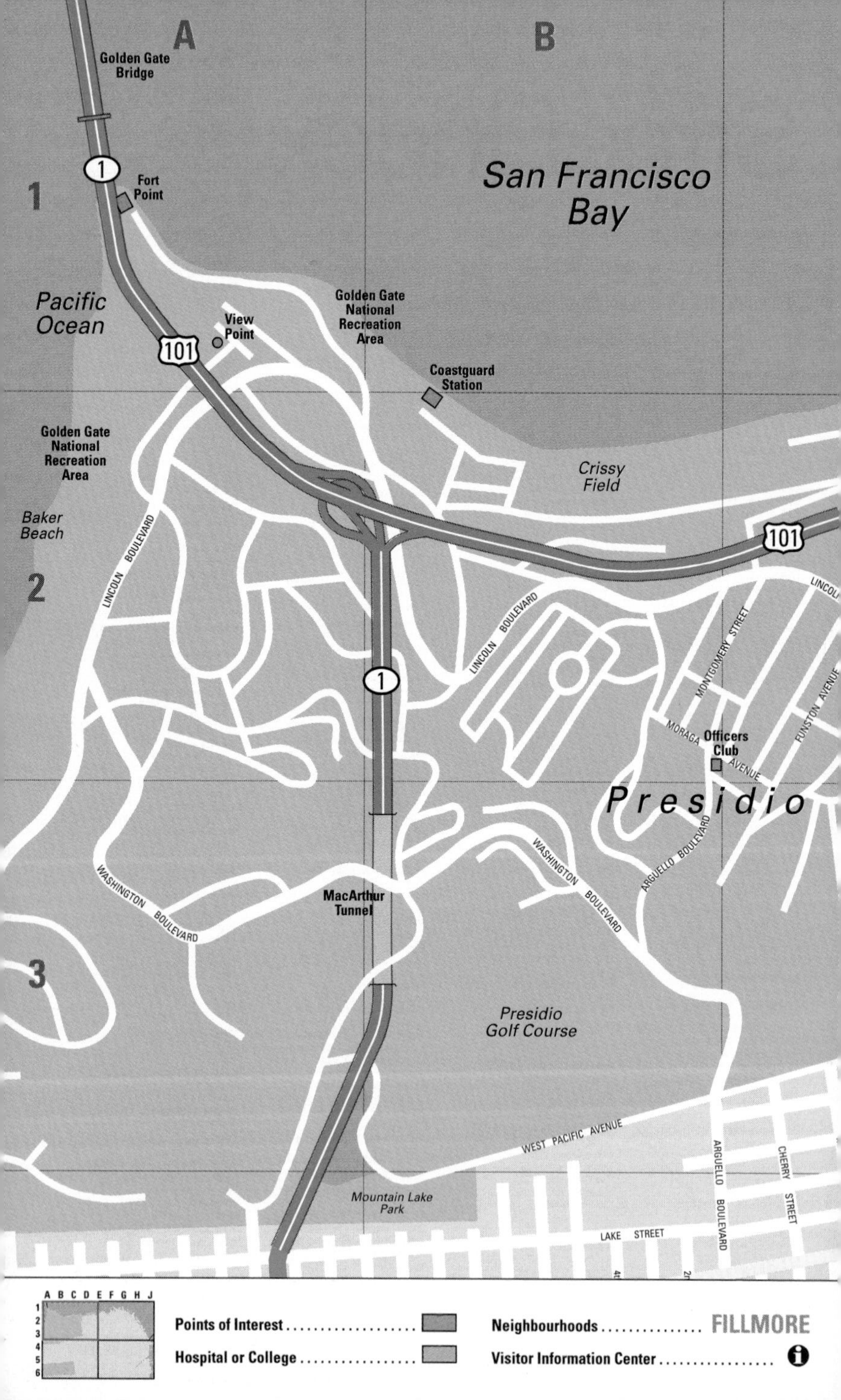
A
B
Golden Gate Bridge
1
Fort Point
San Francisco Bay
Pacific Ocean
View Point
101
Golden Gate National Recreation Area
Coastguard Station
Golden Gate National Recreation Area
Crissy Field
Baker Beach
LINCOLN BOULEVARD
101
2
LINCOLN BOULEVARD
MONTGOMERY STREET
FUNSTON AVENUE
MORAGA
Officers Club
AVENUE
Presidio
WASHINGTON BOULEVARD
ARGUELLO BOULEVARD
WASHINGTON BOULEVARD
MacArthur Tunnel
3
Presidio Golf Course
WEST PACIFIC AVENUE
ARGUELLO BOULEVARD
CHERRY STREET
Mountain Lake Park
LAKE STREET
Points of Interest
Hospital or College
Neighbourhoods
FILLMORE
Visitor Information Center

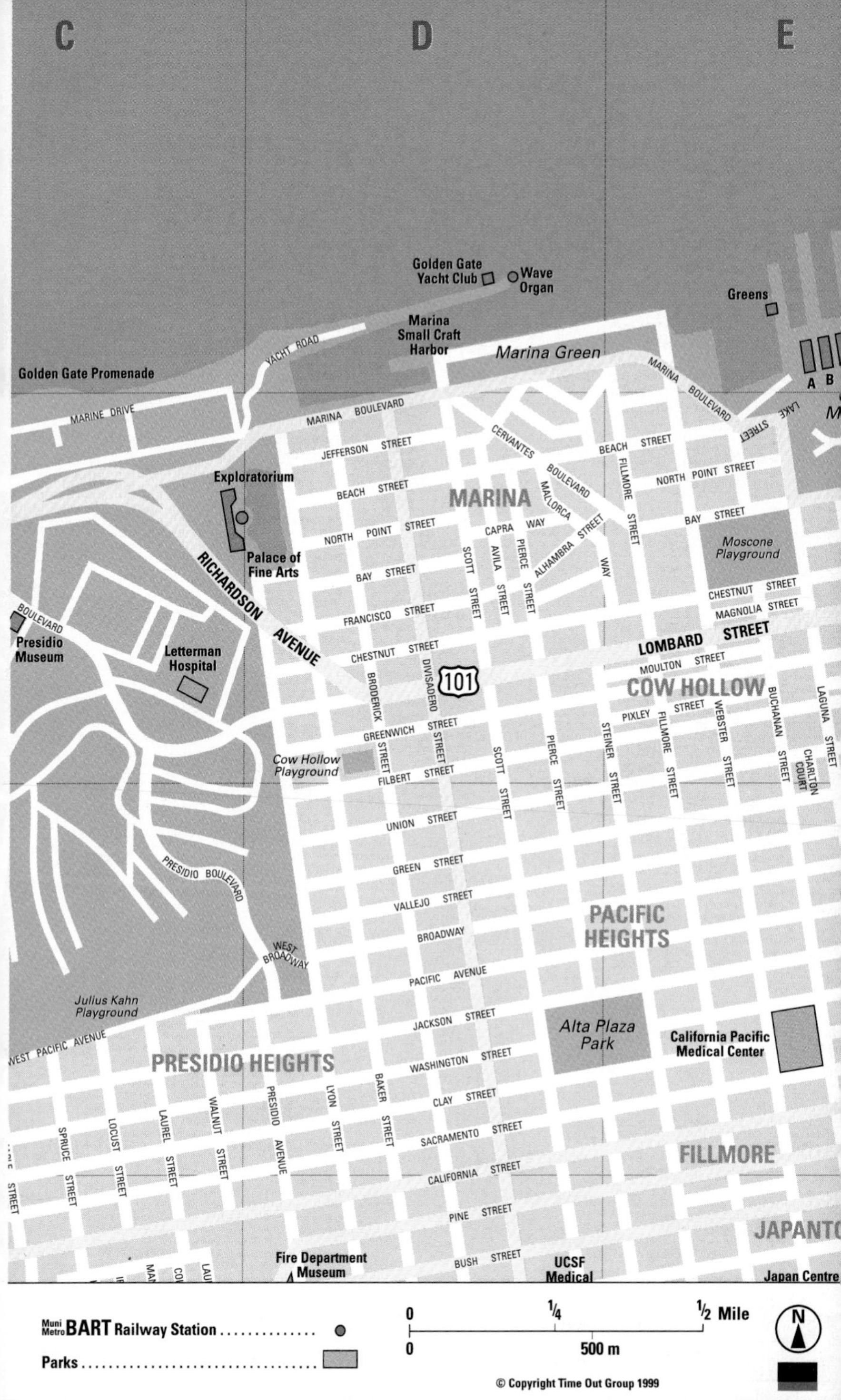

C
D
E
Golden Gate Yacht Club
Wave Organ
Greens
Marina Small Craft Harbor
Marina Green
Golden Gate Promenade
Exploratorium
Palace of Fine Arts
MARINA
Moscone Playground
Presidio Museum
Letterman Hospital
COW HOLLOW
Cow Hollow Playground
PACIFIC HEIGHTS
Julius Kahn Playground
Alta Plaza Park
California Pacific Medical Center
PRESIDIO HEIGHTS
FILLMORE
Fire Department Museum
UCSF Medical
Japan Centre
Muni Metro BART Railway Station
Parks
0 1/4 1/2 Mile
0 500 m
N

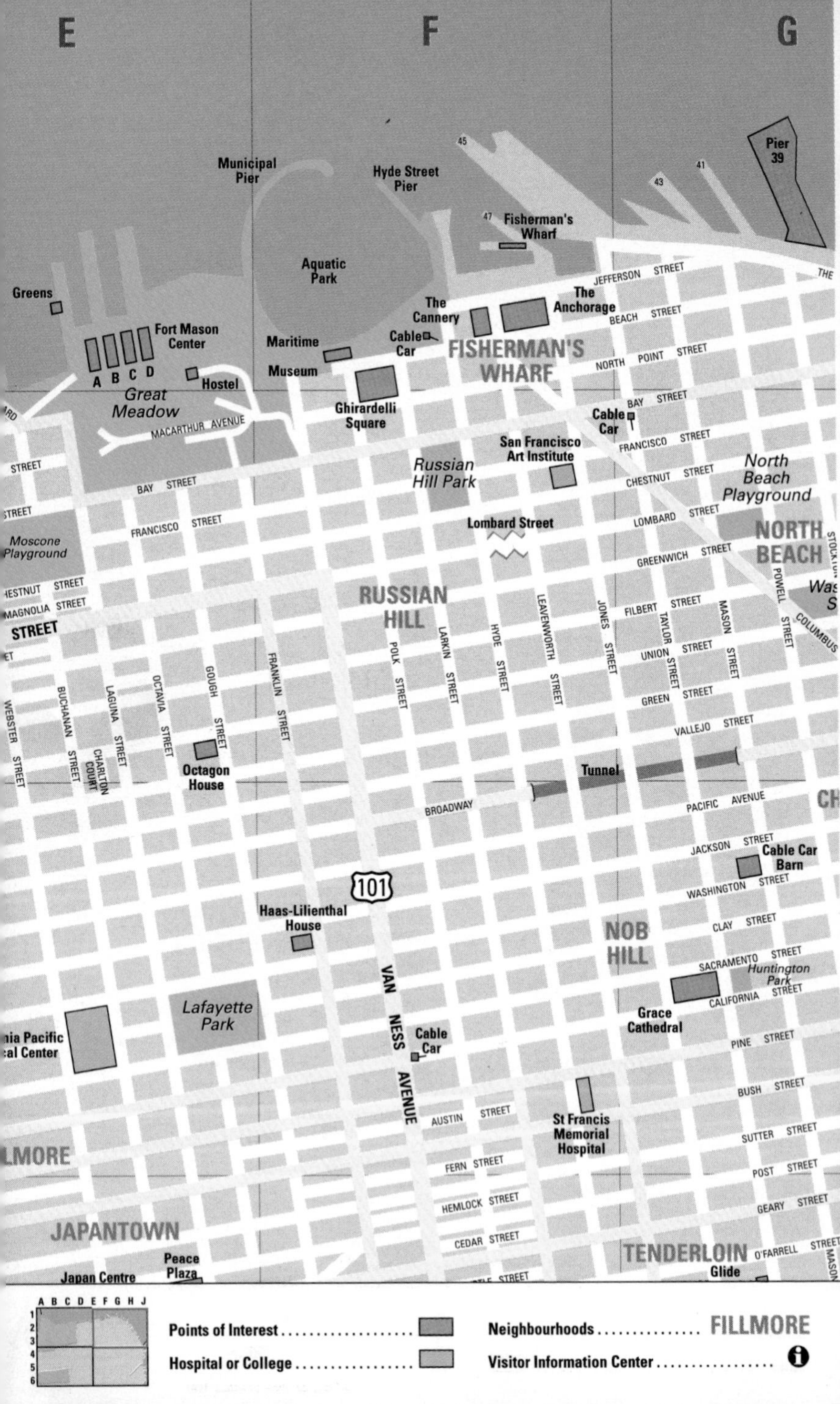

E
F
G
Municipal Pier
Hyde Street Pier
Pier 39
Fisherman's Wharf
Aquatic Park
Greens
Fort Mason Center
A B C D
Hostel
Great Meadow
Maritime Museum
The Cannery
Cable Car
The Anchorage
FISHERMAN'S WHARF
Ghirardelli Square
San Francisco Art Institute
Russian Hill Park
North Beach Playground
Moscone Playground
Lombard Street
NORTH BEACH
RUSSIAN HILL
Octagon House
Tunnel
Cable Car Barn
Haas-Lilienthal House
NOB HILL
Huntington Park
Grace Cathedral
Lafayette Park
Cable Car
St Francis Memorial Hospital
JAPANTOWN
Peace Plaza
Japan Centre
TENDERLOIN
Glide
JEFFERSON STREET
BEACH STREET
NORTH POINT STREET
BAY STREET
FRANCISCO STREET
CHESTNUT STREET
LOMBARD STREET
GREENWICH STREET
FILBERT STREET
UNION STREET
GREEN STREET
VALLEJO STREET
BROADWAY
PACIFIC AVENUE
JACKSON STREET
WASHINGTON STREET
CLAY STREET
SACRAMENTO STREET
CALIFORNIA STREET
PINE STREET
BUSH STREET
SUTTER STREET
POST STREET
GEARY STREET
O'FARRELL STREET
AUSTIN STREET
FERN STREET
HEMLOCK STREET
CEDAR STREET
MACARTHUR AVENUE
VAN NESS AVENUE
101
WEBSTER STREET
BUCHANAN STREET
CHARLTON COURT
LAGUNA STREET
OCTAVIA STREET
GOUGH STREET
FRANKLIN STREET
POLK STREET
LARKIN STREET
HYDE STREET
LEAVENWORTH STREET
JONES STREET
TAYLOR STREET
MASON STREET
POWELL STREET
COLUMBUS
Points of Interest
Hospital or College
Neighbourhoods
FILLMORE
Visitor Information Center

H
J
1
2
3
San Francisco Bay
35 Cruise Ship Terminal
33
31
27
19
17
15
9
7
5
3
1
24
26
28
30
32
EMBARCADERO
TELEGRAPH HILL
Coit Tower
GRANT AVENUE
shington quare
STREET
KEARNY STREET
MONTGOMERY STREET
SANSOME STREET
BATTERY STREET
THE EMBARCADERO
FRONT STREET
DAVIS STREET
AVENUE
BROADWAY
JACK KEROUAC ALLEY
GOLD ST
FINANCIAL DISTRICT
INATOWN
Jackson Square
Golden Gateway Center
DRUMM STREET
Justin Herman Plaza
Ferry Building
Chinese Cultural Center
Transamerica Pyramid
Embarcadero Center
WAVERLY PLACE
Portsmouth Square
COMMERCIAL STREET
Bank of California
Wells Fargo Museum
Cable Car
Rincon Center
Merchant's Exchange
Muni Metro BART Embarcadero
Old St Mary's Cathedral
Bank of America
Stock Exchange
STEUART STREET
SPEAR STREET
MAIN STREET
BEALE STREET
San Francisco Oakland Bay Bridge
80
MARKET STREET
Chinatown Gateway
CLAUDE LANE
Transbay Terminal & Greyhound Bus Depot
FREMONT STREET
Crocker Galleria
1st STREET
Union Square
STOCKTON STREET
MAIDEN LANE
GRANT AVENUE
Muni Metro BART Montgomery St
NEW MONTGOMERY STREET
MISSION STREET
MINNA STREET
NATOMA STREET
2nd STREET
HOWARD STREET
POWELL STREET
Center for the Arts
SFMOMA
Moscone Center
3rd
Muni Metro BART Railway Station
Parks
0
1/4
1/2 Mile
0
500 m
N

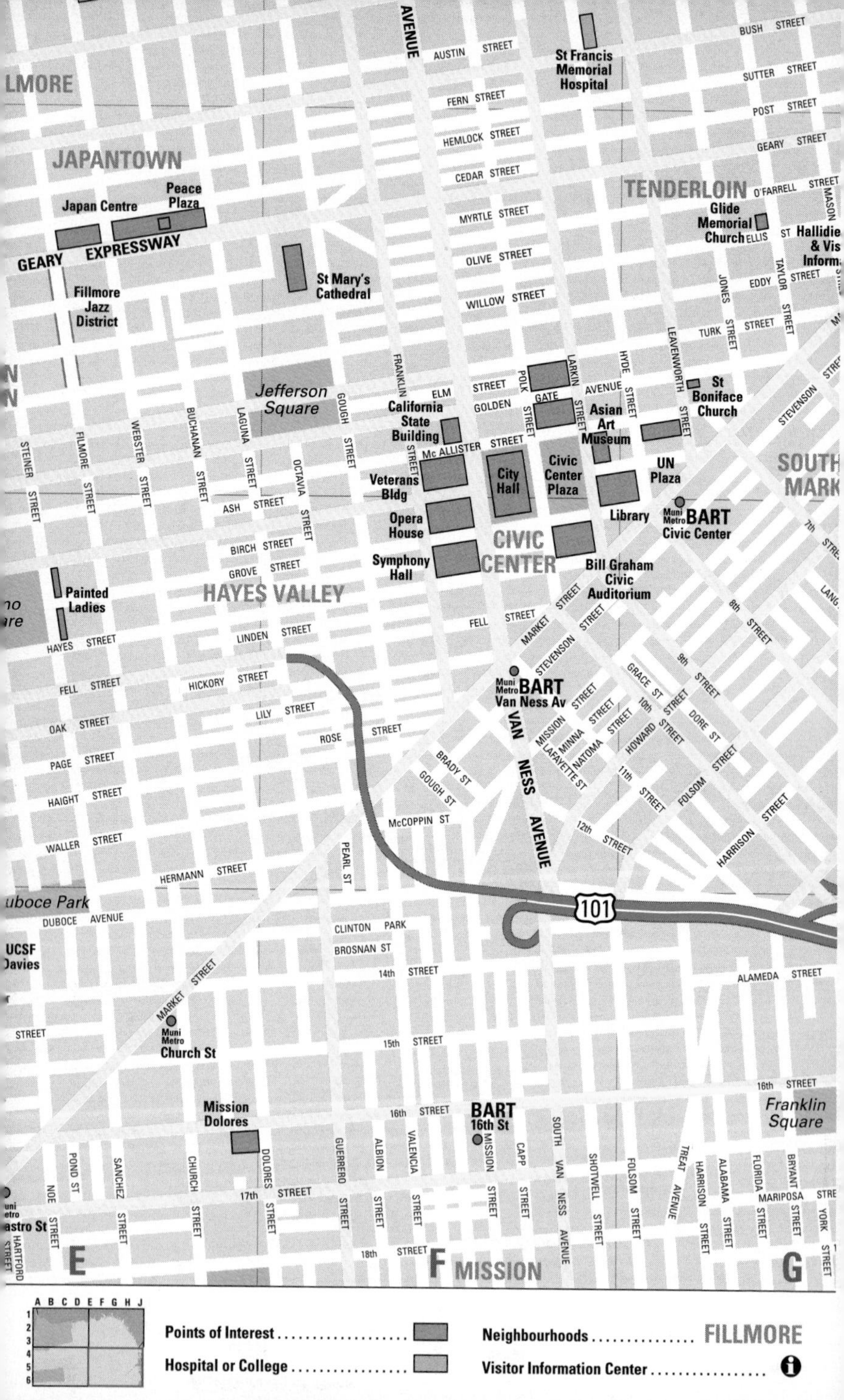

JAPANTOWN
Japan Centre
Peace Plaza
GEARY EXPRESSWAY
St Mary's Cathedral
Fillmore Jazz District
Jefferson Square
HAYES VALLEY
Painted Ladies
TENDERLOIN
St Francis Memorial Hospital
Glide Memorial Church
St Boniface Church
California State Building
Asian Art Museum
Veterans Bldg
City Hall
Civic Center Plaza
UN Plaza
Library
Opera House
Symphony Hall
CIVIC CENTER
Bill Graham Civic Auditorium
BART Civic Center
BART Van Ness Av
BART 16th St
Muni Metro Church St
Mission Dolores
Franklin Square
Duboce Park
MISSION
101
Points of Interest
Hospital or College
Neighbourhoods
FILLMORE
Visitor Information Center

& Greyhound Bus Depot
Crocker Galleria
Union Square
MAIDEN LANE
STOCKTON STREET
POWELL STREET
GRANT AVENUE
Muni Metro BART Montgomery St
NEW MONTGOMERY STREET
MISSION STREET
MINNA STREET
NATOMA STREET
FREMONT STREET
1st STREET
2nd STREET
HOWARD STREET
SFMOMA
Center for the Arts
Moscone Center North (underground)
Yerba Buena Gardens
Metreon
Moscone Center South
Zeum
3rd STREET
4th STREET
5th STREET
6th STREET
Cable Car
Plaza
SF Shopping Centre
Muni Metro BART Powell St
Old Mint
HAWTHORNE STREET
FOLSOM STREET
HARRISON STREET
BRYANT STREET
SOUTH PARK AVENUE
South Park
BRANNAN STREET
TOWNSEND STREET
KING STREET
THE EMBARCADERO
SOUTH BEACH
80
TEHAMA STREET
CLEMENTINA STREET
SHIPLEY STREET
CLARA STREET
South of Market Park
HARRIET ST
MOSS ST
RUSS ST
RITCH STREET
WELSH STREET
FREELON STREET
China Basin Ferry Terminal
BERRY STREET
Pacific Bell Park
China Basin
CalTrain Depot
Hall of Justice & Jail
BOARDMAN ST
GILBERT ST
CHANNEL STREET
CHINA BASIN STREET
Mission Rock Terminal
Concourse Exhibition Center
8th STREET
DIVISION STREET
OWENS STREET
7th STREET
HOOPER STREET
IRWIN STREET
HUBBELL STREET
15th STREET
16th STREET
3rd STREET
ILLINOIS STREET
280
Central Basin
SAN BRUNO STREET
WISCONSIN ST
Jackson Park
17th STREET
HAMPSHIRE STREET
POTRERO AVENUE
UTAH STREET
VERMONT STREET
KANSAS STREET
RHODE ISLAND STREET
DE HARO STREET
CAROLINA STREET
ARKANSAS STREET
CONNECTICUT STREET
MISSOURI STREET
TEXAS STREET
MISSISSIPPI STREET
PENNSYLVANIA AVENUE
INDIANA STREET
MINNESOTA STREET
TENNESSEE STREET
101
POTRERO HILL
19th STREET
H
J
4
5
6
Muni Metro BART Railway Station
Parks
0 1/4 1/2 Mile
0 500 m
N

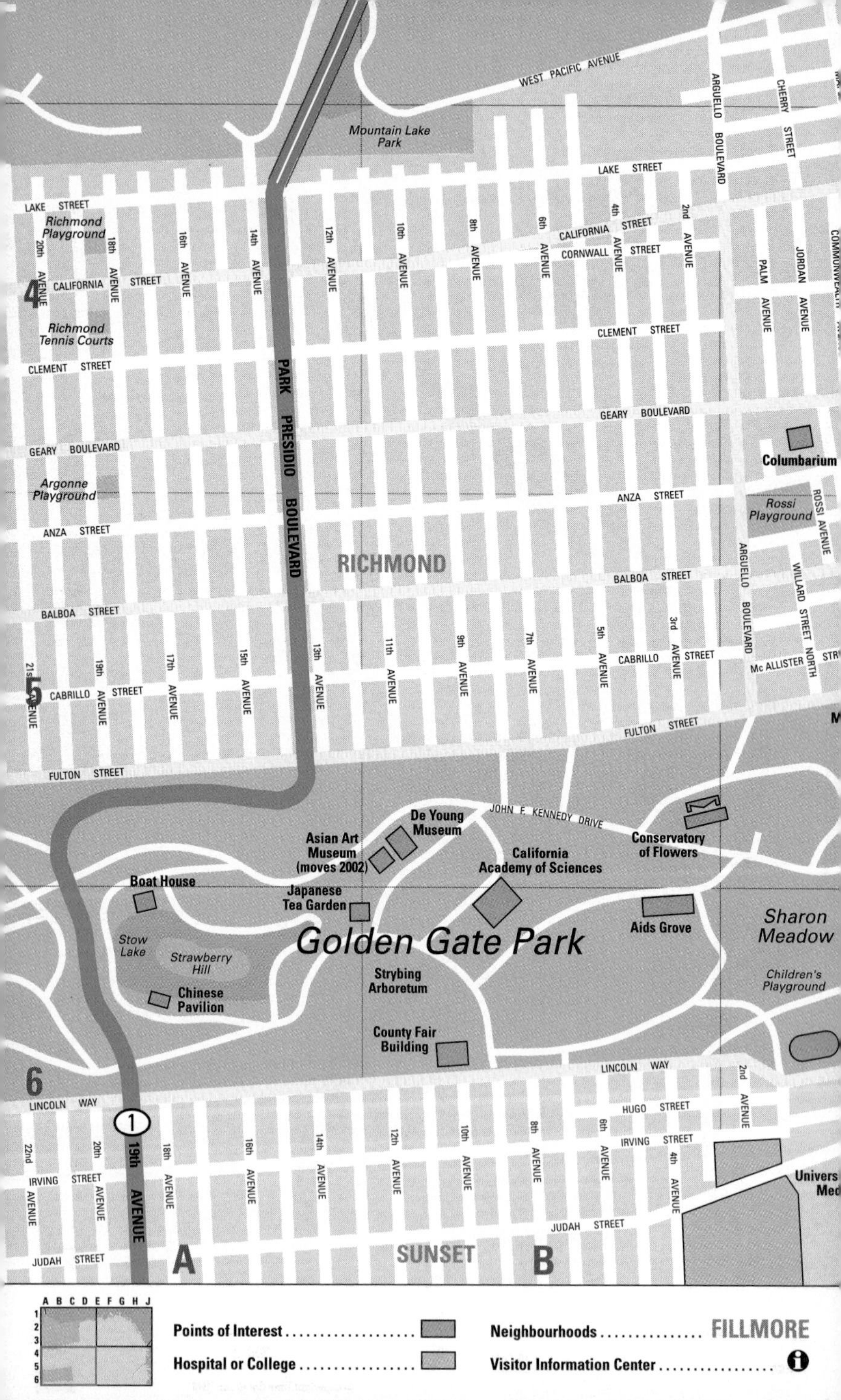

WEST PACIFIC AVENUE
Mountain Lake Park
ARGUELLO BOULEVARD
CHERRY STREET
LAKE STREET
Richmond Playground
20th AVENUE
18th AVENUE
16th AVENUE
14th AVENUE
12th AVENUE
10th AVENUE
8th AVENUE
6th AVENUE
4th AVENUE
2nd AVENUE
CALIFORNIA STREET
CORNWALL STREET
PALM AVENUE
JORDAN AVENUE
4
Richmond Tennis Courts
CLEMENT STREET
PARK PRESIDIO BOULEVARD
GEARY BOULEVARD
Columbarium
Argonne Playground
ANZA STREET
Rossi Playground
ROSSI AVENUE
RICHMOND
BALBOA STREET
WILLARD STREET NORTH
21st AVENUE
19th AVENUE
17th AVENUE
15th AVENUE
13th AVENUE
11th AVENUE
9th AVENUE
7th AVENUE
5th AVENUE
3rd AVENUE
CABRILLO STREET
Mc ALLISTER STREET
5
FULTON STREET
JOHN F. KENNEDY DRIVE
De Young Museum
Asian Art Museum (moves 2002)
Conservatory of Flowers
California Academy of Sciences
Boat House
Japanese Tea Garden
Aids Grove
Sharon Meadow
Stow Lake
Strawberry Hill
Golden Gate Park
Children's Playground
Chinese Pavilion
Strybing Arboretum
County Fair Building
LINCOLN WAY
6
HUGO STREET
IRVING STREET
22nd AVENUE
20th AVENUE
19th AVENUE
1
JUDAH STREET
A
SUNSET
B
Points of Interest
Hospital or College
Neighbourhoods FILLMORE
Visitor Information Center
A B C D E F G H J
1 2 3 4 5 6

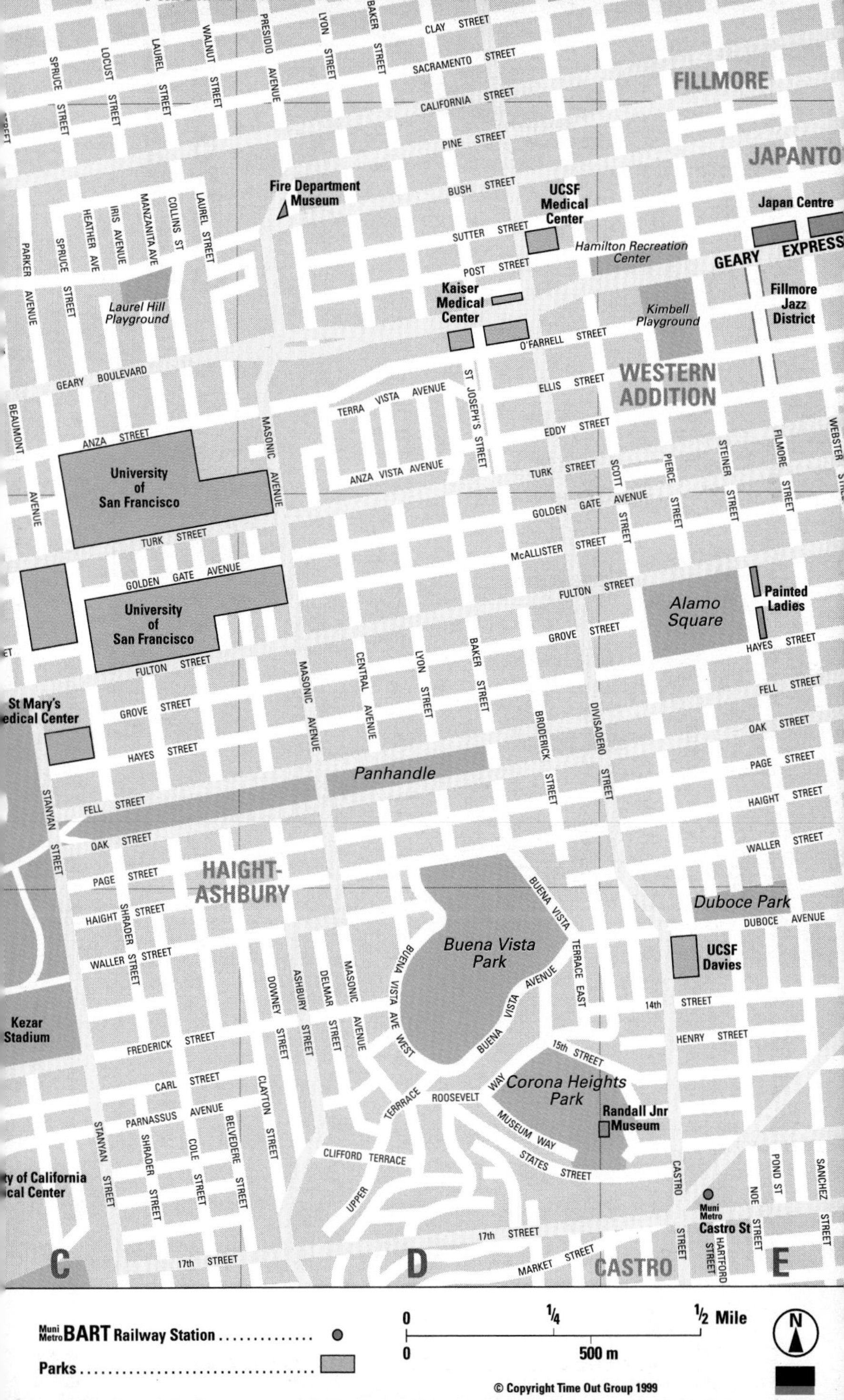
FILLMORE
JAPANTO
WESTERN ADDITION
HAIGHT-ASHBURY
CASTRO
CLAY STREET
SACRAMENTO STREET
CALIFORNIA STREET
PINE STREET
BUSH STREET
SUTTER STREET
POST STREET
O'FARRELL STREET
GEARY BOULEVARD
GEARY EXPRESS
ELLIS STREET
EDDY STREET
TURK STREET
GOLDEN GATE AVENUE
McALLISTER STREET
FULTON STREET
GROVE STREET
HAYES STREET
FELL STREET
OAK STREET
PAGE STREET
HAIGHT STREET
WALLER STREET
DUBOCE AVENUE
14th STREET
HENRY STREET
15th STREET
17th STREET
MARKET STREET
FREDERICK STREET
CARL STREET
PARNASSUS AVENUE
ANZA STREET
TERRA VISTA AVENUE
ANZA VISTA AVENUE
SPRUCE STREET
LOCUST STREET
LAUREL STREET
WALNUT STREET
PRESIDIO AVENUE
LYON STREET
BAKER STREET
PARKER AVENUE
HEATHER AVE
IRIS AVENUE
MANZANITA AVE
COLLINS ST
BEAUMONT AVENUE
MASONIC AVENUE
ST JOSEPH'S STREET
SCOTT STREET
PIERCE STREET
STEINER STREET
FILLMORE STREET
WEBSTER STREET
CENTRAL AVENUE
BRODERICK STREET
DIVISADERO STREET
STANYAN STREET
SHRADER STREET
DOWNEY STREET
ASHBURY STREET
DELMAR STREET
CLAYTON STREET
COLE STREET
BELVEDERE STREET
BUENA VISTA AVE WEST
BUENA VISTA TERRACE EAST
BUENA VISTA AVENUE
ROOSEVELT WAY
TERRACE
CLIFFORD TERRACE
UPPER
MUSEUM WAY
STATES STREET
CASTRO STREET
NOE STREET
POND ST
SANCHEZ STREET
HARTFORD STREET
Fire Department Museum
UCSF Medical Center
Japan Centre
Hamilton Recreation Center
Kaiser Medical Center
Fillmore Jazz District
Laurel Hill Playground
Kimbell Playground
University of San Francisco
University of San Francisco
Alamo Square
Painted Ladies
St Mary's Medical Center
Panhandle
Duboce Park
Buena Vista Park
UCSF Davies
Kezar Stadium
Corona Heights Park
Randall Jnr Museum
Muni Metro Castro St
ty of California ical Center
C
D
E
Muni Metro BART Railway Station
Parks
0 1/4 1/2 Mile
0 500 m
N
© Copyright Time Out Group 1999

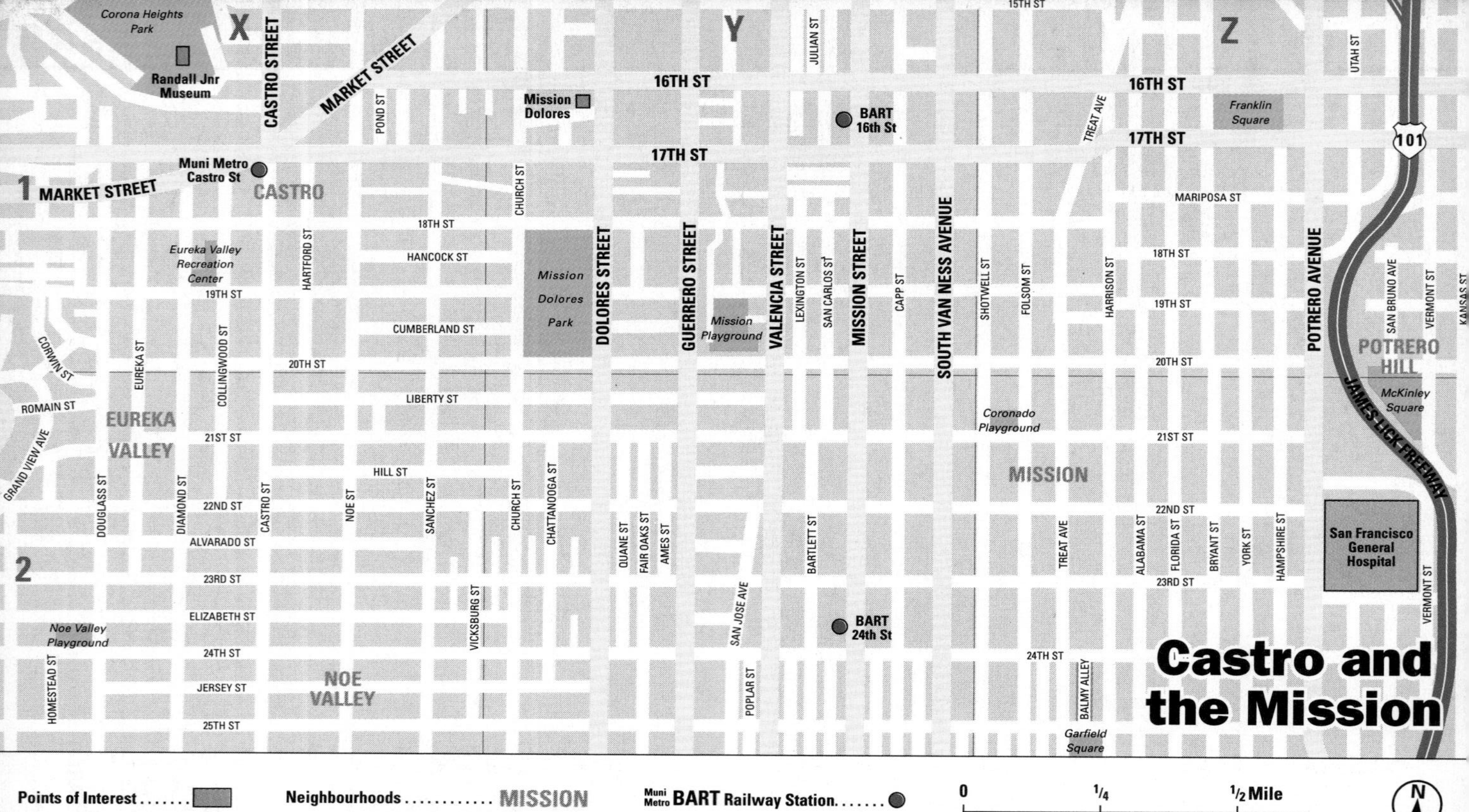
Castro and the Mission
Corona Heights Park
Randall Jnr Museum
X
Y
Z
1
2
CASTRO STREET
MARKET STREET
16TH ST
17TH ST
15TH ST
POND ST
Mission Dolores
JULIAN ST
BART 16th St
TREAT AVE
Franklin Square
UTAH ST
101
Muni Metro Castro St
CASTRO
CHURCH ST
MARIPOSA ST
18TH ST
HANCOCK ST
HARTFORD ST
Eureka Valley Recreation Center
19TH ST
Mission Dolores Park
DOLORES STREET
GUERRERO STREET
Mission Playground
VALENCIA STREET
LEXINGTON ST
SAN CARLOS ST
MISSION STREET
CAPP ST
SOUTH VAN NESS AVENUE
SHOTWELL ST
FOLSOM ST
HARRISON ST
POTRERO AVENUE
SAN BRUNO AVE
VERMONT ST
KANSAS ST
CUMBERLAND ST
CORWIN ST
EUREKA ST
COLLINGWOOD ST
20TH ST
POTRERO HILL
McKinley Square
JAMES LICK FREEWAY
ROMAIN ST
LIBERTY ST
EUREKA VALLEY
GRAND VIEW AVE
21ST ST
Coronado Playground
HILL ST
MISSION
DOUGLASS ST
DIAMOND ST
22ND ST
CASTRO ST
NOE ST
SANCHEZ ST
CHATTANOOGA ST
QUANE ST
FAIR OAKS ST
AMES ST
BARTLETT ST
TREAT AVE
ALABAMA ST
FLORIDA ST
BRYANT ST
YORK ST
HAMPSHIRE ST
San Francisco General Hospital
ALVARADO ST
23RD ST
VICKSBURG ST
SAN JOSE AVE
ELIZABETH ST
Noe Valley Playground
BART 24th St
24TH ST
BALMY ALLEY
HOMESTEAD ST
JERSEY ST
NOE VALLEY
POPLAR ST
25TH ST
Garfield Square
Points of Interest
Parks
Neighbourhoods MISSION
Hospital or College
Muni Metro BART Railway Station
0
1/4
1/2 Mile
1 Km
N
© Copyright Time Out Group 1999